United States Foreign Policy and World Order

United States Foreign Policy and World Order

Second Edition

James A. Nathan
James K. Oliver
University of Delaware

Little, Brown and Company

Boston   Toronto

Library of Congress Catalog Card No. 80-83798

ISBN 0-316-59851-8

9 8 7 6 5 4 3

ALP

Published simultaneously in Canada
by Little Brown & Company (Canada) Limited

Printed in the United States of America

The authors gratefully acknowledge permission to reprint from the following copyrighted works.

Portions of the Introduction are published by permission of Transaction, Inc., from James A. Nathan and James K. Oliver, "Diplomacy of Violence," *Society,* Vol. 11, No. 6, Copyright © 1974 by Transaction, Inc.

Excerpts from Dean Acheson, *Present at the Creation,* are reprinted by permission of W. W. Norton & Company, Inc., and Hughes Massie Limited. Copyright © 1969 by Dean Acheson.

Portions of Chapter 8 are from James A. Nathan, "The Cuban Missile Crisis: His Finest Hour Now," *World Politics,* Vol. 27, No. 2 (January 1975). Copyright © 1975 by Princeton University Press. Reprinted by permission.

Portions of Chapter 10 are from James A. Nathan, "Commitments in Search of a Roost: The Foreign Policy of the Nixon Administration," *Virginia Quarterly Review,* Vol. 50, No. 3 (Summer 1974). Reprinted by permission.

Portions of Chapters 11 and 12 are found in James A. Nathan, "Zbigscam: The Carter Administration's Foreign Policy, 1976–1980," *Virginia Quarterly Review,* Vol. 57, No. 2 (Spring 1981). Reprinted by permission.

Preface

The first edition of this book was published as the Vietnam War ended, the Watergate crisis subsided, and a new administration arrived in Washington. The Carter administration promised new approaches and methods more appropriate to the new era of international relations that seemed to have emerged during the 1970s with the frustration of American military power in Southeast Asia, the acquisition of strategic parity with the United States by the Soviet Union, and the exercise of petropower by OPEC.

The first edition of this book concluded that American foreign policy was, in some respects, suspended between its cold war past and an "interdependent" international future of which it had little vision. The new Carter administration avowed a unique sensitivity to this situation. Secretary of State Cyrus Vance and Secretary of Defense Harold Brown publicly acknowledged the inadequacies of the foreign policies of the Democratic administrations they had served during the 1960s. Andrew Young, a civil rights and anti–Vietnam War activist, a close associate of the slain Dr. Martin Luther King, Jr., and an eloquent proponent of a new— sometimes heretical—approach to the third world, was appointed ambassador to the United Nations. The new Special Assistant for National Security Affairs, Zbigniew Brzezinski, had written of a new "technotronic age" in international relations that required a diplomacy quite different from the neoclassical approach of his predecessor, Henry Kissinger. Further, he expressed an intent to reduce the visibility of his office in policy formulation in deference to the secretary of state. Finally, the new president was inaugurated proclaiming a commitment to reduce the defense budget significantly, stop the proliferation of nuclear weapons and take steps to eliminate them from the earth, as well as place human rights at the very center of American foreign policy.

Yet as the second edition of this book was being written, the Carter administration was in the midst of a difficult—ultimately unsuccessful— reelection campaign in which it proudly emphasized that real military spending had increased more since 1976 than in any comparable period in recent years, that this administration had committed the United States to a $1 trillion increase in defense spending over the next 5 years, and that the United States was now dedicated to the implementation of a new "Carter Doctrine" that anticipated military intervention, if necessary, in the Persian Gulf region to secure American and Western oil supplies. Andrew Young and Secretary of State Vance, both proponents of diplomatic responses and sensitivity to the new conditions of international relations, were gone from the administration. Secretary of Defense Harold Brown presided over the establishment of an American "Rapid Deployment Force" for military intervention anywhere on the globe but especially in the Persian Gulf region. Moreover, Security Adviser Brzezinski played as dominant a role in policy formulation as his predecessor and was the proponent of an even tougher and more confrontationist posture toward the Soviet Union. The second Strategic Arms Limitations Treaty, the avowed keystone of Mr. Carter's approach to arms control, had been set aside, perhaps indefinitely, as Mr. Carter approved a new mobile intercontinental ballistic missile system, a new submarine-launched ballistic missile, cruise missiles, the deployment of new missiles in Europe, and an approach to using these weapons which anticipated their controlled, "war-fighting" employment. In addition Mr. Carter could be found, in the fall of 1980, trying to convince Congress to allow the sale of nuclear fuel to India, which had previously exploded a nuclear device and refused to allow international inspection of its nuclear facilities. Ritual references to human rights were to be heard, but in northeast Asia the Carter administration could only look on in embarrassed acquiescence as yet another South Korean general seized the presidency via assassination, coup d'état, suspension of civil liberties, and imposition of prison sentences on the leadership of the political opposition.

Such seemingly incongruous developments warrant close analysis, and in this edition we have devoted a new chapter to a survey of the Carter administration as well as a new concluding chapter in which we assess the late 1970s in the context of post–World II foreign policy. In addition, we have taken advantage of new materials and memoirs now available on the Nixon-Ford years to rewrite completely the analysis of the early and mid-1970s as well as portions of the discussion of the Vietnam War. The introduction and discussion of the conceptual framework of the analysis have been rewritten, the early chapters on the origins of the cold war condensed somewhat and, where new historical materials have become available, revised.

Undoubtedly, however, the major structural change in this edition of the book is the dropping of the institutional analysis that made up Part II of the first edition. Rather than make what many users of the first edition suggested was an already long book more so, we have devoted the second edition entirely to an overview and analysis of American foreign policy since the Second World War. In this analysis we have retained the first edition's attention to the interrelationship of foreign policy and American domestic politics. The detailed review and analysis of the institutions and processes of policy formulation, executive-legislative relations, public opinion, and the role of nongovernmental and economic actors in American foreign policy making, however, will be taken up in detail in a second book, *Foreign Policy Making in the American Political System: A Decidedly Inferior Form?* Our intent in dividing the analysis in this way is to increase pedagogical flexibility. Those instructors who emphasize the diplomatic history of the cold war and contemporary policy analysis will find this second edition of *United States Foreign Policy and World Order* (corresponding to the coverage in Part I of the first edition) appropriate to their needs; those who focus on institutions and policymaking processes could use *Foreign Policy Making in the American Political System: A Decidedly Inferior Form?* (corresponding to an expanded revision of Part II of the first edition of *United States Foreign Policy and World Order*); and those desiring a more comprehensive survey could employ both books.

As in the first edition, our analytical approach remains eclectic. We have no desire to demonstrate the truth or error of the many philosophical and analytical perspectives contending for the attention and allegiance of the student of American foreign policy. Where traditional analysis seems to us of continuing validity, we employ it, but where a revisionist perspective appears reasonable and warranted by documentation, we are not averse to bringing such analysis to bear. In any event we have tried to make our analytical posture explicit within the range of possible interpretive positions. Similarly, regarding conceptual frameworks, models, and the other accoutrements of contemporary political science and policy analysis, we have searched for and tried to apply those that explain and enlighten. We have not applied, for we do not find available, a single framework, model, perspective, or level of analysis that encompasses the many dimensions and implications of American foreign policy. Thus, as in the first edition, we remain concerned primarily with the perceptions of international relations and America's role in world politics that seem to have dominated American foreign policy since World War II. Our purpose is to understand the origins of the American image of international reality, the resultant policies, the global consequences of these policies, and the interplay with America's domestic institutions and values. In addition, we hope to shed some light on the extent to which the dominant perceptions of America's interests and policy have reached the outer limits of utility.

Acknowledgments

The first edition benefited from the assistance of many people, and the revision is no less encumbered with debt. We have been as explicit as in the first edition in our acknowledgment, through footnotes, of the usefulness of the analysis and insights of other scholars and analysts. We are, however, especially grateful to those who read all or parts of the manuscript and offered their assistance and advice: Robert Art of Brandeis University; John Gilbert of North Carolina State University; John Keeler of the University of Washington (Seattle); David Larson of The University of New Hampshire; Edward L. Morse of the Department of State; Robert E. Osgood of the School of Advanced International Studies, Johns Hopkins University; Read Reading of the University of Pittsburgh; and Hibbert Roberts of Illinois State University. In addition, Neil Chanowski and Harry Temple served as the authors' teaching assistants and as colleagues who provided a valuable stream of commentary and criticism of the first edition as they used it in the classroom. Their written critiques were of the highest professional quality and crucial to our revision efforts. The authors of course accept full responsibility for those conceptual, judgmental, and factual errors that remain.

Finally, William Ethridge, our editor at Little, Brown, provided essential supportive discipline and editorial judgment. His enthusiasm was all the more remarkable in view of the fact that his review and production schedules seemed always to be collapsing under the burden of Nathan and Oliver's crankiness and procrastination. At no time, however, did his patience and encouragement give way—for this we are especially thankful.

Contents

Introduction   1

> Two Views of World Political Reality 1   The Context of World Politics
> and the Course of American Policy 6   Notes 9

Chapter 1: Prelude to the Cold War   11

> Intervention in the Russian Civil War 13   The Coming of World War II
> 18   Conflicting Strategic Concepts 22   Poland and Eastern Europe:
> The Turn Toward Cold War 28   The Administration of Liberation 33
> Truman and the Origins of the Cold War 35   The Atom Bomb, Asia,
> and Europe 38   Notes 48

Chapter 2: The Onset of the Cold War   56

> A World View Takes Shape 56   World View Becomes Policy:
> The Truman Doctrine and the Marshall Plan 64   The Summing Up:
> Containment Is Defined 74   Summary ... and More Questions 76
> Notes 77

Chapter 3: From the Marshall Plan to Global Containment   81

> The Cold War 82   Debate Concerning the Instruments of Containment
> 85   The Marshall Plan as a Politico-Economic Concept 87   The Death of
> Diplomacy 89   Formation of the North Atlantic Treaty Organization 95
> Crisis and Collapse in Asia 100   American Policy Reappraised 104   The
> Policy Reappraisal Appraised 109   Notes 113

Chapter 4: Korea and the Militarization of Containment   118

> The Origins of the First Limited War 118   The "Fog of War" 125   The
> Limited War at Home: Domestic Politics and Rearmament 126
> Conventional Forces for NATO: Plans and Stalemate 133   Up and Down
> the Korean Peninsula 137   The MacArthur Problem 142   The Old Cold

*Warrier Fades Away: The End of the Truman Administration 152
Conclusion 155 Notes 159*

Chapter 5: Conserving Containment 167

*Containing the Republican Right 169 Containment in a Changing
World 179 Containment Through Brinkmanship 192 Negotiating from
Strength and Containing Detente 196 Notes 205*

Chapter 6: Crisis and Salvaging the Status Quo 211

*The Suez Crisis 211 The New Look Challenged 217 Policy Immobility
221 The Opening Toward Detente 223 The Old Reflexes Reemerge 226
The Curious Death of Detente: The U-2 Incident 228 The More Things
Changed . . . 234 Conclusion 235 Transition 238 Notes 241*

Chapter 7: Containment on the New Frontier 250

*The Threatened New Frontier 251 Nation-Building and Counter-
revolution 258 Flexible Response 265 American Aims in the First
Round: The Berlin Crisis 270 Conclusion 278 Notes 280*

Chapter 8: The Apotheosis of Containment 286

*Mastery or Luck? 287 The Domestic Factor 291 Just a Dirty Trick? 293
True Grit and Crisis Diplomacy 295 Cuba and the American Century
299 Cuba and Deterrence 300 The By-Products of Success 303 The
Economics of Containment 306 Conclusion 314 Notes 316*

Chapter 9: Containment "Turns the Corner" . . . into the Swamp 321

*Containment on the Mekong 321 Understanding the Quagmire and the
Stalemate Machine 339 Saving the Stalemate Machine 349 Notes 362*

Chapter 10: The Nixon Doctrine and Beyond 367

*The Nixon-Kissinger Doctrine: Containment and Management 367 The
Limits of Triangular Balance 384 The Limits of Power and Policy in an
Interdependent World 396 Beyond the Nixon Doctrine 404 Notes 406*

Chapter 11: "Commitments in Search of a Roost"   412

  *Interdependence and Containment 413   Carter and the World 421
  Facing the Limits 437   Notes 444*

Chapter 12: Conclusion   447

  *American Power and the Dynamics of the Cold War 447   A Declining
  Prospect for Order? 449   The Road Taken? 454   Notes 458*

Index   461

Introduction

International relations as a distinct mode of inquiry — separate from history, government, philosophy, or law — has achieved independent status and recognition only within the last thirty or forty years. Before this period there were historical narratives of wars or diplomatic machinations, texts and analyses of international law, and philosophical treatments of how people and states should relate to one another. But only the press of the great conflicts of the twentieth century, combined with the rapid rise of universities to a place of prominence in public life, has allowed for the creation of a separate discipline complete with a vast literature, separate schools of thought — even heretics.

So vast has this study of international relations become that simple divisions and distinctions about the study seem facile or incomplete. Yet for all the complexity of the subject matter, it seems that there have arisen several clearly defined alternative frameworks for viewing people's international political behavior and the foreign policy of states. Each of these frameworks emphasizes and illuminates some kinds of activity and passes over and distorts others. These concepts of international relations are like a geographer's map that cannot be true to spatial relations, distance, and shape at all times, but can be fairly accurate to two of the three.

TWO VIEWS
OF WORLD POLITICAL REALITY

The "picture in the head," as Walter Lippman used to say, of most political leaders concerned with international affairs has been to see international relations as if they consisted almost solely of the interaction of nation-states. From this traditional perspective, international society is a separate and dangerous domain of human activity, in contrast to the orderly processes of Anglo-American domestic political life. Wolfers and Martin have explained:

> [D]omestic political conditions stand in striking contrast to the conditions
> . . . nations face in their external relations; the domestic conditions are characterized by order, lawfulness and peace arising from popular consensus on

1

> principle—a consensus so marked that some believe coercion has practically ceased to play a role here; but the external relations continue to be full of bitter struggle, violence, and Machiavellian practices.[1]

The classic conception of traditional statecraft is that in international relations, where there is no force able to regulate disputes, wars occur because there is little to stop them, aside from self-restraint. Foreign policy is conducted in an arena of politics where there is no reliable mechanism for regulating disputes except "self-help." This condition of anarchy necessarily stimulates competition for military power. Military capability is sought to secure states in a domain of threat — international society. This society is such a cockpit of hostility and danger that alliances, conventions, and treaties are all made with the understanding that the ability to defend oneself is never given away. A state must always be sovereign or independent in order to protect its customs, institutions, and inhabitants. As Henry Kissinger once intoned, "No nation can make its survival dependent on the good will of another state if it has any choice about it."[2]

The nature of an international system that is marked by the absence of a superior public monopoly of force is commonly understood by leaders and analysts as a society at the edge of war. Force, in this society, is the common medium of exchange; and power is the only means of gaining interest. It is a realm of politics that recalls Cicero's lament, "What can be done against force without force?"[3] Foreign policy, in such an environment, is above all to protect national interests against the dangerous and hostile forces at loose in a world where there are no international police and no courts with binding authority.

An alternative view of international relations, while not dismissing these traditional concerns, nonetheless urges attention to a host of new forces in world politics that have in some measure made most states more interdependent with one another.[4] In these circumstances military power does not now seem to bring benefits commensurate with its cost; nor does force usually seem an especially useful tool to deal with world economic and social crisis. Military power, moreover, does not always serve its historic function by which states traditionally won their legitimacy. Even the most awesome nuclear power can no longer protect citizens against enemies. Indeed, every American president since Harry Truman has warned the American people that the United States cannot survive an onslaught of nuclear weapons. The state used to be the citizen's fortress against capricious violence. The state would provide for the conditions of order and stability in which citizens could plan for their children or undertake their own livelihood. In this sense, the state used to be a precondition of society's benefits: health, wealth, rectitude or justice. In previous eras, a good life was impossible without a sound, viable state. In turn, the inhabitants of states agreed, at least in theory, to be citizens, to profess allegiance, to pay taxes, and to participate, if necessary, in the state's common defense. But if the state can no longer be counted on to serve as the agent of defense; in fact, if the state becomes an agent of society's ills, then an ancient agreement is shattered as the "roof has been blown off" the historic shelter that nation-states once provided.[5]

The monopolization of military force gave historic states their definition. It was also an instrument of their will. The ability to direct violence against foreign states was a critical element of national greatness. Diplomacy and force were inextricably related. Yet the rise of irregular warfare (both urban and rural) and the expansion of force to the point where the use of force implies suicide has largely paralyzed the greatest military machines. Nuclear weapons have great destructive power; but because world order is delicately balanced, the threat of force seems foolish if the other side can, with assurance, retaliate. To use nuclear weapons and nuclear blackmail seems more and more unreasonable as the threat is disproportionate to almost any conceivable gain. Nuclear weapons have become impotent except as symbols of national greatness and as grim reminders that all humanity is grouped together under the same dark shadow.

Historically military power either begot economic wealth, or economic strength purchased military power. Today, however, there are vast discrepancies between wealth and power. Some countries are all but impoverished yet possess tremendous military potential; others are fabulously wealthy yet militarily feeble.

From this interdependence perspective, the nation-state is seen as caught in a surge of technological change that has brought most aspects of human interaction into closer proximity. There has been an internationalization of social and economic life. In America, for example, the economy has become sensitive to world commodity markets. Economic sovereignty has been breached through the vulnerability of American energy resources. The American inflation that began in the 1970s was triggered and driven not only by the energy crisis, but also by foreign demand for American products made suddenly cheap by dollar devaluations in 1971–1973. Economist and former Treasury Department and National Security Council (NSC) member Fred Bergsten notes the inability of national policy to control inflation. He writes, "[A] U.S. effort to use price controls was subverted in large part by exports of controlled goods, in response to higher prices abroad and the close ties among world markets."[6]

For years economists and politicians were confident that national measures taken by central governments could control inflation and unemployment by priming the national budgetary pump or by changing the costs of borrowing money. Now, however, national remedies are highly dependent for their success on being harmonized with compatible actions in other nations. Complicating such efforts are significant concentrations of private economic power whose activities inevitably link the American economy to the international economy. Thus by the late 1970s, American merchandise exports constituted 10 percent of all the goods produced in the United States, twice the level of the 1950s. The foreign subsidiaries and branches of American multinational corporations were producing 25 percent of the parent firms' production. Americans in foreign countries held some $350 billion in assets while foreigners had invested in the United States $275 billion.[7] Furthermore, by the end of the 1970s international banks held some $666 billion in foreign currency deposits "denominated in a currency other than that of the host country,"[8] of which $436.6 billion were dollars.[9] This European market has for some time been more liquid than the market in New York,[10] and with high interest rates at the end of the 1970s even the most well endowed American corporations, such as IBM, looked not to American bankers to borrow large sums, but to Saudi Arabia or the European dollar markets where funds in the hundreds of millions of dollars could be had at considerable discounts.[11]

These circumstances necessarily place much of the U.S. business world in an interdependent relationship with a global economic system separated from easy national control. Today great corporations nominally based in Delaware, London, or Zurich may have operations in 100 countries. No one national headquarters will contain more than a fraction of its activities. Several such corporations or banks, by shifting their reserves, for instance, out of one currency and into another (this can be done in a paper transaction by calling practically any bank) can cause the value of national currencies to plummet or ascend. All of a nation's fiscal and budgetary policies can thus be undermined by the power of major corporations and banks that exist to some extent beyond national control. The priorities of international corporations and international financial institutions, by making nonpolitical investment decisions, can have dramatic consequences for national governments — as the Chileans, for instance, discovered in September 1973 when the international banks and financial institutions (with American encouragement) took an increasingly dim view of Allende's domestic economic policy and refused to extend credit to Chile. The result fueled a ferocious inflation, which contributed to the regime's brutal removal by the Chilean military. Thus, multinational firms and financial institutions that do not owe allegiance to any particular nation can exert enormous pressure by their attitude toward third world and other countries.[12]

In this way, the United States and most other nations have in some measure become captive to an international financial system from which they can disentangle themselves only at great risk. As Bergsten noted, the old refrain, "let trade wars come, we'll win them," now sounds as ludicrous as Mao Zedong's famous dictum that China would emerge victorious from the ashes of a nuclear holocaust.[13] Increasingly, therefore, all states in international society find themselves in the same leaky craft.

Foreign policy solutions, conceived in traditional terms of military power, do not seem applicable in any self-evident manner to the new kind of problem posed by interdependence.. A *macht politik* based on exhortation seems foolish at best, and leaders have few carrots and sticks with which to inveigle recalcitrant Arabs. The nature of the problem is increasingly one of a rather steady deterrence; that is, as long as the West, for example, needs oil, threats to obtain oil by force can be met by threats to cut production. Moreover, as soon as overt or covert efforts fail, succeeding threats need to become more spectacular. As former Secretary of State Dean Rusk, a long-time advocate of military solutions to military problems, recently observed:

> If you go down [the] trail [of economic sanctions] you face a dismal end. Retaliation breeds counterretaliation. If we withhold food, they will withhold oil. We would have to get the entire Western world to join in that policy and there is no possibility of them agreeing on it.[14]

Indeed, when the United States in 1979 and 1980 sought to mobilize its European and Japanese allies to impose economic sanctions on the revolutionary regime in Iran, to force the release of American diplomatic hostages, these forces of interdependence proved to be major constraints. The Europeans and especially the Japanese, being more dependent upon Iranian oil than the United States, were extremely reluctant to move decisively against the Iranians. Furthermore, the presence of a large American naval task force and a bungled military effort to free the hostages in early 1980 had not secured the release of the hostages by mid-1980 and only underscored the problem of using force in the contemporary world system. Similarly, in neighboring Afghanistan the Soviet Union, despite the insertion of more than 80,000 troops in an effort to suppress an anticommunist insurgency, was faced by mid-1980 with a situation sometimes described as similar to the American intervention in Vietnam more than a decade earlier.

Yet surely, one might retort, security policy — wars and those who threaten them — dominate our attention and the media. If we concentrate on the newer features of interdependence, do we not miss the critical questions of national life and death? Those who maintain that a global systems perspective is useful would not deny the urgent questions of foreign policy — the politics of war and peace. But the ecological or systems view of the globe moves our attention to some of the interactions that are no longer contained or controlled by national policy. Of course, a view of international politics that looks to a kind of primitive global society has limits. It seems best used to illustrate economic, social, and political transnational behavior. The growth of regional economic organizations (e.g., the European Economic Community), multinational economic behavior (ITT or Shell Oil), international nongovernmental organizations (international labor unions and professional organizations), the globalization of questions of poverty (the third world versus the industrialized world), and justice (an international law of the sea): all these are forms of interaction that the global system imagery helps us visualize.

The global systems view does not help us much in understanding Henry Kissinger's secret trip to Peking in 1971, the Israeli move against the Arabs in 1967, the 1973 Middle East War, or the Strategic Arms Limitation Talks (SALT). These politics of power, balance, and strategy are much better illuminated by the classic world view. The transfer of technology from the United States to Japan, the rise of the multinational corporation or transnational economic forces (such as OPEC, Eurodollar markets, or trade wars) are phenomena not highlighted by the classic vision of colliding nation-states which, in Palmerston's words, have no permanent friends or enemies, just interest. But the vision of an increasingly complex and interdependent societal organization on a global scale does help capture some of the rapidly changing complexities of the last quarter of this century. If we recognize that these elements of interdependence have grown out of and coexist with elements of the traditional international politics of the first half of the century, we will have an even more complete image of the context within which American foreign policy has operated during the period surveyed in this book.

THE CONTEXT OF WORLD POLITICS
AND THE COURSE OF AMERICAN POLICY

Finally, it should be noted that this complex international context of new forces and traditional political forms and concerns has frustrated any simple resolution of the problems of world order. American foreign policy has sought for a quarter century or more to build an international order predicated initially on American military and economic superiority, and in recent years, on a balance of military force. From the outset of the postwar period, American policymakers postulated a relationship between American national security and some form of world order. An analysis of the policies designed to define and then establish these postulates as a framework for world politics during the period after World War II is the focus of the narrative that follows.

In late 1945, American policymakers confronted the tasks of reconstructing a world order shattered by three decades of global war, economic dislocation and depression, and political and social revolution. The United States possessed seemingly limitless military power with its monopoly of atomic weapons and was the only national economy of significance to have come through World War II intact. There were concerns about inflation and postwar adjustment, but whereas Europe lay in ruins, the American economy had grown and even prospered as the arsenal for the wartime alliance.

But the postwar international system has proved to be resistant to American political, economic, and military capability. The cold war between the Soviet Union and the United States concerning the political, military, economic, and social structure and dynamics of Europe immediately took the place of World War II. The origins of this conflict lie in the chaotic end of World War I and the American, European, and Japanese attempts to crush the Russian communist revolution of 1917. That intervention failed, but the resultant Soviety anxiety concerning the capitalist world and Western preoccupation with the purported global designs of communist ideology festered throughout the interwar period and were not really suppressed even when a common enemy threw the two worlds together in a superficial alliance between 1941 and 1945 (see Chapter 1).

In the West the greatest threat to international order after World War II was the political and economic chaos of Western Europe. These conditions seemed to provide the opportunity for Soviet expansion beyond a hegemony over Central Europe gained through their defeat of Nazi power in that region during 1944 and 1945. Inasmuch as the immediate postwar European problem was deemed to be primarily economic in origin, economic remedies seemed most appropriate (see Chapter 2). However, because American economic assistance was predicated on the twin necessities of a strong, essentially capitalist Europe and a reconstructed Germany (see Chapters 2 and 3), the Soviets' long-standing fear of a capitalist encirclement on the one hand and the possibility of renewed German aggression on the other could not help but be exacerbated by American policies (see Chapters 1 and 3). The result of this conflict between Soviet security concerns and superior American arms and economic strength directed toward an open, liberal world order was a sustained period of crisis beginning with the Berlin Blockade of 1948–

1949. As crisis followed crisis, the apparent necessity for employing in some fashion — either by threat or demonstrations of "will" — the instrumentalities of force and the American concern for the military imperatives of world order came to override an earlier concern for the international economic order and the economic instrumentalities of the Marshall Plan (see Chapter 3). That a successful diplomacy had to be predicated on military power was a lesson subsequently confirmed by the Korean War (see Chapter 4).

The psychological and material burdens of the Korean conflict seriously eroded domestic support for American conventional military interventions in furtherance of U.S. global activism. But the Eisenhower administration successfully deflected this frustration and built an even larger structure of international obligations. Massive retaliation, the dependence on the threat of ultimate nuclear force, was the temporary response of the Eisenhower administration to uphold far-flung commitments at a reduced cost (see Chapter 5). But during the late 1950s and early 1960s, the Soviet Union's apparent acquisition of a global nuclear capability and the appearance of nationalist upheaval throughout the third world seemed to neutralize this conjoining of nuclear force with an American interest in global order (see Chapters 6 and 7). To meet this challenge, a coalition of scholars and analysts who feared that the possession of nuclear weapons by the Soviet Union and the United States had robbed the threat of force of its credibility developed a conception of limited war. The problem, wrote Henry Kissinger in the late 1950s, was that "since diplomacy which is not related to a plausible employment of force is sterile it must be the task of our military policy to develop a doctrine and capability for the graduated employment of force."[15] A great edifice of strategic theory on how to make military force relevant to diplomacy was subsequently incorporated into the Kennedy administration's concepts of "flexible response." The upper ranges of this strategic doctrine were employed in Cuba in 1962 (see Chapter 8), and the lower ranges were used throughout the third world — especially in Vietnam from the mid-1960s until the end of the decade (see Chapter 9).

By the mid-1960s "graduated response," in the Defense Department's argot, became a kind of article of faith. The *Pentagon Papers* show that the Joint Chiefs of Staff and civilians in the executive branch debating varieties of "squeezes" on Vietnam. There were intervals of "pain" proposed, each with "pauses" that varied in tempo from "low" through "moderate" and proceeded to a fast, "full squeeze" and then to a "blitz" or a "crescendo."[16] Maxwell Taylor, the most prominent military theoretician of the late 1950s and 1960s, echoed the prevailing policy consensus

— that "too much" coercion is as bad as "too little."[17] But by the 1970s it was still an open question whether enormously expanded military power, no matter how "flexible," could be effectively managed to support American security interests (see Chapter 10). More than a decade of American policy had been predicated in large measure on the assumption that force could be productively wedded to diplomacy. It is now apparent, however, that this vast undertaking was perhaps too simple in formulation and too complex in execution.

In the meantime, the conditions of world politics had changed significantly. Prior to the mid-1960s it was at least plausible to view the world as remaining within the traditional image of world politics with its emphasis on military security. By the mid-1960s, however, the newer forces emphasized by the interdependence perspective had begun to emerge, and by the decade of the 1970s they were, if not ascendant, then certainly of no less importance than traditional security problems. The latter had by no means disappeared, for the Soviet Union's achieving of strategic parity or, by some measures, superiority to the United States meant that the context of American national security policy was profoundly changed. At the same time, however, new problems — the Arab oil embargo of 1973–1974, the persistence of global inflation, and an international economic and financial system dominated by concentrations of economic power outside the traditional framework of the industrialized world — confronted the American administration of the 1970s and early 1980s with challenges for which the lessons of the cold war seemed inappropriate (see Chapters 11, 12). Thus, the international system and American foreign policy find themselves in turbulent transition from an era of American predominance to a time of ambiguous interdependence in which the traditional possibilities of either withdrawal or hegemony no longer seem viable. We are at a historic watershed, a time not unlike the early cold war years from 1945 to 1955. It will be a time of learning . . . and possibly even greater peril.

NOTES

1. Arnold Wolfers and Lawrence W. Martin (eds.), *The Anglo American Tradition in Foreign Affairs* (New Haven, Conn.: Yale University Press, 1966), pp. xv–xvi.
2. *Washington Post,* February 5, 1973.
3. Cited by Kenneth W. Waltz, *Man, The State and War: A Theoretical Analysis* (New York: Columbia University Press, 1959), p. 159.

4. The literature on these new forces and on the notion of interdependence is fast becoming unmanageably vast. A useful introduction (and bibliographies) are found in Seyom Brown, *New Forces in World Politics* (Washington, D.C.: The Brookings Institution, 1975), and Robert O. Keohane and Joseph S. Nye, *Power and Interdependence: World Politics in Transition* (Boston: Little, Brown and Co., 1977).

5. John H. Herz, "The Rise and the Demise of the Territorial State," *World Politics,* Vol. IX, No. 4 (July 1957), pp. 473–494.

6. C. Fred Bergsten, "The Response to the Third World," *Foreign Policy,* No. 17 (Winter 1974–1975), p. 13.

7. W. Michael Blumenthal, "Steering in Crowded Waters," *Foreigns Affairs,* Vol. 56, No. 4 (July 1978), p. 729.

8. Ronald I. McKinnon, "The Eurocurrency Market," *Essays in International Finance,* No. 125 (Princeton, N.J.: International Finance Section, Department of Economics, Princeton University, December 1977), p. 1.

9. *50th Annual Report, 1979–1980,* Bank for International Settlements, 1980.

10. International bankers estimated that the Euromarket absorbed 7.8 billion "petrodollars" in the first months of 1974, whereas 4.8 billion went into sterling [Certeris Parabus] (pseudonym), "Vicious Recycling," *Foreign Policy,* No. 17 (Winter 1974–1975), p. 86.

11. *Washington Post,* January 30, 1979.

12. See Raymond Vernon's lucid summary, "Multinationals: No Strings Attached," *Foreign Policy,* No. 33 (Winter 1978–1979), pp. 121–135. See also: C. Fred Bergsten, Thomas Horst, and Theodore Moran, *American Multinationals and American Interests* (Washington, D.C.: The Brookings Institution, 1978) and Robert Gilpin, *U.S. Power and the Multinational Corporation: The Political Economy of Foreign Direct Investment* (New York: Basic Books, 1975), and the earlier and more critical Richard J. Barnett and Ronald E. Muller, *Global Reach: The Power of Multinational Corporations* (New York: Simon and Schuster, 1974).

13. Bergsten, "The Response to the Third World," p. 14.

14. Interview, *Women's Wear Daily,* November 1, 1974.

15. Henry Kissinger, *Nuclear Weapons and Foreign Policy* (New York: W. W. Norton & Company, 1969), p. 54.

16. Neil Sheehan, Hedrick Smith, E. W. Kenworth, and Fox Butterfield, *The Pentagon Papers* (as published in *The New York Times*) (New York: Bantam Books, 1971), pp. 365–371, especially documents no. 85 and 87.

17. Ibid., pp. 294–298, 340–344, 366–367, 369, 377, 392; and Richard C. Barnett, *Roots of War: The Men and Institutions Behind U.S. Foreign Policy* (Baltimore: Penguin Books, 1972), p. 104.

Chapter 1
Prelude to the
Cold War

The origins of the contemporary American view of world order can be traced to the world view of Woodrow Wilson.[1] Wilson believed that America's historic mission was to create an international society where liberal, democratic, and capitalist values of order, law, and harmony would prevail. Thus, just prior to the outbreak of World War I, Wilson identified American ideals and aspirations with those of all mankind:

> My dream is that as the years go by and the world knows more and more of America it . . . will turn to America for those moral inspirations which lie at the basis of all freedom . . . and that America will come into the full light of day when all shall know that she puts human rights above all other rights, and that her flag is the flag not only of America, but of humanity.
>
> I do not know that there will ever be a declaration of independence and of grievances for mankind, but I believe that if any such document is ever drawn it will be drawn in the spirit of the American Declaration of Independence, and that America has lifted high the light which will shine unto all generations and guide the feet of mankind to the goal of justice and liberty and peace.[2]

Yet there was another dimension of Wilson's vision of international order. To Wilson, the internal order of states was a major determinant of state behavior and, hence, world peace. If a state's domestic politics were not marked by democratic institutions and processes, then, to Wilson, that state was a potential threat to world peace. For Wilson held that states characterized by undemocratic domestic institutions almost invariably turn to aggressive behavior for the aggrandizement of their rulers or to deflect the attention of the ruled from their domestic plight. Wilson's beliefs about world politics supported an interventionist policy in two ways: First, the exceptional purity of the American purpose and power allowed America to contribute to the creation of an international order among states. But, second, the Wilsonian vision was necessarily concerned with the undemocratic internal order of those states that might become a threat to the larger international order. Both dimensions are captured in Wilson's famous statement that:

> We are glad ... to fight thus for the ultimate peace of world and for the liberation of its peoples ... for the rights of nations great and small and the privilege of men everywhere to choose their way of life and of obedience. The world must be made safe for democracy. Its peace must be planted upon the tested foundations of political liberty.[3]

There is, however, an important paradox in this vision. People were "to choose their way of life and obedience," but there was the strong implication that unless the outcome of this act of self-determination conformed to Wilsonian standards, intervention would follow. How could it be otherwise if one believed that those "moral inspirations which lie at the basis of all freedom" were somehow uniquely American? Denial of what was to Wilson a self-evident truth necessarily placed the offending state in the camp of the enemy. Wilson, moreover, was prepared to use force in pursuit and potection of his vision. In the case of the Mexican intervention in 1916 and again in World War I, Wilson fought — presumably for some higher notion of the "ultimate peace." And in his conception of the League of Nations after World War I, force was deemed essential to the maintenance of world order.[4] Only now it was to be the "concerted force of the combined action of mankind through the instrumentality of all the enlightened governments of the world."[5] But through all the rhetoric, one assumption remained constant and unchallenged: "the tested foundations of political liberty" were self-evident, and they were "drawn in the spirit of the American Declaration of Independence." To deny this — to deny that America's flag was indeed "the flag of humanity" — marked a state as one of the unenlightened and hence the legitimate target of intervention.

The Soviet view of international politics and Russia's place in the international system that emerged from the Bolshevik Revolution in 1917 challenged Wilson's vision. Indeed, it threatened the very foundations of that vision. Yet, curiously, Lenin's understanding of world politics paralleled some features of American foreign policy. For instance, the Leninist view of world politics carried traces of the traditional Russian sense of mission, which was similar to the American and Wilsonian vision. The sixteenth-century idea of Moscow as a "third Rome" and the nineteenth-century Pan-Slavic movement both saw Russia as possessing a destiny and a duty larger than the mere frontiers of Great Russia. The *Weltanschauung* of the new Soviet leaders, however, was also in sharp contrast to the values of Wilson. Where Wilson viewed consensus as the natural scheme of things, Marxism saw class conflict as the path of social and political development. Where democracy was seen in the liberal tradition as a means for giving expression to the people at large, Marxists thought democracy in the West but an expression of dominant economic/class interest.

Lenin, moreover, felt that his regime was not secure while capitalist values flourished in Europe. He and his followers felt that European leaders would be profoundly hostile to a Soviet Russia. The Soviet Union stood for social revolution; the West stood for orderly progress. As the West questioned the very validity of the political, moral, and intellectual foundation of the Soviet state, the Soviets denied the validity of the Western order. Furthermore, Lenin and his followers believed that the West would attempt, in Churchill's simile, to strangle the Soviet infant in its crib (he called it a "monster"); and therefore the best protection for the October Revolution was an expanding system of states based on the revolutionary principles propounded by the Bolsheviks. As Lenin said in March 1919:

> We live not only in a state, but in a system of states, and the existence of the Soviet Republic side by side with the imperialist states for a prolonged period of time is unthinkable. In the meantime a series of frightful collisions will occur.[6]

Wilson's reaction to the Bolsheviks was predictable in terms of these contradictory world views — they had established, he felt, an illegitimate government. As Wilson proclaimed in July 1919, "The men who ... control ... the affairs of Russia represent nobody but themselves. ... They have no mandate from anybody. ... [A] group of men more cruel than the Czar himself is controlling the destinies of that great people."[7] The loathing of the West for the kind of regime that had come to power in 1917 was intensified by Lenin's successful extrication of Russia from World War I and Trotsky's negotiation of a quick peace favorable to the Germans. The most fundamental source of Wilson's antipathy, however, was the communist vision of humanity's political, economic, and social order that emerged from the revolution of 1917. Wilson therefore sought to interpose American military and economic power against the communists even as they, and all of Russia, were engulfed in civil war.

INTERVENTION IN
THE RUSSIAN CIVIL WAR

Some 70,000 Czechoslovakian soldiers,[8] deserters from the Austrian army, were left in the Soviet Union after the Bolsheviks signed the Treaty of Brest-Litovsk ending hostilities with the Germans. The Czechs, though isolated in Siberia, retained their discipline and organization and represented an important organized military force in Russia during the chaotic civil war that followed the revolution and Russia's departure from World War I. The plight of the Czechs helped fuel anti-Bolshevik sentiment in the West and served as a rationalization for Wilson to contribute to the intervention by Allied troops ostensibly to aid the Czechs to reach the European front. But the Czechs had been joined by Russian anti-Bolshevik forces, so the decision to intervene was known to support the anti-Bolshevik factions in the Russian civil war. In Wilson's words, the intervention would "steady any efforts of the Russians at self-defense, or the establishment of law and order."[9] Such "self-defense" assistance to aid the Russians regain "self-government" left little doubt that the dispatch of troops to help the brave Czechs who had attracted so much attention would also buttress anti-Bolshevik factions.

In the end there were two American interventions in alliance with the British and French, who were as appalled by initial Bolshevik successes as Wilson. One was in European Russia, in the North, above the Arctic Circle. In the summer of 1918, 5000 men went to Murmansk and Archangel in order to see that the vast Allied stores of war goods might not fall into German hands. The American troops were to join an Allied expedition that had already battled Bolshevik troops in an attempt to gain authority over the two important port cities. On arrival, the American troops, plagued by dysentery, confused leadership, and clothing ill-suited for the harsh climate, were placed in the position of defending White Russians and breakaway Bolsheviks against Lenin's regime. As temperatures fell to –50°F and casualties rose to over 500, the Americans neared mutiny.[10] A second American troop contingent entered Siberia in 1918 at just about the same time that the troops destined for Murmansk and Archangel had arrived. There were over 9000 men in Siberia under the command of General Graves, who divided his loathing for Russian politicians equally between Whites and Bolsheviks. The American presence in Siberia was related to Japanese designs on Siberia.[11] But once American troops were in place in Siberia, their presence tended to favor the reactionary anticommunist forces. Indeed, the Russian embassy in Washington, representing the Russian provisional White government, campaigned vigorously to get the American people to support the intervention including sending speakers on tour in the United States and even suggesting logistics to the State Department.[12]

The Intervention and Its Consequences

Although Wilson reached his decision to intervene in the Soviet Union because of his wider image of American interests, he had support from large sections of public opinion. When the Bolsheviks seized power, "most Americans reacted as if the impossible had happened."[13] The Bolsheviks were considered, in Secretary of State Lansing's words, a "usurping gang" of lunatics, anarchists, and Jews. Since they were considered illegitimate in every sense by Americans, it was generally predicted that they would not last. In one study by Walter Lippmann, the demise of Soviet rule was predicted 91 times in the years from 1917 to 1919.[14] If the impossible had happened, it was comfortable to predict that it would soon cease happening. The villification of the new regime in the press was intense. The *Saturday Evening Post* was typical. It editorialized that German despotism was at least practiced by an elite. But Bolshevism was a "despotism by all the lowest."[15] The Bolsheviks came to be characterized as veritable freaks and monsters. *The New York Times,* for instance, reported that in Soviet areas, every eighteen-year-old girl had to register at a "bureau of free love" and was then given a husband without her consent.[16]

Thus American involvement in the intervention had enormous consequences domestically. It froze American attitudes toward the Soviet Union into a kind of hostility that can only be described as bizarre. The famous journalist Lincoln Steffens wrote privately that "Bolshevism means chaos, wholesale murder, the complete destruction of civilization."[17] Senator Myers of Montana spoke for many Americans:

> They have utterly destroyed marriage, the home, the fireside, the family, the cornerstones of all civilization, all society. They have undertaken to destroy what God created and ordained. They defy alike the will of God, the precepts of Christianity, the decrees of civilization, the customs of society. It is hard to realize that such things exist and are tolerated by the civilized world.[18]

The atheism of Bolsheviks repulsed the vast majority of Americans. The influential *Literary Digest* reported that the Soviet government had sponsored ceremonies in which young men dressed as devils and danced about bonfires containing effigies of Jesus, Moses, and Mohammed.[19]

It is important to note the degree of isolation and disruption the Soviets experienced in this period. Its only port, Petrograd, was blockaded by the Allies; foreign trade was reduced to smuggling. Even gold was embargoed. In 1919, the only foreign official in the Soviet Union was a Danish representative of the Red Cross.[20] It is not, therefore, hard to see how the intervention confirmed the suspicion of the Bolsheviks that the West was implacably hostile to the Soviet regime. The nature of these interventions and America's involvement in them are well remembered by Soviet historians. Yet they are all but ignored by Western scholarship.

The scholarly former ambassador to the Soviet Union, George Kennan, confessed that he did not understand the reasons for the contempt and resentment borne by the early Bolsheviks toward the Western powers, until he unearthed the details in his own research.[21]

In the American and Allied intervention, Lenin and the Bolsheviks saw the fulfillment of the communist prophecy of capitalist enmity and aggression. It did not matter that Wilson's aims in the intervention, although undeniably anti-Bolshevik, were pursued with some reluctance. The Americans were clearly part of the range of forces arrayed against the Bolsheviks. Huge sums of money were spent on this adventure. But its cost continued to mount long after Western troops had left. Very probably this intervention aided the coup d'etat of October 1917 in becoming a permanent regime, for as the Russian civil war and the intervention coalesced, the communist leaders played the role of national leaders fighting foreigners. During the struggle, the communists were able to forge an army, a police force, and a party apparatus that enabled them to expand on a very weak base. This power was to become so early entrenched that very soon the Soviet regime was able to undergo the tremendous strain of social transformation under the brutal leadership of Stalin. And the early isolation and encirclement of the new communist state became absorbed in the Soviet mentality. The heroic theme of being subjected to the onslaught of world capitalism and repulsing it was a useful forge on which to build the foundatons of a new Soviet order.

The intervention failed, but it did not fail because the West did not possess superior strength. Clearly it did. Rather the cost of imposing a Western solution was disproportionate to any immediate security interest. Western troops in the Russian intervention never quite understood what their purpose was, and they were several times near mutiny. By mid-1919 outraged parents who had sent their sons to fight the Kaiser caught the ear of Congress, and the troops were withdrawn. But the expansive Wilsonian values of world order based on a comprehensive political capitalism had already contributed much to what would come to the cold war. Wilsonian policy was a precursor of the ideologically motivated decisions of later years and later administrations and, as such, forms the opening phrases of the dialogue of distrust that characterizes the cold war.

Nonrecognition

Throughout the 1920s Soviet-American relations were frozen by an American policy of nonrecognition of the communist regime. Wilson's secretary of state, Bainbridge Colby, explained:

the existing regime in Russia is based upon . . . the negation of every principle of honor and good faith upon which it is possible to base . . . relations. . . .
[S]pokesmen of this power have declared . . . the maintenance of their role
depends . . . upon the occurrence of revolutions in all other great civilized
nations . . . and set up Bolshevist rule in their stead . . . [w]ith a Power whose
conceptions of international relations are so entirely alien . . . so utterly
repugnant . . . we cannot hold official relations.[22]

The United States pressed for Soviet acknowledgment of Czarist
debts. It was clear, however, that the Soviet conception of world order and
the internal regime of states were the dominant bones of contention. Even
as Russia experienced a terrible famine in the spring and summer of 1921,
the emergency relief organized by Secretary of Commerce Herbert
Hoover was tied to preconditions. "It was his view that the Allies should
insist, as a part of the price [for food] . . . the West should insist that the
Bolsheviki cease hostilities against their opponents in Russia and stop
their propaganda abroad."[23] These conditions, concluded George Kennan, although "moderate and reasonable" would be such as to place
before the Soviet government the choice of falling in with general Western desideratum or accepting the onus of denying food to the Russian
people.[24]

The menace of communism waned as Lenin died and Stalin broke
with Trotsky over, in the dictator's words "the idiotic slogan, 'The World
Revolution.' "[25] To Secretary Kellogg, however, lurid reports of Soviet
activity in China, Britain, and the beginnings of Latin American revolutions purported to be Soviet inspired were sufficient cause for restricting
contact with the Bolshevik regime. Thus, in spite of the emerging "peace
offensive" of Soviet foreign minister Litvinov and the expulsion of Trotsky,
the Russians were not invited to sign the Kellogg-Briand agreement,
which outlawed war as an instrument of state relations.

Only global economic depression brought the United States to a reversal of more than a decade of nonrecognition. In 1933, it appeared to
many Americans that Russia offered some economic solace for the depres-
sion-ridden economy. Litvinov was reportedly talking of placing orders of
over an incredible billion dollars with the West.[26] Whereas American
editors appeared five to one to oppose recognition in 1931, a poll in late
1933 showed editors almost three to one favoring relations.[27] There were
objections when Roosevelt and Litvinov exchanged terms of agreement
in November of 1933; but the view of most Americans had become, according to the *Literary Digest,* an agnostic willingness to "see how it all
works out."[28]

THE COMING OF WORLD WAR II

American and especially Western European cooperation with the Soviet regime never moved beyond these tentative contacts. The United States remained preoccupied with the Depression, and the Europeans, especially the British, persisted in a distrustful, even hostile ambivalence toward Stalin. Nowhere was this posture more evident and with greater consequence than regarding the rise of Adolf Hitler in Germany.

Stalin was initially ambivalent — perhaps believing that Hitler was not much more than the anti-Western "national socialist" he (Hitler) proclaimed himself to be. Moreover, Hitler's natural adversaries in Germany, the Social Democrats, were not pro-Soviet in their sentiments. Indeed, they seemed sympathetic to similar regimes in the West, thereby raising the possibility of a formidable alliance against Russia. Stalin was, therefore, passive if not actually supportive of the Nazi's destruction of the Social Democrats.

It became increasingly difficult to ignore, however, that the Nazis were a real menace to the Soviet Union. German officials had begun advocating giving Germany "space for the settlement of its vigorous race" in Russia where "war, revolution and internal decay had made a beginning" and must be stopped.[29] Words like these and the increasing militarization of Germany led Stalin to seek allies in the West, as in the France-Russia mutual assistance treaty in 1935. Furthermore, when the Spanish civil war broke out in 1936, Stalin attempted to enlist the West in aiding the left Republican forces against the fascists led by Franco and equipped by the Italians and Germans. Stalin's intervention in the Spanish civil war resulted, in part, from communist ideology; but Stalin also sought to induce Britain and France to intervene and thus join in containing Germany. The British, however, feared antagonizing the fascists and hoped for a Western settlement that would, by implication, have thrown Hitler against the East and Russia. The unsuccessful effort to enlist the West to aid antifascist forces in Spain and the emerging Western policy of appeasement convinced Stalin that he should make preparations to deal independently with Hitler.[30] For it was not clear if collective security would tempt the West; neither was it apparent that Hitler would be interested in a deal; thus, in Kennan's view, Stalin's diplomacy was increasingly one of "watchful waiting."[31]

Further evidence of Russia's isolation was recorded in Moscow when Hitler moved on Austria in March 1938, raising an obvious security threat to Central Europe. However, France declined to consult with its nominal ally, Russia. Hitler next denounced the Czech government as a staging area for Bolshevism in Central Europe, and charged that Germans living in Czechoslovakia were being oppressed by the Czechs. But when the Soviets urged a multilateral "firm and unambiguous stand," Neville Chamberlain, the British prime minister, told the House of Commons that such a "mutual undertaking" was unacceptable because it would handicap the British government's freedom to maneuver. Paris and London seemed more interested in accommodating themselves to a German plan for partitioning the Czech state than in entertaining the Russian suggestion of concerted resistance to German expansion, perhaps through the machinery of the League of Nations. Only when Hitler demanded an "international guarantee" of the new Czech boundaries and German occupation of Czechoslovakian districts did Chamberlain become alarmed. But his response was a continuation of past policy.

"How horrible, fantastic and incredible," he told a British radio audience, that "we should be digging trenches and trying on gas masks here because of a quarrel in a far-away country between people of whom we know nothing."[32] Hitler gave respite to Chamberlain by inviting him, the French, and Mussolini to confer at Munich. The Czechs and the Soviets were noticeable by their absence even as Chamberlain agreed to all of Hitler's demands. The Soviets protested the Munich aggreements as "monstrous," knowing that the remaining Czech state would be a virtually indefensible vassal of Hitler. The British prime minister knew, however, that the Munich settlement pointed Hitler eastward, and he declared that the agreement signaled "peace in out time."[33]

When, in March of the next year, the German army moved to occupy all of Czechoslovakia, Chamberlain finally became aroused. Chamberlain had staked his reputation on divining the dark corners of Hitler's mind; but now he was convinced that he would have to be more forceful. When it appeared that Poland would be the next victim of Hitler's aggression, Chamberlain, together with the French, guaranteed Polish independence. The Poles, however, did not want the Soviets included in this declaration, harboring an historic anti-Russian and, now, an anticommunist orientation. However, the exclusion of Russia once more from Western security arrangements was hardly encouraging to Moscow and moved Stalin to pursue actively his own arrangement with Hitler. His short-run objectives were not unlike those of Lenin at the end of World War I — to gain a territorial buffer in Eastern Europe and hence, time.

Russia initiated feelers to Germany while continuing attempts to make security arrangements with the West. Stalin's widely reported statement, in the early spring of 1939, that the Soviet Union would not "pull somebody else's chestnut out of the fire" was also intended to indicate that he was still available to the West but that he was open to an agreement with the Germans.[34] In May, London and Paris languidly made an overture to Moscow to discuss a tripartite security pact. But the formula submitted for negotiation contained such caveats as excluding the invasion of the Baltic states by Germany as sufficient cause for France and England coming to the aid of the Soviet Union.[35] On the other hand, Russian demands for transit rights through Poland in the event of war were understandably rejected by the Poles, and the talks stalemated. Moreover, it was known that Stalin was now in formal contact with Hitler. In sum, it might be said, the Allies were less than forthcoming and the Russian negotiating style was ponderous and opaque as Stalin sought to extract the best terms possible from the negotiations.

Finally, in the last days of August 1939, the courtship of the West ended. Stalin gave up on the possibilities of an Anglo-French alliance. There followed a startling and cynical Soviet reversal as Stalin wired Hitler to send his Foreign Minister Ribbentrop to Moscow, where a Nazi-Soviet pact was announced and the Anglo-French mission sent home. Through the agreement Hitler sought to dissuade the West from standing by Poland, now wedged between the so-called German and Soviet allies. This was, of course, Hitler's major miscalculation — the miscalculation that brought on the war. In the short run, however, he had prevented the Soviet opposition to his pending move into Poland. The price was a Soviet sphere of influence in Eastern Poland and Soviet control of the Baltic states under the guise of Moscow as their guarantor. In addition, the two dictators agreed that the Balkan states were to be viewed in a disinterested manner. To the extent that Stalin believed that Hitler would allow him a free hand in this area, he miscalculated as grievously as Hitler concerning Western intentions. In the meantime, however, Stalin now felt that he had bought time to prepare for any future German aggression whether the West assisted or not.

The degree of animosity in the West stemming from the blinding shock of the cynical Nazi-Soviet pact cancelled whatever marginal improvement of Soviet-Western relations might have been garnished by the Litvinov period of diplomacy. The Russians were blamed, with justification, for encouraging the Nazi attack on Poland that brought on the full measure of World War II. Finally, the image of a cynical Soviet Union was fixed in the Western mind — an image that was confirmed as Stalin hastily embarked on a course of strategic consolidation that involved the occupation of the Baltic states of Latvia, Lithuania, and Estonia. Similar moves were initiated against Rumania (with the consent of the Nazis) as well as a clumsy invasion of Finland. By November of 1940, Stalin was demanding of Hitler formal recognition of Soviet control of these areas. No doubt Stalin was buoyed by the success of the British in the battle of Britain and the possibility that the Germans would be preoccupied in the West until well into 1941. Stalin probably figured that even if Hitler, not wanting to fight on two fronts, would not concede a Southeastern European buffer to the Soviets, the Germans would at least proceed cautiously with their claims in the area. But Stalin miscalculated. For instead of continuing the air assault on Britain, Hitler turned to planning a strike on Britain's Mediterranean lifelines. This stratagem required German pressure in the Balkans and an absence there of Hitler's ally, the Russians. By attempting to give himself more of a buffer in the Balkans, Stalin may have hastened Hitler's preparation of his attack on the Soviet Union, which eventually came in 1941.

Soviet policy was now in disarray as Stalin and Russia suffered the consequences of a massively destructive attack on the Soviet Union by his ally Hitler. A second consequence was that Stalin was thrown back into yet another alliance of necessity, this time with the West.

The German attack on Russia in the spring of 1941 was greeted with disbelief by the Russians and relief by the West, especially the British, who had stood alone since the collapse of continental resistance after Dunkirk. Roosevelt's personal reaction to the German attack on Russia was equally unambiguous. He was delighted, and told Churchill that he would support "any announcement that the Prime Minister might make welcoming Russia as an ally."[36] But Roosevelt's policy had considerable opposition in the American government, especially among the Foreign Service officers who had watched the unpleasant paroxysm induced by Stalin's purges in the 1930s and did not want to be associated in the same moral universe as Stalin.[37] Nevertheless, Roosevelt promised more than $1.5 million to Russia by the fall of 1941, and by November had succeeded in the not inconsiderable feat of moving a balky bureaucracy and garnishing Congressional consent to the extension of "lend-lease" aid to Russia.[38] In his letter to the lend-lease administration Roosevelt confirmed that "the defense of the Union of Soviet Socialist Republics is vital to the defense of the United States."[39]

One might conclude from such rhetoric that the emergence of the common enemy in the spring of 1941 was a sufficient basis for overriding the dismal history of distrust of the previous 25 years. In important respects, however, Russia and the West were never joined in alliance during the war. They fought a common enemy simultaneously, and tens of millions of dollars in assistance and material were extended to the Russians by the West. But when we turn to the diplomacy of East-West interactions during the war, we find a continuation of the misunderstandings and real differences that separated Russia and the West before Hitler struck across the Niemen in June 1941. George Kennan has noted that Stalin's objectives and diplomacy during the war were consistent with his efforts before

1941 in that he sought from his new allies what he had sought from Hitler: Soviet influence and control in Eastern Europe and the Balkans.[40] But during World War II also, Stalin's efforts to construct and gain legitimacy for a Soviet presence in Middle Europe were resisted by the West. These same questions preoccupied Stalin after World War II, and Western resistance to Soviet consolidation of their objectives in Europe was to be the central politico-strategic issue of the early cold war.

CONFLICTING STRATEGIC CONCEPTS

The slaughter of World War I seared the memories of the British. They had lost a generation in Flanders, the Marne, and the Somme in a ghoulish holocaust that drained Britain's treasury and enervated its society. A repetition of such sacrifice would not be countenanced by Churchill. He favored, not surprisingly, the use of Britain as if it were a massive aircraft carrier to launch Allied bombers at German industry. Indeed, 50 percent of British production was allocated to the bomber command. Yet he knew that wars are won and lost on the ground.[41] At the first meeting of the combined Chiefs of Staff, Churchill presented his view of a gradual encirclement of Germany; then, when Germany was bled white, the last dagger would be inserted in a continental assault from the west. Churchill pushed for a landing in French North Africa in cooperation with a large American expedition. He also requested that three American divisions be stationed in Northern Ireland as reserves. Germany was to be engaged at a distance in 1942, in a classic grid that guarded historic British interest in the Mediterranean and India while eventually wrestling the weakened Germans to defeat.[42]

Churchill's attention to the periphery of battle was prompted by the bogey of a Japanese-German division of India and the Middle East as a mortal peril, "a measureless disaster."[43] But his strategy of empire was based on a peculiar analogy between the monumental sea power of nineteenth-century Britain and the beleaguered island it had become in the twentieth. In Churchill's mind, the continent was to do its own fighting, as had been British policy in the Napoleonic wars. What was now a difficult point to be reckoned with was the arming of partisans, most of whom were disciplined leftists, on the continent. Armed social revolutionaries and the march of Russia to mid-Europe naturally favored forces inhospitable to British interest; whereas Britain of days past could prevail at the end of a war with a policy of closing the ring, in the twentieth century, it would be severely disadvantaged.

The American military opposed this strategy. General George Marshall thought that Churchill's policy was fraught with risk and was never convinced that the Russians could withstand Hitler unaided by Allied reinforcements. Furthermore, if the Russian army of 8 million was defeated, then the war would be lost. Even if the Russian army withstood the formidable Wehrmacht, Marshall believed that the war would drag on until 1944 or 1945 if a second front were not launched, and the result would be higher, not lower, Allied costs. Therefore, Marshall's plan involved a major buildup in Britain during 1942 and an assault on Europe from England in 1943.

Clearly, these two conceptions of how to proceed with the war were incompatible. It fell to Roosevelt to resolve the issue, for it could only be with American assistance that any strategy would succeed. Roosevelt's decision was in favor of the British concept, thus the invasion of Europe was deferred. Among the factors influencing Roosevelt were his views concerning the as yet incomplete American mobilization and also the inevitability of very high casualties resulting from a frontal assault on the German's continental bastion. Moreover, the British simply refused to participate in any attack upon the continent in 1942. The Russo-German theater of the war remained, therefore, disconnected from the Anglo-American engagement of German power on the periphery of Europe for more than 2 years. However, eventual Soviet victory in the struggle between the two former totalitarian allies was to be the central factor in the postwar configuration of power in Middle Europe. The nature of the victory no doubt intensified Soviet conviction that they alone should structure politically and economically what had been largely their conquest of the eastern portion of the Nazi empire. In the meantime, the issue of Anglo-American assistance to the Soviets by way of a second front poisoned East-West diplomacy.

The Issue of the Second Front

Even before Pearl Harbor, when Britain was weathering a furious air onslaught, Stalin pressed Churchill to open a second front. Churchill turned the pleas aside,[44] perhaps believing that Russia could not hold out, and that a second front would make little sense if he had to face the full might of the German army alone. British Military Intelligence concurred with the German estimates that Russia would be beaten before the famous Russian winter set in. The Germans had fielded 175 divisions and soon raised the number to 232. But they had badly miscalculated; for although Germany gave an initial appearance of success, it was more apparent than real. Hitler's supply lines were badly extended; and when the Russians stood their ground and mobilized remarkable numbers, German casualties assumed staggering proportions. Stalin had defied German General Staff estimates that gave the Soviets 8 weeks. Nevertheless, the Russian situation was grave. On September 15, 1941, Stalin had requested twenty-five or thirty British divisions and suggested Archangel or Iran as access points. Churchill still considered the subject absurd and avoided replying. By October the Germans stood at the bus stops in the outer suburbs of Moscow only 5 miles from the city center.[45] The effect of the initial joyous proclamation of Churchill that the British and Russians were partners in the same glorious enterprise was shaken. But a number of factors conjoined to vitiate the effect of Churchill's obvious reluctance to commit troops to the Russians. First, the vicious Russian winter overtook German troops ill equipped for temperatures that reached 40° below.[46] Second, the Western allies committed themselves to substantial military aid for the Soviets by the middle of the next year.[47] Finally, the Japanese attack on Pearl Harbor and the consolidation of their conquests in Southeast Asia diverted their attention from the Soviet's Asian front and allowed for the transfer of Russian forces to the European front.

Perhaps as important, Roosevelt did not have the abiding dislike of the Soviets that Churchill maintained. He had initiated the first American diplomatic overture to Russia in 1933 and believed that his own personal winning charm could bridge great historic and ideological cleavages. He wrote somewhat arrogantly to Churchill, "I know you will not mind my being brutally frank when I tell you I think I can personally handle Stalin better than either your Foreign Office or my State Department. Stalin hates the guts of all your top people. He thinks he likes me better, and I hope he will continue to do so."[48] Nor did Roosevelt have the same history of anti-Bolshevik efforts and statements that had motivated Churchill since his days as First Lord of the Admiralty in World War I. While many Americans shared Senator Harry Truman's view, "If we see that Germany is winning we ought to help Russia and if Russia is winning, we ought to help Germany and that way let them kill as many as possible . . .,"[49] Roosevelt had somewhat daringly proclaimed: "I think the Russians are perfectly friendly; they aren't trying to gobble up all the rest of Europe or the world."[50]

On the other hand, Churchill's conception of how to proceed with the war ultimately won over Roosevelt; hence the United States was inevitably a target of Soviet distrust during and after the war as a result of the issue of the second front. This distrust was deepened by what must have appeared to the Russians to have been Churchillian duplicity in 1942. When Molotov came to Washington in May 1942, he had elicited a joint declaration that "full understanding was reached with regard to the urgent task of creating a second front in Europe in 1942."[51] Churchill reluctantly endorsed this document and handed Molotov a memorandum that claimed that Britain was "making preparations for a landing on the continent in August or September, 1942."[52] In these same conversations with Molotov, he assured the Soviets that 1.5 million Anglo-American troops would be in Europe by May 1943. But by July of 1942, the British had vetoed the idea of a second front in 1942 in favor of a North African followed by an Italian invasion. Marshall and Admiral King threatened to resign; Eisenhower feared that a North Africa campaign would "not materially assist the Russians in time to save them,"[53] and concluded that this decision could go down as "the blackest day in history."[54]

Roosevelt, understandably, suggested that Churchill himself relate the change of plans to Stalin.[55] Churchill complained, "It was like carrying a large lump of ice to the North Pole."[56] Stalin was predictably furious. Churchill again promised that there would be a second front in 1943. But Stalin was skeptical and claimed to an associate after Churchill's departure, "A campaign in Africa, Italy . . . they want us bled white in order to dictate to us their terms later on . . . They hope that we shall lose Stalingrad and lose the springboard for an offensive."[57]

The landings in North Africa allowed, by Stalin's estimate, more than 27 German divisions — confident that the Allies would not invade that year in Europe — to move to the Eastern front.[58] By Churchill's own embarrassed estimate in early 1943, the West was engaged with, at the most, 12 German divisions, the Russians with 185.[59] The net effect of the North African campaign was to limit the amount of material that could be conveyed to the Soviet Union and increase Soviet suspicions of the West. The dollar value, for instance, of lend-lease shipments to the USSR in the first 6 months of 1943 was 20 percent below the figure for the last 6 months of 1942.[60] The rearrangement of manufacturing in preparation for the desert campaign cut into the production of landing craft and artillery shells, prerequisites for a large landing in France, and the West did not regain their 1942 production levels for this materiel until 1944. In short, the North African campaign precluded a landing in France in 1943 as had been promised, and instead, moved Anglo-American military attention to Italy and the Balkans.

Stalin was enraged. He noted that there was not a single German division in France of any value, a fact confirmed by British Intelligence. The German policy was to station those in the West who suffered disabilities and could not be sent East.[61] Against this rather motley effluvia of the German war machine, Churchill unconvincingly related to Stalin that the British guns and aircraft were keeping the "Germans pinned in Pas de

Calais" across the English Channel.[62] Stalin's lack of appreciation was evident in his reply: "That, I hope, does not imply a renunciation of your Moscow promise to open a second front in Western Europe in the spring of 1943."[63] But the North African campaign could not lead to a landing in France as the West had promised. Instead, the invasion was directed at Italy by the way of Sicily. In spite of the fact that, as the Joint Chiefs had pointed out, the North African campaign precluded an invasion of Europe via France,[64] it was still claimed that a cross-channel attack would be launched "as soon as practicable."

The Anglo-American decision to move into Italy was not, in fact, considered as an effort to relieve Soviet absorption of the majority of German firepower. As Eisenhower noted, the decision to invade Italy might knock the Italians out of the war, but "the difficulty of attacking Germany through the mountainous areas of her southern and southwestern borders was obvious."[65] Stalin understood this: "Fully realizing the importance of Sicily, I must, however, point out that it cannot replace a second front in France." The net result of the landings in Sicily and southern Italy was an early Italian surrender; but the Germans stayed on doggedly in central and northern Italy, and the Allies were bogged down in Italy for almost 2 more years.

Also, at this point, a sharp increase in German submarine activities occurred in the Atlantic. Churchill proposed and Roosevelt concurred that convoys be cancelled for March 1943 and, with some hesitation, Churchill notified Stalin. Convoys, he told Stalin, might resume in September, but shipments would be continued and increased by a southern route. The problem, Stalin answered, was that the southern route had very small clearance capacity and lengthy transport.[66] It was, he said, "catastrophic." Finally, after a Washington meeting in May 1943 between Churchill and Roosevelt, the president sent a message in which was placed in the next to the last paragraph a fateful message, "Under the present plans there should be a sufficiently large concentration of men and material in the British Isles in the spring of 1944 to permit a full-scale invasion of the continent at that time."[67]

The invasion of France would not come until June 1944, less than one year before the war ended and well after a Russian victory in Central Europe became inevitable. Of more immediate importance, it would not come until the Russians were convinced that it was Allied policy to bleed them white. The Allies, for their part, saw themselves as moving with all prudent speed. The gap in mutual perceptions became an open breach by late 1943 as Stalin withdrew his ambassadors from London and Washington.

Fears of a Separate Peace

Exacerbating the distrust generated by the second front issue were persistent rumors and occasional indications that one side or another would seek a separate peace with Hitler. Stalin may have deliberately manipulated the situation in his eagerness to encourage more Anglo-American assistance. On the other hand, in view of the Molotov-Ribbentrop Non-Aggression Pact, one can understand that the Americans and British were not prepared to place the best interpretation on Soviet maneuvering. Furthermore, during 1942 and 1943 there were reported low-level contacts between German and Soviet agents concerning a break-off in the fighting and some form of frontier agreement. And in June 1943, according to some historians, a meeting of Soviet Foreign Minister Molotov and Ribbentrop was held behind German lines to discuss a separate peace and the postwar Russian-Polish frontier.[68] However, all talks were broken off in late 1943 after the Soviet successes at Stalingrad and then at Kursk had signaled the beginning of the Soviet offensive that would end the war in the East.

From the Soviet standpoint, the most suspicious developments were at the end of the war when German, British, and American intelligence and military officers met in early 1945 in Berne, Switzerland, to negotiate the surrender of remaining German troops in Italy. The talks expanded to include all German troops in Western Europe. However, the Russians were not invited to these talks, and they reached the conclusion that the Western Allies were conspiring with the Germans so as to allow rapid movement of Anglo-American forces to the East. The American ambassador to Moscow, Averell Harriman, counseled against letting the talks be broadened. Harriman, with long bitter experience in negotiating with Russians, thought that such a stand would teach the Russians a salutary lesson that they could not always get what they asked for.[69]

Churchill, himself, was later to admit that these talks treaded close to actual negotiations. But Allen Dulles (John Foster Dulles's brother, former head of OSS and CIA), in his memoirs, *Secret Surrender,* while confirming Churchill's observation, also notes that the full extent of these conversations was not at all clear to Roosevelt.[70] Roosevelt, faced with harsh Soviet suspicions, promised that if details of a surrender were talked about, then Soviet leaders would be invited. These were, he emphasized, preliminary discussions and not negotiations. Roosevelt's rationale in refusing the Russians a place came largely from the Joint Chiefs of Staff, who argued that bringing the Russians in would introduce "into what is almost entirely a military matter an unavoidable political element." Roosevelt concurred, fearing that the presence of Soviet officers would unduly discourage German willingness to lay down their arms.[71] Stalin complained, however, that these talks had already allowed the Germans to move three divisions from Italy to the eastern front. Moveover, Stalin wrote:

> My military colleagues . . . are sure negotiations did take place . . . and that they ended in an agreement . . . to open the Front to the Anglo-American troops and let them move east. . . . If the contrary were the case the exclusion . . . of the Soviet command . . . would be explicable.[72]

Roosevelt responded with "astonishment." "Frankly," he said, "I cannot avoid a feeling of bitter resentment toward your informers, whoever they are, for such vile misrepresentations of my actions or those of my trusted subordinates."[73] Nevertheless, Russian fear of a separate peace or settlement primarily or even exclusively beneficial to the West ran throughout the war and was particularly intense at the end of the war. Soviet suspicions intensified and poisoned the atmosphere in which important substantive issues were coming to a head, most notably the inter-related questions of Eastern Europe and the postwar disposition of Germany. In the disputes surrounding these political and strategic issues we find the immediate antecedents to the cold war.

POLAND AND EASTERN EUROPE: THE TURN TOWARD COLD WAR

Eastern Europe and Poland were the incubus in which old distrusts festered. The issue of Poland was, perhaps, the most critical in the wartime and immediate postwar dialogue between the West and the Soviet Union. Poland provided the sharpest challenge to Allied unity because of the seemingly unreconcilable ambitions and interests — a conflict that anticipated and contributed to what was to follow.

The Poles had suffered great privations under the Tsars and Soviets. They had suffered partition, absorption, and various efforts at colonization and, of course, the Soviets had attempted to extinguish Poland in league with the Nazis in the Molotov-Ribbentrop pact. In the West, sympathy was high for the Poles; many refugee Poles fought bravely with the English, and about 20 percent of the pilots who fought the battle of Britain were Polish.[74] Moreover, the Polish-Americans of American cities were an influential minority that merited considerable attention in American electoral politics. For example, there were and are more Polish-speaking persons in Chicago than in Warsaw, and more Polish radio stations and newspapers in the United States than in Poland.

Conflicting Soviet and Western Perspectives

For the Americans at the end of the war, the Polish question had become a symbol of Soviet-Western cooperation.[75] It was, said Harry Hopkins, an issue that "was not important in itself," but he recognized a moral commitment of the West to the Poles and its relation to American domestic politics.

The Soviet's claims in Poland had an entirely different justification. As Stalin noted:

> In the course of twenty-five years the Germans twice invaded Russia via Poland ... These invasions were not warfare but like incursions of the Huns. ... Germany had been able to do this because Poland had been regarded as part of the *cordon sanitaire* around the Soviet Union and that previous European policy had been that Polish governments must be hostile to Russia. In these circumstances either Poland had been too weak to oppose Germany or had let the Germans come through ... Poland's weakness and hostility had been a great source of weakness to the Soviet Union and had permitted the Germans to do what they wished in the East and also the West. ... It is therefore in Russia's vital interest that Poland should be both strong and friendly.[76]

Thus the postwar political future and territorial configuration of Poland was a central concern of Russian wartime diplomacy. In November 1941, in early communications with Churchill, Stalin suggested that one of the aims of the war should be that Germany forever be prevented from provoking aggression. To this end, he suggested that the West recognize the 1941 Polish frontier with Russia. If this were confirmed, he suggested, Poland would be compensated with a piece of partitioned Prussia.

The early Soviet insistence on a different geography for Poland also strained their delicate, newly formed relationship with the London-based Polish government in exile. The London Polish government was recognized by the Soviet Union in July 1941, but the London Poles were in a precarious position. Except for whatever influence they might have with the English or Americans, they were practically powerless. Moreover, the English were less than completely supportive, as the Polish question stood between the Soviets and the British in reaching other understandings and was therefore something of an embarrassment. As Churchill notes rather delicately, "We had the invidious responsibility of recommending [that the London Poles] rely on Soviet good faith in the future settlement of Russian-Polish relations. ... "[77] Yet the Poles refused tenaciously to yield to the Russians their eastern territories. They harbored little good will for the Russians in view of the 1939 pact with the Nazis. About 1.5 million

Poles had been deported from the zone the Soviets occupied after the Molotov-Ribbentrop pact. Their fate greatly concerned the exile government, as they were rumored to be interned in camps and jails. Finally, some 15,000 officers and more soldiers had been captured, and their fate was a cause for great distress.

During 1942 the Russians again claimed Polish territory, and the Allied response became visibly more flexible. The West, not able to deliver a second front and watching the rapid advance of the Soviet army, began to move toward placation of Stalin. As a result, when Churchill and Harriman "could not find the time" to take up certain issues when Churchill visited Stalin in August 1942, the Poles felt abandoned.[78] As the West began to waver in support, the Poles became increasingly unyielding toward Soviet claims in the face of the ever-apparent Russian designs in Poland. Moscow radio in turn assaulted the London Poles as reactionaries, and the Soviet government began to develop a nucleus of its own Poles with the creation of the Union of Polish Patriots who were much more sympathetic to Russian territorial designs and interests than the London Poles. The actual break between the London Poles and the Russians occurred in April 1943, when the Germans discovered the graves of 15,000 Polish officers in the Katyn Forest of Poland. The Germans claimed they were slaughtered by Russia in 1940 — a claim accepted by the London group. Stalin's fury at this immediate Polish acceptance of the Nazi version of the massacre prompted him to break diplomatic relations with the London Poles.

There were, by now, two distinct issues involved. One was the future composition of the Polish government, and the second was the geographic boundaries of Poland. The Soviets argued for an eastern limit of Poland that coincided with the frontier of 1941 resulting from the Molotov-Ribbentrop pact. At Tehran in late 1943 Churchill and Eden initiated a proposal that this line be adopted in the east and Poland be compensated in the west out of former Prussian territory to the River Oder. Thus, they accepted Stalin's suggestions of 1941. Churchill also indicated that he would attempt to convince the London Poles to accept the solution. Roosevelt did not demur in the massive territorial or population adjustments that Stalin was conceded. He said, encouragingly, that he "would like to see the eastern border moved further west and the western border moved to the River Oder." But, the president added, "he could not publicly take part in any such arrangement" because he could not prejudice the "six to seven million Polish-American votes in the upcoming election."[79] Roosevelt's concern about his domestic flank was well taken, for the Republicans would build much of their compaign around charges that Roosevelt's labor support tied him to communist influences. Such Republican "red-baiting" would become commonplace and more effective over the next decade. But even in 1944 its effect was sufficient to undercut Roosevelt's seemingly impregnable position to the point that his electoral margin would be one of the smallest in decades.[80] To have publicly associated himself with the Polish boundary decision, therefore, might well have been diastrous. But in accepting tacitly with Churchill the inevitability of Soviet dominance, Roosevelt undoubtedly contributed to the domestic difficulties to be experienced by his successor. There was probably no alternative available to Roosevelt and Churchill, but by this action they conceded to Stalin both the dominant voice in the future government of Poland and the territorial aggrandizement he desired.

The Tehran plan envisaged a population movement involving at least 6 million people who would have to find homes in Germany. The territory to be taken from Germany stretched 200 miles into Prussia. A future government that displaced so many Germans and held such a vast tract of former German territory could not be but fearful of German claims in the future and dependent on Moscow. As for the new regime to be established in postwar Poland, Stalin now demanded that it be comprised primarily of those Poles acceptable to the Soviet Union. As Soviet troops were marching into Poland, Stalin created the Polish Committee of Liberation, a group that evolved out of the Union of Polish Patriots and that was more clearly than ever the prototype government of Poland. When Soviet troops entered Lublin, Poland, this group was installed, and Lublin was made the administrative center for all of Poland.

But the meaning and full consequences of Soviet policy became clear as the Soviet military action in Poland revealed a kind of record for cynicism. As the Russians reached the Banks of the Vistula within sight of Warsaw in August 1944, Moscow radio urged the Polish Underground or Home Army to revolt. The Poles did, yet the Russians did not advance to drive out the Germans; rather, they watched until January 1945 as the Nazis liquidated the last vestiges of any potential opposition to Soviet domination of the future government of Poland. A quarter of a million Poles were to die in Warsaw fighting Nazis, alone, and the city was destroyed, blown up block by block. Stalin even refused landing rights to Western planes to drop supplies to the beleaguered Poles.

The Allies were horrified but could do little more than tacitly support the Soviet territorial claim in Poland legitimized earlier at Tehran. In October 1944 Churchill came to Moscow to talk about the political shape of postwar Eastern Europe. After gaining Stalin's acceptance of a British free hand in Greece, the conversation turned to Poland, although there was now little left to discuss. The British and the Americans had been presented with an accomplished fact of Soviet power in Poland and Soviet recognition of the Lublin government in spite of protestations that the decision to recognize a Polish government be left until the summit conference at Yalta in February 1945.

Yalta

At the Yalta Conference, Roosevelt extracted vague and ambiguous assurances from Stalin concerning reorganization of the Lublin government and free elections in Poland. Similar weak commitments were made by Stalin concerning all of Soviet-controlled Eastern Europe. Oversight of these elections was left vague and elastic, and when the Soviets later interpreted matters to their advantage, many in the United States would denounce the Yalta agreements as a sellout. But Roosevelt's biographer, Burns, has concluded otherwise:

> He had reached the limit of his bargaining power at Yalta. His position resulted not from naivete, ignorance, illness, or perfidy, but from his acceptance of the facts: Russia occupied Poland. Russia distrusted its Western allies. Russia had a million men who could fight Japan. . . . And Russia was absolutely determined about Poland and always had been.[81]

Moreover, Roosevelt believed — and he may have indulged his vanity to the point of self-deception here — that his personal charm could cut through the ideological differences, accumulated distrust of the preceding decades, as well as the historic Russian interests in Central Europe to capture Stalin's trust and cooperation. If successful, the Wilsonian ideal of an institutionalized world order might yet be fulfilled in the new United Nations, in which case the compromises of Yalta would be mere footnotes on the opening pages of a new era.

On the other hand, the presentation of the Yalta accords to the American people led most Americans to believe that there would be free democratic elections in Eastern Europe. At the same time, Roosevelt understood enough of the realities of the situation to know that in the free hand he had allowed the Soviets since 1943 in Poland and in his acceptance of the "friendly" governments — no matter how cloaked in electoral procedure — he had acknowledged the Soviets their ambitions. Also, he must have known that the military realities of the postwar situation conflicted with what the American people had been led to expect in terms of a new liberal order promised to arise out of the ashes of the war.[82]

It was Harry Truman who was to try to resolve the dilemma of public and private expectations in favor of America's aspirations, rather than acknowledge what increasingly seemed inevitable in the face of Soviet guns and tough interpretations of their security interests. Truman and his advisers were to argue the issue as a breach of faith. Harriman later wrote, Stalin went to "extreme lengths in breaking the Yalta Agreements . . . that the people in these countries were to decide their own government through a free election."[83] However, there was never explicit agreement on the procedure or meaning of free elections or international supervision. These items were kept ambiguous because it was apparent that the declaration of Yalta concerning Poland satisfied different purposes for the West and Stalin. To the West, it helped keep up appearances while Soviet armies that were needed later in the Pacific were still fighting Germans; and to the Russians, it confirmed the obvious. As Stalin was to remark: "This war is not as in the past; whoever occupies territory also imposes his own social system as far as his army can reach. It cannot be otherwise."[84] How could it be otherwise? Once the Lublin group was agreed to as the basis for future government, it was obvious that control would be communist. The inclusion of the London Poles or others could only be decoration for the Western conscience.[85]

THE ADMINISTRATION OF LIBERATION

The issue of the administration of former enemy and enemy-occupied states in Europe was a consistent element of the growing distrust between Russia and the West. It is commonly held that the cold war was a contest between a Western vision of an open-liberal political order and a narrow Soviet definition of security in terms of spheres of interest.[86] But the West accommodated itself to having its own security spheres when military convenience allowed in Europe or when historical ambition demanded it in Latin America. The first evidence of a lack of deep Western commitment to its liberal rhetoric and aspirations was in North Africa, where the United States and the British worked out a surrender deal with the anti-Semitic, collaborationist commander of the Vichy French forces. In return for his surrender, Admiral Jean Darlan was allowed to maintain his political position.[87]

The squalid arrangement with Darlan was viewed as being an unfortunate expediency. Unhappily, it was repeated in the Western action in Italy of negotiating with the rightist regime of General Badoglio. By dealing with the leader of Italy's brutal Ethiopian campaign and leaving much of Mussolini's governmental structure intact, the West indicated the possibility that the Allies would deal with anyone when the time came. But just as importantly, the West, by managing to arrange for a sphere of influence in areas in which Western troops were placed, became poorly positioned to argue against the harsher but functionally equivalent strategy that the Soviets employed in Eastern Europe.

In Greece, German withdrawal touched off fighting between communist and left-wing partisans on the one hand and collaborationists and monarchists on the other. The civil war that was raging by the time Britain entered Athens was settled by the British in favor of a coalition of royalists and collaborationists. But in December 1944, civil war again broke out when the British attempted to disarm the left-wing groups. The left feared the British plan of disarmament would have kept arms in the paramilitary forces of the right as well as in the police and military forces. In the midst of this chaos, the British army supported the rightists, actively attempted to root out the left opposition, disbanded the partisan resistance by extreme methods, and tried to reinstate the king; reportedly 80 percent of the population was opposed to such moves.[88]

It was a blatant and unpopular exercise in reclamation of the British Empire, which brought protest to the House of Commons and great consternation from some Americans who saw liberal principles desecrated. Nevertheless, Roosevelt acquiesced in Churchill's attempt to impose a British solution on Greece. American aid helped in suppressing the civil war as Roosevelt wired Churchill that "I regard my role in this matter as that of a loyal friend and ally whose desire is to be of any help possible in the circumstances." The United States, he confessed, could not take a public stand, but this, he reassured Churchill, was due solely to the "state of public feeling" and did not reflect the official American position.[89]

In spite of the fact that the British army was aimed at the "communistic elements in Greece [who] plan to seize power by force,"[90] not a word of reproach was uttered by the Soviet press, and Stalin was completely silent on the subject. In this, Stalin was conforming to the agreement worked out between Churchill and himself in October 1944 in which Rumania and Bulgaria were conceded to the Soviet sphere of influence and Greece to the British. Yugoslavia and Hungary were to be divided equally. Churchill wrote appreciatively, "I am increasingly impressed, up to date, with the loyalty with which ... Stalin has kept off Greece in accordance with our agreement."[91] The Russians did nothing to help their ideological brethren in Greece and everything possible to discourage them. Stalin even aided the British occupation by offering the British-reconstituted monarchist Greek government Soviet recognition in December 1945. The move caused extreme consternation among the left in Greece; but it was impressive evidence that the Soviets understood the language of power and interest. They had, after all, their own fish to fry in this regard in Germany and Eastern Europe.

In Greece, Italy, and North Africa, the Soviets had precedent for their conduct in Eastern Europe. But the West would not concede that spheres of interest could cohabit the same planet. If they had, then the Soviets and the West might not have undergone the frightful postwar tension that was rapidly strangling the slim neck of wartime amity. But the Western powers were unable or unwilling to reciprocate Stalin's behavior regarding Greece. The harsh Soviet interpretation of their own security needs and Anglo-American resistance to this interpretation (while pursuing a similar policy wherever practicable) became, therefore, the focus of dissension and distrust from which other issues proliferated.

Americans emerged from the war in Europe supremely confident that they could exact the leadership of a new order. Although planning for the postwar period had not been systematic, the State Department envisaged a world where the judicious use of postwar rehabilitation loans would break down trade barriers and establish a prosperous global economy free from imperialism and free from revolutionary socialism. By late 1944, Ambassador Harriman was suggesting that postwar economic reconstruction aid be used to influence Soviet behavior in Eastern Europe. The U.S. Air Force and military planners saw a world where American military power would be so imposing that threats to the peace would have little choice but to yield.[92] The Soviet vision was clearly different. Although the Soviet Union was in ruins, with three-quarters of its industrial plant destroyed and 20 million dead, it nonetheless possessed an immediate challenge to the American vision by the presence of its troops in the heart of Europe and by the affinity of armed partisans for collectivist principles. This, in Stalin's view, could become the basis of a Soviet-controlled central European barrier to future aggression from the West.

TRUMAN AND
THE ORIGINS OF THE COLD WAR

In this context, Harry Truman came to power following President Roosevelt's death little versed in foreign affairs and, in contrast to Roosevelt, heavily dependent on his advisers. Indeed, given Roosevelt's personal diplomacy, Truman had been excluded from major decisions and was relatively ignorant of what had transpired previously. His closest foreign affairs advisers had long and bitter distrust of Soviet ambitions and chafed at Roosevelt's view that good will and yielding to the strongest of Soviet security claims in Eastern Europe could beget a condominium of great powers. The majority of these officials concurred with Kennan's analysis that the Soviets were "Never — neither then nor at any later date . . . a fit ally or associate, actual or potential."[93] They had witnessed the purges and the undeniable excesses and dark features of Soviet life and Stalin's character for long years.[94] These were the people to whom Truman turned when he sought counsel on the great issues before him.

Truman had hardly moved to the White House when the Russians demonstrated to the world that they would brook little interference in excluding unfriendly elements from the new Polish government. At Yalta the Soviets pledged to hold "free and unfettered elections as soon as possible on the basis of universal suffrage and secret ballot. In these elections, all democratic and anti-Nazi parties shall have the right to take part and forward candidates."[95] But the prospects for free elections were dim. There was almost civil war, with the Russians and the Lublin group aligned against the supporters of the London Poles and the remnants of the Polish Resistance.

Ambassador Averell Harriman left the Moscow embassy to George Kennan's care and returned to Washington to advise Truman. Harriman had spent months attempting to resolve the question as to which parties actually constituted "democratic elements" and could take part in a new Polish government. Neither Roosevelt nor Churchill had frankly faced up to the fact that truly free elections might have returned governments manifestly unfriendly to the Soviet Union; and the Soviets were reluctant to provide a structure on which all parties whom the West supported might stand. Harriman was exasperated and told Truman that Russia confronted Eastern Europe with a "barbarian invasion." They could be responded to firmly; for, he held, they needed reconstruction credit for their decimated industry. The tough approach to Russia was seconded by most of Truman's foreign affairs advisers, although some broached the fear that too unyielding an attitude over Poland would break Soviet-American relations completely and endanger the entrance of Russia into the Pacific war.

Truman responded to Harriman that he understood "the Russians need us more than we need them" and though we cannot "expect 100 percent of what he proposed," he did feel "we would be able to get 85 percent."[96] The first step in the march toward 85 percent of U.S. claims was to be taken with Molotov, who was coming to San Francisco in a gesture of good will to the fledgling UN conference and the new American president. In this meeting with the Soviet foreign minister, Truman pointed out in "words of one syllable" the American desire for immediate free elections. Truman stated that Poland had become the symbol of U.S. foreign policy. During the second day of meetings with Molotov, the terse but correct conversation turned into a very undiplomatic diatribe. Truman spoke to the foreign minister as if he were a simple-minded recruit, demanding that elements of the London Poles join the Polish government and that elections be held immediately. Molotov protested, "I have never been talked to like that in my life." Truman snapped, "Carry out your agreements and you won't get talked to like that."[97]

Stalin seemed both puzzled and bitter. In a letter following the April 23, 1945, meeting with Molotov, the Soviet premier protested that "Poland, unlike Great Britain and the United States, had common frontiers with the Soviet Union. . . . 'I do not know whether a truly representative government has been set up in Greece or whether the government in Belgium is truly democratic.' The Soviet Union was not consulted . . . and claimed no right to interfere, 'as it understands the full significance of Belgium and Greece for the security of Great Britain.' "[98]

Truman did not see his policy as the reversal of previous agreements. Instead he seemed to fear that the closing of Eastern Europe would presage its closure economically. In the view of Truman and his advisers, such a political and economic division of East and West would threaten economic chaos in Europe. Moreover, because the dominant belief arising out of World War I was that peace is indivisible, Truman's most fervently held belief was that a "breach of peace anywhere in the world, threatens the peace of the entire world.[99] The Americans began to define Eastern Europe as a launching pad to Western Europe. In contrast, the Russians concluded that the West, because of its concern and claims in Eastern Europe, was involved in a resurrection of the old course of encirclement.

The irony for the West is that it is not clear that security meant expansion for the Russians. To the contrary, there were going to be momentous difficulties in holding the areas where their armies stood. The attitude of the Kremlin at the end of the war was one of panic. The "iron curtain" on which Churchill commented in February 1945 to Truman was a protective shell masking Stalin's concern that the relaxation of ideological control Russia experienced in the "great patriotic war" would accelerate. Moreover, it was feared that the extent of the internal devastation, if it were known, would be an invitation for the West to press its claim. If the Russians had been ready to advance they would not have demobilized nor torn out the rail connections between the Soviet Union and Germany that ran through Poland. The extent of this winding down is even more impressive if one considers the very considerable state of tension in Central Europe in this period and the enormous amount of police supervision required. Yet the West understood the Soviets' fierce defense of their acquisitions and political tactics as preparation for expansion.[100]

Insofar as these communist maneuvers inside the new Soviet empire might be the prelude to Soviet advance, Truman stepped up the pressure. Shortly after Truman's decision to search for 85 percent Soviet agreement with the American understanding of the political future of Eastern Europe, lend-lease was abruptly cancelled. Ships already unloading cargo were packed up and others in the mid-Atlantic turned around in an effort to use economic leverage against the Soviets. As the assistant chief of lend-lease observed, this "decison was taken deliberately and probably was a part of a general squeeze now being put on the USSR."[101] Stalin protested, "the American attitude toward the Soviet Union had perceptibly cooled once it became obvious that Germany was defeated. . . . The Americans were saying that the Russians were no longer needed." Stalin continued that if the cancellation of lend-lease "was designed as a pressure on the Russians in order to soften them up, then it was a fundamental mistake."[102] Although the decision was partially reversed,[103] the damage already done was exacerbated by Truman's decision to implement a "more realistic policy": an approach minimizing financial help to the Russians while agreements were yet to be reached on Eastern Europe to Truman's satisfaction — a satisfaction that demanded a great deal from the Soviets.

THE ATOM BOMB, ASIA, AND EUROPE

Economics were only one part of the strategy of convincing the Russians that they needed to cooperate in Eastern Europe. There was the potential of the atomic bomb, which the secretary of state told Truman "might well put us in the position to dictate our own terms."[104] Or, as Truman himself explained just before the news of the first test reached him, "If it explodes, . . . I'll certainly have a hammer on those boys."[105] The Polish issue and the atomic bomb were conjoined, if not, as some have argued, "inextricably bound together."[106]

To effectuate an ambivalent diplomatic strategy, Truman called on Harry Hopkins, well known as an associate of Roosevelt and a symbol of more cordial times, to go to Moscow, although Hopkins was gravely ill. In Moscow, Hopkins made a substantial concession that granted the Lublin Poles be formally recognized as the basis for a postwar government in Poland in return for the admittance of a few London Poles. On July 5, 1945, pleased with Stalin's promise to insert five independent Poles and the Poles from London into a nucleus of a Warsaw (Lublin) cabinet and pleased with Stalin's reaffirmation of his pledge to hold free elections, Truman extended diplomatic recognition of the Polish provisional government. Nevertheless, this agreement over the composition of the Polish government was not considered final by Truman and his advisers.[107]

There were indications that Stalin, having received a Polish government compatible with Soviet interest, relaxed some controls in most of Eastern Europe. There were concessions granted to the West in the Allied commissions of Hungary and Rumania, and in Hungary the West was even given a veto in the Allied Control Commission. Stalin probably pursued this policy for three reasons. First, it was a conciliatory gesture toward the West. The territory in which he was interested was under the control of Soviet troops, Poland had been accorded recognition, and there were other matters in Central Europe and of economic assistance to which he now felt he could turn. Second, he had, no doubt, no desire to provoke the further ill will of the West. Third, there were administrative limits to the Soviets achieving effective control over such a vast area — if indeed that was their strategy. The nature of that control became quite harsh; but as we shall see, the most unpleasant features of Eastern European life were not established until after the defection of Yugoslavia in 1948. Whether or not totalitarian domination was the long-range vision of Stalin, the immediate tactics of gaining Soviet control were gradualist and unprovocative to center leftist parties in Eastern Europe and conciliatory of Western sensibilities.

When, for example, the Communists of Sofia, Bulgaria, attempted to eastablish a one-party state, Stalin sent Molotov to persuade them to abandon the project. Tito of Yugoslavia was severely chastised for a similar action. Even in the ex-enemy states of Rumania, Bulgaria, and Hungary, the Soviet tactic was to install a coalition of equals between the Communists and the other parties of the center-left. In Rumania, King Michael was praised by the communist press. In Hungary, East Germany, and Czechoslovakia the Communists acknowledged losses in elections and entered into coalition governments. Stalin requested that Truman recognize these regimes; but the Americans refused — stating that the Rumanian, Bulgarian, and Hungarian governments were "neither representative nor responsive to the will of the people." In short, Truman was not prepared to give Stalin the benefit of the doubt — instead he was gradually increasing the pressure on Stalin regarding Eastern Europe in the period before July 1945. Truman and Churchill arrived in a devastated Berlin for their meeting with Stalin at Potsdam, a suburb of Berlin, on the 16th of July, 1945. Truman said that his "immediate purpose was to get the Russians into the war against Japan as soon as possible." It was Truman's contention at the outset that Russia's entry into the war would mean the "saving of hundreds of thousands of American casualties."[108] But the need to substitute Russian casualties for Americans became less apparent when a message arrived from the heat-fused desert of Alamogordo, New Mexico, that the atom bomb had been tested successfully. The success at testing the bomb signaled to the West, in Churchill's words, that "we should not need the Russians. . . . We had no need to ask favors of them."[109] Truman became both confident and visibly more rigid with Stalin after the news of the New Mexico test arrived. He no longer negotiated with the Russians; rather there occurred a sharply barbed exchange of views. As Churchill recalled, "[Truman] stood up to the Russians in a most emphatic and decisive manner, telling them as to certain demands that they absolutely could not have and the United States was entirely against them. . . . He told the Russians just where they could get off and generally bossed the whole meeting."[110] In short, the bomb buoyed the West, for as Churchill told the House of Commons, "we possessed powers which were irresistible"[111] — or so it seemed.

Truman, his advisers, and Churchill determined that the bomb could have several diplomatic and military purposes. First, if it was used quickly, the shock might prompt an immediate surrender of the Japanese and thus be, in Churchill's words "a merciful abridgement of the slaughter."[112] Second, it could now keep Russian participation in the war and hence postwar claims against Japan to a minimum. Moreover, the bomb would present the possibility of rescinding the Yalta understandings regarding Russian claims on territory in China, especially in Manchuria. As Navy Secretary Forrestal recalled in his diary on July 28, 1945, "Byrnes [the secretary of state] said he was most anxious to get the Japanese affairs over with before the Russians get in. . . . Once in there, he felt, it would not be easy to get them out."[113] Third, a significant Russian voice in the internal order of the postwar Japanese government by means of the occupational control agreement might not come into force if Japan could be forced to surrender before Russia managed a significant participation in the war. Truman recalls his determination, on returning from Berlin, "that I would not allow the Russians any part in the control of Japan. . . . I made up my mind that General MacArthur would be given complete command and control of Japan."[114]

Finally, it was hoped, especially by Secretary of State Byrnes and probably by President Truman as well, that the bomb could be exploited to political advantage in Eastern Europe. As Byrnes explained in relation to Eastern Europe in late July, the "New Mexico situation had given us great power, and that in the final analysis, it would control."[115] After the bomb was dropped, Byrnes became increasingly rigid, as Stimson's diary relates:

I took up the question . . . how to handle Russia with the big bomb. I found that Byrnes was very much against any attempt to cooperate with the Russians. . . . He looks to having the presence of the bomb in his pocket.[116]

The official American justification for dropping the bomb has always been in terms of a calculus of military necessity and humanitarian concern. President Truman explained that the bomb was dropped "to shorten the agony of war, in order to save the lives of thousands and thousands of young Americans."[117] But the increasing burden of historical evidence suggests that there were alternatives to dropping the bomb. First, critics point out that the bomb was not necessary to save lives. The Japanese may have wanted to surrender anyway. In mid-June 1945, Foreign Minister Tojo approached the Russians "with a view to terminating the war if possible by September."[118] These overtures became more intense throughout the summer, others were intercepted, and still others were being made directly to the West.[119] The Americans, who had broken the Japanese code years earlier, had easy access to Japanese communications, which were alive with efforts to convince the Russians to intercede on their behalf. In fact, Hopkins advised that these peace overtures be explored, but they were not. Instead, on July 26, 1945, only 13 days before Russia was scheduled to enter the war, China, the United States, and Britain issued an ultimatum to the Japanese to surrender unconditionally or face "prompt and utter destruction."

This insistence on unconditional surrender in the face of Japanese attempts to quit if only the future status of the emperor was clarified is confusing in view of Truman's contention that his sole motive was to end the war with the least bloodshed. If the complete humiliation of Japan was desired, then one can only note that the terms finally offered and accepted did allow for the retention of the emperor and were the same as an important faction of the Japanese Cabinet was prepared to accept in mid-summer 1945. If the minimizing of human suffering alone was the motive, then those terms could have been at least explored; instead, they were ignored until after the bombs were dropped.

Moreover, the bomb was not a military necessity; the most that can be said for the atomic bomb was that it was a military convenience. But not much of one. The fire raids on Tokyo destroyed as much life. American air strikes came and went with no interference — imposing fire storms that incinerated up to 100,000 human beings a raid. The burden of most American military estimates was in agreement with General Curtis LeMay that "even without the atomic bomb and the Russian entry into the war, Japan would have surrendered in two weeks. . . . The atomic bomb has nothing to do with the end of the war." As the authors of the U.S. Strategic Bombing Survey concluded:

> [I]t is the Survey's opinion that . . . in all probability prior to November 31, 1945 Japan would have surrendered even if the atomic bomb had not been dropped, even if Russia had not entered the war, and even if no invasion had been planned or contemplated.[120]

Finally, contemporary critics of the decision to use the bomb have noted that there were any number of other options available to the president the use of which either alone or in combination could have brought Japanese surrender. These included: (1) diplomatic negotiations especially on the terms of surrender; (2) a naval blockade; or (3) the Russian action of declaring war. The use of direct force including the bomb itself could have taken a different form as well. For example, conventional air strikes could have continued given total American air superiority. Concerning the bomb, it has been suggested that Truman might have threatened its use or even demonstrated the bomb rather than use it on civilians with no warning.[121] In each case, of course, these options would have required time and thus increased the possibility or even ensured greater Russian participation and presence in the structuring of postwar Asia. Herbert Feis has concluded that, beyond an immediate end of the war, "some of the men who concurred in the decision to use the bomb discerned other advantages and justifications."[122] More specifically:

> It is likely that Churchill, and probably also Truman, conceived that besides bringing the war to a quick end, it would improve the chances of arranging a satisfactory peace both in Europe and in the Far East. Stimson and Byrnes certainly had that thought in mind. For would not the same dramatic proof of western power that shocked Japan into surrender impress the Russians also? . . . In short, the bomb, it may have been thought or hoped, would not only subdue the Japanese aggressors, but perhaps also monitor Russian behavior.[123]

The bomb seemed to yield benefits: Japan surrendered and the Americans moved quickly to build a "sympathetic Japan . . . in case there should be any aggression by Russia in Manchuria."[124] The attempt to contain Soviet influence in Asia was furthered by the order to the Japanese in Korea, the Philippines, Indochina, and East Asia to surrender only to forces that General Douglas MacArthur would designate. The order was calculated to minimize the possibility that the Japanese would surrender to partisan resistance forces under Mao Zedong, Ho Chi Minh, or others fighting in Indonesia, Korea, and the Philippines, and thereby strengthen the influence of left-led partisans who would presumably have been sympathetic to Russian power. The Russians protested, but they had not been able to establish much of a presence in Asia by dint of arms and, more importantly, their major concern was Central Europe. Thus, although the Russians largely respected the West's claims in Asia, the bomb had probably less to do with it than the discrepancy between the amount of Soviet military personnel and American strength deployed in the Far East at the end of the war. This was, of course, a mirror image of the situation in Central Europe; but in Europe Truman would concede nothing.

Potsdam and Beyond

In the meantime, at Potsdam, Truman proceeded to push claims against the Soviets that denied to the Russians the kind of exclusive arrangement the West had pursued in Greece, Italy, and North Africa. The discussion became increasingly sharp and Truman soon wearied of it, thinking it futile — and, perhaps, believing that soon the great demonstration of American power over Hiroshima and Nagasaki would give the Soviets second thoughts. The issue of whether Eastern Europe was to be open or closed to Western influence remained, however, unaffected by the bomb. This issue turned instead, as we have noted, on the disposition of forces during and immediately after the war. The question of postwar Germany's political and economic future became therefore the most frequently debated issue in the Potsdam conference.

Early in the war Roosevelt had approved of the plan of his secretary of the treasury, Henry Morgenthau, to fragment Germany, "pastoralize it," and bring to Germany the forceful lessons of a Carthaginian peace. When the plan was originally proposed to him, the president endorsed it enthusiastically: "We have to castrate the German people or you have to treat them in such a manner so they can't go on reproducing people who want to go on the way they have in the past."[125] Roosevelt's advisers and Churchill, however, did not fully support this vision, fearing that it would bankrupt European reconstruction, encourage nationalist irredentism, and open the way for communism. By Yalta, in July 1945, the president was also becoming wary of some of the implications of this plan; Roosevelt did not want mass starvation to occur; nor did he want a repetition of the reparations experience after World War I which had contributed to the economic instability of Germany in the 1920s and 1930s. After World War I the United States was forced to pick up Germany's reparations bill. France, Germany, and others who were defaulting on loans to the United States, were being routed millions by these reparations. Subsequently, therefore, Roosevelt rejected the harsh "planned chaos" of the initial

Morgenthau proposal, while accepting other implications of the plan concerning some reduction of the German standard of living. Hence, at Yalta, Roosevelt became committed, as a basis of discussion, to the figure of $20 billion or 50 percent of German wealth drawn from all of Germany as the basic reparations payment. Thus, although divided politically into occupation zones, Germany was to be treated as a single economic unit.

At Postdam, however, the Americans demanded that there be no specific figure set for reparations. It was a harsh blow for the Soviets, who had been promised a $20 billion talking figure. The Russians knew that the action of cutting off lend-lease and of procrastination on Soviet loan requests left reparations drawn from Germany as the only reasonable recourse, in terms of outside assistance, to pursue for postwar reconstruction of Russia. In part, Truman's decison to withdraw reparations from the Russians was prompted by Roosevelt's previous concern that, eventually, Americans would wind up subsidizing the Germans except that in this case their payments would be turned over to the Russians. Moreover, the quandary of how to resuscitate Germany and yet hold down her military potential without Russian cooperation or the long-term stationing of American troops now seemed solvable. America would soon have the ultimate atomic answer. As Truman told DeGaulle after Potsdam, "The German menace should not be exaggerated," for "the United States possessed a new weapon, the atomic bomb, which would defeat any aggressor."[126]

Second, Truman proposed that any reparations that were paid to the allies should be drawn from their respective zones of occupation, rather than from Germany as a whole as envisioned at Yalta. A zonal approach to reparations, it was argued by the Americans, would minimize conflict about what the Germans could or could not afford. The Russians protested, however, that such an arrangement would deprive them of access to the industrialized goods located in the Western zones, especially the Ruhr. East Germany was largely agricultural, and the Russians had removed in a draconian fashion almost all its rolling stock, cattle, a good deal of industrial plant, and even toilets before the Big Three even convened in Berlin. It was, they declared, "war booty" and not part of the reparations calculation. And the Russians also argued that the value of this zonal approach of the Americans would never equal anything like $20 billion. More important: would not this mean, Molotov asked, "that each country would have a free hand in their own zone and would act entirely independent of the other?"[127]

In other words, in the American proposal the outlines of a divided Germany were drawn, one in which Four Power control would be minimized if not eliminated in the respective zones. In view of the Soviet desire to maintain access to and influence on any and all facets of German political and economic reconstruction, this turn of events could not be viewed with optimism in Moscow. The Russians were aware of the need for a German economic reconstruction sufficient to maintain reparations. But they were concerned primarily with the security implications of a Germany, or any part of it, not open to their influence and, if possible, an administrative veto over German policies. At Yalta, Churchill had remarked to Stalin, "If you want a horse to pull a wagon, you have to give it fodder." The Soviet dictator replied, "But care should be taken to see that the horse did not turn around and kick you."[128]

At Potsdam, therefore, the contentious nature of the German question — the pivotal issue of the next crucial 5 years — was drawn. Germany was the key variable in opposing Soviet and American conceptions of a secure and stable Europe. On the other hand, the conference did seem to offer the Soviets a softening of the Western position on Poland. It was not inconceivable, therefore, that the German problem could be worked out by the foreign ministers in the fall of 1945. The Americans, for their part, had extracted the mixed blessing of a Soviet commitment to intervene against Japan. More important, Truman had begun staking out a tougher position on Germany. Finally, of course, the opportunity to apply atomic leverage to the Russians seemed to auger well for the postwar ministers' conference.

Atomic Diplomacy Proves Inadequate

The mushroom clouds from the bombs exploding in the Orient reached silently over the shoulders of the statesmen who sat at the London foreign ministers' meeting, discussing Eastern Europe in the fall of 1945. It was not mentioned in the conference proceedings, but cartoonists drew pictures of it perched on the conference table. As *Time* magazine commented: "at the . . . conference, U.S. diplomats had been reluctant to talk about the bomb. When the subject came up in private conversation they would say something like 'of course, the world knows that the U.S. would never. . . . ' Such sentences usually trailed off in inaudible mumbles."[129] But in the end, the bomb only served to exaggerate the reactions of both sides. Secretary Byrnes's whole negotiating strategy seemed infused with a sense of atomic omnipotence.[130] At London, the tenor of the coming cold war was in evidence as diplomacy turned vitriolic. The conference degenerated into a series of alternating press conferences in which the two sides explained their own positions and castigated each other concerning their respective policies in their European spheres of influence. The atomic threat was always present if unarticulated, but Molotov and the Russians were unmoved — the existing balance of forces in Europe, not the vague if ominous threats of atomic diplomacy, moved the Russians. The conference stalemated.

Byrnes decided to shift his tactics in the next foreign ministers' conference, to be held in Moscow in December 1945. Rather than pursue his London tack of public diplomacy, he undertook a more secretive style and approached Stalin and Molotov with offers of recognition for the Rumanian and Bulgarian regimes if the Russians would agree to a German peace treaty as well as a general set of agreements covering all of Eastern Europe. In Byrnes's scheme, all of these issues would be resolved in a large peace conference which would negotiate the political agreements as well as provide economic access to Central Europe.

The Soviets seemed satisfied[131] but President Truman was not. He was more than a little miffed at Byrnes's secrecy and the latitude exercised by the secretary of state in his negotiations. From all appearances in Washington, Byrnes was free-lancing and making vague concessions to the Russians without presidential approval. Moreover, such diplomacy opened Truman to attacks from conservative Republicans who were labeling Roosevelt's actions at Yalta and Democratic party diplomacy in general a sellout. Byrnes did extract a Soviet pledge of cooperation in Asia and an extremely vague commitment to some form of control of atomic energy, but Truman was privately furious.

It is not clear that Byrnes ever received a direct tongue lashing from Truman, but criticism of the secretary of state became commonplace. Senator Arthur Vandenberg feared that Byrnes's legislative experience in the Senate, which called for compromise and conciliation, would be his "undoing in the international field."[132] Senator Vandenberg grumbled that the conciliatory language of the Moscow meeting and the lack of progress reminded him of "Chamberlain and his umbrella appeasement." House Leader Joe Martin called it a "betrayal of the small nations of the world in the making of peace."[133] And within the Truman administration, Admiral Leahy asserted that the communique of the Moscow conference was "an appeasement document which gives to the Soviet [Union] everything they want and preserves to America nothing. . . . Byrnes was not immune to the communistically inclined advisers in the State Department."[134] Under such attack an already tough Byrnes was pushed even further to the right and into a more inflexible policy line as the postwar conferences began again in 1946. When this posture was juxtaposed against Soviet suspicion and distrust and a crumbling situation in Germany, the postwar prospects could hardly be regarded as bright.

From the Soviet perspective, the American course in Germany was unacceptable. Indeed, it was potentially dangerous, for it implied a reconstituted Germany perhaps ruled by the very class of people who had directed the destruction of 20 million Russians during the preceding 5 years. All in all, it was not a prospect that could win Russian favor or evoke Russian confidence and trust. Western proposals in Germany — an area regarded by the Soviets as the very core of their security interests — were, predictably, rejected. Instead, the Soviets and the Americans turned to the imposition of greater control of their respective zones of occupation. The Allied Control Council for Germany became merely an administrative shell as the military commanders in each occupation zone assumed supreme political as well as military authority. In the American zone, General Lucius Clay pushed for higher industrial production goals; and in December, the Department of State allowed Clay to interpret and use the production ceilings agreed to at Potsdam as production minimums. The Soviets, for their part, destroyed the old land-owning class, nationalized all industry, and imposed Communist party control. The division of Germany seemed assured when, in May 1946, Clay informed the Russians that no more reparations would be paid to them from the Western zones. Similarly, the Soviets, at about the same time, stopped removing machinery from East Germany and apparently decided to regenerate industrial production within the East German zone.

In a highly publicized speech in Stuttgart, on September 4, 1946, Secretary of State Byrnes announced that Germany needed to develop a "self-sustaining" economy and a capacity to export. "Germany is a part of Europe, and European recovery . . . will be slowed with her great resources turned into a poor house," Byrnes explained.[135] Germans, he declared, should be given primary responsibility for running their own affairs. Moreover, the United States would never recognize the Oder-Neisse as the Eastern boundary that separated Poland and East Germany. This was, in the words of one scholar, an historical not a prophetic statement: "it simply summarized the events of the previous eighteen months."[136]

By the fall of 1946, the future outlines of the cold war were plainly established. West Germany would become a state managed by the same class that had supported the Nazis. Few war criminals would be rooted out, as that would not be conducive to the "orderly transition to self-government." Neither the client West Germans nor the West would recognize Polish claims in former German territory, a policy that would, more firmly than ever, rivet the Poles to the Russian embrace. There were over 3.5 million Germans expelled from Poland, living in Western zones. Byrnes's speech gave them hope that they would return, and tied the future German government to that assumption for 25 years. Byrnes's speech also implied that the United States would keep its troops in Germany for "a long time to come," but a provisional government would be set up to manage German contributions to its own and general European recovery. Such a state of affairs, a reconstituted Germany administered by those who had lost the war, could be held up to the Eastern Europeans as a bogey of revenge — and tie the whole area to the Russians.

The East Germans made little pretense at being self-governing. They would be only a hypothetical security threat to Russia's satellites; they had no refugees and were "satisfied." Still, the specter of American troops guarding the Western sectors of a divided Germany with claims to the East promised no immediate reconciliation of the partitioned Germanies. The Americans did not recognize Soviet security interests in Central Europe and feared Soviet designs and Soviet power. Soviet actions were almost without exception interpreted as challenges to the West that had to be met with stern resolve. Unity became an imperative, and the recovery of Europe was only a part of the larger need for sustained resistance to the Soviet threat. In this way a set of conditions were established that were to serve as a persistent flashpoint of East-West contention for the next 25 years.

NOTES

1. N. Gordon Levin, Jr., *Woodrow Wilson and World Politics: America's Response to War and Revolution* (New York: Oxford University Press, 1968).
2. Ray S. Baker and William E. Dodd, *The Public Papers of Woodrow Wilson, III* (New York: 1927), pp. 147–148, as cited by Robert E. Osgood, *Ideals and Self-Interest in America's Foreign Relation: The Great Transformation of the Twentieth Century* (Chicago: University of Chicago Press, 1953), p. 178.
3. Albert Shaw (ed.), *President Wilson's State Papers and Addresses* (New York: George A. Doran Co., 1918), pp. 380–381.
4. A good summary of the literature of Woodrow Wilson's view of world order can be found in Lloyd E. Ambosius, "The Orthodoxy of Revisionism; Woodrow Wilson and the New Left," *Diplomatic History*, Vol. 1, No. 3 (Summer 1977), especially pp. 209–211.
5. Cited by Inis Claude, *Power and International Relations* (New York: Random House, 1962), p. 101.
6. G. H. Stern, "The Foreign Policy of the Soviet Union," in F. S. Northedge (ed.), *The Foreign Policies of the Great Powers* (New York: Praeger Publishers, 1962), p. 77. An exhaustive review of the "Soviet diplomatic method" can be found in Joseph G. Whelan's *Soviet Diplomacy and Negotiating Behavior: Emerging New Context for U.S. Diplomacy*, Special Studies on Foreign Affairs Issues, Congressional Research Service for the Senate Committee on Foreign Relations, July 11, 1979.

7. Woodrow Wilson, Speech at Kansas City, Mo., September 6, 1919, reprinted in Thomas G. Paterson, ed., *Major Problems in American Foreign Policy: Documents and Essays,* Vol. II (since 1914), (Lexington, Mass.: D.C. Heath and Co., 1978), pp. 96–97.

8. The figure is from Betty Miller Unterberger, "President Wilson and the Decision to Send Troops to Siberia," *Pacific Historical Review,* Vol. XXIV (February 1955), pp. 63–74. A good review of the documents and literature is Unterberger, ed., *American Intervention in the Russian Civil War* (Lexington, Mass.: D.C. Heath and Co., 1969).

9. Levin, op. cit., p. 107.

10. One soldier penned a bit of doggerel which captured their misery: "It's the land of the infernal odor, the land of the national smell. The average United States soldier would rather be quartered in L." *Literary Digest,* Vol. LX (February 8, 1919), p. 99, cited in Thomas A. Bailey, *America Faces Russia* (Ithaca, N.Y.: Cornell University Press, 1950), p. 242.

11. See Linda Killen, "The Search for a Democratic Russia," *Diplomatic History,* Vol. 2, No. 3 (Summer 1978), p. 241. Alongside the American military effort, Wilson directed American grains to be sent to the White controlled area since this was a "most effective means of limiting the spread of Bolshevism." The wheat never arrived, however, because its destination, Petrograd, fell to the communists before American ships could deliver the consigned grain.

12. Ibid, p. 251.

13. John G. Stoessinger, *Nations in Darkness* (New York: Random House, 1971), p. 116.

14. Walter Lippmann and Charles Merz, "A Test of the News," *New Republic,* Vol. II (August 4, 1920), pp. 1–42. For an excellent recent summary of the literature on the public's attitudes toward the Soviet Union as a function of official policy, see Ralph B. Levering, *The Public and American Foreign Policy 1918–1978* (New York: William Morrow, 1978).

15. Stoessinger, op. cit., p. 119, citing the *Saturday Evening Post,* July 6, 1918.

16. Ibid.

17. Ibid., p. 120.

18. Ibid., p. 133.

19. Ibid., p. 141.

20. Stephen Pichon, "Allied Policy in Russia," *Current History,* Vol. 10, No. 2 (May 1919), pp. 280–281.

21. George Kennan, *Russia and the West Under Lenin and Stalin* (Boston: Little, Brown and Company, 1961), p. 117.

22. *Foreign Relations of the United States, 1920,* Vol. III, pp. 466–468, cited in perhaps the best study of early Soviet diplomacy, Teddy Uldricks's *Diplomacy and Ideology: The Origins of Soviet Foreign Relations: 1917–1930* (London: Sage, 1978), p. 51.

23. Kennan, op. cit., p. 137.

24. Ibid., 138.

25. Bailey, *America Faces Russia* (Ithaca, N.Y.: Cornell Univ. Press, 1950), p. 257.

26. Stoessinger, op. cit., p. 143.

27. Ibid., p. 143.

28. *Literary Digest,* Vol. CXVI (December 2, 1933), p. 13.

29. Louis Fisher, *Russia's Road from Peace to War* (New York: Harper & Row, 1969), p. 261.

30. Indeed, some have suggested that the brutal purges in 1937 can be seen as a means of ridding the Soviet Union of potential opposition to a *modus vivendi* with Hitler. See Kennan, op. cit., pp. 315–316. Thomas Maddux suggests that Stalin "backed away"

from active cooperation with the West in early 1936. See Maddux, "Watching Stalin Maneuver Between Hitler and the West: American Diplomats and Soviet Diplomacy, 1934–1939," *Diplomatic History,* Vol. 1, No. 2 (Spring 1977).

31. Kennan, op. cit., p. 317.
32. *The Times* (London), September 28, 1938; and John Wheeler-Bennett, *Munich: Prologue to Tragedy* (London: Macmillan Company, 1948), pp. 157–158.
33. The American role was minor but noteworthy for the sense of guilt that it caused. Roosevelt stated to Hitler, just before Munich, that Germany did not have to concern itself about American protest. "The Government of the United States has no political involvements in Europe," Roosevelt declared, "and will assume no obligations in the conduct of the present negotiations." Robert A. Divine, *Roosevelt and World War II* (Baltimore: Johns Hopkins University Press, 1969), p.22.
34. Adam B. Ulam, *Expansion and Coexistence, History of Soviet Foreign Policy, 1917–1967* (New York: Praeger Publishers, 1968), p. 263 *passim.*
35. The British did not want to be responsible for defending the Baltic states but were requesting the Soviets to aid Holland and Belgium.
36. Winston S. Churchill, *The Grand Alliance, Vol. III of the Second World War* (Boston: Houghton Mifflin Company, 1950), p. 369.
37. George F. Kennan, *Memoirs, 1925–1950* (Boston: Little, Brown and Company, 1967), pp. 133–134.
38. Divine, op. cit., p. 81–82.
39. Ibid., p. 84.
40. Kennan, *Russia and the West Under Lenin and Stalin,* pp. 350–351.
41. As the U.S. Chiefs of Staff reported in 1941, "It should be recognized as an almost invariable rule that wars cannot be finally won without the use of land armies." M. Watson, War Department, Chief of Staff; *Pre-War Plans and Preparations (United States Army in World War II).* Washington, D.C.: U.S. Government Printing Office, 1950, pp. 400–410; cited in John Bagguley, "The World War and the Cold War," in David Horowitz (ed.), *Containment and Revolution* (Boston: Beacon Press, 1967), p. 91.
42. Churchill, op. cit., pp. 645–651.
43. James MacGregor Burns, *Roosevelt: The Soldier of Freedom* (New York: Harcourt Brace Jovanovich, 1970), p. 231.
44. Churchill, op. cit., pp. 457–458.
45. Paul Carell, *Hitler Moves East: 1941–1943* (New York: Ballantine Books, 1963), p. 196 *passim.*
46. Ibid., p. 202.
47. Churchill, op. cit., pp. 469–470.
48. Churchill, *The Hinge of Fate, Vol. IV of The Second World War* (Boston: Houghton Mifflin Company, 1950), p. 201.
49. Burns, op. cit., pp. 111–112.
50. John L. Gaddis, *The United States and the Origins of the Cold War, 1941–1947* (New York: Columbia University Press, 1972), p. 7.
51. Robert E. Sherwood, *Roosevelt and Hopkins* (New York: Harper & Brothers, 1948), p. 577.
52. Churchill, *The Hinge of Fate,* p. 342.
53. H. C. Butcher, *The Years with Eisenhower* (New York: Simon & Schuster, 1946), p. 12.
54. Ibid., p. 29; and Stephen Ambrose, *Rise to Globalism: American Foreign Policy Since 1938* (Baltimore: Penguin Books, 1970), p. 53.
55. Burns, op. cit., p. 236.

56. Churchill, *The Hinge of Fate,* p. 475.
57. Cited in Andre Fontaine, *History of the Cold War* (New York: Vintage Books, 1968), p. 160.
58. Bagguley "The World War and the Cold War," in David Horowitz, ed, *Containment and Revolution* (Boston: Beacon Press, 1967), p. 91; and Churchill, *The Hinge of Fate, Vol. IV of the Second World War* (New York: Bantam Books, 1962), Appendix A, Book 2, Memo: Prime Minister to Ismay, January, 1943, p. 806, and March 3 and 4, 1943, p. 816.
59. Churchill, *The Hinge of Fate,* Bantam ed., pp. 663–679, and Memos: Prime Minister to Ismay, March 4, 1943, p. 816.
60. Richard M. Leighton and Robert W. Corkley, *Global Logistics and Strategy: 1943–1945, The United States Army in World War II* (Washington, D.C.: Office of the Chief of Military History, 1968), p. 846.
61. Gordan A. Harrison, *The European Theater of Operations: Cross-Channel Attack (The United States Army in World War II)* (Washington, D.C.: Office of the Chief of Military History, 1951), p. 141.
62. Fontaine, op. cit., p. 160.
63. Ibid., pp. 160–161.
64. Burns, op. cit., pp. 312–316.
65. Bagguley, op. cit., p. 95.
66. Burns, op. cit., p. 328
67. Ibid, p. 371.
68. Basil Liddell Hart, *History of the Second World War, Vol. II* (New York: Capricorn Books, 1972), p. 488; Vojtech Mastny, "Stalin and the Prospects of a Separate Peace in World War II," *The American Historical Review,* Vol. LXXVII, No. 5 (December 1972), pp. 1365–1388; and Lynn Etheridge Davis, *The Cold War Begins: Soviet American Conflict over Eastern Europe* (Princeton, N.J.: Princeton University Press, 1974), pp. 51–52.
69. Herbert Feis, *Churchill, Roosevelt and Stalin* (Princeton, N.J.: Princeton University Press, 1957), p. 584. The Germans, and especially Himmler, were apparently very interested in piquing the Western Allies' interest in a separate deal. Such a move would, at the least, cause disruption in the Allied cause, and might become serious. As Himmler explained to the Swedish diplomat Count Bernadotte, a deal with the Western Allies would save as great a part of Germany as possible from a Russian invasion. "I am willing to capitulate on the Western Front in order to enable the Western Allies to advance to the East." Gar Alperovitz, *Cold War Essays* (Cambridge, Mass.: Schenkman, 1970), p. 26.
70. Allen Dulles, *Secret Surrender* (New York: Harper & Row, 1966), pp. 146–151.
71. Gaddis, op. cit., p. 92.
72. Joseph Stalin, *Correspondence Between the Chairman of the Council of Ministers of the U.S.S.R. with Churchill, Atlee, Roosevelt and Truman, 1941–1945,* Vol. II (New York: Dutton, 1958).
73. Gaddis, op. cit., p. 93.
74. Michael A. Pezke, article in the *Journal of the American Aviation Historical Society,* cited in *The New York Times,* November 8, 1973.
75. Sherwood, op. cit., p. 899.
76. Ibid., pp. 899–900.
77. Churchill, *The Grand Alliance,* p. 391.
78. John A. Lukacs, *The Great Powers and Eastern Europe* (New York: American Book Company, 1953), p. 506.

79. Divine, op. cit., pp. 91–92.
80. Divine, *Foreign Policy and U.S. Presidential Elections 1940–1948* (New York: Franklin Watts, 1974), pp. 130–137.
81. Burns, op. cit., p. 572.
82. Gaddis, op. cit., p. 173.
83. W. Averell Harriman, *America and Russia in a Changing World: A Half Century of Personal Observation* (Garden City, N.Y.: Doubleday & Company, 1971), pp. 35–36.
84. Milovan Djilas, *Conversations with Stalin* (New York: Harcourt, Brace & World, 1962), p. 114.
85. Ronald Steel, "Did Anybody Start the Cold War?" *New York Review,* Vol. 26 (September 2, 1971), p. 26.
86. See Arthur Schlesinger, "The Origins of the Cold War," *Foreign Affairs,* Vol. 46 (October 1967), pp. 22–52.
87. Ambrose, op. cit., pp. 58–59. Jews were still persecuted, unable to practice professions, attend schools, or own property; Arabs continued to be beaten and exploited; the French Generals who had cooperated with the Nazis and fought the Americans lived in splendor amid the squalor that surrounded them.
88. *Times* (London), April 17, 1945.
89. Churchill, *Triumph and Tragedy, Vol. VI of the Second World War* (New York: Bantam Books, 1962), p. 258.
90. Ibid., 247, *passim.*
91. Ibid., p. 610.
92. Perry McCoy Smith, *The Air Force Plans for Peace: 1943–1945* (Baltimore: Johns Hopkins University Press, 1970). American plans at sea were to put U.S. ships "everywhere" so, in the words of one planner, the U.S. fleet would outnumber the fleets of the world. Thomas G. Paterson, *On Every Front* (New York: Norton, 1979), p. 81, and unpublished monograph by James E. King.
93. Kennan, *Memoirs,* p. 57. For Harriman's views see Daniel Yergin, *Shattered Peace: The Origins of the Cold War and the National Security State* (Boston: Houghton Mifflin Co., 1977), pp. 81, 84, and 93.
94. Kennan, op. cit. p. 70.
95. Edward R. Stettinius, *Roosevelt and the Russians* (Garden City, N.Y.: Doubleday & Company, 1949), p. 347.
96. Harry S. Truman, *Memoirs, Vol. II, Year of Decision* (Garden City, N.Y.: Doubleday & Company, 1955), p. 71.
97. Ibid., p. 82. For a milder rendition of this conversation, see Robert J. Donovan, *Conflict and Crisis* (New York: Norton, 1977), p. 42, fn. 33 and p. 445.
98. Churchill, *Triumph and Tragedy,* Bantam Ed., pp. 421–422. This quotation is partly a paraphrase of Stalin's words by Churchill and partly a direct quote of Stalin's message to Churchill.
99. William D. Leahy, *I Was There* (New York: Whittsley House, 1950), pp. 384–385.
100. Gabriel Kolko, *The Politics of War* (New York: Vintage Books, 1968), pp. 439–444; and Schlesinger, op. cit., p. 43.
101. Alperovitz, *Cold War Essays,* p. 98.
102. Sherwood, op. cit. p. 894.
103. And, in the view of some observers, it may have been a bureaucratic mistake: Gaddis, op. cit., p. 219.
104. Truman, op. cit., p. 87.

105. Jonathan Daniels, *The Man of Independence* (Philadelphia: J. B. Lippincott Co., 1950), p. 266. Also see Martin J. Sherwin, *A World Destroyed: The Atomic Bomb and the Grand Alliance* (New York: Alfred A. Knopf, 1975). pp. 188, 191 for a dispute about exactly when the bomb and Poland became bound together as issues.
106. Gar Alperovitz, *Atomic Diplomacy* (New York: Random House, 1965), p. 64. For a critique of Alperovitz's "delayed showdown" thesis, see Martin J. Sherwin "The Atomic Bomb, Scientists, and American Diplomacy During the Second World War" (unpublished doctoral dissertation, University of California, Los Angeles, 1971) pp. 252–269. On the other hand, see Yergin, op. cit., p. 101 and p. 115, who apparently accepts part of Alperovitz's controversial thesis about a showdown with the Soviets until after there was a successful test of the A-bomb. His rather elliptical essay on this point can be found in his notes of p. 433, fn. 19, where he suggests Alperovitz "over-interprets" the data.
107. Gaddis, op. cit., p. 234.
108. Truman, op. cit., p. 314.
109. Churchill, *Triumph and Tragedy* (Houghton Mifflin ed.), p. 639.
110. William A. Williams, *Tragedy of American Diplomacy*, rev. ed. (New York: Delta Books, 1962), p. 249.
111. Ibid.
112. Churchill, *Triumph and Tragedy* (Houghton Mifflin ed.), pp. 545ff.
113. Walter Millis (ed.), *The Forrestal Diaries* (New York: Viking Press, 1951), p. 78.
114. Truman, op. cit., p. 412.
115. Gaddis, op. cit., p. 264.
116. Cited in Alperovitz, *Cold War Essays*, p. 70.
117. Harry S. Truman, *Public Papers of the President — 1945* (Washington, D.C.: U.S. Government Printing Office, 1961), p. 212.
118. Cited in Alperovitz, *Cold War Essays*, p. 54.
119. Herbert Feis, *The Atomic Bomb and the End of World War II* (Princeton, N.J.: Princeton University Press, 1966), pp. 111–116.
120. *The United States Strategic Bombing Survey,* "Japan's Struggle to end the War," War Department, July 1, 1946, p. 13, and Alperovitz, *Cold War Essays,* pp. 62–63. The thesis that the bomb might not have been a military necessity is sharply challenged but not refuted by Professor Edward Shapiro, "The Military Options to Hiroshima: A Critical Examination of Gar Alperovitz," *Naval War College Review,* Vol. 30, No. 4 (Spring 1978), pp. 101–113. The thesis that the Japanese would not have surrendered until at least the first atomic bomb is argued by John Toland, *The Rising Sun: The Decline and Fall of the Japanese Empire, 1936–1945* (New York: Random House, 1970), pp. 809–866.
121. Discussions of these options may be found in Feis, op. cit., and Alperovitz, *Cold War Essays.* Also see the remarks of Isidor Rabi, a Nobel laureate, conversant with both the physics and politics of the decision not to warn the Japanese ahead of time, in Donovan, op. cit., p. 61 and p. 95 for Truman's thinking on this matter.
122. Feis, op. cit., p. 194.
123. Ibid. The decision to use the bomb may have been reinforced by a certain momentum that was somewhat independent of diplomatic or strategic subtleties. Among the elements that could have been at work in this regard, one might note:

    1. The expenditure of $2 billion, in secret, would have to be presumably justified some day.

2. Life was cheap in World War II; thousands had been slaughtered in Europe and Japan in air raids against civilian targets. The raid against Japan did not seem all that extraordinary and was perhaps facilitated by popular racist beliefs about Japan.
3. As Ambrose points out, "The bomb was there ... to use it seemed inevitable." To Truman, it appeared little else than an ace in the flush hand of military capability. It was only after their use, and some reflections, that atomic weapons created the respect they now command for themselves. See also Donovan, op. cit., chaps. 5, 7, and 10.

Still another argument drawing on the implicit momentum of the development process by emphasizing Truman's inexperience is advanced by Kenneth M. Glazier, Jr., "The Decision to Use Atomic Weapons Against Hiroshima and Nagasaki," *Public Policy,* Vol. 18 (Summer 1970), pp. 463–516. See also the important essay by Barton Bernstein, "Roosevelt, Truman and the Atomic Bomb," *Political Science Quarterly,* No. 90 (Spring 1975), pp. 23–29, for some of the uncertainties policymakers harbored regarding the efficacy of the bomb. On balance, however, their hopes for the weapon seem beyond question. See Yergin, op. cit., p. 120.

124. Kolko, op. cit., p. 599.
125. Gaddis, op. cit., p. 119.
126. Charles de Gaulle, *The Salvation: Complete War Memoirs,* Vol. III (New York: Simon and Schuster, 1955–1960), pp. 285–286.
127. Gaddis, op. cit., p. 241.
128. Charles Bohlen, Minutes of Second Meeting, February 5, 1944, *Foreign Relations of the United States, Diplomatic Papers: The Conferences of Malta and Yalta, 1945* (Washington, D.C.: U.S. Government Printing Office, 1955), pp. 620–621.
129. Lloyd C. Gardner, *Architects of Illusion: Men and Ideas in American Foreign Policy, 1941–1949* (Chicago: Quadrangle Books, 1970), p. 98.
130. Atomic scientist Leo Szilard wrote of his conversations with Byrnes at this time, that his "sense of proportion" was appalling. Szilard recalls:

> I shared Byrnes' concern about Russia's throwing around her weight in the post-war period, but I was completely flabbergasted by the assumption that rattling the bomb might make Russia more manageable.
> I began to doubt that there was any way for me to communicate with Byrnes in this matter, and my doubt became certainty when he turned to me and said, "Well, you come from Hungary — you would not want Russia to stay in Hungary indefinitely." I certainly didn't want Russia to stay in Hungary indefinitely, but what Byrnes said offended my sense of proportion. I was concerned at this point that by demonstrating the bomb and using it in the war against Japan, we might start an atomic arms race between America and Russia which was not disposed at this point to worry about what would happen to Hungary.

Leo Szilard, "Reminiscences" in Donald Fleming and Bernard Bailyn (eds.), *Perspectives in American History II* (Cambridge, Mass.: Harvard University Press, 1968), pp. 94–151.
131. Feis, *From Trust to Terror: The Onset of the Cold War 1945–1950* (New York: W. W. Norton & Company, 1970), p. 54.
132. Gaddis, p. 241.

133. Ibid., p. 291.

134. Quoted in Feis, *From Trust to Terror,* p. 55.

135. The Stuttgart Speech, Typescript, National Archives, Washington, D.C., Regional File of the Department of State 740–00119 (Germany), p. 8. For an important dissent on the meaning of the Stuttgart address and review of the literature see John Gimbel, "On the Implementation of the Potsdam Agreement: An Essay on U.S. Post War German Policy," *Political Science Quarterly,* Vol. 87 (June 1972), pp. 242–269.

136. Walter LaFeber, *America, Russia and the Cold War: 1945–1971* (New York: John Wiley and Sons, 1972), p. 34.

Chapter 2
The Onset of the Cold War

By late 1945 it was apparent that Soviet and American policies were no longer joined by even the most tenuous of the strands that had held the wartime alliance together. During the last months of 1945 and throughout 1946 a new and inexperienced American president sought to master American policy even as that policy collided with Soviet interests on a global scale, first in Germany and then simultaneously in the Middle East, Asia, and the United Nations. It was, as former Secretary of State Dean Acheson put it, a time of "learning."[1] And out of it emerged the political culture, reflexes, and some of the most fundamental policy parameters for the next quarter century.

A WORLD VIEW TAKES SHAPE

As positions hardened in Germany, the Soviets and the West issued what Walter LaFeber has called "appropriate declarations of the Cold War."[2] In a speech on February 9, 1946, Stalin took note of the relatively weak position of the Soviet Union and its need, in spite of the hardships of the war, to redouble its efforts to achieve economic recovery. In Stalin's view, the power of the West did not allow the Soviet Union the luxury of returning to a peacetime footing; instead, high industrial production targets and an emphasis on the production of modern weapons systems were to be the order of the day for the next 15 years.[3] Stalin asserted that communism and capitalism were incompatible and that true peace was impossible until the former supplanted the latter. Most people in the United States received the speech as a warlike call to confrontation between communism and the West.[4]

Less than a month later, Winston Churchill replied with his famous "Iron Curtain" speech at Fulton, Missouri, in which he asserted that the Soviets did not want war but rather "they desire . . . the fruits of war and the indefinite expansion of their power and doctrines."[5] The proper response, in Churchill's view, was a show of strength: "There is nothing they admire so much as strength, and there is nothing for which they have less respect than for military weakness."[6] It was the "duty," therefore, of the United States and Great Britain to join in a "fraternal association of the English-speaking peoples" to counter Soviet expansionism. Churchill's position seems to have been quite compatible with a fairly widespread but basically private mood of American policymakers, a mood that had been articulated in an 8000-word telegram from the chargé d'affaires of the Moscow Embassy, George F. Kennan, 2 weeks after Stalin's speech and a week before Churchill's.

The Soviet Threat Defined

The "long telegram" of February 22, 1946, was a response to an exasperated Department of State's request for some explanation of Soviet behavior. Kennan states that he had been trying for the preceding 18 months to get Washington to move toward a firmer policy line. "Now, suddenly, my opinion was being asked. . . . Nothing but the whole truth would do. They had asked for it. Now, by God, they would have it."[7] What they got was an extremely frightening picture of a Soviet Union that would expand inexorably unless opposed:

> Soviet power [is] . . . [i]mpervious to logic of reason, and it is highly sensitive to logic of force. For this reason it can easily withdraw — and usually does — when strong resistance is encountered at any point. Thus, if the adversary has sufficient force and makes clear his readiness to use it, he rarely has to do so."[8]

Although Kennan's recommendations concerning what American policy should be in the face of this threat were rather vague,[9] his description of the horrors and implied horrors of failing to confront Communist power had tremendous impact and was a crucial element in subsequent American foreign policy. The message was read from the president on down and circulated widely in the Department of State and the military. The conclusion seems to have been drawn that the United States was confronted with a multidimensional threat aimed at nothing less than Western civilization. The only apparent remedy to Soviet power was struggle and confrontation because all they understood was force. Negotiations were viewed as being of limited utility if not impossible. Therefore the manipulation of the threat of war had to become the most important facet of diplomacy when dealing with the Soviets.

The inference that force was a primary instrument for dealing with the Russians was drawn, although Kennan claims, in retrospect, to have been uncomfortable with it.[10] A few other officials within the government openly displayed their opposition to the emerging anti-Soviet consensus of the Truman administration. Most prominent was Secretary of Commerce and former Vice President (under Roosevelt) Henry Wallace. Wallace represented a diminishing number of liberal Democrats who continued to advocate a policy of lowered voices and continued negotiation with the Russians.[11] Truman's reaction to these concerns was to ignore them, and when Wallace took a similar position publicly in September 1946, he was fired.[12] The message was clear; the policy of getting tough with the Russians was now official orthodoxy, and those who challenged it did so at their peril. The hard line articulated in Churchill's public warning and Kennan's private epistle was matched by the events of 1946.

"Another War Is in the Making"

In January 1946 a purportedly pro-Soviet government came to power in Iran and began to negotiate with the Soviet-supported Azerbaijanian "autonomous region" in Northern Iran, then occupied by Soviet forces. Truman sent a stiff note to Stalin demanding that all Soviet troops be withdrawn at once and warning that the American fleet and troops were being prepared to move to Iran within 6 weeks.[13] By early April 1946, Stalin had backed away from the confrontation, and under U.S. pressure the internal policy of Iran began to shift. In Turkey the Russians sought throughout 1945 and much of 1946 to fulfill their historic desire to exercise control over the Dardannelles, the link between the Black Sea and the Eastern Mediterranean. Soviet pressure on the Turkish government was met by a display of American arms as Truman dispatched to the area in August the aircraft carrier *Franklin D. Roosevelt* along with a reinforced naval unit including a contingent of marines. Furthermore, in the following month the secretary of defense announced that the navy would maintain a permanent presence in the Eastern Mediterranean.

In the meantime the political situation in China began to deteriorate rapidly. In December 1945 General George C. Marshall had been dispatched to China to work out a reconciliation between the communists under Mao Zedong and Chiang Kai-Shek's Kuomintang. By February 1946 he had succeeded in bringing about a ceasefire, but he could not convince Chiang to enter into a coalition government with Mao. Fighting renewed in April 1946. And by autumn Mao, with the aid of large stores of captured Japanese weapons turned over to him by the Russians as their occupation forces withdrew from Manchuria, had assumed an offensive that would bring victory in less than 2 years.

It was apparent, by late 1946 and early 1947, that Chiang's military ineptitude was exceeded only by the corruption of his civil administration and his consequent loss of popular support. Significant American intervention might have saved Chiang although the Maoist forces fought virtually unaided, excepting the Russian gift of captured Japanese weapons. Mao was, of course, a communist, but Soviet involvement in the Chinese civil war was unenthusiastic. Throughout the war, the Russians continued to recognize Chiang as the head of China. More importantly, there was profound disagreement between Mao and Stalin over the course to political power in China that dated back to the 1920s. Indeed, there is evidence that Stalin feared a postwar China united under the strong leadership of Mao. But Washington's primary concern in 1946 was the Soviet-American confrontation in Europe and the implementation of stiffening U.S. posture vis-à-vis the Russians. Chiang was provided inspiration and limited material aid. He was not given the commitment of American troops probably necessary to save what Marshall reported to be a militarily inept and politically corrupt regime. Nonetheless, as the situation worsened in Europe, the Russians became identified as agents of China's internal agony.

Yet another element in this mix of developments was the total breakdown of efforts to establish some form of international control over atomic energy. The original U.S. position, the so-called Acheson-Lilienthal plan, called for the gradual passing of control of atomic weapons to an international body under the UN. During the proposed transition, the United States would maintain its favored military position while other parties to the agreement would agree to be inspected by international agencies. To make the plan more acceptable to Congress and the American people, Truman decided to entrust Bernard Baruch, a well-known, admired, but vain confidant of public officials, the task of formally making the proposal to the UN. Baruch insisted, however, that the possibility of Soviet veto power, left vague in the control arrangements in the original proposal, be explicitly eliminated in the draft submitted to the UN.

The Soviets rejected Baruch's formulation, calling instead for a reversal of the process being proposed. The first step, they argued, should be the destruction of all atomic weapons and then the evolution by stages of international control within which they would maintain their veto power. Thus, at the very outset of the cold war, the problem of parity and perceived gaps in capability impinged on efforts to control arms. The Soviets, perceiving themselves behind in nuclear weapons technology and thus vulnerable, were not prepared to commit themselves to any scheme of arms control that implied freezing the Soviet Union into a position of permanent inferiority. They would seek a level of equality either through the destruction of existing atomic stockpiles and then discuss the possibilities of control or by building their own atomic weapons. The United States, on the other hand, viewed Soviet fears of the American atomic monopoly as evidence of neurotic stubbornness and as a smokescreen to camouflage their attempts to gain the nuclear secret (an atomic spy ring had been broken in Canada in 1946).[14]

The shift in tenor and tactics begun in late 1945 was complete by the end of 1946. In late 1945, former Secretary of War Henry L. Stimson had cautioned Truman against too blatant a use of American possession of atomic weapons in postwar diplomacy for fear that Russian "distrust of our purposes and motives will increase."[15] A year later he was proposing full production of the weapons.[16] Moreover, in January 1946, Mr. Truman had written to Secretary of State Byrnes:

> There isn't a doubt in my mind that Russia intends an invasion of Turkey and the seizure of the Black Sea Straits to the Mediterranean. Unless Russia is faced with an iron fist and strong language, another war is in the making. Only one language do they understand — "How many divisions have you?"
>
> I do not think we should play compromise any longer. I'm tired of babying the Soviets.[17]

Kennan's long telegram followed in February, Churchill's speech in March, the Iranian confrontation in the same month, the resumption of the Chinese civil war in April, the deterioration of the German situation in April and May, Baruch's proposal in June, and in August the United States reacted to Soviet probes in Turkey with the threat of war. Finally, in September, Secretary of State Byrnes in his Stuttgart speech had made it clear that the United States was prepared to stay in Germany indefinitely — a unified Germany preferably, but a divided one if necessary.

Arranged in this way, the major international political events of 1946 would seem to form a pattern, almost a design. We should not conclude, however, that there was some sort of scheme being worked out by Washington or Moscow. Events retrospectively abstracted from the milieu in which they were embedded invariably appear to have interrelationships that policymakers usually perceived only dimly at the time if at all. On the other hand it would be naive to conclude that there was no relationship among the events. The stiffening and toughening of American policy in 1946 was based on an assessment of Soviet ideology, pronouncements, and activities. The linking by President Truman of an "iron fist" and "strong language" and the aversion of "another war" implies that by 1946 he and others in his administration were drawing parallels between the world of 1946 and the world of 1938 and 1939, when war had come about because the British did not draw the conceptual linkage between force and order now drawn by President Truman. Truman (an avid and voracious reader of history and prone to drawing historical analogies), his advisers, and their British allies had only just brought to a close the horrible consequences of the failure to show an iron fist and strong language to Hitler. That mistake was not going to be repeated by the Truman Administration.

The American Public
and the Onset of Cold War

If there was an element of discontinuity in the initial attempt to define United States-Soviet relations it was due in no small measure to the domestic situation confronting the Truman administration. Apart from the inevitable difficulties surrounding his assumption of the presidency, Truman was faced with an American public whose concerns ran to anything but foreign policy in 1946. The war was over, and most Americans were interested in returning their personal lives to a state of normalcy. What they found in 1946, however, was hardly normal.[18] In April the nation's coal miners went on strike for 40 days, and in May the railroads were struck. Meanwhile unemployment was growing in those industries where wartime contracts were being cancelled. With the removal of wartime price controls the cost of living exploded upward, and by the end of 1946, prices were 33 percent higher than they had been 5 years earlier when Japanese bombs fell on Pearl Harbor. Prices were going up but there was also little to buy. Black markets, under-the-table deals, even bartering reached a scale beyond that undertaken during the war and its attendant rationing.

Socially, "the ill-tempered, the mean, the vicious in human beings pushed to the fore."[19] There were two race riots in the North and six lynchings in the South. Jewish atomic scientists such as Robert Oppenheimer, who had been the architect of the American atomic bomb but became concerned over its implications for mankind, were harassed. At the same time the pent-up desire for luxuries drove people to buy television sets, and the public mood seemed to allow "[a]ny night . . . to burst into New Year's Eve."[20]

The presidency became, as it almost invariably does, the focus of these frustrations and jarring discontinuities. Much of the power of the president stems from his position at the center of the American people's image of their government. But this fact is not only a source of presidential power, it can also become a source of weakness. The man in the White House for the preceding 14 years strode like a giant through the Depression and then World War II. Truman was inevitably the center of invidious comparisons and the enormous expectations following the war; he was also the target of the frustrations that set in. For his own part, Truman seemed unable to gain control of the domestic situation, and although his foreign policy had begun to take shape by the end of 1946, to most Americans foreign affairs were but gathering storm clouds. People worried about the Russians, but the price of meat was understandably more important. All of it, the economic disruption, the social malaise, and the uneasiness concerning foreign affairs, culminated in the 1946 elections. The Republicans, who had not controlled the Congress or the White House since Herbert Hoover, asked the American people, "Had enough?" and the American electorate responded by sending fifty-six new Republicans to the House, putting thirteen new Republican senators in the Senate, and thereby gave the GOP control of both houses of Congress.

The perceptions of and reactions to this domestic situation on the part of the Truman administration are in some respects even more important than the perceptions and reactions to external events during this period. To many of the men around Truman, this unfolding spectacle of public disorientation and self-indulgence seemed to confirm all of their preconceptions concerning the isolationism of the American public. Indeed, Undersecretary of State Acheson was of the view that "focusing the will of 140,000,000 people on problems beyond our shores . . . [when] people are focusing on 140,000,000 other things" was perhaps the most important problem confronting American foreign policy.[21]

There was some basis for the fears of Acheson and others. Public opinion polls taken during this period indicate that throughout 1946, less than 25 percent of the American people felt that foreign problems were the most vital ones confronting the country.[22] On the other hand, one suspects that such a finding need not be surprising given the state of the economy and the understandable expectations of a nation only recently dragged through one of the most intense periods of involvement in foreign affairs in American history. Furthermore, it is not entirely clear that poll findings were indicative of the isolationism feared by those in the Truman administration, who were anxious to exhibit an iron fist and to talk tough with the Russians. It should be recalled that less than one year earlier, the American people and their representatives in Congress had been convinced of the necessity of accepting and participating in one of the greatest efforts at institutionalized multilateralism and internationalism undertaken up to that time, the founding of the UN. Unlike 1919 and 1920, the response was overwhelmingly positive. Beyond this, Winston Churchill's Iron Curtain speech calling for Anglo-American stewardship of world order had not received what could be characterized as universal support. The Department of State, sensing public support for the UN, ordered Undersecretary Acheson to *avoid* appearing on the platform with

Churchill (when he delivered an address in New York 10 days after the Fulton, Missouri, speech) for fear that the undersecretary's presence might imply official acceptance of the former prime minister's position. It may have been the private view of the Truman administration that a shift in policy toward the Soviet Union was needed. But the signals sent to the American people were as yet garbled.[23]

It may well be, therefore, that a portrayal of American public opinion as infected with a deep isolationism is not entirely accurate. There were, in fact, cross currents in American opinion that reflected the ambiguities of American policy. On the one hand, there was a commitment to the UN; but on the other hand, there was popular and congressional reluctance to extend financial assistance to Great Britain and Europe to help them overcome the economic chaos and deprivation of the immediate postwar period. Similarly, the UN had been put across as the curator of the postwar peace; but now Truman was going before Congress and asking for a continuation of the draft and universal manpower training along with a $15 billion defense budget. In point of fact, public opinion at this juncture might be more accurately characterized as confused and disoriented — aware of the world and its problems, but aware of its own immediate problems as well. Furthermore, the Truman administration, although circulating copies of Kennan's long telegram internally, was, at least prior to the summer of 1946, still taking a somewhat conciliatory *public* stance toward the Russians. Indeed, the increasingly bitter negotiations at Yalta, Potsdam, and subsequent meetings of foreign ministers were kept secret —thereby feeding public suspicion and lending credibility to Republican charges of appeasement, sellouts, and secret agreements. In short, the level of public awareness and sensitivity was disoriented and reluctant to accept greater burdens. But as subsequent events were to demonstrate, they were also permissive and accepting of executive leadership when it was provided. "The people react to what the President does," Kenneth Waltz has observed.[24] To many Americans in 1946, the president appeared to be doing very little or, at a minimum, very contradictory things.

To Truman and his closest advisers, there seemed little public awareness of the awesome threat they perceived and with which they had been dealing since early in 1945. The situation was only slightly better in Congress. It was true that Senator Arthur Vandenberg had come around during and immediately after the war to an internationalism that tended to support the stance developing within the Truman administration. But the extent to which the senator's newly gained world view extended to others in the Republican party was questionable. Indeed, what the Truman administration saw, as it confronted the 80th Congress, was a Republican majority that had lambasted the Democrats the previous November for their appeasement of communism but now would cut the administration's budget by $4.5 billion — including significant reductions in the defense budget.

From within the administration, and particularly the Department of State, it seemed that the direction of history was hanging in the balance. The post–World War II international system was perceived as on the verge of being overwhelmed by the onslaught of Soviet expansion. It was felt that this expansion could be checked by the United States; and the events in Iran and Turkey in the preceding months seemed to validate this. "The danger of these Soviet moves," despaired one inside chronicler, "was not generally realized by the American people;"[25] and without such a realization, the full power of the United States could not be mobilized to curb the impending disaster. Thus, when the British informed Washington in February 1947 that they were no longer able economically to deal with the volatile Greek domestic situation, which had once again flared into open civil war, the administration viewed the situation as both a crisis and an opportunity.

WORLD VIEW BECOMES POLICY: THE TRUMAN DOCTRINE AND THE MARSHALL PLAN

The combination of one of the worst winters in history and the economic consequences of World War II had, by February 1947, reduced Great Britain to a state of bankruptcy. Unable to afford even the import of cigarette tobacco, the British informed the United States that they could not continue economic and military assistance to either Greece or Turkey beyond March 31, 1947. The situation in Greece was deemed far more important by the Truman administration in view of the ongoing insurgency, which was purportedly communist led. A communist victory was feared if the British economic relief programs were to break down. All of this was communicated to the Department of State on February 21; and on March 12, 1947, President Truman requested $400 million in economic assistance for Greece and Turkey in a spectacular special message to Congress that is now referred to as the Truman Doctrine.

Joseph M. Jones, one of the drafters of Truman's statement, has observed that the British "had within the hour handed the job of world leadership, with all its burdens and all its glory, to the United States."[26] Yet, "[r]apidly, in an orderly manner, and with virtually no dissent, the executive branch of the government decided to act."[27] The lack of dissent indicates how well established the predisposition was toward U.S. intervention in the face of perceived Soviet expansion. Indeed, by 1947 those who stood in opposition to such a policy had been eliminated from the government or sufficiently intimidated by the experience of Henry Wallace, that they were not prepared to speak up. Thus U.S. involvement in Greece and Turkey was never really in question in the Truman administration. If there was a crisis in the spring of 1947, it concerned whether Congress and the American people could be convinced to enlist in the crusade that had been taking shape within the Truman administration for over a year.

The initial step in moving this policy of American activism was convincing Congress, and Truman sought to do this, first, through consultation with the leadership of Congress; and second, through an appearance before a joint session of the House and Senate.

A meeting with congressional leaders was held on February 27 and assumed dramatic proportions. The newly appointed secretary of state, George C. Marshall, argued for the Greek-Turkish aid program on abstract and broadly humanitarian grounds. Accounts of the meeting all agree that the congressional leadership largely reflected Republican skepticism about the need for U.S. economic assistance and the implication of increasing budgets. The congressmen stood mute after the distinguished secretary's restrained arguments were presented. Then, Undersecretary of State Dean Acheson spoke out and reframed the proposed United States response. Acheson later described the atmosphere of the meeting in terms that convey an image of history breaking open: "I knew we were met at Armageddon," he wrote.[28] His response was appropriately apocalyptic:

> These congressmen had no conception of what challenged them; it was my task to bring it home. . . . Never have I spoken under such a pressing sense that the issue was up to me alone. No time was left for measured appraisal. In the past eighteen months, I said, Soviet pressure on the Straits, on Iran, and on Northern Greece had brought the Balkans to the point where a highly possible Soviet breakthrough might open three continents to Soviet penetration. Like apples in a barrel infected by one rotten one, the corruption of Greece would infect Iran and all to the east. It would also carry infection to Africa through Asia Minor and Egypt, and to Europe through Italy and France, already threatened by the strongest domestic Communist parties in Western Europe. The Soviet Union was playing one of the greatest gambles in history at minimal cost. It did not need to win all the possibilities. Even one or two offered immense gains. We and we alone were in a position to break up the play. These were the stakes that British withdrawal from the Eastern Mediterranean offered to an eager and ruthless opponent.[29]

The members of Congress were stunned by Acheson's presentation, and there seemed to be general agreement that they would support the president if he would go before Congress and the American people and state matters in the same forceful manner as Acheson's presentation.[30] The Department of State, charged with drafting the President's speech, was determined to convince the American people of the existence of a mortal danger and the need for a decisive American response.[31] Thus, from the very outset, the Truman Doctrine had a dual purpose. First, it was a public statement of the foreign policy assumptions and positions that formed the basis of deep consensus within the Truman administration. Second, Truman's statement was aimed at the American public. For in it, he attempted to convince the American people to view world security as jeopardized and then mobilize Americans in support of a world role for the United States.[32] Thus Truman sought and in large measure succeeded in setting forth the idiom of the debate and the central questions of American foreign policy for 25 years. Truman's speech was to be, in Hans Morgenthau's words, the "intellectual capital" of the cold war.[33]

The Truman Doctrine

President Truman's presentation to the Congress centered on what he termed the "broader implications" of U.S. assistance to Greece and Turkey. The world, Truman asserted, was divided between two antithetical ways of life: one based on freedom, the other on coercion.[34]

The president emphasized that it had long been "one of the primary objectives of the foreign policy of the United States [to create] conditions in which we and other nations will be able to work out a way of life free from coercion."[35] He continued:

> We shall not realize our objectives, however, unless we are willing to help free peoples to maintain their free institutions and their national integrity against aggressive movements that seek to impose upon them totalitarian regimes. This is no more than a frank recognition that totalitarian regimes imposed upon free peoples by direct or indirect aggression, undermine the foundations of international peace and hence the security of the United States.[36]

Truman thus displayed the assumptions for post–World War II American foreign policy. The security of the United States, the most basic of foreign policy values, was found only in "international peace," that is, in a system of international order. Unless that international order was secure the United States could not be counted secure; thus it followed that it must be the policy of the United States to support free peoples who are resisting attempted subjugation by armed minorities or by outside pressures.

I believe that we must assist free peoples to work out their own destinies in their own way.[37]

The specific concern of Truman on this day was a request for $400 million in economic and military assistance for Greece and Turkey, but he made it clear that the broader framework articulated in the speech stretched beyond those troubled communities:

> It would be an unspeakable tragedy if these countries which have struggled so long against overwhelming odds, should lose that victory for which they sacrificed so much. Collapse of free institutions and loss of independence would be disastrous not only for them but for the world. Discouragement and possibly failure would quickly be the lot of neighboring peoples striving to maintain their freedom and independence.[38]

Acheson had privately spoken of "rotten apples . . . spreading corruption and infection," the president was now speaking of "confusion and disorder," the "collapse of free institutions," and "discouragement," and future American leaders would warn of falling dominoes—but the underlying premise was the same. Peace and world order were now indivisible. Hence the loss of one country carried with it ominous implications for the entire structure of world order. (This, after all, was the lesson of Munich.) In essence, therefore, the security of the world and the security of the United States were entwined, perhaps synonymous. It was now imperative that the United States build and then maintain a world order congenial to its own values or way of life. In the analysis of Truman and his advisers, if aggression were allowed to proceed, then the fabric of global security would unravel, and American security would inevitably be jeopardized.

Truman's statement implied, however, that U.S. policy involved a great deal more than a simple internationalism. The threat to international security was defined in terms of the regimes and domestic systems of other members of the international system. The internal affairs of other states were now an important component of world order. Whether a country's political, economic, and social system was "totalitarian," "democratic," "communist," or "capitalist" — whether, in short, its way of life conformed to the U.S. vision of what was best or the Soviets' vision — was now central to the question of world order. The internal politics of states were fused with the quality of world order; and intervention in the former was now regarded as legitimate so as to preserve an American vision of the latter.

Although the existence and objectives of the UN were duly noted, they were dismissed with the observation that "the situation is an urgent one requiring immediate action and the UN and its related organizations are not in a position to extend help of the kind that is required."[39] Roosevelt's conception of the nations of the world working through a multilateral structure for the building and preservation of world order (a conception drawn in turn from Wilson) was therefore set aside. A singularly American vision of world order, built and maintained through American instrumentalities, was put in its place. The UN itself had been an American idea, and from the outset the central role of the Security Council with its provision of great-power vetoes ensured a pivotal role for American interests. But now, with the Truman Doctrine, multilateralism became an instrument of American unilateralism.

Important to the Congress was the scope of the Truman Doctrine. Did this new Truman Doctrine mean, the Congress now asked, that we are "adopting a policy where we say the United States of America will be interested all over the world in any country that is seeking democratic freedom?"[40] The administration sought to ease concern that the Truman Doctrine was the opening of a global ideological crusade while at the same time maintaining for itself maximum latitude. Acheson, in soliciting aid to Turkey and Greece before the Senate Foreign Relations Committee, engaged in colloquy with the committee chairman, Senator Vandenberg:

> *Secretary Acheson:* . . . the President . . . was talking specifically about the problem in Greece and Turkey. He laid down this broad principle. He did not state, and I think no one would state that that means that wherever this situation occurs, one must react to it in exactly the same way. The situations of different cases are utterly different, and what you would do in one case you cannot do in another case. But the principle is clear I think. . . . We are concerned where a people already enjoying free institutions are being coerced to give them up. . . .
>
> *The Chairman:* . . . In other words, I think what you are saying is that wherever we find free peoples having difficulty in the maintenance of free institutions, and difficulty in defending against aggressive movements that seek to impose upon them totalitarian regimes, we do not necessarily react in the same way each time, but we propose to react.
>
> *Secretary Acheson:* That, I think, is correct.[41]

The Truman administration's reluctance to extend further aid and/or American combat support to Chiang Kai-Shek and Acheson's staunch refusal to concede under intense questioning in his appearance before the House Foreign Affairs Committee that the Chinese and Greek cases were comparable seems to confirm that there were, indeed, limitations to the scope of the Truman Doctrine. But all in all, Acheson's ready acceptance of Vandenberg's expansive paraphrasing of the president's speech reveals an activist and globalist impulse to American policy that was to transcend the temporary hedging of the American bet in China and play itself out over the next decades in Korea, Lebanon, Berlin, the Bay of Pigs, the Dominican Republic, and Vietnam.

The president seemed relatively unequivocal about the instruments to be employed to buttress this doctrine: "I believe that our help should be primarily through economic and financial aid which is essential to economic stability and orderly political processes."[42] And, at first glance, Truman's request for $400 million was not unlike the loans and credits extended to Belgium, France, the Netherlands, and Norway during 1945 and 1946. Furthermore, the amount requested for Greece and Turkey was small when compared to a $3.4 billion loan extended to Britain the previous year. Thus, the use of economic assistance had well-defined and substantial precedent and was linked to a broad conception of world economic order. Economic recovery had been tied by the Roosevelt and now the Truman administrations to the creation of an international economic order predicated upon the reduction and eventual elimination of tariffs and other obstacles to free trade. A fundamental element in free and expanding international trading systems was stable international monetary affairs, the absence of which during the 1930s had, in this view, brought on the general economic collapse of the Depression and thereby contributed directly to World War II. To prevent a recurrence of this situation and establish the basis for stable world economic order, a set of loosely related institutions had been set up during and after the war: the International Monetary Fund (IMF), the International Bank for Reconstruction and Development (World Bank), and the General Agreement of Tariffs and Trade (GATT).[43] But by 1946 the entire constellation of institutions and processes seemed insufficient to provide needed postwar aid and recovery.

Simple altruism was not the motive force of the Truman economic policy. The brief termination of lend-lease aid to Russia in May of 1945 and the so-called loss of a Soviet request for a billion dollar loan later in 1945 indicated that the Truman administration was prepared to use economic instrumentalities in pursuit of policy ambitions (in these instances, more compliant behavior from Stalin concerning the emerging difficulties in Eastern Europe). A primary thrust of American economic policy prior to the Truman Doctrine can be seen as economic recovery, reconstruction, and ultimately the development of a strong and monetarily stable free-trading international economic system as an end in itself. Yet even then, the central role of the dollar and the solitary strength of the American economy undoubtedly ensured American well-being in and even domination of such a system.[44] Furthermore, given American hegemony in the world economy, one could certainly anticipate the intrusion of American political objectives into the nascent world economic order of 1945 and 1946. Nevertheless, Richard Cooper is probably justified in his contention that the framers of this economic order sought somehow to separate trade and other international economic questions from those political and security issues that comprise what is sometimes referred to as "high diplomacy."[45]

The Truman Doctrine suggested, however, that the perceived imperatives of high policy might transcend the desire or logic of treating international economics and other political questions as separate domains. Truman had asserted that "the seeds of totalitarian regimes are nurtured by misery and want. They spread and grow in the evil soil of poverty and strife."[46] Thus President Truman seemed to view the two tracks of economic and politico-military policy as interrelated. Indeed, his appeal for economic assistance assumed that the relationship of "totalitarian regimes" and the "evil soil of poverty" was reversible, that the instrumentalities and processes of "low foreign policy" could be employed to bring about international order in the realm of high diplomacy. In summary, there was the germ of a grand design implied by the Truman Doctrine: the transformation of a heretofore piecemeal use of economic assistance for recovery into a comprehensive assault on the conditions that gave rise to totalitarian regimes.

The Marshall Plan and the Soviet Union: The Truman Doctrine's Meaning Emerges

Even as Truman spoke and Acheson sought to soothe congressional fears of a far-reaching American involvement, external events and developments within the administration were merging to bring about the "transformation of American foreign policy."[47] During March and April 1947 a special interdepartmental group had tentatively concluded that future United States economic and military assistance would have to proceed within a carefully planned comprehensive framework emphasizing a strong European regional economy including a reconstructed Germany.[48] But the problem of European recovery raised a troublesome issue: What was to be the relationship of the Soviet Union and Eastern Europe to this integrated European economy? How could a continent-wide recovery and integration take place in an atmosphere of deteriorating Soviet-American relations? The idea of giving priority to democratically oriented governments while simultaneously minimizing aid and comfort to "communist-dominated countries" could only contribute to the fears and distrust in the Kremlin. Coupling this to an economically strong Germany could hardly be viewed by the Russians as mere altruism. And finally, to assume and propose that the Soviets and their satellites willingly enter into such a Western-oriented politico-economic structure would seem, at a minimum, illusory, naive, or unserious. At worst, the Soviets might take this posture as support for their assumption that the United States was advancing such proposals so as to economically penetrate and fragment the Soviet's Eastern European hegemony.[49]

An indication of the Soviet reaction to this or similar proposals was the tough position taken by Molotov at the Moscow Foreign Ministers Conference held during March and April 1947. The conference was about the future shape of Germany, its postwar economy, and its relationship with the remainder of Europe. The United States and Great Britain proposed at the outset a federal structure for the German government with limitations on the powers of the central government. Even so, German economic recovery was viewed as a piece with the general economic recovery of Europe. The Russians reacted with suspicion, and attacked the proposals for a weak central German government as protecting the position of former Nazis and other anticommunist elements. In contrast, the Soviets argued for a stronger central government administering an economic recovery directed not at European integration but rather meeting as yet unfulfilled reparations commitments under the Potsdam agreements of 1945. The United States rejected these claims, and the conference dawdled in a maddening stalemate.[50]

Underlying economic claims and counterclaims, however, were bedrock differences over the future political and economic shape of Europe. The United States and Britain sought an economically strong Germany within a context of European economic recovery and integration. The French eventually came to accept much of this view, although at the outset they were reluctant to move too rapidly toward supporting a resurgent German economy. The Soviets' general desire, on the other hand, was to keep Germany in an economically weak and dependent status and hence less likely to reemerge as a threat to their security. Predictably therefore, the conference deadlocked and Secretary of State Marshall returned to the United States with apparent confirmation that the Truman Doctrine accurately portrayed obdurate Soviet behavior. Needless to say, the view from the Kremlin was increasingly a mirror image of that held on the Potomac.

In the meantime, some of the remaining ambiguities of the Truman Doctrine were being removed, as Washington's worst fears — deteriorating economic conditions leading to social and political chaos — seemed ready to bloom with the spring thaw of 1947. The disastrous winter of 1946–1947 had severely reduced coal production in Europe and thus further diminished industrial productivity. European livestock herds were decimated, and projections of reduced crops in the following year were becoming commonplace. In France, the spring saw an extreme government crisis as a lack of supplies led to rationing followed by inflation. French government controls on prices and wages precipitated a dissolution of the coalition of communists and socialists that made up the cabinet; widespread strikes followed. In Italy a similar series of developments seemed imminent. In this environment Acheson indicated the position that had been evolving within the administration.[51]

First, the United States was seen as having to absorb large quantities of imports so as to stimulate productivity abroad. Second, further emergency U.S. financing would be necessary. Furthermore, he stated: "We must take whatever action is possible immediately, *even without full Four Power agreement, to effect a larger measure of European, including German,* recovery."[52] In calling for European recovery and including West German recovery and participation, Soviet objections notwithstanding, the opportunity for avoiding a further deterioration of Soviet-American relations was reduced. Acheson's emphasis on using American assistance to promote and defend democratic institutions when they were subjected to totalitarian pressure indicated an acceptance, even encouragement, of a bifurcated Europe, and by implication a divided Germany as well.

International economic instrumentalities and processes were, therefore, absorbed into the national security equation of the Truman Doctrine. International political and economic order, American national security, totalitarian (Soviet) threats to American national security were all integrated by Acheson into a statement of American "duty" and "privilege."[53]

The fully elaborated European Recovery Program was proclaimed by Secretary Marshall at the Harvard University commencement in early June 1947. The secretary's speech restated the nexus of political and economic order at the heart of the administration's policy: "It is logical that the United States should do whatever it is able to do to assist in the return of normal economic health in the world, without which there can be no political stability and no assured peace."[54] From this it followed that American policy "should be the revival of a working economy in the world so as to permit the emergence of political and social conditions in which free institutions can exist."[55] The substance of Marshall's speech was a proposal for European economic integration rather than a piecemeal aid program. It required that the Europeans assume the initiative in establishing the structure within which they would receive Amercian aid. At the same time, the Europeans could hardly refuse the American offer — and preconditions. Thus the United States might realize its postwar objective of an integrated economic system encompassing most of the market economies of the world. Still, there was an unspoken dilemma: How were the Soviets to fit into this scheme?

Soviet participation in the Marshall Plan seemed inconsistent with the explicit linkage of economic instrumentalities and American national security drawn by Acheson. Furthermore, members of the Department of State feared that allowing Soviet participation in the planning and administration of the program would lead to Soviet disruption of European integration and political exploitation of the continuing economic stagnation. In addition, there was some concern that Soviet and Eastern European participation could undercut congressional support for the billions of dollars that would have to be requested. Nevertheless, there were disadvantages in not at least inviting the Russians: the onus for precipitating the inevitable political and economic division of Europe would fall on the United States and the Western Europeans if the Russians were snubbed. The resolution of the dilemma lay in a course of action proposed by Kennan: The Soviets would be invited to participate (hence Marshall's statement: "Our policy is directed not against any country or doctrine ..."),[56] but only on the condition that they would contribute raw materials and abide by any arrangements for mutual planning and economic integration that emerged.[57]

In other words, the Soviets were to be asked to open up their economic planning and control and the economies of Eastern Europe to the scrutiny and implied control of capitalistic Western Europeans and ultimately the United States. Furthermore, they were to contribute raw materials to the reconstruction of these same Western states, including Germany. The prospect was breathtaking. For the Soviets were being asked, in effect, to accept absorption into the American vision of world economic and political order. "If they were unwilling to do this," Kennan said, "we would simply let them exclude themselves. But we would not ourselves draw a line of division through Europe."[58] Of course, one cannot help but wonder if there was any real possibility that the Soviets could do anything else but exclude themselves and thereby place themselves in the position of being blamed for the division of Europe.

Rather unexpectedly and to the dismay of much of Washington, the Soviets, under Molotov's leadership, arrived at the initial planning sessions in Paris in late June 1947 with scores of economic experts, thus indicating interest in the program. Perhaps they felt that the position set forth by the Americans was an initial bargaining point that might be changed; or perhaps the plan genuinely interested them in view of possible assistance for their own beleaguered economy.[59] In any event, they came and participated in initial discussions and urged a plan that, though continental in scope, would nevertheless preserve the integrity of sovereign prerogatives concerning domestic economic planning. When it became apparent that the American preconditions were not negotiable and that Soviet participation would have to be on American terms, there was really little else for Molotov to do except walk out. As Molotov left, he issued an angry warning that acceptance of the American plan would mean the imposition on Europe of a supranational planning body with the power to intervene in domestic economic and, by extension, political affairs; the resurgence of West Germany; and the eventual domination of the European economy by American capital and corporations. Molotov returned home. And immediately afterward, the Soviets proposed their own rather uninspiring plan for the economic integration of Eastern Europe and established the Cominform — a uniting of the ruling parties of Eastern Europe and the Communist parties of France and Italy.

The Soviets had been maneuvered precisely as Kennan had projected; thus post–Marshall Plan diplomacy may be viewed as a brilliant tactical victory for American diplomacy. But in the long run it proved to be a decisive turn toward the depths of the cold war. The Soviets now seemed convinced that American policy was committed to European hegemony and ultimately the political and economic penetration of Eastern Europe.[60] With the formation of Cominform, the Communist parties of France and Italy moved from the collaborationist posture they had adopted immediately after the war to one of resistance to the Marshall Plan. All of this was viewed in the West as evidence of an ideological offensive.[61] The American reaction was a redoubling of efforts to bring about European economic integration, including a decision to go ahead with West German redevelopment and European partnership. In early December, the French entered into discussions with the British and the Americans concerning the integration of the French zone of occupation into the previously merged British and American zones. Further steps were therefore taken towards the creation of an independent West German state. In Herbert Feis's words, "The rift over Germany became an irreparable rupture."[62] On December 19, 1947, a Marshall Plan request for $17 billion was submitted to Congress for approval, and at the end of the month informal talks were begun on the formation of some kind of Western European defense arrangement.

THE SUMMING UP:
CONTAINMENT IS DEFINED

In the summer of 1947, George Kennan, writing under the pseudonym "X," published a public restatement of his earlier theses concerning Soviet behavior and added a somewhat more distilled set of policy prescriptions.[63] There is perhaps no better summary statement of official thinking at this time than Kennan's article; for it encompasses most of the prevailing American assumptions concerning Soviet behavior and the appropriate American response to the situation.

As with the 1946 telegram, Kennan emphasizes his perception of the internal weaknesses of the Soviet political system. From this vantage point he sees a Soviet foreign policy that emphasizes flexibility of means: Soviet policy is "a fluid stream which moves constantly, wherever it is permitted to move, toward a given goal. Its main concern is to make sure that it has filled every nook and cranny available to it in the basin of world power."[64]

The flexibility of Soviet policy suggested dangers, but the internal weaknesses of their system also provided opportunities. In the first place, Soviet pressure would be ongoing and not easily discouraged; rather, "if it finds unassailable barriers in its path, it accepts these philosophically and accommodates itself to them."[65] Kennan felt, however, that

> the United States has it in its power to increase enormously the strains under which Soviet policy must operate, to force upon the Kremlin a far greater degree of moderation and circumspection than it has had to observe in recent years, and in this way to promote tendencies which must eventually find their outlet in either the break-up or the gradual mellowing of Soviet power.[66]

This was so because "no mystical, Messianic movement — and particularly not that of the Kremlin — can face frustration indefinitely without eventually adjusting itself in one way or another to the logic of that state of affairs."[67] The manner whereby these "frustrations" and "strains" were to be induced and "moderation" and "circumspection" brought about is the prescriptive core of Kennan's argument:

> In these circumstances it is clear that the main element of any United States policy toward the Soviet Union must be that of a long-term vigilant containment of Russian expansive tendencies.... The Soviet pressure against the free institutions of the Western world is something that can be contained by the adroit and vigilant application of counter-force at a series of constantly shifting geographical and political points, corresponding to the shifts and maneuvers of Soviet policy.[68]

Kennan's statement provided a coherent summation of the policy and assumptions that had been developing incrementally over the preceding 2 years. It was, in some respects, a more subtle and moderate assessment of Soviet behavior and prescription for American behavior than the public statements of other members of the Truman administration. One suspects, for example, that Kennan's admonition "that such a policy has nothing to do with outward histrionics; with threats or blustering or superfluous gestures of outward 'toughness' "[69] was directed at no less a figure than the president himself; for Kennan and others (notably Secretary of State Marshall) were known to have reacted negatively to the ideologically belligerent tone of the Truman Doctrine.

Nevertheless, because the article was a reflection of a consensus about the roots of Soviet behavior and a suitable response, Kennan's statement was also characterized by much of the expansive optimism and vague rhetoric of officials in the Truman administration. Thus he, like Acheson, offered his "gratitude to a Providence which, by providing the American people with this implacable challenge, has made their entire security as a nation dependent on their pulling themselves together and accepting the responsibilities of moral and political leadership that history plainly intended them to bear."[70]

More important, in retrospect, his language about a "firm containment designed to confront the Russians with unalterable counter-force at every point where they show signs of encroaching upon the interests of a peaceful and stable world," was more than a faint echo of Truman's and Acheson's rhetoric. The interrelated motifs of containment, confrontation, and "unalterable counter-force at every point" were sufficiently open-ended as to allow more militant prosecutors of American policy to recast Kennan's vision of political and economic containment of Soviet power in Europe to one of global military containment.[71]

SUMMARY ... AND MORE QUESTIONS

Thus Kennan's public "X" article reaffirmed publicly the doctrine that had been developing within the Truman administration since the end of the war: Early Soviet-American disagreements over Germany contributed to a growing predisposition toward toughness within the administration — a predisposition supported by Kennan's extended analysis of Soviet international behavior in the long telegram. Events in Iran, Turkey, and to a lesser extent, China seemed to support Kennan's analysis. Thus, by early 1947 President Truman was prepared to move America into a posture of confrontation with the Soviet Union. American public opinion, however, did not seem to allow such a departure. A popular as well as congressional isolationist mood seemed in evidence. Acheson and others concluded that only a dramatic statement, even overstatement, of the Soviet threat was necessary to expand the limits of public permissability. The Greek-Turkish crisis of early 1947 provided such an opportunity, and the president dramatically set forth a concept of American national security that required that America — alone if necessary — build and then maintain global order. Indeed, American national security was deemed synonymous with that global order.

Questions concerning the means and scope of American policy remained. The Marshall Plan proposal seemed to clarify the issue in that it expanded the initial Truman Doctrine's foreign assistance proposal to a comprehensive program of European economic redevelopment. However, the structure of the program consciously precluded Soviet participation on any but American terms. The Soviets' worst fears — fears that American policy, now embracing German recovery, was directed at the economic and political penetration of their Eastern European empire — were therefore confirmed. Thus a program subsequently heralded by Winston Churchill as the "most unsordid act in history"[72] stands as an ambiguous marker at an important fork along the road to the cold war.

The economic recovery and integration of Western Europe is undoubtedly a worthy, perhaps noble, end in itself. But we should realize that in the view of the world held by the Truman administration it was also an instrument of the containment of Soviet power. For their part, however, the Soviets viewed both the Marshall Plan and Kennan's concept as something more than a defensive Western posture. These policies were perhaps seen by men such as Truman, Acheson, and Marshall as limited, well-intentioned, and ultimately peaceful responses to Soviet expansion. But by the time Kennan published his exposition of American policy, the Soviets were no longer able or willing to view the deteriorating relationship in this light. The Soviet-American relationship moved, therefore, from the crumbling edge of a tenuous wartime alliance into a crevice of distrust, fear, and, ultimately, terror.

NOTES

1. Dean Acheson, *Present at the Creation* (New York: W. W. Norton & Company, 1969), p. 196.
2. Walter LaFeber, *America, Russia and the Cold War 1945–1971* (New York: John Wiley & Sons, 1972), p. 30.
3. Marshall Shulman, *Stalin's Foreign Policy Reappraised* (New York: Atheneum Publishers, 1963), pp. 13–21.
4. For examples of American reaction see John L. Gaddis' discussion of the speech and its aftermath in *The United States and the Origins of the Cold War, 1941–1947* (New York: Columbia University Press, 1972), pp. 299–302.
5. Winston Churchill, "The Sinews of Peace," March 5, 1946, *Vital Speeches of the Day*, Vol. 12 (March 15, 1946), p. 332.

6. Ibid.
7. George F. Kennan, *Memoirs, 1925–1950* (Boston: Little, Brown and Company, 1967), p. 293.
8. Kennan, "Excerpts from Telegraphic Message from Moscow of February 22, 1946," in *Memoirs, 1925–1950*, pp. 557–558. Kennan has admitted that he now reads the long telegram with "horrified amusement" in that "it reads like one of those primers put out by alarmed congressional committees or by the Daughters of the American Revolution, designed to arouse the citizenry to the dangers of the Communist conspiracy" (Ibid., p. 294).
9. Kennan's recommendations in this regard are not unlike the proposals of Senator J. William Fulbright two decades later, that America should become "an intelligent example to the world" [Fulbright, *The Arrogance of Power* (New York: Vintage Books, 1967), p. 257.] Kennan suggested, for example, that the United States should "apprehend, and recognize [the Soviet Union] for what it is," "see that our public is educated to the realities," take "courageous and incisive measure[s] to solve internal problems of our own society," "formulate and put forward for other nations a much more positive and constructive picture of the sort of world we would like to see," and "have courage and self-confidence to cling to our own methods and conceptions of human society" (Kennan, op. cit., pp. 558–559).
10. See, for example, Kennan's admonition in the "long telegram" that the United States approach the problem of dealing with the Soviets "calmly" and "with good heart" and avoiding "prestige-engaging showdowns" (Kennan, op. cit., p. 558). For recent scholarly debate about Kennan's view of military strength and its utility at this time see John Lewis Gaddis, "Containment: A Reassessment," *Foreign Affairs*, Vol. 55, No. 4 (July 1977), pp. 873–887, and Edward Mark, "The Question of Containment: A Reply to John Lewis Gaddis," *Foreign Affairs*, Vol. 56, No. 2 (January 1978), pp. 430–440 and Gaddis' response in Ibid., pp. 440–441. There is a final minisalvo between these two in the *Newsletter* of the Society for Historians of American Foreign Relations, Vol. IX, No. 3, (September 1978), pp. 28–31.
11. Harry S. Truman, *Memoirs I: Year of Decisions* (Garden City, N.Y.: Doubleday & Co. Inc. 1955), p. 555; and D. F. Fleming, *The Cold War and Its Origins*, Vol. II (London: Callen & Unwin, 1961), pp. 420–421.
12. Truman, *Year of Decisions*, p. 556. Interestingly enough, Wallace had personally cleared his speech with Truman before delivering it. Truman, either through oversight or incomprehension, did not glean its departure from the tougher line he wished to establish with the Soviets. Truman did not fire Wallace, however, until Byrnes, his secretary of state, in Paris at a foreign minister's meeting threatened to resign "immediately." Richard Walton, *Henry Wallace, Harry Truman and the Cold War* (New York: The Viking Press, 1976), and Robert J. Donovan, *Conflict and Crisis: The Presidency of Harry S. Truman, 1945–1948* (New York: Norton, 1977), pp. 224–228.
13. Herbert Feis, *From Trust to Terror: The Onset of the Cold War, 1945–1950* (New York: W. W. Norton & Company, 1970), p. 84.
14. See Shulman, op. cit., pp. 21–24, and Thomas W. Wolfe, *Soviet Power and Europe, 1945–1970* (Baltimore: Johns Hopkins University Press, 1970), p. 37. David Holloway, "Entering the Nuclear Arms Race: The Soviet Decision to Build the Atomic Bomb, 1939–1945," *Working Papers, The Wilson Center* (Washington, D.C., July 25, 1979), p. 47. Most of the supposed secrets delivered to Soviet agents during the war were already known to Soviet physicists, ibid., fn. 76, p. 58.
15. Quoted in LaFeber, op. cit., p. 21.
16. Gaddis, op. cit., p. 335.
17. Harry S. Truman, *Memoirs: Year of Decisions*, p. 552, and Gaddis, op. cit., p. 289.

18. Eric F. Goldman, *The Crucial Decade — And After: America, 1945–1960* (New York: Vintage Books, 1960), pp. 25–41.
19. Ibid., p. 42.
20. Ibid., p. 41.
21. *Department of State Bulletin,* Vol. 14, No. 363 (June 16, 1946), p. 1045.
22. See Gabriel Almond, *The American People and Foreign Policy* (New York: Praeger Publishers, 1960), p. 73.
23. For a review of the Acheson incident, see Gaddis, op. cit., p. 309.
24. Kenneth N. Waltz, "Electoral Punishment and Foreign Policy Crises," in James N. Rosenan (ed.), *Domestic Sources of Foreign Policy* (New York: The Free Press, 1967), p. 293.
25. Joseph M. Jones, *The Fifteen Weeks* (New York: Harcourt, Brace & World, 1965), p. 47. For some idea of the world as viewed from within the Department of State at this time see pp. 39–47.
26. Ibid., p. 7.
27. Ibid., p. 11.
28. Reprinted from *Present at the Creation* by Dean Acheson. By permission of W. W. Norton & Company, Inc., and Hamish Hamilton, Ltd. Copyright © 1969 by Dean Acheson.
29. Ibid.
30. There is some disagreement concerning exactly what Vandenberg said. Acheson recalls Vandenberg saying: "Mr. President, if you will say that to the Congress and the country, I will support you and I believe that most of its members will do the same" (p. 219). Goldman, on the other hand, has Vandenberg saying: "Mr. President, if that's what you want, there's only one way to get it. That is to make a personal appearance before Congress and scare the hell out of the country" (Goldman, op. cit., p. 59).
31. Jones reports that the interdepartmental committee responsible for an initial draft of the speech indicated that there were three primary objectives of the speech: "1. To make possible the formulation of intelligent opinions by the American people on the problems created by the present situation in Greece through the furnishing of full and frank information by the government. 2. To portray the world conflict between free and totalitarian or imposed forms of government. 3. To bring about an understanding by the American people of the world strategic situation" (Jones, op. cit., p. 152).
32. For an extended discussion of the Truman Doctrine as essentially domestic propaganda, see Richard M. Freeland, *The Truman Doctrine and the Origins of McCarthyism: Foreign Policy, Domestic Policies, and Internal Security, 1946–1948* (New York: Schocken Books, 1974).
33. Hans J. Morgenthau, *A New Foreign Policy for the United States* (New York: Praeger Publishers, 1969), p. 1.
34. Harry S. Truman, "The Truman Doctrine: Special Message to the Congress on Greece and Turkey, March 12, 1947," *Public Papers of the Presidents of the United States.* Harry S. Truman, 1947 (Washington, D.C.: U.S. Government Printing Office), p. 178.
35. Ibid.
36. Ibid.
37. Ibid., pp. 178–179.
38. Ibid., p. 179.
39. Ibid., p. 177.
40. U.S., Congress, Senate Foreign Relations committee, *Hearings on S. 938 Assistance to Greece and Turkey,* 180th Cong., 1st Sess., March 24, 1947, p. 19.
41. Ibid., pp. 30–31.
42. Truman, "The Truman Doctrine: Special Message to the Congress . . .," p. 179.

43. For a straightforward introduction to the often baffling world of international economic policy the reader is referred to Joan Spero, *The Politics of International Economics* (New York: St. Martins Press, Inc., 1977).

44. See Harry Magdoff, *The Age of Imperialism: The Economics of U.S. Foreign Policy* (New York: Monthly Review Press, 1968), esp. pp. 54–113, for a Marxist exposition of this thesis. William Diebold's *The United States and the Industrial World: American Foreign Economic Policy in the 1970's* (New York: Praeger Publishers, 1972) provides the conventional and more benign view of American policy. David P. Calleo and Benjamin Rowland's *America and the World Political Economy: Atlantic Dreams and National Realities* (Bloomington, Ind.: Indiana University Press, 1973) is somewhat less conventional in its assessment.

45. Richard Cooper, "Trade Policy is Foreign Policy," *Foreign Policy,* No. 9 (Winter 1972–73), pp. 18–21.

46. Truman, "The Truman Doctrine," p. 180.

47. See Charles Bohlen, *The Transformation of American Foreign Policy* (New York: W. W. Norton & Company, 1969).

48. For a detailed account of the formation, activities, and recommendations of the Special Committee, see Jones, op. cit., pp. 199–209.

49. Ibid., 205.

50. For a more detailed consideration of the Conference, see Feis, op. cit., pp. 208–220.

51. Once again, a good detailed account of these developments is in Jones, op. cit., pp. 206–213.

52. Dean Acheson, "The Requirements of Reconstruction," *Department of State Bulletin,* Vol. 16 (May 18, 1947), p. 994 (emphasis added).

53. Ibid.

54. George C. Marshall, "European Initiative Essential to Economic Recovery," *Department of State Bulletin,* Vol. 16 (June 15, 1947), p. 1160.

55. Ibid.

56. Ibid.

57. Accounts of Kennan's position are numerous but essentially alike. See Kennan, *Memoirs, 1925–1950,* p. 342; and Feis, op. cit., pp. 242–243. See also Jones, op. cit., p. 253.

58. Kennan, *Memoirs, 1925–1950,* p. 342.

59. Adam Ulam, *The Rivals* (New York: Praeger Publishers, 1973), pp. 128–129.

60. Shulman, op. cit., pp. 14–15, and Ulam, op. cit., p. 130.

61. See Ulam, op. cit., p. 133.

62. Feis, op. cit., p. 281.

63. "X" (George F. Kennan), "The Sources of Soviet Conduct," *Foreign Affairs,* Vol. 25 (July 1947), pp. 566–582.

64. Ibid., p. 575.

65. Ibid.

66. Ibid., p. 582.

67. Ibid.

68. Ibid., p. 575–576.

69. Ibid., p. 575.

70. Ibid., p. 582.

71. See Kennan, *Memoirs; 1925–1950,* pp. 364–365; and Ronald Steel, "Man Without a Country," in his *Imperialists and Other Heroes: A Chronicle of the American Empire* (New York: Vintage Books, 1973), pp. 53–55.

72. Cited in Jones, op. cit., p. 256.

Chapter 3
From the
Marshall Plan to
Global Containment

The distrust generated by the initial clashes of antithetical Soviet and American visions of world order hardened into confrontation and cold war during the thirty months between the winter of 1947–1948 and June 1950. Throughout most of the period, as in the immediate postwar years, the cockpit was Europe and specifically Germany as the Truman administration sought to make the Marshall Plan — European recovery including a reconstituted Germany — the central component in the policy of containment. Stalin reacted with a brutal consolidation of his East European empire, including the termination of limited Czechoslovakian democracy, and increasingly anxious protests concerning the West's efforts to create a new German state free of the Four Power administration agreed to at the Potsdam meeting of 1945. In a last desperate effort to forestall this disaster for Soviet foreign and security policy, Stalin blockaded Western surface access to Berlin in 1948 and demanded a reversal of the Western thrust toward a West German state.

With the blockade, East–West relations turned, perhaps irrevocably, into the darkest days of cold war. The West responded by redoubling its efforts to bring about the creation of the Federal Republic of Germany. Even more important, the previously somewhat amorphous economic structure of containment in Europe crystallized into a military alliance, the North Atlantic Treaty Organization (NATO) in mid-1949. Almost simultaneously, in late 1949, Mao Zedong's communist revolution achieved victory on the Chinese mainland and the Soviets exploded their first atomic device. These events contributed to a top-level reassessment of American policy in late 1949 and early 1950. The outcome was a call for a decisive shift away from dependence on the political and economic instruments of containment embodied in European reconstruction and a weak NATO to a remobilization of American political and military power equal to the tasks of global containment. Indeed, American domestic priorities were to yield to the demands of a confrontation of indefinite length.

In retrospect these events seem to have about them a decisive, almost inevitable directionality. In fact, there was much uncertainty and internal debate within the United States. There were similar uncertainties and perhaps an even greater sense of vulnerability in the Soviet Union, and these fears contributed directly to the evolution of Western policy. Most of this chapter will be concerned with an overview and analysis of the playing-out of these uncertainties into the hard-edged confrontation of cold war.

THE COLD WAR

If the view of the world from Washington was grim in the winter of 1947–1948, it was no less so from Moscow. Under American leadership, the capitalist countries seemed to be consolidating their position. Stalin may have surmised that American political and economic hegemony of the West would be the first step in forming a strong base for bringing pressure to bear on the Soviet dominance of Eastern Europe. The initial pressure on the Soviets may have been limited to economic enticements, but then again the Americans would in time perhaps become sufficiently bold to instigate and support unrest in Eastern Europe. In sum, Soviet security seemed to require the maintenance of a strong Soviet political, economic, and military presence in the Eastern European countries occupied after the war.[1]

The Red Army, though reduced in size,[2] was adequate to whatever immediate external military threat may have existed. Internally, however, Stalin felt compelled to strengthen his hand. He purged Eastern European regimes of anticommunist elements as well as nationalist communist parties that were unwilling to subordinate themselves to the Soviet vision of the future. Stalin's policy collided most spectacularly with that of Tito in Yugoslavia. Tito's desire for regional hegemony in the Balkans undercut Stalin's drive for consolidation of Eastern Europe. Consequently, tensions heightened, replete with veiled threats and border incidents, and eventually, in mid-1948, Tito broke with Stalin.[3]

In the meantime, replication of this insolence and insubordination had to be anticipated. A quick crushing of the Yugoslavs might have served Stalin's ends, but there seems to have been some doubt on Stalin's part that he could end the matter quickly. The possibility of resource-consuming guerrilla conflict with Yugoslav communists led by the same Tito who had two and a half years earlier successfully prosecuted a largely partisan war against the Germans, could not have been appealing to Stalin. Stalin is said to have boasted that he could "shake my little finger and there will be no more Tito" — but he did not behave as if he believed it. The

image of the Russian bear grappling perhaps ineffectually with the Yugoslav midget would not inspire awe on the part of other Eastern Europeans.
The Yugoslav situation deteriorated slowly while more decisive moves
were made elsewhere. In Hungary, Bulgaria, and the other communist
countries "potential Titos were tracked down, demoted, tried, and often
executed. In none of the other satellites was there in fact that combination
of factors which had enabled Yugoslavia to launch her defiance, but the
Soviets were not taking chances."[4]

The Czechoslovakian Coup

Nowhere was this militancy more manifest and with greater consequence
for the future of East-West relations than in Czechoslovakia. Prior to 1948,
Czech opposition parties coexisted in a coalition government with the
Communists maintaining a slight popular plurality entitling them to nine
cabinet positions including that of prime minister. By February of 1948,
however, the Communists were instructed to eliminate independent parties, thereby consolidating Communist control in a country whose borders
touched western and eastern Germany, Poland, Hungary, and the Soviet
Union. Czechoslovakia was perhaps the most industrialized of the Central
European states, and unlike eastern Germany and Poland, its industrial
base had come through the war more or less intact. In short, Czechoslovakia was the geographic and industrial heart of the Soviet Central European glacis.

But the avowed American intention to integrate Western Europe,
including Germany, into the Marshall Plan (which was received favorably
among noncommunist Czechs), the fears of the possible magnetic effect
of Western European recovery and even future political and economic
penetration, intimations of a Western European alliance, and now the
intra-empire Titoist threat were apparently seen by Stalin as dangerously
cumulative. In such an environment he felt that he could not tolerate a
Czech government whose president, Eduard Benes, had proclaimed in
May 1946, "Culturally we are Europeans. We will never range ourselves
with East alone, or with the West alone, but always with East and West
simultaneously."[5] Accordingly, on February 25, 1948, with the Russian
army arrayed on the border and local Communists poised in and around
Prague, the Czech Communist party took control of the government.

Stalin now had the desired leverage on Central European politics;
Tito was a problem, but Yugoslavia was geographically separated from the
Soviet Union by Hungary and Rumania and was therefore not the strategic
threat a neutral Czechoslovakia could have become. In summary: Stalin,
with the establishment of the Cominform, the purging of East European
regimes, and the Czech coup, seemed to have consolidated his position.

The West Reacts

In the West, however, Stalin's actions were seen as anything but defensive. The elimination of a few Eastern European Communists with nationalist visions was one thing — but the Czechs being bullied into submission created "coursing emotion" and "gave an emotional tone to the Western reaction."[6] General Lucius Clay, the military commander of American occupation forces in Germany, informed the Pentagon that he perceived a subtle but ominous change in the Soviet attitude — a change that might presage the onset of war. Clay was to concede later that he never had any confirming evidence that war was on the horizon.[7]

Nevertheless, the immediate reaction was an intensification of tentative discussion among the Western Europeans and Americans concerning some form of defensive alliance. With the coup, matters quickly came to a head; and by the third week in March, Britain, France, the Netherlands, Belgium and Luxembourg signed in Brussels a fifty-year mutual assistance pact "clearly directed at the Soviet Union."[8] On March 17, 1948, President Truman informed Congress that the growing menace of the Soviet Union was threatening the reconstruction of Europe. He called upon Congress to provide full support for Western Europe and especially those countries that were, as Truman spoke, linking themselves through the Brussels accord. But there remained the question of the appropriate means, in President Truman's words, "to help them to protect themselves."

Still, Truman and his top advisers moved cautiously. For even though there was agreement within the upper levels of the administration on the general direction of American policy, there was disagreement concerning the instrumentalities to be employed. Second, there was also broad and deep concern about support from a Republican-dominated Congress for the imminent departure in policy toward a peacetime military alliance. Finally, we should not overlook Truman's domestic political circumstances in the spring of 1948: the fall of 1948 was to be a national time of reckoning. And in view of the Republican majorities in both houses of Congress, which had resulted from the 1946 election, and the generally held opinion that the Republicans were already ahead in the race for the White House, it is understandable that Truman was uncertain of his base for a bold foreign policy.

President Truman's ultimately successful but prodigious electoral effort vied for his attention and energy throughout much of 1948. In the meantime, he had to build support in a hostile Congress, and especially in the Senate, for the Marshall Plan and presidential discretion in working out the as yet ambiguous relationship with Western Europe. The memory of Wilson's humiliation over the League at the hands of Congress inspired

Truman to instruct Undersecretary of State Robert Lovett during April and May of 1948 to work with Senator Vandenberg to produce a declaration of senatorial support for an American–Western European alliance. Simultaneously, the State Department entered into preliminary talks with the British, Canadians, and other representatives of the Brussels Pact concerning the structure and obligations of signatories of such an arrangement.[9] On May 19, Vandenberg, well briefed by high State Department officials, introduced his resolution; three weeks later, on June 11, 1948, the Senate passed the Vandenberg Resolution by a margin of 64–4. President Truman could now claim bipartisan support for whatever course he chose.

DEBATE CONCERNING THE INSTRUMENTS OF CONTAINMENT

The successful steering of the Vandenberg Resolution through the Senate seemed to confirm the existence of some operational latitude for President Truman. Within the administration some, notably in the newly formed Defense Department led by James Forrestal, felt that the United States should strengthen its military capacity, particularly the air force. This view clashed, however, with those led by Marshall, who advocated primary reliance upon the economic instrumentalities embodied in the European Recovery Program. More important, the cost implications of Forrestal's approach proved incompatible with the president's domestic interests in an election year, his desire for a balanced budget, and his commitment to the Marshall Plan. Thus even as the rhetoric of cold war was escalating in late 1946 and 1947, President Truman was reducing the size of the military establishment and demanding the observance of strict spending ceilings.[10]

Truman, therefore, faced seemingly irreconcilable, conflicting demands. His sense of fiscal needs and his domestic political strategy compelled him to advance his domestic programs aggressively yet within a framework of fiscal responsibility. On the other side, however, was the ominous drift of events in Europe, which seemed to confirm the need for some kind of unified Western response, presumably underwritten by the United States. Indeed, the president had encouraged this in his March speech supporting the Brussels Pact and his subsequent effort to get a Senate resolution of support for his European policy. But now he was being warned that a significant increase or the mere consideration of new defense spending could so inflate the economy that extensive controls on the economy would be inevitable — an unpleasant prospect in an election year.

Complicating matters further was that as of early 1948, no clear-cut strategic policy had yet emerged. The air force and congressional air-power advocates were urging reliance on an atomic-armed, long-range air force as the basis for the American defense posture. However, there was a good deal of skepticism concerning the viability of this posture.[11] The production of American atomic warheads was lagging due to shortages and problems of uranium delivery, and there were doubts concerning bomb potency during this early period. There was also limited confidence in the delivery systems available to the United States. The B-29 bomber was the only long-range aircraft available to the air force from 1946 until 1949, and it did not have sufficient range to strike Soviet targets from North America on any other than one-way suicide missions.[12]

It is probable, therefore, that in the event President Truman had been predisposed to rely heavily on military instrumentalities and sought to develop a carefully integrated politico-military approach to problems of American policy, the means were not available. In fact, Truman's approach to postwar defense requests indicates that the president was not so predisposed. His rhetoric was tough, even belligerent, but in the aftermath of the Czech coup it was Marshall's Economic Recovery Program that received the president's support as the best means for filling out the American relationship with the Europeans. He would support some increase in the defense budget, but not the $9 billion being requested. In contrast to the Marshall Plan, which received complete and intensive support when it went before Congress, Truman cut the Defense Department's supplemental request by two-thirds.

An identifiable structure of policy and programmatic assumptions seemed to be crystallizing. The most fundamental assumption set forth by Marshall, and apparently accepted by Truman, was that there was not going to be a war with the Soviet Union in the forseeable future. The recent behavior of Stalin suggested that the Soviets would seek an oppressive politico-economic control of Eastern Europe, undergirded by Soviet conventional military strength. But it was also assumed that the Soviets did not then have and were unlikely to possess atomic weapons within the next five years. American strategic superiority was not in question. Prudence and the need for bureaucratic compromise might dictate that the Department of Defense be allowed to develop and maintain the ability to deal with a theoretical Soviet strategic threat. However, Marshall and the president did not perceive the threat as imminent. Indeed, the Soviet threat was deemed manageable within the resources provided by a $15 billion-a-year defense budget, less than fifty bomber groups (which would be about fifty more bomber groups that the Russians would possess), an army of less than 600,000 men, and a navy equipped very much as it had been at the end of the war. Far more important to the American posture envisioned by Truman and Marshall at this time was the economic reconstruction of Europe.

THE MARSHALL PLAN AS A POLITICO-ECONOMIC CONCEPT

The idea of European recovery as the foundation of American policy had many appealing qualities. Not the least of these was the possibility that through European recovery the United States might simultaneously frustrate the Soviets, unify all of Europe, and reduce or even eliminate the future need for massive U.S. economic assistance appropriations.[13] There were collateral benefits. A productive and economically integrated Western European economy might prove irresistible to Eastern Europeans and ultimately the Soviets themselves. Further, containment, and perhaps the eventual taming of communist excesses, could be implemented while avoiding the domestic dislocations brought on by the development and maintenance of a large military establishment. Thus, the response to Truman's call for international commitment and involvement could be both dynamic and economically finite.

In the longer run, a growing capitalist Western Europe promised benefits for the postwar American economy. European recovery through the Marshall Plan held out the promise of an Atlantic community. This American–European relationship might become the basis of an even larger global economic system. In such a liberal, free-trading, and essentially capitalistic world, the United States, its economy unscathed by World War II, could not help but benefit, indeed, predominate.

In 1948, American efforts focused on the short-run dimensions of this Atlantic vision. The immediate problem had been set forth in the Truman Doctrine and was reiterated by Secretary of State Marshall: "economic distress is to be employed to further political ends."[14] In Marshall's view, Europe's desperate economic straits, brought on for the most part by the war, were now being exploited by "those small groups who aspire to dominate by the method of police states."[15] The prevailing and largely bipartisan understanding of this crisis[16] was that European cooperation and even unification were the only means for using U.S. aid effectively and thus retrieving the political situation.[17]

In line with these sentiments were the crucial decisions in 1947 to formally merge the economics of the American and British zones of western Germany into "Bizonia," and the relaxation of the rigid occupation directives of 1945. Thus, the denazification programs instituted immediately after the war would be eased; similarly, the dismantling of German industrial capacity, and decartelization — the elimination of monopolistic industrial organizations — was slowed. Those measures once viewed essential for preventing the resurgence of German political and military power were now viewed as contradictory to German and, more importantly, European recovery. In January 1948, German officials were urged to consider the formation of more centralized government structures that might assume some political functions.[18] And on January 22, 1948, the British called a meeting for the following month in London to discuss the future of Germany. Invitations were extended to the Americans, the French, and the Benelux countries. Pointedly, the Russians were not invited.

West German Statehood Is Ratified

Decisions were reached in three broad areas at London. First, the earlier implicit moves toward full German participation in the European Recovery Program were ratified. Moreover, it was agreed that not only would Bizonia participate, but also the French zone. Finally, the London conference urged the Western zones to move quickly toward the establishment of West German political institutions and processes which would allow the West Germans to assume control of their own political and, in large measure, economic affairs.[19] The means whereby this West German federal constitution was to be drawn up, ratified, and its relationship to the three occupation administrations were to remain points of some contention until early 1949. Communists as well as some conservatives in the French Parliament were especially reluctant to accept the degree of German autonomy implied by the conference recommendations and urged that greater power be reserved to the occupation powers. Their fears were predictably centered on the specter of yet another *Wehrmacht* growing out of an economically resurgent Germany. Not the least of the problems from the French standpoint were the conference recommendations for international control of the Ruhr Valley industrial complex,[20] long considered the heart of Germany's industrial and thus potential military power.

Despite French ambivalence, the London conference summarized and institutionalized the developments of the preceding two years. The Western powers had now officially recognized "that German reconstruction is essential to the well-being of Europe."[21] And in the establishment of an international authority for the control of the Ruhr, the United States won acceptance for the view that the Ruhr "constitutes the economic heart of Europe. [And] Europe cannot possibly achieve our ideals for her unless this area becomes productive ... and unless its productivity is integrated into the economic life of Europe including Germany."[22] Of equal importance, the commitment to the formation of a West German state and the exclusion of Soviet interests in that decision marks yet another intensification in the reciprocating dynamics of East–West distrust.

THE DEATH OF DIPLOMACY

The thrust and specifics of the Marshall Plan proved discomforting to the French; to the Russians they must have been appalling. As events unfolded in late 1947 and early 1948, Stalin's worst fears were materializing: There were internal problems in Eastern Europe. Now the Western powers were moving resolutely toward the reestablishment of the European political economy. Perhaps more distressing to Stalin, the seed of a new German state had finally sprouted with the completion of the London conference. Prior to mid-1947, U.S. policy had been rhetorically tough, but there had been limited action to go with American posturing. Now, however, the United States had initiated a comprehensive and apparently long-run program of economic assistance designed to set in motion Western European economic integration and the creation of a new West German state that would eventually control the important Ruhr Valley industrial complex. Moreover, the Soviets were isolated from and unable to influence these events directly.

The diplomatic dialogue essential to the operation of Four Power control of Germany envisioned at Potsdam was at the breaking point. The Soviets and the West maintained only the shadow of multilateral control and participation through the vestigial Allied Control Council in Berlin.[23] In a very real sense, the Soviet's isolation was a product of their own actions beginning with Molotov's walk-out at the Paris conference in June 1947. But the United States was not entirely displeased with Soviet behavior, and in the development of the Marshall Plan had sought to structure the proposal, its promulgation, and its operation so as to make it unacceptable to the Soviets.[24]

The London Conference of early 1948 was itself the culmination of Western unilateralism[25] in that it expressly excluded Soviet participation. The communique of the London Conference stated that "The present recommendations ... in no way preclude and on the contrary should facilitate eventual 4-power agreement on the German problem...."[26] However, the establishment of guidelines for the creation of the West German state, trizonal economic integration, and especially the recommendations on the Ruhr, all without Soviet participation, could not help but communicate a message to the contrary. And if there was any uncertainty concerning the intentions of the West, it was made clear that any future Four Power agreements would have to be consonant with the measures the West was initiating.[27]

In sum, both sides shared responsibility for the breakdown of diplomacy. Insofar as both sides were using the Control Council and foreign ministers' meetings for little more than public posturing, they both debased the medium of diplomatic exchange. The early postwar period had been marked by tough negotiations and sometimes bitter diplomatic exchanges; nevertheless, there had been more than the semblance of diplomatic interaction as the two sides felt their respective ways through the ambiguities of the new postwar world. Now things were taking an uglier turn, for East–West relations "had begun to assume the proportions of a struggle between two competing theologies. It had passed out of the realm of ambiguity into a period of moral clichés based on absolute definitions of good and evil that were to blight relations between the super powers for over a decade."[28]

The increasing diminution of diplomacy left each side with the crudest and most dangerous of means for communicating with the other: threat, counterthreat, confrontation, and the escalation of confrontation. The actions and intentions of the adversary were to be evaluated in the worst light. The modalities of interaction were now to be played out within a syndrome of tests and demonstrations of will, a reciprocating and mutually reinforcing diplomacy of threat.

The Berlin Blockade

The prototypical example of what was to become the norm of East–West interaction emerged from Stalin's efforts to check what he now perceived to be a concerted Western effort to undermine Soviet security. First he turned to the remaining point of institutionalized diplomatic contact in what may have been at best a half-hearted attempt to communicate his concerns about what was, to him, a deteriorating German situation. In February 1948, he filed a formal protest in the Control Council before the London talks began and again in March when the conference ended. When, during the March meeting, the Russians were unable to get information on or a discussion of the London meeting, they broke off the talks. Stalin now turned to more direct means in an attempt to communicate his position and influence Western behavior so that the German question could be reopened.

In April 1948 Stalin halted Western military supplies to West Berlin, located deep within the Russian zone. The Western reaction was to press on with the plans laid out at the London Conference. Specifically, the West approved in early June the initial step in the formation of the West German state. The Russians responded in turn with further interference with traffic into Berlin. Finally, in mid-June, at precisely the moment Tito's heresy broke into a total rupture with Stalin culminating in Tito's formal expulsion from the Cominform (after a Russian-inspired coup directed at Tito had failed), the Western powers initiated a currency reform in all their sectors except Berlin. This seemingly innocuous move was regarded by the Soviets as a precursor to economic chaos in their zone because they envisioned the old devalued German currency being dumped in the Eastern zone. The initial Soviet reaction was to initiate a currency change of their own, but when the new Western reform was extended to West Berlin, they responded on June 24, 1948, with a full blockade of Berlin. The West countered with their own economic blockade of the entire Eastern zone.

All surface movement in and out of Berlin was at a complete standstill, and both sides quickly defined the situation as a mutual testing of will. General Clay, in messages described as "pulsating," implored the president to resist and break the blockade with force; others advised conceding Berlin to the Russians. Truman never seriously contemplated the latter; Forrestal noted in his diary:

> When the specific question was discussed as to what our future policy in Germany was to be — namely, were we to stay in Berlin or not? — the President interrupted to say that there was no discussion on that point. We were going to stay, period.[29]

On the other hand, Truman did not adopt the bold course of action proposed by Clay. Instead, he ordered an airlift of supplies into West Berlin. Two weeks later he ordered two groups of atomic-capable B-29's to England, although it is not clear that nuclear weapons were in fact deployed outside the United States. Nevertheless, by the end of July more than sixty B-29's were in Europe, and there was no effort to conceal the fact.[30]

In August 1948 Stalin granted an interview with the ambassadors of the Western Allies. The Allied ambassadors were interested in reasserting Western access routes to West Berlin, whereas Stalin sought to shift negotiations to the broader question of recent events in West Germany, most notably the outcome of the London Conference. He wanted nothing less than the cessation of efforts to form a West German government and the full restoration of Four Power control of Germany, in which case the Western powers were welcome back in Berlin. It seems, therefore, that Stalin was attempting to use the blockade as leverage to get at the far more salient issue of Germany's political future. The West, on the other hand, was now committed to a diametrically opposed course; for the West Germans were to begin drafting a constitution within weeks. The West's response to the Stalin proposal, therefore, was to try to shift discussion back to the narrower questions of access rights. Talks deadlocked, and the situation in Germany reached a perilous state as Truman asked his advisors in early September to "brief me on bases, bombs, Moscow, Leningrad, etc. I have a terrible feeling . . . that we are close to war. I hope not . . . Berlin is a mess."[31]

Any number of circumstances could have been seized upon to initiate fighting if either the Soviets or the Americans had so desired. Border incidents or conflict in and around Berlin were available if either side had wanted to fight. The airlift itself provided ample opportunity. From June–July 1948 until February 1949, food and fuel deliveries increased to more than 7000 tons daily. To accomplish this, the Western Allies were landing a plane in West Berlin every two minutes. There was no lack of targets for the Soviets if they had sought an igniting incident. Harassment continued, but no provocative incident occurred.

The unwillingness or inability of the Soviets to provoke open conflict may be attributed to the ambiguous threat posed by the American B-29's. More likely is the fact that Stalin was simply not interested in pushing the West out of Berlin. Rather, he hoped by blockading Berlin to force the West to negotiate about security interests, such as the political and economic future of all Germany. Simple diplomacy had proved inadequate during the preceding months, for the Western Allies had gone ahead unilaterally with their plans for the integration of a West German state into the European Recovery Program. Stalin undertook, therefore, the slow strangulation of West Berlin as a means for dramatizing his own demands.

If this was Stalin's intent, he misread feelings in Washington, London, Paris, and Ottawa. Officials in these capitals responded to Stalin's actions by accelerating the very trends the Soviet dictator sought to deflect.[32] From July through early September 1948, military and diplomatic representatives of the Brussels Pact met with counterparts from the United States and Canada and began developing a concrete proposal for joining the North Atlantic countries in a defense pact. In December 1948, the language of a draft treaty was prepared. In January 1949, Truman made passing reference to the new defense treaty in his State of the Union message. By February 1949, a three-month process of trilateral negotiations on the final language of the treaty was underway among the Department of State, representatives of the Brussels Pact and Canada, and the U.S. Senate. Paralleling these events, a West German Parliamentary

Council was elected in August 1948 and began drafting a West German constitution in September 1948. Simultaneously, the Americans, British, and French began developing terms for the international authority for the Ruhr as well as drafting a new occupation statute, which would define Allied authority once the new West German state was in place.

The negotiations on the Ruhr and occupation statutes confirmed the division of Germany that Stalin sought to prevent. During November and December 1948, in the face of considerable French opposition, an international authority for the Ruhr was established. A law concerning trusteeship of the Ruhr industries decreed after the London conference was also accepted. These arrangements included German management and in some instances German ownership of the Ruhr industries. Moreover, rules of exclusion for former Nazis, although included in the statutes, were now little more than symbolic inasmuch as some of the men recommended for trusteeship positions had been involved with the management of German industry during the war. As historian Herbert Feis notes, "a test of usefulness" was now the measure of a man's role in the new German state, not his past political affiliation.[33] Agreement on the West German constitution moved more slowly, but by the spring of 1949 a constitution or basic law was approved by the military governors in the three Western zones. The new basic law was accepted on the same day, May 12, 1949, that the Soviets lifted their blockade.

The correspondence of these two events, the lifting of the blockade and the approval of the basic law, is an important benchmark. The basic law or West German constitution was what the blockade had been all about from the outset. The lifting of the blockade, even as the basic law was accepted in principle is, therefore, an especially strong indication of how desperate the Soviet diplomatic position had become by mid-1949. It must have been clear to Stalin by early 1949 that the blockade would fail and that its effect had been totally unproductive. Rather than split the Western Allies and hasten the resumption of negotiations on Germany's future, the blockade brought the Allies together and probably facilitated intra-Allied bargaining on such contentious questions as the Ruhr authority and occupation rights.[34] In addition, the Western powers, when confronted with the blockade, had moved quickly to extend the Brussels Pact into a North Atlantic defense arrangement that now included the United States. All of this activity pointed to a divided Germany with the West German state increasingly a part of an economically integrated Western Europe operating under an as yet undefined American military commitment.

Faced with these cumulating reverses, Stalin sought a way back from the confrontation of the blockade while at the same time trying to hold off the formation of West Germany. The blockade had originally been used as a stick with which Stalin sought to prod the West into acceptance of his position. Now he would try unsuccessfully to use the removal of the blockade as a carrot.

The Blockade
Is Lifted — The West Ascendant

In January and February 1949 the Russians made public overtures through press conferences followed by secret contacts at the United Nations proposing that if the formation of West Germany could be delayed until after a foreign ministers meeting, the Soviets would consider lifting the blockade. Acheson, who had taken over as secretary of state in the second Truman administration, agreed only to "simultaneously lifting the blockade and counterblockade, and fixing a date for a meeting of the Council of Foreign Ministers."[35] There was to be no commitment to do or not do anything concerning West Germany. Acheson was aware of the thrust of Stalin's diplomacy:

> We . . . saw the danger in allowing Stalin to edge his way into the incomplete and delicate negotiations among us regarding our relations among ourselves and with the Germans in our zones, which could lead to disunity among us and no progress in lifting the blockade. The greatest danger of disunity lay in any postponement of our tripartite preparations together and with the Germans.[36]

The Soviets continued the secret contacts throughout April 1949, seeking some form of commitment to postpone preparations for the formation of the West German government, but the West would not yield. On May 4 the Russians finally agreed to go ahead with the lifting of the blockade on May 12, 1949, because it was clear now that private negotiations could take them no further. Perhaps Stalin concluded that public negotiations would bring pressure to bear on the West to make concessions. At a minimum, Stalin could end the blockade and perhaps save face.[37]

In the meantime, Secretary of State Acheson was working almost feverishly to ensure the complete isolation of the Soviets. In April 1949, while negotiations on the lifting of the blockade were underway, the NATO pact was completed and the German constitution drafted. In addition, the Western Allies hammered out agreements on virtually all outstanding issues concerning Germany: the Ruhr, their respective occupation rights, agreements on Berlin and its relationship to the new West German state, future reparations, unresolved boundary questions, and a memorandum of main principles of policy toward Germany.[38] Moreover, just prior to the foreign ministers' meeting, a common understanding concerning tactics and procedures at the conference was reached. The Western powers' consensus hinged on the idea that they would turn down any Soviet proposal concerning Germany's political and economic future if that proposal was based on any other than Western policy and procedure.[39] In summary, the only things the Soviets wanted to discuss were to be nonnegotiable; or, as at Paris in 1947, negotiable only on Western terms.

The West expected very little from the conference, and in putting forward (in Acheson's words) "our requirements for a 'good opportunity' " which were admittedly "severe,"[40] the prophecy became a reality. "Our requirements" were deemed "not impossible"[41] by Acheson, but the Russians found them so, and the Paris meeting quickly settled into mutual recrimination. By all accounts, President Truman was not unhappy with the results of the conference. He publicly applauded Acheson for the skill with which he had carried off the tasks of ending the blockade while simultaneously maintaining the thrust of American policy in Europe. For the Russians, however, the dismal end of the conference marked the collapse of their effort to counter the Marshall Plan, the formation of West Germany, and NATO. It was, as Professor Marshall Shulman has noted, the "low point of Soviet diplomacy."[42] Washington's attention was now free to focus on the problem of institutionalizing and providing resources for the alliance that had been struck in the heat of the Berlin crisis — and the deteriorating situation in Asia.

FORMATION OF THE NORTH ATLANTIC TREATY ORGANIZATION

The passage of the Vandenberg Resolution and the imposition of the blockade gave impetus to a period of intense contacts between U.S. representatives and members of the Brussels Pact. By December 1948 there was general agreement on one point: the geographic scope of the pact should include Scandinavian, North Atlantic, and Mediterranean powers so as to provide protection for the flanks of the main powers.[43] A second and more difficult point concerned the substance of the pact.

Conflicting Concepts of Alliance Emerge—and Are Compromised

Robert E. Osgood, in his definitive study of the NATO alliance,[44] has suggested that two conflicting concepts of the NATO alliance emerged in late 1948 and persisted even after the signing in April and ratification of the treaty in July 1949. First there was the view, held for the most part by American and European military planners, that NATO should be a large and fully integrated "trans-Atlantic military coalition."[45] In line with this view, the defense ministers of the Brussels Pact countries had agreed that the alliance should proceed with a common defense policy under some sort of integrated command buttressed by a permanent group concerned with logistical and supply problems.[46] The American Joint Chiefs of Staff were already on record as supporting such a concept, including an American supreme commander if fighting actually occurred.[47] Furthermore, this concept of the alliance carried with it the implication of a local and forward defense of Western Europe. This was necessary because it was assumed that the most basic threat to European security was the large standing army of the Soviet Union. Moreover, from a continental perspective, there was the concern that unless the alliance formally committed to the forward defense of the continent, the Americans and/or the British might revert to the kind of peripheral strategy they had adopted in World War II. The continental powers and especially France did not look forward to another prolonged liberation struggle. The logic of this position, therefore, was to commit the alliance partners and especially the Americans and the British to an automatic response to external aggression.[48]

There was opposition to this view in the Department of State, the White House, and the Congress. Instead of viewing the alliance as an American military trip wire, the treaty was interpreted as "intending to provide political and psychological reinforcement in the continuing political warfare of the Cold War."[49] This view held that it was the political, economic, and social weakness of Western Europe itself that opened up subversive opportunities for Soviet communism. The purported propensity for the Soviets to use force, as displayed in Czechoslovakia and Berlin, was viewed as "defensive reactions on the Soviet side to the initial success of the Marshall Plan initiative and to the preparations ... to set up a separate German government in West Germany." Critics of a well-reinforced military "plate glass" shield to Europe saw the communist-inspired strikes in France and Italy in the autumn of 1947 as "Moscow's attempt to play, before it was too late, the various political cards it still possessed on the European continent."[50]

Many advocates of a more political concept of NATO believed that communist political and economic pressure in the shadow of Soviet conventional military strength might force the Western Europeans into a neutral stance between East and West (in the jargon of a later time, they might be "Finlandized"), thereby threatening the Marshall Plan. But in this view the response was the intensification and success of the Marshall Plan itself, not a comprehensive and expensive U.S. military commitment to Europe's defense. At most, NATO was to be a "modest military shield" behind which the primary task of economic construction would go forward and European self-confidence reestablished.[51] From the perspective of many in the U.S. Congress, such a political and economic commitment should not entail an automatic commitment of U.S. military involvement.

The procedural question of automatic commitment was to be the most contentious issue in the drafting of the final language of the treaty. The Senate, with Acheson serving as both advocate and mediator, and the Western ambassadors struggled over this point during February and March 1949 and produced a short-run compromise acceptable to them all, although in some measure unsatisfactory to each. The United States was not automatically committed to war if the treaty[52] came into force, thereby satisfying American minimalists, particularly those in the Senate. On the other hand, by signing the treaty the United States was committed to its provisions, which implied certain obligations on the part of the United States, including mutual aid, but what those obligations were and how they were to be fulfilled were not yet clear. But then precision was not required in the spring of 1949, for in the heat of the Berlin crisis, a show of unity and agreement in broadest principle was all that was deemed necessary; operational specifics could be resolved later.

In his memoirs, Acheson noted that the April 4, 1949, NATO treaty signing ceremony was "dignified and colorful." He adds: "The Marine Band added a note of unexpected realism as we waited for the ceremony to begin by playing songs from the currently popular musical play *Porgy and Bess,* 'I've Got Plenty of Nothin' and 'It Ain't Necessarily So.' "[53]

Support for NATO and More Compromise on Strategic Concepts and Means

The debate on the $1.3 billion Mutual Defense Assistance Program (MDAP), which was conceived by the Truman administration as the first installment on the NATO agreement, in no way clarifed the strategic thinking underlying U.S. policy. Indeed, the administration's efforts to justify the program suggest that although President Truman conceived of the MDAP as implementing America's commitment, his administration had not yet conceived of NATO within a detailed strategic concept. The administration remained satisfied (and the successful outcome of the Berlin crisis must have reinforced this conviction) to maintain a political image of NATO, to limit overall defense spending, and to continue emphasizing the European Recovery Program as the primary basis of containment.

The NATO treaty was described by Acheson to the Senate as limited in its commitment of assistance. Indeed, the administration presented the request for the MDAP only after the treaty was approved in July 1949, thereby separating the more explosive question of material support from the principle of the alliance. When asked by Republican Senator Bourke Hickenlooper of Iowa whether the treaty would lead to the United States sending large numbers of troops to Europe "as a more or less permanent contribution to the development of these countries' capacity to resist," Acheson replied, "The answer to that question, Senator, is a clear and absolute 'no.' "[54]

Acheson was to eat these words eighteen months later. The administration's gambit in the Senate was to minimize the apparent costs of the commitments under the NATO agreement; but this was, in the final analysis, a tactical extension of their own belief that the material cost and implications of the treaty could be minimized. That such a view was shortsighted, contradictory, and ultimately wrong is not proof that the view was not, in fact, held. It does suggest that the Truman administration persisted in its belief that the mission of the Truman Doctrine could be fulfilled without diverting or distorting the allocation of resources within American domestic society. The best evidence of this lies in the budget President Truman had recommended to Congress in January 1949, the midpoint of the Berlin crisis.

President Truman's less than $15 billion defense budget suggests that he was not overly concerned with balancing the armed services either in terms of their budgets or missions. He was prepared to live with dependence upon strategic air power as the basis of American security policy. The MDAP was designed to meet broader alliance needs and the argument for some form of forward strategy in Europe, for MDAP did envisage the reconstruction of European conventional strength. Congress seemed amenable to the first part of this argument in that it cut the requests for the army and navy and added an additional $800 million for the air force. In the meantime, the logic of the fiscal year 1950 budget was being carried forward with even greater vigor in the planning for fiscal year 1951.

Louis Johnson replaced Forrestal in the Defense Department in 1949,[55] bringing with him the belief that by reorganizing and carefully overseeing the department, defense spending could be held even more closely in check. Johnson and the Bureau of the Budget agreed that the fiscal year 1951 budget should be held to a $13.5 billion ceiling, and the Secretary of Defense chose as the target of his reductions the army and especially the navy's desire to maintain a hold on the strategic bombing mission. His efforts during mid-1949 to cut the size of the navy's air arm led to an explosion within the military as the navy fought back by forcing a congressional investigation of the air force's new strategic B-36 bomber. These hearings during August and October 1949, although beginning with allegations concerning procurement of the B-36, ultimately moved to the broader strategic questions of which service branch could best carry out a strategy of maximum atomic retaliation on the Soviet Union.[56] Congressional sentiment tended to run with the air power advocates, however, and the thrust of Truman's policy remained intact.

The MDAP was received less enthusiastically, however, for it implied that the alliance was based on a doctrine of large-scale land war in Europe supported by U.S. strategic air power. Opponents argued that the president's defense budget was deceptively low and the MDAP inconsistent with the strategic doctrine that supposedly underlay the budget request. Moreover, the services, especially the army, did not show much enthusiasm for the proposal, for the military assistance program had been and continued to be a competitor for funds.

The upshot was that the MDAP stalled in Congress and was passed only after being reduced to $1 billion and only after the president announced in late September that the Soviets had exploded their own atomic bomb. The effect of Truman's announcement was described in *Atomics Magazine* as "a minor panic; many radio commentators have the country practically at war with Russia."[57] However, its passage in this manner, resulting in large measure from the perceived urgency of the moment, obscured and left unanswered the many questions raised in the preceding months.[58] Nevertheless, alliance planning went forward in the months after MDAP's passage and the explosion of the Soviet's A-bomb. The specifics of initial NATO planning were not published, but Osgood has speculated that they involved the assignment of strategic bombardment and protection of sea lines of supply and communication to the United States and foresaw Europe providing the basis of conventional land forces.[59]

Summary

By 1950 the reactions and departures set in motion by the Marshall Plan and the crises of early 1948 must have seemed to the Truman administration as having evolved into mature policy. The political and economic reconstruction of Europe encompassing that of West Germany was now well underway. Furthermore, an alliance structure had been established with Western Europe and a modicum of defense integration achieved that anticipated the reconstruction of European conventional capability by means of U.S. assistance. In the meantime, U.S. strategic superiority, coupled with the accelerating success of the Marshall Plan, was deemed adequate to the task of containing Soviet power in Europe.

In the long run, however, the possession of the A-bomb by the Soviets struck at a fundamental assumption of Western policy — the strategic imbalance between the United States and the Soviet Union. If American strategic superiority could be eliminated, even as its monopoly on atomic power was now broken, then the prospect of some form of mutual atomic deterrence arose in which a conventional balance of forces would assume more and perhaps decisive importance. This was especially disturbing in view of the undeniable Soviet superiority along this dimension of the East-West military relationship.[60] In this event, the United States' NATO guarantee would no longer be convincing.

Of course, an erosion of American atomic superiority was not going to occur overnight, given the paucity of Soviet intercontinental delivery aircraft. Furthermore, it is by no means clear that Stalin ever intended or even contemplated strategic warfare five years after the appalling losses of World War II. Indeed, Stalin's primary concern at this time was his vulnerability to the West's nuclear advantage.[61] No one in the administration, in short, saw war with the Soviets as imminent.

Nevertheless, the explosion of the Soviet A-bomb contributed to the cross-currents and implicit contradictions that underlay the compromises and apparent success of American European policy in late 1949. In addition, the Chinese civil war built to a climax in late 1949, and with the collapse of the Nationalist Chinese a chain of events was set in motion that eventually consumed the Truman administration.

CRISIS AND COLLAPSE IN ASIA

The momentous events in China did not take the Truman administration unawares. In view of American involvement in China during and immediately after World War II, it cannot be said the administration lacked information or concern about events in China. It is true, however, that the evolution of events in China was a lower-priority item for the Truman administration. China, indeed Asia, was felt to be on the periphery of the "basin of world power" of which Kennan had written. If countries or continents were to be reconstructed by and in the likeness of America, better that they be at the epicenter of world politics. On the periphery America would, in Acheson's words, "wait until the dust settles," and then concern itself with the emergent balance of forces. But this was not enough for those in America who thought they had heard a call for world ideological confrontation and crusade in the Truman Doctrine.

The Civil War in China — and in Congress

Marshall had spent a good deal of 1946 in China trying to bring about some kind of reconciliation between the communists and Chiang Kai-Shek. By the end of the year, however, negotiations had collapsed and Marshall had been recalled to Washington to assume direction of the Department of State. In January 1947, Marshall's report on the Chinese situation was made public. In it, Marshall pronounced a plague on both the Communist and Nationalist Chinese houses for their mutual distrust and extremism. By the end of January, the United States terminated all efforts at mediating the struggle; and in February and March 1947, full-scale fighting was renewed.

American policy was characterized by ambivalence, incrementalism, and what must have appeared to both the communist Chinese and the conservatives in Congress as disingenuousness. In June 1947, more than $6 million in ammunition was provided the Nationalists, while Marshall claimed that the sale did not signify U.S. support for Chiang's regime. In July 1947, Marshall noted U.S. concern over the economic conditions in China and asserted that U.S. assistance would be forthcoming only as conditions developed that seemed to promise that such assistance would be beneficial. To evaluate conditions, Lieutenant General Albert Wedemeyer was sent to China on a fact-finding mission and to inform Chiang that future assistance would be predicated upon internal reform and under American supervision. Wedemeyer's report was unfavorable to the Nationalists and suggested that the Nationalists could succeed only by undertaking far-reaching political and economic reforms to correct what Wedemeyer saw as widespread corruption and inefficiency. Nevertheless, the Truman administration found itself unable or unwilling to cut Chiang's regime completely adrift. Thus, in November 1947 Marshall announced a new $300 million economic assistance program for China to begin the following year, although he conceded that the United States was finding it difficult to develop a course of action in which American funds could be expended with expectations of "getting about a 70-percent return in effectiveness of use."[62]

Increasingly, therefore, the Truman administration found itself in Asia in the position of a gambler faced with a run of bad cards and a crowd of jeering kibitzers — in this case, a growing band of conservative Republicans who were charging that the Truman administration was doing too little. The gambler knows that the probabilities are that the next cards will be as bad as his previous hands. Indeed, he begins to suspect that the game might be rigged. However, although his losses have begun to mount, they are not yet unacceptable and there is the hope that one more play might recoup those losses; thus, yet another bet is made.

The Truman administration seemed to have convinced itself that the best strategy in 1947 and early 1948 was to stay in the Chinese game by means of economic assistance. No one seems to have been terribly optimistic — but then maybe something would turn up. The alternatives seemed unpleasant: China would fall to the Communists and the administration would be open to a merciless attack — in an election year — from the Republicans that even as Roosevelt had sold out Eastern Europe at Yalta, Truman and the Democrats had now lost China. Moreover, cutting the Nationalists loose might threaten the bipartisan support so carefully nurtured for the administration's policy in Europe.[63] The important thing in the short run, therefore, was not to lose nerve — press on, commit the minimum resources necessary to keep in the game in Asia and simultaneously hold domestic critics at arm's length until after the election in November. Once the election was over, the entire situation could be reassessed.

In the meantime, this incremental holding strategy could never satisfy the Republicans, who were calling for an all-out commitment similar to that in Europe. More important in the long run, the provision of *any* aid to Chiang, no matter how symbolic, could only reinforce Mao's suspicion and distrust, thereby complicating any future effort at reconciliation. By Christmas of 1947 Mao was publicly calling the Nationalists "reactionary forces" and "running dogs of American imperialism." Simultaneously Chiang's regime and the Republicans were blaming President Truman for increasing communist control in Manchuria. Throughout the first half of 1948 political pulling-and-hauling over the size and conditions to be attached to American aid to Chiang persisted in the Congress. The game was not unlike the one to be played out 20 years later in Southeast Asia by another Democratic president — for both gamblers, the good hand was never dealt.

But nothing changed in China, as the military reverses accumulated. On September 24, Tsinan fell; on October 20, the Manchurian capital of Changchun; and on November 1, 1948, Mukden, the key to all of Manchuria, fell. In October 1948 a report of the House Foreign Affairs Subcommittee on World Communism had called for an American guarantee "of territorial and political integrity"[64] of China. But while the House committee was demanding a firm position, Secretary Marshall and the State Department remained ambivalent. Earlier in August, Secretary Marshall had advised the American embassy in China that the United States would not support a coalition government that included communists. On the other hand, the United States would not try to mediate the civil war again. Beyond the provision of some economic and military assistance, Mr. Marshall advised the embassy that it was "not likely that the situation will make it possible for us at this juncture to formulate any rigid plans for our future policy in China."[65]

A Decision to "Let the Great Tree Fall"

President Truman's reelection in 1948 allowed the administration to resist a commitment of full support for Chiang. Thus, when two weeks after the election Chiang requested an increase in aid to save his regime, President Truman was noncommittal. Moreover, when Chiang's wife arrived in Washington in December with a request for $3 billion in aid, she was ignored by the administration. Just prior to her arrival the administration had received the report of Major General David Barr, Director of the U.S. Military Advisory Group to the Government of China. General Barr's feeling was that:

> The military situation has deteriorated to the point where only the active participation of United States troops could effect a remedy. . . . No battle has been lost since my arrival due to lack of ammunition or equipment. Their military debacles in my opinion can all be attributed to the world's worst leadership and many other morale destroying factors that lead to a complete loss of will to fight. . . . The Generalissimo has lost much of his political and popular support.[66]

Secretary Marshall agreed that the only way to save Chiang's regime was to commit American troops, but he would not recommend such a course.

The inference was clear: the administration would now attempt to put even more distance between itself and the Nationalist Chinese although not moving to a position of real neutrality. To do so would have further provoked those conservative Republicans who were urging higher levels of assistance and U.S. commitment. Thus, during January and February 1949, when the Nationalist government was being forced to move from Nanking to Canton in the face of advancing Communist forces, the White House instructed the State Department "that in order not to discourage Chinese resistance to communist aggression, military aid should not be suspended, but no effort should be made to expedite it."[67] Congressional pressure continued, but Acheson persistently reiterated that there would be no change in American policy.

Throughout May, June, and much of July 1949, major cities in southern China continued to fall to the Communists, but the administration stood fast in its refusal to intervene. Earlier, in February 1949, Acheson had been asked by a group of Congress members to predict the course of events in China and had responded that "when a great tree falls in the forest one cannot see the extent of the damage until the dust settles."[68]

Acheson insists that his "waiting until the dust settles" was not a description of American policy, but it was taken as such.[69] Certainly Acheson's willingness to watch mutely the chain of Nationalist disasters in China stood in marked contrast to his feverish activity during this same period concerning American European policy. He was clearly not prepared to let the great European tree fall.

With the NATO treaty ratified in mid-July 1949 and the MDAP submitted to Congress, Acheson prepared to go to the public with what had been American policy for months. On July 27 he announced that American policy in Asia would be subjected to a full review. Ten days later the Department of State released a White Paper of more than 1000 pages that sought to absolve the United States of all responsibility for the impending collapse of the Nationalist Chinese. The White Paper emphasized that the only manner in which the Nationalists could be saved would be through American intervention but noted that such an intervention would have been "resented by the mass of the Chinese people, would have diametrically reversed our historic policy, and would have been condemned by the American people."[70]

The report was met with a firestorm of criticism from all sides but especially from the right, where Senators Bridges, Knowland, and Wherry — all Republicans — and Democratic Senator McCarran labeled it "a 1,054-page whitewash of a wishful, do-nothing policy which has succeeded only in placing Asia in danger of Soviet conquest."[71] But the rage of Nationalist China's supporters in the Congress was not sufficient to prevent what Acheson was prepared to accept when he took office. On September 21, 1949, the Nationalist Chinese tree crashed to the ground as the People's Republic of China was proclaimed. On October 1, Mao Zedong's new government was inaugurated in Peking with Chou En-Lai as premier and foreign minister. By the end of the year Chiang Kai-Shek had ensconced himself on Taiwan and was calling for American aid.

AMERICAN POLICY REAPPRAISED

The combined reverberations of the Nationalist Chinese collapse and the Soviet's atomic explosion gave impetus to a reassessment of American policy. The result in early 1950 was Policy Paper Number 68 of the National Security Council, "United States Objectives and Programs for National Security," or NSC-68, which became an overarching conceptual framework incorporating past American policy up to 1950 and establishing important parameters for future policy.[72] Before it was completed, however, one of the questions of late 1949 was resolved, for on January

31, 1950, the president decided to go forward with the development of the hydrogen bomb.

The Hydrogen Bomb Decision

One of the most immediate effects of the Soviet A-bomb explosion was a debate within the American foreign and defense policymaking community over how the United States might maintain its pre-1949 nuclear superiority. The debate was intensified by the fact that moving up to the next level of nuclear weaponry, the hydrogen bomb, would involve a truly awesome increase in explosive capacity — a thousandfold increase over the atomic weapons used at Hiroshima and Nagasaki. The military advantages seemed more decisive than had been the case with atomic weapons, hence the military attractiveness of technological escalation. But this very fact of a quantum leap in destructiveness made the weapon especially repugnant to many in the scientific community. Within the government all of the members of the General Advisory Committee to the Atomic Energy Commission (AEC), as well as a majority of the commission itself, opposed going forward. The Defense Department favored going forward on a crash basis, but AEC Chairman David Lilienthal refused to move until all the foreign-policy implications of the H-bomb had been considered. This meant, of course, that the Department of State was brought into the debate, but within the department there was also disagreement.

George Kennan, who was leaving as Director of the Planning Staff, had prepared a memorandum on the question of the hydrogen bomb and more broadly, U.S. nuclear policy as it related to international control.[73] In this memorandum Kennan underscored what he regarded as extreme ambiguity and confusion in American policy on nuclear weapons and their use. He urged, therefore, that there be a complete review of the entire question of the "first use" of these weapons by the United States, and emphasized that he was opposed to any doctrine of "first use." He did not challenge the necessity of maintaining such weapons until some form of disarmament arrangements could be worked out. In the meantime, however, Kennan urged that "we remain prepared to go very far, to show considerable confidence in others, and to accept certain risks for ourselves, in order to achieve international agreement on their removal from international arsenals."[74] In opposition to this position were Paul Nitze, the new Director of the State Department's Policy Planning Staff, and Dean Acheson. Both were joined in "measuring the risks on a different scale,"[75] and seemed persuaded that immediate research and development should begin, given the likelihood that Soviet research was undoubtedly proceeding.[76] President Truman concurred with Acheson's view that further delay would not be wise, and announced on January 31, 1950, that the United States would proceed with the development of the hydrogen bomb.

Thus, on the H-bomb decision the worst-case assumption concerning Soviet capabilities and behavior was made and assumed primary importance in the American decision. George Kennan and others on the Policy Planning Staff were prone to considering first what the Soviet's intentions were and using this as the basis or, at a minimum, a fundamental part of American policy. Now, however, Kennan sensed a "growing tendency in Washington ... to base our own plans and calculations solely on the *capabilities* of a potential adversary, assuming him to be desirous of doing anything he could to bring injury to us, and to exclude from consideration, as something unsusceptible to exact determination, the whole question of that adversary's real *intentions*."[77] Kennan's concerns were regarded by Acheson and Nitze as "obscure argument" based on a kind of intuitive approach to policy making. Such an approach, Acheson conceded, had great utility and applicability in foreign operations; however, in his view, "its value ... was limited in Washington."[78] In Acheson's opinion, "what [the president] needed was communicable wisdom, not mere conclusions, however soundly based in experience or intuition...."[79] Acheson saw himself providing such "communicable wisdom" in the H-bomb decision, and he sought to do the same in the drafting and promotion of NSC-68.

NSC-68

The drafting of NSC-68 was undertaken by a group of Department of State and Department of Defense planners working under the immediate direction of Paul Nitze and the Policy Planning Staff. Not unlike the authors of the Truman Doctrine, the authors of NSC-68 saw the world as essentially bipolar, only now there were no vague references to antithetical ways of life. The polarization of world politics and power was not a temporary one, but rather a "fundamentally altered" distribution of world power such that two nations, the United States and the Soviet Union, confronted one another with profoundly antithetical objectives and ideals in an international system in which "conflict has become endemic."[80] The Soviet's objectives were threefold and involved: (1) consolidation of its hold on the Soviet Union as the ideological and political center of world communism; (2) consolidation of control over existing and extension of control to new satellites; and (3) the "complete abolition or forcible destruction" of power centers that opposed the Soviet aspiration for world hegemony.

"The fundamental design of those who control the Soviet Union and the international communist movement," the report argued, is "the complete subversion or forcible destruction ... of the non-Soviet world and their replacement by an apparatus and structure subservient to and controlled from the Kremlin." Soviet objectives were "wholly irreconcilable" with the objectives of a free society. Moreover, "the assault on free institutions is worldwide now, and in the context of the present polarization of power a defeat of free institutions anywhere is a defeat everywhere. . . ." "In a shrinking world which now faces the threat of atomic warfare, it is not an adequate objective merely to seek to check the Kremlin design, for the absence of order among nations is becoming less and less tolerable. This fact imposes on us, in our own interest, the responsibility of world leadership,"[81] which would require "a much more rapid and concerted build-up of the actual strength of both the United States and the other nations of the free world. . . .[T]his will be costly and will involve significant domestic financial and economic adjustments."[82]

NSC-68 provided a generally bleak assessment of the respective capabilities of the United States and the Soviet Union in this total struggle between "free society" and the "implacable purpose of the slave state." First, the nuclear superiority of the United States was deemed to be of limited duration with a stalemate of nuclear power anticipated in 1954, although the United States might extend its advantage if hydrogen weapons were perfected rapidly. But the Joint Chiefs of Staff were cited as concluding that the Soviets would be able by 1950 to overrun most of Western Europe, drive into the Middle East, consolidate control of Asia, and initiate air and sea attacks in the Atlantic basin including attacks on "selected targets with atomic weapons, now including targets in Alaska, Canada, and the United States."[83]

Faced with this grim prospect, what should the West, and especially the United States, do? First, Western European recovery and the NATO alliance should be fully implemented, for only in this way could the purported Soviet conventional military advantage be countered. But the prospect was long-run unrelieved tension and danger, and under these circumstances the framers of NSC-68 recommended "a rapid build-up of political, economic, and military strength in the free world" with the United States as the center of the effort. Furthermore, the reconstructed military capability of the United States and the West should be such that it surpassed that of the Soviet Union, and the West should be prepared to employ the capability in a clear-cut, unequivocal, and even "offensive" manner when challenged by communist power.[84]

The authors of NSC-68 were fully cognizant of the domestic implications of this proposal:

> Budgetary considerations will need to be subordinated to the stark fact that our very independence as a nation may be at stake.

A comprehensive and decisive program to win the peace and frustrate the Kremlin design should be so designed that it can be sustained for as long as necessary to achieve our national objectives. It would probably involve . . . :

(2) A substantial increase in expenditures for military purposes. . . .

(3) A substantial increase in military assistance programs. . . .

(10) Reduction of Federal expenditures for purposes other than defense and foreign assistance, if necessary by the deferment of certain desirable programs.

(11) Increased taxes.[85]

More specifically, the paper argued that the national economy was sufficiently dynamic that "in an emergency the United States could devote upward of 50 percent of its gross national product . . ." to national security if necessary. That is, rather than the $13–15 billion defense budgets of the postwar years, military budgets proportionate to those of World War II were acceptable — and perhaps essential in view of the threat confronting the United States and the Free World.[86]

Summary

The picture painted by Nitze's group was, to say the least, a dark one. Past American policy was not criticized, but the inference was that the policies developed within the Marshall Plan framework were no longer adequate. For the fall of China and the acquisition of nuclear weapons by the Soviets suggested "a permanent and fundamental alteration in the shape of international relations."[87] "The issues that face us are momentous, involving the fulfillment or destruction not only of this Republic but of civilization itself."[88] Under these circumstances, if the ideals and objectives of "American life" were to be protected and furthered, an equally permanent and fundamental change in American policy must occur. Significantly, NSC-68 concluded that in such a transformation of American policy, negotiations and especially negotiations concerned with nuclear weapons, mutual arms reduction, or the control of atomic energy were not likely to be beneficial.

Negotiation is not a possible separate course of action but rather a means of gaining support for a program of building strength, or recording, where necessary and desirable, progress in the cold war, and of facilitating further progress while helping to minimize the risk of war. Ultimately, our objective [is] to negotiate a settlement with the Soviet Union . . . on which the world can place reliance as an enforceable instrument of peace. But it is important to emphasize that such a settlement can only record the progress which the free world will have made in creating a political and economic system in the

world so successful that the frustration of the Kremlin's design for world
domination will be complete.[89]

In sum, negotiations were conceived not as viable good faith instruments
of Soviet-American interaction, but rather as benchmarks of or ratifica-
tions of "progress in the cold war." In any event:

> The present world situation, . . . is one which militates against successful
> negotiations with the Kremlin — for the terms of agreements on important
> pending issues would reflect present realities and would therefore be unac-
> ceptable, if not disastrous, to the United States and the rest of the free world.
> After a decision and a start on building up the strength of the free world has
> been made, it might then be desirable for the United States to take an
> initiative in seeking negotiations in the hope that it might facilitate the
> process of accommodation by the Kremlin to the new situation. Failing that,
> the unwillingness of the Kremlin to accept equitable terms or its bad faith
> in observing them would assist in consolidating popular opinion in the free
> world in support of the measures necessary to sustain the build-up.[90]

In view of this jaundiced and narrowly instrumental conception of
negotiations, it is not surprising that the thrust of the proposal was that the
United States and the West must seek and maintain military superiority
over the Soviet Union so as to confront and override the inevitability of
Soviet aggression at each turn. Indeed, NSC-68 refused to rule out the first
use of nuclear weapons by the United States.[91] Finally, such superiority
would have to be maintained even at the expense of other elements on
the national public policy agenda.

THE POLICY REAPPRAISAL APPRAISED

Thinking at the top of the Department of State had turned very nearly 180
degrees in less than 2 years. Whereas Marshall concerned himself, to an
extent, with how the Russians might perceive and react to an American
action, Acheson seemed to care primarily about Russian capabilities. Attempts to evaluate Soviet intentions were deemed "interesting," but not
really applicable to the task confronting the new secretary of state. The
task as Acheson saw it was a redirecting of American policy away from the
"soft" political and economic containment of the Marshall Plan. World
politics was now cast in harsh relief — the grim remorseless struggle of
nuclear-armed and ideologically driven combatants: "our analysis of the
threat combined the ideology of communist doctrine and the power of the
Russian state into an aggressive expansionist drive, which found its chief

opponent and, therefore, target in the antithetic ideas and power of our own country."[92]

In Secretary Acheson's view, and the view of the other men who drafted NSC-68, however, the power of America was not yet realized. That power was not realized because too many in the United States persisted in two outmoded beliefs: The first had been held by Marshall when he was secretary of state — that the primary threat to world peace was the social and economic chaos of Western Europe, a threat that could be eliminated through American economic and moral assistance culminating in the economic unification of Europe. "This I did not believe," Acheson asserts.

> The threat to Western Europe seemed to me singularly like that which Islam had posed centuries before, with its combination of ideological zeal and fighting power. Then it had taken the same combination to meet it: Germanic power in the east and Frankish in Spain, both energized by a great outthrust of military power and social organization in Europe. This time it would need the added power and energy of America, for the drama was now played on a world stage.[93]

The crisis was not mere economic recovery; the barbarian was once again quite literally at the gates of Europe. And once again it would require "a great outburst of military power and social organization" — a reconstructed Europe but, most importantly, NATO (including "Germanic power") — in order that civilization might hold. Mobilizing Europe was necessary, but not sufficient, for the barbarian was at the gates everywhere and in this global confrontation American "energy and power" was also necessary. Acheson and his colleagues were convinced that this energy and power, if mobilized, would also be sufficient.

But the mobilization of American power on the scale deemed necessary ran up against the second of the great misconceptions thought to be widely held in Washington — that domestic ruin would follow on the heels of the reallocation of resources proposed by Secretary Acheson. The problem was complicated by the fact that no less a figure than the president and his White House staff seemed somewhat sympathetic to this view, for the president was in early 1950 sticking to his $13 billion ceiling for the Defense Department's fiscal 1951 budget and, as Paul Hammond notes, "Talk of even a $10 billion budget ceiling for fiscal 1952 was serious enough to have prompted preliminary soundings on it."[94]

On the other hand, the administration was obviously not of one mind. NSC-68 had been, after all, presidentially commissioned and signed, and Truman was certainly not unaware of his new secretary of state's predispositions concerning the Soviets and the threat they posed. Moreover, the rationale for his H-bomb decision indicated Truman's receptivity to the views that were set forth in the document even though his economic instincts may have forced him to recoil. Acheson did not suffer from any indecisiveness. Hence, he relates, "The purpose of NSC-68 was to so bludgeon the mass mind of 'top government' that not only could the President make a decision but that the decision could be carried out."[95] Indeed, much of the emphasis on and overstatement of the Soviet threat can and has been explained as a rhetorical tactic adopted by Nitze and Acheson as a means for stating the case for an increased American defense effort as persuasively as possible.[96]

> The task of a public officer seeking to explain and gain support for a major policy is not that of the writer of a doctoral thesis. Qualification must give way to simplicity of statement, nicety and nuance to bluntness, almost brutality, in carrying home a point. It is better to carry the hearer or reader into the quadrant of one's thought than merely to make a noise or to mislead him utterly.[97]

The perspective and policies to which the listeners were to be persuaded were not without their detractors. Within the Department of State, Kennan and Charles Bohlen, the two foremost Soviet experts in the U.S. government, were skeptical of both the analysis of Soviet policy set forth in the NSC-68 and the way in which the analysis was to be employed. Kennan persisted in a more subtle and complex view of Soviet behavior and viewed Nitze's statement of Soviet intent as simplistic. Both Bohlen and Kennan regarded Soviet behavior as being too complex to encompass in such a planning document. Indeed, they expressed reservations concerning the entire exercise because it forced extremely complex and delicate considerations of policy into the sterile abstractions of a planning document. From such a statement, higher officials lacking perspective and a sense of nuance, would be prone to draw even more simple-minded conclusions.[98] Acheson's perceived need for serving as militant missionary among the beknighted of the Truman administration underscores and extends Kennan's point. For, having bludgeoned the top minds of government, can one realistically expect that same government to respond to the ambiguity and change of world politics with sophistication and conceptual elegance?

Let us reemphasize, however, that there were fundamental substantive differences between the positions represented by Kennan and Acheson. To Kennan the real threat confronting the West was political and economic. He saw no real military threat either to Western Europe or Western ideals. Ironically, as we have traced in this chapter, the policies developed and pursued by Marshall, although he may have regarded them as limited and no real threat to Soviet security, were taken as such by Stalin. An economically strong Western Europe, including a new German state, when combined with his own difficulties in Eastern Europe and at home, were unacceptable pressures from Stalin's increasingly isolated standpoint. Moreover, the means adopted by the West for implementing their policies excluded Soviet participation, hence Stalin through the Berlin crisis tried to force his way into the West's decisions on Germany. The Berlin crisis became in turn the opportunity for the emergence of the position represented by Acheson: the threat to Western Europe was essentially military and Stalin's moves were not — as Kennan argued — desperate, but limited actions by an isolated Soviet dictator playing his last cards. The fall of China and the explosion of the atomic bomb by the Soviets seemed to confirm that Stalin represented a deeper and darker threat, a dislocation of history, to which NATO, the Mutual Defense Assistance Program, the hydrogen bomb, and a massive increase in U.S. military preparedness were the answers.

In summary, the president, the bureaucracy, Congress, and the country were suspended in mid-1950 between a past that was captured in Kennan's admonition that American policy must be "that of a long-term vigilant containment" of Soviet power which avoided "outward histrionics: without threats or blustering or superfluous gestures of outward 'toughness' " and Acheson's Wagnerian vision of "the road to freedom and to peace," which was "a hard one." In Acheson's view:

> The times in which we live must be painted in the dark sombre values of Rembrandt. The background is dark, the shadows deep. Outlines are obscure. The central point, however, glows with light; and, though it often brings out the glint of steel, it touches colors of unimaginable beauty. For us, that central point is the growing unity of free men the world over. This is our shaft of light, our hope, and our promise.[99]

The main difference in these perspectives lay in their proposals for action. Kennan, like Acheson, saw a prolonged confrontation, but it was to be one of political and economic containment, like the Marshall Plan, a largely symbolic alliance, and even taking risks to bring about arms control and broader negotiations. Acheson feared world domination by Soviet ideology and military power, the containment of which would require a full-fledged military alliance with Europe abroad and a subordination of domestic priorities to national security needs, which were in fact indistinguishable from global security needs. Moreover, meaningful negotiations were deemed unlikely except when carried out in the presence of Western political, economic, but above all, military strength — in short, "the glint of steel."

President Truman apparently stood somewhere between those perspectives/prescriptions. Perhaps by mid-1950 he was somewhere closer to Acheson's view of the threat, but unwilling to pursue vigorously its implementation.[100] The policy proposed in NSC-68 remained, therefore, tentative. But on June 24, 1950, the North Korean army crossed the 38th parallel into South Korea, and most of the remaining uncertainties vanished. Acheson's road would be taken.

NOTES

1. Adam Ulam, *The Rivals: America and Russia: Since World War II* (New York: Viking Press, 1971) and Marshall D. Shulman, *Stalin's Foreign Policy Reappraised* (New York: Atheneum Publishers, 1965), pp. 14–15, 258.
2. The actual size of the Soviet military at this time is a question of some dispute. For a review of the issue and the numerous estimates see Thomas W. Wolfe, *Soviet Power and Europe, 1945–1970* (Baltimore: Johns Hopkins University Press, 1970) pp. 9–11.
3. Ulam, op. cit., pp. 139–140.
4. Ibid., pp. 140–141. Ulam notes that Stalin's boast concerning Tito's destruction is probably not a literal quotation, but Professor Ulam observes, "that is how he felt" (p. 140).
5. Quoted by Herbert Feis, *From Trust to Terror: The Onset of the Cold War, 1945–1950* (New York: W. W. Norton & Company, 1970,) p. 292.
6. Ibid., p. 294.
7. See Clay's biography, *Decision in Germany* (Garden City, N.Y.: Doubleday & Company, 1950), p. 354, and Feis, op. cit., p. 296.
8. Ibid.
9. Truman's careful preparation was not always successful. The *sine qua non* of a meaningful alliance was seen by the army as a sufficient standing army. The first time that universal conscription was suggested to Congress, it was voted down. There were reports, as the *Chicago Tribune* put it, that "in March, apparently in desperation, the Army handed President Truman a false intelligence report which 'pictured the Soviet Army as on the move,' when 'actually the Soviets were redistributing their troops to spring training stations'" (*Chicago Tribune*, June 19, 1948). Thus, when Truman called a joint emergency session of Congress to consider issues of defense, he had "evidence" that aided the passage of conscription as well as the Vandenberg Resolution.
10. For the most thorough analysis of the Truman administration's fiscal policy and its relationship to defense spending see Warner R. Schilling, "The Politics of National Defense: Fiscal 1950," in Warner R. Schilling, Paul Y. Hammond, and Glenn H. Snyder, *Strategy, Politics, and Defense Budgets* (New York: Columbia University Press, 1962). Most accounts of Truman's planning and budgeting eventually draw upon this excellent set of essays; the following analysis is no exception.
11. For a full account see George H. Quester, *Nuclear Diplomacy: The First Twenty-Five Years* (New York: Dunellen Co., 1970), p. 6 *passim*.

12. Ibid., pp. 5–6, 34–36 and Report of the President's Air Policy Commission, *Survival in the Air Age* (Washington, D.C.: U.S. Government Printing Office, 1948) and David MacIsacc, "The Air Force and Strategic Thought 1945–1951," *Working Paper* No. 8, The Wilson Center, International Security Studies Program, June 21, 1979, Washington, D.C., p. 27.

13. See the testimony of Undersecretary of State Robert Lovett before U.S. Congress, Senate Committee on Foreign Relations, *Interim Aid for Europe*, 80th Congress, 1st Session, 1947. The following exchange is especially revealing (p. 99):

   The Chairman [Vandenberg]: The thing I was trying to highlight at the moment was simply the general concept that we are approaching . . . this subject this time in a totally different fashion than ever before.

   Secretary Lovett: Absolutely, completely different.

   The Chairman: And that it does involve an attempt to set down an effective *quid pro quo* and to produce an ultimate emancipation of the obligation of the United States for any further relief.

   Secretary Lovett: That is its purpose.

14. Testimony of Secretary George C. Marshall before U.S. Congress, Senate Committee on Foreign Relations, *U.S. Assistance to European Economic Recovery*, 80th Congress, 2nd Session, 1948, p. 4.

15. Ibid.

16. Ibid., pp. 589, 591.

17. Ibid., p. 591. John Foster Dulles, a prominent Republican attorney and close adviser to the Department of State, reflected administration assumptions and thinking when he testified in support of the Marshall Plan:

   The importance of unity is clearly brought out by the fact that Western European unity is the feature of the Marshall idea which has particularly aroused Soviet leaders to attack. They are supremely confident that if western Europe can be kept divided, the governments can, one by one, be discredited and economic conditions made so hopeless that the people will, in despair, accept a Soviet-dictated peace. On the other hand, they know that a unity of upward of 250,000,000 people in Western Europe, industrious and educated as they are, could not easily be reduced even by Soviet power.

   Unity is thus a vital aspect of the present struggle. So long as it is not achieved, Soviet expectations will justifiably be high and their efforts will be prolonged. Once unity is achieved, their struggle will be lost and efforts to prolong it will be abandoned (p. 588).

   But, Dulles emphasized — again reflecting a growing sentiment within the administration — German recovery was essential to European recovery.

18. John Gimbel, *The American Occupation of Germany: Politics and the Military, 1945–1949* (Stanford, Calif.: Stanford University Press, 1968) pp. 195–196. Gimbel notes that relations within the Bizonal Economic Council had deteriorated through the latter half of 1947 as internal German political disagreements between the Social Democratic party and the Christian Democrats–Christian Socialists concerning the control of the council and struggles growing out of food shortages brought decision making to a standstill (pp. 186–194).

19. "London Conference Recommendations on Germany: Text of Communique," *Department of State Bulletin*, Vol. 18 (June 20, 1948), p. 808. This discussion is drawn, for the most part, from Gimbel, op. cit., and from Feis, op. cit., pp. 318–323.

20. "London Conference Recommendations on Germany: Explanation of the Conference," *Department of State Bulletin,* Vol. 18 (June 20, 1948), p. 812. The "explanation" under its section on "security" noted French concern explicitly: "The French Government in particular has been acutely aware of the possible dangers inherent in the reconstruction of a German state and the substantial revival of German economy."

21. Ibid., p. 811.

22. Testimony of John Foster Dulles in Hearings before U.S. Congress, Senate Committee on Foreign Relations, *U.S. Assistance to European Economic Recovery,* 80th Congress, 2nd Session, 1948, p. 589.

23. Actually, the confrontation at the November–December 1947 foreign ministers' conference was forecast by Marshall Sokolovsky's vitriolic attacks on the West during a meeting of the control council on November 21. See Feis, op. cit., pp. 276–277.

24. See the preceding chapter, and Feis, op. cit., pp. 267–274.

25. Testimony of Secretary of State George C. Marshall before U.S. Congress, Senate Committee on Foreign Relations, *U.S. Assistance to European Economic Recovery,* 80th Congress, 2nd Session, 1948, p. 12.

26. "London Conference Recommendations on Germany: Text of Communique," p. 808.

27. Ibid.; Feis, op. cit., pp. 320–321.

28. John G. Stoessinger, *Nations in Darkness* (New York: Vintage Press, Random House, 1971), p. 148.

29. Walter Millis (ed.), *The Forrestal Diaries* (New York: Viking Press, 1951), entry dated June 28, 1948, p. 454; quoted by Feis, op. cit., p. 342.

30. Quester, op. cit., 48–49.

31. Quoted by Feis, op. cit., p. 352.

32. This historical review is reconstructed from ibid., pp. 366–383.

33. Ibid., pp. 370–371.

34. Ibid., p. 373.

35. Reprinted from *Present at the Creation* by Dean Acheson. By permission of W. W. Norton & Company, Inc., and Hamish Hamilton, Ltd. Copyright © 1969 by Dean Acheson, p. 272.

36. Ibid., p. 272.

37. Shulman, p. 73.

38. See Acheson, op. cit., 286–292.

39. Ibid., p. 292.

40. Ibid.

41. See ibid.

42. Shulman, op. cit., p. 77.

43. Feis, op. cit., p. 377. Feis' conclusion is drawn from his conversations with many of the participants in these talks carried out during late 1948.

44. Robert E. Osgood, NATO: *The Entangling Alliance* (Chicago: University of Chicago Press, 1962).

45. Ibid., p. 33.

46. Feis, op. cit., p. 377.

47. Walter Millis, *Arms and the State* (New York: The Twentieth Century Fund, 1958), p. 237.

48. Osgood, op. cit., pp. 29–31, 36–39.

49. Ibid., p. 30.

50. George Kennan, *Memoirs, 1925–1950* (Boston: Little, Brown and Company, 1967) p. 401.

51. Osgood, op. cit., p. 35.

52. U.S. Congress, House Committee on Foreign Affairs, "North Atlantic Treaty Between the United States of America and Other Governments," *Collective Defense Treaties,* 91st Congress, 1st Session, 1969, p. 77.
53. Acheson, op. cit., p. 284.
54. U.S. Congress, Senate Committee on Foreign Relations, *Hearings on the North Atlantic Treaty,* 81st Congress, 1st Session, 1949, p. 47.
55. According to psychohistorian Arnold Rogow, James Forrestal, the first secretary of defense, "regarded the final outcome of the 1948 defense debate as both a personal defeat and conclusive evidence that the nation lacked the leadership and stamina necessary for victory in the Cold War. The personal defeat, he felt, had been administered less by Congress than by Truman, and [Secretary of the Air Force] Symington." On March 28, 1948, Forrestal resigned. On April 2, 1948, he was formally admitted to Bethesda Naval Hospital in Washington. On Sunday, May 22, despondent that what he regarded as a coalition of high administration dupes of Jews and communists had chosen him "as their Number One target for liquidation as a consequence of his efforts to alert Americans to the Communist menace," Forrestal leapt to his death from his sixteenth-floor suite at the hospital. Arnold A. Rogow, *James Forrestal: A Study of Personality, Politics and Policy* (New York: Macmillan Company, 1963), pp. 6–7 and 299.
56. See Paul Y. Hammond, "NSC-68: Prologue to Rearmament," in Schilling et. al., op. cit., pp. 280–282.
57. Cited by Robert Sherrill, "The War Machine," *Playboy,* Vol. 17 (No. 5, 1970), p. 220.
58. Osgood, op. cit., p. 45.
59. Ibid., pp. 46–47.
60. For a discussion of the scenarios thus presented, see Quester, op. cit., p. 32.
61. Wolfe, op. cit., p. 32.
62. Committee on Foreign Affairs, U.S. Congress, *Hearings on Emergency Foreign Aid,* 80th Congress, 1st Session, 1947, p. 14.
63. See Acheson, op. cit., pp. 303–304.
64. Quoted in *China and U.S. Far East Policy 1945–1967* (Washington, D.C.: Congressional Quarterly Service, 1967) p. 45.
65. Quoted in Ibid.
66. U.S. Department of State, *United States Relations with China with Special Reference to the Period 1944–1949* (Washington, D. C.: U.S. Government Printing Office, 1949), pp. 358–359.
67. Acheson, op. cit., p. 306.
68. Ibid.
69. Mr. Acheson contends that the analogy was used to emphasize his inability to peer into the future. He continues: "Of course, any stick is good enough to beat a dog, but this was an example of my unhappy ability — if I may mix a metaphor — to coin a stick" (p. 306).
70. Letter of transmittal, *United States Relations with China,* p. xvi.
71. *China and U.S. Far East Policy,* p. 47.
72. NSC-68, described by Dean Acheson as one of the most important documents of American history, has now been declassified after more than twenty years of secrecy: NSC-68, A Report to the National Security Council: *United States Objectives and Programs for National Security* (Washington, D.C.: Xeroxed, April 14, 1950). Hereafter cited as "NSC-68." Previously analyses of it had to be drawn from secondary sources. Of these, there is wide consensus that the account of Paul Y. Hammond, "NSC-68: Prologue to Rearmament," in Schilling et al., op. cit., pp. 305–

308, is the best review. Acheson's autobiography is also useful, especially pp. 344–349 and 373–381.

73. A full review of the memorandum, described by Kennan as "in its implications one of the most important, if not the most important, of all the documents I ever wrote in government," may be found in his *Memoirs, 1925–1950,* pp. 471–476.

74. Ibid., p. 474.

75. Acheson, op. cit., p. 347 and Robert J. Donovan, "The Devastating Times: The Hydrogen Bomb, China, and Korea," *Working Paper* No. 6, The Wilson Center, International Security Studies Program, Washington, D.C., April 19, 1979, p. 23.

76. Acheson, op. cit., p. 349.

77. Kennan, op. cit., p. 475 (emphasis in original).

78. Acheson, op. cit., p. 347.

79. Ibid. and Samuel Wells, Jr., "Sounding the Tocsin: NSC-68 and the Soviet Threat," *Working Paper* No. 7, The Wilson Center, International Security Studies Program, Washington, D.C., September 26, 1979, p. 11.

80. "NSC-68," p. 4.

81. Ibid., pp. 6–9.

82. Ibid., pp. 63–64.

83. Ibid., pp. 17–18.

84. Ibid., pp. 54–55.

85. Ibid., pp. 56–57.

86. Ibid., p. 58.

87. Ibid., p. 3.

88. Ibid., p. 4.

89. Ibid., p. 48.

90. Ibid., p. 64.

91. Ibid., pp. 39–40.

92. Acheson, op. cit., p. 375.

93. Ibid., p. 376.

94. Hammond, op. cit., p. 331.

95. Acheson, op. cit., p. 374.

96. Hammond, op. cit., pp. 309–318.

97. Acheson, op. cit., p. 375.

98. Hammond, op. cit.

99. Acheson, op. cit., p. 380.

100. Hammond, op. cit., pp. 340–341. As RAND Analyst Paul Hammond notes, there was some effort to incorporate NSC-68 guidelines into Defense Department budgeting in early 1950.

Chapter 4
Korea and the Militarization of Containment

More than anything else, two events, the first successful atomic test in the fall of 1949 and the Korean War beginning in the late spring of 1950, confirmed the increasingly military definition of America's global role. Although the Soviet test foretold the eventual end to one-sided nuclear diplomacy and was the cause of public consternation, the Soviet test was seen privately as something of a blessing. Acheson relates not fear but relief: "once again the Russians had come to the aid of an imperiled nonpartisan foreign policy, binding wounds and rallying the divided Congress."[1]

The other seminal event of the cold war was the American response to the Korean conflict. The U.S. military reaction confirmed the transformation of the scope and means of containment. The crisis of communist military action in Asia pushed forward the rearmament advocated in NSC-68. One of Acheson's aides remembered the trepidation which the administration felt when contemplating the "sale" of NSC-68 to the American people: "We were sweating over it, and then . . . thank God, Korea came along."[2]

THE ORIGINS
OF THE FIRST LIMITED WAR

The focus of containment was vague in NSC-68. Apparently Dean Acheson had not intended that its ambit circumscribe much of Asia. As Acheson explained American interests on January 12, 1950, to the National Press Club, "this defensive perimeter runs along the Aleutians to Japan and then goes to the Ryukus . . . [then] . . . runs from the Ryukus to the Philippine Islands."[3] In defining American interests in this manner, Acheson's analysis seemed like an ambiguous call for local self-help from countries on the mainland. If military attacks were to come, "the initial reliance must be on the people attacked to resist it and then upon the commitments of the

118

entire civilized world under the Charter of the United Nations."⁴ The primary threat in these areas was not direct military aggression, but rather "subversion and penetration that cannot be stopped by military means."⁵

Conspicuous by its absence in this outline of American security interests in Asia was Taiwan. The week before Acheson's speech to the National Press Club, the president had made it clear that the United States had no intention of providing more than economic assistance to Chiang Kai-Shek's government.⁶ Indeed, the eventual fall of Taiwan was assumed by the Department of State, which was so certain of Chiang's doom and the fall of Taiwan that ". . . [it] had already prepared and distributed an information paper to be used as a guide for information officers on what they were to say after the Chinese Communists had overrun the islands."⁷

Korea seemed an even more remote concern than Taiwan. Under the postwar occupation agreements the United States had been responsible for the administration of South Korea until reunification under UN auspices could take place. When the Soviets refused to submit the question of Korean reunification to the United Nations, separate administrations were established. As early as 1947, President Truman asked the Joint Chiefs to evaluate the military significance of Korea. In September 1947 they reported "that, from the standpoint of military security, the United States has little strategic interests in maintaining the present troops and bases in Korea."⁸

However, both Soviet and American assistance continued to their respective clients during 1948 and 1949. But by 1950 Syngman Rhee, the president of the South Korean regime, was becoming something of an embarrassment to the Americans. He severely restricted civil liberties, balked at holding elections, and did so only after withdrawal of American aid was threatened. Between September 1948 and April 1949 over 80,000 people were arrested in South Korea. There were sporadic demonstrations in the capital and by October 1949, 7 percent of the National Assembly had been jailed by Rhee. By spring of 1950 economic conditions had worsened dramatically. Although Rhee arrested more than two dozen of his opponents prior to the May 30, 1950, elections, he lost heavily, and more than half of the new assembly favored a move toward reunification with the North.⁹

To many in the Truman administration, Rhee was taking on all the attributes of a lesser Chiang Kai-Shek. The most explicit public statement of growing ambivalence toward the South Koreans came from Democratic Senator Tom Connally of Texas, the chairman of the Senate Committee on Foreign Relations. Just after the elections, in an interview Senator Connally asserted that South Korea might have to be abandoned. He noted that "of course any position like that is of some strategic importance. But I don't think it is very greatly important."[10] Secretary of State Acheson refused to comment on the Connally interview, thereby heightening the uncertainty, or at a minimum, seeming indifference, of American policy in early May of 1950.

There is little or no evidence that Peking was in any way involved in the North Korean attack on the South that came in late June. The North Koreans were armed with Soviet weapons and had been trained by Soviet advisers, leading most observers to regard the North Koreans as a Soviet satellite.[11] A victory by the North Korean communists might benefit the Chinese in that it would undercut the image of American power in Asia. Still, for Peking, the main military problems remained the conquest of Taiwan and Tibet, the pacification of southern and central China, and the reduction of military expenditures so as to relieve inflationary pressures.[12]

Soviet interest in Korea was long-standing and focused in part on its proximity to Japan and the geopolitical centrality of the peninsula in East Asian politics. It was possible that a communist victory in Korea might lead the Japanese to reconsider their relationship with the Americans. Even if the Americans responded by intensifying their commitment to Japan, the Russians may have reckoned that this would require a drawing down of the American presence in Europe. Then, too, an increased American presence in Asia would contribute to increased Chinese dependence on the Soviets.[13] Thus, for the Soviets, the benefits to be gained from encouraging and/or allowing a North Korean attack on the South seemed significant, the costs quite acceptable.

The evidence that the Soviets *directed* the attack is inconclusive at best. Next to speculation in the West that Stalin instigated the Korean adventure (he may well have known about it), there is Khrushchev's testimony: "I must stress that war wasn't Stalin's idea, but Kim Il-Sung's. Kim was the initiator."[14] Khrushchev's accusation can be supported. There had been, since 1948, a declining number of Russian advisers in North Korea who might have exercised an effective veto on Kim's action. In 1948 there were 150 Russians per North Korean army division, but by spring 1950 a State Department historian estimates that there were only from three to eight Russians to advise each North Korean division,[15] perhaps a total of less than forty[16] at the moment of attack. Soviet intentions, as interpreted in Washington, were, in the words of Assistant Secretary for Far Eastern Affairs Dean Rusk, "fuzzy."[17] And as Harvard Kremlinologist Adam Ulam speculates:

> The American reaction to the North Korean invasion on June 25 must have been one of the greatest surprises of Stalin's life. Having acquiesced in the loss of China, these unpredictable people now balked at the loss of a territory

they themselves had characterized as unimportant. . . . Had there been any inkling . . . the Soviet delegate would not have boycotted the Security Council since January . . . and Moscow would have been ready with diplomatic notes and propaganda campaigns. . . . Between June 27 and July 3, the news from Korea was tucked in the back pages of the Soviet press.[18]

If Korea's place in the U.S. defense perimeter had been left ambiguous in January by Secretary of State Acheson, and very nearly disavowed by his silence in May,[19] then why was it a security interest in June? In part, Korea was seen as an overt communist military attack; that is, the form of communist aggression had changed decisively.[20] But also, the North Korean attack was deemed a Soviet probe by proxy, aimed at Japan. And Japan was most definitely a well-marked American interest. If Korea was perceived by mainland Asians as a bridge for Japanese aggression, the Japanese had historically conceived of Korea as a dagger pointed at their heart. The combination of a weak South Korean regime and a strong Soviet-backed North Korean government, in the analysis of President Truman and his advisers, provided the means for extending communist control of the peninsula at minimal cost.

But to President Truman and his advisers that danger was more than specific to any country. The menace was now aggression and its attendant dangers to global order. This was clearly in Truman's mind as he flew back to Washington on the 26th of June upon learning of the intense military action along the 38th parallel:

> Communism was acting in Korea just as Hitler, Mussolini, and the Japanese had acted ten, fifteen, and twenty years earlier. I felt certain that if South Korea was allowed to fall Communist leaders would be emboldened to override nations closer to our own shores. If the communists were permitted to force their war into the Republic of Korea without opposition from the free world, no small nation would have the courage to resist threats and aggression by stronger communist neighbors. If this was allowed to go unchallenged it would mean a third world war, just as similar incidents had brought on the second world war.[21]

Thus President Truman's decision to seek a UN mandate for military assistance to the South Koreans, the immediate interpositioning of the Seventh Fleet between Taiwan and the mainland, and increases in assistance to the Philippines and the French in Indochina which grew out of the Korean crisis, were acts to demonstrate American will. In so acting, "the safety and prospects for [the] peace of the free world would be increased."[22] The rationale and the rhetoric should be familiar, for they are virtually synonymous with that of March 1947 . . . or August 1964.

Even if the substantive essence of the Truman Doctrine might remain European, its applicable limits now became global.

NSC-68 summarized this notion about the integrity of world order and also predicted military probes and feints by the Soviets that had to be answered. Otherwise, as Acheson explained, "To back away from this challenge [in Korea] would be highly destructive of the power and prestige of the United States. By prestige I mean the shadow cast by power, which is of great deterrent importance."[23] Prestige, "the shadow of power," was seen by Acheson as crucial to the deterrence of communist aggression. The United States would escalate its commitment, for if the aggressor was not stopped on the frontiers of containment, then the integrity of the entire concept would be compromised. If the commitment were debased, it would indicate a lack of will to defend the heart of the system — Europe. Korea was not, therefore, essential in the same sense as Germany or Britain. Nonetheless, President Truman and his advisers were convinced that "the Korean situation [was] vital as a *symbol of the strength and determination of the West.*"[24]

To President Truman and his advisers, intervention in Korea held great dangers. First, there was the danger of world war. Once the decision had been made to use force, the possibility increased that the violence might get out of hand and escalate into a Soviet-American confrontation. Consequently, an overriding consideration was keeping the Soviets out of the conflict. At the very outset, therefore, the United States took careful note of Soviet sensibilities. The Soviets were not accused of starting the war. They were simply asked to disavow any responsibility for the attack. Some observers have suggested that this approach by the United States, when combined with President Truman's reluctance to equate explicitly the Soviet Union with communism in his June 27 statement, indicates that the United States was not convinced that the Soviets had started the war.[25] In any event, the Soviets replied that the South Koreans had started the fight and that they (the Soviets) advocated a policy of noninterference by outside powers in Korea. Secretary Acheson and the State Department's Russian experts took this response, the lack of any further follow-up by the Soviets, and the cumulating string of North Korean victories as conclusive evidence that the Soviets would not intervene in the short run.[26]

Then, too, how might U.S. policy avoid confusing the symbol, Korea and American action in Asia, with the more important object of the symbolic action, containment and the defense of Europe? American action in Korea had to be kept limited because it was taken to be the means to the larger end of maintaining the integrity of the system of containment.

There was also concern about Chinese intervention, although here the immediate threat was perceived to be an attack on Taiwan. Ostensibly this eventuality was the basis for the decision to move the Seventh Fleet into the Taiwan Strait. President Truman recognized, however, that Communist Chinese intervention might be provoked by Chiang Kai-Shek's actions. Consequently, he called upon Chiang to cease all actions against the mainland and declined, on Secretary Acheson's advice, the offer by Chiang and General Douglas MacArthur of some 30,000 Chinese Nationalist troops.

The delicacy of the Nationalist Chinese position in the crisis was compounded by the militancy of the China lobby in the United States, and also by the presence in Asia of General MacArthur, who had long disagreed with the European focus of American policy. Ironically, this European orientation of U.S. policymakers allowed General MacArthur to build for himself, in Asia after the war, a position of considerable personal power and a network of personal contacts and confidences among East Asian anticommunists including a strong attachment to Chiang and his cause. A European-oriented White House, State Department, and Defense Department were prepared to leave the administration of American policy — which was primarily occupation policy — to the Supreme Commander of the Allied Powers in Tokyo. From his Pacific command in Tokyo, General MacArthur possessed power and authority comparable to that of a head of state, powers never before possessed by an American military man. Indeed, his staff compared him to Napoleon and Alexander.[27] As President Truman put it later, "there was never anybody around him to keep him in line. . . . He just wouldn't let anybody near him who wouldn't kiss his ass . . . there were many times when he was . . . out of his head."[28]

From his position of virtual control of American military and political policy in Asia, General MacArthur was uniquely situated to assist Chiang and Rhee in their struggle for survival. In late 1949 Rhee had sought out General MacArthur's help in obtaining an increase in American arms. Almost simultaneously the South Korean defense minister stated after a conference with General MacArthur "that he would gladly march on Pyongyang," the North Korean capital. Also in early 1950, Rhee visited General MacArthur in Tokyo, outlined his increasingly desperate position, and reportedly called for an Asian anticommunist crusade under General MacArthur's leadership.[29]

The MacArthur problem would eventually dominate war and domestic policy, but in the meantime a buildup of military forces was culminating on both sides of the 38th parallel. From March 1949 until June 1950, Rhee expanded his military forces from 114,000 to more than 150,000 men. Rhee's American arms were light weapons, perhaps reflecting U.S. anxiety concerning his intentions.[30] In contrast, the North Koreans began a rapid buildup of their forces to a level of 135,000 men after January 1950, with large shipments of Soviet equipment, including armor, arriving as late as April and May. Despite the North Korean advantages in armor, American intelligence, fully aware of the mini-arms race then underway, reported that Rhee was fully capable of defending the South.[31]

Tensions between the two Korean governments grew steadily. Philip Jessup, a State Department official, declared in April 1950 that "the boundary at the 38th parallel . . . is a real front line. There is constant fighting. . . . There are very real battles, involving one or two thousand men."[32] As one authority on Korea, Robert Simmons, summed up the situation: "Koreans were accustomed to the fighting and the possibility of war; each side believed that an early unification was worth a war."[33] As tensions and arms increased along the 38th parallel, John Foster Dulles (then acting as Republican special consultant to the State Department) visited Asia. In a speech before the South Korean national assembly on June 18, 1950, Dulles struck a rather different note than indicated by Secretary of State Acheson in his January "defense perimeter" speech. Dulles denounced the North Koreans and then added, concerning South Korea, "you are not alone. You will never be alone as long as you continue to play worthily your part in the great design of human freedom."[34] Dulles did not promise any specific form of aid. But these statements before a National Assembly controlled by Rhee's opponents must have encouraged Rhee — and frightened the North Koreans. After leaving Korea, Dulles traveled to Tokyo, and after meeting with General MacArthur made vague references to positive action by the United States in the future.

Thus the circumstances surrounding the outbreak of fighting in Korea remain, after three decades, confusing. The American perception of the importance of the peninsula was deeply divided between MacArthur's desire for action and Washington's ambivalence, which was resolved only when the fighting began. The calculus of interests regarding the motives of the Soviet Union, China, and the two Koreas is no less controversial. But the hazy facts now surrounding the origins of the Korean War did not inhibit the crystallization of a policy consensus that allowed President Truman to insert swiftly an American military presence in Korea when the apparent North Korean attack came on June 25, 1950.[35] Stewart Alsop remembered that even George Kennan (now, in 1950, seen as an iconoclast in his views about how to manage Soviet power) did a "jig of delight" on hearing that the United States would now confront "Stalin's carefully calculated challenge in Korea."[36]

THE "FOG OF WAR"

On the morning of June 24, 1950 (June 25, Korean time), about 90,000 men of the Korean People's Army of North Korea (KPA), supported by more than one hundred Russian-built T-34 tanks, crossed the 38th parallel, the border between North and South Korea.[37] Within hours the North Koreans were claiming that their forces had pushed 10 to 15 miles into the Republic of Korea. Confusion as to what was happening was extensive. At least one official in General MacArthur's headquarters in Tokyo believed that the South Koreans had attacked the North Koreans. Some observers characterized events as a complete surprise followed by the fairly rapid collapse of South Korean resistance. Other, more skeptical analysts have suggested that the Republic of Korea (ROK) Army recovered quickly from a North Korean surprise attack, launched a counterattack, and had established a more or less stable defensive line by June 26.[38]

In any case, news in Washington throughout the 27th and 28th of June was still confused. General MacArthur and Syngman Rhee predicted imminent collapse. But other journalistic sources suggested that any report from the battlefield had to be viewed cautiously.[39] Hanson Baldwin, military correspondent of *The New York Times*, reported on June 29: "The normal fog of war — greatly accentuated in the Korean campaign by the paucity of communications — has left Washington with insufficient information to determine with precision our future course."[40]

The response in Washington to these perplexing reports was nonetheless, decisive. Secretary of State Acheson had received the news from Korea, and before contacting the president — who was in Independence, Missouri, on family business — requested that the UN Security Council be called into session. The council met on the afternoon of June 25. Absent was the Russian delegate, who was boycotting the council over the issue of its exclusion of the People's Republic of China as the legitimate representative of China to the United Nations. An American-drafted resolution was quickly passed, which labeled the North Koreans aggressors and demanded their withdrawal from the South.[41]

By June 26 President Truman had returned to Washington. There he received an alarming message from General MacArthur: "South Korean units unable to resist determined Northern offensive.... [O]ur estimate is that a complete collapse is imminent."[42] Mr. Truman has recorded his reaction to this message:

> There was now no doubt! The Republic of Korea needed help at once if it was not to be overrun.... I told my advisers that what was developing in Korea seemed to me like a repetition on a large scale of what had happened

in Berlin. The Reds were probing for weaknesses in our armor; we had to meet their thrust without getting embroiled in a world-wide war.[43]

President Truman was prepared, in short, to assume the worst, draw what were becoming the conventional analogies of his administration, and move.

The president ordered American air and naval forces into action in support of what were assumed, in Washington, to be retreating South Korean units. The President then requested that the UN Security Council meet again the next day, June 27, and recommend that the member states provide assistance to South Korea. The council was thus put in the position of meeting to consider whether it should approve sanctions against the North Koreans that the United States had already initiated. Inasmuch as the council had already declared the North Koreans aggressors on June 25, the decision was a foregone conclusion. The Security Council passed a resolution that recommended that "members of the United Nations furnish such assistance to the Republic of Korea as may be necessary to repel the armed attack and to restore international peace and security in the area."[44]

The command and control of UN forces were structured in such a manner that the United States had total control. All forces committed to the UN effort were to operate under U.S. command and a U.S.–designated commander, who would be Douglas MacArthur. The UN flag was to be used, but the UN resolution in no way required that the U.S. commander report to the United Nations. Indeed, the Security Council established no machinery for administering the military effort. It was clear, therefore, that the UN effort in Korea would be United States conceived, administered, and implemented.

THE LIMITED WAR AT HOME:
DOMESTIC POLITICS AND REARMAMENT

The Korean War cannot be understood as merely a military operation, a case study in the problems of limited war[45] or primarily a problem of civil-military relations.[46] It was also seen by the Truman administration as a crucial part of the complex and interrelated domestic and foreign milieu of 1950.

Domestic Politics

The concept of a limited war was never completely understood by the American people. This was due in some measure to the combination of

President Truman's actions and his hyperbolic rhetoric. As the war progressed, the public grew uneasy with the notion that the United States was circumscribing its military activities both geographically and in terms of the means employed. Discontent was perhaps increased by the fact that many of the men called upon to carry the brunt of this limited war had only 5 years earlier brought to a successful close a massive total war effort. Moreover, World War II had been conducted so as to crush the same forces of aggression that were said now to be loose again.

Exacerbating the domestic situation immeasurably was a second factor: an executive-legislative struggle with conservative Republicans pitched against President Truman and Secretary of State Acheson. The battle was engaged by men with mixed motives, who had not held the presidency and had held a congressional majority only once in 20 years. Conservatives such as senators Knowland, Bridges, Jenner, Wherry, Taft, and McCarthy are frequently identified as isolationists in that they attacked the Truman administration's deepening involvement in Europe. Curiously, however, these same men assailed Truman, Marshall, and Acheson for not doing enough in Asia to stop the spread of communism. The inconsistency is striking and confusing unless one admits the possibiity that the majority of congressional Republicans as well as a significant portion of congressional Democrats were simply ideological conservatives opposed to every facet of Truman's public policy as crypto–New Dealism.

There was an avowedly internationalist thrust of the administration's foreign policy symbolized by its support of the United Nations, increasing foreign assistance budgets brought on by the ERA, NATO, and new economic assistance programs in the Third World, and all of it epitomized by the anglophilic presence of Dean Acheson as secretary of state. The backdrop of conservative suspicion was what they saw as Roosevelt's "treasonous maneuvering" over Eastern Europe. The only remedy suggested by Republicans to amend Roosevelt's perfidy was liberation, not containment. Containment was seen as involving coexistence with, and thus the continuation of communism — not its destruction. And to many conservatives the final proof that containment would not work could now be found in Asia: first in Mao Zedong's success in China and now in the attack on South Korea.

Under these circumstances, Truman administration policy in Asia became a target of criticism from the right. Republicans reproached Truman not for any love they may have had for Asia (although this was undoubtedly the case for a few of Truman's critics such as Congressman Walter Judd, who had a long personal attachment as a missionary doctor in China prior to Mao's victory), but simply because containment in Asia was beset by difficulties in contrast with the apparent success of containment in Europe.

The expediency of the conservative position is apparent: Republicans could support Truman's decision to intervene in Korea while simultaneously criticizing the administration's policy for having brought on the attack in the first place. They charged that all of this could have been avoided if the Truman administration had been willing to commit U.S. troops and greater aid to save China and support Asian anticommunists such as Syngman Rhee. Ironically these were the same conservatives who supported Truman's reduction of U.S. conventional military strength and advocated a greater reliance upon air power.

The Senator from
Wisconsin: "A Pig in a Minefield"[47]

Perhaps the best example of the political opportunism underlying much of the attack from the right is to be found in the rise of Senator Joseph McCarthy to national prominence. Beginning in February 1950 and continuing until December 1954, Senator McCarthy maintained that the U.S. government was and had been for a decade infiltrated with communists, former communists, communist sympathizers, and unknowing instruments of communism. Their presence throughout the government, but especially in the Department of State, was the explanation for all the failures of American foreign policy during the preceding decade. Their influence explained the willingness of the Roosevelt administration to accept the Soviets in middle Europe and, above all, communist influence among the Department of State's Asian experts explained the loss of China.[48]

On February 9, 1950, Senator McCarthy unveiled his blunderbuss: "While I cannot take the time to name all the men in the State Department who had been named as members of the Communist Party and members of a spy ring, I have here in my hand a list of two hundred and five that were known to the Secretary of State as being members of the Communist Party and who, nevertheless, are still working and shaping policy in the State Department."[49] On other occasions Senator McCarthy referred to 207, 57, 10, 116, 121, 106, and 81 communists in "foggy bottom," and sometimes he merely spoke of a "lot" of subversives. In July a Senate committee and then a full vote of Congress attested that there was nothing to Senator McCarthy's charges. But Republicans, as journalist David Halberstam writes, "welcomed him; the more they assaulted the Democrats the better for the Republicans." "Joe," said John Bricker, one of the more traditional conservatives and a candidate for vice president in 1944, "You're a real SOB. But sometimes it is useful to have SOB's around to do the dirty work."[50]

The assault on Democratic and State Department integrity and patriotism was a clever strategy. It explained how it was that Americans were now fighting a curious war in Asia without confronting the complexities and ambiguities of world politics and American policies: there were traitors in high places. Moreover, it appealed to America's alienated and preyed on an endemic fear deeply rooted in American society: the fear that America might not be equal to the task of global involvement.[51] Senator McCarthy's answer was reassuring: America's difficulties were not the product of inexperience and naivete, but rather treason.

Senator McCarthy was a much-sought speaker. He coveted the publicity that rapidly came to him. His simplistic views articulated the fears and confusion of many Americans. In time, it would be demonstrated that he "was in many ways the most gifted demagogue that ever lived on these shores. No bolder seditionist ever moved among us — nor any politician with a surer, swifter access to the dark places of the American mind."[52] But even in early 1954, as he neared censure in the U.S. Senate, 50 percent of the American people held a favorable opinion of him; only 29 percent reacted negatively. "It was a melancholy time," Richard Rovere has observed, "and the Chief Justice of the United States was probably right when he said at the time that if the 'Bill of Rights were put to a vote, it would lose.' "[53]

His meteoric rise made him the rallying point for the rather large number of Americans who found American foreign policy under Harry Truman confusing and burdensome. It was this characteristic that made Senator McCarthy attractive to the Republican leadership in the Senate, including "Mr. Republican," Senator Robert A. Taft.

Senator Taft's association with McCarthy is striking in view of Taft's reputation for conservative probity and sensitivity to civil liberties, all of which was in contrast with McCarthy's insensitivity and demagogic excesses. However, Senator Taft wanted the Republican presidential nomination in 1952, and he was going to do nothing that would cost him the support of conservative Senate Republicans. When it became clear that the center of Republican opinion, searching for any means to strike at Truman, had begun to move with or was at least willing to tolerate McCarthy, Taft abandoned his early uneasiness with McCarthy and began to support him. Senator Taft began castigating "the pro-communist group in the State Department who surrendered to every demand of Russia at Yalta and Potsdam, and promoted at every opportunity the communist cause in China."[54] Taft's biographer, William W. White, has said of the senator at this time, "it seemed to some of his friends and admirers that he began, if unconsciously, to adopt the notion that almost *any* way to defeat or discredit the Truman plans was acceptable. There was ... a blood in the nostrils approach."[55]

On June 2, 1950, Senator Margaret Chase Smith, Republican of Maine, issued what she termed a "Declaration of Conscience" in which she attacked the Republican leadership. She noted, "The nation sorely needs a Republican victory. But I do not want to see the Republican Party ride to political victory on the Four Horsemen of Calumny — fear, ignorance, bigotry, and smear."[56] It is a mark of the effects of Truman's stunning victory in 1948 on Robert Taft and the Republican party, Taft's personal ambition, and the fear and the polarization brought about by McCarthy, that Senator Taft could not or would not associate himself with Senator Smith's declaration.[57]

Rearmament

Against this backdrop of increasing vitriolic conservative opposition, President Truman sought to use the emergency of Korea and, subsequently, Chinese intervention in the war, to flesh out the framework of NSC-68. The task was made no easier by losses in the 1950 elections, which cut Democratic majorities in both the Senate and House. Nevertheless, as Paul Nitze, chairman of the committee that drafted NSC-68, recalled:

> The dilemma involved in choosing between an unbalanced budget, higher taxes, and more stringent economic controls on the one hand, and an adequate military posture on the other was not resolved at the policy decision level until some three months prior to the outbreak of the North Korean aggression. Those decisions were translated into specific action *only after* the aggression into South Korea had given *concrete and bloody confirmation to the conclusions already produced by* analysis.[58]

By the end of 1951 total requests for defense spending had reached $74 billion. NSC-68 had argued that American defense spending expand from $13.5 billion to $50 billion. The added difference of some $24 billion represented the cost of Korea *per se* and a sudden inflationary surge to the economy under the impact of war. The sheer magnitude of this defense spending is awesome given the defense budgets and philosophy that had existed for the past several years. Even more important, however, was the programmatic content of the requests, for what was being funded carried implications far beyond Korea.

The fiscal year 1952 budget request reflected the administration's decision to go over to a basically conscript army. The president asked that draft authority be extended to 1955 and a permanent military obligation of 8 years total and 2 years active duty be imposed on all males between the ages of 18 and 26. Expansion of the American overseas military base system was proposed to Congress. More than seventy new bases and support facilities were to be constructed in the United States, North Africa, and the Middle East. The air force was to be placed within striking range of the Soviet Union, to be expanded, and its strike capability to be augmented by the decision to deploy a new bomber, the B-47. The construction of atomic weapons forged ahead to the point that the secretary of the air force could claim in November 1951 that the United States had entered the age of atomic plenty. At the same time, the last technical problems standing in the way of a thermonuclear device or H-bomb were surmounted in the spring of 1951. The navy was in no sense left out of this quantum jump in American global military capability. With virtually no opposition, the Congress approved $2.4 billion in fleet construction and modernization. Included in this program was the first super-carrier, the 57,000-ton *Forrestal,* and the first nuclear submarine, the *Nautilus.* If, as envisaged in NSC-68, a "year of maximum peril" was closing on the United States in 1953 or 1954, the Truman administration would be ready.

In 1951 there was also established the foundations for a permanent U.S. defense presence in Asia. Most important was the Japanese peace treaty signed in September 1951. The treaty simultaneously excluded any Russian involvement in the future of Japan and ensured future American basing. The Japanese treaty was supplemented by a similar arrangement with the Philippines and a third mutual security treaty with Australia and New Zealand. An increase in aid to the French in Indochina was also extended. Finally, the administration moved toward permanent support of Chiang Kai-Shek's regime on Taiwan as U.S. military assistance increased.

In short, the fiscal year 1952 budget that went before and was approved by Congress in 1951 provided the basis for the expanded military capability envisaged by NSC-68. But there was more to Truman's budget than a request for increased spending; he also proposed increasing the number of American troops stationed in Europe. In so doing, Truman sparked a great debate on both sides of the Atlantic: with Senator Taft, on the one hand, as he attacked the premises of President Truman's policy, and on the other hand with the Europeans, concerning the future of NATO.

The Great Debate

Truman's announcement on December 19, 1950, that now U.S. troops would be needed in Europe prompted Senator Taft to argue for a "reexamination" of the entire course of postwar foreign policy. Taft charged that Truman, "without authority . . . involved us in the Korean War. Without authority he is now attempting a similar policy in Europe. This matter must be debated."[59] Taft did not wish to return to the old isolationism of one hemisphere hegemony. The Senator disagreed with President Truman not about the scope of American interests; rather Taft was bothered by the financial and constitutional costs involved in securing and maintaining a global role. Thus Senator Taft regarded the two U.S. divisions then stationed in Europe as a sufficient guarantee of America's commitment to the NATO alliance. This ensured, in Taft's view, American involvement in the event of a Russian attack. In the meantime, "an all-powerful air force [was] the best possible defense for the United States, [and] . . . also the greatest deterrent to war."[60] Moreover, he implored the Truman administration to "not assume obligations by treaty or otherwise which require any extensive use of American land forces."[61] The defense of Japan and an unequivocal commitment to Chiang Kai-Shek were to be exceptions to Senator Taft's security coverage, but not Europe. In Taft's opinion, the American obligation to Europe was fulfilled with the mere existence of NATO — nothing else was mandated. Otherwise the country's economy would be seriously distorted through a disastrously inflated economy, deficit spending, and hence a mortgaged future. To control a spiraling arms budget would require, according to Senator Taft, wage and price controls — controls that would eventually extend to other dimensions of American life. In short, Senator Taft anticipated a political economy that was the very antithesis of the free-market capitalist domestic system that comprised the ideological bedrock for conservatives such as himself.[62]

The only recourse, to Senator Taft and his followers, was a defense policy predicated upon air and naval superiority. Taft also called for an aggressive effort to sell the American system abroad by means of propaganda and where necessary clandestine infiltration and support of "those millions who yearn for liberty in satellite countries. . . ."[63] Sympathetic elements of Soviet-bloc nations would be cultivated, for Taft hoped that they "may be organized to seize power wherever they have support of their fellow citizens."[64] Senator Taft recognized the irony implicit in this policy: it would rely on the very methods of those he would fight.[65] But it was essential, he believed, to pursue a course of subversion and propaganda if a limited military posture was to succeed.

Three days after Senator Taft spoke, a resolution was introduced into the Senate by the conservatives that would require congressional action before any troops could be moved to Europe. During February and March of 1951 the administration sent a parade of witnesses before the Senate Foreign Relations Committee to counter Senator Taft's position, including his proposition that the president did not, in fact, already have the authority to move the troops to Europe. Similarly, military leaders including General Dwight Eisenhower testified in favor of European deployment. Administration officials led by Acheson and Marshall emphasized that the United States was thinking in terms of four to six divisions. Since 60,000 to 100,000 troops fell within limits that Taft had previously found acceptable, the conservative opposition began to diminish.[66]

In April 1951 the Senate acted on President Truman's request, passing a retroactive endorsement of the president's decision and approving the appointment of General Eisenhower as NATO commander. An amendment was added reflecting Senator Taft's influence, which stated that no more than four divisions could be sent to Europe without the approval of the Senate. Nevertheless, President Truman ignored the amendment and characterized the Senate's action as an endorsement of his foreign policy and his prerogatives as commander-in-chief.

CONVENTIONAL FORCES
FOR NATO: PLANS AND STALEMATE

Parallelling the great debate in the United States was another within NATO. The outbreak of fighting in Korea provided the Truman Administration with some leverage on the stalemated situation within the NATO alliance. Prior to the Soviets acquiring atomic weapons, American planning for the defense of Europe was based solely on the deterrent capacity of American atomic superiority. The Soviets' test explosion in 1949 brought American deterrence into question. The American nuclear umbrella to others, now, at least potentially, was a risk. First, the umbrella could be swept away if the Soviets ever attained the ability to launch a disarming blow. Second, sharing the American umbrella implied that an ally was not only a target but also, perhaps, a negotiable asset. After all, the French, Germans, and British would muse, why would America want to risk Chicago for Dusseldorf or Lyon? Could not European targets become chips of a great power poker game unless the Europeans became equipped to play the game too and obtained nuclear weapons for themselves?

The questions were still hypothetical. Most Europeans continued to believe, and correctly, that American military predominance would not be effectively undercut for some time to come. The problem was viewed with greater urgency in the United States and especially by Secretary of State Acheson. The conclusion of NSC-68 — that rearmament should begin immediately in both the United States and NATO — was in anticipation of a nuclear stalemate predicted to materialize in the mid-1950s. By then, it was estimated, the balance of conventional forces would assume overriding importance.

Consequently the American position at the foreign ministers' meeting of the North Atlantic Council in May 1950 was that planning for increased European conventional forces was essential. For their part, the Europeans were reluctant to move rapidly toward reinvigorating their military establishments. They feared that an emphasis on rearmament would divert scarce resources away from the continuing economic reconstruction of Europe. European preoccupation with the economic needs of the alliance emerged just prior to the May meetings of 1950. The French advanced a proposal for integrating the coal and steel industries of Europe, but especially those of France and Germany, under supranational control. This plan had been developed by Jean Monnet and French Foreign Minister Robert Schumann and was seen as "the setting-up of common foundations for economic development as a first step in the federation of Europe."[67] Clearly European priorities and problems were economic. Although they recognized impending military difficulties, they, with the exception of the British, were not anxious to devote time or resources to such matters.

Nevertheless, Secretary of State Acheson persisted and was able to forge an amorphous agreement that NATO force planning should go forward on a basis of balanced *collective* forces rather than equilibrated *national* forces. In the abstract, the approach seemed economically sound in avoiding wasteful duplication. However, when the foreign ministers turned to how the member states would contribute to a balanced collective force structure, problems arose immediately. First the Americans and the British sought to define their contribution in terms of their nuclear deterrent role. But this meant that the continental nations would have to provide the bulk of the conventional manpower, at least to start with. However, arms are expensive and so are the paychecks and supplies of even conscript armies. And, of course, this was the kind of economic commitment that the Europeans wanted to avoid. Moreover, from the standpoint of those Europeans who were attempting to maintain a colonial empire, a second problem was raised by the concept of balanced collective forces. Imperial powers such as the French, Dutch, Belgians, and Portuguese demanded independent control over their manpower contribution to the ostensibly integrated NATO structure in order to meet the exigencies of empire maintenance. The problem was especially acute for the French, given their deteriorating situation in Indochina.

From the very outset the concept upon which NATO conventional force planning was based was weakened by what proved to be an irresolvable tension. In the end, the May 1950 conference did not attempt to deal with the contradiction between the needs to retain control of crumbling empires and the requirements of a collective grand force. Rather, the NATO allies settled for a vague statement of principle and an equally vague concession from the Americans and the British that they would increase their levels of participation in the defense of the continent. Obviously, there was another source of manpower — Germany. But the idea of German rearmament was still very nearly unmentionable given French sensitivity to a new *Wehrmacht*.[68] Hence on the eve of the Korean War the NATO allies were forced to admit that there were grave differences between their rhetoric and the resources they were willing to commit to any collective effort.

The outbreak of the Korean War caused temporary movement toward reconciliation of these problems. American assistance was now predicated upon an increased effort on the part of the Europeans.[69] The French demanded in return for this subordination of their priorities (economic recovery) a greater contribution by the Americans to the conventional defense of Europe. This demand, in turn, became part of Truman's reason for his announcement of an increase in the number of American divisions to be stationed in West Germany. However, Truman anticipated the issues around which the great debate about European defense would turn. He called for a matching manpower effort on the part of the Europeans. Once again, the question of European manpower above that to be supplied by the Anglo-Americans was before the alliance. Truman had skillfully forced the issue by linking his announcement of the increased American contribution to NATO with an insistence that the question of a German contribution be confronted at the September 1950 NATO conference.

The Korean War was, in this way, a catalyst for the explicit consideration of what NATO military planners had thought for some time was inevitable: German rearmament. The issue of German participation was considered at the September 1950 NATO council meeting and formal adoption of a forward strategy for the defense of Europe was undertaken. A conventional defense of Western Europe as far east as possible clearly required augmented troop levels beyond those that the Europeans were prepared to raise. Thus the NATO council also accepted, as a matter of great urgency, the consideration of how the Germans might best be integrated into the common effort and formally approved the idea of an integrated military force under a centralized command structure. Still, the precise nature of German participation in all of this was not resolved. Nor could the issue be forced by the Americans in view of European uneasiness with the entire notion of German rearmament. However, it was clear that the Germans would be integrated in some way into the European army concept that now seemed to be emerging.

Both Marshall and Acheson sought to underscore as much for the Europeans as for the members of the Senate in early 1951 that the American contribution was not sufficient to meet the needs of the forward strategy adopted in the September 1950 council meeting. Six American divisions and American superior air power provided a short-run advantage, but in time this advantage was forecast to disappear. The time purchased by the six divisions to be stationed in Europe and the U.S. strategic advantage was, therefore, best spent developing the balanced forces agreed upon earlier in May and September 1950. Yet, as one authority, Robert Osgood, has noted, there was great uncertainty as to just what kind of aggression would be deterred by the NATO structure, whether skeletal or fully muscled. Acheson does not seem to have believed that the Russians could be matched along every military dimension, but he and the Joint Chiefs clearly sought to avoid Europe's being overrun. However, this seemed to require a NATO force of almost 100 divisions. As Robert Osgood observes, "Yet in 1951 it was already obvious that only the fear of imminent invasion, . . . could conceivably inspire the Europeans to make sufficient contribution of men, money, and equipment to support a strategic objective which the United States herself expected to support primarily with airpower."[70]

Even as the Truman administration was winning its great debate in Congress, the Europeans perceived that the crisis that had brought it about was waning. The Korean emergency lost its catalytic force as negotiations for a cease fire began in June 1951. Moreover, the second half of 1951 saw the emergence of serious economic problems in Western Europe. The Korean-inspired U.S. inflation and rearmament contributed to European inflation, particularly with respect to raw material imports. This rise in prices was reflected in a deterioration of Western Europe's export position. Britain was especially vulnerable and suffered a severe balance-of-payments deficit. Throughout Europe, rearmament cut into the social welfare efforts of European governments and brought on the defeat of the Labor government in Britain and the reassumption of power by Winston Churchill in October 1951. Churchill immediately emphasized his belief that nuclear deterrence was still quite valid. Although he agreed that NATO's conventional forces were a problem, he stated that the British would have to stretch out their general armament plan; similar problems and sentiments emerged throughout Western Europe. When the Truman administration announced that its fiscal year 1953 budget would show some cuts in defense spending, it was a clear signal to Europeans that military imperatives could be compromised in the face of domestic political and economic realities.[71]

UP AND DOWN
THE KOREAN PENINSULA

In the meantime, the military events that had given rise to the great debate and the parallel intra-alliance negotiations were approaching a turning point. General MacArthur had consolidated the UN position at the tip of the South Korean peninsula around Pusan and was preparing to take the offensive–an offensive that would crush the North Korean army, pull the Chinese into the war, and bring the general and the president into conflict *mano a mano.*

MacArthur Takes the Offensive

By September 1950 four American divisions had been committed to Korea — twice what General MacArthur had first requested — and they had been driven with their backs to the sea in the Pusan perimeter. Nevertheless, UN troop strength began to mount until it surpassed that of the North Koreans. Total UN air superiority complicated the North Koreans' position, for their lines of supply now stretched the length of the peninsula and were therefore very vulnerable to air interdiction. Even as the North Koreans pushed deep into the South, General MacArthur had begun planning for an amphibious landing far in their rear at the port city of Inchon on the west coast of the Korean peninsula just west of Seoul below the 38th parallel. Simultaneously, UN forces would break out of the Pusan perimeter, push up the peninsula, and link up with General MacArthur's forces at the 38th parallel. The landing at Inchon would be extremely dangerous: one military planner said, "We drew up a list of every conceivable natural and geographic handicap and Inchon had 'em all."[72] But General MacArthur did not heed nearly unanimous advice. Instead, in his own words, he heard "the voice of his father telling him years before 'Doug, councils of war breed timidity. . . .' " And General MacArthur was nothing if he was not bold.[73]

The Joint Chiefs came to Korea to counsel against the adventure and refused General MacArthur what he considered an adequate number of marines for the assault. Rear Admiral Doyle, his amphibious commander, said, "I have not been asked . . . my opinion about this landing. If I were asked however, the best I can say is that Inchon is not possible."[74] Inchon had incredible tides. Water would rise and then fall some thirty feet each day. As the tide came wooshing out, vast banks of mud reaching some three miles from shore were exposed. Some landing assault and troop vehicles drew 29 feet of water; there were only two days each year when high tide would be up enough to allow the vessels to port at the harbor of Inchon. Even then the LST's would have only two or three hours to debark their marines — not on the beach, for there was none, but on a concrete seawall—before they would be pounded into the the murky slime of Inchon. Not only were the logistics difficult, the purported advantage of surprise, the key to the operation, had been lost for some time. In Japan the plans for the assault had become a topic of barroom conversation, where it was termed "operation common knowledge." Indeed, the landing preceded a Korean mine-laying effort by a hairsbreadth. Yet it was undeniable that if the two phases of the operation, the assault from the sea and the drive from the South, could be carried out, the North Korean army would be trapped between the pincers of General MacArthur's UN force. If it worked, the original objectives of the UN action would be attained.

On September 15, 1950, the Inchon landing was effected with remarkably low casualties. Within two days, the port was secured and the push toward Seoul began as UN troops began to rush up from their enclave in the South. By September 23 North Korean resistance was collapsing. And by September 26 virtually the entire North Korean army had been cut off and destroyed, with only 30,000 North Koreans able to retreat across the 38th parallel. On September 27, 1950, Seoul was retaken after terrible destruction, described by one historian as "apocalyptic" — the result of massive U.S. firepower turned on the city.[75] By the end of September UN forces were back on the 38th parallel.

After Inchon, the military momentum grew infectiously. General MacArthur apparently assumed from the outset that his mandate extended to the military reunification of Korea.[76] But after the collapse of the North Korean army resistance his ambitious designs for Korea became the Western norm. Louis Halle was commuting between Western capitals at the time. He remembered:

> The political leaders in Washington, in London, and elsewhere were themselves in a state of *hubris* brought on by success after long failure. They were themselves swept along by the momentum of victory, and they allowed themselves to be swept along the more readily because anything else was politically impossible for them.[77]

With victory, Washington now believed that American power could control events beyond the 38th parallel. The geographic restrictions imposed on non-Korean military units and the absolute prohibition on military activity against Manchuria and the Soviet Union would be sufficient, it was believed, to assure the Chinese and the Russians that the new U.S. objectives were limited. Nevertheless, Washington now found itself in an increasingly dangerous situation, for President Truman was now preparing to go beyond containment into the uncharted terrain of liberation.

There were, of course, domestic political considerations that undoubtedly influenced Truman's decision. The Republican leadership had already announced that it would regard failure of the administration to go north of the 38th parallel as evidence of appeasement. In addition, there were midterm elections coming up in November. Total victory in Korea on the eve of the elections would, perhaps, undercut the McCarthyites. Domestic realities, therefore, limited Truman's ability or willingness to respond to Chinese hints of a desire for a political settlement or take seriously similar Soviet proposals in early October 1950.

The forward dynamic of policy was gathering and on September 30, 1950, UN Ambassador Austin submitted a US–drafted resolution calling on UN forces to take measures "to ensure conditions of stability throughout Korea."[78] The UN General Assembly approved overwhelmingly the motion, which sanctified the destruction of North Korean military forces and unifying the country under a UN command led by General MacArthur.

There is some evidence that George Kennan and others at the Department of State did have reservations about the American advance toward China.[79] However, these men were precisely those toward whom McCarthy was then directing his withering fire. It was a time, as one inside observer could remember, when "a noble boldness, rather than a craven timidity, became the order of the day — and everyone wanted to be identified with it."[80] Sinologist and former intelligence official Harold Hinton described how the Chinese must have felt about events in Korea:

[O]ne need only imagine American reaction if a large Soviet army, under an especially anti-American commander, were to move up the Lower California peninsula toward the California frontier. The analogy is improved if one further imagines that Southern California is the main heavy industrial region in the United States, as Manchuria was (and is) in the CPR.[81]

The Chinese were not coy or hesitant in airing their view of the imminent collapse of North Korea. In late September the chief of staff of the Chinese People's Liberation Army informed the Indian ambassador to China that the People's Republic would not "sit back with folded hands and let the Americans come to the border." Again, on September 30, Chou En-Lai gave a public warning: "The Chinese people . . . will not supinely tolerate seeing their neighbors being savagely invaded by the imperialists." Chinese warnings were accompanied by a redeployment of their best troops into the Yalu frontier area. American intelligence was aware of the troops, although their exact disposition and intentions remained unclear.[82] Finally, on October 1, when ROK units entered North Korea, the Indian ambassador was called. In a midnight meeting he was informed by Chou En-Lai that although the Chinese were not concerned about the

South Koreans, the movement of U.S. troops north of the 38th parallel would be regarded by the Chinese as a reason for Chinese entry into the war. Professor Allen S. Whiting, a former State Department official, notes, "In the next few days Washington received additional reports of Chou's warning through allied and neutral channels and through American embassies in Moscow, Stockholm, London and New Delhi."[83] Evidently, President Truman brushed aside Chou En-Lai's warnings by discounting the credibility of the Indian ambassador who served as the channel of communication: "Mr. Panikkar had in the past played the game of the Chinese Communists fairly regularly, so that his statement could not be taken as that of an impartial observer."[84] And Secretary of State Acheson, astonishingly, asserted that, in any case, Chou En-Lai was not an authoritative spokesman.[85]

On October 1 the first South Korean units crossed the 38th parallel as General MacArthur called for the unconditional surrender of all communist forces in the north. On October 7 the first American units of the Eighth Army crossed the frontier and began moving toward the North Korean capital of Pyongyang.

Mao Zedong, General MacArthur, and Harry Truman: Three's a Crowd

The political *hubris* that attended General MacArthur's punch toward the north seemed to sweep away doubts about Chinese ability or interest in Korea. The peninsula would be unified by the victorious UN juggernaut. On October 9, President Truman informed General MacArthur:

> Hereafter in the event of the open or covert employment anywhere in Korea of major Chinese Communist units, without prior announcement, you should continue the action as long as, in your judgment, action by forces now under your control offers a reasonable chance of success.[86]

Moreover, Truman also seemed ready at least to consider actions against the PRC itself. In place of the earlier absolute prohibition on operations against China, the commander-in-chief closed his October 9 dispatch to General MacArthur with the cryptic statement: "In any case you will obtain authorization from Washington prior to taking any military action against objectives in Chinese Territory."[87]

Since the North Koreans had been beaten, China made repeated attempts to explain that they were concerned about their own security more than they fretted over the future of a fraternal communist state. The Chinese even hinted that they might be able to live with the conquest of

North Korea, providing that North Korea were occupied by South Koreans and the Americans stayed below the 38th parallel. Even after U.S. troops crossed the 38th parallel, the Chinese indicated that they could live with a rump North Korean state that would buffer China's Manchurian boundary. The United States would be allowed to be ensconsed with its client South Korean regime up to 39°30' north latitude, or the neck of the Korean peninsula.[88] On October 15, 1950, a confident General MacArthur remarked that the American boys would be home before Christmas. Mao Zedong, it has been reported, was up 72 hours before making his decision, which took effect October 16, when Chinese General Lin Biao's Fourth Field Army began crossing the Yalu at night and in secret.

On October 19 the North Korean capital of Pyongyang fell to American forces and General MacArthur prepared to press on for his much-heralded quick victory. North Korean Premier Kim fled to the Yalu, leaving behind vast supplies of military equipment. Soon the North Korean defeat turned into a rout. U.S. soldiers parachuted in front of the retreating Koreans and Kim's forces began to surrender *en masse.* By the end of October over 135,000 North Koreans had been captured.

General MacArthur's plan called for the Eighth Army to move up the west coast of Korea to the Yalu River and the Tenth Corps to move toward the Yalu somewhat further east. But the spine of mountains running down the middle of the peninsula separated the two elements of General MacArthur's force by more than 50 guerrilla-filled miles. The Chinese would exploit this tactical blunder within weeks. But in mid-October General MacArthur and his commanding general were eyeing an early and easy victory. Lt. General Walton H. Walker, the commander of the Eighth Army, for instance, thought the entire advance was not unlike a quail shoot in his native Texas.[89] On October 24, 1950, General MacArthur ordered his commanders to move all units, Korean and non-Korean, forward to the Yalu, thus violating JCS directives of late September. When reminded of this by Washington, General MacArthur cited a personal message of Marshall's giving MacArthur tactical and strategic discretion. The matter was dropped. Was it reasonable, Washington pondered, to countermand the man who had masterminded the amazing Inchon landing? By the 26th of October, elements of a South Korean division on the American Eighth Army's eastern flank reached the Yalu; that night they were surrounded by Chinese communist troops, ambushed, and sent fleeing south, encountering Chinese ambushes throughout the withdrawal.

By November 1, U.S. forces were heavily engaged by Chinese troops. Yet, on November 7, curiously, almost as swiftly as the Chinese had attacked, they broke off contact. During this two-week period MacArthur's analysis of what was taking place along the front swung from optimism to deep pessimism. He urgently requested and received permission to bomb the Yalu River bridges, and then, once his request was satisfied, he manifested a kind of befuddled optimism. General MacArthur was still not prepared to view those initial, sharp contacts with the Chinese as conclusive proof of Chinese intervention.

On November 15 he proposed to the Joint Chiefs that he press forward with his advance. But November 15 was the date the Communist Chinese had been invited to the United Nations to discuss the Taiwan situation and perhaps Korea as well. Nevertheless, Washington approved MacArthur's advance. In the meantime, the Chinese announced that their arrival at the United Nations would be delayed until the 24th of November. Inexplicably, MacArthur delayed his attack until the 24th, and on that date he pressed forward again announcing that the "boys would be home by Christmas." Needless to say, the Chinese diplomats refused to proceed with negotiations as the UN offensive churned ahead.

General MacArthur's final blow had only a day's momentum when the Eighth Army was hit by a strong Chinese attack. By the 26th of November it was clear that a full-scale counterattack was underway by six Chinese armies. In two days, the entire right flank of the UN force was collapsing. During the next eight days the UN forces fought heroically for their lives as they retreated south. Pyongyang was evacuated by UN forces in early December, and by Christmas the boys were back on the 38th parallel.[90]

As the military defeat began to unfold, the tenuous politico-military consensus that had marked the onset of the campaign disintegrated. While victorious armies had marched north, all parties sought identification with General MacArthur's successes. Now, however, politicians and generals alike sought to disassociate themselves from each other and of course the deepening disaster on the Korean peninsula. This self-serving and confused scramble revealed the deep disagreements between Washington and UN military headquarters in Tokyo, brought into the open Europe's unease, and, of course, exacerbated the profound domestic frustration with the war and President Truman's foreign policy.

THE MACARTHUR PROBLEM

If there were any worries within the highest levels of the Truman administration about expanding the war, they centered on General MacArthur and not his mission. These misgivings were reflected in the hedged, frequently contradictory language of the directives sent to the general. Both the White House and the Pentagon were sensitive to General MacArthur's domestic following and his personal vanity. Indeed, during World War II, the general's independence came to be thought of as the "MacArthur problem."[91] Consequently, it was deemed necessary to qualify heavily most of his orders to ensure control of his military activities.

With the outbreak of the Korean War, the MacArthur problem resurfaced. One example occurred on July 31, 1950, when General MacArthur paid a visit to Chiang Kai-Shek on Taiwan, ostensibly to inform him of the progress of the fighting in Korea and explain the decision not to use his troops. However, General MacArthur pointedly refused to invite a State Department representative to the talks, claiming that only military matters were to be discussed. Nevertheless, both MacArthur and Chiang issued statements after the conference was over in which they praised one another's great leadership and called for closer Sino–American cooperation. Washington was upset, given the implications of these statements, i.e., that the United States should support Chiang's desire to return to the mainland.

MacArthur's position was that the United States remove its prohibition against Taiwan's attacks on the mainland. To clarify Washington's position, Averell Harriman was immediately sent to Tokyo to discuss matters with General MacArthur. MacArthur told Harriman, "We should fight the communists every place — fight them like hell!"[92] After Harriman left, MacArthur issued a public statement defending his talks with Chiang and charged that his purpose was being "maliciously misrepresented to the public by those who invariably in the past have propagandized a policy of defeatism and appeasement in the Pacific."[93]

Again on August 17, 1950, MacArthur lashed out at the Truman administration. In a letter to the Veterans of Foreign Wars to be read at their annual meeting on August 28 and also printed in *U.S. News & World Report,* General MacArthur stated that it was merely his intent to evaluate the strategic position of the United States in Asia. However, the letter, which was never cleared in Washington, went on to emphasize the vital position of Taiwan in America's strategic posture. General MacArthur asserted: "Nothing could be more fallacious than the threadbare argument by those who advocate appeasement and defeatism in the Pacific that if we defend [Taiwan] we alienate Continental Asia."[94] President Truman and his advisers reacted, in Truman's words, with "surprise and shock," and Truman apparently considered relieving MacArthur of his command.[95] In the end, however, Truman merely ordered MacArthur on August 26 to withdraw the statement, although the action came too late to prevent its public appearance in *U.S. News & World Report.* By late August the plans for the Inchon landing were well advanced, as was the decision to invade North Korea. To have fired MacArthur at the end of

August 1950 would have destroyed the building momentum. Moreover, Truman's decision to invade the north brought him into line with MacArthur's aggressive spirit. And given the sense of forward movement after months of retreat, forcing the issue of MacArthur's independence could be politically disastrous. An ultimate confrontation was, therefore, avoided. By October, however, Truman felt compelled once again to discuss the relationship of his political objectives to the general's military activities. On October 9 two U.S. Air Force aircraft had attacked a Soviet airfield near Vladivostok, some 62 miles inside the Soviet Union. This was hardly a routine cold war border incident, and this was precisely the kind of event that could provoke the larger conflict Truman hoped to avoid. It was certainly the sort of thing that might heighten Truman's distrust of MacArthur and trigger any latent desire of the president to communicate face to face with the general.[96]

On October 10, 1950, three days after American troops had crossed the 38th parallel, President Truman announced that he would be flying to Wake Island in the Pacific to discuss the military effort with General MacArthur. However, the hasty manner in which the conference was arranged and its brevity once undertaken — the talks lasted only five hours — have puzzled observers. Truman has stated that he went to Wake simply because he had never met MacArthur personally and felt that the general should have a better appreciation of the "situation at home."[97] It would seem, however, that such matters and the establishment of personal contacts would have been more appropriate prior to the launching of the northern invasion. What now seems likely is that some emergency had arisen, perhaps caused by MacArthur or members of his command — such as the Vladivostok incident — that precipitated a meeting Truman may indeed have wanted for some time.

Although the meeting was brief and, on the surface, somewhat *pro forma*, it nevertheless betrayed some of the tension between the men. When, for example, the president stepped from the plane, General MacArthur greeted him cordially. But the general was dressed in a casual manner and did not salute the president, his commander-in-chief. Truman, on the other hand, planted an eavesdropping secretary behind a partially opened door adjacent to private conversations between the president and the general, who, supplied with legal pad and pen, automatically took down everything she overheard. Later when relations between Truman and MacArthur collapsed over the crisis brought on by the Chinese intervention, MacArthur's assurances that the Chinese would face the "greatest slaughter" if they intervened, were released.

Truman seemed, said the *New York Times* reporter who covered the conference, "like an insurance salesman who has signed up an important tory measures on China and reiterated the directive of December 29. But MacArthur persisted in additional requests to the JCS based on pessimistic analyses of the situation in Korea. On January 13, 1951, the administration opened a counteroffensive as President Truman sent a personal letter to MacArthur urging him to hold his position or, at a minimum, only withdraw to islands off the coast of Korea. For emphasis, Truman sent Generals Collins and Hoyt Vandenberg of the JCS to Korea.

The Collins-Vandenberg visit confirmed what the Truman administration had come to suspect. General MacArthur was consciously overestimating the threat to his command in an effort to gain approval for an attack on the Chinese mainland. As soon as Collins and Vandenberg made this report, Truman responded — sacking General O'Donnell of the Far East Air Force Bomber Command and a well-known advocate of bombing China. It was a clear signal to MacArthur to keep his own advocacy of attacks on China to himself and support the counteroffensive soon to be launched by General Matthew Ridgeway. Ridgeway's willingness to stand and fight *in* Korea marked him as more responsive to Washington's concept of how the war should be fought. Moreover, as military historian David Rees noted, "Henceforward, MacArthur [located in Tokyo], who had now ceased to exercise close supervision over the Eighth Army, was increasingly bypassed by Truman and the JCS in dealing with Ridgeway."[104]

In mid-February the general went public again. MacArthur branded Ridgeway and Washington's strategy "wholy unrealistic and illusory."[105] On March 7 in a press statement, General MacArthur called the prevailing limited approach to the war as "Die for [a] Tie"[106] and pointed to Washington as being responsible for the "savage slaughter that the current strategy would bring about."

By March 12 Ridgeway reached the 38th parallel and Seoul was retaken. President Truman now prepared a diplomatic initiative that anticipated the beginnings of cease-fire negotiations and a settlement of the entire Korean question. Moreover, this was to be followed, in turn, by consideration of other problems in Asia. Presumably this referred to the entire China question, including recognition and UN representation.[107] When the news of this overture to China was sent to General MacArthur, he was requested not to initiate any major advance north of the parallel while negotiations were in the offing. MacArthur sullenly agreed.

But suddenly, without any forewarning, General MacArthur thundered his own public ultimatum to the Chinese before the President had taken his planned initiative. The general arrogantly pointed out to the Chinese their "complete inability to accomplish by force of arms the conquest of Korea" and then threatened them with an expansion of the war. Whatever might be the others' idea of a settlement, MacArthur plainly marked his terms for negotiations:

> there should be no insuperable difficulty in arriving at decisions on the Korean problem if the issues are resolved on their own merits, without being burdened by extraneous matters not directly related to Korea, such as [Taiwan], or China's seat in the United Nations.[108]

The legendary warrior then, magnanimously, offered his services as a negotiating partner to end the war — on Western terms.[109]

The fact of the matter was that President Truman's pending offer would have signaled that he was tacitly offering the Chinese the opportunity to discuss their broader concerns in Asia if they would begin negotiations on a cease fire. General MacArthur's ultimatum explicitly precluded Truman's offer and indicated to the Chinese instead that they could expect a general war if they would not come to the negotiating table. MacArthur must have known that this was utterly unacceptable to the Chinese. He must also have known that his ultimatum would so complicate matters for the administration that it would be unable to proceed with its diplomatic effort. Finally, it has been suggested that he was also aware that his action would jeopardize his career; for in making this public statement he was clearly in violation of Truman's December 6, 1950, directive that all public statements by theater commanders be cleared by Washington.

The man in the White House was infuriated. "By this act MacArthur left me no choice — I could no longer tolerate his insubordination. . . . [O]nce again General MacArthur had openly defied the policy of his Commander in Chief, the President of the United States."[110] Still, Truman did not yet relieve MacArthur. Instead the president reminded MacArthur of his December order concerning public statements and awaited the general's response.

His response came in a letter to Congressman Joseph Martin, the House Minority Leader, who had said earlier that he had "good reason" to believe that MacArthur and the Pentagon had favored using "800,000" Chinese Nationalist troops in Taiwan to fight with the United States in Korea. "If we are not in Korea to win," Martin concluded, "then Truman's administration should be indicted for the murder of thousands of American boys." Martin sent a copy of the speech to MacArthur and asked for the general's comments. On March 20, MacArthur congratulated the Republican leader for having "lost none of your old time punch" and ended by writing:

> It seems strangely difficult for some to realize that here in Asia is where the communist conspirators have elected to make their play for global conquest, and that we have joined the issue thus raised on the battlefield; that here we fight Europe's war with arms while the diplomats there still fight it with words; that if we lose this war to communism in Asia the fall of Europe is inevitable; win it and Europe most probably would avoid war and yet preserve freedom. As you have pointed out, we must win. There is no substitute for victory.[111]

The breaking point had now been reached. Truman initiated a week-long round of discussions with his top advisers concerning his next step. All agreed the president had but one course of action open to him: the removal of MacArthur and his replacement by Ridgeway. The announcement was made on April 11, and the nation was immediately caught up in one of the great spectacles of U.S. history as the general came home.

Truman was vilified throughout the country. He and Acheson were burned in effigy, and his public approval ratings dropped to less than 30 percent according to the Gallup poll. In Congress, calls for impeachment of Truman, Acheson, and Marshall were commonplace. Senator Richard Nixon characterized Truman's action as "appeasement of communism" and demanded that Truman be censured if the general were not reinstated. Others were less discreet. Senator McCarthy declared that the president was a "son-of-a-bitch,"[112] and Senator Jenner of Indiana spoke for many when he charged on the floor of the Senate:

> This country today is in the hands of a secret inner coterie which is directed by agents of the Soviet Union. We must cut this whole cancerous conspiracy out of our government at once. [Applause from the public gallery.] Our only course is to impeach President Truman and find out who is the secret invisible government which has so cleverly led our country down the road to destruction.[113]

The general and his wife arrived in San Francisco on April 17, 1951, and paraded 14 miles in 2 hours to their hotel. The next day the general told a crowd that "he was not running for President. . . . The only politics I have is contained in a single phrase well known to you — God Save America."[114] On the 19th of April he appeared in the House of Representatives for his farewell address. He described the global communist menace and reviewed his proposals for ending the war in Korea. Next MacArthur hammered away at his conception of war — a conception shared by millions of Americans — and its relationship to events in Asia:

[O]nce war is forced upon us, there is no other alternative than to apply every available means to bring it to a swift end.... War's very object is victory, not prolonged indecision.

He concluded, choked with tears:

I am closing my 52 years of military service. When I joined the Army even before the turn of the century, it was the fulfillment of all my boyish hopes and dreams. The world has turned over many times since I took the oath on the Plains at West Point, and the hopes and dreams have long since vanished. But I still remember the refrain of one of the most popular barracks ballads of that day which proclaimed most proudly that, "Old Soldiers never die; they just fade away." And like the old soldier of that ballad, I now close my military career and just fade away — an old soldier who has tried to do his duty as God gave him the light to see that duty.
    Good-by.[115]

The scene on the floor of the House of Representatives was pandemonium. Senators, members of Congress, and spectators leaped to their feet, many with tears streaming down their faces. Afterwards, Harvard-educated Congressman Dewey Short proclaimed, "We saw a great hunk of God in the flesh, and we heard the voice of God."[116] Former President Herbert Hoover saw only a "reincarnation of St. Paul into a great General of the Army."[117] A distinguished senator was overheard to remark after the speech, "I have never feared more for the institutions of the country. I honestly felt . . . that if [the General's] speech had gone on much longer there might have been a march on the White House."[118] If the senator had been outside he would have been concerned that the march had in fact begun. For as David Rees noted:

In the afternoon MacArthur drove down Pennsylvania Avenue to be given the freedom of the City of Washington. It was a public holiday and, as hundreds of thousands watched, bombers and jet fighters flew overhead and artillery boomed out over the capital.[119]

The next step for the legendary American general, who had led American troops into one of the greatest military disasters since the first battle of Bull Run and openly flouted his oath of office with his insubordination of his commander-in-chief, was New York. The city gave him a 6-hour and 5-minute parade, longer and larger than any in its history, including those given for Lindbergh in 1927, and twice as large as Eisenhower's victorious return in 1945. The New York Police Department estimated that there were more than 7 million people along the parade route. Signs along the way read, "God Save Us from Acheson," and the city hired sky-writing fliers who spelled in 2-mile-long heavenly script, "Welcome Home" and "Well Done."[120]

The MacArthur Hearings:
Denouement of Domestic Confrontation

Clearly the general was not just fading away. There followed a series of speeches throughout the country. MacArthur extolled the simple virtues of a pastoral America he hadn't seen for over 15 years. Yet the years of his absence, especially the 5 years since the war, were among the most crucial in America's history.[121] During this time Americans had begun to adjust to the demands of a new world role being thrust upon them by their political leadership. Containment, Truman, Marshall, and Acheson had argued, was a commitment to world involvement and expensive military strength. But power had to be employed in a limited and controlled manner lest events elude them and war ensue.

By the time of Korea, Americans had begun to accommodate themselves to this new situation. But Korea ripped at the emerging consensus. In the resultant disorientations, General MacArthur represented, for many Americans, a needed point of reference and seeming stability. It must have been reassuring for the general to state: "though without authority or responsibility, I am the possessor of the proudest of titles. I am an American."[122] In city after city MacArthur appeared with one arm around Mrs. MacArthur, another around his son Arthur. The general seemed the unabashed symbol of home and patriotism and what he delighted in calling the simple eternal truths of the American way.[123]

But for tens of millions of other Americans the Depression, World War II, and the onset of the cold war had proved that there were no more simple eternal truths. Truman recognized this and counterattacked effectively by using the forum presented in the Joint Senate Foreign Relations and Armed Services Committee hearings on MacArthur's dismissal and the conduct of the war. MacArthur led off the hearings and stated once again his objection to any concept of a limited war under the close control of political leadership.[124]

The Truman administration responded as it had in meeting Taft's challenge. A solid phalanx of administration officials — Marshall, all of the Joint Chiefs, and Acheson — carefully detailed MacArthur's insubordination and attacked his notion of all political control shifting to a theater commander once war began as beyond the pale of the American civil-military tradition and the Constitution. Moreover, MacArthur's broader strategic vision was deemed dangerously in error in that his proposals would not result in an end to the war, but a wider war that would divert American resources from the truly fundamental confrontation with the Soviet Union. Finally, the administration witnesses instructed the Congress that a commitment to a full-scale Asian conflict was opposed by our European allies. Therefore, pursuing the course advocated by the general might drive a wedge between us and the Europeans. The spectre of a weakened or collapsed NATO was outlined, and the fulfillment of Soviet objectives in Europe were detailed.

The result of Truman's effort was to deflect MacArthur's simplistic appeal to patriotism, which masked a notion of civil-military relations subversive of the American Constitution. The Joint Chiefs supported Truman's conception of American priorities and would not allow wedges to be driven between them and the civilian leadership of the administration. Most important, however, was the united front maintained on the issue of civilian supremacy and agreement on MacArthur's violation of this precept. Because the administration was generally successful in framing much of the debate largely in terms of this issue, it was also successful in shifting the ground on which confrontation rested. Questions of grand strategy would and did provoke disagreement. But the principle of civilian supremacy was broadly accepted. Once the issue was set in these terms, the emotion of the general's return began to settle, and public opinion shifted away from MacArthur.

Moreover, as the hearings ended, negotiations finally got underway in Korea. The Chinese advance south finally stalled under the combined weight of appalling casualties inflicted by American firepower and overextended lines of supply, vulnerable to UN air superiority. The burst of optimism that greeted the opening of talks and military success would turn to growing cynicism in the fall and winter of 1951 as the talks deadlocked and stalemated fighting resumed. But in the summer of 1951 the news of negotiations in a domestic context of a booming, if inflated, economy produced an atmosphere little conducive to MacArthur's case.

THE OLD COLD WARRIOR
FADES AWAY: THE END OF
THE TRUMAN ADMINISTRATION

In the longer view, however, President Truman's success in exploiting the MacArthur hearings was but a holding action for he was never able to translate his victory into increased support for himself. He may have been able to convince a majority of the American people that Douglas MacArthur and the conservative Republicans did not possess a prudent and constitutionally acceptable way out of the cold war and Korea, but neither could he convince the same group that Harry Truman knew where the exit lay.

The November 1950 elections had left Truman with the barest of Democratic margins in the House and Senate. Joseph McCarthy had demonstrated his own personal political clout by campaigning against important Democratic supporters of the president in both the House and the Senate who were defeated in the 1950 election. The frustrations of containment, the Korean War, and the purported domestic subversion were all linked during the 1950 election, and the result was a two-vote Democratic margin (down from twelve) in the Senate and thirty-six (down from ninety-two) in the House. More important, the men and women who returned to Congress in early 1951 were unlikely to challenge McCarthy frontally.

Further diminishing Truman's domestic support was a series of revelations beginning in 1950 and running throughout 1951 of deficient and even corrupt administration within many agencies of the government.[125] The succession of scandals and Truman's announcement in March of 1952 that he would not seek reelection reduced the Truman administration to virtual caretaker status unable to conclude the war through negotiations or force. Senator McCarthy unleashed a renewed attack on the members of the Truman administration, starting with General Marshall, whom he characterized as being a member of "a conspiracy so immense, an infamy so black, as to dwarf any in the history of man."[126] The vilification of Acheson grew, and one commentator noted that "many people burst into profanity at the mere mention of Truman's name."[127]

In July 1952 the parties nominated their candidates and went to the American people. Adlai Stevenson and the Democrats told the nation for the next 3 months that they "never had it so good" and raised the spectre of another depression if the Republicans were elected. The Republicans behind Eisenhower, who had defeated Taft for the nomination, systematically attacked the Democrats concerning Korea, communism, and corruption. The Democrats, it was charged, had given the American people a corrupt administration at home, compounded by subversion by communists and communist sympathizers. The endless war in Korea was proof that containment as a foreign policy was, in the words of the Republican platform (drafted largely by John Foster Dulles, who was assumed to be the next secretary of state if Eisenhower was elected), "Negative, futile and immoral."

As the campaign seemed to be gaining momentum for the Republicans, it was revealed that Richard Nixon, the Republicans' vice presidential nominee, had been the beneficiary of an $18,000 special fund established for him by some wealthy California businessmen. General Eisenhower was furious and demanded that Nixon explain matters to the American people if he was going to remain on the ticket. Senator Nixon then went before the nation through a televised address on September 23, 1952, and delivered his now famous Checkers speech, in which he denied that he had ever used any of the money for his personal use; it had all been used to clean out the communists and crooks in Washington. He emphasized that he, like many Americans, had found it difficult to meet payments on his car and his mortgage, and that he and Pat were struggling financially. He did admit to one gift, however:

> Do you know what it was? It was a little cocker spaniel dog in a crate . . . sent all the way from Texas. Black and white spotted. And our little girl — Trisha, the six year old — named it Checkers. And you know the kids love the dog, and I just want to say this right now, that regardless of what they say about it, we're going to keep it.

They did not have very much, the senator summarized, but:

> Pat and I have the satisfaction that every dime that we've got is honestly ours. I should say this — that Pat doesn't have a mink coat. But she does have a respectable Republican cloth coat. And I always tell her that she'd look good in anything. . . .
>
> And now, finally, I know that you wonder whether or not I am going to stay on the Republican ticket or resign. Let me say this: I don't believe that I ought to quit because I'm not a quitter. And incidentally, Pat's not a quitter. After all, her name was Patricia Ryan and she was born on St. Patricks's Day, and you know the Irish never quit.[128]

The public response was overwhelmingly positive, for Nixon succeeded in aligning himself and the Republican party with the little man struggling with inflation, the war, the corruption, and the desire for a better life.[129] It may have been corny, tear-jerking stuff, but in the domestic malaise of 1952, it was devastating electoral politics.

A month later General Eisenhower, whose attacks on Truman had become more and more pointed and slashing, announced that the first thing he would do, if elected, was make a trip to Korea for a personal assessment of the situation. This promise and a stunningly effective nationally televised speech by General MacArthur on October 27 brought the campaign to an end. A week later, 20 years of Democratic party rule came to an end in the landslide election of Dwight Eisenhower.

CONCLUSION

The Korean experience was critical in a number of ways. As Professor Robert Tucker has noted:

> In the decade following the initiation of containment, Korea stands out as the decisive event in the evolution of American policy. The Korean experience largely determined the form and course that the great transformation in American foreign policy eventually took. . . . In Europe, the Korean conflict led to the reestablishment of American forces, the establishment of an integrated command structure, the decision to rearm Germany, and the agreement on a common defense strategy. In Asia, the Korean War led to American intervention in the Chinese civil conflict and prompted the conclusion of a series of bilateral and multilateral alliances that continue today roughly to define the extent of the American commitment in that area.[130]

In the end, this effort was widely adjudged by American academic and policy makers to be a success. Professor Osgood, for instance, observes that "one can hardly overestimate the importance of the United States achievment in containing the Communist attack on South Korea without precipitating total war. By this achievement the nation went a long way toward demonstrating that it could successfully resist direct military aggression locally by limited war in the secondary strategic areas. . . ."[131] Yet if the war was limited, it was only in some rather specific aspects. It was limited geographically, and nuclear weapons were not used on the peninsula. Beyond this, however, Korea was one of the most destructive wars ever fought. An estimated 4 million Koreans were killed out of a population of about 30 million.

General (Rosie) Emmett O'Donnell, head of the U.S. Bomber Command in the Far East, testified: "I would say that the entire, almost the entire Korean peninsula, is just a terrible mess. Everything is destroyed. There is nothing standing worthy of the name." Just before the Chinese came in, he elaborated, "We were grounded. There were no more targets in Korea." General MacArthur testified on May 3, 1951, "The war in Korea already almost destroyed that nation. . . . I have never seen such devastation. I have seen, I guess, as much blood and disaster as any living man, and it just curdled my stomach, the last time I was there. After I looked at that wreckage and those thousands of women and children and everything, I vomited."[132] The authoritative military publication, *The Armed Forces Yearbook,* said in its 1951 edition:

The war was fought without regard for the South Koreans, and their unfortunate country was regarded as an arena rather than a country to be liberated. As a consequence, fighting was quite ruthless, and it is no exaggeration to state that South Korea no longer exists . . . its towns have been destroyed . . . its people reduced to a sullen mass dependent on charity. . . . Few attempts were made to explain to the American soldier why they were fighting. . . . The South Korean . . . was regarded as a "gook" like his cousins North.[133]

The war also introduced the notion of relating force to political objectives prior to achieving a thorough military victory. Negotiating while fighting was obviously not congruent with the "unconditional" military posture employed by U.S. Forces just 6 years earlier. As Professor Thomas Schelling elaborates, "the war in Korea [was] a 'negotiation' over the political status of the country. But, as in most bargaining processes, there was also implicit bargaining about the rules of behavior, about what one would do, or stop doing, according to how the other side behaved."[134] Or as Dean Rusk observed recently, "in the Korean war there came a point when the other side was ready to negotiate. . . . [I]n the Korean war . . . we . . . tried to use the amount of force that [was] required to achieve the essential objectives without letting it escalate."[135] Thus, "diplomacy of violence"[136] received its conceptual baptism in Korea. The Truman administration's response in Korea consummated a trend toward primary reliance upon military instrumentalities and the use of the threat of war as the basis of containment. The economic tools of the Marshall Plan and global economic cooperation were now subordinated to military assistance and the use of force.

The war reversed an emerging policy of differentiating between the new Communist Chinese regime and the Soviet Union. After American troops were committed to Korea, and the Seventh Fleet blocked Mao from storming the Nationalist redoubt on Taiwan, and especially after Chinese and American forces began to bloody each other, normal relations became almost impossible to contemplate. Indeed, the domestic distortions and convulsions of the Korean experience — epitomized by the antics of Senator McCarthy — would scar the American consciousness. Communism, not just Soviet power, but a sinister conspiracy, became the whipping boy of ruthless men and the fear of Americans great and small.

The war also had the effect of being something of a self-fulfilling prophecy. Earlier, Dean Acheson in his January 12, 1950, "defense perimeter" remarks to the National Press Club, had tried to distinguish between historic Chinese and Russian aspirations by asserting that eventually Chinese nationalism would turn against Soviet imperialism. After the Korean conflict had begun, Assistant Secretary of State Dean Rusk would say of China in 1951:

The Peiping Regime may be a colonial Russian government — a Slovanic Manchukuo on a larger scale. It is not the government of China. It does not pass the first test. It is not Chinese.[137]

But early relations between Mao's new China and the Soviet Union were not those of partners. The initial formal state instrument between Communist China and Soviet Russia was negotiated by Mao in Moscow in February 1950. It took Mao 3 months to secure the treaty, and he was gone so long "that rumors arose about Mao being detained against his will."[138] Stalin, according to Professor Ulam, "was . . . incredibly stingy," negotiating an "embarrassingly small loan," a "pittance." Even the European satellites had "received . . . credits greater than now extended to the most populous country in the world."[139]

After the Korean War had begun, however, China became increasingly dependent on the Soviet Union. The Chinese were forced to borrow at least $2 billion in order to finance the Korean War, and the Soviets charged interest.[140] The Soviets became a deterrent force on which the Chinese were forced to rely, and it was the Soviet Union that now was the voice of the Chinese position in international councils. Occasionally, the Soviets did not always inform the Chinese as to how they were proceeding in the Chinese interest, but the Chinese, in a period of profound isolation, had little choice but to use Moscow as their intermediary.

The Korean War served ultimately to debase the United Nations by employing expedient stratagems to avoid the processes elaborated in the charter. Using the Soviet absence from the Security Council to vote UN sanctions against a Soviet client, although of questionable legality, would not likely be precedent if the Soviets remained alert in the future. But using the General Assembly to obtain a warrant to move north would come to haunt the United States when the character of the General Assembly was to dramatically change in the early 1970s. The Uniting for Peace Resolution, proposed by Acheson, "provid[ed] for an emergency session of the General Assembly upon twenty-four hours' notice if the Security Council should be prevented from acting."[141] Under the charter the assembly can only "recommend," not authorize action. But the Uniting for Peace Resolution blurred the distinction between recommendation and authorization.* By the mid-1960s, when the number of members of the UN Assembly had expanded enormously and proved unresponsive to U.S. pressure, the United States tried to move important decisions back

---

*Thus when the assembly recommended that "all appropriate steps be taken to ensure conditions of stability throughout the whole of Korea," it was taken as a legal justification by the United States for crossing the 38th parallel.

to the Security Council. Bit by bit, however, the General Assembly slipped from U.S. control and influence.

The decision to go into Korea was predicated on the perception that American will was being tested. Although the arena was peripheral, the United States, it was believed, must respond in order to establish a reputation for action that would deter probes at the center. The perception may have been in error given the murky origins of the Korean civil war. Yet having committed American reputation or honor on the periphery, the principle of containment was instantly extended to that periphery and, in theory at least, virtually everything within it.

In February of 1950, Secretary of State Acheson observed:

> The only way to deal with the Soviet Union, we have found from hard experience, is to create situations of strength. Wherever the Soviet detects weakness or disunity — and it is quick to detect them — it exploits them to the full. . . . [W]hen we have eliminated all of the areas of weakness that we can — we will be able to evolve working agreements with the Russians.[142]

During the Korean war, the Truman administration set about creating situations of strength on a global scale. Thus the Japanese Peace Treaty, encompassing military basing rights as well as similar arrangements in Australia, New Zealand, the Philippines, the Middle East, and North Africa, began the process of institutionalizing global containment. Likewise, support of the French in Indochina, the Dutch in Indonesia, or extension of aid to Chiang Kai-Shek could be rationalized as essential to this process of establishing a global network of situations of strength.

However, as Coral Bell has emphasized in her analysis of the 1950s, negotiating from strength is elusive at best and probably a contradiction in terms, especially if strength is conceived of as superiority — as seems to have been the case in NSC-68.

> The idea of negotiation from strength has had . . . the true mirage-like quality of some of the most effective political myths: shimmering promisingly, always a little farther off, across a stony waste of effort, keeping its distance at each apparent advance.[143]

If the United States found superiority and strength to be the only prudent posture from which to negotiate, why should the Soviet Union settle for less? Why should it be prudent for the Soviets to negotiate from relative weakness?

The Korean War caused profound distortions at home. Arms expenditures reached 67 percent of the budget by 1952. There were dramatic price rises and shortages, and wage/price controls were imposed as wholesale prices began to rise at the rate of 25 percent a year. In September 1950 Congress passed the McCarran Act, banning aliens who had belonged to "totalitarian organizations." In June 1951, in the case of *Dennis v. U.S.*, the Supreme Court held that, given the state of tension in the world, advocating or teaching revolutionary philosophy constituted a crime. The State Department began to lose some of its best people — especially in Asian affairs — as experienced diplomats were asked if they had ever dealt with communists. After all, communism was killing American sons in Korea; why should those who truck with it at home, or on the job abroad, be given the benefit of the doubt?

Finally, the United States became tied to a client regime with a reputation for terror that gnawed the conscience of jurists and journalists who witnessed the political conditions of South Korea. The American effort to liberate North and South Korea has contributed to the maintenance of highly militarized, authoritarian regimes: North Korea, according to Amnesty International, is the most closed society in the world, and in South Korea, documentation about the abuse of human rights is abundant.[144] Professor Thomas Schelling is, no doubt, correct when he points out: "We lost thirty thousand dead in Korea to save face for the United States and the United Nations, not to save South Korea for the South Koreans." Schelling's conclusion is, however, at the least, debatable: "It was," he writes, "undoubtedly worth it."[145]

NOTES

1. Reprinted from *Present at the Creation* by Dean Acheson. By permission of W. W. Norton & Company, Inc., and Hamish Hamilton, Ltd. Copyright © 1969 by Dean Acheson.

2. Edward W. Barrett in a debriefing seminar for Acheson and his close associates, Princeton University, October 10–11, 1953. Box 65, Acheson Papers, cited by Thomas G. Paterson, *On Every Front* (New York: W. W. Norton, 1979). p. 171.

3. Dean Acheson, "Crisis in Asia — An Examination of U.S. Policy," *Department of State Bulletin*, Vol. 22 (January 23, 1950), p. 116. Acheson was paraphrasing MacArthur's observation of the preceding year: "Our defensive dispositions against Asiatic aggression ... starts from the Philippines and continues through the Ryuku Archipelago, which includes its main bastion, Okinawa. Then it bends back through Japan and the Aleutian chain to Alaska." *The New York Times*, March 2, 1949, quoted in Acheson, *Present at the Creation*, p. 357.

4. Acheson, "Crisis in Asia," p. 116.

5. Ibid.

6. "Statement: United States Policy Towards Formosa," *Department of State Bulletin*, Vol. 22 (January 16, 1950), p. 79.
7. John Spanier, *The Truman MacArthur Controversy and the Korean War* (New York: W. W. Norton & Company, 1965), p. 56. For an exegesis of recently declassified documents confirming that the U.S. fully expected Taiwan to fall, see Robert R. Simmons, "Contradictions in 'Fraternal Relationships': Moscow, Peking, P'yongyang and the Korean War," *Conference on Security Arrangements in Northeast Asia from 1945 to Present*, Harvard University, June 19–23, 1978, pp. 7–8.
8. Quoted in Merle Miller, *Plain Speaking: An Oral Biography of Harry Truman* (New York: Berkeley, Medallion, 1974), pp. 286–287. See also the testimony of General L. Bolte, Director of Plans and Operations in testimony for the Korean Assistance Act, June 16, 1950, *United States Policy in the Far East*, Vol. VIII, Historical Series of the Committee on Foreign Relations, United States Senate, 1976, p. 46. A good review of Acheson's view of the significance of Korea is in David S. McLellan, *Dean Acheson: The State Department Years* (New York: Dodd, Mead and Co., 1977), pp. 209–211.
9. Robert R. Simmons, "The Korean Civil War," in Frank Baldwin (ed.), *Without Parallel* (New York: Pantheon Books, 1974), p. 149.
10. World Policy and Bipartisanship: An Interview with Senator Tom Connally," *U.S. News & World Report*, Vol. 28 (May 5, 1950), p. 30.
11. Allen S. Whiting, *China Crosses the Yalu: The Decision to Enter the Korean War* (Stanford, Calif.: Stanford University Press, 1960), pp. 42–43.
12. Ibid., p. 45.
13. Harrison E. Salisbury, "Image and Reality in Indochina," *Foreign Affairs*, Vol. 49 (No. 3, April 1971), p. 388. Mr. Salisbury has speculated that the real target of the North Korean offense, "instigated" by Stalin, was Communist China. He writes: "I think it reasonable to assume that Stalin felt he could take Washington's word — that we did not feel obligated to rise to the defense of South Korea. . . . [I]f he could overrun all of Korea he would be able to dominate Peking from positions in Mongolia, Manchuria and Korea. He would possess the power to deal with Mao as he once said he would deal with Tito. . . ."
14. Strobe Talbott (tr. and ed.), *Khrushchev Remembers* (Boston: Little, Brown and Company, 1970), p. 378. See also, Robert M. Slusser, "Soviet Far Eastern Policy, 1945–1950; Stalin's Goals in Korea," in *The Origins of the Cold War in Asia* edited by Yonosuke Nagai and Akira Iriye (Tokyo and New York: University of Tokyo Press, 1977), pp. 141–142, 146.
15. U.S. Department of State, *North Korea: A Case Study in the Technique of Takeover* (Washington, D.C.: U.S. Department of State, 1961), p. 114.
16. According to a purported defector, Lt. Col. Kyril Kalinov, "How Russia Built the North Korean People's Army," *Reporter Magazine* (September 26, 1950), pp. 4–8. Also see Robert R. Simmons, *The Strained Alliance: Peking, P'yongyang, Moscow and the Politics of the Korean War* (New York: The Free Press, 1975), p. 120 *passim*.
17. Glenn D. Paige, *The Korean Decision, June 24–30, 1950* (New York: The Free Press, 1968), p. 97. (Paige is citing an interview he had with Rusk in 1955.)
18. Adam B. Ulam, *The Rivals: America and Russia Since World War II* (New York: Random House, Viking ed., 1971), p. 171.
19. Moreover, the year before, Truman was extraordinarily cautious when arguing for a $150 million military aid bill: "It is a question of defense by the Southern Korean government . . . against Koreans from the North. I do not think our forces should be mixed up in that. The Russians would love to see that. . . . They would sit back and laugh their heads off if we got our forces engaged at all . . . and the one thing that causes

me some surprise is that the Russians have not realized how much damage they could do if they really did begin to let military events start in Southern Korea. I will feel relieved when we get these [American troops] out of there" (*United States Policy in the Far East, Part II, Korean Assistance Act,* Vol. VIII, U.S. House, Committee on International Relations, Historical Series, 1976, pp. 33, 46).

20. Statement by President Truman, "U.S. Air and Sea Forces Ordered into Supporting Action," *Department of State Bulletin,* Vol. 23 (July 3, 1950), p. 5.
21. Harry S. Truman, *Memoirs: Years of Trial and Hope* (Garden City, N.Y.: Doubleday & Company, 1956), p. 333.
22. Ibid., p. 340.
23. Acheson, *Present at the Creation,* p. 405.
24. Truman, op. cit., p. 339 (emphasis added).
25. Joyce and Gabriel Kolko, *The Limits of Power: The World and United States Foreign Policy* (New York: Harper & Row, 1972), pp. 579–582. In any event, even if they did not initiate the conflict, there is good reason to believe that: (1) they probably knew about it in advance and did not attempt to prevent the conflict and (2) they probably could have had the North Koreans withdrawn early and with honor if they were willing to exercise sufficient influence. In this sense the Soviets' relation to the North Koreans may have been similar to Russian–Syrian and –Egyptian relations in 1973. The Soviets may not have provoked the Arab attack *per se,* but the Arab attack was preceded by large arms delivery and Soviet advisers were at Arab command headquarters and with Arab field units. (3) No matter what the initial Soviet reason for acquiescence in the North Korean adventure, there is some evidence that the Soviets made it clear that they would not become involved in what they called a "Korean *civil* war" (emphasis added) but that the Chinese had more direct interests. The Chinese, in turn, tried to implicate the Soviets without success. See Simmons, "Contradictions in 'Fraternal Friendships,' " pp. 11–13.
26. Ulam, *Expansion and Coexistence* (New York: Praeger, 1968) pp. 523–525, and Acheson, *Present at the Creation,* pp. 408–412.
27. David Rees, *Korea: The Limited War* (Baltimore: Penguin Books, 1964), pp. 67–69.
28. Quoted in Miller, op. cit., p. 313.
29. Kolko and Kolko, op. cit., p. 572.
30. Ibid., and *The New York Times,* February 17, 1950.
31. Kolko and Kolko, op. cit., pp. 573–574.
32. Philip Jessup, in *Department of State Bulletin,* Vol. 22, No. 564 (April 24, 1950), p. 627.
33. Simmons, op. cit., p. 152.
34. John Foster Dulles, "The Korean Experiment in Representative Government," *Department of State Bulletin,* Vol. 23 (July 23, 1950), esp. p. 13.
35. Some observers, notably journalist I. F. Stone and historian Gabriel Kolko, have drawn from these events in Seoul and Tokyo an interesting hypothesis combining the circumstances in the months before the war with the confusion and curiously contradictory reports emanating from the battlefield during the week of June 25. Specifically, the U.S. command in Tokyo is viewed as being quite aware of the North Korean buildup and seeking to provoke a fight or perhaps maneuver the North Koreans into attacking. Thus, Dulles, as a representative of Republican conservatism, along with General MacArthur, publicly supported an increasingly belligerent Rhee. Such support, it is argued, could only have increased tensions and fears in the North, perhaps raising the fear that American military assistance was about to increase dramatically. If there was a new rapid buildup in the South, then the North Koreans would lose their recently acquired arms advantage. Once the attack occurred, whether started by South Korean

incursions (as Stone suggests) or as the result of a preemptive strike (Kolko), General MacArthur and Syngman Rhee, the revisionists suggest, allowed the situation to deteriorate so as to ensure a significant U.S. intervention. Washington was, in this analysis, rather ignorant of this maneuvering. President Truman and his advisers were more or less dependent upon General MacArthur for information as to what was going on in Asia. Having been misled by General MacArthur, they were pulled into the involvement and consequent redirection of American policy in Asia desired by General MacArthur, Syngman Rhee, and Chiang Kai-Shek. See I. F. Stone, *The Hidden History of the Korean War,* Second Modern Reader Edition (New York: Monthly Review Press, 1952), esp. pp. 1–107.

36. Cited by George F. Will, "Right Out of the '30s," *Washington Post,* January 17, 1980, p. A27.
37. Numerous accounts of the Korean War are available. Among the more concise yet comprehensive are David Rees, op. cit., and John Spanier, op. cit. Also important and provocative is the revisionist I. F. Stone, op. cit. Shorter but useful accounts and analyses are provided by Bernard Brodie, *War and Politics* (New York: Macmillan Company, 1973), pp. 57–112, and Martin Licterman, "Korea: Problems in Limited Wars," in Gordon B. Turner and Richard D. Challener (eds.), *National Security in the Nuclear Age* (New York: Praeger Publishers, 1960), pp. 31–58. The major documentary source on the war is U.S. Congress, Senate Committee on Armed Services and Committee on Foreign Relations, *Military Situation in the Far East,* 82nd Congress, 1st Session, 1951. Finally the civilian–military implications are dealt with in Spanier, op. cit., and also in Walter Millis, *Arms and the State* (New York: Twentieth Century Fund, 1958), pp. 259–332.
38. Rees, op. cit., pp. 3–7, 21–26 and Kolko and Kolko, op. cit. pp. 579–582. Recently debate concerning the origins of the war resurfaced in the pages of *China Quarterly.* Karwnakar Gupta argues that South Korean forces attacked first at the North Korean border city of Haeju on June 25, 1950, and that the North Korean onslaught was a response. See Gupta's "How Did The Korean War Begin," *China Quarterly* (October–December 1972), pp. 699–716. This article prompted a refutation and a rejoinder by Gupta. See Chang-sik Lee, W. E. Skilend, and Robert Simmons, "Comment," *China Quarterly* (April–June 1973), pp. 354–368.
39. *The Times* (London), June 29, 1950, quoted in Kolko and Kolko, op. cit., p. 583.
40. Hanson Baldwin, "Ground Aid in Korea," *The New York Times,* June 29, 1950, p. 4.
41. *Department of State Bulletin,* Vol. 23 (July 3, 1950), pp. 4–5.
42. Quoted in Truman, op. cit., p. 337.
43. Ibid., p. 337.
44. "Text of Security Council Resolution," *Department of State Bulletin* (July 3, 1950), p. 7.
45. See Brodie, op. cit., or Licterman, op. cit.
46. See Spanier, op. cit.
47. David Halberstam, *The Best and the Brightest* (New York: Random House, 1972), p. 119.
48. Perhaps the best short analysis of McCarthy is Richard H. Rovere's *Senator Joe McCarthy* (New York: Harper & Row, 1959).
49. Halberstam, op. cit., p. 118.
50. Ibid., p. 119.
51. Hans J. Morgenthau, *The Purpose of American Politics* (New York: Random House, Vintage Books, 1960), p. 146.
52. Rovere, op. cit., p. 3.

53. Ibid., p. 23. McCarthy's influence had a half-life of over a generation. Even after his name had become an oath, in 1968 when *Eugene* McCarthy challenged Lyndon Johnson in the snows of a New Hampshire primary as an anti-Vietnam War peace candidate, many of his supporting votes were cast in the belief that he was *Joe* McCarthy.

54. Richard P. Stebbins, *The United States in World Affairs, 1950* (New York: Harper & Row, 1951), p. 57.

55. William S. White, *The Taft Story* (New York, Harper & Row, 1954), pp. 84–85.

56. Margaret Chase Smith, "Declaration of Conscience," *Congressional Record,* Vol. 96, Part 6 (June 1, 1950), p. 7894.

57. Indeed, only six other Republicans did: Tobey of New Hampshire, Aiken of Vermont, Morse of Oregon, Ives of New York, Thye of Minnesota, and Hendrickson of New Jersey.

58. Paul H. Nitze, "The United States in the Face of the Communist Challenge," in C. Grove Haines (ed.), *The Threat of Soviet Imperialism* (Baltimore: Johns Hopkins University Press, 1954), p. 374 (emphasis added).

59. Senator Robert A. Taft, *Congressional Record,* January 5, 1951, 82nd Congress, 1st Session, p. 59.

60. Ibid., p. 58.

61. Ibid.

62. Ibid., p. 60.

63. Ibid., p. 61.

64. Ibid.

65. Ibid.

66. See Acheson, *Present at the Creation,* pp. 494–495 on this point. However, Acheson quoted Taft as saying "[I] would not object to a few more divisions simply to show the Europeans that we are interested and will participate in the more difficult job of land warfare while we carry out also our larger obligations" (p. 495).

67. Announcement of the French government, May 9, 1950, quoted in Acheson, *Present at the Creation,* p. 384. The Schumann Plan envisaged that the integration of German heavy industrial capacity would make more difficult the development of independent military power. The French and any other Europeans who chose to join would sacrifice some of their sovereignty, but in return they would gain an unprecedented margin of control over German productive capability.

A split immediately developed between the British and the French. The British perceived problems with the Schumann Plan apart from their ancient ambivalence concerning the continent and the more recent notion that the British possessed a special relationship with the Americans that would be diminished as the result of close political and economic ties with the continent. Specifically, the Labor government in power in the spring of 1950 feared that entering into any such supranational arrangement would diminish their capacity to exercise socialist principles of domestic economic planning. All this was sufficient to keep the British out of the new European economic integration for almost two decades.

68. Ibid., p. 399.

69. See Robert E. Osgood, *NATO, The Entangling Alliance* (Chicago: University of Chicago Press, 1962) for further elaboration.

70. Ibid., pp. 80–81.

71. Ibid., *passim.*

72. Malcolm W. Cagle and Frank Manson, *The Sea War in Korea* (Annapolis, Md.: U.S. Naval Institute, 1957), p. 81.

73. Robert Leckie, *The Wars of America, Vol. II: San Juan Hill to Tonkin* (New York: Bantam Books, 1969), pp. 357–358.
74. Capt. Walter Karig, Comdr. Malcolm Cagle, and Lt. Cmdr. Frank A. Manson, *The War in Korea Battle Report,* Vol. VI (New York: Holt, Rinehart & Winston, 1952), p. 5.
75. This description is drawn from Rees, op. cit., pp. 77–97; see esp. pp. 90–92 for an account of the fighting in and around Seoul.
76. Millis, op. cit., p. 274.
77. Louis J. Halle, *The Cold War as History* (New York: Harper & Row, 1967), p. 220.
78. *Department of State Bulletin,* Vol. 23 (October 9, 1950), p. 580.
79. Halle, op. cit., p. 220.
80. Ibid.
81. Harold C. Hinton, *Communist China in World Politics* (Boston: Houghton Mifflin Company, 1966), p. 213.
82. Rees, op. cit., p. 109.
83. Whiting, op. cit., pp. 108–109.
84. Truman, op. cit., p. 362.
85. Acheson, *Present at the Creation,* p. 452.
86. Truman, op. cit., p. 362.
87. Ibid.
88. This offer was conditional on a withdrawal of diplomatic recognition, protection, and aid to the Nationalists on Taiwan. *Manchester Guardian,* November 18, 1950, cited by Harold Hinton, op. cit., p. 213.
89. Rees, op. cit., p. 128.
90. The best short account of the military action from October 19 through the Chinese intervention is Rees, op. cit., pp. 123–177. The classic study of the Chinese offensive is S. L. A. Marshall, *The River and the Gauntlet* (New York: William Morrow & Co., 1953). There has been some speculation that MacArthur's battle plan had been betrayed by the now notorious British spy "Kim" Philby and his associates. Philby was a Soviet mole in the British Embassy in Washington and a liaison between the British Soviet Intelligence Service and the Central Intelligence Service. The British had a commonwealth brigade under MacArthur's command; much information regarding common concerns was channeled through the British Embassy. See William Manchester, *American Ceasar: Douglas MacArthur, 1880–1964* (New York: Dell Publishers, 1979), pp. 711–713.
91. Millis, op. cit., p. 267, although Truman was fairly successful in his relationship with the general while MacArthur was SCAP.
92. Quoted by Harriman in Truman, op. cit., p. 353.
93. Quoted by Spanier, op. cit., p. 73.
94. Douglas MacArthur, "Formosa Must Be Defended," *U.S. News & World Report,* Vol. XXIX (No. 9, September 1, 1950), p. 34.
95. Truman, op. cit., pp. 355–356.
96. Stone, op. cit., pp. 145–150.
97. Truman, op. cit., pp. 362–363.
98. Manchester, op. cit., pp. 706–709.
99. Richard H. Rovere and Arthur M. Schlesinger, Jr., *The General and the President* (New York: Farrar, Straus & Young, 1951), p. 258.
100. "MacArthur's Own Story," *U.S. News & World Report,* Vol. 29 (December 8, 1950), p. 17.
101. Ibid., p. 384.

102. Ibid.
103. Douglas MacArthur, "Reply to the Joint Chiefs of Staff, December 30, 1950," in U.S. Congress, Senate Committee on Armed Services and Committee on Foreign Relations, *Hearings on the Military Situation in the Far East,* 82nd Congress, 1st Session, 1951, p. 2180; and Gaddis Smith, "After 25 Years — The Parallel," *The New York Times Magazine,* June 22, 1975, p. 20.
104. Rees, op. cit., p. 183.
105. Quoted in ibid., p. 206.
106. Ibid., p. 207.
107. Truman, op. cit., pp. 439–440.
108. Ibid., p. 441.
109. Ibid.
110. Ibid., p. 442.
111. Manchester, op. cit., p. 736, and Rees, op. cit., p. 213.
112. John Spanier, op. cit., p. 212.
113. Rees, op. cit., p. 222.
114. Quoted in ibid., p. 224.
115. Quoted in ibid., p. 226.
116. Spanier, op. cit., p. 220.
117. Ibid.
118. Quoted in William S. White, *Citadel: The Story of the U.S. Senate* (New York: Harper & Row, 1957), p. 244.
119. Rees, op. cit., p. 227.
120. Spanier, op. cit., p. 217.
121. See Eric Goldman, *The Crucial Decade and After: America 1945–1960* (New York: Vintage Books, 1960).
122. Ibid., p. 208.
123. Ibid., pp. 208–209.
124. MacArthur, *Hearings,* p. 45.
125. For a review of the details, see Cabell Phillips, *The Truman Presidency: The History of a Triumphant Succession* (Baltimore: Penguin Books, 1969), pp. 402–414.
126. Senator Joseph McCarthy, *Congressional Record,* June 14, 1951, Vol. 97, Part 5, p. 6556.
127. Quoted by Rees, op. cit., p. 386.
128. Richard M. Nixon, "My Side of the Story," *Vital Speeches of the Day,* October 15, 1952, pp. 11–15.
129. Goldman, op. cit., p. 232.
130. Robert W. Tucker, *Nation or Empire? The Debate over American Foreign Policy* (Baltimore: Johns Hopkins University Press, 1968), p. 28.
131. Robert E. Osgood, *Limited War: A Challenge to American Strategy* (Chicago: University of Chicago Press, 1957), p. 178.
132. U.S. Congress, Senate Committee on Armed Services and Committee on Foreign Relations, *Hearings on the Military Situation in the Far East,* 82nd Congress, 1st Session, 1951, pp. 3075, 3082.
133. Cited in Stone, op. cit., p. 313.
134. Thomas C. Schelling, *Arms and Influence* (New Haven, Conn.: Yale University Press, 1966), p. 136.
135. Dean Rusk, "The Revisionist Historians," *Firing Line* (transcript), PBS broadcast,

January 27, 1974 (Columbia, S.C.: Southern Educational Communications Associations, 1974), pp. 7–8.

136. See James A. Nathan and James K. Oliver, "The Diplomacy of Violence," *Society*, Vol. 11 (September/October 1974), pp. 32–40.

137. Marvin Kalb and Elie Abel, *Roots of Involvement: The U.S. in Asia, 1784–1971* (New York: W. W. Norton & Company), p. 65.

138. Adam Ulam, *Expansion and Co-Existence,* p. 493.

139. Ibid., p. 495; see also Salisbury, op. cit.

140. Allen S. Whiting," 'Contradictions' in the Moscow-Peking Axis," *Journal of Politics,* Vol. 20, No. 1 (February 1958), p. 120. Apparently, for instance, when Soviet Ambassador Malik made his speech of June 23, 1951, calling for negotiations to bring the war to a close, the Chinese were surprised, not having been informed prior to Malik's proposal (Simmons, op. cit., p. 165).

141. Acheson, *Present at the Creation,* p. 450.

142. Dean Acheson, *Department of State Bulletin,* Vol. 22, No. 559 (March 20, 1950), pp. 427, 429.

143. Coral Bell, *Negotiations from Strength* (New York: Alfred A. Knopf, 1963), p. 5.

144. Amnesty International, *Report on Torture* (London: Duckworth & Co., 1973), pp. 143–145 and for an updated precis of events, see Gregory Henderson, "The 'Other Boot' in Seoul," *New York Times,* January 16, 1980.

145. Schelling, op. cit., p. 124.

Chapter 5
Conserving
Containment

The two dominant figures in the formulation of American foreign policy during the Eisenhower years were the president and his secretary of state. The two men had come to power as the result of deep national and partisan disaffection. Most of the animus was directed toward the Democratic architects of a foreign policy that had been served by both Dulles and Eisenhower with considerable distinction during and after World War II. The fact that they had helped build and served that policy explains much of the continuity underlying the campaign rhetoric announcing the new administration.

Eisenhower's wartime and immediate postwar role is well known to most Americans. As commander of Allied forces in Europe during World War II he had directed the closing of Churchill's ring — thus destroying the Nazis — a deed in itself sufficient to guarantee his place in his nation's and the world's pantheon of heroes. But there had been much more: postwar commander of U.S. forces in the European theater; governor of the American zone of occupation; army chief of staff; president of Columbia University; and finally, supreme commander of NATO. As military chief of NATO, he had gone before the Senate as an advocate of President Truman's plan to increase the American presence in Europe. This associated him with the European-centered policies of the Truman administration, created deep suspicion of him within the right wing of the Republican Party and guaranteed the struggle with Robert Taft for the presidential nomination in 1952.

With his resounding victory over Taft, it seemed that the globalism of the preceding years would continue. But there were some counter indications, among them: Richard Nixon, a partisan of the right, as the vice presidential nominee; the inevitable association with Senator McCarthy during the campaign; and most troublesome to Republican and Democratic internationalists, Eisenhower's long meeting with Taft in September out of which came Taft's assertion that he and Eisenhower were in "full agreement" on virtually every aspect of domestic and foreign policy. These concessions to the right were, perhaps, politically essential given the make-up of the Republican party, but intimated a major constraint during the crucial first two years of the Eisenhower administration. Only during this period would the Republicans control the House and Senate, but the leadership of the congressional Republicans would be in the hands of the right. His enormous popularity notwithstanding, Eisenhower would repeatedly display ambivalence toward this ideological block within his own party. The result, in the eyes of his more moderate advisers, was a lamentable tendency upon occasion to compromise or suppress his own instincts and yield before what he feared would be disruptive attacks from the right.[1] Nevertheless, Eisenhower was personally committed to the global structure of containment and the commitments that were implied by this doctrine. Indeed, he was vastly to enlarge the scope of these commitments.

The designation of John Foster Dulles as secretary of state may have had, in view of Dulles's background as a member of the postwar foreign policy establishment, a certain air of inevitability about it.[2] However, attention to the convoluted career of Dulles, especially during the Truman administration, indicates that he, like Eisenhower, seemed to be swimming against strong currents within the Republican party. Dulles, despite the almost frothing partisanship he displayed in drafting the foreign policy statement in the 1952 Republican platform, undeniably represented the internationalist Republican party of Thomas Dewey. His intensely moralistic conception of the postwar Soviet-American confrontation set him apart from the more pragmatic tone of the Democratic secretaries of state he served as a special consultant. Nevertheless, he had served them in the development and defense of the Marshall Plan and the negotiation of the Japanese Peace Treaty and as a general symbol of bipartisanship. But to the extent that he was successful in his role of "house Republican," he was suspect in the intensely partisan Republican party of Taft, Knowland, Jenner, and McCarthy. Furthermore, as a high-level adviser to the State Department he had watched Acheson and Truman attempt with only partial success to shield the department and its foreign policy from the onslaught of what Acheson termed "the primitives."[3] Consequently, achieving the stewardship of American foreign policy required careful timing in joining the Eisenhower bandwagon, a delicate feat of ideological nimbleness, and a fine sensitivity to the policy preferences and political power of the right. Moreover, maintaining one's stewardship in the face of these men would require no less political skill.

But if Dulles was necessarily concerned about his domestic front, was it not also in large measure true of Eisenhower as well? Eisenhower's past military involvement with the Roosevelt and Truman administrations was as suspect to the right as Dulles's diplomatic service to the political and diplomatic architects of containment. Eisenhower's immense personal popularity provided him with a fund of political capital that Dulles never could possess, but Eisenhower was no less sensitive than Dulles to what had happened to the Truman administration. The Republican party was under the thrall of Joseph McCarthy, the man who had viciously attacked Eisenhower's mentor and commander-in-arms, General George Marshall, a man of enormous prestige.[4] Could McCarthy, would he do less to Eisenhower? Thus from the very outset, Eisenhower and Dulles were lined up in a mutual effort to contain the Republican right.

CONTAINING THE REPUBLICAN RIGHT

During the first 2 years of his administration, President Eisenhower refused to rebut Senator McCarthy's brutalizing of the foreign service and State Department. Instead the president adopted a strategy of waiting for McCarthy's excesses to double back on the senator and destroy him.[5] In the meantime, John Foster Dulles would proclaim the rhetoric of rolling back communist power and liberating so-called captive peoples, while appeasing Senator McCarthy by allowing him and his cohorts virtual freedom to investigate and vilify the foreign service.

Dulles approved the appointment of a McCarthy confidant, Scott McCleod, as Chief of Personnel Security — a man who had a plaque on his desk with his personal motto: "an ounce of loyalty is worth a pound of brains." When Charles Bohlen, the distinguished diplomat and friend of President Eisenhower, was appointed by the new president to be American ambassador to the Soviet Union, he underwent a brutal hectoring at Senator McCarthy's hands because of his association with the Roosevelt and Truman administrations. President Eisenhower remained aloof, however, and it fell to Secretary Dulles to steer Bohlen's nomination through the Senate over the objections of McLeod and McCarthy. Dulles did so but with trepidation lest he (Dulles) be personally associated with the nomination. So great was Dulles's fear that at one point he asked Bohlen that the two of them not be photographed together. Finally, when the nomination ordeal was over and Bohlen indicated that he would be traveling to the Soviet Union in advance of his family, Dulles, ever fearful, cautioned against the plan because "such a circumstance could open him to veiled charges of homosexuality no matter how baseless such charges might be."[6]

Similarly, Dulles allowed John Carter Vincent and John Paton Davies to be fired although he personally concluded that both men were not security risks as charged by McCleod. Both men were among those foreign service officers who had warned that Chiang Kai-Shek was corrupt and must inevitably fall before Mao Zedong's revolutionaries. From the standpoint of Senator McCarthy and his followers, however, they were responsible for what had happened, and would have to go. Dulles acquiesced, although in both instances he officially refused to reinstate the men not because they were security risks, but because they had not demonstrated "sound judgment" — a standard that was never defined by Dulles.[7] Years later Bohlen, in reflecting on these early months of the Eisenhower administration, said that he had

> the strong impression that Dulles was a man who lived in mortal terror that events would conspire to turn the McCarthy attack on him, that "... so strong were his preoccupations with his job and staying in it, that this affected his attitudes and actions" in nearly every realm. Dulles was a man with "one obsession: to remain Secretary of State."[8]

President Eisenhower probably did not feel these pressures as intensely. However, it is clear that he, too, was not prepared to take the initiative and engage McCarthy and McCarthyism publicly.[9] This reluctance on President Eisenhower's part has engaged the analysis of many of those who worked with or studied the man and his administration. Many, including his vice president, have concluded that Eisenhower was simply naive and inexperienced in the ways of political warfare.[10] Thus he could be absolved of responsibility for his lack of response because of his innocence and a justified concern for his personal reputation. But Nixon's analysis is not accepted by other observers. Gary Wills points out that Eisenhower

> rose in the peacetime professional army, where ambition is thwarted of its natural object (excellence in war) and falls back on jealousy and intrigue. Eisenhower climbed that slippery ladder of bayonets with a sure step and rare instinct for survival.[11]

He was a soldier, but unlike a Patton, he did not romanticize war. He was above all a realist who was conserving and deliberate in the use of his resources, not a man to come out swinging against a McCarthy. In 1953 he assumed the presidency of a country that was torn by suspicion and hysteria. He would in later life assert that his greatest domestic accomplishment as president was the calming of this mood.[12] Insofar as Eisenhower is justified in his claim, he "got the job done, without trumpets."[13] Similarly, with Senator McCarthy, who more than any other individual, simultaneously caused and symbolized domestic foment, the president's attitude seemed to be one of "this too will pass."

This temperate attitude and approach was institutionalized in his staff system.[14] Especially in the areas of foreign and defense policy, President

Eisenhower replicated the elaborate staff system to which he had become accustomed and employed so successfully in the army. The National Security Council (NSC) expanded dramatically, as committees and subcommittees proliferated. The NSC was managed by a proper Bostonian, Robert Cutler, who dampened dissent and diffused accountability by firmly insisting on the confidentiality of both the substance of recommendations and the process of arriving at decisions in the NSC. Congress, Cutler believed, was not a proper party to this process. Undoubtedly, as it would be charged later, this slowed the decision process; decision papers moved at a more measured pace. But it was Eisenhower's view that the frantic effort to build the wall of containment in the preceding administration had led to the overextension of American power, and the accompanying tense and charged domestic atmosphere had led to the destruction of whatever authority President Truman might have possessed, thus threatening containment itself.

Perhaps Gary Wills is correct: "Eisenhower had the true professional's instinct for making things look easy. He appeared to be performing less work than he actually did. And he wanted it that way. An air of ease inspires confidence."[15] Futhermore, as Wills perceptively notes, "it allowed him to evade responsibilities, in the sense that if any head had to roll, it would not be his."[16]

The relationship of Dulles and Eisenhower, though perhaps strained at first, came to embody this approach and style. To many who observed the Eisenhower administration, Dulles totally dominated American foreign policy.[17] Dulles always seemed out front and belligerently proselytizing his moralistic message of a new "political offensive" within "a policy of boldness."[18] The front page of the morning papers seemed at times permanently highlighted with a picture of the secretary of state grimly boarding or deplaning either in Washington or some other world capital, the picture captioned with his travel itinerary for the week. President Eisenhower, in contrast, was affable, relaxed, always smiling. His speeches on foreign policy frequently emphasized the positive, the opportunities for relaxing East-West tensions, or, at a minimum, he articulated a deep and seemingly genuine desire to end the confrontation of Soviet and American power that now dominated world politics. And if Dulles's photographs seemed to come from the travel section, Eisenhower's came from the sports pages, for the president seemed to be perpetually teeing-off at Burning Tree or Augusta.

There were undoubtedly important differences of approach and emphasis between the two men. There may also have been disagreements as to the long-term opportunities and probabilities of coexistence with the Soviet Union. But there seemed to be agreement concerning the immediate national security problems before the Eisenhower administration: Korea, and beyond that, retrenchment and consolidation of America's defense posture. Both men knew that their own party would be harassing them as they dealt with these problems. In retrospect, however, Eisenhower's style and especially his relationship with Dulles were admirably suited to dealing with his priorities of Korea and conserving containment within the politically dangerous domestic environment confronting this administration.

Regarding Korea, Eisenhower had reached some very definite conclusions. He had carried out his campaign pledge of visiting Korea during the first week of December 1952. He came away with the conviction that further offensive military action would be enormously costly and ultimately fruitless given the strong defensive positions established by the Chinese and North Koreans during the year of stalemated negotiations.[19] But Eisenhower also seems to have concluded that he would not go for total victory.[20] To go for anything less than total victory, however, risked bringing the wrath of the Republican right down upon the administration. Unless the fact that Eisenhower was now pursuing the same war aims as Truman could be in some way masked, the Eisenhower administration might suffer the same political fate. Yet Eisenhower possessed in his secretary of state exactly what he needed. By allowing Dulles to take the public initiative with his tough and belligerent rhetoric and, in some instances, adopting the same stance publicly and privately himself, President Eisenhower and his administration put forth an image that many in Congress and America wanted to see. Dulles's and Eisenhower's willingness to sacrifice the careers of many in the foreign service, though morally repugnant and ultimately destructive of the State Department, also contributed to the functional equivalent of a smoke screen. In the meantime, Eisenhower moved to end the war in Korea in a manner for which President Truman might well have been impeached.

A Korean Truce: Continuing
Containment along the 38th Parallel

On returning to the United States from Korea, Eisenhower noted that America was dealing with an enemy that could not be impressed by words "however eloquent, but only deeds — executed under circumstances of our own choosing."[21]

The deeds came very quickly, a pattern of escalating military pressure that would be replicated in another Asian war almost two decades later. In his State of the Union Address in February 1953, Eisenhower announced that the Seventh Fleet would be removed from the Taiwan Strait — a clear threat to the mainland Chinese, for Eisenhower was indicating a willingness to allow the Nationalists to step up their guerrilla activities against the mainland and perhaps go even further. There seems to have been little belief that Chiang Kai-Shek could launch a full-scale attack; but to the Communists, Eisenhower's action could be read as a toughening of America's posture. It could also be read in the same light by those in Congress who sought total victory, in spite of the fact that Eisenhower had no intentions of seeking such an outcome.

Eisenhower was prepared to use threats and words as well as deeds, and the threat that followed was, therefore, blunt and awesome, though quietly communicated.[22] "In February, at his orders," Peter Lyons reports, "word had been discreetly passed that if the truce negotiations did not begin to show results, a few atomic weapons might, to use the jargon of the military, be 'wasted.' "[23]

Eisenhower and others in his administration believed that these threats were responsible for subsequent movement in the peace talks in March. This may or may not have been the case, for an event of monumental importance for the communist world occurred at the end of March — Stalin died. Suddenly the symbol of Soviet and communist power and intransigence was gone. An extended period of transition followed in the communist world during which long-standing policies underwent important change. Among these changes was undoubtedly some increase in the policy latitude available to Beijing. Within weeks the Chinese decided to move to end the Korean War. In April 1953, an exchange of sick and wounded took place, but negotiations bogged down on the repatriation issue. The problem, as always, was how to handle those prisoners in the hands of the South Koreans who might choose to stay in the South after an armistice.

Once again Eisenhower privately threatened the use of nuclear weapons and simultaneously bombed the only remaining strategic targets in North Korea. On May 10 and 11, hydroelectric dams on the Yalu River were attacked, followed on May 13, 1953, by attacks on five irrigation dams in North Korea. The May 13 attacks were directed at civilian populations although such raids had been undertaken by the Nazis in Holland in 1944 and 1945 and "as all military leaders everywhere well knew, [had] been stigmatized as a war crime by the Nuremberg Tribunal."[24] A dozen or more dams remained, but the message was clear — the United States was prepared to do virtually anything, including the starvation and/or incineration of North Korea (and China?), to end the war.[25] On June 8, 1953, the Communists signed an agreement that seemed to meet most of the objectives of the Americans.

In the meantime, however, Syngman Rhee was digging in his heels. The spectre of a settlement that left him little better off than in 1950 now loomed before him. Indeed, Rhee would now confront a strong Chinese presence in addition to a war-devastated South Korea. In April and May 1953, Rhee denounced the negotiations, called instead for yet another march to the Yalu, said he would withdraw his troops from the UN force if the Chinese remained in the North, boycotted the talks at Panmunjom, and when it was announced that the repatriation obstacle had been surmounted, organized street demonstrations against the impending settlement. Finally, on June 18, 1953, Rhee started releasing more than 25,000 prisoners in the hope that North Koreans would be sufficiently embarrassed by the reality of thousands of their former soldiers choosing to stay in the south that they and the Chinese would break off the talks and resume fighting. Rhee's action received support from some military men in Korea, notably General Clark. In Congress, Senator McCarthy commented that "freedom-loving people throughout the world should applaud" Rhee's actions.[26]

Eisenhower did not applaud. In fact an air of crisis settled on the White House as the president feared that the Chinese would ("and, I must confess, with some right") simply refuse to participate in any further talks given the American's apparent inability to control their ally. But the Chinese, having made a firm decision to end the war, proved patient and waited for the Americans to bring Rhee in line. By July 12, 1953, the Americans had succeeded, but only after promising Rhee a mutual security treaty, hundreds of millions of dollars in military assistance and economic aid, a voice in any postwar conferences concerning Korea, and according to recently declassified documents thinly veiled threats to remove Rhee from power.[27]

In the meantime, the Chinese were applying their own stick to go with the American carrot and stick. On July 13 and 14 the Chinese struck at South Korean units, pushing them back several miles and inflicting thousands of casualties. The American Eighth Army stood by while Rhee's forces took a terrific pounding. As Eisenhower notes: "One possibly useful result was to remind President Rhee of the vulnerability of his forces if deprived of United Nations support."[28] On July 19 the chief UN negotiator informed the Chinese that the UN command would honor any armistice reached no matter what the ROK did.[29] Final arrangements were quickly worked out for the repatriation of remaining prisoners, and the truce was signed on July 27.

Hot war had ended, but now the president asked the American people to harken to the persistent drum of cold war. A year earlier the secretary of state had written into the Republican platform strong words concerning "hampering orders" on the part of the Truman administration leading to "stalemate and ignominious bartering with our enemies . . . (with) no hope of victory" in Korea.[30] The Eisenhower administration had countermanded some of the hampering orders and allowed the bombing of irrigation dams and threatened the use of nuclear weapons, thereby providing the appearance of having decisively forced the end of the war. But in the end there had been no victory. Moreover, what Dulles called some of the most "ignominious bartering" of the war was of necessity carried out between America and its South Korean allies. And finally, when the war ended the Eisenhower administration found itself agreeing, through the truce and promise of massive aid to South Korea, to accept a militarily stalemated line not unlike the one that had existed in June 1950.[31] In summary, the use of escalating force and the threat of nuclear weapons combined with even more important changes in the communist world had the net effect of formalizing the preexisting balance of political and military power on the Korean peninsula.

Reassessment and Continuity

When the Eisenhower administration entered office it found a study prepared by the outgoing administration providing its assessment of what American national security needs would be in coming years. The paper was an updated distillation of the world view contained in NSC-68. Under the urging of Senator Taft and his own economic advisers, President Eisenhower reduced the outgoing Truman administration budget by more than $6 billion. At the same time, Eisenhower announced what he termed a radical departure in his first defense budget, which would be sent to Congress in January 1954. The so-called radical nature of this approach referred to Eisenhower's rejection of the year of crisis concept that had appeared in NSC-68 and other planning documents of the Truman administration. In its place Eisenhower would substitute the notion of the long haul or long pull: "providing a strong military position which can be maintained over the extended period of uneasy peace."[32] The implication was that the older planning concepts were unsound because they introduced into military budgets and planning a feast or famine cycle rather than the substained effort envisioned by Eisenhower.[33]

In fact, Eisenhower's rhetoric represented something of a misrepresentation of Truman's policies.[34] President Truman's rearmament proposals were presented to a Congress that was, prior to June 1950, reluctant to proceed as the president desired. The notion of a year of maximum peril, 1954, served as a device to emphasize and dramatize the target date for completion of the buildup. The years between 1952 and 1954 were portrayed as the crucial period for American rearmament to gain a position of strength, but there was no intention of reversing the process after 1954.[35] If there was a difference, it lay in the fact that the Eisenhower administration felt that it could stretch out the build-up in military capability called for in NSC-68, achieving its target levels in 1957 rather than the end of 1955. Of perhaps greater importance, however, Eisenhower gave to his defense planning the image of a new departure. It was after all essential — as in Korea — that the appearance of change be maintained. At a minimum, Eisenhower's own party had to be convinced that a transformation was taking place.

In summary, the Eisenhower administration's assumptions and expectations concerning a period of extended Soviet-American confrontation were very similar to those held by the Truman administration. However, the Eisenhower administration held that the rearmament effort, already well under way as a result of the Korean War, could be completed and sustained at a lower rate of expenditure than planned by Truman. This contention was drawn in turn from the underlying and fundamental principle of Eisenhower's planning — that the national security was first and foremost a function of a balanced budget and that these economic principles must be incorporated into all military planning including that undertaken by the services and the new Joint Chiefs of Staff. The new chiefs had been selected by Eisenhower (and with the approval of Taft) so as to ensure that they would be totally responsive to the new administration's defense priorities and concepts. Ironically, however, the broad foreign policy concepts on which the defense posture rested were increasingly similar to those held by Truman's administration.

As in the case of defense policy, Eisenhower had set in motion a parallel reassessment of foreign policy. Task forces were established to study and make recommendations concerning three alternative politico-military strategies:

1. *Containment*: a continuation of the basic structure of policy during the Truman years.
2. A policy of *global deterrence* in which American commitments would be actually extended and communist transgressions met with severe punishment.
3. *Liberation:* political, psychological, economic and even paramilitary warfare designed to penetrate the communist empire, "roll it back," and liberate the captive peoples.

The last two options clearly bore the stamp of John Foster Dulles, who had previously called for heavy reliance upon the threat of nuclear weapons as the best means for checking the threat of communist military aggression. Global deterrence was a defensive or deterrent military posture; but if aggression occurred, the response of the West would not be confined to a limited conventional response *à la* Korea. If American interests were global and indistinguishable, and the threat to those interests was monolithic, undifferentiated Soviet Communist aggression, then the United States and the free world now felt free to direct its response directly against the Soviets (or any other communist aggressor such as China). Moreover, Dulles claimed that having thus resolved the problem of military defense, the free world "can undertake what has been too long delayed — a political offensive:"[36] — liberation.

Eisenhower, however, was perplexed and skeptical concerning Dulles's notion of liberation. He did not understand how Dulles could ever effectively implement his political offensive. In fact, as the planning exercise was underway, the first opportunity for liberation occurred in June 1953 as East Berlin workers, ostensibly reacting to the imposition of higher production quotas, rioted. The United States did nothing beyond an offer of free food and the establishment of soup kitchens in West Berlin. The uprising was crushed and the detonation in August 1953 of the Soviet's first hydrogen bomb made explicit what Eisenhower and, one suspects, Dulles knew all along: given the Soviets' growing military capacity and the importance of Eastern Europe to their security designs, liberation was at best an incredibly dangerous policy. The option was "firmly rejected."[37] In contrast, the deterrence option, with its emphasis on air and sea power, was clearly looked upon favorably by Eisenhower. The appointment of Radford ("whose maxim as a carrier Admiral in the war against Japan had been 'kill the bastards scientifically' "[38]) as chairman of the Joint Chiefs and the economic constraints issued him with his initial planning directives led almost inevitably to support for a less manpower-intensive defense posture.

Thus, the outcome of a policy review set in motion by President Eisenhower was the rejection of Secretary Dulles's proposed policy of boldness and political offensive, and confirmation of the posture advocated by Eisenhower from the very outset: the continuation of containment but with a shift in the instrumentalities away from conventional force and toward the technology of air and sea power. This was, of course, Senator Taft's conception of what American military policy ought to be, and not that of Dulles.

The New Look and Massive Retaliation

In October 1953 the crucial task of integrating foreign policy assumptions and defense planning into the first Eisenhower budget was begun. The president approved an NSC paper that allowed the services to "plan on using nuclear weapons, tactical as well as strategic, whenever their use would be desirable from a military standpoint."[39] Apart from small brush fire conflicts, all wars were now assumed to be, at a minimum, tactical nuclear wars. Moreover, massive retaliatory capability rather than ground troops was now regarded as the major deterrent to Soviet aggression, although what specifically the form of aggression might be was never made explicit. It was agreed that some American ground forces should be available to deter local aggression, but here again there was a certain vagueness concerning the planning assumption that local indigenous forces would be employed. These decisions, especially reductions in the size of the army, opened the way for a reduction in the military budget not only in the fiscal 1955 period but also through to 1957, when the administration intended to complete the implementation of the new look.[40]

On January 12, 1954, Dulles, in a speech before the Council on Foreign Relations, explained the outcome of the new administration's policy deliberations and planning. The speech included criticism of what Dulles regarded as the defensive, reactive, and expensive character of Truman's containment.[41] The Eisenhower administration was advancing a new conception of American policy — "a maximum deterrent at a bearable cost,"[42] in which

> local defenses must be reinforced by the further deterrent of massive retaliatory power.... The way to deter aggression is for the free community to be willing and able to respond vigorously at places and with means of its own choosing.[43]

Dulles succeeded through the massive retaliation speech in projecting an American policy with a tough and rigid image that obscured the administration's decision to continue American policy within the framework of containment developed by the Truman administration. The continuities with the past are striking. Despite Dulles's rhetoric concerning the flexibility provided by the new look and massive retaliation, the structure of American military policy became even more rigid. If anything, the options were now fewer in number; in the event of local aggression the United States would rely on local forces, perhaps backed by American air and sea support, but if that was not sufficient or if the aggression was major, there remained only nuclear war. In fact, as Robert Bowie, the head of the Policy Planning Council under Dulles from 1953 to 1957, observed:

Fundamentally those basic lines of policy, in terms of security, of economic interests, of relations with allies and relations with the Soviet Union and relations in the Far East, were the product of the external conditions, as they were perceived, and the American sense of its interests, which really weren't partisan.... There wasn't anywhere near as much room for maneuver as some campaign oratory might have suggested.[44]

CONTAINMENT IN A CHANGING WORLD

The first of the Eisenhower years, from 1953 through mid-1955, was a time of vigorous activity directed at preserving and formalizing the status quo in a period of revolutionary change. The rapid contraction of British power in the Middle East and the French in Southeast Asia accelerated the struggle for national independence in the non-Western world. To Eisenhower and Dulles, these momentous changes were understood by means of the metaphors drawn from the quasi-theological dogma of confrontation between communism and the free world. The Middle East, Latin America, and Vietnam were, therefore, "vacuums" into which Soviet and Chinese communism would move unless anticipated by a free world — that is, American — presence. The remnants of the Chinese civil war in and around the Taiwan Straits were formalized as the eastern frontier of the cold war and the testing ground for the notion of deterrence.

There was also a continuation of economic motives in U.S. policy in these years. The Truman Doctrine and the development of the Marshall Plan underscored the interdependence (and interpenetration) of economic, political, and military considerations in the formulation and implementation of American policy in Europe. Eisenhower and his secretary of state generally framed their policies in the lofty rhetoric of ideological confrontation. But, as was the case in the Truman administration, the freedom that American power was to protect usually encompassed a notion of a particular way of life, and at the heart of this concept was the particular variety of political economy found in the United States. Moreover, that way of life — its political forms and, inseparably, its economic essence — was deemed appropriate to the rest of the world.

Thus, concerning Vietnam and Indochina, Eisenhower stated:

The loss of all Vietnam, together with Laos in the west and Cambodia in the southwest, would have meant the surrender to Communist enslavement of millions. On the material side, it would have spelled the loss of valuable deposits of tin and prodigious supplies of rubber and rice. It would have meant that Thailand, enjoying buffer territory between itself and Red China, would be exposed on its entire eastern border to infiltration or attack.

And if Indochina fell, not only Thailand but Burma and Malaya would be threatened, with added risks to East Pakistan and South Asia as well as to all Indonesia.[45]

All the elements of the world view developed after World War II are here: the enslavement of millions, raw materials, and the strategic concern for buffer territory and proliferating threats to others. One element might assume dominance in a particular case. Yet whether it was an economic or strategic question or a matter of the internal political regime of other nations, it always stood inseparably in the context of the other elements and of the ideological whole.

During the Eisenhower administration, a primary objective was to protect world economic and ideological order in the emerging third world of the 1950s. The containment doctrine developed in and for Central Europe in the late 1940s was extended and consolidated. However, this effort reflected a profound misunderstanding of the forces at work, not only in the Middle East and Southeast Asia, but also in East Asia and Latin America. To Eisenhower and his advisers, the revolutionary changes that seemed to be activated all over the globe by the collapse of European colonial empires were not viewed as the result of complex and fragile traditional societies being thrust into the crucible of rapid decolonization and modernization. Instead, the often violent unrest was regarded as merely the newest form of world communist aggression, requiring an American response not unlike that undertaken in Europe.

The effort to restructure emerging societies in the American image had three consequences: First, the frequently brusque shouldering aside of America's European allies as they proved unable to deal with what was perceived as communist penetration of the non-Western world intro-duced near irreconcilable strains in the NATO alliance. Second, this as-sumption of the postcolonial Western presence in the non-Western world also meant that the Americans would now be confronted with social, political, and economic forces they did not and perhaps could not under-stand until the United States was itself tragically and irretrievably en-meshed in a colonial war in Asia. Finally, the preoccupation with formalizing containment outside of Europe contributed to the inability of Eisenhower and Dulles to explore developments in Soviet-American rela-tions that might have allowed movement into a postcontainment phase of world politics. It was, in short, a pivotal time requiring a substantive as well as formal new look. Unhappily, form prevailed over substance, and American foreign policy found itself set against the revolutionary forces of the postwar international system.

Vietnam

By the early 1950s and after 7 years of bloody counterrevolutionary warfare in Indochina it was inescapably apparent that French colonial control was not to be reestablished. American economic and military assistance were substantial but could not offset the material and psychological costs of the war the French had been waging against the Viet Minh, a communist-led coalition of Vietnamese revolutionaries under the direction of Ho Chi Minh. The Viet Minh, with the active support of the American OSS (the forerunner of the CIA), had fought the Japanese effort to impose their political and economic order on Indochina during World War II. When the French attempted to reimpose colonial rule after the war, the Viet Minh continued to fight for national independence. By 1954, the price the French were paying to deny self-government to the Viet Minh had become inordinate. The French suffered 92,000 dead and 114,000 wounded.[46] But many in the French government feared that to grant Vietnamese independence would cost even more. For it might encourage revolutionary activity in other colonial areas such as Morocco, Tunisia, or most important, Algeria.

The dilemma was a painful juxtaposition of national pride and waning imperial glory against a hemorrhage of blood and treasure. In early 1954 the French, with a 15,000-person garrison surrounded at Dien Bien Phu accepted a Russian proposal for a five-power foreign ministers conference — to include the Soviet Union, United States, Britain, France, and Communist China — that would discuss both the Korean and Indochinese situations. Secretary Dulles and the president were quite concerned that an important and vital front in the cold war was about to be compromised. Both worried that the outcome of negotiated withdrawal of France would lead to "shift[s] in the power relations throughout Asia and the Pacific [that] could be disastrous. . . ."[47] Neither man viewed what was going on in Vietnam as the continuation of a struggle for independence. To Eisenhower, "Ho Chi Minh was, of course, a hard-core Communist, while the Viet Minh, the forces under his command, were supported by the Chinese Communists in the north."[48] The Eisenhower administration came to see the imminent collapse of French power as the breaching of the dike holding back the tide of Chinese communist-promoted aggression throughout southeast Asia. As the president explained in April 1954:

> First of all, you have the specific value of a locality in its production of materials that the world needs.

Then you have the possibility that many human beings pass under a dictatorship that is inimical to the free world.

Finally, you have ... what you would call the "falling domino" principle. You have a row of dominoes set up, you knock over the first one, and what will happen to the last one is the certainty that it will go over very quickly.[49]

With the Geneva Conference beginning at the end of April 1954, an air of crisis developed in Washington. The immediate reaction, especially on the part of the head of the Joint Chiefs of Staff, Admiral Radford, was for military intervention by means of an air strike, with nuclear weapons if necessary, on the Viet Minh positions around Dien Bien Phu. Dulles was no less prone to intervention, although he announced publicly that any U.S. action should be within the context of "united action." This ambiguous notion — united action — reflected Eisenhower's view that any U.S. intervention would have to meet certain preconditions. First, American intervention would have to have the support of Congress, and second, any intervention would have to be undertaken in concert with the Southeast Asians and the British.[50]

Eisenhower wanted a victory as intensely as anyone in Washington. But Eisenhower, perhaps more than most, was aware of the domestic limits in the situation. Korea had ended less than a year earlier, and the military situation in Vietnam seemed to require a commitment of American manpower similar to Truman's effort at military containment in Asia. Aside from the fact that the manpower necessary for such an engagement would not be available under the new look, Eisenhower sensed that there was no national stomach for another fight and probably knew that Congress, the Republican right wing notwithstanding, would not support another engagement in Asia. In fact, the congressional leadership, when consulted, further strengthened the president's hand against immediate military intervention by echoing his precondition of British approval and support for military involvement.

To meet Eisenhower's and Congress' preconditions would require a considerable diplomatic effort which precluded a quick intervention; therefore Dulles set about the tasks of getting British and Southeast Asian support against Ho Chi Minh and minimizing the possible damage growing out of the Geneva Conference. Eisenhower and Dulles wanted no involvement in any negotiated settlement of the Indochinese situation that resulted in a *de facto* communist victory. The way to avoid this, according to Eisenhower, would be the creation of "a new, *ad hoc* grouping or coalition" comprised of the United States, Britain, France, the Associated States in Southeast Asia (Cambodia and Laos), Australia, New Zealand, Thailand, and the Philippines. This coalition would provide material and moral support, and "it must be willing to join the fight if necessary."[51] In short, the coalition would provide the French with the wherewithal to avoid having to negotiate any agreement at Geneva. Eisenhower and Dulles simply did not want the French to give up.

Dulles was sent to London and immediately encountered British resistance to the idea of hastily trying to construct an alliance or coalition before the Geneva talks. The reticent French suggested that they were interested; but they wanted to take no action that would compromise a settlement at the Geneva Conference. Thus, they were not willing to discuss any form of defense agreement until the Geneva Conference had ended.

The Indochina phase of the Geneva Conference began the day after the commander of Dien Bien Phu, on May 7, after 57 days of siege, surrendered all his remaining men to the Vietnamese leader, General Giap. Dulles and Eisenhower persisted in their view that the United States had to prevent any settlement that undercut the containment of communism in Southeast Asia. Thus, they refused to participate formally in the talks or state an unambiguous position concerning the outcome. American policy was one of no participation in any agreement and limiting to the maximum extent possible any communist gains made through the negotiations. The sum of the American position was to impede any progress toward a settlement at Geneva; and if this failed, to refuse any ratification of the agreement.

This obstructionist position ran counter to all other participants, especially the British, who under Foreign Minister Anthony Eden's skilled direction attempted to move the conference toward a settlement. In the meantime, Washington persisted in its private contacts with the French concerning the possibilities and conditions of intervention including, then French Premier Bideault would later claim, the possibility of using nuclear weapons. These overtures only served to inhibit French willingness to come to an agreement with the Viet Minh and further exacerbated American relations with the British, who were attempting to move matters to a settlement. By late May 1954, the conference had stalemated, the French government fell, and the talks were suspended pending French elections.

By the end of June 1954 the French had elected as premier Pierre Mendes-France, who assumed direct responsibility for the negotiations and promised to have a settlement within 30 days. The Geneva Conference now moved quickly to a conclusion. The substance of the agreement was to provide for a resolution of the military conflict by means of a temporary partition of the country at the 17th parallel. The final declaration of the conference explicitly rejected the notion that the provisional demarcation line was a political boundary:

> The conference recognizes that the essential purpose of the agreement relating to Vietnam is to settle military questions with a view to ending hostilities and that the military demarcation line is provisional and should not in any way be interpreted as constituting a political or territorial boundary.[52]

The political future of the country was to be resolved in 1956 in national elections.

In summary, two countries were not formed and there were no political preconditions established for the elections. Subsequent South Vietnamese and U.S. justifications for refusing to undertake or carry out the election provisions of the Geneva Accords rests on the assertion that "conditions in North Vietnam during that period were such as to make impossible any free and meaningful expression of popular will."[53] In fact, the participants in the talks agreed that the establishment of democratic institutions or the free and meaningful expression of popular will was not something to be guaranteed by the Geneva Accords. Rather, democratic institutions and processes would be a product of elections. The elections were not dependent upon any specified political conditions in the provisional regroupment zones. And the zones were clearly not viewed as political units or nascent nation-states.[54]

On the understanding and misunderstanding of these agreements rest the respective claims concerning American intervention in Vietnam. If one construes the Geneva Accords to have established two Vietnamese states, then American involvement appears legally unexceptional. If, on the other hand, the language of the final declaration is interpreted as above, then subsequent development of the Vietnam War is clearly a civil war and not a case of aggression as insisted by the Eisenhower, Kennedy, Johnson, Nixon, and Ford administrations.

The immediate response of the Eisenhower administration in 1954 was consistent with their refusal to participate in the talks or final accords. Dulles and Eisenhower moved to undo the results of the Geneva agreement on Indochina. "The important thing," Dulles said, shortly after the conference broke up, "is not to mourn the past but to seize the future opportunity to prevent the loss in Northern Vietnam from leading to the extension of Communism throughout Southeast Asia and the Southwest Pacific."[55]

Within 6 weeks Dulles convened a meeting in Manila of representatives of the United States, Britain, France, Australia, New Zealand, Pakistan, Thailand, and the Philippines for the purpose of establishing a Southeast Asia Treaty Organization (SEATO) to prevent the extension of Communism. Dulles sought but could not get, either from the participants in the conference or from the Congress, the kind of precommitments to the defense of the area embodied in the NATO agreement. All that Dulles could get was agreement that each member of SEATO would "meet the common danger in accordance with its constitutional processes ... ;" beyond this were equally vague agreements to consult in the event of subversion, guerrilla warfare, or similar kinds of activity.[56]

Dulles also sought to include the French Associated States of Laos, Cambodia, and the state of Vietnam in SEATO. This was resisted vigorously by the French. The French pointed out that such an act would violate the Geneva Accords proscription against Vietnam or the other associated states from entering into alliances. However, Dulles persisted and got everyone to agree to at least a protocol to the SEATO agreement that extended the protection of the treaty to Laos, Cambodia, and the "free territory under the jurisdiction of the state of Vietnam."[57] In other words, within weeks after the completion of the Geneva conference, Dulles and Eisenhower had set in motion a line of policy designed to end the ambiguous and fluid situation in Indochina. What had been left by the signatories as a nonpolitical provisional separation of the parties in Vietnam pending elections, Dulles and Eisenhower set out to make politically permanent. The United States had failed to stop the Geneva Conference, but the SEATO agreement and the reference in the protocol to the treaty to the "free territory" in Vietnam was a clear indication of Eisenhower and Dulles's intent to transform the 17th parallel into a permanent political boundary with American support going to a separate state of South Vietnam. Indeed, the SEATO protocol extended protection to that state even before it existed. During and immediately after the Geneva Conference a confused struggle for power developed in the southern part of Vietnam. Ho Chi Minh was in firm control in Hanoi, but in Saigon the locus of power was in doubt, at least until the United States entered the picture. The government of the Vietnamese chief of state, Emperor Bao Dai, had served as a front for French colonial control since 1948. With the impending collapse of French power Bao Dai had left Vietnam seeking refuge in France, and in 1954 Ngo Dinh Diem became prime minister. Diem, a Catholic, had spent much of the preceding 4 years in the United States and gained the support of the American Friends of Vietnam, an analogue of the China lobby. He was also supported by a collection of American politicians including such senators as Mike Mansfield, Hubert Humphrey, and John F. Kennedy; a spectrum of academics; and Catholic religious leaders, most notably Cardinal Spellman.

In November of 1954 full U.S. support for Diem was announced and, with the removal of those Vietnamese military leaders opposed to Diem, the way was cleared for the consolidation of Diem's power in Saigon. To ensure Diem's control, more than $325 million in economic and military assistance was pumped into the South. Included in this aid were, by some accounts, more than $12 million which Diem employed in early 1955 to bribe the leadership of the remaining domestic political opposition.[58] In October 1955, Diem organized a referendum in which the South Vietnamese had to choose between Diem and Bao Dai. Diem won more than 98 percent of the vote, and on October 26, 1955, the prime minister proclaimed the founding of the Republic of Vietnam and himself the first president.

Meanwhile, Diem had refused to begin negotiations with the Viet Minh concerning elections. In July 1955, Diem asserted that he had not signed the Geneva agreements and that he could not therefore be bound by them. In this, Diem was merely reflecting the position of Dulles, who had claimed, in June 1955, that the preconditions for free elections did not exist in the North. Hence, there was no obligation on Diem's part to proceed. Instead, Diem continued his consolidation of control and, with the establishment of the Republic of Vietnam, provided the United States with a political entity in name as well as fact. The United States thus extended and formalized its militant anticommunist and antirevolutionary presence into the turbulent milieu of Vietnamese politics.

Iran

As in Southeast Asia, American intervention in the Middle East was related to the collapse of colonial control on the part of an American ally, in this case Great Britain. In 1951 the Iranians had nationalized the Anglo-Iranian Oil Company. The major oil companies had subsequently boycotted Iranian oil, bringing on a near-impossible economic situation in the country. The Truman administration had tried to straddle the issue. Fearing Soviet involvement if the Iranian economic structure collapsed, Truman had maintained a low-level economic assistance program even as he refused to prevent the oil companies from trying to bring Iran and the nationalist government of Premier Mohammed Mossadegh to their knees.

Eisenhower and Dulles decided very early in their administration that American policy would change — Mossadegh would have to go. Significantly, however, it was not Eisenhower's intention merely to retrieve British interests and influence in the area. Rather, the president sought to replace the British in Iran even as he replaced the French in Indochina and would try to replace the British throughout the Middle East during 1956 and 1957. There was, to be sure, the conviction that British power was forever broken, thereby leaving a politico-strategic vacuum in the area, but literally underlying these balance of power abstractions were the realities of oil. Eisenhower's election had been heavily financed by the American oil industry; and of the men Eisenhower counted as his closest friends numerous oil men, investment bankers, and other titans of the corporate world constituted a clear majority. He was, therefore, intuitively responsive to their interests and concerns, and his entire conception of the national economy and America's role in the global economy was pervaded with their views concerning free enterprise, access to raw materials, and world markets.[59] It seemed unlikely, therefore, that the dangerous implications of a nationalist success in Iran for American oil interests throughout the Middle East escaped him. And finally, the situation in Iran, if carefully orchestrated, provided an opportunity for replacing not only British political power but also its economic presence. The multiple arguments for intervention were too compelling to resist.

In March 1953 Eisenhower, Dulles, and Undersecretary Walter Bedell Smith had agreed with Eden to seek "alternatives to Mossadegh."[60] This understanding was reached after the United States had tried and failed in the first weeks of the Eisenhower administration to bring Mossadegh in line with a threatened cut-off in U.S. economic assistance. Mossadegh had responded that he would turn to the Soviet Union for assistance if need be, although he would prefer to work with the Americans. The Americans urged the Iranian premier to settle with the British, then the United States would consider further assistance. Mossadegh refused, and in early August 1953, Kermit Roosevelt, Theodore Roosevelt's grandson and the Central Intelligence Agency's primary operative in the Middle East, was despatched to Iran for the purpose of bringing down Mossadegh's government and turning U.S. support to the Shah.

The situation in Iran was seething by this time and amenable to Roosevelt's efforts. On August 19 Roosevelt, using a Teheran basement as a command post, engineered a coup.

> One authority has it that Kim Roosevelt's Iranian agents emptied the athletic clubs and steam rooms of Teheran, producing a pride of weight-lifters, gymnasts, wrestlers, and assorted musclemen who paraded through the bazaars braying pro-Shah slogans and gathering great crowds along their way. Another authority speaks of "a lumpenproletarian mob, armed with knives and clubs" moving on the center of the city. There is no essential discord. All agree the uprising brought riots, terror, violence, bloodshed, death.[61]

Within 3 days, Mossadegh had been arrested and the Shah returned from Rome where he had been consulting with Allen Dulles, the head of the CIA. Earlier on August 21 Eisenhower received a note, probably from Roosevelt, which read in part: "The Shah is a new man. For the first time, he believes in himself because he feels that he is king of his people's choice and not by arbitrary decision of a foreign power."[62] Iran was immediately extended $45 million in economic assistance, and a month later Kermit Roosevelt was awarded the National Security Medal by Eisenhower.[63]

Next the United States undertook the negotiation of a new oil arrangement which reduced substantially the British position while increasing the American share. The five major American oil companies — New Jersey Standard, Mobil, Texaco, Gulf, and Standard Oil of California — received 40 percent of a new international consortium developed to exploit Iranian oil. British Petroleum received 40 percent, Royal Dutch Shell 14 percent, and the French 6 percent. American antitrust laws were adjusted to permit the formulation of the American portion of the cartel, and Iranian oil production was carefully controlled by the consortium to avoid a reduction of world oil prices.[64]

Guatemala

The situation in Guatemala a year later was somewhat different than the Iranian case in that the regime of Jocobo Arbenz Guzmán accepted and depended upon domestic communists for support.[65] The existence of leftist and Marxist politics in Guatemala should not have been surprising, however, in view of the country's postwar history. Prior to 1954 a series of dictators had served as a governmental front for a vast concentration of private American political and economic power, the United Fruit Company. The company virtually owned the country. Since the late nineteenth century it had bought hundreds of square miles of banana-producing and nonproducing acreage, employed forced labor, and controlled the only railroad in the country. In 1944, however, the last dictator, General Jorge Ubico, who admired and compared himself favorably to Hitler, was overthrown and replaced by a military junta which included Arbenz.

Arbenz was subsequently elected president in 1951, and Marxist activity increased as the communists formed a national party in 1951 and were taken into the government. Moreover, during 1952 and 1953 heavy-handed suppression of anticommunist labor and political leaders became commonplace, although this activity cannot be dissociated from the ongoing antigovernment and anticommunist activities of United Fruit, which included the end of tourism promotion by American companies and, more important, the reduction of both international and bilateral economic assistance from the United States. In March 1953 matters came to a head as Arbenz expropriated more than 230,000 acres of uncultivated land for which United Fruit was compensated $600,000 in long-term interest-bearing bonds — the low valuation previously placed on the land by

United Fruit to escape Guatemalan taxes. The president of United Fruit reportedly remarked at this time: "From here on out it's not a matter of the people of Guatemala against the United Fruit Company; the question is going to be communism against the right of property, the life and security of the Western Hemisphere."[66]

Washington saw matters in a similar light. As U.S. Ambassador to Guatemala John E. Peurifoy described his first impression of Arbenz in 1953:

> It seemed to me that the man thought like a Communist and talked like a Communist, and if not actually one, would do until one came along. I so reported to Secretary Dulles, who informed the President; and I expressed to them the view that unless the Communist influences in Guatemala were counteracted, Guatemala would within six months fall completely under Communist control.[67]

This was hardly news to Eisenhower and Dulles. They had, in fact, sent Peurifoy to Guatemala to coordinate the activities of the CIA and other U.S. ambassadors in Central America — activities explicitly directed at the overthrow of the Arbenz regime.[68] Dulles had prepared the way in March 1953 by getting the Tenth Inter-American Conference to pass a resolution declaring that intervention against a state whose political institutions were dominated or controlled by "the international Communist movement" would not constitute an abrogation of hemisphere principles of political and territorial integrity.[69]

The coup itself did not come until June 1954, for the liberation army had to be prepared. The CIA employed Carlos Castillo Armas, a graduate of the U.S. Army Command and General Staff School, to lead a band of mercenaries from their base camp in Honduras with air support flown by American CIA pilots out of Managua International Airport in Nicaragua. Eisenhower closed a personal review of the coup d'etat plans on June 16, 1954, with the observation, "I want all of you to be damn good and sure you succeed. I'm prepared to take any steps that are necessary to see that it succeeds. When you commit the flag, you commit it to win."[70]

On June 18, 1954, Castillo Armas, driven in an old station wagon, led his would be army across the border as the CIA's rebel air force of four P-47 Thunderbolts bombed the Guatemalan capital. Little progress was made, however, as no popular uprising occurred and half the CIA's planes were knocked out of action. On June 20 Eisenhower approved the sale of two P-51 fighter bombers to Nicaragua; the planes promptly entered the liberation struggle. On the ground Castillo Armas was making little headway, but Arbenz, facing possible rebellion in his own army, capitulated

and turned over control of the government to an army colonel named
Diaz, who proved reluctant to go much beyond the abolition of the communist party.

Peurifoy, who had displayed singular anticommunist skills in similar
operations in Greece while he was an ambassador there, had had enough.
Strapping a .45 pistol to his hip and taking along his marine embassy guard,
the ambassador strode down the street to meet with the new Guatemalan
leader. As the conference proceeded, American pilots bombed the radio
station and army headquarters. Diaz then agreed that another governmental change would be in order. Within a week Castillo Armas arrived
in Peurifoy's private plane and assumed power.

The first act of Castillo Armas in the aftermath of the coup was disen-
franchisement of about 70 percent of the population. Next, an election was
held in which Castillo Armas received 99.9 percent of the votes cast.
There was no opposition. Eisenhower noted in his memoirs:

> Castillo Armas was . . . confirmed . . . by a thundering majority, as President.
> He proved to be far more then a mere rebel; he was a farseeing and able
> statesman.. . .he enjoyed the devotion of his people.[71]

This "farseeing and able statesman" proceeded to suspend Congress and
all constitutional rights, end agrarian reform thereby returning all land to
United Fruit, and end all rights and privileges of labor organizations.
Finally, Castillo Armas established a committee for defense that could
secretly name anyone, without appeal, a communist who was in turn
subject to arrest and death; 72,000 people were so named within 4
months.[72] For this display of leadership the Castillo Armas regime received $90 million in American aid over the next 2 years. In contrast, from
1944 through 1953 the leftist regimes received — apart from road-build-
ing subsidies — less than $1 million in economic assistance.[73]

Intervention and Containment

In April 1953 the President had proclaimed that among the "few clear
precepts, which govern its conduct in world affairs, the United States
counted:

... Any nation's right to form a government and an economic system of its
own choosing is *inalienable.*

... Any nation's attempt to dictate to other nations their form of government is *indefensible.*"[74]

In view of the preliminary planning then underway for both the Iranian and Guatemalan coups, how are we to explain the gross inconsistency of this statement with contrary policies already in motion?

One answer might be simply to discuss the Iranian and Guatemalan coups as sordid but nonetheless deviant cases designed to protect the particular interests of political benefactors, past business associates, present investments, or future employment opportunities. Eisenhower's connection with American oil interests has been noted. As a lawyer, John Foster Dulles had drawn up the contracts between United Fruit and the Guatemalan government by which whole provinces were turned over to the company; the assistant secretary of state for inter-American affairs at the time of the coup held a significant block of United Fruit stock; Allen Dulles, the head of the CIA, had been president of the company; and Walter Bedell Smith, the undersecretary of state, would join the board of directors of United Fruit upon leaving the State Department.

Although this line of analysis is straightforward and on its face powerful, the Guatemalan and Iranian coups must be placed in a broader context of policy development during the early Eisenhower administration. Viewed in relation to parallel events in Vietnam there is apparent a more generalized and yet systematic set of attitudes and pattern of policy with respect to political and economic change in the non-Western world. In all these instances, anti-Western nationalism and/or revolutionary leftist political activity was viewed by Washington as externally derived, the product of international communist penetration. Men such as Eisenhower and Dulles found it impossible to accept that revolutionary change in the non-Western world could result solely or even primarily from indigenous conditions. And if they did accept the possibility, such change was nevertheless a threat to their conception of acceptable political and economic order. Moreover, even if they had regarded such revolutionary change as legitimate — and there is no evidence whatsoever that they did — perceived domestic political constraints were such that they could not admit it.

In summary, then, the Eisenhower administration had begun during its first years in office to develop and elaborate a conception of containment in those non-Western areas regarded as peripheral by Kennan, Acheson, and the other framers of the containment policy. The modalities of containment in the non-Western world were as yet crude — these early coups were in most respects frenetic affairs conducted by romantic types straight out of contemporary fiction. Indeed, Eisenhower recorded in his personal diary concerning the Iranian coup, "our agent there, a member of the CIA, worked intelligently, courageously and tirelessly. I listened to his detailed report, and it seemed more like a dime novel than an historical fact."[75] The image of a Kermit Roosevelt directing a nation's destiny from a basement or an American ambassador personally conducting a coup d'etat with a gun appended to his hip is almost comical until we reflect on the consequences of their actions for the people of the countries in question. Nevertheless, their activities were consistent with Eisenhower's view that containment must be carried out at lower cost than in the Truman years if it was to be domestically acceptable. From this standpoint the immediate ends achieved, the salaries, bribe funds, limited equipment required by a Roosevelt or Peurifoy and subsequently a few hundred million dollars in military and economic assistance compared favorably to the tens of thousands of casualities and billions of dollars consumed by containment in Korea.

CONTAINMENT
THROUGH BRINKMANSHIP

The crisis of the Taiwan Strait during 1954 and 1955 is another example of the Eisenhower view of global containment. Because the crisis involved the Chinese civil war, the situation was perhaps as dangerous domestically as it was internationally. On no other issue was the Republican right more vocal; indeed, it had emerged as an important political force because of the China issue. Consequently, the contours and outcome of the crisis were shaped in part by Eisenhower's concern for this domestic right flank. The crisis is also important for through it the Eisenhower administration confirmed once again its willingness to threaten nuclear war. By the end of the crisis, Dulles would formalize nuclear threats as the preeminent component of an American-constructed peace.

The Onset of Crisis

The Taiwan crises of 1954 and 1955 did not emerge suddenly. The tensions of 1954 were in fact the ongoing essence of the relationship between Chiang's regime on Taiwan and Mao's in Beijing. During 1953 and early 1954, the Eisenhower administration announced that it was removing the Seventh Fleet from the Taiwan Straits, and, in response to strong lobbying, increasing American economic and military assistance to Chiang. The Chinese communists, anticipating increased military pressure from Taiwan, felt compelled to signal their disfavor. By midyear 1954, the communists and Chiang were exchanging threats of invasion. Air and naval incidents had gradually intensified and increased in number. In August

1954, Syngman Rhee, speaking in the U.S. House of Representatives, called for the United States to join him and Chiang Kai-Shek in a full-scale invasion of the mainland. In September 1954 the communists began shelling the offshore Nationalist island of Quemoy two miles off the mainland and the confrontation was joined.

Perhaps the most difficult aspect of this early phase of the escalating confrontation was in Washington, where Senate hawks demanded a decisive response to the communists' use of force. The Joint Chiefs recommended that the offshore islands be defended and that Chiang be allowed to bomb communist gun emplacements on the mainland as well as further inland if necessary. If this brought on a communist invasion, then the United States should join the battle. Eisenhower emphasized, however, that such a step could not be kept limited. He foresaw only two likely outcomes of such a course of action — a Korea-type engagement or world war; both were unacceptable. Nevertheless, he had to respond to the domestic pressures and his own inclination that Dulles was correct in his assessment of the situation: "The Chinese communists, Dulles said, were probing; unless we stopped them, we faced disaster in the Far East."[76] The initial American response was a proposal to submit the issue to the United Nations, but Chiang refused, fearing that the United Nations might resolve the broader question of the civil war against him. The only apparent remaining course, therefore, was the defense treaty with Chiang that was negotiated and eventually signed on December 2, 1954.

The communists may have begun their escalation as an essentially "preemptive or spoiling attack."[77] By the end of the year, however, they were confronted with a U.S. guarantee of mutual assistance to Chiang. Moreover, the public agreement remained totally ambiguous concerning the American commitment to the defense of the offshore islands and the use of force by Chiang. It is probable that this ambiguity was inevitable and consciously contrived. Eisenhower and Dulles sought simultaneously to balance the pressures of the congressional hawks who would have been infuriated by any withdrawal of U.S. support; Chiang's desire to extend U.S. commitment and involvement; and the administration's private wish to avoid precisely such involvement and commitment.[78] Eisenhower had, therefore, succeeded in the manipulation of an extremely ambiguous diplomatic and domestic political situation. But from the Communists' standpoint, the situation remained unclear, and they continued their probing. In this instance, however, their actions included the bombing of the strategically insignificant Tachen Island and an amphibious assault on the island of Ichiang near the Tachens, routing in the process a garrison of Nationalist irregulars. The Eisenhower administration now had to deal with a seemingly more dramatic escalation of the crisis. The mutual security treaty may have contained the home front, but clearly it had not stabilized the situation in East Asia.

The Crisis Goes to the Brink

Eisenhower resolved that the most appropriate response would be an embellishment of the treaty — a precommitment on the part of Congress to give the president considerable discretion in the implementation of the treaty and in meeting the renewed crisis. The resulting "Formosa [i.e., Taiwan] Resolution" found the Congress affirming Eisenhower's "inherent powers" to deal with the situation as he saw fit.[79]

The specifics were left vague and ominous, a condition heightened by Secretary Dulles in a press conference on January 24, 1955:

> Well are you going to nail your flag to this little bit of rock . . . which in fact could be pretty easily pulverized by artillery fire from the Mainland, and make that into a Dien Bien Phu? You certainly wouldn't want to do that. Nor would you want to give a notice to the communists that they can come in and pick it up without a fight.[80]

Ambiguity and its manipulation were, however, the essence of the American position. By confronting the communists with uncertainty, Dulles and Eisenhower hoped to induce caution into their behavior. Still, there was more to the Eisenhower-Dulles policy. It also sought a confirmation of the status quo in the Taiwan Straits — a cease fire — something the communists seemed reluctant to grant while the United States continued increasing the pressure.

After a trip through Southeast and East Asia, Dulles returned to Washington in March 1955, and informed President Eisenhower that the odds were even that the crisis could not be resolved without war and that war would require the use of nuclear weapons. Vice President Nixon publicly noted that "tactical atomic explosives [are] now conventional"[81] and Eisenhower seemed to agree: "I see no reason why they shouldn't be used just exactly as you would use a bullet."[82] The president's statement was qualified with disclaimers as to the difficulties of using these weapons on a battlefield; however, this orchestration of ambiguity and threat brought the crisis to a peak. The Joint Chiefs, through a public statement by Admiral Carney, chief of naval operations, recommended a preemptive strike, but American allies such as Britain and Canada stated flatly that they would not join in any fight to protect the offshore islands.

Eisenhower now found himself caught between his administration's rhetoric and domestic hawks urging escalation and America's allies who were quickly placing distance between themselves and the United States. Eisenhower reacted as he had in September of the previous year. The position of the Joint Chiefs was skillfully undercut by leaking a statement denying dire predictions of imminent aggression from the mainland (and subsequently not reappointing Carney to the JCS). Moreover, in April 1955 Eisenhower tried to deescalate the crisis diplomatically by urging Chiang to withdraw his troops from Quemoy and Matsu in exchange for an increase in the American military presence on Taiwan. Chiang demured but there was in fact no further escalation and the crisis petered out in late April 1955. The communists, like the United States, were under pressure from third parties, in this case third world countries urging a reduction in tension. Desiring greater influence with these countries and perhaps concerned about American threats, the communists relaxed the pressure on the offshore islands.[83]

An Appraisal

Dulles, would, in subsequent months, take this as evidence that the threat of massive retaliation was a viable foundation for American policy. Creating an atmosphere of risk and ambiguity was by definition dangerous, the secretary of state would argue, but it could be managed to deter your opponent:

> You have to take chances for peace just as you must take chances in war. Some say that we were brought to the verge of war. Of course we were brought to the verge of war. The ability to get to the verge without getting into the war is the necessary art. If you cannot master it, you inevitably get into war. If you try to run away from it, if you are scared to go the brink, you are lost. We've had to look it square in the face — on the question of enlarging the Korean War, on the question of getting into the Indochina War, on the question of Formosa. We walked to the brink and we looked it in the face. We took strong action.[84]

Dulles's brinkmanship in the Taiwan crisis seems to have been directed as much toward American and world opinion as toward China.[85] Dulles, it is true, tried to force a cease fire with his nuclear brinkmanship, but he also attempted to demonstrate the administration's willingness to work at the outer limits of the diplomacy of violence. A reputation for recklessness was a weapon with many surfaces. Its psychological purpose was not meant to be limited to just Quemoy and Matsu.

The pay-off in East Asia was, in fact, quite limited. Eisenhower gained through the treaty with Chiang nothing more than a formal restatement of the relationship and balance of forces that had existed prior to the crisis, an institutionalization of the status quo as it were. More important, perhaps, Eisenhower and Dulles were able to put on display in early 1955 the operational crux of the new look — deterrence by means of threatening massive nuclear retaliation. The dramatic display of will, the bold walking to the brink assumed added importance. For in the early spring of 1955, the pressures on the United States to meet the Soviets at the summit were becoming irresistible. Eisenhower and Dulles agreed with the general assessment of Truman and Acheson that if there were to be negotiations then they should be conducted from positions of strength.

NEGOTIATING FROM STRENGTH AND CONTAINING DETENTE

In mid-1955, the Eisenhower administration seemed to be making considerable headway in its effort to consolidate global containment. Paradoxically, the presumed source of America's and the free world's danger was undergoing significant changes. Stalin's death released great anxiety and confusion within the Soviet ruling elite. Fears of a coup prompted the dispersal of security troops throughout Moscow, and the members of the Presidium sought to avoid disintegration of the government by agreeing to form a fragile collective dictatorship with Georgi M. Malenkov as prime minister. By July 1953, an uneasy equilibrium of ambition and power seemed to have developed.[86] In the meantime, Malenkov and the Presidium started to de-Stalinize Soviet life and Soviet foreign policy. Ten days after Stalin's death Malenkov proclaimed that there were no disagreements or disputes between the Soviet Union and other states, but especially the United States, that could not be resolved by peaceful means. Moreover, Malenkov and the Presidium indicated in speeches to the Supreme Soviet that Stalin's preoccupation with heavy industry should give way to more attention to the production of consumer goods as well as stimulation of the Soviet Union's chronically inadequate agriculture system.

The View from Washington

Washington's reaction to the death of Stalin was, at the outset, as confusing as the events in Moscow. By the end of March 1953, Eisenhower had decided that a public acknowledgement and review of the changed circumstances was in order. In private conversations with Emmet John Hughes, a presidential adviser and speech writer, Eisenhower asserted, "Look, I am tired — and I think everyone is tired — of just plain indictments of the Soviet regime. I think it would be wrong — in fact, asinine — for me to get up before the world now to make another one of those indictments."[87] In contrast to Eisenhower's instinct to respond positively, to see in the momentous turn of events an opportunity to be seized, Secretary Dulles was prepared to stand Eisenhower's argument on its head. Yes, there was indeed an opportunity available to the United States in Stalin's demise — an opportunity to take advantage of what we saw as the fatal weakness of the Soviet or any totalitarian society — the problem of leadership transition. Dulles argued that any apparent concessions on the Soviets' part resulted "because of outside pressures, and I don't know anything better we can do than to keep up these pressures right now."[88] For months after news of Stalin's death Dulles seemed preoccupied and enthusiastic about the possibility that the new leadership would devour itself as its members struggled for power.[89]

Accordingly, Dulles fought a vigorous rearguard action against the speech. When it was clear that the president intended to give it anyway, Dulles worked to make its tone as tough and uncompromising as possible and/or to qualify it so as to render it meaningless. When the speech was finally delivered on April 16, 1954, it emerged as a mix of new hope and cold war gamesmanship.

President Eisenhower, while proclaiming that "[t]his is one of [the] times in the affairs of nations when the gravest choices must be made, if there is to be a turning toward a just and lasting peace,"[90] required of the Soviets nothing less than a renunciation and reversal of their entire foreign policy since the end of the war. He demanded that the Soviets halt revolutionary activity in Asia and Korea, all of which assumed a control of events on the part of the Soviets that they did not possess. Preconditions of on-sight inspection of any disarmament proposal ran directly counter to the known position of the Soviet Union. He tied West Germany's future to that of NATO[91] and thereby could not help but raise Soviet fears. Finally, his prerequisites concerning Germany and Eastern Europe, "free choice of their own forms of government," clearly reflected the thinking of John Foster Dulles and involved nothing less than the removal of the foundations of Soviet postwar security policy. On balance, therefore, Eisenhower saw a "chance for peace" only if the Soviets would concede — as "genuine evidence of peaceful purpose" — every point at issue in the cold war.

It is rather difficult to evaluate the seriousness of Eisenhower's overture — if it was that. Significantly, the Soviets published the Eisenhower speech in its entirety and publicly responded to it on April 25, 1953, using the front page of *Pravda* to do so.[92] But nothing else followed; perhaps it was too much to expect a breakthrough. Both governments were caught up in their respective periods of governmental transition, with the Soviets perhaps facing the more difficult task.[93] In any event, Eisenhower seems not to have expected an immediate response and suggests that the speech was as much for the record as it was a serious effort to indicate negotiations.[94] The Soviets in their response indicated a willingness to proceed to "serious businesslike discussions," but as Lyon notes, "in the White House nobody picked up the telephone."[95]

An Opportunity Missed?

Some students of American and Soviet foreign policy have suggested that this period was one of those rare moments when serious Soviet-American negotiations on the future of Europe could have been undertaken.[96] The Soviets seemed willing to negotiate, especially on the future of Germany. Even prior to Stalin's death the Soviet Union on March 10, 1952, had proposed Four Power talks on a German peace treaty and the question of reunification and agreed to the rearmament of a reunified Germany if it accepted strict neutrality and nonalignment with any block or coalition.[97] A neutralized Germany, though rearmed, was clearly more appealing to the Russians than a rearmed West Germany integrated into an avowedly anti-Soviet military alliance. Stalin's proposal for a neutral, rearmed Germany made in his last days may have been mere propaganda, but as Professor Adam Ulam emphasizes:

> the fear of a German Army backed by the United States and on the borders of the Soviet empire was a real fear felt by the Soviet policy-makers, unlike the fear, partly the product of genuine apprehension but also a bogey for propaganda purposes, of the evil machinations of American Capitalists. And to conjure away his real fears Stalin was ready to pay highly.[98]

Of near equal importance in evaluating this period of Soviet-American relations was the nature of the strategic balance between the two countries. Perhaps at no other time than between 1952 and late 1953 did the United States possess greater strategic superiority over the Soviet Union. The Soviets possessed a very limited supply of atomic weapons and no intercontinental bombers with which to deliver them. Moreover, even the Soviet explosion of a thermonuclear device, in August 1953, did not transform this situation, for it would be still another year or more before the Russians would acquire credible intercontinental delivery capability.[99] Thus, if there ever was a situation in which the United States could negotiate from strength it was during the last year of the Truman Administration and the first year to 2 years of the Eisenhower administration.

Churchill clearly thought the time was auspicious, for on May 11, 1953, he made a major speech to the House of Commons in which he called for a summit conference to seize the moment. "The great Khan is dead," he exclaimed as he suggested that although some settlement of outstanding issues as a prelude to such a meeting might be desirable, nevertheless, "It would be a mistake to assume that nothing could be settled with Soviet Russia unless or until everything is settled."[100] Churchill thought he saw "a profound movement of Russian feeling" and hoped that the West would move to encourage the positive development of this situation. During both 1953 and 1954 Soviet budgetary allocation for defense declined.[101] In Washington, however, detente would have to contend with Dulles and a curiously reluctant Eisenhower. The whole thing, Dulles grumbled, was a "phony peace campaign."[102]

By early 1954, however, the opportunity, if it had ever existed, began to slip away. The understandable American preoccupation with ending the Korean War, and Churchill's severe illness in mid-1953, worked to slow whatever thrust toward negotiations may have existed in the West. By the end of the year Eisenhower and Dulles agreed to participate in a foreign minister's conference on Germany to be held in Berlin in early 1954, but by the time the conference was under way a subtle but important shift had begun within the Soviet Union. During the Berlin conference the Russians removed their offer of a unified but neutralized Germany of 2 years standing and now advocated a settlement that would maintain the two Germanies.[103]

It is not clear in any event that the American delegation, headed by Secretary of State Dulles, was in any frame of mind to negotiate. One cannot discount the intangible impact of the ghost of Yalta on Dulles, the man who in the Republican platform had called for the repudiation of secret understandings assumed to have been made in 1945 with the Russians.[104] An incident observed by Ambassador Bohlen, who attended the Berlin conference,[105] indicates the spirit of Dulles's approach:

> At this meeting, Dulles had a Russian-speaking lip-reader watching the Soviet delegation. The idea was to find out what the Russians were talking about and possibly to pick up some secrets. I do not believe the lip-reader learned anything of importance.[106]

The Twilight of Opportunity

The stiffening Soviet posture at Berlin may have been a reflection of an evolving debate within the Presidium. Malenkov's priorities had their opponents among the military, and there were those within the

Presidium, notably Nikita Khrushchev, the leader of the Soviet Communist party, who were prepared to use these disagreements to their own personal ends.

The debate in the Kremlin leadership centered on Malenkov's downgrading of the traditional Soviet emphasis on heavy industry and his denigration of nuclear weapons as realistic war-fighting implements. In contrast, Khrushchev, though accepting the necessity for reform of the agricultural system and a better balancing of heavy industry and consumer-oriented production, nevertheless opposed Malenkov's overall priorities. Khrushchev sided with those in the collective leadership who remained skeptical of Malenkov's contention that the use of nuclear weapons had become unthinkable. As the debate gained momentum in the Soviet Union, it was fed by Dulles's statement concerning "massive retaliation" in January 1954, the rumblings of nuclear intervention in Vietnam during April and May, and then similar overtones to the Quemoy-Matsu crisis as it developed during late 1954.

Moreover, developments within NATO confirmed the central role of nuclear weapons in American strategy. In view of the new look, it was clear that the United States would not be providing increased manpower. Furthermore, the political and economic evolution of the other NATO members made it equally clear that they were not going to support higher manpower levels. The only recourse, therefore, was the implementation of the new look in Europe, that is, "a strategy based upon a tactical nuclear response to conventional aggression in order to support this objective [the defense of Western Europe] at a level of economic and manpower contributions that the allies were willing to pay"[107] — and the rearmament of Germany. The Germans unilaterally pledged not to manufacture nuclear, chemical, or biological weapons or missiles, warships, or long-range bombers, thereby making German rearmament more palatable to the French. In return, the German Federal Republic regained full sovereign status. Finally, the United States and Great Britain agreed to maintain their own military presence on the continent.[108]

In the Soviet Union, the new look, the evolving strategy of brinkmanship, a nuclear strategy for NATO, and the prospect of German rearmament could not help but reinforce those within the Presidium who argued against Malenkov. Throughout 1954 the debate intensified, and by the end of the year the alternative views were being aired openly in the Soviet press.[109] Ambassador Bohlen in Moscow reported throughout the year that Khrushchev's prominence was increasing,[110] and added that he believed the question of German rearmament might well be the decisive test of the collective leadership given the extreme sensitivity of the Soviets to the reemergence of West German military potential.[111] Bohlen advised that unless Eisenhower and Dulles approached the issue circumspectly, the Soviets would respond, perhaps in kind.

This is, in fact, what happened. With the announcement in December 1954 of West German rearmament, the Soviets moved to formalize in 1955 their military presence in Eastern Europe with the formation of the Warsaw Pact — in many respects a more tightly integrated image of NATO.[112] The debate within the Presidium came to an end, with Khrushchev supplanting Malenkov as the primary spokesman for the collective leadership. With the shift of control in early 1955, the odds in favor of serious negotiations about Germany, arms control, or any other issues may have decreased decisively. Whereas Malenkov seemed willing to accept for the foreseeable future the implications of Soviet strategic inferiority and work toward a minimum deterrence posture, Khrushchev was not. In time, Khruschev would come to display ambivalence concerning the costs of achieving anything near parity with the United States. But in 1955 one of his first acts was to increase the defense budget by 12 percent.

Simultaneously, Khrushchev sought to minimize the image of Soviet weakness. Khrushchev knew that the prospects were good that the Soviet Union would make considerable progress in developing long-range rocket capability in the immediate future.[113] Therefore, within the next few years the Soviets would be able to pursue seriously an intercontinental ballistic missile capability that might cut into the gap between the Soviet Union and the United States.[114] In the meantime, Soviet strategic capability was inferior. But Khrushchev was prepared to exploit the limited Soviet strategic capability then available to create an image of strength.

By early 1955 the Soviets had developed a marginal intercontinental bomber capability in the form of a handful of heavy bombers. In July 1955 these were dramatically put on display during Aviation Day in what seemed to be great numbers, and sufficiently impressed Western observers that they calculated that the Soviets had secretly built up a large bomber fleet. In fact, the Soviets were not building large numbers of bombers, for they were sinking their resources into missile technology. The CIA has since concluded that the image of large numbers of strategic bombers at the Aviation Day display was accomplished by overflying the same squadron of rather short-ranged Bison bombers repeatedly in a large circle at the May Day parade to impress Western military observers.[115]

The fact that the West could be so easily deceived into overestimating Soviet capability was not lost on Khrushchev. His willingness to gamble on and exploit Western gullibility and suspicion is revealing of the problem now before American diplomacy. By not vigorously exploiting the opportunities presented after Stalin's death, Eisenhower and Dulles may have undercut forces working for detente. In the place of Malenkov, they got

Khrushchev, a man who was prepared to use every opportunity including, in a figurative sense, mirrors, to gain for the Soviet Union a position of strength from which he might negotiate. This is not to say that Khrushchev was never serious in his off-and-on pursuit of detente over the next decade. However, he was clearly a far tougher adversary than Malenkov might have been simply because he, like Dulles and Eisenhower, did not believe in negotiating from a position of apparent weakness. Consequently, after February 1955 the United States and the Soviet Union were once again led by men whose behavior would, as in the late 1940s, reinforce their respective suspicions about one another.[116]

The "Spirit of Geneva"

Following the 1954 elections, in which the Democrats recaptured the House and Senate, the new Democratic leadership in Congress was urging Eisenhower toward the summit.[117] Since Eisenhower was now dependent upon the Democrats for support of his programs, he found it difficult to resist their urgings for a Soviet-American meeting. Furthermore, Khrushchev began to maneuver in early 1955 to cut away some of the preconditions thrown up by Dulles and Eisenhower. There were two simultaneous and dramatic Soviet actions. In April 1955, the Soviets requested that the foreign ministers of the four major powers meet in Vienna to work out a treaty to end the occupation of Austria, thereby neatly removing one of Dulles's preconditions to negotiations. Dulles held, however, that the neutralization treaty was one more piece of evidence that the hard line worked, for he took the treaty as evidence of the liberation of Austria.

The second major Soviet overture concerned disarmament and involved the Soviets' accepting positions of the disarmament position previously adopted by the United States. The Soviets dramatically reversed their previous policy: dropping their demand for the abolition of nuclear weapons at the outset and accepting Western European (but not U.S.) proposals on manpower level reduction formulas. Finally, they accepted the notion of international control, including some form of inspection and access to internal military budgetary processes and defense installations.[118] There were "jokers" in the Soviet proposal: a ban on nuclear testing at the outset (unacceptable to the West); the use of nuclear weapons would have to be approved by the UN Security Council (thereby subject to Soviet veto); force levels would be conditional upon the end of all overseas bases (thus the end of U.S. bases in NATO, SEATO, North Africa, and Japan); and uncertainties concerning inspection.[119] Nevertheless, they caught the United States absolutely unprepared.

There followed a good deal of embarrassed obfuscating on the part of President Eisenhower as his administration scrambled to prepare a fall-back position. The outcome was the administration's "open skies" inspection proposal. It called for the exchange of detailed information about the respective defense establishments and open aerial inspection of each other's territory. However, such information about the American defense establishment was relatively available and information about the Soviet's was not. Thus, the Soviet Union had little to gain by accepting the American proposal. Indeed, open aerial inspection might reveal the magnitude of Soviet weakness and make impossible the kind of deception engaged in during the Aviation Day fly-by.[120] The plan was unacceptable to the Russians, and Eisenhower and Dulles apparently anticipated that it would be. Eisenhower recalled: "We knew the Soviets wouldn't accept, we were sure of that."[121]

Thus both the United States and the Soviet Union approached a summit conference that had been gestating for years with limited expectations and skepticism: the Soviets in the hope that they could gain time to close the strategic gap with the United States[122] and the United States because they could not gracefully avoid going and because of their difficult propaganda position. Dulles was, as might be expected, extremely concerned that the United States not be taken in at the conference.[123] But by mid-May 1955 a summit conference became inevitable. Dulles urged that Eisenhower avoid any substantive negotiating, arguing the conference be considered the beginning of a process of negotiations, the technical details to be left to the experts (Dulles). Dulles even suggested at one point that Vice President Nixon should go instead of the president. Furthermore, it was Dulles's view that the president suppress his instinct for relaxed and open socializing, avoid being photographed with the Soviets, and where it was inevitable maintain "an austere countenance."[124] "[T]he wolf was to put on a new set of sheep's clothing," said Dulles, and then confusing the menagerie a bit, "while it is better to have a sheep's clothing on than a bear's clothing on, because sheep don't have claws, I think the policy remains the same."[125]

Under the circumstances, the conference — at least as a public relations exercise — would have to be counted something of a success. Eisenhower's open skies proposal, dropped extemporaneously and unannounced into a formal discussion on disarmament, had the desired effect: maximum press coverage, minimum Soviet response apart from momentary confusion, and a vague commitment to study the proposal. There was no movement on other agenda items, as virtually all substantive items were deferred to a foreign ministers' conference to follow in the fall. Moreover, informal discussions outside the conference meetings did not go especially well, as Eisenhower held to a minimum his social contacts with the Russians.[126] Nonetheless, in those formal and the few informal contacts that did occur, one American observer notes that the president, to the chagrin of Dulles, succeeded in "project[ing] an earnest and pacific intent, a serious yearning for conciliation, a readiness to grant the other side a rectitude no less than his own."[127] The Soviets responded with what Eden termed a "new found. . .enthusiasm for free and easy methods."[128] Virtually all observers agree that at a minimum it was a refreshing change in style for all concerned and that there was indeed a new spirit of discourse among the heads of state. On the issues, however, there was no movement either at the Geneva Conference or later at the foreign ministers' conference in October 1955.

The notion of a *spirit* of Geneva is therefore appropriate, for it conveys the idea of something ethereal and lacking in substance. There may have been opportunities for serious negotiations at the Geneva Conference. However, given the attitude with which the United States and the Soviet Union approached the conference, they were extremely narrow. In fact, Dulles was expressly opposed to substantive negotiations. It would have required a remarkable act of will on Eisenhower's part to move East-West relations beyond the exchange of good feelings and reassurances. Of course, not all the obstacles were imposed by the United States. There is good reason to believe that the Soviets sought to foster and exploit the spirit of detente not as an end in itself but rather as a defensive gambit. A *spirit* of relaxing cold war tensions is probably all that was possible after Khrushchev's faction won out and the Eisenhower-Dulles team had gone through the fires of coup d'etat and crisis during 1954 and early 1955.

The period of opportunity passed when the Soviets achieved thermonuclear status and began moving toward building their own positions of strength in 1954. Earlier, during the period of leadership transition in both countries, the United States seemed to possess the strength, even superiority, that it had deemed the necessary prerequisite for negotiations since the end of the war.[129] Kennan, in his long telegram, had argued that it was incumbent upon the United States to be able to respond to what he thought would be the inevitable domestic changes in the Soviet Union. In the early 1950s the United States possessed the military superiority to have risked a testing of the Soviets' responsiveness. But the signal that the United States was willing to move into a postcontainment era was at best ambiguous and perhaps unwillingly sent. Once Khrushchev began consolidating his power, it was no longer clear that anyone was listening. By then, Khrushchev sought to anticipate and contain the pressures in Soviet foreign and domestic policy foreseen by Kennan.

NOTES

1. Perhaps this interpretation of President Eisenhower's early administration is most thoroughly and eloquently developed by Emmet John Hughes, *The Ordeal of Power* (New York: Dell Publishing Co., 1964), especially Chaps. 3 and 4.

2. Dulles came from a family long associated with the formulation and administration of American foreign policy. His grandfather had served briefly as secretary of state during 1892 and 1893. In 1907 he accompanied his grandfather, then an adviser to the Chinese government, to the Second Hague Peace Conference of 1907. In 1917 he performed diplomatic service in Latin America for his uncle, Robert Lansing, President Wilson's secretary of state, and served with distinction as a legal adviser to the American delegation to the Versailles Peace Conference following World War I. For a complete review of Dulles' early life see Townsend Hoopes, *The Devil and John Foster Dulles* (Boston: Little, Brown and Company, 1973), pp. 9–61.

3. Hans J. Morgenthau, "John Foster Dulles: 1953–1959," in Norman A. Graebner (ed.), *An Uncertain Tradition: American Secretaries of State in the Twentieth Century* (New York: McGraw-Hill Book Company, 1961), p. 293.

4. Eisenhower's concern for his domestic flank, and specifically Joseph McCarthy, was apparent during the campaign. While speaking in Wisconsin, Eisenhower had carefully deleted an intended tribute to General Marshall. Some accounts have it that Eisenhower did this only under the most intense pressure from Republican politicians who trembled before the junior senator from Wisconsin. Nevertheless, Eisenhower would not risk McCarthy's ire, even though the man for whom the tribute was intended had fostered Eisenhower's military career throughout the war. See the account of this incident in Peter Lyon, *Eisenhower: Portrait of the Hero* (Boston: Little, Brown and Company, 1974), p. 522.

5. Hughes, op. cit., pp. 81–83.

6. Hoopes, op. cit., p. 160, paraphrasing an oral history interview with Bohlen, See also Bohlen's account of these events in Charles E. Bohlen, *Witness to History, 1929–1969* (New York: W. W. Norton & Company, 1973), pp. 309–336.

7. Joseph C. Harsch, "John Foster Dulles: A Very Complicated Man," *Harpers Magazine,* Vol. 213, No. 1276 (September 1956), p. 30. It is reported that when Dulles held his final interview with Vincent, he offered his name as a reference if Vincent wanted to use it in the future. Dulles confided to the departing official that the chief problem had been simply that "Mr. Vincent's critics in the Senate talked louder than his supporters."

8. Hoopes. op. cit., p. 160, quoting and paraphrasing an oral history interview with Bohlen.

9. Lyon, op. cit., p. 524.

10. See Richard M. Nixon, *Six Crises* (Garden City, N.Y.: Doubleday & Company, 1962), p. 97.

11. Gary Wills, *Nixon Agonistes: The Crisis of the Self-Made Man* (Boston: Houghton Mifflin Company, 1970), p. 119. Wills' essay on Eisenhower is a brilliant and perceptive piece.

12. Ibid., and Lyon quoting CBS Reports, Eisenhower on the Presidency, Part I, October 12, 1961, on p. 851.

13. Wills, op. cit., p. 133.

14. See James A. Nathan and James K. Oliver, *Foreign Policy Making in the American Political System* (Boston: Little, Brown & Co., 1981), Chapter 2.
15. Wills, op. cit., p. 131.
16. Ibid., p. 132.
17. See Morgenthau, op. cit.
18. See John Foster Dulles, "A Policy of Boldness," *Life*, Vol. 32, No. 20 (May 10, 1952), pp. 146–160.
19. Eisenhower, *Mandate For Change* (Garden City, N.Y.: Doubleday & Co., 1963), p. 95.
20. General Mark Clark, *From the Danube to the Yalu* (London: Harrap, 1954), p. 221, quoted in David Rees, *Korea: The Limited War* (Baltimore: Penguin Books, 1964), p. 402.
21. Lyon, op. cit., p. 472.
22. Eisenhower, op. cit., p. 181.
23. Lyon, op. cit., p. 534.
24. Ibid., p. 536.
25. See ibid., and Joyce Kolko and Gabriel Kolko, *The Limits of Power: The World and United States Foreign Policy, 1945–1954* (New York: Harper & Row, 1972), p. 681. Kolko adds that in view of these attacks the communist charges of bacteriological warfare assumed added credibility (ibid., fn. 10, p. 794).
26. Quoted in Lyon, op. cit., p. 541.
27. Eisenhower, op. cit., p. 185, and *The New York Times*, August 4, 1975.
28. Ibid., p. 189.
29. At the same time, however, the South Koreans were informed that the United Nations would not use force to stop them from breaking an armistice. What really emerged in the unspoken agreement between the two sides on July 19 was that if Rhee's army was foolish enough to attack the communists, the war need not be expanded if the Chinese merely pulverized the South Korean forces without involving the UNC's western divisions.
30. Republican Platform in *National Party Platforms, 1840–1968*, compiled by Kirk H. Porter and Donald Bruce Johnson (Urbana, Ill.: University of Illinois Press, 1970), pp. 497–498.
31. There had been some adjustment of the border between North and South Korea as the result of the fighting. The ROK had gained some 2350 square miles on the eastern end of the main line of resistance but lost 850 square miles to the west. Military historian David Rees is of the view that the newer line was more defensible than the old boundary (Rees, op. cit., p. 431).
32. "Message of the President: National Security," *The Budget of the United States Government for the Fiscal Year Ending June 30, 1955* (Washington, D.C.: U.S. Government Printing Office, 1954), p. M-38.
33. Ibid., p. M-39.
34. This analysis is drawn from Glenn H. Snyder, "The New Look of 1953," in Warner Schilling, Paul G. Hammond, and Glenn H. Snyder, *Strategy, Politics, and Defense Budgets* (New York: Columbia University Press, 1962), pp. 401–406.
35. Although Eisenhower and the Republicans had implied this in the campaign.
36. Dulles, op. cit., p. 152.
37. Hoopes, op. cit., p. 195, and Snyder, op. cit., pp. 408–409.
38. Quoted by Hoopes, op. cit., p. 194.
39. Snyder, op. cit., p. 436.

40. A complete account of the struggle of the army against these cuts can be found in ibid., pp. 443–455. See also Hanson W. Baldwin, " 'New Look' of the U.S. Armed Forces Is Emerging at the Pentagon," *The New York Times*, December 13, 1953, p. 5E, the *Budget for FY 1955*, op. cit., p. M-45, and Snyder, op. cit., pp. 457–460. See also the testimony of Secretary of Defense Wilson and Admiral Radford before U.S. Congress, Senate Committee on Appropriations, *Department of Defense Appropriations, 1955*, 83rd Congress, 2nd Session, 1954, pp. 2–15 and 79–91.

41. John Foster Dulles, "The Evolution of Foreign Policy," Speech made to Council on Foreign Relations, January 12, 1954, *Department of State Bulletin*, Vol. 30, No. 761 (January 25, 1954), p. 107.

42. Ibid., p. 108.

43. Ibid.

44. Robert R. Bowie interview, Oral History Research Office, Columbia University, quoted in Lyon, op. cit., footnote on p. 520.

45. Eisenhower, op. cit., p. 333.

46. Joseph Buttinger, *Vietnam: A Dragon Embattled, Vol. II: Vietnam at War* (New York: Frederick A. Praeger, 1967), pp. 797–798, and Lauran Paine, *Viet Nam* (London: Robert Hale, 1965).

47. Eisenhower, op. cit., p. 346.

48. Ibid., p. 333.

49. News Conference, April 7, 1954, *Public Papers of the Presidents, Dwight D. Eisenhower, 1954* (Washington, D.C.: U.S. Government Printing Office, 1960), pp. 382–383.

50. Eisenhower, op. cit., pp. 340–341.

51. Ibid., p. 347.

52. "United States Declaration on Indochina," July 21, 1954, in Richard A. Falk (ed.), *The Vietnam War and International Law* (Princeton, N.J.: Princeton University Press, sponsored by the American Society of International Law, 1968), p. 558. Though refusing to sign the agreement, the United States did make a "unilateral declaration in which Under Secretary of State Walter B. Smith stated that the United States will refrain from the threat or the use of force to disturb" the agreements. Smith made no reference to a North or South Vietnam, and although he refused to sign any documents the American declaration could certainly be taken as American acceptance of the politically provisional nature of the agreement.

53. "The Legality of United States Participation in the Defense of Viet Nam, March 4, 1966," in ibid., p. 596.

54. See the excellent discussion of this point in George M. T. Kahin and John W. Lewis, *The United States in Vietnam*, rev. ed. (New York: Dell Publishing Co., 1969), pp. 48–57.

55. Marvin Kalb and Elie Abel, *Roots of Involvement: The U.S. in Asia, 1784–1971* (New York: W. W. Norton & Company, 1971), p. 89.

56. Southeast Asia Collective Defense Treaty, Article IV, in Falk, op. cit., p. 562.

57. Protocol to the Southeast Asia Collective Defense Treaty, in Falk, op. cit., p. 564.

58. Kahin and Lewis, op. cit., p. 70.

59. Lyon, op. cit., pp. 497–499 and 513–514.

60. Eden, op. cit., p. 236.

61. Lyon, op. cit., p. 551.

62. Quoted in ibid., p. 552, and drawn from *Mandate for Change*, p. 165. Eisenhower claims that he did not know who had written the memorandum, ibid., p. 164.

63. Ibid., and see also Richard Barnet, *Intervention and Revolution,* rev. ed. (New York: Mentor Books, 1972), pp. 264–268.

64. See Leonard Mosely, *Power Play: Oil in the Middle East* (New York: Random House, 1973), pp. 219–222, and Lyon, op. cit., pp. 553–554.

65. Throughout the Iranian crisis, Eisenhower and Dulles had tried to tie Mossadegh's activities to the influence of the Iranian Communist Party, the Tudeh. The effort was transparent. Mossadegh's National Front coalition had repeatedly refused to include the communists. In fact, in 1951 the premier turned the army on a Tudeh demonstration against the oil companies, killing 100 and injuring another 500 communists. Once again, during the American-inspired coup attempts of mid-August, 1953, Mossadegh unleashed the army against Tudeh demonstrators. Manfred Halprin, "The Middle East and North Africa," in *Communism and Revolution: Uses of Political Violence* (Princeton, N.J.: Princeton University Press, 1964), pp. 316–319, and Barnet, op. cit.

66. Quoted by Lyon, op. cit., p. 590.

67. Testimony before U.S. Congress, House Select Committee on Communist Aggression, Hearings Before the Subcommittee on Latin America, 83rd Congress, 2nd Session, 1954, pp. 24–26.

68. See the testimony of Ambassador Whiting Willauer before the Senate Internal Security Subcommittee, 87th Congress, 1st Session, 1961, as quoted by Lyon, op. cit., pp. 590ff.

69. See "Declaration of Solidarity for the Preservation of the Political Integrity of the American States Against the Intervention of International Communism," in U.S. Department of State, *Tenth Inter-American Conference* (Washington, D.C.: U.S. Government Printing Office, 1955), pp. 156–157, and Philip B. Taylor, Jr., "The Guatemalan Affair: A Critique of United States Foreign Policy," *American Political Science Review,* Vol. L, No. 3 (September 1956), pp. 790–792.

70. Quoted in Lyon, op. cit., p. 611.

71. Eisenhower, op. cit., p. 426.

72. Lyon, op. cit., p. 614, and Barnet, op. cit., pp. 275–276.

73. Barnet, op. cit., p. 275.

74. Dwight D. Eisenhower, "The Chance for Peace," an address delivered before the American Society for Newspaper Editors, April 16, 1953, in *Public Papers of the Presidents, Dwight D. Eisenhower, 1953* (Washington, D.C.: U.S. Government Printing Office, 1960), p. 180, and Barnet, op. cit.

75. Dwight David Eisenhower's Personal Diary, entry of October 8, 1953, quoted by Lyon, op. cit., p. 552.

76. Eisenhower, *Mandate for Change,* p. 464.

77. Harold C. Hinton, *China's Turbulent Quest* (Bloomington, Ind.: Indiana University Press, 1972), p. 67.

78. See Hoopes' discussion of these factors, op. cit., pp. 268–272. The latter position was confirmed in an exchange of private understandings between Dulles and the Nationalist foreign minister that the use of force from territory controlled by the Nationalists would have to be approved by the United States.

79. "The Formosa Resolution," 69 Stat. 5, January 29, 1955.

80. Dulles press conference of January 24, 1955, quoted in Hoopes, op. cit., p. 273.

81. *The New York Times,* March 18, 1954.

82. Eisenhower press conference, March 16, 1955. *Public Papers of the Presidents, Dwight D. Eisenhower, 1955* (Washington, D.C.: U.S. Government Printing Office, 1959), p. 332.

83. See Hinton, op. cit., pp. 68–69, and Hoopes, op. cit., pp. 282–283.

84. James Shepley, "How Dulles Averted War," *Life*, Vol. 40, No. 3 (January 19, 1956), p. 78.

    In contrast to Dulles's explication of the necessary art of war prevention in the straits crisis is the note Eisenhower penned to himself when the crisis seemed most intense: "hostilities are not so imminent as is indicated by the forebodings of a number of my associates" (*Mandate for Change*, pp. 478–479) and his leak to the press in April that "the best political and military intelligence reaching the White House is that the Chinese Reds have not yet undertaken the kind of military and aviation buildup that would make an attack likely in the near future." (Attributed to Eisenhower by Hoopes, op. cit., p. 281.) Furthermore, after January the Communists had not again increased their level of threat. In fact, the probability is that they could not escalate further short of launching air strikes against Quemoy or Matsu. And, as Eisenhower noted, Chinese Communist ability to engage in aerial warfare was limited at best.

85. Hoopes, op. cit., p. 277.

86. Adam Ulam, *Expansion and Coexistence: Soviet Foreign Policy 1917–1973*, rev. ed. (New York: Praeger Publishers, 1974), pp. 539–540, and Bohlen, op. cit., pp. 354–355.

87. Hughes, op. cit., p. 90.

88. Ibid., p. 96.

89. Bohlen, op. cit., p. 356.

90. Eisenhower, "The Chance for Peace," p. 183.

91. Ibid.

92. Lyon, op. cit., pp. 533–534.

93. Ulam, op. cit., pp. 540–541.

94. Eisenhower, *Mandate for Change*, p. 148.

95. Lyon, op. cit., p. 534.

96. See especially Coral Bell, *Negotiation from Strength: A Study in the Politics of Power* (New York: Alfred A. Knopf, 1963), pp. 100–136, for perhaps the best treatment of this subject and also Ulam, op. cit., pp. 534–571. The following discussion is drawn primarily from these analyses and that of Bohlen, who was the American ambassador to the Soviet Union during this crucial period.

97. See Ulam's analysis, op. cit., pp. 535–536, and the text of the Soviet proposal in *Documents on International Affairs, 1952* (London: Royal Institute for International Affairs, 1955), p. 88.

98. Ulam, op. cit., p. 537.

99. Arnold L. Horelick and Myron Rush, *Strategic Power and Soviet Foreign Policy* (Chicago: University of Chicago Press, 1966), p. 17.

100. Winston Churchill, House of Commons debate, 5th Series, Vol. 515, cols. 896–897, quoted in Bell, op. cit., p. 106.

101. Raymond L. Garthoff, *Soviet Strategy in the Nuclear Age* (New York: Praeger Publishers, 1958), p. 23, and Horelick and Rush, op. cit., pp. 18–20.

102. Private memorandum, late April 1953, Dulles Papers. Quoted by Hoopes, op. cit., p. 173. See also Bohlen, op. cit., p. 371.

103. Ulam, op. cit., pp. 551–552.

104. Hoopes, op. cit., pp. 176–177. There was no such agreement.

105. Although he notes that he had no substantial role to play, it is noteworthy, of course, that he had been at Yalta as an adviser and interpreter, and this fact was used against him in his struggle for nomination as ambassador.

106. Bohlen, op. cit., p. 362.

107. This strategy was formally ratified in December 1954. It promptly generated turmoil within NATO over control of the nuclear trigger, an issue that would plague the

alliance for the next two decades. See Robert Osgood, *NATO: The Entangling Alliance* (Chicago: University of Chicago Press, 1962), p. 116.

108. Ibid., pp. 95–98.
109. Horelick and Rush provide a useful review of this aspect of the debate, pp. 23–26; also Mackintosh, op. cit., pp. 90–97.
110. Bohlen, p. 366; Horelick and Rush note that Malenkov was upon occasion now retreating publicly from his earlier position, p. 21.
111. Bohlen, op. cit.
112. See Malcolm Mackintosh, *The Evolution of the Warsaw Pact*, Adelphi Paper No. 58, June 1969 (London: International Institute for Strategic Studies). For Bohlen's reporting during this period see Bohlen, op. cit., pp. 366–367.
113. Horelick and Rush, op. cit., pp. 27–31.
114. Ulam, op. cit., pp. 560–562.
115. Allen Dulles, *The Craft of Intelligence* (New York: Harper & Row, 1963), p. 149.
116. Bohlen, op. cit., p. 371.
117. Alfred Steinberg, *Sam Johnson's Boy* (New York: Macmillan Company, 1968), p. 402.
118. One of the best detailed reviews of these proposals is in John W. Spanier and Joseph L. Nogee, *The Politics of Disarmament: A Study in Soviet-American Gamesmanship* (New York: Praeger Publishers, 1962), pp. 86–92.
119. Ibid., pp. 88–89.
120. Ibid., for a review of "open skies," esp. p. 92.
121. Lyon, op. cit., p. 653 fn.
122. A strong statement of this view can be found in Malcolm Mackintosh, "Three Detentes: 1955–1964," in Eleanor Lansing Dulles and Robert Dickson Crane (eds.), *Detente: Cold War Stategies in Transition* (New York: Praeger Publishers, 1965), pp. 103–120.
123. On Dulles' attitude see Hoopes, op. cit., pp. 290–295.
124. Briefing memorandum for Eisenhower, June 18, 1955, Dulles Papers, quoted in Hoopes, op. cit., p. 295.
125. Dulles Press Conference, May 15, 1955, quoted in Lyon, op. cit., p. 653.
126. Eden was especially concerned about this. See Eden, op. cit., pp. 341–342.
127. Hoopes, op. cit., p. 297.
128. Eden, op. cit., p. 341.
129. Ibid., p. 215.

Chapter 6
Crisis
and Salvaging
the Status Quo

If the vision and spirit was perhaps emerging at Geneva, the body of one of the participants soon failed. Upon returning from Geneva, Eisenhower, now 65 years of age, took a long vacation in Colorado that included strenuous and extended rounds of golf, sometimes twenty-seven or thirty-six holes a day. Suddenly, after days of trout fishing, golf, and a few hours work, the president suffered a heart attack. On September 23, 1955, the president lay near death in Fitzsimmons General Hospital in Denver. And for almost a year, the effects of the heart attack and an intervening attack of ileitis were to be apparent. In the meantime, perhaps the greatest crisis of his administration was set in motion in the Middle East.

THE SUEZ CRISIS

The Suez crisis had its origins in Dulles's and Eisenhower's obsession with international communism and their inability to grasp fully non-Western nationalism. In early 1955 the British, sensing that their hold on their base at Suez was increasingly tenuous, sought to shore up their Middle East military presence. Anthony Eden chose Iraq as the focus of his efforts in isolating the nationalist views of Egyptian President Gamal Abdel Nasser. American interests paralleled those of the British. Dulles wanted to replicate the SEATO arrangement in the Middle East to prevent communist penetration of the area. At length, in February and April 1955, an alliance — "The Baghdad Pact" — was completed that linked the so-called northern tier of states in the region, Turkey, Iraq, Iran, and Pakistan, with Britain. The United States declined formal association only in deference to the Israelis. Nasser was deeply disturbed by this instrusion of what he took to be neocolonialist meddling directed at him personally and launched a vigorous propaganda campaign against the alliance. Nasser calculated that British influence might best be offset by going to the Soviets for military assistance. After long negotiation, a Soviet-Egyptian arms deal was consummated in September 1955 — almost the very day Eisenhower had his heart attack. The Russians now had leapfrogged the Baghdad Pact defensive alliance.

Nasser attempted to maintain his image of neutrality by approaching the World Bank and the United States to gain financing for the construction of a high dam across the Nile River at Aswan. The Soviets had also offered to provide aid, but Nasser preferred to work with the West. The dam was to be the centerpiece of Nasser's plans to modernize Egypt; and, at least at the outset, the fact that he turned to the West for financing impressed the usually skeptical Dulles with Nasser's protestations of neutrality. On December 19, 1955, a tentative American decision to loan the Egyptians the money was made and negotiations were opened. Yet Nasser, suspicious of losing control of the Aswan project to his creditors, bargained slowly, a delay that was reciprocated on the American side.

Nasser now grew anxious about his loan and hedged his bet. He turned East. Nasser extended recognition to the Chinese communists as a possible alternative source of arms. Dulles, grumbling that Nasser was playing both sides,[1] informed the Egyptians on July 19, 1956, that the United States would withdraw its support from the Aswan project.[2] Dulles reportedly handled the matter with insensitivity to Egyptian pride, accusing them of blackmail and making gratuitous comments on the state of the Egyptian economy.[3] A week later, a deeply hurt and furious Nasser, in an impassioned speech, announced that he was nationalizing the Suez Canal and would operate it himself.

A crisis was now all but inevitable. Both the British and the French protested that Nasser's foot was on their necks. For Anthony Eden, his health and domestic political base deteriorating,[4] the canal seizure seemed more than adequate justification for the use of force to eliminate a menace he compared to Mussolini. But Eden's bellicosity ran counter to Eisenhower's political needs of the moment, for the last thing Eisenhower needed going into a presidential campaign was a war in the Middle East in which two NATO allies were acting in clear violation of international law. Eden, however, had lost control of his own emotions and was determined to push the issue through to a definitive conclusion.

There followed throughout August, September, and most of October 1956 frantic diplomatic activity. The Americans sought to prevent Anglo-French intervention, and Eden, in a near frenzy of persistence, pushed the crisis forward.[5] Dulles's role was that of ambivalent middleman between a president who absolutely refused to countenance Anglo-French military intervention (but seemed to acquiesce in other forms) and the British and French, who sought to pull the United States into the intervention in some form or, if they could not gain American support, insure noninterference. Dulles's ambivalence stemmed from his sympathy for the Anglo-French position, for he shared their antipathy toward Nasser's action and ideology. Moreover, he tended to view Nasser's Arab nationalism as being, if not communistic, then vulnerable to cummunist penetration. Against these forces pushing him toward intervention, however, was Dulles's position as an advocate of Eisenhower's interest, which was quite simply — no war.

The only way out of the box was to try to buy time through delay and the development of a negotiated settlement that would be nevertheless beneficial to the British and the French. Dulles proposed the establishment of a Suez Canal Users Association (SCUA) in which the users of the canal would not take over the canal but would simply join together, provide their own canal pilots, and pay tolls to SCUA. Some portion of these funds would be passed on to the Egyptians. The plan was "as any casual observer could confirm . . . possessed [of] a transparently grotesque, unreal quality,"[6] for Dulles's proposal simply ignored the political and economic claims of Egyptian sovereignty. Nasser rejected the proposal out of hand and suggested with bitter irony that in its place there be established "an association of the users of the Port of London and all ships bound for London would pay to it."[7] Eden was not sure what Dulles's SCUA proposal meant.[8] However, the British ambassador communicated to Eden that Dulles had given assurances that "the United States would *do* everything required to assert the authority of the Suez Canal Users Association."[9]

Dulles's view seems to have been designed to allow the Europeans to put whatever interpretation they desired on his ambiguous assurances as he tried to buy time and save the situation. Eden, thinking that the Americans had finally committed themselves to the elimination of Nasser, by force if necessary, adopted the proposal for a users association and took it to Parliament. During a heated two-day debate in Parliament on the crisis, Eden defended the scheme by alluding to the apparent willingness of Dulles to use force in support of the association.

Dulles, now realizing that Eden's statement placed him (Dulles) in opposition to the president, publicly reversed the ambiguous position he had taken in his private diplomacy with the British. Eden and his foreign minister, Harold MacMillan, now looking quite foolish, were plunged into a black fury. More important, Dulles's actions strained the alliance to the point of collapse, for "it cut the last remaining strands of trust and engendered an enduring bitterness."[10] The British and French now felt free to go their own way.

In late September 1956, the French, who had been supplying the Israelis with arms in anticipation of a major Israeli attack in the Sinai, decided to use the Israeli attack as a pretext for their own involvement.

By mid-October the Franco-Israeli plans had neared completion and the British were brought into the conspiracy. Between October 16 and 24, 1956, the three countries agreed on a plan that would have the Israelis attack Egypt's Sinai positions and push toward the canal. The British and French would then issue an ultimatum for the fighting to stop. The Israelis would "fail" to respond, and the British and French would then "intervene" to "protect," that is, seize the canal. On October 16 the British and French cut off the flow of normal communications with Washington, and the president was forced to employ high-altitude U-2 aerial surveillance flights over the Middle East to gain generally inconclusive information as to what was going on.

On October 23 the confusion of Anglo-French silence, a brewing crisis, and a presidential election was compounded by the eruption of an uprising in Hungary against Soviet power. For a week Dulles and Eisenhower watched what Dulles hoped would be the fulfillment of his wish for liberation, but there was little else that could be done for events were surging to a climax in the Middle East. The Israelis launched the attack against Egypt on October 29, the British and French vetoed a U.S. and Soviet cease-fire resolution in the Security Council, and joined the assault on October 31. The fighting continued for another 5 days as the Israelis routed the Egyptians and the insertion of British and French troops was carried out. While the assault on Egypt was underway, the Russians crushed the Hungarian revolt; and, on the night of November 2, Dulles, in extreme pain, entered the hospital for abdominal surgery that revealed the presence of cancer which would kill him in a little over 2 years.

At the height of the crisis, Eisenhower employed diplomatic and economic instruments against both the Israelis and the Anglo-French effort. The French and British sensibilities were important, for Eisenhower was concerned about the impact of the crisis on the alliance. The problem, then, was to end the intervention but simultaneously salvage the alliance. However, the delicacy of the situation did not prevent extreme anger and toughness on Eisenhower's part when he learned that the British and French were using force on a mere pretext without consulting their major NATO benefactor. Eden and Eisenhower had exchanged lengthy communications in the days prior to the Israeli attack, but Eden, of course, never mentioned the Anglo-French plans. When Eisenhower pieced together the Anglo-French collusion on October 30, Lyon reports, his "amiability" turned to "flint," and "the air in the oval office became briefly a blue haze. . . . The President was very angry, but it was a carefully frigerated wrath. From that moment Eden's ambitions were destined to go smash."[11] It is reported that on the next morning, October 31, Eisenhower placed a personal call to Eden and in "less official and tougher army life, tongue lashing language told the Prime Minister of his 'deep concern' over the drastic action implied by the ultimatum and its probable consequences. The Prime Minister burst into tears."[12] Three weeks later, his health broken, Eden would be ordered by his doctors to take a three week rest.

Eisenhower, in addition to verbal abuse, hit the British at their most vulnerable point — their economy. As October turned to November it became apparent that the pound sterling was under immense pressure and the United States was not only doing nothing to help but may, in fact, have encouraged the drain of reserves. Specifically, in the week of November 5 the Bank of England was forced to draw down its gold and dollar reserves by some 15 percent to meet the demands for gold and dollars from holders of sterling — more than $250 million. Much of the large-block selling was taking place in New York, and there was speculation that it was being initiated by the Treasury Department at Eisenhower's direction. Foreign Secretary MacMillan now warned Prime Minister Eden of British economic collapse. MacMillan knew that there was no help in Washington.[13] The British knew that they would receive a financial transfusion only if there was an immediate cease fire. It came on November 6.

As the crisis waned in late November and early December, American diplomacy turned to the task of patching up the damage, especially in NATO. The damage within the alliance was a complex mix of personal bitterness and the inevitable sensitivity of those who had once possessed great imperial power now being confronted with the reality of their impotence. Nevertheless, during February and March 1957, talks were held with the French and British in which much of the personal rancor was dispelled. It was clear, however, that the French, and especially the British, were rethinking the nature and magnitude of their NATO commitment. The French had withdrawn most of their conventional combat units from NATO to deal with a new colonial struggle in Algeria, and now in March the British, for economic reasons, were moving toward similar reductions in their conventional forces.

The other area in which the pre-Suez crisis status quo was threatened was the Middle East itself. As the result of Eden's foolishness, Dulles's bungling, and Eisenhower's pressure during the preceding months, British power and credibility had collapsed in the area. Eisenhower concluded that an American presence was urgently required even as the lingering problem of Israeli withdrawal was being dealt with. Thus the president went before Congress and urged the adoption of a special program of economic and military assistance in the Middle East. He asked for a congressional prior commitment "to use armed forces to assist any nation or group of such nations requesting assistance against armed aggression from any nation controlled by international Communism." This presidential discretion to use force was essential, Eisenhower argued, because the Middle Eastern vacuum had to be "filled by the United States before it is filled by Russia."[14] However, a Democrat-controlled Congress refused to move quickly on what was now referred to as the Eisenhower Doctrine.

Extensive hearings provided a forum for criticizing Dulles's behavior during the Suez crisis and the resultant disarray in the alliance. Dulles's alarmism about an imminent penetration of the area by international communism no longer rang true to some in a Congress that had been asked to prepare for the coming of the wolf almost daily for 4 years. In fact, the State Department and Dulles were forced to concede that there were no nations in the Middle East controlled by communism. Moreover, Congress, under intense pressure from American Jewish groups, refused to legitimize any effort to force the Israelis out of the Sinai. The onus fell, therefore, on Eisenhower, who publicly avowed his intention of cutting off U.S. assistance to Israel as well as eliminating tax loopholes for private American contributors to Israel's welfare. On March 1, 1957, the Israelis gave way and withdrew. Only after the Israelis moved out of Sinai did Congress pass the Middle East Resolution.

It had been a desperate fall and winter. Yet as the Washington spring of 1957 blossomed the Eisenhower administration seemed to have come through the crisis in fairly good shape. The NATO alliance had gone through a traumatic and wrenching experience, and Dulles had earned the everlasting enmity of many Europeans, but the 1957 springtime NATO conferences provided some reason to believe that relations were on the mend. Even more impressive was the way Eisenhower had moved to expand the American presence in the Middle East. Indeed, Dulles could point out before the Senate Foreign Relations Committee that with the Eisenhower Doctrine, the United States had now succeeded in closing a ring of American power, alliances, and commitments about the communist world: NATO in Europe; the Eisenhower Doctrine and Baghdad Pact in the Middle East; SEATO; the Korean and Taiwan mutual security agreements; the treaties Dulles had negotiated in the late Truman years — ANZUS and the Japanese arrangements; and finally, of course, the revised Rio Pact with its heightened defenses against communist subversion.[15] In sum, Eisenhower and Dulles seemed to have succeeded by early 1957 in institutionalizing containment on a global scale.

But beneath the image of a carefully nurtured and now stable system of containment there were signs that all was not well. The most distressing feature of this policy was the inability to grasp the magnitude and nature of revolutionary change in the non-Western world. Militant anti-Western and anti-American nationalism was consistently equated with international communism and therefore subject to unilateral American policing under such abstract rationales as the Eisenhower Doctrine. Thus, when a relatively minor domestic upheaval occurred in Jordan in April 1957 and similar unrest, at the same time, in Syria (coupled with a Syrian-Soviet arms deal), Dulles sniffed communism and Eisenhower moved the Sixth Fleet into position to intervene.

In neither Jordan nor Syria, however, did overt intervention occur. In the more serious case of Syria conservative Arab states withdrew their support of U.S. plans, pointing out to Washington that intervention against leftist Syria would merely make states such as Saudia Arabia and Jordan the next targets of Nasser-inspired Arab nationalism. There was no power vacuum and no external communist threat — both Syria and Egypt had jailed the members of their indigenous communist parties — and the conservative Arab leaders indicated that Washington might best let the Arabs work out their own respective regional *modus vivendi.* Dulles was apparently upset and puzzled by this attitude.[16] But without Arab support, American intervention would look painfully like the Anglo-French disaster of the previous year. Prudence and the need for continued American credibility seemed to dictate, therefore, a temporary tactical adjustment of the American position away from intervention and toward restraint.

THE NEW LOOK CHALLENGED

In August 1957, the Soviet Union announced that it had successfully tested a long-range intercontinental ballistic rocket. In October the Soviets orbited the first artificial earth satellite, Sputnik I; in November 1957 and May 1958, the second and third Soviet satellites went into orbit. In the meantime Khrushchev made sure, through a seemingly endless stream of interviews and public statements, that the strategic implications of this feat would not be lost on the West.[17]

The point was a simple one: Soviet space accomplishments were evidence that the Soviet Union now possessed strategic weapons delivery technology equal to and perhaps even surpassing that of the West. The fact of the matter was that this was untrue. But from 1955 to 1961 Khrushchev exploited the American tendency to overestimate Soviet weapons capability first revealed in mid-1955. Khrushchev's ability to deceive the United States was aided by the inability of the United States to penetrate with certainty Soviet secrecy.[18] Soviet rocket development seemed instantly to have compromised the entire structure of the new look. By all appearances the Soviets could now equal the American threat of massive retaliation. If this were the case, was the nuclear threat that constituted the underpinning of Eisenhower and Dulles's foreign policy any longer credible? Was it not necessary to reexamine the entire question of force in the nuclear age? Sputnik provided, therefore, the immediate fillip to a reexamination of American defense posture.

The Attack on Massive Retaliation

As early as 1956 the sophisticated army chief of staff, Maxwell Taylor, had been lobbying diligently for an army role and capability to deal with the changed strategic environment.[19] Taylor was concerned that the army was being dangerously shortchanged by the reliance on an airborne deterrent. Strategic weapons might prevent a massive general war but they could not be used believably, especially with the advent of potential Soviet retaliation, as an instrument of policy for controlling local pressures. Coup d'etats in the Middle East, insurgencies in Asia, Soviet pressure on Berlin could not be credibly countered by brandishing atomic weapons. Containment by nuclear weapons at the points where communism pressed would be like a housewife using a shotgun on a hornet that was about to enter her kitchen. It might work; but even if it did, the effects on the environment — the hornet's and the housewife's — might be disproportionate. Then again, it might not work. In which case the sting might not only be painful, but would also show the kitchen vulnerable to all kinds of similar pests.

General Taylor explained:

> In a period when the atomic air fleets of the opposing power blocs offset one another by their countervailing threats, it would seem increasingly likely that the dynamism of Communism will become more likely than ever to seek an outlet in the form of aggression with limited objectives. If such pressures are unresisted, the Free World will be exposed to loss through piecemeal erosion; if resisted, there will be the danger of general war developing out of a local "brush fire."[20]

In short, there had to be a rethinking of the concepts of warfare and diplomacy in the nuclear age.

Among the leaders of concerned scholars in this area was a young Harvard instructor, Henry Kissinger, who became director of a study group formed in 1954 of "exceptionally qualified individuals" whose mandate was to "explore all factors involved in making and implementing foreign policy in the nuclear age."[21] In a 1956 *Foreign Affairs* article, "Force and Diplomacy in the Nuclear Age," Kissinger anticipated many of the arguments he was to use later in his widely read volume, *Nuclear*

Weapons and Foreign Policy. In his article, his basic assumption was that the use of nuclear weapons was inevitable if war were to break out between the Soviet Union and the United States. The question, therefore, was how to limit the scope of the war.[22]

In *Nuclear Weapons and Foreign Policy,* Kissinger argued for a spectrum of military capability available to American policymakers: "a twentieth century equivalent of 'showing the flag,' an ability and a readiness to make our power felt quickly and decisively, not only to deter Soviet aggression but also to impress the uncommitted without capacity for decisive action." In short, a willingness to meet any level of force with at least an equivalent response,[23] including a strategy of limited war, using tactical nuclear weapons which promised "the best chance to bring about strategic changes favorable to our side" from Indochina and Korea, to eastern Europe and Berlin.[24] Kissinger wrote:

> The key problem of present-day strategy is to devise a spectrum of capabilities with which to resist Soviet challenges. These capabilities should enable us to confront the opponent with contingencies from which he can extricate himself only by all-out war, while deterring him from this step by a superior retaliatory capacity. Since the most difficult decision for a statesman is whether to risk the national substance by unleashing an all-out war, the psychological advantage will always be on the side of the power which can shift to its opponent the decision to initiate all-out war. All Soviet moves in the post-war period have had this character. They have faced us with problems which by themselves did not seem worth an all-out war, but with which we could not deal by an alternative capability. We refused to defeat the Chinese in Korea because we were unwilling to risk an all-out conflict. We saw no military solution to the Indochinese crisis without accepting risks which we were reluctant to confront. We recoiled before the suggestion of intervening in Hungary lest it unleash a thermonuclear holocaust. A strategy of limited war might reverse or at least arrest this trend. Limited war is thus not an alternative to massive retaliation, but its complement. It is the capability for massive retaliation which provides the sanction against expanding the war.[25]

By the end of 1958, most strategists in the scholarly community had written off massive retaliation as a viable strategic concept. They agreed that the United States needed a massive substrategic capability, the capacity and will to fight limited wars.[26] The only contention left centered on the point at which nuclear weapons should be introduced into a "local war." By early 1960, Henry Kissinger abjured the early use of tactical weapons and argued, instead, for a wide-ranging conventional capability so that the nuclear option "becomes the *last* and not the *only* recourse."[27]

The Notables Bless "Flexible Response"

The Gaither report, prepared in 1958 by the head of the Ford Foundation, H. Rowan Gaither, and assisted by great industrialists, eminent educators, scientists, and former high-level officials, pronounced America's defense capability to be in a desperate condition.[28] The report argued that the Soviet Union's economic strength was growing at a pace twice as fast as the American economy and that Soviet expenditures for arms were presently at least equal to American expenditures. By 1959, the report forecast, the Soviet Union would have 100 ICBM's and be in a position to attack preemptively the vulnerable U.S. strategic bomber force, docked on crowded airfields.[29] The committee recommendations implied "that the government was dangerously underestimating the gravity of the Soviet threat."[30] The Gaither Committee called for a massive defense build-up including a multibillion dollar fall-out shelter program, shelters housing U.S. strategic aircraft dispersed on civilian and military fields, and a large but unspecified sum to be spent on arms research and development. The report was laden with contingencies that pushed the total recommendation for increased spending on missile forces, strategic air command dispersion, and ground forces to over $60 billion, an increase of some $25 billion over what the Eisenhower administration had expected to spend.[31]

Eisenhower and Dulles Hold the Line

The Gaither report and the defense intellectuals were proposing an immediate shift in the American defense posture requiring billions of dollars beyond the conservative ceilings acceptable to Eisenhower. Many of those who were pushing for a reenergized defense posture were Democrats associated with the cold war from the earliest days of the Truman administration. No doubt this ingredient, plus the deep suspicion Eisenhower harbored of an unbalanced budget and what he later termed the military-industrial complex, allowed him to resist the burgeoning pressure for an increased American military capability. Eisenhower did, however, initiate a long-term process of transforming the American strategic posture by authorizing the development of a new sea-based nuclear deterrent based on nuclear submarines and the new, solid-fueled Minuteman missile. At the November 1957 NATO conference the United States urged an increase in the number of tactical nuclear weapons and intermediate-range ballistic missiles in Europe. Many in West Europe were now inclined to pursue some kind of negotiated settlement with the Russians, but Eisenhower and Dulles would not yield significantly. It was increasingly clear that "[i]nitiative had passed to the adversary. Washington was governed by old, tired, unimaginative men. It seemed a time of twilight."[32]

POLICY IMMOBILITY

All about the Eisenhower administration change was accelerating, dramatically transforming the terrain of world politics. Most important was the momentous schism within the communist world as Khrushchev's concern for Soviet strategic inferiority and preoccupation with Europe brought him into conflict with his ideologically intense and more bellicose Chinese brethren.

The last year of the Eisenhower-Dulles partnership was marked by a predictable sameness. The observer of the events in the Middle East and Asia in 1958 experienced a sensation of *déjà vu.* In May pro-Nasser Lebanese nationalists rebelled against a conservative government that announced that it would remain in power beyond its constitutional term. The Lebanese and Jordanian governments were in a state of panic, fearing imminent intervention from Iraq and/or Syria. They urged immediate Anglo-American intervention. Eisenhower decided to go in: "the question was whether it would be better to incur the deep resentment of nearly all of the Arab world (and some of the rest of the Free World) and in doing so to risk general war with the Soviet Union or to do something worse — which was to do nothing."[33] On July 15 the United States landed the first of 14,300 troops in Lebanon and the British put more than 3,000 troops into Jordan. But the crisis was more intense in Washington than in Lebanon:

> Combat marines came ashore across the bathing beaches in front of Beirut's expensive hotels. One private looked at the cluster of bikini-clad young women who were taking the sun, idly watching the operation or wholly indifferent. He put down his rifle, thoughtfully scanned the scene, and proclaimed in tones of wonder and appreciation: "So this is Eye-Rack."[34]

A compromise arrangement was worked out. The Lebanese government stepped down and was replaced by another acceptable to all parties. Indeed, Nasser had suggested precisely such a solution a month earlier. Coming from Nasser it was *a priori* unacceptable; only terms arrived at by the State Department could be regarded as legitimate. In the meantime, hatred of the United States was increased and the Arab left was driven closer to the Russians.

During the summer and fall of 1958 the Taiwan Straits crisis was rerun as the communists resumed the shelling of Quemoy and Chiang Kai-Shek dispatched a frenzied call for help to Washington. As in the earlier crisis, Dulles marched to the brink, claiming that the American commitment to the defense of the offshore islands was unequivocal and total. And once again, Eisenhower let matters ride at the outset as Dulles and the Joint Chiefs of Staff began talking privately of "no more than small air bursts without fallout. That is of course an unpleasant prospect, but one I think we must face up to."[35] Khrushchev added his ambiguous threats; naval and air incidents increased, and the world became extremely nervous. At the same time Khrushchev refused to provide Mao Zedong with a guarantee of support up to and including the use of nuclear weapons. Thus, Mao's capacity to escalate the crisis was truncated, as was in fact the entire Sino-Soviet relationship. The crisis became in turn a decisive turning point in the eventual dissolution of the Sino-Soviet alliance. In the United States, congressional and allied support for Dulles's tough posture began to break, Eisenhower apparently intervened, and Dulles reversed himself publicly and drew back from the brink. There was, the president stated, no commitment to defend the offshore islands or, for that matter, to help Chiang return to the mainland. The fundamental structure and assumptions of U.S. foreign policy remained unchanged, however.[36]

In Europe, Khrushchev had grown anxious to resolve what was for him the dangerously ambiguous question of Germany. Khrushchev's concern by late 1958 was that the West Germans, as they were integrated into NATO, would gain access to nuclear weapons. To counter this, Khrushchev had backed the proposal made in late 1957 by the Polish foreign minister, Adam Rapacki, that Central Europe be transformed into a nuclear-free area. In January 1958, Rapacki had issued through Soviet Premier Bulganin a call for a summit to discuss this and other issues.

The Rapacki proposal posed a number of difficulties for NATO planners. The elimination of nuclear weapons without a parallel reduction of manpower by the Warsaw Pact threw NATO defenses into what was deemed to be an impossible disadvantage. Nevertheless, the Soviet call for a summit conference was viewed favorably by many in Europe, especially the British. Khrushchev took dead aim at this soft spot by declaring on November 27, 1958, that he would turn over all remaining Soviet occupation functions in Berlin to the East Germans within 6 months unless there was a summit conference to create a normal situation in Germany. The image of a renewed Berlin blockade ran through Europe. Only now the confrontation would be even more dangerous. Demands for a conference rose throughout Western Europe.

Dulles and Eisenhower, once more on the defensive, sought to hold the alliance in line. Dulles was now only 6 months away from death. All who saw him were struck by his declining physical appearance.[37] Yet in December 1958 and February 1959 Dulles made two trips to Europe in an effort to hold things together. Those who met with him were awed by his courage but they, and one suspects Dulles as well, knew that he would no longer captain containment. The initiative was now in the hands of the more pliant and pragmatic MacMillan. The British prime minister, in an 11 day visit to Moscow in February and March 1959,[38] found Khrushchev willing to defer the crisis deadline as long as diplomatic movement was in evidence. Later in March, MacMillan arrived in Washington to get American consent to the arrangements. His substantive talks were all with Eisenhower who, although distracted by Dulles's desperate situation at Walter Reed Hospital, ratified MacMillan's diplomacy. A new and final phase of the Eisenhower presidency had begun.

THE OPENING TOWARD DETENTE

With John Foster Dulles dead, Eisenhower assumed personal control of American foreign policy and sought, through sheer force of his personality, to redirect American policy in the time left to his administration. The result, according to one student of the Eisenhower years, was "a turn so swift and sharp that the pattern of six years was utterly broken and the world was left in startled wonder."[39] Eisenhower's attempt to exploit personal diplomacy was paralleled by his Soviet counterpart. Khrushchev, although prone to mercurial theatricality and even boorishness, was also attempting to impose his own personal stamp on a Soviet foreign and defense bureaucracy that was, in many respects, the mirror image of that in the United States. Thus, Khrushchev's domestic needs, the bitter fight with the Chinese, and perhaps his own personal instincts as well, moved him toward a positive response to Eisenhower's new departure.

The Confluence of Personal Diplomacies

In December 1959 Eisenhower "began to reexamine the image of America across the world" and discovered that he "did not like much of what he saw."[40] Eisenhower's global perusal had mixed motivations. The 1958 election had not been successful for the Republicans, the economy was in the third and deepest recession of his administration, and Eisenhower's personal prestige among independent voters and the press had been eroded by his ambivalence toward the black civil rights movements in the

South. Sometimes reporters laughed at his circumlocutions at press conferences. References to the "program of the President" drew laughter
from members of Congress and staffers.[41] And there were jokes on television about the Eisenhower doll: you would wind it up and it wouldn't do
anything. Then, too, there was the contrast of the Russians and the Chinese, both actively on the offensive in the third world pursuing nonaligned
nations with aid offered at nominal interest and with no visible strings
attached. Khrushchev became the first Soviet leader to make diplomatic
travels abroad, leaving in his wake major loans for projects with high
visibility.[42] Similarly, China had broken her diplomatic isolation and had
begun a small, but increasingly effective effort to convince neutralist nations of Chinese good intentions.

Given the seeming loss of *elan* in America and a declining prestige
abroad, Eisenhower prepared to undertake a series of global tours of good
will. Eisenhower's itinerary took him to Europe, Asia, and, less successfully, to Latin America. It was motived by a desire to assert an image of
American leadership for the benefit of the increasingly disoriented American people and the Republican party.[43] Perhaps Eisenhower believed that
he could combat expanding communist influence by the force of his enormous personal prestige in four separate visits to all corners of the globe,
and to arrange, if possible, the beginnings of detente with the Soviets.

It was clear to Eisenhower that the ultimate extension of personal
diplomacy would have to be talks with the Soviets themselves. Khrushchev was prepared to stake much prestige and a good deal of his reputation on his ability to deal with Eisenhower. By January 1960, for example,
Khrushchev would use his relationship with Eisenhower to convince the
Soviet military to accept a cutback of about one-third of Soviet forces.[44]
But Khrushchev had significant domestic opposition to a detente with the
United States.[45] Molotov, ideologically not unlike a Soviet Dulles, writing
from exile as ambassador to Mongolia, sent an article to *Kommunnist* that
recounted the older themes of the inevitable incompatibility of communism and capitalism and the need for vigilance.[46] The Chinese proclaimed
that they were "able to see no substantial change in the imperialist war
policy, the policy of the United States Government and of Eisenhower
himself."[47] The Western press began to report the Soviet Union's internal
disagreements, and Khrushchev indicated that there was considerable
truth in them. He complained bitterly about the "libelous tales" that
"other socialist countries [China and Albania] are demanding that the
Soviet Union abandon its policy of detente." Khrushchev objected that it
was "the silliest inventions . . . that officers and generals who lost their jobs
owing to a cut-back in the armed forces are opposed to [peaceful coexistence.]."[48]

The Spirit of Camp David

Clearly, therefore, Khrushchev was taking a chance in his pursuit of detente through personal diplomacy. But his hugely successful trip through the United States in September 1959 seemed to justify the risks. Indeed, the talks at the presidential retreat at Camp David, Maryland, may have led Khrushchev, and perhaps the president as well to believe that a duopolistically managed detente was after all possible.[49] For a time, it seemed that the crucial territorial issues of the cold war might be arranged by a series of summit conferences. First there was the remarkable meeting of Khrushchev and Eisenhower at Camp David, then a series of consultations among the allies of both camps, followed by a meeting of the Big Four scheduled to take place in Paris in the spring of 1960. The planned capstone of all this activity was to be Eisenhower's visit to Moscow, scheduled to take place in the summer of 1960. It was, in short, a curious harbinger of the manner in which detente would unfold some 14 years later. In 1960, however, almost as soon as detente assumed an identifiable shape, it shattered. The most dramatic fracture was to occur with the downing of an American aerial surveillance aircraft, the U-2. For after the plane and its pilot, Francis Gary Powers, appeared in a field near the Soviet city of Sverdlovsk, the cold war reemerged as detente's nascent form suddenly evaporated — almost without a trace.

Nikita Khrushchev's 1959 visit had startled Americans.* On his arrival Khrushchev behaved as if he were running for office. He lunched with Hollywood stars Bob Hope, Marilyn Monroe, and Frank Sinatra, and had his picture taken laughing and joking with corn farmers in Iowa. Then, at the end of his journey, Khrushchev visited the Eisenhower farm at Gettysburg and played with the Eisenhower grandchildren. Both the press and the public had the impression that these two benign men, both grandfathers, had become partners for peace.

About to leave, Khrushchev delivered an amazing farewell to the American people over national television. The speech was almost completely devoid of what the Soviet premier termed the "old boring arguments of the Cold War period." "Good evening, American friends" he began. After complimenting America's "beautiful cities and kind-hearted people," the nominal leader of the world communist movement referred to scripture and Christ to explain to the American people Soviet socialism. Then, in English, Khrushchev concluded his farewell speech, "Goodbye,

*Most of the argument from here to page 235 is adapted from James A. Nathan, "A Fragile Detente: The U-2 Incident Re-examined," *Military Affairs*, October 1975, pp. 97–104, with permission. Copyright 1975 by the American Military Institute. No additional copies may be made without the express permission of the author and of the editor of *Military Affairs*.

good luck, friends."[50] Historian and former State Department official Louis Halle commented: "All this is not a dream. The record of the visit is there."[51]

It was a remarkable break with the past. Senator Stuart Symington, then a potential presidential candidate, in contrasting the domestic change that accompanied the Soviet premier's visit, averred that if Harry Truman had invited Stalin to dinner at the White House, he would have been impeached.[52] To Halle, the Khrushchev trip signified no less than the end of the cold war. "All that remained," Halle wrote, "was to put it into practice."[53]

THE OLD REFLEXES REEMERGE

Yet almost as soon as Khrushchev departed, the spirit of Camp David appeared steadily less substantial. To be sure, there was some initial appearance of forward movement at the disarmament meeting in Geneva. On February 16, 1960, the Soviets proposed that Western inspection teams be allowed to visit "the site of virtually any earth tremor in the Soviet Union in order to see if this was due to natural causes or an atomic test." To the British prime minister, Harold MacMillan, this offer seemed to be a "complete reversal of the previous Soviet position." But MacMillan sensed an inexplicable lack of interest by the United States.[54] By March the reaction of many American officials to the prospect of negotiation seemed increasingly unenthusiastic. Secretary of State Christian Herter confessed to the Senate Foreign Relations Committee on March 22, 1960, that "I am frank to admit I'm not too optimistic that the summit will produce very great results."[55] Herter told the Senate the most that could be reasonably expected from a summit meeting would be the beginning of the shaping of the guidelines that would set the framework for protracted negotiations, at lower levels, on substantive matters. Herter emphasized, however, that even in the context of a very tentative first step, the May summit was a "gamble."[56] Clearly, the atmosphere of good will at Camp David had begun to dissipate.

In part, the hardening of the American position was a response to pressure from America's allies. The French were apparently most responsible for the delay between Khrushchev's visit in September 1959 and the Paris Summit in May 1960. Both Eisenhower and Khrushchev had expected to meet again soon, first in Paris and then in Moscow sometime in early summer. But President De Gaulle wanted time to consolidate his domestic position and, moreover, he wished to negotiate only after there had been a successful test of France's new atomic bomb. De Gaulle did not want to be excluded from great conferences and, following the reasoning of British labor leader Aneurin Bevan, who had argued earlier that the British bomb allowed England not to stand "naked at the conference chamber,"[57] De Gaulle, too, desired a nuclear fig leaf.[58] De Gaulle's principal purpose, however, in seeking the delay was to undercut the beginnings of a great power condominium — a situation in which France, in or out of an atomic loin cloth, would not be relevant. De Gaulle calculated that he could successfully delay the summit so that it would have to be placed in the shadow of a presidential election in order that it would be less likely that a lame duck president could be able to undertake any startling innovation with the Russians.

In the meantime, Khrushchev let the timing of his November 1958 6 month deadline on Berlin become ambiguous.[59] He told the East Germans that "the conditions are not yet ripe for a new scheme of things." The date for a final settlement had become open-ended with the September 1959 meeting at Camp David. But instead of seizing upon this element of apparent retreat, the State Department, concerned about how to ameliorate fissures in the alliance and worried about long-range Soviet intentions, chose to respond as if a final treaty might still be signed by Khrushchev. A final treaty meant that Germany would be permanently divided, and that Soviet claims in Eastern Europe would gather some additional legitimacy. But to acknowledge the Soviet position in Eastern Europe threatened Western unity because it could weaken the German Federal Republic under Konrad Adenauer. Adenauer's Germany held an enormous number of displaced Germans who had fled before the Russians entered middle Europe in the last days of World War II and who had escaped the comparatively harsh conditions of East Germany via Berlin. Each year some 300,000 East Germans had escaped to the miraculously prosperous West Germany of the late 1950s. By late 1959 some 3 million East Germans had come to West Germany by the Berlin route alone. The West's nonrecognition of the Soviet position in East Germany and Poland, but tactical inaction about pushing the Russians out, stabilized internal West German affairs by pacifying somewhat Germans separated from their traditional lands, and yet managed to dangle in front of displaced Germans the image of a Russian conqueror who held these territories, making it seem that the only remedy could be found in the context of a Western alliance. But whenever talk in the West turned to "disengagement" or some other form of settling World War II, Adenauer conjured up the memory of Rapallo, the startling Soviet-German relationship of the 1920s. And nobody in Western Europe or the United States desired that kind of reversal.[60] Adenauer did not even want the issue of Berlin brought up, and counseled that the only permissable and fruitful issue that might be discussed at Paris would be disarmament.[61]

To meet these fears, real and imagined, Undersecretary of State C. Douglas Dillon spoke before the AFL-CIO conference on world affairs and warned Khrushchev that by threatening a separate peace with the GDR he was "skating on very thin ice:"

> Germany . . . represents a critical test of Soviet good faith. . . . [T]he problem of Germany and Berlin can only be solved through German reunification. This the Soviets have so far rejected. . . . But we cannot abandon our goals. . . . It would be highly optimistic to pretend that the prospects of . . . agreement are bright. . . . [But i]s the Soviet Union willing to remove its forces from East Germany and the East European countries on which they are imposed? Is it willing to grant self-determination to the East Germans and to permit the people of the Soviet-dominated states in East Europe to choose their destiny? Is it willing to abandon the fiction of a separate north Korea and permit the entire Korean peoples to reunite? We . . . know that to the Soviet Union "peaceful coexistence" . . . includes the use of military force whenever it suits their purpose.[62]

The tone of Dillon's speech seemed to indicate that Berlin would be placed in the context of all the outstanding issues between the Soviets and the United States since World War II — even the nature of world order itself was on the table. Similar statements made by Secretary of State Herter and Vice President Nixon made it obvious that the United States intended in no way to move away from its Berlin stand of the past. The Soviets, through a variety of channels, expressed dismay at this toughening of the American position in the wake of Camp David and on the eve of the Paris summit.[63]

THE CURIOUS DEATH
OF DETENTE: THE U-2 INCIDENT

Fourteen days before the scheduled conference in Paris, on the morning of May 1, over Sverdlovsk, a large industrial area in the Urals, 1200 miles deep in the Soviet Union, there appeared a black plane with a peculiarly large tail and enormous wings. The pilot, Francis Gary Powers, carried two military identification cards, a U.S. and an international driving license, a Selective Service card, a Social Security card, a PX ration card, a medical certificate, two flying licenses, American dollars, French francs, Turkish currency, Italian lira, German marks, Soviet rubles, two gold watches, gold coins, and seven gold rings, as Khrushchev put it sarcastically, "for the ladies."[64] Indeed, Powers was a multilingual billboard for

American espionage. Along with his pistol with a silencer, morphine, and flares, he also carried a "large silk American flag poster" in fourteen languages reading "I am an American and do not speak your language. I need food, shelter and assistance. I will not harm you. I bear no malice toward your people. If you help me, you will be rewarded."[65] Somewhat incongruously, he also had a needle dipped in curare. The U-2 also contained a destructor unit with 2½ pounds of plastic explosive activated by a delayed timing switch. If the pilot were to use his ejection seat, the destructor button would be set off automatically.[66]

It is not clear how the plane descended to earth. The Soviets claim that they shot it down. But the photographs of the wreckage showed neither bullet nor rocket damage. So much of the plane was intact that the lettering U-2 could plainly be seen on the huge fragment of the plane's fuselage and tail displayed in Gorky Park in Moscow. Eisenhower was told by the Joint Chiefs and the CIA that the plane "would virtually disintegrate" in the event of a "mishap," so "fragile" was the plane's construction.[67] When Khrushchev announced that "the uninjured pilot of a reconnaissance plane, along with much of his equipment was intact, was in Soviet hands," Eisenhower was flabbergasted. It was, he wrote, "unbelievable."[68]

Powers was paid a salary of almost $30,000 a year to steer an aircraft from Pakistan to Norway by way of the Soviet Union.[69] His high pay was presumably a reflection as much of the risks of his profession as his skill. Moreover, *Aviation Week,* the prestigious aerospace trade journal, noted that Powers's "embarrassing survival was not in the best tradition of the USAF which trained him or the CIA who employed him."[70] When Powers parachuted to earth he should have had, by the code of his profession, only two possible distinguishing characteristics. He could have been "deniable" and he could have been dead — or, and perhaps preferably, he could have been both. Powers contends that his instructions were that if he were caught he could "tell them everything" he knew, because they could probably get it out of him anyway. The non-use of the curare needle with which Powers was supplied was also supported in the CIA public statement upon his release.[71] In any case, he should not have been caught, and if caught he should not have talked and talked and talked.

The Paris Summit Is Aborted

On May 5 Khrushchev announced to the Supreme Soviet that an aircraft had penetrated Soviet airspace but neglected to mention that Powers or much of his plane and equipment were intact and in Soviet hands. Khrushchev asked, "Who sent this aircraft across the Soviet frontier? Was it the

... President? Or was this token aggressive act carried out by Pentagon militants?"[72] Lincoln White, the Department of State spokesman, responded to Khrushchev emphatically, "There was absolutely no — n–o —, no deliberate attempt to violate Soviet airspace. There has never been."[73] But on May 7, Powers was shockingly produced, alive. Khrushchev claimed, however, that he was prepared to grant that the president had no knowledge of a plane being dispatched to the Soviet Union and failing to return.[74]

The American response was hardly a disavowal.[75] On May 11, just 4 days before the conference was scheduled to open and 6 days after Khrushchev had asked the president to tell him it was not true that it was he who was responsible, Eisenhower spoke to the American people saying the U-2 flight and flights like it were a "vital necessity" because the Russians "make a fetish of secrecy and concealment." And echoing a statement by Secretary of State Herter on May 9, he indicated that the flights would be continued.[76] Walter Lippman commented, *"To avow* [emphasis his] that we intend to violate Soviet sovereignty ... makes it impossible for the Soviet government to play down this particular incident because now it is challenged openly in the face of the world. It is compelled to react because no nation can remain passive when it is the avowed policy of another to intrude upon its territory."[77] Nonetheless, Khrushchev still insisted that he would come to Paris. When asked in an informal conference in Moscow on May 11 if "this plane incident [will] influence Soviet public opinion when Mr. Eisenhower visits Moscow," Khrushchev replied, "I can only say the Soviet people ... are very polite, so there will be no excesses, but questions will be asked. . . . The people will say, 'Are you nuts?' " But, he assured the president again, "our people are courteous, they let off steam in words and leave the government to act. They will not indulge insulting behavior."[78]

But on May 16, Khrushchev, pale and with shaking hands, appeared in front of world television at a Paris news conference side by side with his splendidly decorated defense minister, Marshall Rodin Malinovsky, and proceeded to roast President Eisenhower, who Khrushchev claimed was like "a thief caught red-handed in his theft. . . . The President," Khrushchev demanded heatedly, "must apologize for his wrong and punish his responsible confederates, if a meeting would proceed." It was not certain, by now, if Khrushchev could have proceeded even if he had wished. According to Bohlen, who was at Paris, "Khrushchev had come to Paris determined to get an apology."[79] And if he could not elicit Eisenhower's regrets, then Khrushchev, speculated Bohlen, "was not authorized to participate in the conference."[80] Khrushchev recalled in his memoirs that "I went out of my way not to accuse President Eisenhower in my own statements. As long as [he] was dissociated from the U-2 affair, we could continue our policy of strengthening Soviet-U.S. relations." But Eisenhower publicly acknowledged that "he had known about the U-2 flight in advance and he had approved it. . . . It was no longer possible for us to spare the President. He had, so to speak, offered us his back end, and we obliged him by kicking it as hard as we could."[81]

At Paris when Khrushchev personally demanded of Eisenhower a formal apology and assurances of no more American reconnaissance flights over Russia, he said his interpreter overheard Eisenhower ask Secretary of State Herter, "Well, why not? Why don't we go ahead and make a statement of apology?" Herter said no — and he said it in such a way, with such a grimace on his face, that he left no room for argument on the issue. Khrushchev said that this incident demonstrated that "if Eisenhower had followed his own good instincts and used his considerable intelligence, he would have done the right thing and given in to our demand . . . but unfortunately Eisenhower wasn't the only one who determined foreign policy for the United States."[82]

Eisenhower did start to edge away from his position of May 11, that espionage was "a distasteful but vital necessity."[83] But it was too late. Khrushchev had already asked in a press conference that Eisenhower's visit be "postponed" until "conditions for the visit . . . mature."[84] After a 36-hour delay, perhaps waiting for Eisenhower to change his position, Khrushchev departed, saying that he hoped he would be able to deal with the new administration more successfully than he had with Eisenhower.[85]

The whole period from the meeting at Camp David, Maryland, to the Paris spring seems, in retrospect, almost fantastic. Suddenly, the promise of peace was dashed and Eisenhower would write: "the Paris summit, had it been held, would have proved to be a failure and thus would have brought the free world only further disillusionment."[86] Eisenhower may have meant by this cryptic remark that the Russians were given little choice after his May 11 speech except to break off discussion or make vastly increased demands; thus the conference could not have been a success, for it could not attend to the mutual interests of both nations. Eisenhower tried not to appear overly agitated that no conference took place. And it was with obvious pride that Secretary of State Herter told the Senate Foreign Relations Committee: "One of the most impressive things I have ever seen was the meeting of NATO that took place after the aborted, so-called summit conference. I have never seen such unanimity, such firmness, such determination, as exhibited at that meeting."[87]

The Strange Odyssey of Francis Gary Powers

Did the U-2 rescue Americans from a conference with which they had decided not to go forward? Adlai Stevenson summarized the Paris conference: "We handed Khrushchev that crowbar and sledge-hammer to wreck the meeting."[88] Is it plausible that the U-2, to use a favorite expression of Marshall Stalin, was "not accidental"? This was clearly one of the suspicions of Khrushchev. He recalls that he was "haunted by the fact that just prior to this meeting the United States had dared to send its U-2 reconnaissance plane against us. It was as though the Americans had deliberately tried to place a time bomb under the meeting, set to go off just as we were about to sit down with them at the negotiation table."[89]

The anomalies surrounding the U-2 flight are numerous. First, there are unanswered questions concerning the altitude of the plane, whether it was in fact shot down, and why it landed in such pristine condition.[90] Second, there is the problem of the curious timing of the flight, shortly before a summit conference, a schedule all the more strange because previous U-2 flights had been cancelled before and during no more important diplomatic events than the Paris conference.[91] Third, Powers told all to a crowded courtroom full of reporters, but 21 months later was retrieved by the CIA in exchange for Rudolph Abel, widely reported to be the most important Soviet agent ever captured in the United States.[92] Finally, few questions were asked by Congress on the day Powers gave public testimony to the Senate about his performance, testimony preceded by a still secret briefing provided by CIA chief John McCone. Moreover, Gary Powers was rewarded on returning home with the highest honor the CIA can bestow — the Intelligence Star — and given a comfortable job that lasted some years as a test pilot for the Lockheed Aircraft Corporation, which built the U-2.[93] As MacMillan noticed on May 8, 1960, "It seemed a very queer story," to say the least.[94] The complex truth of the U-2 incident and the Paris conference may never be known. MacMillan felt that the situation might have been "retrieved" if it had not been for Eisenhower's "unlucky admission."[95] It is reasonable to suppose that Eisenhower felt he had little choice but to confess that he had responsibility for the flights; after all, he was the top civilian and military administrator. Nevertheless, suspicion remains that the conference was one that Americans had apparently initiated and then took advantage of every device to see that it was unsuccessful. Investigative reporters Wise and Ross concluded: "By lying, when it could have remained silent, by admitting it had lied, by disclaiming Presidential responsibility, then admitting Presidential responsibility, and finally by implying the flights would continue, the United States all but made it impossible for the summit meeting to take place."[96] As De Gaulle summarized, "Khrushchev *does* want detente — *does* want disarmament; ... but ... except perhaps for Eisenhower, the Americans want neither."[97]

Nor has the passage of time diminished the curious nature of the U-2 incident. Thus as he was leaving the Senate in 1975, Senator J. William Fulbright observed:

> [W]hen Khrushchev came here in '60, he had it in mind to seek what we would now call detente, so as to devote more Soviet resources to Soviet development. I often wondered why, in the midst of these efforts by President Eisenhower and Khrushchev to come to some understanding, the U-2 incident was allowed to take place. No one will ever know whether it was accidental or intentional.[98]

Gary Powers seemed like a human monkey wrench tossed into the emerging East-West relationship and then, later, unaccountably retrieved and refurbished. When the U-2 went down, there was indeed some private speculation, in Eisenhower's words, that the president had been the "victim of overzealous subordinates." Eisenhower denied this. "After all," he pointed out, since he had approved the flights in principle he "did not want it to appear that [he] could not, in important matters ... speak authoritatively" for the United States.[99]

Denouement

The effect of the U-2 was dramatically and immediately apparent. On May 14, *the day before* the conference ended, but when all the heads of government were in Paris, the American secretary of defense announced a worldwide military alert as a "sound precautionary measure."[100] In Washington, the Joint Chiefs interpreted Gates' message to mean that a "type 3" nuclear alert was called for.[101] Walter Lippman despaired:

> On Sunday night Mr. MacMillan and General De Gaulle were still struggling to find some way out of the affair of the spy plane. Yet this was the time chosen by the Secretary of Defense to stage a worldwide readiness exercise which, though not the last stage before actual war, is one of the preliminary stages to it.
> Why Sunday of all days? ... The timing of the exercise was just a shade worse than sending off the U-2 on its perilous mission 2 weeks before the summit. The timing of the so-called exercise makes no sense whatever. For if the alert was concerned with a possible surprise attack, when in the name of common sense could there be less danger of a surprise attack on the Western World than when Mr. K. in person was in Paris?[102]

On Tuesday, May 18, an irate Khrushchev, with Malinovsky at his side, berated Eisenhower: he was ready, he boomed, "to divest the Western powers of the right to have occupation troops in Western Berlin. And when we see fit we shall take up our fountain pens from our pockets — the drafts are all ready — sit down, sign and make the announcement."[103] Khrushchev's parting shot at Paris apparently terrified Western leaders. He used incredibly insulting language, being particularly abusive toward the German "bastards" of the Adenauer regime. MacMillan reported to the cabinet that British correspondents, "especially the Left Wing papers [were] really shocked."[104] To MacMillan and the British press it was reminiscent of Hitler at his worst.

The position of the United States and the West hardened to what appeared to be a renewed Soviet offensive led by a man whose posture as an effective diplomatist paled beside the memory of his insults at Paris delivered with an unblinking and obviously approving representative of Soviet military power at his side. Indeed, enthusiasts for all-out preparedness such as columnist Joe Alsop used the incident to demand that the "facts be faced . . . appropriations are needed to speed . . . reconnaissance satellites . . . and the B52H bomber."[105] To some, the results of the Paris meeting seemed no surprise. Defense Secretary Gates testified at the official summit post mortem, "In January I repeat[edly] stated we didn't expect to have any significant substantive conclusions. We believe there was a tactic on the part of the Soviet Union. We didn't know how long it would last . . .[106] [so] as late as April we went back with a major revision in our military programs to the appropriations committees."[107]

THE MORE THINGS CHANGED . . .

With the collapse of the Paris summit conference, the Eisenhower administration's capacity to pursue detente or, for that matter, his personal diplomacy vis-à-vis America's allies was circumscribed. Anti-American demonstrations in Tokyo forced cancellation of his trip to Japan. His ability to deal with the Russians on any basis other than by means of the traditional cold war modalities had ended. The opening of lines of communication by means of personal diplomacy required above all else the credibility of the instrument of personal diplomacy. But Eisenhower's personal credibility with Khrushchev had been shattered by the U-2 incident. Indeed, continued positive interaction with Eisenhower was a liability for Khrushchev: the U-2 and the aborted summit conference made Khrushchev's personal diplomatic efforts suspect to Soviet hardliners and to the Chinese, who were now prepared to bring their feud with Moscow into the open.

Moreover, the Twenty-second Amendment, with its prohibition on presidential succession after two terms, now decisively entered into the picture. The Eisenhower administration would, of necessity, pass from the scene within a matter of months. In the meantime, Khrushchev could simultaneously refuse to deal with Eisenhower and attack him, thereby underscoring the president's impotence. Khrushchev's ebullient and sometimes belligerent personality had, therefore, a clear field during the election and transition period. And he exploited the situation to its fullest by berating Eisenhower but also trying to replace detente on the agenda of the incoming administration.

For its part, "the Eisenhower administration ran steadily down like a tired clock, its energies spent, its coherence blurred."[108] Under the circumstances, it fell back reflexively upon the cold war stance of the Dulles years. A potential reversal of the idiom of the cold war had been halted by the peculiar events leading to the May summit meeting of 1960. The U-2 scuttled a conference from which many in the West had concluded that no profit could be secured. But given the competitive East-West relationship, the symbolic importance of Berlin, the reliance of NATO on West Germany's ground forces, and the massive reassurances continually required by Adenauer, it was surprising that a fruitful meeting in Paris could have been contemplated.

CONCLUSION

All diplomatic innovations contain dangers. Eisenhower's attempt to reach a settlement of the major issues of the cold war was a great departure. But Eisenhower's effort risked fracturing the Atlantic alliance. And Eisenhower's pursuit of detente had the potential of reawakening domestic sensitivities dormant since Senator McCarthy's censure. A healthy, although somnolent tone had been restored to American domestic political life. Eisenhower's new moves toward rapproachment exposed his administration to charges at home that he was betraying the widely accepted American vision of world order based on containment for a vague arrangement with the Kremlin. Thus, it may be that even Eisenhower was relieved that a fruitful dialogue at the Paris conference was precluded by the U-2 incident. In any case, Eisenhower was locked in by events and his advisers into making the best of the situation. After all, the last years of Eisenhower's administration were plagued with charges that the president did not or could not take active charge of policy. Rather than succumb to these humiliating allegations and unwilling to gamble rupturing the consensus of his administration or risk fissures in the Atlantic alliance,

Eisenhower perhaps decided to foreclose the possibility that the cold war would be ended during his tenure.

In this respect the last phase of the Eisenhower presidency was the captive of its earlier successes. It was Eisenhower's objective to preserve containment not only in the face of the perceived threat of international communism but at home as well. Domestically, the threat was twofold. Eisenhower defended, on the one hand, against anticommunist zealots whose militancy was ultimately rooted in an isolationism that wanted to get what seemed to be an inevitable struggle with the devil over with and then retire behind the oceans. On the other hand, there was the economic and spiritual weariness of a country that wanted no part of containment if it meant more Koreas.

To preserve containment, Eisenhower and Dulles constructed a ring of commitments around the perimeter of a communist world that, by the end of the 1950s, was fractious and preoccupied with its internal problems but perceived by the United States as being monolithic and expansive. The circle of treaties, guarantees, and bases were predicated on clear American strategic superiority. The United States seemed to possess, especially at the outset of the Eisenhower and Dulles years, the requisite strength to negotiate the issues of the cold war, but the second phase of containment by Kennan never took place:

> The failure consisted in the fact that our government, finding it difficult to understand a political threat as such and to deal with it in other than military terms, and grievously misled, in particular, by its own faulty interpretations of the significance of the Korean War, failed to take advantage of the opportunities for useful political discussion when, in later years, such opportunities began to open up, and exerted itself, in its military preoccupations, to seal and to perpetuate the very division of Europe which it should have been concerned to remove. It was not "containment" that failed; it was the intended follow-up that never occurred.[109]

But in relying on the maintenance of a policy implemented through the threat of war, Eisenhower, perhaps unwittingly, institutionalized the very thing against which he would warn the nation in his farewell address:

> We have been compelled to create a permanent armaments industry of vast proportions. . . .
> This conjunction of an immense military establishment and a large arms industry is new in the American experience. The total influence — economic, political, even spiritual — is felt in every city, every statehouse, every office of the federal government. We recognize the imperative need for this development. Yet we must not fail to comprehend its grave implications.

Our toil, resources, and livelihood are all involved; so is the very structure of our society.

In the councils of government we must guard against the acquisition of unwarranted influence, whether sought or unsought, by the military-industrial complex. The potential for the disastrous use of misplaced power exists and will persist.[110]

An irony of the Eisenhower-Dulles era, therefore, is that although there was no war during their stewardship, their most significant legacy to America was an institutionalized cold war. And not the least of its manifestations and consequences was the massive and potent union of U.S. government and private politico-economic power necessary to wage that cold war and man the defenses of containment — a joining of public and private power that would, as Eisenhower, Dulles, and Taft feared, come to dominate the institutions and spirit of America during the next decade.

There was an additional, external legacy in Eisenhower and Dulles's policy of institutionalized and globalized containment. By failing to distinguish international communism and nationalist and/or anticolonial revolution, by seeing the latter as indistinguishable from the former, Eisenhower and Dulles set American policy against the nationalist revolutions of the non-Western world. There was much of real and imagined economic necessity in this: the presumed need for raw materials, export markets, and the implied integrated world economy built on low tariffs and the free flow of U.S. private investment.[111] But this was very quickly subordinated to the incompatible imperatives of what was thought to be a more immediate threat: the penetration of the global political economy by international communism *through* these anti-Western nationalist revolutions. Thus, Ho, Nasser, Mossadegh, Arbenz, and the mobs that attacked Richard Nixon in Venezuela in 1958 were not viewed as primarily products of a collapsing colonial and traditional milieu, they were instead the political and even military instruments of communism.

The threat of massive or tactical nuclear retaliation based on U.S. strategic superiority could check communist expansion in Europe or the Taiwan Straits, but in the third world something else was required if Korea was not to be replicated. The answer was intervention in a counterrevolutionary mode. The form of intervention was often crude, as in Lebanon, Iran, or Guatemala. Such intervention, although it did not always work, was nevertheless relatively cheap. But by the end of the Eisenhower-Dulles era, a somewhat more sophisticated range of instrumentalities was being employed, including the use between 1952 and 1959 of $37.3 billion in foreign aid, of which almost $21 billion was military assistance in support of essentially counterrevolutionary regimes on the periphery of the communist world and incorporated into Dulles's alliance system. Moreover, the economic aid was usually structured, as in Vietnam after 1956, to benefit those most likely to resist revolutionary activity.[112]

Nevertheless, the thrust of the Dulles-Eisenhower effort was the politico-military containment and suppression of non-Western political, social, and economic revolution. Economic instruments were simply not, in the emerging view of the 1950s, sufficient in themselves to this great task. As in Europe and Japan, American power supplemented by economic and military aid would establish the political preconditions for world economic order, integration, and stability. In this respect, what Eisenhower and Dulles tried to do in the non-Western world was merely an extension of what Truman, Marshall, and Acheson saw themselves doing in Europe after World War II. The legacy for the 1960s was that insofar as Eisenhower and Dulles succeeded, they set their faces and the face of American power against history. They were, at least superficially, successful in the short run of their 8 years. But in the meantime, revolutionary forces were growing, and the 1960s would demonstrate that American political and military power was ultimately and tragically limited in its ability to contain them.

TRANSITION

During the 7 months following the collapse of the Paris summit conference, Khrushchev held the diplomatic initiative. As the attention of the American people turned to the presidential campaign between Richard Nixon and John Kennedy, the Soviet leader unleashed a frequently vicious diplomatic offensive directed at the hapless Eisenhower administration. At the same time Khrushchev indicated a willingness to renew the quest of detente with a new administration, especially if it was Democratic.

For the balance of 1960, however, the Eisenhower administration fought a diplomatic holding action in a world that seemed perpetually in turmoil. The worst of it exploded in the newly independent Congo, where rape, riot, murder, mayhem, and eventually civil war accompanied the departure of Belgian colonial rule. The flood of anarchy in the Congo, it was feared, might spread to any one of the recently independent nations of Africa. Seventeen nations gained independence in 1960 alone, and the precedence of chaos and savagery in the Congo appeared to incite great power conflict.

When the Congolese army mutinied, Prime Minister Patrice Lumumba appealed to the United Nations to restore order. He also appealed to the Soviet Union, which MacMillan believed was "sinister evidence of his sympathies."[113] Acting under a Security Council resolution, in which the Soviets concurred, the United States airlifted Tunisian and Moroccan troops into the Congo and provided these troops with relief food, airplanes, and helicopters and sent a U.S. aircraft carrier to the mouth of the Congo River. In September, UN Secretary General Dag Hammarskjold reported that Soviet flyers and military personnel might begin operations to support Lumumba. To Eisenhower, the Soviet presence was "an invasion" that the United Nations, shored up by American support, was obligated to resist.[114] More UN peace-keeping troops arrived and attempted to keep order between the central government of the Congo and the secessionist factions. In this confused situation the pro-Western Colonel Joseph Mobutu gained power and demanded that the Russian advisers leave, in MacMillan's words, "Lock, stock and barrel . . .; it is too good to be true!"[115]

The situation in the Congo sputtered on but at the high point of the crisis, MacMillan, known for his unflappability, brooded, "ever since the breakdown of the summit in Paris I have felt uneasy about the summer of 1960. It has a terrible similarity to 1914. Now Congo may play the role of Serbia. Except for the terror of the nuclear power on both sides, we might easily slide into the 1914 situation."[116] The Russians, losing politically in the Congo, attempted to recoup by refusing to recognize the Mobutu government and claimed with many African and other nonaligned nations that Lumumba was the legitimate head of state. Simultaneously, the Soviet pressed for the removal of Secretary Hammarskjold and a reorganization of the United Nations.

Khrushchev next took his attack on the United Nations and the lame duck Eisenhower administration to the United Nations itself when he announced that he would return to the United States to head the Soviet delegation to the General Assembly on September 20, 1960. The visit would also place him precisely in the middle of the American presidential election campaign. While at the United Nations Khrushchev conspicuously conferred with Afro-Asian and other leaders of the third world, notably Fidel Castro, the new leader of the increasingly anti-American Cuban regime. During debate in the General Assembly Khrushchev pressed his attack on the West and Hammarskjold's purportedly pro-Western UN leadership. This performance reached its peak during a speech by MacMillan as Khrushchev's rather startling and discourteous interruptions were climaxed by the Soviet leader removing his shoe and alternately banging on his desk and waving it at the imperturbable British leader.[117] It was a shocking and frightening spectacle in which the Kremlin appeared to be headed by a man so reminiscent of earlier totalitarians that the world of negotiation seemed barely applicable.

In marked contrast with this behavior, however, was Khrushchev's attitude toward the American election and the new president-elect. During the campaign, Khrushchev made references to the unacceptability of Richard Nixon as the next president — an oblique endorsement of Kennedy that nonetheless contributed to much discomfort in the young senator's camp.[118] And following Kennedy's victory, Khrushchev's persistent overtures to the president-elect during the interregnal period between November 1960 and the inauguration in January 1961 sounded the refrain of harmony and new opportunities for detente.

However, during the postelection period, the Soviets were confronted with and seemed to have been somewhat perplexed, even chagrined, by Kennedy's cool but correct silence.[119] Khrushchev undoubtedly hoped for some reinforcement for his effort to renew detente — but there was at best an ambiguous response. Perhaps little else could be expected from the president-elect. Kennedy had earlier emphasized that the responsibility for policy making remained with President Eisenhower until January 20, and that he (Kennedy) had no intention of usurping it. Reaction to the Russian overtures was determined in part, therefore, by Kennedy's conception of a president-elect's status. An additional inhibiting factor was the enormity of the administrative changeover itself. Although the Eisenhower administration willingly extended itself in order to facilitate the orientation of Kennedy's appointees, those appointees, particularly in the top decision-making positions, still were faced with the formidable job of grasping the magnitude of their particular positions. Thus, even if Kennedy had been inclined to respond to the Russian approaches at this time, a considered response would have been difficult to construct.

More fundamental, however, was that the incoming Kennedy administration was no less an advocate of negotiating from strength than its predecessors. On October 8, 1960, during the second of the famous televised debates between Kennedy and Nixon, Kennedy had agreed completely with Nixon concerning the preconditions of negotiation with the Soviets:

> Before we go into the summit, before we ever meet again, I think it's important that the United States build its strength — that it build its military strength, as well as its own economic strength.
>
> If we negotiate from a position where the power balance or wave is moving away from us, it's extremely difficult to reach a successful decision on Berlin, as well as the other questions.[120]

This statement was more than mere campaign puffery designed to demonstrate that the youthful senator was as tough as his experienced

Republican opponent. One would be hard-pressed to find a more straight-forward statement of this most fundamental conception of world politics and Soviet-American relations during the cold war. John Kennedy, along with the "best and the brightest" he brought to the presidency, would continue the vigorous pursuit of military superiority before any serious effort would be made to negotiate the outstanding issues of the cold war. Thus Kennedy's conception of America's world role, and the hostile nature of the international system within which that role would have to be played out, was consistent with the principles that had guided American foreign and national security policy during the preceding 15 years.

NOTES

1. Townsend Hoopes, *The Devil and John Foster Dulles* (Boston: Little, Brown and Company, 1973), p. 337.
2. Eisenhower's role in this decision seems to have been minimal. In early June he suffered a recurrence of the ileitis. His intestinal problem required major surgery and during the crucial 5-week period that the Suez Crisis was set in motion, Dulles had near total control of policy.
3. Hoopes, op. cit., pp. 341–342.
4. Anthony Nutting, *No End of a Lesson: The Story of Suez* (New York: Clarkson Potter, 1967), pp. 32–33.
5. Among the accounts of the crisis perhaps the standard analysis has been that of Herman Finer, *Dulles' Own Suez: The Theory and Practice of His Diplomacy* (Chicago: Quadrangle Books, 1964). However, Finer's book was, of necessity, written without benefit of access to Dulles' papers. For an account that does have benefit of this primary source, see Hoopes, op. cit., pp. 318–414. The following analysis draws most heavily on the latter.
6. Hoopes, op. cit., p. 359.
7. Kenneth Love, quoting Nasser in *Suez: The Twice Fought War* (New York: McGraw-Hill Book Company, 1960), p. 429.
8. Finer, op. cit., p. 218.
9. Ibid., pp. 217–218 (emphasis in the original).
10. Hoopes, op. cit., p. 361.
11. Peter Lyon, *Eisenhower: Portrait of the Hero* (Boston: Little, Brown and Company, 1974), p. 715.
12. Finer, op. cit., p. 386.
13. His request that a portion of British capitalization in the International Monetary Fund be rebased in order to support the pound had been referred to the I.M.F. in Washington and rejected.
14. Dwight D. Eisenhower, *Waging Peace* (Garden City, N.Y.: Doubleday & Company, 1965), p. 178.
15. Notes for testimony before the Senate Foreign Relations Committee, February 1957, in the Dulles Papers, quoted by Hoopes, op. cit., p. 408.
16. Hoopes, op. cit., p. 413.

17. For a review of Khrushchev's claims see Arnold L. Horelick and Myron Rush. *Strategic Power and Soviet Foreign Policy* (Chicago: University of Chicago Press, 1966), pp. 42–50.
18. Ibid., p. 110.
19. His efforts are recounted in Maxwell D. Taylor, *The Uncertain Trumpet* (New York: Harper & Row, 1960).
20. Ibid., p. 185.
21. Gordon Dean, former head of the Atomic Energy Commission, writing in the foreword of Henry Kissinger's *Nuclear Weapons and Foreign Policy* (New York: W. W. Norton & Company, 1957), p. vii.
22. Henry Kissinger, "Force and Diplomacy in the Nuclear Age," *Foreign Affairs*, Vol. XXXIV (April 1956), pp. 349–366.
23. Kissinger, *Nuclear Weapons and Foreign Policy*, p. 264.
24. Ibid., p. 147.
25. Ibid., pp. 144–145.
26. Morton Halperin, *Limited War in the Nuclear Age* (New York: John Wiley & Sons, 1963), p. 62.
27. Henry Kissinger, "Limited War: Conventional or Nuclear? A Reappraisal," in Donald G. Brennan (ed.), *Arms Control, Disarmament and National Security* (New York: George Braziller, 1961), pp. 138–152, p. 146. Italics in the original.
28. This report was declassified in February 1973. It is entitled "Deterrence and Survival in the Nuclear Age," Security Resources Panel of the Science Advisory Committee, NSC Cover Sheet 5724, November 7, 1957, Office of Presidential Libraries, Reference Copy No. 43.
29. Ibid., p. 6.
30. Morton L. Halperin, "The Gaither Committee and the Policy Process," *World Politics*, Vol. 13 (April 1961), pp. 360–384.
31. See the Gaither Report, op. cit., table "C." For Eisenhower reaction see *Waging Peace*, pp. 220–221.
32. Hoopes, op. cit., p. 430.
33. Eisenhower, op. cit., p. 274.
34. Hoopes, op. cit., p. 436.
35. Harold MacMillan, *Riding the Storm* (London: Macmillan Company, 1971), pp. 547–548. The Joint Chiefs' inclination to use atomic weapons became almost a fixation according to Morton Halperin, a Defense Department official in the Johnson administration.
36. Hoopes, op. cit., pp. 442–457.
37. MacMillan, op. cit., p. 587.
38. Ibid., pp. 592–632.
39. Hoopes, op. cit., p. 492.
40. See Hoopes, pp. 492–494. See also Emmett John Hughes, *The Ordeal of Power* (New York: Dell Books, 1964), pp. 247–248 and Merriman Smith, *A President's Odyssey* (New York: Harper & Row, 1961), p. 250.
41. Richard Neustadt, *Presidential Power* (New York: Signet Books, 1964), p. 83.
42. Marshall Goldman, *Soviet Foreign Aid* (New York: Praeger Publishers, 1967), p. 116.
43. Hoopes, op. cit., p. 493.
44. Michael Tatu, *Power in the Kremlin: From Khrushchev to Kosygin,* translated by Helen Katel (New York: Viking Press, 1969), p. 50.
45. Ibid., pp. 49–52.
46. Ibid., p. 51.

47. Ibid., p. 48.
48. Ibid., p. 44.
49. Hoopes, op. cit., p. 496.
50. Text reprinted in *The New York Times,* September 28, 1959; see also Khrushchev's Press Conference, *The New York Times,* September 28, 1959.
51. Louis Halle, *The Cold War as History* (New York: Harper & Row, 1967), p. 366.
52. *The New York Times,* September 28, 1959.
53. Louis Halle, op. cit., p. 367.
54. Harold MacMillan, *Pointing the Way* (London: Macmillan Company, 1972), p. 179. MacMillan wrote that he was "concerned at the slow American reaction to these undoubted advances."
55. *The New York Times,* March 23, 1960.
56. Ibid.
57. *The Times (London),* October 4, 1957, quoted in Robert E. Osgood, *NATO, The Entangling Alliance,* (Chicago: University of Chicago Press, 1962), p. 242.
58. Coral Bell, *Negotiation from Strength* (New York: Alfred A. Knopf, 1963), p. 203, and *Le Monde,* October 22, 1959.
59. Adam Ulam, *Expansion and Coexistence: Soviet Foreign Policy* 1917–1967 (New York: Praeger Publishers, 1968), pp. 626–627.
60. See James Richardson, *Germany and the Atlantic Alliance: The Interaction of Strategy and Politics* (Cambridge, Mass.: Harvard University Press, 1966), pp. 33–34.
61. Bell, op. cit., p. 204 and *The New York Times,* November 22, 1959.
62. C. Douglas Dillon, "American Foreign Policy Today," *Department of State Bulletin,* Vol. 42, Speech of April 20, 1960, pp. 724–725, 727.
63. See Charles E. Bohlen, *Witness to History, 1929–1969* (New York: W. W. Norton & Company, 1973), p. 451; David Wise and Thomas B. Ross, *The U-2 Affair* (New York: Random House, 1962), p. 141; and *Current Digest of the Soviet Press,* Vol. 12 (May 25, 1960), p. 7.
64. See Khrushchev's remarks as reported in *The New York Times,* May 8, 1960, and Wise and Ross, op. cit., pp. 125–126.
65. Francis G. Powers and Curt Gentry, *Operation Overflight* (New York: Holt, Rinehart and Winston, 1970), p. 45.
66. L. Fletcher Prouty, *The Secret Team* (Englewood Cliffs, N.J.: Prentice-Hall, 1974), p. 374. Prouty maintains that procedure for these flights invariably included a "skin search," where pilots were stripped naked and then given a flying costume without pockets. "The zipper might be made in Denmark, the shoes in India, and the underclothes in Hong Kong," Prouty told James Nathan in a telephone interview, June 3, 1974.

   Powers contends in *Operation Overflight* that curare is a "horrible" death (like self strangulation) [p. 143]. (This is correct.) But, Powers says, he refused to take the proferred cyanide capsule (which toxicologists indicate to be the suicide "drug of choice") because he was afraid it would break in his pocket [p. 53]. (Checking with the chief toxicologist and former army chemical warfare researcher at the Du Pont Company's Haskell Laboratory we find that cyanide capsules are not gelatin coated but "hard as walnuts" and have to be cracked with the back teeth. There is no chance they will break in one's pocket.) Nevertheless, Powers tossed away the silver dollar covering of a poorly constructed [p. 144] and poorly sheathed curare plunger and put it in his pocket where it remained undetected for several days [p. 88] until he revealed its presence to the KGB even though he claims that he still feared torture [pp. 102–107]. In any case, he took this needle, he says, not as a suicide device, but as a weapon.

However, his ostentatiously silenced "extra long barreled" [p. 146] semi-automatic pistol with the initials U.S.A. on the handle [p. 77] was, he contends, only for hunting game.

One speculation arising from these contradictions might be that the curare needle and the gun were but mere dramatizations of Powers' role as a spy. Powers explained that he did not "reach for the destruct switches ... but I thought I had better see if I can get out of here before using this. I knew that there was a seventy second time switch delay." Powers was worried the seventy seconds was not enough time and maintains, to this day, that he simply bailed out. David Wise and Thomas R. Ross, *The Invisible Government* (New York: Bantam Books, 1964), p. 132, citing Hearings, Francis G. Powers, U-2 pilot, Senate Committee on the Armed Services, March 6, 1962.

67. Eisenhower, op. cit., p. 546. Indeed, in September 1956 a U-2 "simply disintegrated" in mid-air when passed by two curious Canadian jets and caught in the wake of the interceptors. Powers and Gentry, *op. cit.,* pp. 49–50.

68. Eisenhower, op. cit., pp. 549–550. Some former intelligence men have speculated that the plane simply ran out of fuel. Prouty, op. cit., p. 424. Although Powers radioed on May 1 an "engine flame out," he later became insistent that he was, in fact, shot down. See Eisenhower, op. cit., pp. 543 and 558, and Powers and Gentry, op. cit., p. 82. Powers claims that his radio could not reach over 400 miles and he did not radio back. There is some reason to believe that Powers may well not have radioed back as Eisenhower recalls in *Waging Peace,* for Undersecretary of State Douglas Dillon testified, "But we did not have any specific information that it was down in the Soviet Union ... until Mr. Khrushchev made the statement of Thursday morning [May 5]." *Events Incident to the Summit Conference,* Hearings before the Senate Committee on Foreign Relations, 86th Congress, 2nd Session, May 27, June 1 and 2, 1960, p. 48; hereafter cited as *Events.*

69. Powers' 1956 contract for employment was a complex arrangement between Lockheed, NASA, and the CIA. See Wise and Ross, *The Invisible Government,* p. 240.

70. *Aviation Week,* Vol. 72, No. 20 (May 16, 1960), p. 21; see also *Newsweek,* May 23, 1960, p. 29.

71. Cited by Powers and Gentry op. cit., p. 315. It is instructive to compare Powers's cooperative attitude with that of Navy Commander Lloyd Bucher of the *Pueblo,* captured off North Korea in 1968. Bucher resisted, but, unlike Powers, was tortured and collaborated only marginally with his captors. The navy, however, court-martialled, reprimanded, and consigned him to the ignominy of commanding a minesweeper. One of the presiding admirals investigating the *Pueblo* incident explained, "I know that when I put on a blue uniform, I'm expected to stand in harm's way." (Admiral Bergner, quoted in Trevor Armbrister, *A Matter of Accountability* (New York: Coward McCann, 1970), p. 385.) Bucher's "failure to put up any resistance ... was incredible ... shocking ... and unforgivable." (According to one senior admiral of the court, ibid., p. 387.)

72. *The New York Times,* May 6, 1960.

73. *Events,* p. 49.

74. *The New York Times,* May 8, 1960. Speech of May 7, 1960.

75. Wise and Ross, *The U-2 Affair,* p. 100 and Jack Shick, *The Berlin Crisis, 1958–1962* (Philadelphia: University of Pennsylvania Press, 1971), p. 114, and *The New York Times,* May 8, 1960.

76. *The New York Times,* May 12, 1960; one unexplored possibility was simply to claim that Powers was unauthorized to intrude on Russian air space and that he had simply disobeyed orders. The U.S. government could have then stuck by its denial enough

so as not to have been embarrassed, "apologized," and asked the "insubordinate" or "demented" pilot to be returned for punishment. This kind of line is fairly frequent. One of the best-known examples occurred at the height of the Cuban missile crisis when a U-2 "strayed" into Soviet air space.

77. Cited by Wise and Ross, *The U-2 Affair,* p. 132 (emphasis added). Similarly, Emmett Hughes, Eisenhower's biographer, speech writer, and friend, wrote later, scathingly, that the president had claimed espionage was "a sovereign right." (Hughes, op. cit., p. 361.)

78. *The New York Times,* May 13, 1960, reprinted in *Events,* p. 204 and 208. And there were other favorable signs. For after some hesitation, a Soviet military delegation accepted an invitation to visit the United States the same day that Khrushchev averred that the Soviet people would think him mad that he was keeping open his invitation for the president to visit Russia.

79. Apologies for spying, even insincere apologies, are not an uncommon practice in international affairs. A ceremonial declaration of regrets was insisted upon when Japan in 1937 "mistakenly" bombed for 3 hours the American ship *Panay.* A similar formal apology was elicted from the Israelis when they "mistakenly" sank the U.S. "Elint" [electronic intelligence] vessel *Liberty,* in the 1967 Middle East War. On December 23, 1968, Major General Gilbert Woodward signed a document prepared by North Korea which stated that the United States "solemnly apologizes for the grave acts of espionage committed by the U.S. Ship *Pueblo* . . . and gives firm assurance that no U.S. ships will intrude again . . . into the territorial waters . . . of North Korea." Woodward proclaimed as he signed: "My signature will not and cannot alter the facts. I will sign . . . only to free the crew" (Armbrister, op. cit., p. 340).

80. Charles Bohlen, op. cit., p. 470.

81. Nikita Khrushchev, *Khrushchev Remembers: The Last Testament,* translated and edited by Strobe Talbott (Boston: Little, Brown and Company, 1974), pp. 447–448. For Khrushchev's insistence that Powers was shot down, see p. 445. It was always in the Soviet interest to maintain, as Khrushchev does in his memoirs, that the Russians possessed "surface to air missiles" that were literally "rolling off the production line." Khrushchev maintains that Powers "ejected from his plane when hit and parachuted to earth." Given the characteristics of the plane and the altitude (21,000 meters) at which he hints the U-2 was operating (although he does not come out and directly claim that it was hit at that altitude), it is unrealistic that Powers or his plane could have made it to earth in such pristine condition. As translator Talbott explains, Khrushchev's recollections are marked with "deliberate deceptions" as well as "revelations" (p. xxii). If Powers were not "shot down" and the Soviets did not possess an antiaircraft capability of reaching a U-2 and Khrushchev revealed this, he would have, in the words of Edward Crankshaw, "subjected [himself] and his heirs to charges of disloyalty and the laws governing state secrets" (p. xviii).

82. Ibid., pp. 454–455.

83. *The New York Times,* May 12, 1960.

84. *Events,* p. 244; *The New York Times,* May 17, 1960.

85. *Events,* pp. 238–248.

86. Eisenhower, op. cit., p. 558.

87. *Events,* p. 47.

88. *The New York Times,* May 30, 1960.

89. Khrushchev, op. cit., pp. 450–451.

90. It was said that the plane flew well over 80,000 feet, yet the CIA is also reported to have concluded that it was downed by remarkably accurate SA-2 missiles. Powers, in his "recollections," claims that he was "shot down at his assigned altitude" (implying

that it was well over 75,000 feet), and he rejected Khrushchev's claim that the plane was shot down at 20,000 meters or 65,616 feet. However, SA-2 missiles of 1960 vintage had a ceiling of only 60,000 feet. But there is a curious and unexplained loss of 10,000 to 15,000 feet under the plane's normal height [*Military Review,* Vol. XLI, No. 5 (May 1961), p. 105; Ross and Wise, op. cit., pp. 130–31]. *Aviation Week* claimed that some U-2's could fly over 100,000 feet and that the version Powers was flying could do at least 90,000 feet [*Aviation Week,* Vol. 72, No. 20 (May 16, 1960, p. 26)]. *Aviation Week* puzzled over the details of the incident for 4 weeks. Why were the pilot, plane, and gear, the editors wondered, in such "exceptionally clean" condition? After 30 days, the journal concluded that Powers must have made a "belly landing," and that no other explanation fit the facts. (See ibid., pp. 33–34 and *Aviation Week,* Vol. 72, No. 22, June 6, 1960, p. 28.) Although Powers insisted that he was "shot down" above 68,000 feet, the administration clearly did not believe at the time that he was struck by a Soviet rocket at high altitude. Secretary Herter told the Foreign Relations Committee, "We are very skeptical and there are certain evidences that it was not shot down from [its maximum] altitude." Senator Aiken then asked, "Does it seem unlikely to you that the U-2 was brought down with a one shot rocket?" Secretary Herter responded, "It seems very unlikely." (*Events,* p. 37 and p. 41.) Secretary Herter went on, "I am not skilled enough in the techniques of shooting down planes. But I should think it is very doubtful if he was hit by a rocket whether either he or the plane would have come down intact" (*Events,* p. 61). Eisenhower was equally skeptical. He said, "In the Soviet allegations there are many discrepancies. For example, there is some reason to believe that the plane in question was not shot down in high altitude" (ibid., p. 199). Russian radar would have had to have been superior to the then-existing state of the art in American electronics for the Russians to have successfully tracked the U-2. When the U-2 was being tested against the "probability of being detected" in the United States, American radar, "even when warned of strange airplanes flying over national territory," could not see or if picked up could not track the plane at the U-2's operating altitude. Moreover, neither American nor Soviet interceptors could then reach an altitude beyond 50,000 feet (Eisenhower, op. cit., pp. 545–546).

91.   The official explanation for the flight is controversial. Notwithstanding the claim that there was good weather forecast for the day of the flight, there were many clear days over the Urals in the spring. Moreover, it was claimed that Russian radar would be reduced in the area because of a holiday. Yet on this same festive day it was claimed that there was to be an important test launch of a new missile, surveillance of which required Powers's flight. And would Soviet radar operators go on holiday no matter what the occasion? Finally, there is evidence that there had been no missile activity in the Sverdlovsk area for the preceding 2 years, and there is some doubt if there had ever been any there at all. (Sanche de Gramont, *The Secret War Since World War II* (New York: G. P. Putnam's Sons, 1962), p. 256; Fletcher Prouty, op. cit., p. 422; Jack Anderson, "United States Heard Russians Chasing U-2," *Washington Post,* May 11, 1960. Gramont gives no source, Anderson cites only "official reports." Apparently this was the official explanation given to the press. See *Newsweek,* May 16, 1960, and *Time,* May 16, 1960. See Horelick and Rush, op. cit., pp. 74–75).

Powers, in his book, claims that this was the first trans-Russian flight. All others had been relatively short incursions. The Powers flight was to cover 3800 miles in all, 2900 inside Soviet airspace, giving the Soviets a long time, indeed, to notice it. The men who ordered the U-2 flights and controlled the flight schedules fully realized that the Soviets knew of them and that a U-2 had been lost over Russia a year earlier. (Powers and Gentry, op. cit., p. 74). Powers claims that this particular flight was personally approved by Eisenhower, and, in fact, the flight was delayed 30 minutes before communication from the White House was secured. (Ibid., p. 78). The flights had been going on since August 1955, but the Russians could not profit from revealing their existence until a live pilot unavoidably descended on them. Indeed, when Air Force General Nathan Twining was invited to visit the Soviet Union in 1956, Khrushchev revealed (on May 9, 1960), that a U-2 had penetrated Soviet airspace as far as Kiev but the Russians did not protest (Tatu, op. cit., p. 54). And just three weeks prior to the May Summit Conference on April 9, 1960, another U-2 transversed the Soviet Union, and Khrushchev "for his own reasons . . . said nothing of it" (Chalmers Roberts, *Washington Post,* May 27, 1960, and Eisenhower, op. cit., p. 547). According to one account at the time, Eisenhower had cancelled the U-2 flights before and during delicate negotiations. For example, he ordered the flights stopped in September 1956 while engaged in talks with the Egyptians and the Russians at the height of the Suez crisis. Overflights were also halted during Khrushchev's trip to the United States in September 1959. So the diplomatic implications of the flights were not unknown to the administration.

Eisenhower complained that he was the "only principal" who feared the repercussions of a U-2 failure over Soviet territory:

> Secretary Dulles, for instance, would say laughingly, "If the Soviets ever capture one of these planes, I'm sure they will never admit it. To do so would make it necessary for them to admit also that for years we had been carrying on flights over their territory while the Soviets had been helpless to do anything about the matter" (Eisenhower, op. cit., p. 546).

Eisenhower then adds, tartly, "When the text of Khrushchev's revelation was released the theory that Khrushchev would never admit such an occurrence was demolished." (Ibid., p. 548).

92. It seemed extraordinary that a young technician of the cold war should be traded for a seasoned master spy — especially when the technician had failed so spectacularly in his mission. There was considerable public speculation about Powers's courage, character, and ability. Indeed, there were stories in the press that former Assistant U.S. Attorney General W. F. Tompkins, the prosecutor of Abel, had complained, "It's like trading Mickey Mantle for the average ball player" (Powers and Gentry, op. cit., p. 296). Rudolph Abel's lawyer concurred. He described Powers as a kind of calm, likable mercenary hillbilly but not in the same class as Col. Abel. "Suppose you wished to recruit an American to sail a shaky espionage glider over the heart of hostile Russia at 75,000 feet. . . . Powers was a man, who, for adequate pay, would do it; and as he passed over Minsk, would calmly reach for a salami sandwich [James B. Donovan, *Strangers On A Bridge: The Case of Colonel Abel* (New York: Atheneum Publishers, 1964), p. 421].

93. The CIA issued an unusual statement even before he took the stand. The dispatch said that Powers had fulfilled his contract, lived up to "his obligations as an American," and would get $52,500 back pay. (Statement concerning Francis Gary Powers, Central Intelligence Agency, March 6, 1962, released by Carl Vinson (Dem., Georgia), Chairman of the House Armed Services Committee, partially quoted in Powers and Gentry, op. cit., pp. 300–301 and Ross and Wise, *The U-2 Affair,* p. 257.) Senator Russell set the tone of the hearing, "I understand from Senator Byrd that you are a Virginia boy." Ninety minutes of gentle questions later, the official inquest into the incident was over and Powers was on his way, leaving in the words of a *Time Magazine* reporter, a

"persistent feeling that some of his story remains untold" ([Time] March 16, 1962, p. 19).

The report of the CIA released upon Powers's return was obviously less than frank. For instance, in an attempt to explain that even if the destructor unit had been detonated, the U-2 would have been identifiable and the pilot would have survived, the CIA said, "The purpose of the destruct mechanism was to render inoperable the precision camera and other equipment, not to destroy them or the plane." But as Wise and Ross note, "Army ordinance . . . describes cyclonite . . . as one of the most powerful explosives in the world. Three pounds . . . could blow up four trucks" (Wise and Ross, *The U-2 Affair*, p. 18, fn. 2).

Although there was not inconsiderable speculation in the press about why Powers had used neither his needle nor his destruct button, the terms of the discussion were captured by one headline, which read "Hero or Bum?" Powers adds, interestingly, that Attorney General Robert Kennedy opposed the Powers-Abel trade and wanted him tried for treason (Powers and Gentry, op. cit., p. 302). The Lockheed Aircraft Corporation announced on November 3, 1962, that Powers had "taken a routine test pilot job . . . checking out the U-2's that are modified, maintained and overhauled" — a plane that was obsolete and was being phased out. Powers worked for Lockheed until the company hit a stretch of financial trouble in 1970 and was layed off. He later worked as a helicopter pilot for the Los Angeles Police Department (Wise and Ross, *The Invisible Government*, p. 240).

94. MacMillan, op. cit., p. 197.
95. Ibid., p. 201.
96. Wise and Ross, *The U-2 Affair*, p. 261.
97. MacMillan, op. cit., p. 193; April 5, 1960. MacMillan is citing a conversation with De Gaulle (emphasis MacMillan's, paraphrasing De Gaulle in an official dispatch).
98. J. William Fulbright: "Reflections on a Troubled World," interview conducted by Warren Howe and Sarah Trott, *Saturday Review*, January 11, 1975, p. 14.
99. Eisenhower, op. cit., p. 553. No less than pilot Powers confessed to suspicions that the U-2 was betrayed. To Powers, it now seems curious that official approval for his flight was given over an open telephone line because radio communications between Germany and Turkey broke down. Thus, Powers concludes, "there is a possibility that the Russians knew I would be taking off even before I did." Powers also feels that defectors, including Lee Harvey Oswald, might have given the Soviets the technical capacity to track the U-2. This seems a bit fanciful at best, and Powers' demonstration of the connection is only by the assertion that Oswald had access to height-finding equipment while in the marines and that six months after he defected, the U-2 was shot down. Powers and Gentry, op. cit., pp. 356–358.
100. *Aviation Week*, Vol. 72, No. 23 (June 6, 1960), p. 26.
101. Wise and Ross, *The U-2 Affair*, p. 146.
102. Walter Lippmann, "First of All," *Washington Post*, May 19, 1960.
103. "Press Conference of N. S. Khrushchev in Paris on May 18," *Current Digest of the Soviet Press*, Vol. 12, No. 20 (June 15, 1960), p. 9.
104. MacMillan, *Pointing the Way*, p. 212.
105. *Chicago Sun Times*, May 22, 1960.
106. But on May 10, 1960, Khrushchev had pointed out that in the last 18 months he had "unilaterally cut the armed forces in the Soviet Union by one-third . . . to 24 million men." *The New York Times*, May 10, 1960. Between 1955 and 1960 the armed services had been cut by 2 million, and an additional 1.2 million cut had been announced for 1960–1961. CIA Report, May 1960, reprinted in *Events*, p. 288.

107. *Events,* p. 134.
108. Hoopes, op. cit., p. 504.
109. George Kennan, *Memoirs: 1925–1950* (Boston: Little, Brown and Company, 1967), p. 365.
110. Eisenhower, op. cit., p. 616.
111. See Joyce and Gabriel Kolko, *The Limits of Power, 1945–1954* (New York: Harper & Row, 1972), esp. the "Introduction" and "Conclusion."
112. U.S. Congress, Senate Committee on Foreign Relations, *Some Important Issues in Foreign Aid,* 89th Congress, 2nd Session, 1966, pp. 6–7 and table 1.
113. MacMillan, op. cit. p. 261.
114. A supplemental appropriation of $100 million was sought from Congress. Eisenhower, op. cit., p. 575.
115. Dispatch of January 16, 1960, in MacMillan, op. cit., p. 269.
116. Ibid., pp. 264–265.
117. *The New York Times,* September 30, 1960.
118. Arthur M. Schlesinger, Jr., *A Thousand Days: John F. Kennedy in the White House* (Boston: Houghton Mifflin Company, 1965), p. 50.
119. *The New York Times,* December 29, 1960. See also Schlesinger, op. cit., pp. 126–127.
120. "Transcript of the Second Nixon-Kennedy Debate on Nation-Wide Television," *The New York Times,* October 8, 1960, p. 11.

Chapter 7
Containment on
the New Frontier

John F. Kennedy and his administration had a flair and style that set them apart from the generation that had shaped American policy during the late 1940s and then institutionalized the cold war during the mid-1950s. As he eloquently proclaimed in his inaugural address, "The torch has been passed to a new generation of Americans." Nevertheless, it was a generation "tempered by war, disciplined by a hard and bitter peace, proud of our ancient heritage." Not the least of the elements retained from that heritage were the old objectives and reflexes of the "hard and bitter peace."

When the Democratic nominee, John Kennedy, rose to give his acceptance speech, his central theme was the interrelationship between world affairs and the American mission. It seemed an almost cosmic challenge, "a new frontier" where we would be asked "more sacrifice instead of more security." "Can a nation organized and governed such as ours endure?" asked Kennedy. "Have we the nerve and the will? . . . Can we carry through in . . . a race . . . for mastery of the sky and the oceans and the tides the far side of space and the inside of men's minds?"[1] The American people, declared Kennedy, stood "at a turning point in history," and must choose "between the public interest and private comfort, between national greatness and national decline . . . all mankind awaits upon our decision."[2]

The Kennedy victory in the 1960 election was razor thin; but the sense of power and vitality that the young president brought to the tasks thus won was almost contagious. On Inauguration Day Kennedy stood before the American people and called them to their destiny: "Let every nation know, whether it wishes us well or ill, that we shall pay any price, bear any burden, meet any hardship, support any friend, oppose any foe to assure the survival and success of liberty. We will do all this and more." Thus the first message of the new administration was an eloquent reaffirmation of the Truman Doctrine. It was containment with vigor. The problem, as Kennedy saw it, was not the objectives of the Eisenhower administration but its reluctance to develop and exploit a full range of American instrumentalities to implement containment. "Eisenhower,"

Kennedy complained, "had escaped" the burden of making good on the far-flung commitments rendered during his administration. Kennedy, however, had premonitions that "all the pigeons are coming home on the next President."[3]

THE THREATENED NEW FRONTIER

The view from the new frontier was frightening. The domestic preoccupations of the communists during the mid-1950s had provided the Eisenhower administration a respite. But during that time deep and consequential forces had been at work throughout the international system. By the end of the decade the Kennedy administration thought they could discern the shape of these forces. Indeed, they felt that the Eisenhower administration had seen them as well, especially those in the third world, but had chosen to ignore them or confront them with the inapplicable rigidities of the new look and massive retaliation. The years since 1957 were viewed as an unrelieved succession of cumulating disasters. Soviet missile strength seemed to grow, and the pressure on Berlin became very nearly unbearable. Simultaneously the Soviets and the Chinese expanded their activities in the Middle East, South and Southeast Asia, as well as Africa. Castro's victory in the Cuban civil war marked the penetration of the western hemisphere.

In the face of this burgeoning assault on 15 years of American order, America seemed no longer able to respond either spiritually or materially. Thus, the Kennedy administration moved immediately to reinvigorate American will through the bedazzling rhetoric and energy of the New Frontier. It was, however, but an eloquent reaffirmation of the absolutism of John Foster Dulles and the sense of mission of Dean Acheson. As for the instruments of containment on the new frontier, they would have to be commensurate with the scope of the purported challenge. Since the challenges were apparent at every level of potential conflict, then it seemed imperative that the United States be able to respond at all levels and arenas of potential conflict. "We are moving," Kennedy told Americans, "into a period of uncertain risk and great commitment . . . thus we must be able to respond with discrimination and speed, to any problem at any spot on the globe at any moment's notice."[4]

This search for a wide-spectrum response to the far-ranging demands of containment prompted the development of interrelated instrumentalities and doctrine ranging from general nuclear war to the problems of public health in the third world. Military forces were conceived and designed for a flexible response: to fight total thermonuclear war, limited nuclear war, conventional wars in Europe or Asia, or unconventional warfare anywhere in the world. At the same time, the Kennedy administration sought to expand American military and economic assistance programs in an effort to anticipate and defeat communist efforts in the third world. The problem of building nations that reflected American political and economic values was but a natural extension of the effort to maintain an international strategic environment conducive to historic American purposes and principles. Indeed, American involvement in nation-building, whether by means of military or politico-economic intervention, constituted a demonstration of the will and commitment deemed crucial to the maintenance of the strategic balance.

The Kennedy administration's concern with the problem of nation-building resulted in part from the circumstances existing in the third world when Kennedy assumed office. The situation in the Congo, insurgencies in Laos and Vietnam, and Castro's success in Cuba meant that in virtually every corner of the third world the Kennedy administration felt compelled to deal with revolutionary developments. This concern was given even more urgency by the prevailing view of the nature of the Soviet and Chinese relationship to these events. The American perception of these events was complicated by the Sino-Soviet schism. But disputes within the communist world notwithstanding, the conclusion was drawn that the third world was to be a major if not the primary testing ground of communist and American will. Consequently, nation-building within the third world revolutionary context became much more than an end in itself. It was to become a major element in the overarching global struggle.

The Sino-Soviet Dispute, Revolutionary War, and American Policy

By the early 1960s American officials knew that communism was no monolith. The Sino-Soviet dispute was apparent to all but the most insensitive observer even by the late 1950s. In the wake of Khrushchev's refusal to back the Chinese during the last Taiwan crisis in 1958, what had been latent Sino-Soviet tension broke into open conflict. Khrushchev withdrew all technical advisers. Unfinished cement factories were abandoned as Russian engineers returned to the Soviet Union, taking their architectural drawings with them. China was militarily deprived of the Soviet nuclear shield and at supposedly fraternal international conclaves was denounced as "irresponsible" by the Soviets. The Chinese were bitter in the extreme. They had expected that the appearance of a Soviet retaliatory capability as manifested by the launching of Sputniks and working model ICBMs and large thermonuclear explosions could be used to contain American pressure on China. When their hopes did not materialize, the Chinese rhetorically reverted to a kind of exorcism of danger. The Americans with their atomic bombs, they declared, as much to Russia as to the United States, were paper tigers. War with the capitalists, they pointed out, was inevitable, and although other societies might perish, "victorious peoples would create very swiftly a civilization thousands of times higher than the capitalist system and a truly beautiful future for themselves."[5] To believe otherwise was proof of declining ideological purity, revolutionary will, and capacity for leadership of the communist world.

Official Washington, as well as alert readers of *The New York Times*, were aware therefore that the one-time "Sino-Soviet monolith" was cracking.[6] But the Kennedy administration, ever sensitive to the memory of Truman's difficulties in trying to differentiate between Moscow and Peking, though perhaps accepting that the two powers were now analytically distinct, nevertheless dealt with them as functional equivalents. In the young president's first State of the Union message, only 10 days after his inauguration, Kennedy told the nation that "each day we draw near the hour of maximum danger" in foreign affairs. The "great obstacle," proclaimed Kennedy, was the Soviet Union and Communist China. "We must never be lulled into believing that either power has yielded its ambitions for world domination. . . . On the contrary, our task is to convince them that aggression and subversion will not be profitable routes to pursue these ends."[7] Secretary of State Dean Rusk made the same point some 6 months later when he told the National Press Club: "The central issue . . . is the announced determination to impose a world of coercion upon those not already subject to it . . . it is posed between the Sino-Soviet empire and the rest, whether allied or neutral; and it is posed on every continent."[8]

Sino-Soviet Enthusiasm for Emerging Nations

The consequence of this image of the Sino-Soviet relationship held by the new administration and the Sino-Soviet perception of revolutionary war is critical to the history of this period. The military doctrine of the Soviet Union traditionally had showed little attention to the third world.[9] But in 1955, as part of the new effort at world activism assumed by the Khrushchev regime, Moscow made new overtures to the developing nations. Yet rather than working to promote revolution, Soviet strategy, after the Bandung Conference of 1955, strove toward detaching former colonial areas from the imperialist bloc by working with the national bourgeoisie. Indeed, the nonaligned nations might jail local communists and still count on Soviet moral and material development assistance.[10]

By the end of 1960, however, the ebullient and chimerical Khrushchev began to propound a theory of "wars of national liberation" which neatly mirrored the analysis of American defense intellectuals who were arguing for a capacity to wage limited war. The Soviets announced that they were prepared to sponsor and promote insurgencies. Although they had refrained from military activity previous to 1960 in the third world, support would now be forthcoming: first, in the form of doctrinal approval; and, second, with economic assistance. This policy was articulated on January 6, 1961, 2 weeks before Kennedy's inauguration, in which Khrushchev reviewed the full range and dangers of modern war and declared:

> The armed struggle by the Vietnamese people or the war of the Algerian people, which is already in its seventh year, serve as the latest examples of national liberation wars. These wars began as an uprising by the colonial peoples against their oppressors and changed into guerrilla warfare. Liberation wars will continue to exist as long as imperialism exists, as long as colonialism exists. These are revolutionary wars. Such wars are not only admissible but inevitable, since the colonialists do not grant independence voluntarily. Therefore, the peoples can attain their freedom and independence only by struggle, including armed struggle. . . .
>   What is the attitude of the Marxists toward such uprisings? A most positive one.[11]

But Khrushchev's analysis of the need to support wars of national liberation was tempered by his awareness of the need for caution in the face of the potential price.[12] Thus, Khrushchev's redefinition of Soviet strategy was part of his rejection of the traditional historical inevitability of communism's triumph in any circumstance — even war. But Khrushchev's call to support wars of national liberation helped him counter Chinese charges that Russia had grown too soft to challenge capitalism. Nevertheless, he remained essentially cautious; he circumspectly chastened the Chinese:

> We must be realistic in our thinking and understand the contemporary situation. Of course, this does not in any way mean that if we are so strong, we should test the stability of the capitalist system by force. This would be wrong. The peoples would not understand and would never support those who took it into their heads to act in such a way. We have always been against predatory wars. Marxists have recognized and still do recognize only wars of liberation, wars that are just, and have condemned and still do condemn wars that are predatory and imperialistic.[13]

China, it was widely purported, held markedly more activists and militant doctrines.[14] But it is debatable that Mao Zedong's notion of "people's war" was a grand design for world conquest. However, Mao's writings on guerrilla warfare, penned from the perspective of his defensive war against the Japanese and civil war against Chiang Kai-Shek, were not taken as a description of a defensive effort carried out by indigenous nationalist revolutionaries. Rather, Dean Rusk and others in the policy-making community believed that the resurrection of Mao's writings on people's war was an advocacy of a formula for aggressive Chinese communist expansion. In fact, however, from 1949 there was a 17 year hiatus in which Chinese officials made almost no statements that could be interpreted as actively encouraging wars of national liberation, and Lin Biao's 1965 statement concerning revolutionary war (called a Chinese *Mein Kampf* by Secretary Rusk) had ambiguous support at best. As Arthur Huck, an Australian scholar working at London's International Institute for Strategic Studies, wrote: "Far from being a blue print for the direct expansion of Chinese influence [Lin Biao's] 'Long Live the Victory of People's War'[15] argues that revolution cannot be exported and that the peoples forces must be almost entirely self-reliant."[16]

The American Misperception

But American policy makers chose to believe that China's militant rhetoric of the late 1950s and early 1960s, although directed at Moscow and primarily the product of the Sino-Soviet ideological and political dispute, was indicative of an intensely aggressive nature, especially with respect to South and Southeast Asia. The threat of insurgent communist war as articulated by Khrushchev was therefore interpreted to be as much a Chinese menace to world order as were the purported designs of Stalin and his successors.

The trumpet of worldwide testing, then, had been sounded over the issue of the expansion of power from *either* the Soviets or the Chinese. The issue was, as it had been since the days of Woodrow Wilson, whether aggression was tolerable in an orderly world environment where American ideals and institutions would prosper. In this way, it made no difference what its source or instruments, disorder had to be contained. It was this conviction that could lead Dean Rusk to explain to the Senate Foreign Relations Committee that the differences among the great communist rivals did not erase their fundamental similarities.

> *Secretary Rusk:* It was said here the other day that Hitler was a unique phenomenon. Well, there were some unique aspects. An airedale and a great dane are different but they are both dogs.
> Now, we have this phenomenon of aggression.
> *Senator Aiken:* They bite you in different places.

Secretary Rusk: That is right. We have the phenomenon of aggression. Hitler could see that the Japanese militarists in Manchuria were not stopped. He saw that Mussolini was not stopped in Ethiopia. This encouraged him.

Now, what happens here in Southeast Asia, if Peiping discovers that Hanoi can move without risk or can move with success? What further decisions are they going to make? What difference will that make in Moscow about what would happen to our commitments elsewhere, whether they should make choices as between peaceful coexistence and a more militant policy of world revolution?[17]

Secretary Rusk's response to an assumed communist challenge was one in which Sino-Soviet differences did not really matter.[18] Intellectually, therefore, Americans had by 1960 changed very little from the view expressed by Truman that global order was a seamless web, which if threatened by aggression anywhere was liable to collapse into Armageddon. As President Truman stated the notion of American policy matters in a radio talk April 11, 1951:

If history has taught us anything, it is that aggression anywhere in the world is a threat to peace everywhere in the world. When that aggression is supported by the cruel and selfish rulers of a powerful nation who are bent on conquest, it becomes a clear and present danger to the security and independence of every free nation.[19]

The instruments of aggression were different, for now as Robert McNamara observed:

The faces of *World Communism* operate in the twilight zone. Their military tactics are those of the sniper, the ambush and the raid, their political tactics are terror and assassination. We must help the people of threatened nations to resist these tactics.[20]

Moreover, a new and in some ways more perplexing arena of conflict had been opened up in the emergence of revolutionary political and economic dynamics in the third world. But if there was the slightest doubt as to the necessity of a multifaceted response, they were dispelled by events in Cuba and the failure of Kennedy's first crude attempt at counter-revolution in the style of the 1950s.

The Bay of Pigs

In Cuba, a handful of men under the leadership of Fidel Castro had arrived by boat in 1956 to begin a successful 3 year struggle to topple a dictator who was an American client. After seizing power on New Year's Day in 1959, Castro had begun to restructure Cuban institutions while professing a socialist-revolutionary ideology profoundly disturbing to Americans. Almost at a stroke, one of the most advanced nations in Latin America had been converted to socialism. If only a few dozen men or so could manage such a feat in a traditional zone of American preeminence, then what, American policymakers despaired, would be the fate of countries in areas that were in dispute among the superpowers? The Kennedy administration saw the third world symbolically interlaced in a structure of political and economic order in want of an American guarantee to maintain order.

It is not surprising, therefore, that Kennedy did not stop the preparations set in motion by the CIA with Eisenhower's approval for an invasion of the island by Cuban exiles to overthrow Castro's regime. Arthur Schlesinger and Theodore Sorensen have tried to portray Kennedy as being misled about the operation by the Eisenhower holdovers in the CIA and Defense Department.[21] And it may well be that Kennedy was unclear concerning the details of the intervention. But Kennedy did approve the intervention. That is to say, he accepted the underlying premise of Eisenhower's policy — the Castro regime should be destroyed.

The operation itself was an absolute disaster. Somewhat less than 1500 Cuban exiles hit the beaches at the Bay of Pigs, and some 500 men were promptly and efficiently cut to pieces by Castro's well-disciplined forces. The remaining 1000 men were ignominiously captured. Contrary to what the CIA had confidently predicted, there was no uprising of the Cuban people to greet the invaders and provide the necessary assistance.[22] The full dimensions of the disaster were apparent and Kennedy accepted complete responsibility for the failure. Kennedy's candor and remarkable rapport with the press and the willingness of the American people to rally around the presidency at moments of crisis eased the administration's handling of the failure at home. Covertly, however, the Kennedy administration established an extensive clandestine operation against the Castro regime using the Cuban exile community in south Florida as a source of manpower under CIA direction. This harassment and several attempts to assassinate Castro would continue until Kennedy's assassination more than 2 years later.

The Bay of Pigs fiasco is important for what it tells us of the Kennedy administration's attitude toward revolution and intervention. In a speech only hours after it was clear that the invasion had failed, Kennedy warned of the dangers posed by the "menace of external communist intervention and domination in Cuba."[23] Kennedy reemphasized the intention of his administration to reorient American force structure to be able to counter the revolutionary challenge to American power. "We dare not fail," he asserted, "to see the insidious nature of this new and deeper struggle. We dare not fail to grasp the new concepts, the new tools, the new sense of urgency we will need to combat it — whether in Cuba or South Vietnam."[24] This was essential if "the United States was to win in a struggle in many ways more difficult than war, where disappointment will often accompany us."[25] Kennedy concluded with reaffirmation of the grim vision of the inaugural address:

> I am convinced . . . that history will record the fact that the bitter struggle reached its climax in the late 1950s and the early 1960s. Let me then make it clear as the President of the United States that I am determined upon our system's survival and success, regardless of the cost and regardless of the peril![26]

Activism and American involvement were absolutely essential and, as in Europe after World War II, the United States was prepared to act with or without the assistance of others.

> Let the record show that our restraint is not inexhaustible. Should it ever appear that the inter-American doctrine of noninterference merely conceals or excuses a policy of nonaction — if the nations of this hemisphere should fail to meet their commitments against outside communist penetration — then I want it clearly understood that this government will not hesitate in meeting its primary obligations which are to the security of our nation![27]

The possibility of American intervention remained; indeed, Kennedy had proclaimed that the national security of the United States required that the "right" of intervention be retained by the United States. In the meantime, "any free nation under outside attack of any kind can be assured that all of our resources stand ready to respond to any request for assistance."[28]

NATION-BUILDING
AND COUNTERREVOLUTION

The preoccupation of the Kennedy administration with the role of communism in the third world led to a search for economic, cultural, and social instrumentalities that could parallel military counterinsurgent tactics and lead to a stabilizing of revolutionary situations in the under-developed world. Communism would not be allowed a foothold or would be stifled while it was little more than an idea. Revolution was perhaps inevitable, but the Kennedy administration sought a way to redirect revolution away from a communist conclusion.

Nation-Building

Khrushchev's January speech about "sacred wars of national liberation" prompted Kennedy to reconvene in February 1961 one of his transition task forces under the leadership of Adolph Berle and Thomas Mann with a mandate "to develop politics and programs which channel the revolution ... in Latin America ... and prevent it being taken over by the Sino-Soviet bloc."[29] Earlier the task force had reported to the new president that the social revolutionaries were targets for "capture by Communist power politics."[30] According to the report, the communists intended "to convert the Latin American social revolutionaries into a Marxist attack on the United States itself." This threat, the report warned, "is more dangerous than ... the Nazi Fascist threat."[31] The report held that the primary threat was of armed revolutionaries and the essential remedy was a combination of military action and development aid.

The report, stimulated by the relationship Castro had established with Moscow, was the foundation of Kennedy's March proposal for "a vast new ten-year plan for the Americas." The Alliance for Progress was envisioned as a $20 billion development assistance program whereby the nations of Latin America would establish a new legitimacy through reforms of archaic tax and land systems and through expanded assistance to the public sector: education, housing, and health. But there was more to the proposal than an economic assistance program having as its objective simply the economic development of Latin America or the third world. The entire national security establishment was coordinated by a special interdepartmental task force chaired by the attorney general, Robert Kennedy, who in turn reported to his brother after each meeting. The resources detailed to the Special Counterinsurgency Group constituted a massive undertaking "blazing new and uncharted paths in the tradition of such recent triumphs as the Marshall Plan."[32]

There evolved with the Alliance for Progress and the revitalized aid program an infusion of governmental funds to universities and think tanks designed to foster a body of scholarship that was to support the policy objectives of the Kennedy administration in the third world. Political development or political modernization was to emerge in the early 1960s as a distinct subfield of social science, bridging such diverse disciplines as psychology, sociology, political science, and economics. The purpose of this study was to describe, predict, and ultimately assist in the management of the process of development.

Nation-building was a heady undertaking. Yet few government officials or academics hesitated before the exhilarating prospect of social architecture.

> As a house can be built from timber, bricks, and mortar, in different patterns, . . . according to the choice, will and power of its builders, so a nation can be built according to different plans, from various materials, rapidly or gradually, by different sequences of steps, and in partial independence from its environment.[33]

The prescriptive elements and the tools of the study of nation-building are a bit chaotic to summarize easily; but, essentially, they shared a belief that the poor nations of the world would achieve a modest prosperity without succumbing to what Walt Rostow called "the scavengers of modernization," communism.[34] As a society modernized, became more Western, urbanized, and literate in its attitudes, there was an assumption that liberal governmental and capitalist economic forms would take hold. In short, in winning the battle of modernization in the developing societies the developing countries would expunge communism and, perforce, attune themselves to a process of building a stable, orderly community where American ideals would be vindicated and would flourish. As one academic put it to a War College audience in 1963:

> Here is one place where "winning over communism" has clear and specific meaning. When we look ahead over the next ten years our aim should be to have laid the foundation for good relations with those countries *after* they have passed through the first rude stages of transition from colony to nation, from asleep to awake, from medieval to twentieth century. Our investment today in these countries is in many ways a great gamble, with very real costs of which the financial is only one.
>
> The only meaningful payoff to this great investment is in the establishment of societies in the new countries that will be friendly to us, democratic in political complexion, and preferably capitalist rather than socialist in their economic structure.[35]

The search for the secret of how to make developing societies compatible with the historic American purpose was the essential endeavor of the theorists and practitioners of modernization. To many of the academic devotees of nation-building, a developed society was cohesive. Tribalism, multiethnicity, or autonomous regions were not believed to be congruent with development. The growth of a city-dwelling population was deemed especially important. Urbanization was seen as a function of integration and the beginning of differentiation where urban dwellers begin to have specialized services, market facilities, access to societal agents of socialization, and political learning. Further, urban environments bring security from the unpredictable, overpopulated, and perhaps insecure countryside. Moreover, urbanization provides the setting for the building of strong central institutions. After all, what could be more useful than a recognizable capital with some ambit of control and the possibility of diffusing its control outward from a central policy. To development theorist Samuel Huntington, "modernization is, in large part, measured by the growth of the city."[36] Professor Huntington praises the great serendipity that:

> In an absent-minded way the United States in Vietnam may well have stumbled upon the answers to "wars of national liberation." The effective response lies neither in the quest for conventional military victory nor in the esoteric doctrines and gimmicks of counterinsurgency warfare. It is instead forced-draft urbanization and modernization which rapidly brings the country in question out of the phase in which a rural revolutionary movement can hope to generate sufficient strength to come to power.[37]

Paralleling integration — purportedly the by-product of urbanization — was the need for strong institutions: "A society with weak institutions lacks the ability to curb the excesses of personal and parochial desires."[38] Almost by definition, weak institutions lack authority and cannot do their job. They are "immoral in the same sense in which a corrupt judge, a cowardly soldier or an ignorant teacher is immoral."[39] But also by definition, there are few strong institutions in developing societies — with one exception: in developing societies, one almost universally strong institution is the military. The purpose, therefore, of American military and economic assistance was to strengthen the most logical central institution that has been widely conceived of as providing the *sine qua non* of development — security and order.

> All nation-building efforts will encounter resistances requiring a combination of persuasion and coercion. In the earliest stages, coercion must be a primary instrument and nation-builders must give prime attention to improving organizational capability (e.g., army, police, foreign assistance) in this area. The degree of coercion will vary with the degree of heterogeneity (e.g., class, religion, ideology, economic development) a would-be national territory manifests.[40]

The support of military regimes seemed an almost inexorable conclusion of the nation-builders because

> contemporary coups in Asia and Africa may be regarded as providing necessary and tolerable periods of transition. The coup is a necessary link in the process of modernization. For the new nations, it seems far better to accept a military government that preserves law and order than to face radical subversives or guerrilla warfare.[41]

Thus, in order to rival the appeals of communism in the third world, the prescription of many American development theorists and practitioners was to search for strong leadership in command of well-functioning institutions who could form alternatives to communism.[42] This, then, was the struggle that development theorists saw between revolution and collectivist doctrines on the one hand and "liberal development" on the other.[43] It was the same Manichean struggle of the Truman doctrine given new terms: *WHAM* — Winning Hearts and Minds.

Counterrevolution

The ultimately counterrevolutionary thrust of nation-building is apparent in the Alliance for Progress, the 10-year, $20 billion economic assistance program established to counter the influence of Castro throughout Latin America. Schlesinger has written that Kennedy was quite sensitive to the need to remain responsive to revolutionary demands if reform and development were to take place.[44] But then the court historian of Camelot, Arthur Schlesinger, Jr., also recounts that Kennedy employed a revealing criteria to test whether a regime could be supported:

> There are three possibilities in a descending order of preference: a decent democratic regime, a continuation of the Trujillo regime [a right-wing dictatorship], or a Castro regime. We ought to aim at the first, but we really can't renounce the second until we are sure that we can avoid the third.[45]

Decent democratic regimes were clearly desirable, but it is clear from this arraying of preferences that Kennedy would settle for a good deal less if there was a chance he might get a replication of Castro.

Kennedy sought through the alliance to bring about a 5.5 percent annual economic growth rate in Latin America, but the conditions under which the program was implemented included the provision that American aid had to be spent on American goods and services, which were more expensive than could be obtained elsewhere. The real infusion of resources was therefore correspondingly reduced. The alliance was, however, successful in encouraging private American corporations to expand their holdings in Latin America during the period.[46] Finally, and most indicative of the purpose of the alliance, was that even as the economic assistance programs were receiving special attention, the Department of Defense was emphasizing the training of Latin American units in counterinsurgency and counterguerrilla activity at Fort Bragg, North Carolina, home of the Green Berets, and in the Jungle Warfare School in the American-controlled Panama Canal Zone. In addition, hundreds of Latin American policemen were given special instruction in pacification and civic action at an Agency for International Development school also based in the Canal Zone.

Kennedy, in effect, simultaneously supported economic and (presumably) democratic political development, but would not risk Latin America's extant social structure and pattern of privilege if the cost might include revolution from the left. The former was, of course, the declaratory policy of the alliance. However, if development took an unfavorable turn to the left, then the Kennedy administration wanted to be able to draw upon those indigenous forces that would be able to stem or channel the revolutionary tide. Furthermore, if U.S. intervention was necessary, there would be available material to construct a pro-American regime.

The Dominican case is illustrative. Following Trujillo's ouster by assassination, Juan Bosch, a leftist but noncommunist writer who had been in exile for 20 years, was elected president. Bosch appeared weak, however. He was described by Schlesinger as a "literary figure, better as short story writer than as statesman."[47] Consequently, Kennedy maintained support of the Dominican military, which subsequently overthrew Bosch in 1963 just before Kennedy's death. Theodore Draper summarizes Kennedy's policy and problems succinctly: "When the latter decided to stage the coup, this double bookkeeping proved to be the undoing both of Bosch's regime and Kennedy's Dominican policy."[48]

Beset by such anomalies and contradictions, the alliance did not prosper. The hoped-for 5.5 percent growth projections could not be achieved until the fifth year of the program, and then it required a good deal of prodding and juggling of indicators. It was apparent that the countries of the alliance would not respond to the simplistic notion that growth would come about primarily as the result of the infusion of American capital. Social and political transformation were essential to the development effort. But transformation implied a disruption of class structures and patterns of privilege. How could those who had the most to lose be expected to lead a campaign that would enervate their power? In nations where survival looked almost like comfort, and in countries where personalist rule prevailed and a civic culture was but a transplanted social science fantasy, the whole notion of a ruling elite being a party to its own enfeeblement was absurd. Moreover, forceful removal of these elites would have placed Kennedy in the quadrant of the collectivists and revolutionary elements he opposed. Thus, Kennedy was forced to fall back on the contradictory notion that:

> The men of wealth and power in poor nations "must lead the fight for those basic reforms which alone can preserve the fabric of their own societies. Those who make peaceful revolution impossible will make violent revolution inevitable. These social reforms are at the heart of the Alliance for Progress."[49]

It might be said that Kennedy's developmental programs saw three possibilities in descending order of preference: development in all its dimensions was desirable; stability was the minimum that was acceptable; and leftist revolution was simply unacceptable. The Kennedy administration would aim for development, but under no circumstances would the second be surrendered in the face of the third possibility. Kennedy's warning to the elites of Latin America and the third world that they might well be crushed by violent revolution if they stood in the way of reform reflects an important ambivalence in Kennedy and his administration. He was, on the one hand, sensitive and perhaps emotionally responsive to the revolutionary ferment of the third world. On the other, however, he saw America locked in mortal struggle with world communism, and from this higher strategic vantage point, revolutionary ferment was conceived as more of a threat than an opportunity. Accordingly, revolution was to be anticipated by means of development.

But the effect of such an approach was the subordination of development as an end in itself. Development assistance became an instrument in the larger strategic struggle and was justified to Congress primarily as an instrument in the cold war. Indeed, a report prepared for the Senate Foreign Relations Committee in 1966 concluded that among the numerous rationales advanced by all administrations since 1950, the most common were first, the enhancement of American national security; second, containment of communist aggression; and then, third, "to assist economic development in the less-developed countries." Moreover, American foreign assistance has been concentrated — more than 75 percent in most years — in a handful of forward or confrontation countries on the periphery of the Soviet Union and China.[50] Contrary to the charge that American aid has been distributed indiscriminately in pursuit of unrealistic altruistic ends, it has in fact served as an instrument of American national security policy.

Thinking of nation-building in this way meant that the American attitude toward development in the third world was and would be marked by a perhaps irreconcilable ambivalence. On the one hand, decent democratic development could be, was, and continues to be thought of by many Americans as an end in itself — the ultimate long-run preemption of communism in the third world. At the same time, however, Kennedy and his successor saw an immediate problem of revolutionary unrest that had to be stabilized through support of strong institutions if the perceived Sino-Soviet threat was to be contained.

One cannot be sure that the elimination of this ambivalence would have ensured the success of American aid as an instrument of nation-building and development. Indeed, it is now increasingly apparent that the development of so-called decent regimes in the third world is an immensely more complex task than envisioned by the proponents of nation-building. In any event, development was at best one, and probably not the primary, objective of nation-building. As an objective it has always competed with another generally overriding objective — the containment of communism's advance in the third world. Thought of in this way, nation-building is understood as a major addition to the spectrum of political, economic, unconventional and conventional military and strategic capability — otherwise known as flexible response — that the Kennedy administration sought to develop and employ during the decade of the 1960s.

FLEXIBLE RESPONSE

At the other end of this spectrum of capability was the realm of conventional and strategic military power. And as with nation-building, Kennedy called for a reappraisal and augmentation of American potential. In his first State of the Union message the new president noted:

> *We must strengthen our military tools.* ... In the past, lack of consistent, coherent military strategy ... [has] made it difficult to assess accurately how adequate — or inadequate — our defenses really are. I have, therefore, instructed the Secretary of Defense to reappraise our entire defense strategy.[51]

The signal that a massive infusion of funds would be available to the various defense agencies set off an internal wrangle over the allotment of funds among the various services. The air force asked for 3000 new solid-fuel Minuteman missiles to replace the huge, liquid-fueled Titan. The air force had approximately fifty such Titan missiles. They were comparatively vulnerable, and were enormously expensive. A squadron of nine Titan II's cost hundreds of millions of dollars.[52] Some requests for new missiles apparently went as high as 10,000 missiles. McNamara "compromised" and submitted a request for appropriation to build 950 new Minutemen.[53]

The air force insistence on massive superiority illuminates a remarkable coincidence of manipulation of information for bureaucratic reasons and the Kennedy administration's sense that the way to deal with the Russians was to outdistance them at every level of armaments. Indeed, the notion of a missile gap originated with inspired leaks from the air force. *The New York Times,* on January 17, 1959, based an article on interviews with "numerous persons having intimate knowledge of the defense effort" and estimated that by 1962 Soviet ICBMs would outnumber American missiles by 1000 to 130 and would increase in 1964 to 2000 to 130.

But in his farewell speech President Eisenhower told Congress that the missile gap showed every sign of being a fiction.[54] Eisenhower's evidence was fairly conclusive. The U-2 flight of May 1, 1960, was the last of a series that had revealed, according to Eisenhower, "information of the greatest importance to the nation's security. In fact, their success has been nothing short of remarkable."[55] What the U-2 flights (and other intelligence means) had demonstrated was that there were only a handful of Soviet missiles, perhaps 30 to 35. More important, there was no massive build-up underway.

By the end of 1960 Khrushchev knew that the United States probably was aware that there was no missile gap, and he made several attempts to signal the incoming administration of the possibility of limiting deployment on both sides. In the December 1960 "Pugwash" Conference on disarmament, W. W. Kuznetsov worriedly approached the American representatives, Walt Rostow and Jerome Wisner, about the campaign rhetoric concerning the missile gap. Kuznetsov suggested that if the new administration went in for massive rearmament, it could not expect the Russians to sit still. Rostow told the Soviet official "that any Kennedy rearmament would be designed to improve the stability of the deterrent, and the Soviet Union should recognize this as in the interests of peace."[56]

Schlesinger despairs that Kuznetsov, "innocent of the higher calculus of deterrence recently developed in the United States, brusquely dismissed [Rostow's] explanation."[57] Apparently the higher calculus was one of overwhelming American superiority. For as the prestigious International Institute for Strategic Studies (IISS) has noted, the acceleration of United States ICBM and submarine-launched ballistic missile (SLBM) production during the first 2 years of the Kennedy administration created a missile gap — but a gap clearly advantageous to the United States. The

IISS comparisons of American and Soviet strategic missile deployment at the end of the Eisenhower years and during the Kennedy Administration are shown in Table 7-1.

As the Kennedy administration assumed office in early 1961, they found already in place a two- or three-to-one American advantage in strategic weapons. Moreover, the Eisenhower administration had provided the basis for maintaining such an advantage for the immediate future. It will be recalled that the response of Eisenhower to the ferment of the late 1950s following the launch of Sputnik and the reappraisal of massive retaliation was a modest increase in American strategic weapons programs, especially the Polaris and Minuteman systems. By 1960–1961 these strategic systems had been moved from the research, development, and testing phase to actual procurement. Therefore, at least at the stategic level, Eisenhower had provided Kennedy with more than ample resources to deal with whatever threat might have existed.

Indeed, it was argued by McNamara that the Eisenhower approved strategic bomber, the B-70, was unnecessary and perhaps obsolete strategic capability. Professor Schlesinger suggests that McNamara accepted the arguments for massive ICBM superiority because the new defense secretary

> was already engaged in a bitter fight with the Air Force over his effort to disengage from the B-70, a costly, high-altitude manned bomber rendered obsolescent by the improvement in the Soviet ground-to-air missiles. After cutting down the original Air Force missile demands considerably, he perhaps felt that he could not do more without risking public conflict with the Joint Chiefs and the vociferous B-70 lobby in Congress. As a result, the President went along with the policy of multiplying Polaris and Minuteman missiles.[58]

But even if one grants this bureaucratic political necessity, one should not lose sight of the fact that Kennedy and McNamara sought to maintain

TABLE 7-1. *GROWTH OF ICBM/SLBM STRENGTH, 1960–1964 (MID YEARS)*

		1960	1961	1962	1963	1964
USA	ICBM	18	63	294	424	834
	SLBM	32	96	144	224	416
USSR	ICBM	35	50	75	100	200
	SLBM	—	some	some	100	120

Source: The Military Balance 1970–1971 (London: International Institute for Strategic Studies, 1971), p. 106. Reprinted by permission.

overwhelming strategic superiority over the Soviets. Thus, in spite of some administration doubts and perhaps abetted by some administration log-rolling, the first 10 months of the Kennedy administration witnessed a $6 billion increase in the military budget, from $43,685,000 to $49,878,000. The capacity to produce Minuteman missiles was increased 100 percent, and the number of Polaris subs to be produced by 1964 was increased by 50 percent. Moreover, about one-quarter of the Strategic Air Command bomber force was put on 50 percent alert, thus increasing by 50 percent the number of long-range bombers on alert status. This build-up was undertaken although, as Schlesinger has pointed out, Kennedy and the White House staff "wondered whether the new budget was not providing more missiles than national security required" and thereby threatened the Soviets' retaliatory capability. But the "President," reports Schlesinger, "was not prepared to overrule" the recommendation of Secretary McNamara.[59]

Considering the level of strategic superiority when Kennedy took office, these increases were awesome. Congressman Melvin Laird entered into the *Congressional Record* some estimates of the considerable baseline from which the Kennedy team advanced:

> ... two Polaris submarines with a combined total of 32 missiles, each missile capable of much more destruction than was rained upon Hiroshima.
> ... about 16 Atlas ICBM's.
> ... over 600 long-range B-52 jet bombers, each carrying more destructive explosive power, than that used by all the combatants in World War II.
> ... nearly 1400 B-47 medium-range jet bombers based abroad and at home with a 4500-mile range and distances beyond with air-to-air refueling.
> ... B-58 Hustlers, the first U.S. supersonic medium-range jet bombers.
> ... Fourteen aircraft carriers able to launch more aircraft than the entire Soviet heavy bomber force.
> ... eighteen wings of tactical aircraft, each wing with a substantial nuclear attack capability deployed globally.
> ... Sixty Thor IRBM's (intermediate-range ballistic missiles) deployed in England, capable of raining nuclear destruction on Russia, and thirty Jupiter IRBM's being installed at bases in Italy, from which Russia can be hit.

or "well over 2000 nuclear carrying vehicles capable of reaching Russia."[60]

Kennedy was also willing to move toward expansion of American military capability at the subnuclear level. "Flexible response," as Henry Kissinger had indicated in the late 1950s, required superiority not only at the strategic level but at all levels of potential conflict. Thus at the same time as American strategic forces were being augmented, Kennedy and McNamara moved to build up the conventional capability that Eisenhower had cut back. During the first eighteen months of the Kennedy administration, McNamara strove to increase the size of the army, the navy, and the air force. By mid-1962, after a year of intense and escalating crises (to be described below), McNamara would have available sixteen combat-ready divisions (up from eleven), along with twenty-one tactical air wings (up from eighteen), three marine divisions and their air wings, or the equivalent of a ten-division strategic reserve. William Kaufmann notes:

> With it, he could handle a Korean size engagement and still have several divisions left over for another emergency. Alternatively, he could triple the size of the American forces in Europe, and do so in fairly short order, since he had prepositioned in Europe the equipment for two divisions and was continuing to expand the airlift and sealift to move the strategic reserve. . . . His conventional options were expanding steadily.[61]

The interfaces between strategic nuclear and conventional war on the one hand and conventional war and nation-building on the other were not ignored. The basis for a graduated response between conventional war and strategic nuclear war was already present in the Eisenhower administration's tactical nuclear capability. Apart from improving existing systems, therefore, all that remained to be done was the development of a doctrine of controlled use and/or graduated escalation from conventional war up to and through limited or tactical nuclear war to, finally, general war. But throughout this spectrum of force McNamara sought options:

> Our new policy gives us the flexibility to choose among several operational plans, but does not require that we make any advance commitment with respect to doctrine or targets. We shall be committed only to a system that gives us the ability to use our forces in a controlled and deliberate way.[62]

Finally, McNamara developed an American potential for dealing with what he termed the "gray areas" of the third world. Nation-building was conceived as an anticipation of unconventional military conflict. But if conflict or what Khrushchev had called wars of national liberation broke out, the United States was to be prepared to respond in kind. Specifically, McNamara called for a more than $1.5 billion increase in military assistance, and soon noted proudly that the ability to fight guerrilla wars had been augmented by a 150 percent increase in antiguerrilla forces in all services but especially the army special forces or Green Berets.[63]

In time McNamara would come to question elements of this doctrine, especially the notion of the controlled and limited use of nuclear weapons. By the late 1960s McNamara would be publicly warning that neither the United States nor the Soviet Union possessed or could attain the capacity for a nuclear first strike against the other without inviting the certainty of unacceptable nuclear destruction in retaliation.[64] By the mid and late 1960s, McNamara would shift to an advocacy of deterrence grounded in "assured destruction capability" as the basis of American strategic planning and forces. But in 1961 and 1962, nuclear weapons were viewed as but one of several instrumentalities to be employed — a "complement" to nonnuclear antiguerrilla forces which, taken together, "aimed at achieving the best balance of military capabilities — over the entire range of potential conflict, in the various areas of the globe where the Free World has vital interests, and over the years, as far ahead as we can reasonably plan."[65]

In summary, the Kennedy administration feverishly prepared for confrontation with communist aggression at whatever level of conflict or wherever it appeared. In the meantime, however, Khrushchev continued to pursue the more moderate diplomacy that had marked his overtures to Kennedy during the interregnal period.

AMERICAN AIMS IN THE
FIRST ROUND: THE BERLIN CRISIS

Immediately following Kennedy's inauguration, Khrushchev moved dramatically to demonstrate his desire to improve communications between the United States and the Soviet Union. On January 21, 1961, Khrushchev met for 2 hours with U.S. Ambassador Llewellyn E. Thompson and informed him that he earnestly desired an improvement in communications between the United States and the USSR. To demonstrate this, Khrushchev announced to Thompson that he would release the two survivors of the RB-47 shot down in July 1960. Khrushchev noted that he had deliberately waited until now so as to benefit Kennedy rather than the Republicans.[66] Finally, Khrushchev made it clear to Thompson that he was very interested in a meeting with Kennedy as soon as possible.[67] This Russian overture, announced by Kennedy in his first news conference on January 25, was taken by the new administration as an indication that the Russians wanted a reduction in tensions, but Khrushchev's "Wars of National Liberation" speech of January 6 was not overlooked. Khrushchev's gesture was therefore accepted, but with a note of caution. Secretary of

State Dean Rusk echoed Kennedy's reserved appraisal of the Russian move in his news conference of February 6.[68]

Kennedy's cautious receipt of Khrushchev's overture indicated a basic need of the new administration at this stage in the transition — time. Kennedy had been in office less than a week. He was confronted with a crush of demands, including the preparation of numerous messages for the new Congress and the completion of his legislative program. Furthermore, Kennedy had not yet had an opportunity to confer with his Soviet experts as to a future course of action. An immediate and dramatic response to Khrushchev at this point was, therefore, not forthcoming, although Kennedy did announce during his January 25 news conference that during his administration, the U-2 flights would not be resumed.

The new administration's need for time and its intention to avoid an immediate meeting with Khrushchev at an early date was also apparent in its attitude and approach toward diplomacy in general. The State Department in particular advocated the use of traditional means of diplomacy, although it would be inaccurate to characterize Secretary of State Rusk's and the State Department's attitude as being absolutely in opposition to high-level meetings.

The door was not, therefore, closed on a meeting between Kennedy and Khrushchev, but at this point Kennedy did want more time before moving to the summit level of negotiations. This point was communicated to Khrushchev by Ambassador Thompson in his meeting with the Russian premier on January 21, and apparently Khrushchev did not challenge Kennedy's request. Rather, he restricted himself to an expression of his wish that lines of communication might be reopened.[69]

Russian reaction to Kennedy's February announcement of a stepped-up strategic armaments program was noticeably restrained. *Pravda,* for example, confined itself to a bland denunciation of the defense passages in the address and urged that the new administration follow a course of peaceful coexistence.[70] Beyond this there was little official reaction on the part of the Kremlin. The Russians seemed content to exercise a degree of restraint until Kennedy's position was more clearly spelled out.

In the meantime, events were transpiring which upon first examination appeared to endanger the still-developing contacts between the Soviet Union and the United States. The civil strife in Laos was an explosive situation given the presence of Russian aid and a commitment of American prestige. Kennedy moved to demonstrate to Khrushchev that he was willing to commit U.S. troops in order to ensure in Laos what he called in his first press conference a "peaceful country — an independent country not dominated by either side."[71] The communist-backed Pathet

Lao forces launched an offensive against Vientiane in early March, and Kennedy on March 23 gravely warned that there could be no peace unless the external support of the Pathet Lao was halted.[72] Kennedy followed up his warning by moving American troops into neighboring Thailand across the Mekong River from Vientiane. Apparently the show of force had its desired effect; for by April Khrushchev had agreed to discuss proposals for the neutralization of the country.

An earlier event in February, which also implied difficulties for Soviet-American relations, was the very peculiar murder of Patrice Lumumba in the Congo.[73] The Russian reaction to the event indicated, however, that they would confine their attacks to charges against Secretary-General Dag Hammarskjold and the United Nations, while avoiding direct attacks against the United States. Indeed, on the day of the incident, February 13, Khrushchev, in a reply to a congratulatory telegram from Kennedy (on the occasion of the launching of a Soviet Venus probe), indicated that he was interested in exploring joint Soviet-United States space efforts.

The event that evoked the greatest concern for Soviet-American relations, however, was the abortive Bay of Pigs invasion. If the Russian actions with respect to Laos and the Lumumba murder provided some hope that Soviet-American relations might be improving, the sharp diplomatic exchange between Kennedy and Khrushchev over Cuba seemingly returned those relations to their preinauguration status.[74] Within 3 weeks following the U.S. Caribbean failure, however, events were to take a dramatic turn as Khrushchev renewed his request for a summit meeting and Kennedy replied positively and agreed to meet with Khrushchev in Vienna on June 3 and 4, 1961.

It was generally believed at the time of the announcement that Kennedy's decision to go to Vienna on June 3 could be attributed to the deterioration of the position of the United States resulting from the Bay of Pigs disaster. Kennedy feared that Khrushchev might miscalculate the strength and position of the United States and thereby dangerously overestimate his position, thus the opportunity for talks was sized by Kennedy as a means for making the U.S. position clear. Khrushchev's motivations were, however, somewhat problematic. His letter of May 12 restated his position on Cuba but also repeated a Soviet desire for improved relations with the United States. Khrushchev listed disarmament, Laos, and Germany as major areas for discussion if Kennedy decided to accept the offer. Furthermore, one might surmise that Khrushchev was as anxious as Kennedy to take the measure of his counterpart. Khrushchev may also have felt that the American president's position had been sufficiently weakened by the Cuban affair as to make him prone to bullying — a tactic that

Khrushchev had shown some propensity to use in the past.[75] There is also evidence that Khrushchev's specific intent was to attempt to force the German question to a solution.[76] Khrushchev reportedly informed the American ambassador, Llewellyn Thompson, that he had waited long enough on the Berlin question, and noted that the matter of his own prestige was involved. Thompson reported in turn that Khrushchev was faced with a Communist party congress in the fall and needed some action on the Berlin question to protect himself.[77]

Kennedy's desire that he enter into negotiations from a position of apparent strength manifested itself in a disconcertingly tough speech to Congress on May 25, less than 2 weeks before the Vienna summit. The title of his message was "On Urgent National Needs." He explained his appearance by declaring: "These are extraordinary times . . . and . . . I am here to promote the doctrine of freedom." The Soviets, he declared, "possess a powerful intercontinental striking force, large forces for executing war, a well trained underground in nearly every country . . . the capacity for quick decision, a . . . society without dissent . . . and long experience in the techniques of violence and subversion."[78] The challenge was formidable. But the young president proceeded to describe a wide range of strategies to meet it. Along with his request for increased conventional and unconventional war capability, Kennedy also announced a new national fall-out shelter program. Every federal, state, and local building, and even private homes, were to be subsidized by an immediate tripling of the then-pending budget request. A great civil defense effort had been advocated by civilian strategists, notably Harvard's Henry Kissinger and Herman Kahn, then at RAND.

This school of strategists believed that a massive fall-out shelter program and new methods for quick evacuation of cities and dealing with the results of thermonuclear destruction by improved communication capabilities would prepare for the worst and could well save millions of lives; and, more important, would demonstrate the United States' willingness to take the worst the Soviets had to offer, if the stakes were high enough. In short, fall-out shelters were a concrete, burlap, and sandbag symbol of national will to uphold commitments at any level of violence necessary. Critics, however, pointed out that shelters could also be interpreted by the Soviets as a preparation for an American first strike. Given the number of missiles and planes that the Soviets could send to the United States after they had been hit by a disarming blow, fall-out shelters would minimize damage to an extent where an American victory could be contemplated without the thought of a mountain of American corpses. To that extent, critics held, the program was provocative. Political scientist J. David Singer wrote worriedly in the *Bulletin of Atomic Scientists:*

[T]he Kremlin strategists might well want to ask how useful a shelter program would be to the nation whose doctrine is a purely retaliatory one. More specifically, how many lives would be saved by such a program if we were the victims of a surprise attack?

If the [surprise] attack were against our cities, it is evident that very few people would be able to get to their shelters in time, and those that did would not find them particularly protective. . . . [Therefore] the Soviets must begin to wonder whether the shelters are for protection against [a] surprise attack, or whether they may not reflect a first-strike strategy.[79]

Kennedy and McNamara were later to yield to these arguments. But in the meantime, so near to the summit, the announcement of vastly enlarged civil defense programs had a clear and immediate diplomatic purpose. "Our greatest asset," Kennedy concluded "in this struggle [for freedom] is the American people['s] willingness to pay any price. . . . It is heartening to know, as I journey abroad, that our country . . . is ready to do its duty."[80]

The Vienna Conference

The Vienna Conference, described as "useful" in the joint communique issued at the conclusion of the meetings on June 4, produced substantive agreement on only one point, Laos. Agreement was reached on the second day of the talks that the conclusion on a cease fire should be a "priority matter."[81] The remainder of the conference produced frank, well-defined, but courteous disagreement.

The first day of the conference was devoted to a thorough airing of the world views of both leaders. By becoming involved in such an ideological debate, Kennedy was forced to talk on Khrushchev's grounds, hence Khrushchev apparently held the initiative throughout this initial day of talks. Such ideological debate was, as Schlesinger has pointed out, inevitably fruitless.[82] Kennedy sought, therefore, in the second day of the talks, to turn the discussion to more concrete matters. On disarmament a complete stalemate was reached. The discussion then turned to Berlin and the German question, and in so doing the first great confrontation on the new frontier was initiated.

Khrushchev repeated the oft-stated position of the Soviet Union that a peace treaty had to be signed so as to eradicate the threat of the West German militarists starting a third world war. He wanted agreement with the West, but if none was forthcoming he would sign a separate treaty with East Germany. A free city of West Berlin would be established, with control of all access in the hands of the German Democratic Republic.

Kennedy replied that, unlike Laos, Berlin was considered by the United States to be a point of vital interest. The position of the United States vis-à-vis Berlin and Germany was the result of legal contractual rights as decided by World War II. If the United States withdrew from Berlin, it would ultimately mean the abandonment of the rest of Europe. In summary, Kennedy made it clear to Khrushchev that he would not accept an ultimatum from the Soviet Union. He would not "acquiesce in the isolation of his country."[83]

Khrushchev now became considerably more harsh. He repeated that he only wanted to assure that the "most dangerous spot in the world" would not cause war. He in effect closed the question as he noted that nothing could possibly prevent him from signing a peace treaty with East Germany by the end of the year;[84] and from that time on, any infringement on the sovereignty of the German Democratic Republic would be considered as an act of aggression.[85]

The Berlin Crisis: Emergence from Transition

Khrushchev had given to Kennedy at Vienna two *aide-memoires* which restated in more formal diplomatic language the position advanced by Khrushchev during his conversations with Kennedy.[86] The memoranda did not include Khrushchev's pledge that he would sign a peace treaty by the end of the year, but his television and radio talk to the Russian people on June 15, 1961, did state the pledge clearly.[87] Kennedy's statement a week earlier was

> I made it clear to Mr. Khrushchev that the security of Western Europe and therefore our own security are deeply involved in our presence and our access rights to West Berlin, that those rights are based on law and not on sufferance, and that we are determined to maintain those rights at any risk.[88]

When joined with Khrushchev's pronouncement, this announced to the world that another Berlin crisis was full blown.

Throughout the summer the crisis was gradually escalated. On June 21 Khrushchev noted that the United States was increasing its appropriations for military expenditures. The Soviet leader indicated that such a move might necessitate a similar increase on the part of the Soviet Union. Khrushchev went further and threatened to resume nuclear testing if the United States did so.[89]

On the following day, Secretary of State Rusk reaffirmed the intention of the United States to stay in Berlin, and refused to consider the Russian peace treaty as valid.[90] The president, in his news conference of June 28, solemnly restated the position of the United States to honor its commitments and warned the Russians not to "underestimate the will and unity of democratic societies where vital interests are concerned."[91] Khrushchev reciprocated these sentiments and stepped up the pressure. On July 8 he announced that, in response to increased U.S. defense expenditures, the Soviet Union would be forced to increase its own defense preparations by suspending all proposed reductions in the size of the Soviet armed forces until the German question was resolved and increasing defense spending of 3,144,000,000 rubles.[92]

The initial reaction of the United States to this new Soviet move came in the form of a note given to the Soviet Union on July 17. This note was, in fact, a reply to the Soviet *aide-memoires* of June 4, and was comprised of a legalistic point-by-point refutation of that document.[93] The White House seems to have been disappointed by the document, particularly with the "maddening" slowness with which it had been produced by the State Department.[94] Kennedy was reportedly dismayed that the document was only a "compilation of stale, tedious, and negative phrases, none of them very new."[95] Kennedy felt that a new and more dynamic statement of the United States was needed; a clear delineation of the over-all response of the United States to the German question had to be presented to the American people and the world.

Kennedy's new response was delivered in a televised report to the American people on July 25, 1961. At the outset the president repeated the intention and right of the United States to be in Berlin. Again he restated that the U.S. position was considered as being vital to the national interest:

> We cannot and will not permit the Communists to drive us out of Berlin, either gradually or by force. For the fulfillment of our pledge to that city is essential to the morale and security of Western Germany, to the unity of Western Europe, and to the faith of the entire Free World.[96]

Kennedy next set forth his specific proposals, which were to constitute his response to Khrushchev's escalation of the crisis. The president called for an additional $3,247,000,000 in defense appropriations. He asked for an increase in the size of the army from 875,000 men to approximately one million, an increase in the navy and air force of respectively 29,000 and 63,000 men. The draft was to be doubled and then tripled within the near future, and Kennedy announced that he was requesting authority to call upon reserve units. The numbers required were unstated, but soon over 150,000 men, veterans of Korea and World War II, and National Guardsmen, were called from their jobs to active service. Also, the planned deactivation of ships and aircraft such as the B-47 was to be delayed. Fifty percent of "our missile power . . . and of our B-52 and B-47 bombers" were on "ground alert which would send them on their way with 15 minutes warning." Moreover, Kennedy announced that $1.8 billion of the funds he had requested would be spent for the procurement of nonnuclear war materials.[97] Defense programs were to be enlarged yet another $205 million. The year's appropriation of $3.5 billion for civilian defense was to be applied toward procuring adequate food, water, first aid kits, household warning kits to detect dangerous levels of home radiation, and a national air raid warning system ranging from sirens to telecommunications systems.

The Berlin crisis did not, of course, end with Kennedy's speech. In the tension-filled weeks following Kennedy's talk, the exodus of refugees from East Berlin was to increase, thereby prompting Khrushchev to seal off East Berlin on the night of August 12 and, in the days that followed, to construct the Berlin wall. Possibly this cessation of the flow of refugees to the West was seen by Khrushchev as his only obtainable goal (other than using the circumstances as a pretext for renewing atmospheric testing); for after inconclusive negotiations had been initiated, Khrushchev announced, in a 6-hour report to the 22nd Congress of the Communist party, that he would no longer insist on a peace treaty.[98]

Just before Khrushchev rose to make his speech, the probability of a Soviet-American showdown seemed unusually high. The calling up of 150,000 American reservists, the increase in the American arms budget, the inauguration of a nationwide fall-out shelter system that indicated Americans would be prepared to accept the worst from the Soviets and still, in the words of the Pentagon's second in command, "not be defeated," all indicated an assurance that America's full might could well be called into play in Berlin. Reports of the wall — the sordid details of land mines, barbed wire, and watchtowers — reached the morning papers in Washington on an especially inauspicious Friday the 13th of October, 1961. General Lucius Clay, the U.S. military governor general of Berlin, who was largely responsible for the Berlin airlift, returned to the city. As he arrived, White House spokesmen announced that a battle group of 1500 men was heading down the Autobahn to reinforce the American garrison in Berlin.

While the 22nd Congress was being held in Moscow, the East German authorities began to slow Western traffic, including American armored columns, headed for Berlin. On October 26 Soviet tanks moved in the East Berlin sector so as to be separated by a strip less than 75 yards from the position of American tanks. There were reports that American bulldozers had joined the American tank columns and infantry positions. In his memoirs, Khrushchev claims that Marshall Konev reported to him that the Americans were preparing to cross the frontier and destroy the wall.[99] But on October 27 Khrushchev spoke to the 22nd Congress: "What counts most," he declared, "is not the particular date" of the settlement of the German problem, "but a businesslike and honest settlement of the question."[100] Soviet tanks withdrew as Khrushchev finished speaking.

The apparent successful manipulation of threats and signals again indicated Soviet susceptibility to the diplomacy of threat. After the Cuban missile crisis, this lesson seemed to displace almost all other alternative approaches for dealing with America's most powerful adversary. Soviet power was depreciated. For a while, Americans believed that an American-constructed international system would endure without challenge for the foreseeable future. Yet the Berlin crisis and the successful installation of the Berlin wall had further significance. Khrushchev was probably correct in pointing out that Western acquiescence to the implied permanent division of Germany that the wall portended also prepared the ground for future German leaders to live with the results of World War II. Khrushchev claims that he "forced Kennedy and the Western Allies to swallow a bitter pill."[101] In the long run, the medicine did not seem pernicious. In the short run, both the patient and the good Soviet doctor almost died as the cold war moved to a climax in the waters off Cuba.

CONCLUSION

Nation-building and a flexible response provided the Kennedy administration with a policy construct predisposed toward activism. Flexible response, of course, was in part rooted in the concepts of the past. However, the thrust of the Kennedy administration was to free itself of the "reactive elements" that to them characterized the massive retaliation of the Eisenhower years. That is to say, Kennedy, through Robert McNamara and his collection of defense intellectuals, sought to develop a spectrum of usable force in addition to an expanded and embellished strategic retaliatory capacity at the upper end of the scale of possible violence. Indeed, with the incorporation into the Kennedy Department of Defense of many of the men who had criticized the massive retaliation doctrines of the 1950s, American nuclear forces began to reflect a limited nuclear war potential as well as an expansion of conventional capability. Nowhere is the propensity toward an activist interventionist posture more apparent than in the area of unconventional warfare. In fact, the doctrines of insurgency and counterinsurgency stand as a kind of conceptual and practical bridge between the diplomacy of violence embodied in the doctrines of flexible response and the ostensibly peaceful activism of nation-building.

Nation-building as a concept and policy was clearly activist and interventionist. Whether the intervention was to be by means of a Peace Corps volunteer or a massive aid grant, the objective was the same. Forces of economic, social, and cultural development were to be set in motion and then monitored so as to allow the country to take off toward self-sustaining economic growth. At the same time, however, this economic growth "should aim at the strategic goals of a stronger national independence, an increased concentration on domestic affairs, greater democracy and a *long-run association with the West.*"[102] President Kennedy concerned himself with the development of a world marked by "diversity and independence," but "above all, 'this emerging world is incompatible with the communist world order.' "[103] The direction of history, Kennedy asserted, "represent[ed] the very essence of our view of the future of the world."[104]

But like the Truman administration, the Kennedy administration could not leave the historical process alone. America was now thought to be benefactor and monitor of the development process. This was the corollary of the mission set forth in the Truman Doctrine: to build and maintain a global order among great powers such that American values of political economy might flourish. Moreover, the burden was now doubly great, for had not Khrushchev proclaimed support of national wars of liberation a primary thrust of Soviet policy? Previously, external aggression was clear warrant for American intervention. Now the presence of armed insurgents was *ipso facto* grounds for intervention. The Kennedy administration accepted wholeheartedly, therefore, the somewhat enigmatic charge of the Truman Doctrine that we must help others "work out their own destiny in their own way."

Yet this was a slippery slope; for intervention pulled the United States into a process inevitably marked by enormous social, cultural, and economic discontinuity. Traditional structures were, of necessity, cracked open, often violently. But the mechanistic concepts and policies of nation-building were marked by a naive belief that somehow violence could be avoided. Indeed, if violence persisted, it was not unreasonable to assume that it was related in some way to Khrushchev's January 2, 1961, pledge, in which case reliance upon military force either indigenous or external was perfectly appropriate to the development process. The paradox was that in turning to the military and others of a conservative bent in the developing world, the United States was aligning itself with those least predisposed to a world of diversity and social justice. Moreover, it is notable that despite his protestation of willingness to allow pluralistic forces to work, Kennedy adopted and maintained intense personal interest in the Green Berets, that elite group of men responsible for insurgency and counterinsurgency — the gray nether world that joined nation-building to flexible response.

The doctrinal basis of the Kennedy administration foreign and defense policy was, therefore, a return to the activism of the late Truman administration. By adopting many of the modalities implied by NSC-68, the Kennedy administration worked to build and maintain an international system not unlike that envisioned in the 1950s as well as the 1940s. Indeed, what is commonly regarded as the finest hour of the Kennedy administration, the Cuban missile crisis, was in a way a classic example of the brinkmanship of the 1950s.

NOTES

1. Theodore H. White, *The Making of the President: 1960* (New York: The New American Library, Signet Edition, 1967), pp. 204–205.
2. Theodore C. Sorensen, *Kennedy* (New York: Bantam Books, 1966), p. 189.
3. Ibid., p. 256.
4. John F. Kennedy, "Annual Message to the Congress on the State of the Union, January 30, 1961," *Public Papers of the President, 1961* (Washington, D.C.: U.S. Government Printing Office, 1962), pp. 23–24.
5. "Long Live Leninism!" *Red Flag*, April 16, 1960, translated in *Peking Review*, No. 17 (1960).
6. Bernard S. Morris, *International Communism and American Policy* (New York: Atheneum Press, 1968), pp. 133–148.
7. Kennedy, op. cit., p. 23.
8. Cited by John Kenneth Galbraith, "The Moderate Solution" in John R. Boettiger (ed.), *Vietnam and American Foreign Policy* (Lexington, Mass.: D.C. Heath, 1968), p. 130.
9. For a good review, see Herbert Dinerstein's classic *War and the Soviet Union*, rev. ed. (New York: Praeger Publishers, 1962). There had been some writing on partisan warfare and some attention by Trotsky and Lenin to the revolutionary potential in the third world, but the dominant part of Soviet intellectual energy had been to diagnose the nature of capitalist ambitions and capacities and prepare a deep defense. Soviet diplomatic and revolutionary activity in Asia were especially muted as Stalin's campaign began in the late 1920s to build "socialism in one country" after disastrous attempts to bestir communist revolution in the colonial world.
10. John A. Armstrong, "Soviet Policy in the Middle East," in Kurt London (ed.), *The Soviet Union: A Half-Century of Communism* (Baltimore: Johns Hopkins University Press, (1968), pp. 423–454, esp. pp. 440–450.
11. Reprinted in "Selected Readings: Counter Insurgency" (U.S. Army War College, Carlisle Barracks, Pa., 1962), and in *Selected Readings in Guerrilla and Counter Guerrilla Operations* (U.S. Infantry School, Fort Benning, Ga., July 1967), pp. 54–62. Also see his speech reprinted in *World Marxist Review*, January 1961, and Robert McNamara's exegesis of it in his speech given to the Fellows of the American Bar Association, February 17, 1962, reprinted in *Selected Reading in Guerrilla and Counter Guerrilla Operations*, pp. 9–17.
12. Khrushchev in January 6, 1961, "Za Novye Pobedy Mirovogo Kommunisticheskogo Dvizheniia Kommunist (January 1961), p. 20; cited by Michel P. Gehlen, *The Politics*

of Coexistence: Soviet Methods and Motives (Bloomington, Ind.: Indiana University Press, 1967), p. 105.

13. Cited in Gehlen, op. cit., pp. 105–106.
14. Especially important in perpetuating this understanding was the influential translation of Mao Zedong, *On Guerrilla Warfare* by Brig. Gen. Samuel Griffith (New York: Praeger Publishers, 1961), especially page 4 where Griffith equates a statement made in November 1949 by Liu Shaoqi to the effect that other Asian revolutions "would follow the Chinese pattern," to Khrushchev's remarks in December 1960 and January 1961 on national liberation wars. Griffith's translation was considered "classic," and the Praeger distribution was the first major dissemination of Mao's thought in English by an American publishing firm.
15. *Peking Review,* No. 36 (September 3, 1965) for the full text.
16. Arthur Huck, *The Security of China: Chinese Approaches to Problems of War and Strategy* (New York: Columbia University Press, 1970), p. 50.
17. Dean Rusk, in U.S. Congress, Hearings before the Committee on Foreign Relations, *Supplemental Foreign Assistance, Fiscal Year 1966, Vietnam,* U.S. 89th Congress, 2nd Session, p. 596.
18. But this view was not confined to policy makers. It was also a perception widely shared by academics. As Professor Frank Trager of New York University wrote, "To support this view of the communist challenge in Southeast Asia, one does not have to argue for a supposed total identity of Sino-Soviet objectives, strategies and tactics in the area: that is, for world monolithicism ... [v]ariations help make it possible for Moscow and Peking to advance their overriding communist objectives. Separately or together, they acquire more strings to their respective bows for the greater success of the communist symphony ... there should be no doubt that basic purpose of the exercise in both Moscow and Peking is to overwhelm, that is to communize Southeast Asia." Frank N. Trager, in William Henderson (ed.), *Southeast Asia: Problems of United States Policy* (Cambridge, Mass.: The M.I.T. Press, 1963), pp. 163–164.
19. *Public Papers of the President of the United States: Harry S. Truman — 1951* (Washington, D.C.: U.S. Government Printing Office, 1965), p. 224.
20. Secretary Robert McNamara, February 17, 1962, speech to the American Bar Association in Chicago, p. 11 (emphasis ours), cited in *Selected Readings in Guerrilla and Counter Guerrilla Operations.*
21. Arthur Schlesinger, Jr., *A Thousand Days* (Boston: Houghton Mifflin Company, 1965), pp. 296–297; and Sorensen, op. cit., pp. 332–333.
22. Richard J. Walton, *Cold War and the Counterrevolution: The Foreign Policy of John F. Kennedy* (New York: Viking Press, 1972), pp. 44–45. In a press conference 5 days before the invasion on April 17, Kennedy skillfully dissembled when asked about American support for any such invasion, rumors of which had been in the press for weeks.
23. "Speech to American Society of Newspaper Editors," in *Public Papers of the President of the United States: John F. Kennedy — 1961* (Washington, D.C.: U.S. Government Printing Office, 1962), p. 305.
24. Ibid., p. 306.
25. Ibid.
26. Ibid.
27. Ibid., p. 304.
28. Ibid., p. 305.
29. Schlesinger, op. cit., p. 202.
30. Ibid., p. 195.

31. Ibid.

32. Douglas A. Blaufarb, *The Counter-Insurgency Era: U.S. Doctrine and Performance, 1950 to Present* (New York: Free Press, 1977), p. 88.

33. Karl W. Deutsch and William J. Foltz, *Nation-Building* (New York: Atherton Press, 1966), p. 3.

34. "Guerrilla Warfare in the Underdeveloped Areas," address made at graduation ceremonies at the U.S. Army Special Warfare School, Ft. Bragg, N.C., June 28, 1961, *Department of State Bulletin*, Vol. XLV, No. 1154 (August 7, 1961), p. 234.

35. Lincoln S. Bloomfield, "Vital Interests and Objectives of the United States," paper delivered to the Naval War College on August 26, 1963, reprinted in Wesley Posvar et al. (eds.), *American Defense Policy* (Baltimore: Johns Hopkins University Press, 1965), pp. 18–19 (emphasis in the original).

36. Samuel Huntington, *Political Order in Changing Societies* (New Haven, Conn.: Yale University Press, 1968), p. 72.

37. Samuel P. Huntington, "The Bases of Accommodation," *Foreign Affairs*, Vol. 46 (July 1968), p. 652.

38. Huntington, *Political Order in Changing Societies*, p. 24.

39. Ibid., p. 28.

40. Joseph La Palombara, "Political Science and the Engineering of National Development," in Monte Polner and Larry Stern (eds.), *Political Development in Changing Societies: An Analysis of Modernization* (Lexington, Mass.: D.C. Heath, Lexington Books, 1971), p. 52.

41. David W. Chang, "The Military and Nation Building in Korea, Burma and Pakistan," *Asian Survey*, Vol. 9, No. 11 (November 1969), p. 830.

42. See especially Charles Wolf, Jr., *The United States Policy and the Third World: Problems and Analysis* (Boston: Little, Brown and Company, 1967), for an elaborate panegyric to the military contribution to development.

43. See Gabriel Almond and J. S. Coleman (eds.), *The Politics of the Developing Areas* (Princeton, N.J.: Princeton Univ. Press, 1960), or Edward C. Banfield, *American Foreign Aid Doctrines* (Washington, D.C.: American Enterprise Institute, 1963).

44. Schlesinger, op. cit., p. 201. Professor Schlesinger writes:

> But the revolutionary point remained primary. For Kennedy fully understood — this was, indeed, the mainspring of all his thinking about Latin America — that, with all its pretensions to realism, the militant anti-revolutionary line represented the policy most likely to strengthen the communists and lose the hemisphere. He believed that, to maintain contact with a continent seized by the course of revolutionary change, a policy of social idealism was the only true realism for the United States.

45. Ibid., p. 769.

46. See, for example, *U.S. Department of Commerce, Statistical Abstract of the United States, 1971* (Washington, D.C.: U.S. Government Printing Office, 1972), p. 755.

47. Schlesinger, op. cit., p. 773.

48. Theodore Draper, "The Dominican Crisis: A Case Study in American Policy," *Commentary*, Vol. 40, No. 6 (December 1965), p. 34.

49. Schlesinger, op. cit. quoting Kennedy, p. 789.

50. Legislative Reference Service, Library of Congress, *Some Important Issues in Foreign Aid*, A Report Prepared for the Senate Committee on Foreign Relations (Washington, D.C.: U.S. Government Printing Office, 1966), pp. 10–13 and Agency for International Development, *U.S. Overseas Loans and Grants and Assistance from International*

Organizations: Obligations and Loan Authorizations, July 1, 1945–June 30, 1972 (Washington, D.C.: U.S. Government Printing Office, 1973), *passim.*

51. Annual Message to the Congress on the State of the Union, January 30, 1961, in *Public Papers of the Presidents, John F. Kennedy, 1961* (Washington, D.C.: U.S. Government Printing Office, 1962), p. 24 (emphasis added).
52. Louis Fitzsimmons, *The Kennedy Doctrine* (New York: Random House, 1972), p. 233, citing an oral history interview with Doctor Herbert York.
53. Ibid., pp. 233–234.
54. *The New York Times,* January 12, 1961.
55. Television and Radio Address of May 25, 1960, *Department of State Bulletin,* Vol. XLII, No. 1093 (June 6, 1960), p. 900.
56. Schlesinger, op. cit., p. 301.
57. Ibid.; I. F. Stone, in *New York Review of Books,* April 23, 1970, p. 21.
58. Schlesinger, op. cit., p. 500.
59. Ibid., pp. 499–500.
60. Melvin Laird, *Congressional Record,* January 25, 1961, House p. 1228; also cited by I. F. Stone, *New York Review of Books,* April 23, 1970, p. 22. In addition, Stone notes that Republicans pointed out that under the final Eisenhower budgets, there would be "600 Minuteman missiles by the end of 1964; 129 Atlas and 126 Titan ICBM's by the end of 1962; 4 more Polarises in service by the end of 1961, with 64 more missiles; and . . . 15 Jupiter IRBMs."
61. William W. Kaufmann, *The McNamara Strategy* (New York: Harper & Row, 1964), pp. 79–80.
62. Robert S. McNamara's Address in Atlanta, Ga., November 11, 1961, quoted in ibid., p. 75.
63. Ibid., pp. 69–72.
64. See, for example, McNamara's speech before the annual convention of United Press International editors and publishers at San Francisco, Calif., on Steptember 18, 1967, printed in *Department of State Bulletin,* Vol. LVII, No. 1476 (October 9, 1967), pp. 443–451.
65. Quoted in Kaufmann, op. cit., p. 76.
66. Schlesinger, op. cit., pp. 301–302. See also Seymour Topping, "Kremlin Initiation Step," *The New York Times,* January 22, 1961, pp. 1–3.
67. Sorensen, op. cit., p. 541.
68. "Secretary Rusk's News Conference of February 6," *Department of State Bulletin,* Vol. 44, No. 1131 (February 27, 1961), p. 302.
69. There does exist some disagreement on the question of whether Khrushchev forcefully pushed for an immediate meeting with Kennedy. Sorensen, as we have noted, merely states that Khrushchev expressed a desire for such a meeting. Others, notably Dana Schmidt, "Kennedy to Seek Delay in Parley and Atom Test Ban," *The New York Times,* January 25, 1961, p. 1, and William Jorden, "U.S.-Soviet Approaches Studied," *The New York Times,* January 25, 1961, p. 2, report that Khrushchev was not forceful in his expression of a desire for talks. Apparently the wish was expressed but not pushed.
70. "Only Sane Course Is Peaceful Coexistence," *Current Digest of the Soviet Press,* Vol. 13 (March 1, 1961), pp. 29–31.
71. "The President's News Conference of January 25, 1961," *Public Papers of the President, 1961,* p. 16.
72. "The President's News Conference of March 23, 1961," *Public Papers of the President, 1961,* pp. 213–214.

73. The authors of a Senate investigation some 15 years later wrote: "The chain of events revealed by the documents and testimony is strong enough to permit a reasonable inference that [a] plot to assassinate Lumumba was authorized by President Eisenhower." But even though "[t]he Congo station had advanced knowledge of the Central Government's plans to transport Lumumba into the hands of his bitterest enemies, where he was likely to be killed, . . . there is no evidentiary basis for concluding that the CIA conspired in *this* plan. . . ." U.S. Congress, Select Committee on Governmental Operations with Respect to Intelligence Activities, *Alleged Assassination Plots Involving Foreign Leaders,* Report No. 94–463, November 20, 1975, pp. 48 and 51.

74. "Message from N. S. Khrushchev, Chairman of the U.S.S.R. Council of Ministers, to U.S. President John F. Kennedy," *Current Digest of the Soviet Press,* Vol. 13 (May 17, 1961), pp. 4–5; and "Message to Chairman Khrushchev Concerning the Meaning of Events in Cuba, April 18, 1961," *Public Papers of the President, 1961,* pp. 286–287. Also in "United States and Soviet Union Exchange Messages in Regard to Events in Cuba," *Department of State Bulletin,* Vol. 44, No. 1141 (May 8, 1961), pp. 661–667.

75. Schlesinger, op. cit., p. 344. Schlesinger is the only person who has spoken of the exact contents of Khrushchev's letter and Louis J. Halle, "The Job to Be Done at the Summit," *The New York Times Magazine,* May 28, 1961, p. 48.

76. "For New Victories of the World Communist Movement," 2 parts, *Current Digest of the Soviet Press,* Vol. 13 (February 22, 1961), p. 10.

77. Schlesinger, op. cit., p. 347.

78. "Special Message to the Congress on Urgent National Needs, May 25, 1961," *Public Papers of the President, 1961,* pp. 396–397.

79. Ibid., pp. 402–403; and J. David Singer, "Deterrence and Shelters," *Bulletin of the Atomic Scientists,* Vol. XVII, No. 8 (October 1961), p. 313.

80. "Special Message, May 25, 1961," p. 406.

81. Schlesinger, op. cit., pp. 367–368; and Sorensen, op. cit., pp. 548–549.

82. Schlesinger, op. cit., p. 367.

83. Ibid., p. 371.

84. Sorensen, op. cit., p. 585. There is some disagreement between Sorensen and Schlesinger on chronology here. Schlesinger does not mention Khrushchev's pledge of an end-of-the-year treaty until after lunch of the second day. Sorensen records the pledge as being made during the morning talks.

85. Schlesinger, op. cit., pp. 370–374; and Sorensen, op. cit., pp. 584–586.

86. "On the Memorandum Handed by N. S. Khrushchev to U.S. President Kennedy," *Current Digest of the Soviet Press,* Vol. 13 (July 5, 1961), pp. 4–7.

87. "Radio and Television Address by N. S. Khrushchev on June 15, 1961," *Current Digest of the Soviet Press,* Vol. 13 (July 12, 1961), pp. 3–8. The East German leader Walter Ulbricht added emphasis to Khrushchev's statement by noting that he intended to maintain absolute control of access when the treaty was signed. "Ulbricht Warns on Berlin Access," *The New York Times,* June 16, 1961, pp. 1–2.

88. "Radio and Television Report to the American People on Returning from Europe, June 6, 1961," *Public Papers of the President, 1961,* p. 444.

89. "Speech by Comrade N. S. Khrushchev at Meeting of the Representatives of Moscow Public Park to Mark 20th Anniversary of Beginning of Great Patriotic War, June 21, 1961," *Current Digest of the Soviet Press,* Vol. 13 (July 19, 1961), p. 20.

90. "Secretary Rusk's News Conference of June 22," *Department of State Bulletin,* Vol. 45, No. 1150 (July 10, 1961), p. 51.

91. "The President's News Conference of June 28, 1961," *Public Papers of the President, 1961,* p. 477.
92. "Speech by Comrade N. S. Khrushchev at Reception for Graduates of Military Academies of U.S.S.R. Armed Forces, July 18, 1961," *Current Digest of the Soviet Press,* Vol. 13 (August 2, 1961), p. 5.
93. "Note from the United States to the Soviet Union, Replying to the Soviet Aide-Memoire Handed to President Kennedy at Vienna, July 17, 1961," *Department of State Bulletin,* Vol. 45 (August 7, 1961), p. 224.
94. Schlesinger, op. cit., p. 406.
95. Sorensen, op. cit., p. 587. Schlesinger describes the reply as "a tired and turgid rehash of documents left over from the Berlin crisis of 1958–1959," p. 384.
96. "Radio and Television Report to the American People on the Berlin Crisis, July 25, 1961," *Public Papers of the President, 1961,* p. 534.
97. Ibid., pp. 535–536.
98. "Report of the Central Committee of the Communist Party of the Soviet Union to the 22nd Congress — II," *Current Digest of the Soviet Press,* Vol. 13 (November 3, 1961), p. 5.
99. Nikita Khrushchev, *Khrushchev Remembers: The Last Testament,* Strobe Talbott (ed.) (Boston: Little, Brown and Company, 1974), pp. 506–507.
100. "Concluding Remarks by Comrade N.S. Khrushchev at the 22nd Party Congress, October 27, 1961," *Current Digest of the Soviet Press,* Vol. 13, No. 46 (December 13, 1961), p. 24.
101. Khrushchev, *Khrushchev Remembers,* p. 509.
102. Schlesinger, op. cit., p. 588 (emphasis added).
103. Schlesinger noting Kennedy, op. cit., p. 617.
104. "Address in Berkeley at the University of California, March 23, 1962," *Public Papers of the President, 1962,* p. 265.

Chapter 8
The Apotheosis
of Containment

Historians know there is a rhythm to their craft. Events are examined, and orthodoxies are established. Then comes a chipping away of previously held convictions. New understandings emerge and stand — for a while; and then comes another tide of reevaluation. The Kennedy administration's shimmering hour — the Cuban crisis — has just begun to have its luster tarnished by critics. Yet few have subjected the event to a complex review of its meaning in terms of the assumptions, policy processes, and relationships of the cold war.[1] Our contention is that the crisis became something of a misleading model of the foreign-policy process and diverted attention from profound changes under way in the world political economy.

Concerning the former model there are seven central tenets, each of which was confirmed by the lessons of the Cuban crisis:

1. Crisis is typical of international relations. The international environment is a constant collision of wills that is, at once, both a surrogate of war and takes place at the doorstep of war. Crises are objective elements of the international system — but they also have a profoundly psychological element of will and resolve.
2. Crises are assumed to be manageable. Those skills of personality, training, and organizational expertise that had developed in the national security machinery during the previous 25 years could be orchestrated by a vast bureaucracy in controlled and responsive movements.
3. Although crises are a characteristic of the international system, the domestic system is one of order and consensus and is insulated from the necessities of international politics. Public opinion, in this view, can be controlled to lend support for a particular foreign policy; but rarely do appurtenances of the domestic sector have their own imperatives.
4. Diplomacy is a mixture of the instrumentation of force and bargaining. An essential element of crisis management is the ability to reconcile the inherent forward dynamic of violence, threats of violence, and the instruments of violence with negotiation.

5. The Americans can control the process of crisis negotiation to win. Winning ends with the events themselves. Political crises then, almost like a medical crisis, terminate by definition.
6. The Soviets seldom negotiate serious matters except under extreme duress.
7. Military questions are too critical to be left in the hands of strictly military men and organizations that are not in step with the needs of crisis management. Crisis management can and must be a civilian enterprise.

After the crisis, there were the beginnings of detente with the Soviet Union. The test ban treaty, the hot line, and a more civil exchange between the two powers are widely believed to stem from the favorable resolution of the missile crisis. Yet the model and its inherent assumptions on the meaning of Cuba can be challenged. Cuba does indeed stand as a watershed in the cold war and the history of the international system. But it is properly understood as a part and product of the cold war; indeed, the Cuban crisis was in many ways the climax of the cold war.

Even as the crisis occurred, evidence was emerging that the structure of the world's political economy was changing irrevocably and in a manner that would constrain the future exercise of American political and military power. More than a decade of American foreign military spending could no longer be dismissed as temporary or nonrecurring. The surfeit of American dollars in foreign hands — formerly the necessary liquidity for a rebuilding Western economy — was by the early 1960s regarded by Europeans as a threat to their new prosperity. But the Americans, now reinvigorated by the successful management of the Cuban crisis, saw such concerns as secondary. Granted that communism had been faced down at the brink of nuclear Armageddon, there was now a new crisis in the rice paddies of Southeast Asia.

MASTERY OR LUCK?

By far the most intense experience in East-West relations occurred in October 1962, when the Russians were discovered to have placed forty-two medium-range missiles in Cuba. In Khrushchev's apt description, it was a time when "a smell of burning hung heavy" in the air.[2] Kennedy's apparently controlled and masterful way of forcing Khrushchev to withdraw the missiles in the 13-day crisis has become a paradigmatic example of the way force can be harnessed to a policy by an elaborate manipulation of threats and gambits, negotiation and intimidation. Academic and government analysts have viewed Kennedy's response as a highly calibrated dissection of alternatives instead of seeing his actions as largely an intuitive response to a threat to his administration's electoral future, pride, and strategic posture. As Hans J. Morgenthau, the eminent scholar and a critic of the Kennedy administration, concluded: "The Cuban Crisis of 1962 . . . was the distillation of a collective intellectual effort of a high order, the like of which must be rare in history."[3] Much of this analysis — so drenched in the cool light of hindsight — bears a suspicious resemblance to the logical and psychological fallacy of reasoning *post hoc ergo propter hoc.*[4] Nevertheless, the dominant lesson Americans have drawn from the Cuban experience has been a joyous sense of the United States regaining mastery over history.

For many years Americans had felt threatened by the Soviet challenge to world order — especially since that challenge had been reinforced by growing Russian strategic capability. But after Cuba, the fears of precipitate expansion of a Soviet-American dispute into a final paroxysm of nuclear dust were dissipated. After Cuba, escalation became the *idée fixe* of academics and policymakers — a vision of a ladder of force with rungs separated by equivalent spaces of destruction, each with its own "value," running out toward darkness. Escalation became the dominant metaphor of American officialdom. Each rung could be ascended or descended with the proper increment of will and control. Events and military machines could be mastered for diplomatic ends. As Robert McNamara exalted after the exciting and frightening Cuban climax: "There is no longer any such thing as strategy, only crisis management."[5] Dennis Healy, the British Labor party "shadow" defense minister, called the Kennedy administration's performance a "model in any textbook on diplomacy."[6] Journalist Henry Pachter described Kennedy's execution of crisis management as "a feat whose technical elegance compelled the professionals' admiration."[7] Similarly, the Wohlstetters made Cuba into a general historical principle about the use of force in times of great stress: "where the alternative is to be ruled by events with such enormous consequences, the head of a great state is likely to examine his acts of choice in crisis and during it to subdivide these possible acts in ways that make it feasible to continue exercising choice."[8]

The decisions as to what steps should be taken to deal with the implantation of the missiles were hammered out in the Executive Committee (ExCom) meetings. Although court chroniclers of the Kennedy administration have pored over each detail, the impression now is not one of all choices having been carefully weighed and considered. Rather, in retrospect, there appears to have been a gripping feeling of uncertainty and pressure. Robert Kennedy, for instance, at the height of the crisis, looked across at his brother and almost fainted at the horror of what they were contemplating: "Inexplicably, I thought of when he was ill and almost died; when he lost his child, when we learned that our oldest brother had been killed; of personal times of strain and hurt. The voices droned on, but I didn't seem to hear anything."[9]

There were reports that one assistant secretary was so disconcerted and fatigued that he drove into a tree at 4 A.M. Robert Kennedy recalled, "The strain and the hours without sleep were beginning to take their toll. . . . That kind of pressure does strange things to a human being, even to brilliant, self-confident, mature, experienced men." Robert Kennedy suspected that Dean Rusk, the secretary of state, "had a virtually complete breakdown mentally and physically."[10] And President Kennedy, although deliberately pacing himself, wondered how many of his principal advisors might suffer mental collapse from the long hours and pressure. Tense, fearful, and exhausted men planned and held together the American policy response to the Russian missiles.

The consensus of most behavioral research is that men operating under such acute stress are scarcely capable of considered judgment. Strain and fatigue commonly produce actions that are "caricatures of day-to-day behavior."[11] Although the stress of crisis decisionmaking concentrates and focuses the collective mind, it does not allow for the kind of elegant dissection of events that is now read into the Cuban affair. Events can take charge of decision makers; on October 25, 1962, Robert Kennedy reported that he felt, as Soviet ships drew near the edge of the American quarantine, that "[W]e were on the edge of a precipice with no way off. . . . President Kennedy had initiated the course of events, but he no longer had control over them."[12] John F. Kennedy's calm public face, discipline, and cool control gave a sense of intellectual engagement in the crisis that yielded no hint of the mute wasteland he was contemplating. But his private anxiety is well recorded, and a case can be made that dispassionate analysis or problem solving was all but precluded by the psychology of the situation.

It was very close. The military and the "hawks" — a term coined by journalistic descriptions of the ExCom deliberations — were pushing for actions ranging from a "surgical strike" to an all-out invasion of Cuba. Such options would have demanded the stark choice of an even greater Soviet humiliation or a Soviet response in kind. Ironically, a surgical strike was not really practical, for there was no guarantee that more than 90 percent of the missiles could be extirpated. Even after an American air attack, some of the missiles could have survived and been launched. And "surgical" always was a misnomer to describe an estimated 25,000 Cuban fatalities, not to speak of the 500 sorties that American planes would have had to run in order to destroy the Soviet missiles and bombers. Nevertheless, if six out of fourteen members of the ExCom group had had their way, the blockade of Cuba would have been an attack, which Robert Kennedy called a "Pearl Harbor in reverse." It is no wonder that President Kennedy estimated the world's chance of avoiding war at between one out of three and even.[13]

The illusion of control derived from the crisis was perniciously misleading. Although many Americans shared the belief of historian Arthur Schlesinger that the Cuban crisis displayed to the "whole world . . . the ripening of an American leadership unsurpassed in the responsible management of power . . . [a] combination of toughness . . . nerve and wisdom, so brilliantly controlled, so matchlessly calibrated that [it] dazzled the world,"[14] President Kennedy's control was in fact far from complete.

McNamara had sensed the navy's lack of responsiveness to civilian commands and had gone to the "Flag Plot," or Naval Operations Center, where he could talk to ship commanders directly by voice-scrambled radio. McNamara pointed to a map symbol indicating that a ship was in a spot where he had not wanted it. "What's that ship doing there?" he asked. Chief of Naval Operations Admiral Anderson confessed, "I don't know, but I have faith in my officers."[15] McNamara's unease with the apparent lack of responsiveness of the navy to civilian command prompted him to inquire what would happen if a Soviet captain refused to divulge his cargo to a boarding American officer. Anderson picked up a Manual of Naval Regulations and rose to defend the navy against any implied slight about navy procedure. "It's all in there," Anderson asserted. McNamara retorted, "I don't give a damn what John Paul Jones would have done. I want to know what you are going to do, now!" The last word — again — however, was the navy's: Admiral Anderson patronizingly soothed the fuming defense secretary, "Now, Mr. Secretary, if you and your deputy will go to your offices, the Navy will run the blockade."[16] As McNamara and his entourage turned to leave, Anderson called to him, "Don't worry, Mr. Secretary, we know what we are doing here."[17]

Just when the first Soviet-American encounter at sea seemed imminent, William Knox, the president of Westinghouse International, who happened to be in Moscow, was surprised by an abrupt summons from Premier Khrushchev. The voluble Soviet leader, perhaps half-convinced that Wall Street really manipulated American policy, gave a frightening summary of the strategic situation in the Caribbean. He warned that if the U.S. navy began stopping Soviet ships, Soviet subs would start sinking American ships. That, Khrushchev explained, would lead to World War III.[18]

Only a little later, the navy began to force Soviet subs to the surface in order to defend its blockade — well before Kennedy had authorized contact with surface vessels. Kennedy was appalled when he learned that military imperatives are distinct from diplomatic necessities and can, all too often, conflict. When he found out that the navy was intent on surfacing ships, he was horrified: "Isn't there some way we can avoid having our first exchange with a Russian submarine — almost anything but that?" McNamara replied flintily, "No, there's too much danger to our ships. There is no alternative." The president's brother wrote that "all six Russian submarines then in the area or moving toward Cuba from the Atlantic were followed and harassed and, at one time or another, forced to surface in the presence of U.S. military ships."[19] One can only wonder what would have happened if one of the Russian subs had refused to surface and had instead turned on its pursuers.

Events were only barely under control when, at the height of the crisis, on October 26, an American U-2 plane fixed on the wrong star and headed back from the North Pole to Alaska via Siberia. To compound matters the Alaskan Air Command sent fighter-bombers to escort the plane home, and the U.S. fighters and the spy plane met over Soviet territory before proceeding back.[20] To survive a Strangelove series of incidents like these, even given the assumptions of the day, can hardly be characterized as more than luck. It would not seem to be the mastery that Schlesinger and other court scribes delight in recalling and extolling.

THE DOMESTIC FACTOR

Why was there a crisis in the first place? The answer was found, in part, in one of the unacknowledged necessities in the conduct of American international affairs — domestic political considerations.[21] The Kennedy administration's sense of its own precarious electoral position, the coming of the November mid-term elections, and the place Cuba had occupied in public debate, all augured for an immediate and forceful response, no matter what the strategic reality was of having Russian missiles near American borders. The imperatives of American domestic politics during an election year had been building for some time. On August 27, 1962, for example, Republican Senator Homer E. Capehart of Indiana declared, "It is high time that the American people demand that President Kennedy quit 'examining the situation' and start protecting the interests of the United States."[22] Former Vice President Nixon, on the gubernatorial campaign stump in California, proposed that Cuban communism be "quarantined" by a naval blockade.[23] Republicans in both Houses had warned the administration that Cuba would be "the dominant issue of the 1962 campaign."[24] The chairman of the Republican national committee jabbed at Kennedy's most sensitive spot–his concern for foreign policy resolve: "If we are asked to state the issue in one word, that word would be Cuba — symbol of the tragic irresolution of the administration."[25]

The pressure mounted. As the political campaign began, one observer spotted a sign at a Kennedy rally in Chicago that read, "Less Profile — More Courage."[26] The widely respected and conservative London *Economist* reported that America had become "obsessed" by the "problem" of Cuba;[27] and I. F. Stone despaired in his *Weekly* that Cuba was a bogey that shook Americans, in the autumn of 1962, even more than the thought of war.[28] The domestic pressure on the American president was so intense that one member of Camelot, former Ambassador John Kenneth Galbraith, wrote: "Once they [the missiles] were there, the political needs of the Kennedy administration urged it to take almost any risk to get them out."[29] This skeptical view was shared by none other than former President Eisenhower, who suspected "that Kennedy might be playing politics with Cuba on the eve of Congressional elections."[30]

Nor, as Ronald Steel pointed out, were the principals — the ExCom — insulated from domestic considerations in their deliberations.[31] One Republican member of the crisis planners sent Theodore Sorensen — Kennedy's alter ego — a note that read: "Ted — have you considered the very real possibility that if we allow Cuba to complete installation and operational readiness of missile bases, the next House of Representatives is likely to have a Republican majority?"[32] Similarly, McGeorge Bundy, chief adviser to two presidents, wondered, when the missiles were first reported, whether action could be deferred until after the election.[33] If the missile installations were completed earlier, there would be, arguably, both a strategic and an electoral problem facing the administration.

What was the worrisome substance of change in the strategic balance represented by the placement of forty-two missiles? To Robert McNamara, the secretary of defense, it seemed that "a missile is a missile. It makes no great difference whether you are killed by a missile from the Soviet Union or from Cuba."[34] About 2 weeks later, on television, Deputy Secretary of Defense Roswell Gilpatric confirmed the debatable meaning of the missiles: "I don't believe that we were under any greater threat from the Soviet Union's power, taken in totality, after this than before."[35] Indeed, Theodore Sorensen wrote in a memorandum to the president on October 17, 1962 — 5 days before the blockade was ordered — that the presence of missiles in Cuba did not "significantly alter the balance of power." Sorensen explained, "They do not significantly increase the po-

tential megatonnage capable of being unleashed on American soil, even
after a surprise American nuclear strike." Sorensen confessed, in conclusion, that "Soviet motives were not understood."[36]

JUST A DIRTY TRICK?

To Khrushchev, the missiles offered the appearance of what former State
Department analyst Roger Hilsman called a "quick fix" to the Soviet
problem of strategic inferiority. Khrushchev was under enormous pressure from the Russian military, who rejected his promise of "goulash
communism" and were pushing for a vast increase in the Soviet arms
budget.[37] The Cuban missile ploy was probably Khrushchev's response to
the prospect of Russian strategic inferiority, which was reported by the
Kennedy administration as it admitted that the Democratic preelection
charge of a missile gap had not been based on fact. The American announcement that the gap had been closed was accompanied by a Defense
Department plan, dated October 19, 1961, for production of over 1000
missiles by 1964.

One purpose of the Soviet moves in Cuba was, therefore, to gain the
appearance of parity with the Americans. The employment of twenty-
four MRBM's and eighteen IRBM's *seemed* to be a dramatic movement
in that direction. But such an increase posed no real threat to American
retaliatory strength, or to increasing American superiority. As Henry Kissinger noted at the time: "The bases were of only marginal use in a defensive war. In an offensive war their effectiveness was reduced by the
enormous difficulty — if not impossibility — of coordination of a first strike
from the Soviet Union and Cuba."[38]

The U.S. administration knew that the Soviets were not striving for
more than an appearance of strategic equality. As Kennedy later reflected,
they were not "intending to fire them, because if they were going to get
into a nuclear struggle, they have their own missiles in the Soviet Union.
But it would have politically changed the balance of power. It would have
appeared to, and appearances contribute to reality."[39] In the 1970s, by
contrast, appearances were less important while the Americans were ar-
ranging a complex international order that verged on duopoly. Indeed,
beginning in 1970, Soviet missile-firing submarines and tenders began to
visit Cuban ports.[40] What protest there was by the Nixon administration
seemed so muted as to be almost inaudible.[41]

Why was Kennedy so concerned about appearances? Perhaps he felt
that the American people demanded an energetic response, given their
purported frustration over Cuba. The administration's evaluation of the

public mood supported the notion that firmness was a requisite of policy. Although repeated Gallup polls before the crisis showed 90 percent of Americans opposing actual armed intervention in Cuba,[42] Kennedy's own sense was, as his brother pointed out, that if he did not act, he would be impeached.[43]

Another explanation for Kennedy's concern that he would not appear credible to Khrushchev dates from the time, less than 2 years earlier, when he decided not to use air support for the Bay of Pigs invasion. According to James Reston's impression upon seeing Kennedy 10 minutes after the two leaders had met in Vienna, "Khrushchev had studied the events of the Bay of Pigs; he would have understood if Kennedy had left Castro alone or destroyed him; but when Kennedy was rash enough to strike at Cuba but not bold enough to finish the job, Khrushchev decided he was dealing with an inexperienced young leader who could be intimidated and blackmailed."[44] Similarly, George F. Kennan, then the U.S. ambassador to Yugoslavia, met the president after the Vienna summit session and reported that he found Kennedy "strangely tongue-tied" during these talks. Later, he recalled for a Harvard oral history interviewer:

> I felt that he had not acquitted himself well on this occasion and that he had permitted Khrushchev to say many things which should have been challenged right there on the spot.
> I think this was definitely a mistake. I think it definitely misled Khrushchev; I think Khrushchev failed to realize on the occasion what a man he was up against and also that he'd gotten away with many of these talking points; that he had placed President Kennedy in a state of confusion where he had nothing to say in return.[45]

Kennedy expressed concern to Reston and others that Khrushchev considered him a callow, inexperienced youth and that he soon expected a test. "It will be a cold winter," he was heard to mutter as he left the Vienna meeting. Khrushchev may indeed have been surprised at the forceful reaction of Kennedy, particularly after the young president had accepted the Berlin wall in August 1961 with no military response and had temporized in Laos in 1961 and 1962.

Perhaps, as Hilsman has argued, the Soviets assumed that the fine American distinctions between "offensive and defensive" missiles were really a *de facto* acknowledgment of the Soviet effort in Cuba. One could conjecture that this was what led Khrushchev to promise, and to believe that Kennedy understood, that no initiatives would be taken before the elections. In any case, Kennedy's concern about his appearance and the national appearance of strength kept him from searching very far for

Soviet motivation. His interpretation was that it was a personal injury to him and his credibility, as well as to American power. He explained this sentiment to *New York Post* reporter James Wechsler:

> What worried him was that Khrushchev might interpret his reluctance to wage nuclear war as a symptom of an American loss of nerve. Some day, he said, the time might come when he would have to run the supreme risk to convince Khrushchev that conciliation did not mean humiliation. "If Khrushchev wants to rub my nose in the dirt," he told Wechsler, "it's all over." But how to convince Khrushchev short of a showdown? "That son of a bitch won't pay any attention to words," the President said bitterly on another occasion. "He has to see you move."[46]

TRUE GRIT AND CRISIS DIPLOMACY

The missile crisis illuminates a feature of the American character that came to be considered a requisite personality trait of the cold war: being tough. Gritty American determination had become the respected and expected stance of American leaders under stress in confrontations with the Soviets from the earliest days of the cold war. When Truman, for example, dispatched an aircraft carrier, four cruisers, a destroyer flotilla, and the battleship *Missouri* to counter Soviet pressure on the Turkish Straits, he told Acheson, "We might as well find out whether the Russians [are] bent on world conquest now as in five or ten years."[47] Clark Clifford gave more formal expression to this sentiment when he advised Harry Truman, in a memo, in late 1946: "The language of military power is the only language which disciples of power politics understand. The United States must use that language in order that Soviet leaders will realize that our government is determined to uphold the interest of its citizens and the rights of small nations. Compromise and concessions are considered, by the Soviets, to be evidence of weakness and they are encouraged by our 'retreats' to make new and greater demands."[48]

The American concern with its appearance of strength was a mark of the Kennedy administration. One White House aide recalled that, especially after the failure of the Bay of Pigs, "Nobody in the White House wanted to be soft. . . . Everybody wanted to show they were just as daring and bold as everybody else."[49]

In the Cuban crisis, the cold war ethic of being tough exacerbated the discrepancies between the necessities of force and the necessities of diplomacy and negotiation. As a result, diplomacy was almost entirely eclipsed. In fact, it was hardly tried. According to Adam Yarmolinsky, an inside observer of the executive committee of the National Security Council, "90 percent of its time" was spent studying alternative uses of troops, bombers and warships. Although the possibility of seeking withdrawal of the missiles by straightforward diplomatic negotiation received some attention within the State Department, it seems hardly to have been aired in the ExCom." Yarmolinsky confesses that it is curious that no negotiations were considered. Nor were economic pressures ever suggested by the foreign affairs bureaucracy. Only a series of military plans emerged, and they varied from a blockade to a preemptive strike.[50]

Kennedy knew the Russians had deployed missiles on October 16. But instead of facing Soviet Foreign Secretary Gromyko with the evidence while the Russian was giving the president false assurances that missiles were not being installed, the president blandly listened without comment. Whether or not the Russians believed that Kennedy must have known, the effect of the charade was an absence of serious negotiations. Instead of using private channels to warn the Russians that he knew and intended to act, Kennedy chose to give notice to the Russians in a nationwide TV address. After that, a Soviet withdrawal had to be in public, and it almost had to be a humiliation. When the Soviets attempted nonetheless to bargain for a graceful retreat, their path was blocked. Kennedy refused Khrushchev's offer of a summit meeting "until Khrushchev first accepted, as a result *of our deeds* as well as our statements, the U.S. determination in the matter."[51] A summit meeting, Kennedy concluded, had to be rejected; for he was intent on offering the Russians "nothing that would tie our hands." We would only negotiate with that which would "strengthen our stand."[52] If there were to be any deals, Kennedy wanted them to seem a part of American munificence. He did not want a compromise to be tied to the central issue of what he conceived to be a test of American will and resolve. "[W]e must stand absolutely firm now. Concessions must come at the end of negotiation, not at the beginning," Robert Kennedy cautioned.[53]

In other words, the Soviets had to submit to American strength before any real concessions could take place. When Khrushchev offered to exchange the Cuban missiles for the Jupiter missiles stationed in Turkey, Kennedy demurred, even though he had ordered the missiles out months earlier; in fact, he had thought they were out when Khrushchev brought them to his attention. (The Jupiters were all but worthless. A marksman with a high-powered rifle could knock them out. They took a day to ready for firing, and the Turks did not want them.)[54] Kennedy, however, did not want to appear to yield to Soviet pressure even when he might give little and receive a great deal. An agreement would have confounded the issue of will. As Kennedy's Boswell put it, the president wanted to "concentrate on a single issue — the enormity of the introduction of the missiles and the absolute necessity of their removal."[55]

In the final act of the crisis, Kennedy accepted one of two letters sent almost simultaneously by Khrushchev. One contained the demand for removal of the Turkish missiles; the other did not. Kennedy accepted the latter. Khrushchev's second letter began with a long, heartfelt, personal communication and made no mention of a *quid pro quo*. Kennedy's response was a public letter to Khrushchev, temperate in tone, in which he accepted the more favorable terms he preferred and further detailed American conditions. It is said that Kennedy published his response "in the interests of both speed and psychology."[56] But this procedure of publishing the private terms of an interchange with another head of state was a considerable departure from diplomacy. It was not negotiation; it was, in this context, a public demand. Public statements during a crisis lack flexibility. Compromise is almost foreclosed by such a device, because any bargaining after the terms have been stated seems to be a retreat that would diminish a statesman's reputation. Because reputation was the stake in Cuba as much as anything else, Kennedy's response was hardly more than a polite ultimatum. In private, Kennedy was even more forceful. Robert Kennedy told Soviet Ambassador Dobrynin: "We had to have a commitment by tomorrow that those bases would be removed. . . . If they did not remove those bases, we would remove them. . . . Time was running out. We had only a few more hours — we needed an answer immediately from the Soviet Union. . . . We must have it the next day."[57]

As a result of the crisis, force and toughness became enshrined as instruments of policy. George Kennan observed, as he left 40 years of diplomatic service: "There is no presumption more terrifying than that of those who would blow up the world on the basis of their personal judgment of a transient situation. I do not propose to let the future of mankind be settled, or ended, by a group of men operating on the basis of limited perspectives and short-run calculations."[58]

In spite of occasional epistles from the older diplomatist, the new managers who proliferated after Cuba routed those who most favored negotiations. In an article in the *Saturday Evening Post,* one of the last moderates of the Kennedy administration, Adlai Stevenson, was attacked for advocating "a Munich." The source of the story, it was widely rumored, was President Kennedy himself.[59]

The policy of toughness became dogma to such an extent that nonmilitary solutions to political problems were excluded. A moderate in this circumstance was restricted to suggesting limited violence. Former Undersecretary of State Ball explained his "devil advocacy" in Vietnam, in which he suggested that there be a troop ceiling of 70,000 men and bombing be restricted to the South: "What I was proposing was something which I thought had a fair chance of being persuasive . . . if I had said let's pull out overnight or do something of this kind, I obviously wouldn't have been persuasive at all. They'd have said 'the man's mad.'"[60]

This peculiar search for the middle ground of a policy defined in terms of force was abetted by the sudden sense on the part of Kennedy's national security managers that the military was filled with Dr. Strangeloves. There was some warrant for this fear. Time and time again, during the crisis, the military seemed obsessed by the opportunity to demonstrate its potential. When asked what the Soviet reaction would be to a surgical raid on their missiles and men, General Lemay snapped, "There will be no reaction." When the crisis ended on Sunday, October 25, one of the Joint Chiefs suggested that they go ahead with a massive bombing the following Monday in any case. "[T]he military are mad," concluded President Kennedy.[61] Robert Kennedy recalled acidly that "many times . . . I heard the military take positions which, if wrong, had the advantage that no one would be around at the end to know."[62]

In part, it was a result of the Cuban crisis that the civilians of the American defense and foreign policy bureaucracy grew to despise the military. Hilsman reports that later in the Kennedy administration, an official prepared a mock account of a high-level meeting on Vietnam in which Averell Harriman "stated that he had disagreed for twenty years with General [Brute] Krulak [commandant of the marines] and disagreed today, reluctantly, more than ever; he was sorry to say that he felt General Krulak was a fool and had always thought so." It is reported that President Kennedy roared with laughter upon reading this fictitious account.[63] Hilsman also delighted in telling a story about General Lemnitzer, chairman of the Joint Chiefs of Staff, who once briefed President Kennedy on Vietnam: "This is the Mekong Valley. Pointer tip hit the map. Hilsman, watching, noticed something, the pointer tip was not on the Mekong Valley, it was on the Yangtze Valley."[64] Hilsman's recollection of the general's error became a common office story.

Ironically, while the military was increasingly thought to be rather loutish and ill-prepared, civilians were starting to rely more and more on military instrumentalities in the application of which, with few exceptions, they were not trained, and whose command structure they depised as being second-rate at best. Civilian crisis managers felt, after Cuba, that they should have control and that the military could not be trusted and had to be made more responsive to the political and civilian considerations of policy. To many observers, as well as to these managers, the failures of the Cuban missile crisis were not failures of civilian judgment but of organizational responsiveness. The intelligence establishment, for instance, had not discovered the missiles until the last minute. McNamara never really secured control over the navy. U-2 flights were sent near the Soviet Union to excite Soviet radar at the height of the crisis. Until Kennedy ordered their dispersal, American fighters and bombers were wing to wing on the ground, almost inviting a preemptive Soviet blow. Moreover, American tactical nuclear weapons and nuclear-tipped IRBMs in Turkey and Italy were discovered to be unlocked and lightly guarded.[65] All this led observers and policy makers to believe that crisis management demanded the president's organizational dominance and control, because the military and intelligence organizations were inept and their judgment was not reliable or at times even sane.

CUBA AND THE AMERICAN CENTURY

After Cuba, confidence in the ability of U.S. armed superiority to command solutions to crises in a way that would favor American interests expanded in such a way that Americans again began to speak of the American century. For a period before the crisis there had been a national reexamination. There were fears of national decline in the face of startling Soviet economic growth. Advances in Russian rocketry had led Americans to believe that not only were they in a mortal competition with the Soviets, but that the outcome was uncertain. Now, however, most of these doubts seemed to have dissipated.

The Cuban missile crisis revived the sense of the American mission. Henry R. Luce once rhapsodized in a widely circulated *Life* editorial that Americans must "accept wholeheartedly our duty and opportunity as the most powerful and vital nation in the world and in consequence to exert upon the world the full impact of our influence for such purposes as we see fit, and by such means as we see fit."[66] After the crisis, Arthur Schlesinger could lyrically resurrect this tradition: "But the ultimate impact of the missile crisis was wider than Cuba, wider than even the western hemisphere. . . . Before the missile crisis people might have feared that we would use our power extravagantly or not use it at all. But the thirteen days gave the world — even the Soviet Union — a sense of American determination and responsibility in the use of power which, if sustained, might indeed become a turning point in the history of the relations between east and west."[67]

Similarly, Professor Zbigniew Brzezinski, then a member of the Planning Council of the Department of State, proclaimed that American paramountcy was the lesson of Cuba. Brzezinski explained, "The U.S. is today the only effective global military power in the world."[68] In contrast to the

United States, Brzezinski declared, the Soviets were not a global power. Although Khrushchev may at one time have believed otherwise, the Cuban crisis demonstrated the limits of Soviet capabilities. "The Soviet leaders were forced, because of the energetic response by the United States, to the conclusion that their apocalyptic power [nuclear deterrent power] was insufficient to make the Soviet Union a global power. Faced with a showdown, the Soviet Union didn't dare to respond even in an area of its regional predominance — in Berlin. . . . It had no military capacity to fight in Cuba, or in Vietnam, or to protect its interests in the Congo." No doubt the historic American sense of divine purpose and the almost Jungian need to be the guarantor of global order received a strong fillip from the Cuban crisis. Brzezinski concluded: "What should be the role of the United States in this period? To use our power responsibly and constructively so that when the American paramountcy ends, the world will have been launched on a constructive pattern of development towards international stability. . . . The ultimate objective ought to be the shaping of a world of cooperative communities."[69]

The overwhelming belief of policymakers in American superiority seriously eroded deterrence. The Soviet Union reached the same conclusion as the United States — that a preponderance of military power, ranging across the spectrum of force from PT craft to advanced nuclear delivery systems, was the *sine qua non* of the successful exercise of political will. Before fall of 1962, Khrushchev's strategic policy, in the words of a RAND Kremlinologist, "amounted to settling for a second-best strategic posture."[70] The missile crisis, however, manifestly demonstrated Soviet strategic weakness and exposed every Soviet debility that Khrushchev's verbal proclamation of superiority had previously covered.

CUBA AND DETERRENCE

After Cuba, the Soviet military, responding to the humiliating American stimulus, demanded a higher priority to strategic arms and a cutback on the agricultural and consumer sectors of the Soviet economy. Although Khrushchev and Kennedy were by then moving toward a detente — best symbolized by the signing of the test-ban accords of mid-1963 — many in the Kremlin saw this as but a breathing spell in which the Chinese might be isolated and Soviet arms could catch up. Naval preparations, especially the building of Polaris-type submarines, were intensified.[71] Soviet amphibious landing capability — something in which the Soviets had shown little interest before — was revitalized and expanded. As Wolfe noted: "From the time of the first test-launching . . . of 1957 to mid-1961 only a handful of ICBM's had been deployed. . . . After Cuba, the pace of deployment picked up, bringing the total number of operational ICBM launchers to around 200 by the time of Khrushchev's ouster."[72] Although the West still outnumbered the Russians by four to one in numbers of launchers at the time, the Russians worked furiously and by September 1968 they commanded a larger force than the United States.[73] Worldwide "blue water" Soviet submarine patrols were initiated; and a decision was made under Brezhnev and Kosygin to extend the Soviet navy to "remote areas of the world's oceans previously considered a zone of supremacy of the fleets of the imperialist powers."[74]

After the missile crisis, the cold war establishmentarian John McCloy, representing President Kennedy, was host to Soviet Deputy Foreign Minister V. V. Kuznetzov. McCloy secured an affirmation from Kuznetzov that the Soviets would indeed observe their part of the agreement to remove the missiles and bombers from Cuba. But the Soviet leader warned, "Never will we be caught like this again."[75]

The Soviets were to yield again to U.S. strength in Vietnam and the Middle East. But each time, the usable strategic leverage of the United States grew weaker. Thus the structure of the international system and international stability was shaken in three ways.

First, the United States became confident that its power would prevail because global politics had become "unifocal."[76] But American military primacy began to erode as soon as it was proclaimed, when the Soviets fought to gain at least a rough strategic parity.

Second, nations, once cowed, are likely to be less timid in the next confrontation. As Kennedy admitted some time later, referring to the Cuban missile crisis, "You can't have too many of those."[77] Just as Kennedy feared that he had appeared callow and faint-hearted in successive Berlin crises and thus had to be tough over Cuba, the Soviets were likely to calculate that they must appear as the more rigid party in future confrontations or risk a reputation of capitulationism. For weeks after the missile crisis, the Chinese broadcast their charges of Russian stupidity and weakness to the four corners of the globe. The Chinese labeled Khrushchev an "adventurist" as well as a capitulationist," and therefore not fit for world communist leadership. The Russian answer was to accuse the Chinese of being even "softer" than they for tolerating the Western enclaves of Macao and Hong Kong.[78] The charge of who was the most capitulationist, the Chinese or the Russians, grew almost silly; but these puerile exchanges had their own dangers in terms of deterrence.

Third, once a threat is not carried out — even after an appearance of a willingness to carry it out has been demonstrated — the ante is upped just a bit more. Morgenthau described a two-step process in nuclear gamesmanship, "diminishing credibility of the threat and ever bolder challenges to make good on it. . . . [T]he psychological capital of deterrence has been nearly expended and the policy of deterrence will be close to bankruptcy. When they reach that point, the nations concerned can choose one of three alternatives: resort to nuclear war, retreat, or resort to conventional war."[79]

Morgenthau's observation captured the dilemma of American policy makers after Cuba. The problem was that nuclear superiority had been useful, but each succeeding threat (because no nuclear threat has ever been carried out) would necessarily be weaker than the last. Yet how could security managers translate military power into political objectives without such threats? Daniel Ellsberg recalled the quandary of U.S. security managers:

> McNamara's tireless and shrewd efforts in the early sixties, largely hidden from the public to this day, [were to] gradually control the forces within the military bureaucracy that pressed for the threat and use of nuclear weapons. [He had] a creditable motive for proposing alternatives to nuclear threats. . . . [I]n this hidden debate, there was strong incentive — indeed it seemed necessary — for the civilian leaders to demonstrate that success was possible in Indochina without the need either to compromise Cold War objectives or to threaten or use nuclear weapons.
>
> Such concerns remained semi-covert: (for it was seen as dangerous to lend substance to the active suspicions of military staffs and their Congressional allies that there were high Administration officials who didn't love the Bomb)."[80]

But after the Cuban crisis, the option of low-level violence became more and more attractive. Conventional and limited deployments of force became increasingly necessary as conventional force was considered less forbidding than the nuclear abyss. After all, the symbolic or psychological capital of deterrence rested on the notion of resolve. And one way to demonstrate political will was through the resurrection of conventional force as an instrument of demonstrating commitment — a commitment whose alternative form was a threat of nuclear holocaust. The latter was bound to deteriorate with the advent of a viable Soviet retaliatory capability and the knowledge that the Soviets had collapsed once under a nuclear threat and might not be willing to be quite so passive again. Many national security managers found they could navigate between the Scylla of nuclear war and the Charybdis of surrender with the serendipitous discovery of the lifeboat of the 1960s — limited war. It would not prove to be a sturdy craft.

Of course, the assumptions of the planners of limited war — as they emerged victorious from the Cuban crisis — were as old as the cold war. They dated from the Truman Doctrine's Manichean presentation of a bipolar global confrontation where a gain to one party necessarily would be a loss to the other. A world order of diverse centers of power, with elements of superpower cooperation, where gains and losses would be less easily demonstrable, was not so demanding of military remedy. A multipolar world would be less congenial to the belief that the only options available to policymakers were either military force or retreat. Maneuver and negotiation, in such a world, would again become part of diplomacy. But such a development was to come about only after the tragic failure of the military remedy had been demonstrated in Vietnam.

THE BY-PRODUCTS OF SUCCESS

There were other effects related to the exuberant reaction to the Cuban crisis. As the United States began to feel that power and force were successful solvents to the more sticky problems of the cold war, the role of international law declined precipitously.[81]

Hypocrisy, in the words of H. L. Mencken, "runs, like a hair in a hotdog, through the otherwise beautiful fabric of American life."[82] Moral pontifications appeared increasingly hypocritical after Cuba. The participants in the crisis knew the blockade was an act of war that had little basis in international law. After the crisis was over, even lawyers began to see law as but another instrumentality of American policy. The conclusion reached by American academics was that "International law is . . . a tool, not a guide to action. . . . It does not have a valid life of its own; it is a mere instrument available to political leaders for their own ends, be they good or evil, peaceful or aggressive. . . . [The Cuban missile crisis] merely reconfirms the irrelevance of international law in major political disputes."[83]

Dean Acheson summarized the code of the cold war as it was confirmed by the Cuban experience: "The power, prestige and position of the United States had been challenged. . . . Law simply does not deal with such questions of ultimate power. . . . The survival of states is not a matter of law."[84]

George Ball, former undersecretary of state, wrote: "No one can seriously contend that we now live under a universal system or, in any realistic sense, under the 'rule of law.' We maintain the peace by preserving a precarious balance of power between ourselves and the Soviet Union — a process we used to call 'containment' before the word went out of style.

It is the preservation of that balance which, regardless of how we express it, is the central guiding principle of American foreign policy."[85]

The United Nations was used in the Cuban crisis, not as Kennedy had told the General Assembly the year before, as "the only true alternative to war,"[86] but as a platform where Adlai Stevenson, the eloquent American representative, could deal "a final blow to the Soviet case before world opinion."[87]

Epitomized by Cuba, crisis after crisis pointed out the stark irony: Americans, who had so long stroked the talisman of international law, now seemed to do so only when their interests were not jeopardized. Otherwise, law became merely a rhetorical flourish of U.S. policy. International law was still a part of the admonition that armed aggression and breaches of the peace cease and desist. But behind these legalistic and moralistic injunctions, the armed cop became more and more apparent. As General de Gaulle had observed earlier, the conclusion that American idealism was but a reflection of the American will to power became almost inescapable after the Cuban crisis.[88] Few obeisances about the need for law in international society disguised the sense that America had abandoned her ancient, liberal inheritance in the zesty pursuit of world order.

Another effect of the crisis was to differentiate the great powers — the United States and the Soviet Union — from other states, which were literally frozen out of a major role in structuring global politics. After all, the major chips of big-power poker were simply not accessible to other governments — even those with modest and nominally independent nuclear forces. For no other nations had the capability of making even plausible calculations of either preemptive or second-strike blows against a great power, much less basing national strategies on such possibilities. As a result, Europeans were offered the appearance of some control in their nuclear lot with the ill-fated multilateral force. But the nuclear trigger was still in the hands of the United States, and so was the final squeeze. Not only were the weapons of great-power diplomacy increasingly inaccessible to other states, but the other tools of statecraft also receded from the grasp of those with modest resources. The spy, for instance, was largely replaced by satellite reconnaisance. Intellectual musings on great-power conflict became differentiated from other strategic thinking. Gradually, the Soviets and the Americans created a shared private idiom of force; and a curious dialogue began between the congressional budget messages of the secretary of defense and the periodic revisions of *Military Strategy* by Marshal Sokolovsky.[89]

Allies became mere appurtenances of power whose purpose, in the duopolistic structure of international society, was increasingly symbolic. Thus, for example, the Organization of American States was asked to validate the U.S. blockade at the same time the American quarantine was announced.

Similarly, Dean Acheson flew to Paris and other European capitals to confer with American allies about the coming confrontation over Cuba.

"Your President does me great honor," de Gaulle said, "to send me so distinguished an emissary. I assume the occasion to be of appropriate importance." Acheson delivered President Kennedy's letter, with the text of the speech to be delivered at P-hour, 7 P.M. Washington time. He offered to summarize it. De Gaulle raised his hand in a delaying gesture that the long-departed Kings of France might have envied. "May we be clear before you start," he said. "Are you consulting or informing me?" Acheson confessed that he was there to inform, not to consult. "I am in favor of independent decisions," de Gaulle acknowledged.[90]

For the Europeans, Gaullists and leftists alike, it appeared that there was a high likelihood of nuclear annihilation without representation.[91] In spite of European gestures of support, the alliance received a shock from which it did not recover. The British, in the midst of a vicious internal debate about whether or not to abandon nuclear weapons, decided they were necessary to buy even minimum consideration from their American allies. The French did not debate; they accelerated their nuclear programs while withdrawing from a military role in the alliance in 1964. Henceforth, NATO would be, in Henry Kissinger's words, a "troubled partnership."[92]

On the Soviet side, it was equally apparent that Russian interests would not be sacrificed to sister socialist states. Castro was plainly sold out. The weak promise tendered by the Kennedy administration not to invade the island was probably cold comfort as Castro saw his military benefactors beat a hasty retreat from American power. Embarrassingly, Castro began to echo the capitulationist theme of Chinese broadcasts. Privately Castro said that if he could, he would have beaten Khrushchev to within an inch of his life for what he did. Soviet Foreign Minister Mikoyan was dispatched to Cuba and stayed there for weeks, not even returning to the bedside of his dying wife, but Castro's fury was unabated. Whatever the motive for Khrushchev's moves in Cuba, the Chinese were also enraged.[93] Any attempts the Soviets had made to dissuade the Chinese from assuming a nuclear role prior to October 1962 lost their validity when it became obvious that the Russians would not risk their own destruction for an associate.

By 1963 a new era of East-West relations was unfolding. The Americans still cultivated the asymetrical assumptions of the cold war, but the

Soviet Union was at least admitted as a junior partner in a duopolistic international system that was now increasingly characterized as one marked by detente.

Indications of this new spirit appeared in the administration's desire for improved economic relations with the Soviet Union. This effort extended into the early years of the Johnson administration as Johnson spoke enthusiastically of improved East-West economic relations as a bridge-building exercise and Zbigniew Brzezinski would write early in 1965 in his book, *Alternative to Partition,* sponsored by the prestigious Council on Foreign Relations, "The Cold War in Europe has lost its old meaning. There was a vitality and a passion to it as long as either side had reason to believe that it could prevail and as long as either side felt genuinely threatened by the other. Neither condition truly exists today."[94] The relaxation was favorable to Kennedy, who wanted to begin to deal with the Soviets without the ideological rancor that had poisoned previous relations and who had a vision of Soviet responsibility that would be enlarged upon by succeeding administrations. The Soviets too sought a detente. Another series of confrontations, given their acknowledged strategic inferiority, could hardly be successful. Moreover, the Chinese began to present formidable ideological and political difficulties for the Soviets. The Soviets' new interest in improved relations with the Americans brought intense fears from China of American-Soviet collusion. At the same time, the Soviets began to fear a Sino-American agreement that would be detrimental to their interest. As chief ideologue of the Soviet Union, Michael Suslov explained, in early 1964:

> With a stubbornness worthy of a better cause the Chinese leaders attempt to prevent the improvement of Soviet-American relations, representing this as "plotting with the imperialists." At the same time the Chinese government makes feverish attempts to improve relations with Britain, France, Japan, West Germany, and Italy. It is quite clear that they would not refuse to improve relations with the United States but as yet do not see favorable circumstances for such an endeavor.[95]

THE ECONOMICS OF CONTAINMENT

The events of October 1962 and the euphoria and renewed sense of American power that followed this great climax of the cold war also had as a by-product the obscuring of other economic elements of the new era of world politics that seemed to be opening up. By 1961 and 1962 the international position of the American dollar had begun to weaken markedly. A favorable balance of payments situation in the years after World War II had turned to a small but nagging deficit of around $1.4 billion a year by 1956. Between 1958 and 1960 this average annual deficit had jumped to more than $3.5 billion and during the early 1960s persisted at just over $2.5 billion annually.[96]

Making this situation especially perplexing was the fact that this deteriorating U.S. balance of payments position could not be readily explained in a conventional manner. Normally a persistent deficit in a nation's balance of payments situation can be attributed to domestic circumstances, usually inflation, leading to its goods and services being too expensive to maintain a competitive position on world markets. Under these circumstances (and assuming relatively low barriers to trade) a nation imports more than it exports, leading to a net outflow of wealth and a deficit in its balance of payments. Another source of such a deficit might be an export of currency to finance foreign investment, but in this case the return of profits, fees, and royalties should in the long-run equal or even exceed outflow, leading ultimately to a net gain for balance of payments.

Recent analysis of the American international economic position during the cold war years suggests that the growing balance of payments problem cannot be explained in these traditional terms. Indeed, for the 15 years following World War II, U.S. private sector transactions showed an annual average surplus. Between 1960 and 1964 these private transactions slipped slightly into deficit (less than $400 million a year on the average), then recovered to a surplus of more than $1.2 billion in 1965 and 1966, before sliding into deficit again between 1967 and 1970. However, even in the troubled decade of 1960 to 1970, the more than $2.0 billion annual average deficit cannot be explained easily by conventional economic factors. Throughout the late 1950s and well into 1963 and 1964 the American domestic economy was actually in recession, the recovery from which during late 1963, 1964, and 1965 was marked by sustained economic growth without significant inflation. Thus, it would not seem that American goods were priced out of the world market, leading to an excess of imports. Moreover, American export strength has never rested with low-price goods, but rather with relatively high-priced but technologically sophisticated goods and agricultural commodities.

International conditions facilitating the movement of private capital developed after 1958 and led to an outflow of American private investment in the late 1950s and early 1960s, especially to Europe. But it is not clear that these seemingly negative short-run transactions were detrimental to the American balance of payments situation in the long run. Thus, Raymond Vernon, a foremost student of American multinational corporations and their investment behavior has noted[97] that one outcome of this investment activity in the late 1950s and early 1960s has been development of substantial American claims on the assets of other countries. Moreover, by the end of the 1960s much of what the United States was exporting to the world was in the form of services:[98] "The rewards to the U.S. economy from these activities are to be found not in the merchandise balance, but in sales of business services, in interest and dividends, and in the build-up of the earnings left abroad in subsidiaries and branches. When these are taken into account, the U.S. performance appears a good deal less bleak."[99] Thus it would seem that the balance of payments problems of the 1950s and early 1960s cannot be easily explained by focusing on private foreign economic transactions. Instead, we must turn our attention to the foreign expenditures of the U.S. government, and in so doing we are drawn to the economic dimension of the diplomacy of violence.

America's International Economic Position in the 1960s

The underlying causes of the balance of payments crisis that confronted the Kennedy administration in the early 1960s seem best understood in terms of the long-run and accumulating costs of containment increasingly dependent on the instruments of military threat and capability. Containment relied originally on the Marshall Plan and then in time came to rest on NATO, military intervention in Korea, and subsequently large economic and military assistance to Europe and the third world — in short, foreign expenditures by the U.S. government that in most instances did not have a financial return as private foreign investment might have yielded. The upshot was, logically and in practice, a net deficit in American balance of payments. It is, of course, accurate to respond that these expenditures purchased something of great value for the United States—national security. However, this is a form of transaction that cannot be factored into a balance of payments statement.

These large public expenditures contributed decisively to a negative balance and accumulating quantities of American dollars in the hands of foreigners. Moreover, during the 1950s and 1960s, as this quantity of dollars grew steadily, the amount of gold backing them remained relatively unchanged. As long as those governments and traders holding dollars maintained their confidence in the capacity and willingness of the U.S. government to back these dollars, they might be content to hold and use the currency. By 1960, however, foreign confidence in the recession-ridden American economy's ability to sustain growth (while the Eisenhower administration continued to expand military assistance and other forms of foreign expenditure) dwindled. By October 1960, the American deficit had become sufficiently large that many of those holding dollars were willing to gamble that the United States would have to devalue the dollar. Accordingly, dollars were exchanged for gold on the London free gold market, forcing up the price of gold from $35 to $41 an ounce. This speculative surge was fueled in some measure by expressions of official concern about the balance of payments situation.

The roots of this situation go back to the Marshall Plan. During the late 1940s, the reconstruction of Western Europe — the bedrock of containment — required a large infusion of American foreign assistance to the West Europeans so that they might finance the purchase of American goods and services necessary to European recovery. Similarly, between 1949 and the early 1950s, the United States provided large amounts of assistance to fund the startup of NATO through the MDAP and, subsequently, spent billions extending containment to Asia. This combination of economic and military assistance meant that the United States was running slight deficits in its balance of payments by 1956, although net private transactions were in the black by more than $3 billion annually. Nevertheless, these government expenditures were not regarded in the early years of the cold war as normal transactions, and they were not, therefore, viewed with alarm. By and large, they were seen as temporary and, over the long-run, nonrecurring.[100] In any event, they were thought essential to the national security and acceptable as long as the annual deficit remained, as it did, around $1.5 billion a year.

Between 1958 and 1960, however, the deficits increased dramatically — up to an average of $3.7 billion per year. A combination of factors contributed to some deterioration (although not a net deficit) in private transactions. For the most part, these events marked the culmination of trends set in motion by the Marshall Plan. Thus, between 1958 and 1960 the industrialized economies of Western Europe had recovered sufficiently to be able to enter into export competition with the United States. At the same time and with the encouragement of the United States, Europeans moved forward with the creation in 1958 of the European Economic Community (EEC) or the Common Market. A key element of the Common Market included some tariff protection to encourage even more rapid development of a truly European economy. At the same time all European currencies became convertible with one another so as to facilitate the movement of capital for investment purposes. Finally, this combination of economic growth and internationalization of capital *behind* the Common Market tariff wall served as incentives for American investment to move behind these tariff barriers. Trade through these tariffs proved difficult, but on the other hand the internationalization of capital within Europe and growing European economies led to American businessmen "discovering" Europe, and there occurred a tripling of their investment there in the late 1950s and early 1960s.[101]

In the short run, therefore, there was a draw down of the positive private transactions balance. Far more important, however, was the fact that American foreign and military expenditures could no longer be regarded as temporary. Indeed, if anything, increased Soviet activism implied an indefinite and perhaps growing level of such expenditures. As this fact began to sink in during the late 1950s, concern with the constantly growing deficit began to increase in official American circles and, inevitably, abroad. This concern was high in Western Europe and especially in France, where this seemingly unending stream of U.S. government spending came to be viewed as a potential threat to new-found prosperity.

The European position was paradoxical in that in the past they had encouraged U.S. foreign assistance to stimulate their own growth. Similarly, during the late 1940s and early 1950s and even at the start of the 1960s, the Europeans benefited from the American military presence. At the same time, however, the European economy was now being forced to absorb large quantities of public as well as private investment dollars — dollars that seemed to have less and less gold to back them. The problems posed for the Europeans were twofold. First, of course, was the growing doubt that the Americans would be able to exchange gold for their dollars, and as the number of dollars increased, the doubts could only increase. Nevertheless, if governments and international traders were willing to continue using the dollars as if they had backing, i.e., as the international money rather than the gold to which the dollar was theoretically pegged in value under the postwar Bretton Woods system of monetary agreements, there need not be an international monetary crisis. However, for this forebearance, the Europeans had to pay an increasing price in terms of their own domestic economies.

Insofar as the Europeans remained faithful to the postwar international monetary agreements, they were obligated to maintain the value of their currencies at a fixed rate of exchange against the dollar. Sudden devaluations or revaluations upward were not permitted under International Monetary Fund rules. Thus, for example, the German or French or British governments were obligated to exchange their currencies for dollars at a fixed rate whenever the holders of dollars (e.g., a French, British, or German merchant engaged in export-import trade) wanted to convert them into francs, pounds, or marks. As long as the holders of dollars were willing to use them, there was little consequence for European domestic economies. But as confidence in the dollar began to slip, the demand for other, seemingly stronger currencies or gold would increase. The governments responsible for the currencies in demand were obligated to supply the marks, francs, or whatever.

The net effect of this process was an increasing supply of the Europeans' currencies in their own economies as they sought to sop up the steady stream of dollars and maintain the fixed exchange rate system. To the extent that their own economies grew faster than this supply of money, inflation might be controllable. But it was apparent to European national bankers and economic planners that the expanding presence of dollars constituted a virtually uncontrollable inflationary pressure both in the short and especially in the long term. As long as the fixed exchange rate system remained in place, the European domestic money supply would have to increase, not necessarily because of real growth in the production of their own goods and services (although this was taking place as well), but in response to diminishing confidence in the bloated quantity of dollars sloshing about in the European and world economy.

Thus, by the end of the 1950s, American economic policy had finally succeeded in fostering the rebirth of the European economy but, paradoxically, the decline of European confidence in the dollar. At the same time, the American foreign and defense policymaking community was not prepared to forego what it regarded as an essential instrument of containment — U.S. foreign and military assistance — at the very moment the cold war seemed to be reaching a point of tolerable adjustment.

Sound and Fury . . . and More of the Same

The American response did not attempt to remove the source of the balance of payments problem — American economic assistance and military spending abroad. Instead, during the last 2 years of the Eisenhower administration, conditions were attached to these programs that were designed to increase American exports and otherwise reverse or restrain the flow of dollars abroad. First, in the case of economic assistance, recipient countries were required to use their American economic assistance dollars to purchase American goods and services. Second, military expenditure regulations were restructured so as to emphasize a "Buy American" approach. By the 1960s, these latter provisions required that government agencies purchase American goods, although this meant frequently paying as much as 50 percent more for goods and services than would have been the case if purchased from foreign suppliers. By the late 1960s, more than 90 percent of U.S. economic assistance funds were being spent in the United States. In many instances, however, this meant that the cost of aid projects increased by as much as 30 percent to recipient countries.[102]

In summary, the cost of the Buy America measures led to the cost of government overseas programs increasing for the American taxpayer. At the same time, American economic assistance recipients being forced to spend their receipts on more expensive American goods and services were actually receiving less for their aid dollar. Moreover, aid recipients were frequently subsidizing noncompetitive American exporters. In terms of balance of payments, however, these measures combined with loan repayments from previous years, allowed the United States actually to make money on much of its economic program in the 1960s. Nevertheless, military assistance spending remained high, and the net flow of U.S. government–generated dollars was, therefore, only slowed but not stopped.

The Kennedy administration maintained the "tied aid" concept and undertook a number of scattered measures including minor adjustments in the tax laws and interest rates in an effort to repatriate more U.S. private dollars. When these actions did little to change the rate of private investment by the mid-1960s, President Johnson introduced a program of voluntary constraints that were subsequently made mandatory. Moreover, Presidents Kennedy and Johnson initiated vigorous arms sales programs abroad in an effort to improve the American export picture.

In the area of export expansion, Kennedy sought and received new trade legislation from Congress, the Trade Expansion Act of 1962. The negotiating authority under the Trade Expansion Act (TEA) was to be used by the administration to bring about significant mutual reduction in tariffs between the United States and Europe so as to allow for the expansion of U.S. exports. There were, however, other motives involved. Specifically, the TEA gave the president the authority to negotiate tariff reductions of 50 percent across the board and to eliminate tariffs altogether on those product groups where U.S. and EEC exports equaled 80 percent or more of world exports.[103] In the latter case, however, this "dominant supplier" provision was meaningful only if the British were in the Common Market, for otherwise there were very few EEC–U.S. traded product groups that could meet the 80 percent requirement.

Thus the TEA of 1962 was oriented toward export expansion, but the United States was also trying to use the TEA's dominant supplier provision as an inducement to the EEC countries to admit the British into the EEC. It was the Kennedy administration's hope that British entry would offset the economically and politically troublesome French and transform the EEC into an outward-looking Europe more open to U.S. exports. De Gaulle saw through the American effort, however, and fearing that Britain would serve as an American Trojan horse in Europe, vetoed British entry into the EEC in 1962.[104] Kennedy's "grand design" for export expansion, British entry into the Common Market, and the diminution of de Gaulle's political and economic influence in Europe was never consummated.

Some tariff reductions were brought about over the extended "Kennedy round" of negotiations, but, generally the EEC turned increasingly inward and fostered expansion of its internal trade.[105] American exports did increase, but only rapidly enough to very nearly balance American imports— and certainly not enough to offset the continued export of American dollars associated with U.S. military spending.

Indecision and Marginal Measures

By the mid-1960s, therefore, the various American efforts to check or reverse the U.S. balance of payments deficits could claim only the most marginal success. Indeed, after 1965 and 1966, the deficit began to creep back up toward $2 billion plus, in spite of a booming U.S. economy in which U.S. exports were increasing. American military spending continued to expand at a rate far in excess of the surplus generated by private trade and investment income. And, of course, a major source of this growing hemorrhage of dollars was the escalating conflict in Southeast Asia. Moreover, once the war became thoroughly Americanized after 1966, the costs of military spending cut even deeper. Not only did the export of dollars directly attributable to military spending increase to more than $3.2 billion annually, but the domestic inflation set in motion by the war undercut the American competitive position abroad as the prices of American exports increased.

Choosing 1967 as a typical year for the international economic position of the United States during the 1960s, economist Robert Stevens summarizes the conditions underlying the American balance of payments situation:

> When we compare the gross and net impacts on the figures of these three major types of outflow, we find that in 1967 Pentagon-inspired arms exports offset only 29 percent of gross foreign military spending, whereas 86 percent of U.S. foreign aid was offset by purchases made in the United States and 133 percent of private investment outflows were offset by return flows of foreign investment income. Thus, viewed in this context, the government's net foreign military spending has had a much more deleterious effect on the balance of payments than foreign aid or private foreign investment.[106]

This situation could always be rationalized domestically, however, for the outflow of dollars was presumably buying security and, until very late in the 1960s, the American economy felt no negative effects of this spending.

The situation abroad, especially in Europe, was of course quite different, for they were more or less compelled to absorb the exported American dollars. Insofar as the dollar was the basis of the industrialized world's economy, serving as the key currency (and the United States as a kind of banker for the system), the United States could, unlike other countries, escape until very late the need to settle its deficits. As the banker, the United States possessed seemingly unlimited credit symbolized by an unending series of deficits, which the rest of the world and primarily Europe were asked to assume by holding rather than converting American dollars. In time, however, the feared inflation of European economies began, and pressure for international action increased.

During the 1960s a series of short-run measures were developed to deal with speculative pressures as currency swaps, short-term credit arrangements, and an international gold pool were established. In addition, the United States created a new form of credit with issuance of medium-term securities (Roosa bonds) designed to repatriate some of the excess dollar assets in European and other central banks. For a while, these arrangements stemmed somewhat the short-term flow of dollars and diminishing American gold into Europe. Nonetheless, these measures did not get at the fundamental weakness of the dollar's position — a currency that was serving as the key international currency even as it was being used to finance global containment. This patched-up system stumbled through most of the 1960s, then staggered under the added burden of even more military spending in the late 1960s and, along with the foreign policy it was to finance, collapsed in the swamp of Vietnam.

By the end of the 1960s it was increasingly clear, therefore, that the American dollar could no longer be viewed as an instrument simultaneously serving American foreign policy and the international economic system. The actors comprising this system now had economic and political interests of their own. It mattered not that American balance of payments deficits had in large measure financed the development of those interests. For they were no longer congruent with an American foreign policy that seemed to require that industrialized countries of the world passively and indefinitely absorb American dollars as their own economies inflated.

CONCLUSION

Thus, by the mid 1960s, the beginning of the end of the cold war had precipitated a change in the global structure of power even as it deflected attention from another growing crisis. American paramountcy had been self-proclaimed, the seeds of detente were sown by a shared vision of nuclear oblivion, and the ingredients for a great power condominium were becoming clear. Tragically and ironically, however, the lessons of the Cuban missile crisis — that success in international crisis was largely a matter of national guts; that the opponent would yield to superior force; that presidential control of force can be suitable, selective, swift, effective, and responsive to civilian authority; and that crisis management and execution is too dangerous and events move too rapidly for anything but the tightest secrecy — all these inferences contributed to the Johnson decision to use American air power against Hanoi in 1965. Even the language of the Gulf of Tonkin resolution was almost identical to that which Kennedy's legal advisers had drawn up for the OAS in October 1962.[107]

The Cuban crisis changed the international environment but riveted American expectations to the necessities of the diplomacy of violence. Although the Cuban crisis created substantial changes in distinguishing superpowers from other states, the realization both of the parity of the superpowers and of the indications that they could join in a relationship that had some elements of condominium and other elements of the classic balance of power was suppressed until the end of the Vietnam War.

Finally, the shimmering image of the "American century" blinded American policy makers to the magnitude of an emerging crisis in the industrialized world's political economy. The construction of containment and the surmounting of the apparent strategic crisis of 1961 and 1962 were all immensely costly, requiring a steady flow of American capital into the reconstruction of the industrialized world's political economy. Just as the Soviet-American political-military confrontation at the center of the cold war climaxed in Berlin and in the waters off Cuba, the political economic dynamics that the Marshall Plan and the flow of American government dollars had sought to set in motion finally took hold in Europe. The eventual result would be the establishment of an international political economy of interdependence that no single government could control. But reflection, modesty, and humility were not characteristic traits of the activists who had just managed one of the great turning points of history. Thus, the importance of the opportunities and risks attendant to these new transnational economic forces seems to have been misunderstood or, if comprehended, deemed manageable as the missile crisis had been managed.

In retrospect, therefore, the great cold war strategic crisis of 1961 and 1962 and the economic crisis of the early and mid-1960s seem to mark the beginning of a major transformation of the international system and American foreign policy. The realization of this profound fact was obscured in some measure by the management of the crises themselves. In any event, the full implications of this transformation could not be dealt with until the American agony in Vietnam drew to a close.

NOTES

1. Revisionist critiques of the Cuban crisis are becoming more frequent. But most are rather polemical and thin. For a sample of some of the better ones, see Richard J. Walton, "The Cuban Missile Crisis" in *Cold War and Counter Revolution* (Baltimore: Penguin Books, 1972), pp. 103–43; Leslie Dewart, "The Cuban Crisis Revisited," *Studies on the Left,* Vol. V. (Spring 1965), pp. 15–40; John Kenneth Galbraith, "Storm over Havana: Who Were the Real Heroes?" (review of *Thirteen Days* by Robert F. Kennedy), *Book World,* January 19, 1969, p. 16; Ronald Steel, "Endgame," (review of *The Missile Crisis* by Elie Abel), *New York Review of Books,* March 13, 1969, reprinted in Ronald Steel, *Imperialists and Other Heroes* (New York: Vintage Books, 1971), p. 115; Louise FitzSimmons, *The Kennedy Doctrine* (New York: Random House, 1972), pp. 126–173.

2. Roger Hilsman, *To Move a Nation* (New York: Dell Books, 1967), p. 48, p. 157; also cited in Steel, op. cit., p. 115.

3. Hans J. Morgenthau, *Truth and Power, Essays of a Decade, 1960–1970* (New York: Praeger Publishers, 1970), p. 158.

4. A current review of this enormous literature is contained in Charles F. Hermann (ed.), *International Crises: Insights from Behavioral Research* (New York: The Free Press, 1972).

5. Cited by Coral Bell, *The Conventions of Crisis: A Study in Diplomatic Management* (London: Oxford University Press, 1971), p. 2.

6. Alexander George et al., *The Limits of Coercive Diplomacy* (Boston: Little, Brown and Company, 1971), p. 132.

7. Henry Pachter, "J. F. K. as an Equestrian Statue: On Myths and Myth Makers," *Salmagundi* (Spring 1966), cited in George, op. cit.

8. Albert and Roberta Wohlstetter, "Controlling the Risks in Cuba," *Adelphi Paper No. 17* (London: Institute for Strategic Studies, April 1965), p. 19.

9. Robert F. Kennedy, *Thirteen Days: A Memoir of the Cuban Missile Crisis* (with Afterword by Richard Neustadt and Graham T. Allison) (New York: W. W. Norton & Company, 1971), p. 48.

10. Ibid., p. 22; Theodore C. Sorensen, *Kennedy* (New York: Bantam Books, 1969), p. 705. Hermann, op. cit., p. 33 and Arthur M. Schlesinger, Jr., *Robert Kennedy and His Times* (New York: Ballantine Books edition, 1979), pp. 546–547.

11. See Thomas W. Milburn, "The Management of Crisis," in Herman, op. cit. esp. pp. 263–266.

12. Kennedy, op. cit., pp. 48–49.

13. Sorensen, op. cit., p. 705.

14. Arthur M. Schlesinger, Jr., *A Thousand Days* (Boston: Houghton Mifflin Company, 1965), pp. 840–841.

15. Jack Raymond, *Power at the Pentagon* (New York: Harper & Row, 1964), pp. 285–286.

16. Elie Abel, *The Missile Crisis* (Philadelphia: J. B. Lippincott Co., 1969). Abel interviewed the witnesses to this episode, some of whom did not agree as to Anderson's exact words. Anderson, Abel reports, could not recall ever having said this.

17. William A. Hamilton, III, "The Decline and Fall of the Joint Chiefs of Staff," *The Naval War College Review,* Vol. XXIV (April 1972), p. 47.

18. Abel, op. cit., p. 151–152; Hilsman, op. cit., p. 214; W. E. Knox, "Close-up of Khrushchev During a Crisis," *The New York Times Magazine,* November 18, 1962, p. 128.

19. Kennedy, op. cit., p. 55.

20. Irving Janis, *Victims of Group Think* (Boston: Houghton Mifflin Company, 1972), p. 163; Henry Pachter, *Collision Course* (New York: Praeger Publishers, 1963), p. 58.
21. Leslie Gelb and Morton Halperin, "The Ten Commandments of the Foreign Affairs Bureaucracy," *Harpers*, Vol. 244 (June 1972), pp. 28–37; Leslie Gelb, "The Essential Domino: American Politics and Vietnam," *Foreign Affairs*, Vol. L. (April 1972), pp. 459–476.
22. Homer E. Capehart: "U.S. Should Act, Stop 'Examining Cuba,'" *U.S. News & World Report*, September 10, 1962, p. 45.
23. *The New York Times*, September 19, 1962.
24. "Cuban Crisis," *Data Digest* (New York: Keynote Publications, 1963), p. 35, cited by Thomas Halper, *Foreign Policy Crisis: Appearance and Reality in Decision Making* (Columbus, Ohio: Charles E. Merrill Publishers, 1971), p. 132.
25. "Notes of the Month: Cuba: A U.S. Election Issue," *World Today*, Vol. XVIII, (November 1962), p. 543; Halper, op. cit., p. 132.
26. Quincy Wright, "The Cuban Quarantine of 1962," in John G. Stoessinger and Alan Westin (eds.), *Power and Order* (New York: Harcourt, Brace and World, 1964), p. 186.
27. *Economist*, October 6, 1962, p. 15.
28. "Afraid of Everything but War," *I. F. Stone's Weekly*, September 17, 1962, p. I.
29. Quoted in Steel, op. cit., p. 119.
30. Abel, op. cit., p. 78.
31. Steel, op. cit., p. 121.
32. Sorensen, op. cit., p. 688.
33. George et al., op. cit., p. 89.
34. Hilsman, op. cit., p. 195.
35. *The New York Times*, November 12, 1962.
36. *Wilmington Morning News*, January 25, 1974.
37. Walter W. Layson, "The Political and Strategic Aspects of the 1962 Cuban Missile Crisis," unpub. Ph.D. Diss. (University of Virginia, 1969), pp. 18–87; Thomas W. Wolfe, *Soviet Power and Europe, 1945–1970* (Baltimore: Johns Hopkins University Press, 1970), pp. 73–99, 100–194.
38. Henry Kissinger, "Reflections on Cuba," *The Reporter*, Vol. XXVII (November 22, 1962), p. 22.
39. Interview, December 17, 1962, *Public Papers of the Presidents, John F. Kennedy* (Washington, D.C.: U.S. Government Printing Office, 1963), p. 898.
40. *The New York Times*, December 6, 1970. According to the authoritative *Aviation Week*, the Russians also began to schedule regular stops of long-range aircraft at about the same time. December 21, 1970, pp. 16–17.
41. For a description and forceful but private insistence that the building of the Soviet submarine base at Cienfuegos, Cuba, be halted, see Henry Kissinger, *The White House Years* (Boston: Little, Brown and Co., 1979), pp. 636–651. Nevertheless, sporadic press reports indicate that missile-firing Soviet submarines were putting into Cuba long afterwards; see Barry Blechman and Stephanie Levinson, "U.S. Policy and Soviet Subs," *New York Times*, October 22, 1974; *Washington Post*, October 26, 1974, and Walter Pincus, "Hanging at Soviet Anchor," *Washington Post*, October 12, 1979, p. A15. Pincus reports that in 1972, a nuclear armed "Golf II" submarine anchored off Cuba and was serviced by a Soviet tender. Another visit was made in May of 1974, by another "Golf II"—a submarine which usually carries three missiles. Neither time were the visits protested.
42. "How U.S. Voters Feel about Cuba," *Newsweek*, October 13, 1962, p. 138; Halper, op cit., p. 133.

43. Kennedy, op. cit., p. 45, and "Afterword," p. 114.
44. Reston, "What Was Killed Was Not Only the President but the Promise," *The New York Times Magazine,* November 15, 1964, p. 126.
45. *The New York Times,* September 1, 1970; *New York Daily News,* August 31, 1970.
46. Schlesinger, *Thousand Days;* op. cit., p. 391.
47. Walter Millis (ed.), *The Forrestal Diaries* (New York: Viking Press, 1951), p. 192.
48. Arthur Krock, *Memoirs* (London: Cassel and Co., 1968), pp. 228–229.
49. Hugh Sidey, *John F. Kennedy, President* (New York: Atheneum Publishers, 1964), p. 127.
50. Adam Yarmolinsky, *The Military Establishment* (New York: Harper & Row, 1971), p. 127.
51. Kennedy, op. cit., pp. 44–45 (emphasis added).
52. Sorensen, op. cit., p. 699.
53. Schlesinger, op. cit., p. 811.
54. Hilsman, op. cit., p. 202. Donald F. Hafner, a State Department officer, in an article, "Bureaucratic Politics and those 'Frigging Missiles': JFK, Cuba and U.S. Missiles in Turkey," *Orbis,* vol. 21 (Summer 1977), p. 313, claims that Kennedy was not surprised that the missiles were in place and that the assertion that Kennedy refused to negotiate is a "myth." More recently, however, Arthur Schlesinger, in *Robert Kennedy and His Times,* supports that idea that Kennedy was surprised (p. 559) and engaged in "no *quid pro quos"* but thought that in 4 or 5 months "matters would be resolved." (p. 563).
55. Schlesinger, *A Thousand Days,* op. cit., p. 810.
56. Sorensen, op. cit., p. 714.
57. Kennedy, op. cit., p. 87.
58. Schlesinger, op. cit., p. 397; also cited by I. F. Stone, *In a Time of Torment* (New York: Random House, 1968), p. 23.
59. Walton, op. cit., p. 119. The article was by Stewart Alsop and Charles Bartlett, "In Time of Crisis," *Saturday Evening Post,* December 8, 1962.
60. Gelb and Halperin, op. cit., p. 36.
61. Schlesinger, op. cit., p. 831; Neustadt and Allison, in "Afterword," in Kennedy, op. cit., p. 126.
62. Ibid., p. 26.
63. Hilsman, op. cit., pp. 512–513; John McDermott, "Crisis Manager," *New York Review of Books,* Vol. IX (September 14, 1967), pp. 4–10. The fictitious paper, written by James Thompson, also took on the whole Vietnam decision-making team.
64. David Halberstam. *The Best and the Brightest* (New York: Random House, 1972), p. 255.
65. *Washington Post,* May 26, 1974.
66. Luce, *The American Century* (New York: Farrar and Rinehart, 1941), p. 23; and *Life,* February 17, 1941, p. 63. Actually, Luce had been on record with this message from the age of twenty. See W. A. Swanberg, *Luce and His Empire* (New York: Dell Books, 1972).
67. Schlesinger, op. cit., pp. 840–841.
68. "Background" remarks to a conference for editors and broadcasters, May 22, 1967, cited in Hans J. Morgenthau, *A New Foreign Policy for the United States* (New York: Praeger Publishers, 1969), p. 19. For Brzezinski's edited remarks, see "The Implications of Change for United States Foreign Policy," *Department of State Bulletin,* Vol. LVII (July 3, 1967), pp. 19–23.
69. Ibid.
70. Wolfe, op. cit., p. 134.

71. David Woodward, *The Russians at Sea: A History of the Russian Navy* (New York: Praeger Publishers, 1964), pp. 229–230.
72. Wolfe, op. cit., pp. 182–183.
73. Statement by Secretary of Defense Clark M. Clifford, *The Fiscal Year 1970–1974 Defense Program and Defense Budget,* Department of Defense, January 15, 1969, p. 35.
74. Fleet Admiral V. Kasatonov, "On Battle Watch," *Krasnaia Zvezda,* July 30, 1967; cited in Wolfe, op. cit., p. 446.
75. John Newhouse, *Cold Dawn: The Story of SALT* (New York: Holt, Rinehart and Winston, 1973), p. 68.
76. George Liska, *Imperial America: The International Politics of Primacy* (Baltimore: Johns Hopkins University Press, 1967), pp. 36ff.
77. K. J. Holsti, *International Politics,* 2nd ed. (Englewood Cliffs, N.J.: Prentice-Hall, 1972), p. 325.
78. Michel Tatu, *Power in the Kremlin: From Khrushchev to Kosygin* (New York: Viking Press, 1968), pp. 319–320.
79. Hans J. Morgenthau, *A New Foreign Policy for the United States,* pp. 212–213.
80. Daniel Ellsberg, *Papers on the War* (New York: Simon and Schuster, 1972), pp. 292–293.
81. Dean Rusk reflected earlier, obligatory American statements about international legal order and American foreign policy when he declared:

> Our foreign policy has been reflected in our willingness to submit atomic weapons to international law, in feeding and clothing those stricken by war, in supporting free elections and government by consent, in building factories and dams, power plants and railways, schools and hospitals, in improving seed and stock and fertilizer, in stimulating markets and improving the skills and techniques of others in a hundred different ways. Let these things stand in contrast to a foreign policy directed towards the extension of tyranny and using the big lie, sabotage, suspicion, riot and assassination as its tools. The great strength of the United States is devoted to the peaceful pursuits of our people and to the decent opinions of mankind. But it is not healthy for any regime or group of regimes to incur, by their lawless and aggressive conduct, the implacable opposition of the American people. The lawbreaker, unfortunately in the nature of things, always has the initiative, but the peace-making peoples of the world can and will make themselves strong enough to insist upon peace. [Cited in Halberstam, op. cit., p. 327.]

82. H. L. Mencken, "Editorial," *American Mercury,* Vol. IX (November 1926), p. 287. Cited in Halper, op. cit., p. 157.
83. William P. Gerberding, "International Law and the Cuban Crisis," in Lawrence Scheinman and David Wilkinson (eds.), *International Law and Political Crisis: An Analytic Casebook* (Boston: Little, Brown and Company, 1968), pp. 209–210
84. Richard J. Barnet and Marcus Raskin, *After Twenty Years* (New York: Random House, 1965), p. 229n.
85. George Ball, "Slogans and Realities," *Foreign Affairs,* Vol. 47 (July 1969), p. 624.
86. John F. Kennedy, "Let Us Call a Truce to Terror," address to the General Assembly of the United Nations, September 23, 1961, *Department of State Bulletin,* October 16, 1961, p. 619.
87. Schlesinger, op. cit., p. 824.

88. For General de Gaulle's analysis, see his *Memoires de Guerre,* Vol. II, *L'Unite* (Paris: Libraire Plon, 1956), pp. 97–98.
89. Marshal Z. D. Sokolovsky, *Military Strategy: Soviet Doctrine and Concepts* (Introduction by Raymond Garthoff) (New York: Praeger Publishers, 1963). (Subsequent editions were translated by RAND for internal use by government officials.)
90. Abel, op. cit., p. 112.
91. Amitai Etzioni, *Winning Without War* (Garden City, N.Y.: Doubleday & Company, 1965), p. 46.
92. Henry Kissinger, *The Troubled Partnership: A Reappraisal of the Atlantic Alliance* (Garden City, N.Y.: Doubleday & Company, 1966).
93. Adam Ulam, *Expansion and Coexistence* (New York: Praeger Publishers, 1968), p. 675. Ulam (pp. 668–670) suggested that Khrushchev aimed at precluding both Chinese and German acquisition of nuclear weapons.
94. Zbigniew Brzezinski, *Alternative to Partition: For a Broader Conception of America's Role in Europe* (New York: McGraw-Hill Book Company for the Council on Foreign Relations, 1965), p. vii.
95. Cited by Ulam, op. cit., p. 691.
96. These figures and much of the following review of the deteriorating American international economic situation are based on the refreshingly clear analysis of Robert Warren Stevens in *A Primer on the Dollar in the World Economy: United States Balance of Payments and International Monetary Reform* (New York: Random House, 1972), esp. pp. 108–174. See also Lawrence Krause, *Sequel to Bretton Woods: A Proposal to Reform the World Monetary System* (Washington, D.C.: Brookings Institution, 1971).
97. Raymond Vernon, "A Skeptic Looks at the Balance of Payments," *Foreign Policy,* No. 5 (Winter 1971–1972), pp. 52–65.
98. See Lawrence Krause, "Why Exports Are Becoming Irrelevant," *Foreign Policy,* No. 3 (Summer 1971), pp. 62–70.
99. Vernon, op. cit., p. 60.
100. On this point see Stevens, op. cit., pp. 119–121.
101. Ibid., and David P. Calleo and Benjamin M. Rowland, *America and the World Political Economy: Atlantic Dreams and National Realities.* (Bloomington, Ind.: Indiana University Press, 1973), pp. 118–192.
102. Stevens, op. cit., p. 130.
103. For a detailed analysis of the TEA of 1962, see Ernest H. Prieg, *Traders and Diplomats* (Washington, D.C.: Brookings Institution, 1970).
104. See Nora Beloff, *The General Says No: Britain's Exclusion from Europe* (Baltimore: Penguin Books, 1963), *passim.*
105. See Calleo and Rowland, op. cit., pp. 123ff.
106. Stevens, op. cit., p. 138.
107. Remarks by William P. Bundy, October 16, 1973, University of Delaware, Newark, Del.

Chapter 9
Containment
"Turns the Corner"
... into the Swamp

By the onset of the 1980s, the running sore of the Vietnam War had become a scar. Vietnam, no longer a subject of sometimes violent public debate and confrontation, had become the object of cinematic art, the novel, the memoir, and the historian. But those foreign policy analysts of this period who still surveyed the smoke and ruin of Vietnam and the concomitant domestic turmoil and near disintegration, like the ancient Mediterranean oracles who opened the bellies of oxen and burned their entrails to understand the past and predict the future,[1] asked: How did it happen and what did it mean?

CONTAINMENT ON THE MEKONG

To write of American combat involvement in the Indochina War in the past tense strikes the authors as somewhat odd. Both were politicized during the truncated Kennedy years and then lived through what seemed to be an interminable succession of presidential statements and news conferences in which corners were turned and light seen at the end of the tunnel. One fought to maintain some sense of the human implications of the dehumanized jargon of the decade: "gooks" and "slopes," "search and destroy," "free fire zones," "pacification," and that omnipresent obscenity of the late 1960s, the daily "body count." And yet in retrospect, what appeared to be an endless torrent of indistinguishable days, weeks, months, and years can be seen to have fallen into more or less definable periods or phases containing specific and crucial decision points. In this way the war seems to have had an identifiable structure and, more important for our purposes, was an intellectual and historical culmination of the fundamental elements of American foreign policy mapped out in previous chapters.

The Period of Limited
but Escalating Commitment

John Kennedy's investment in the problem of Vietnam was unusual. He was one of the founding members of the American Friends of Vietnam. The Friends were established in the fall of 1955 in order, as then-Senator Kennedy explained at one of their meetings, to offer an alternative to "revolution — a political and social revolution far superior to anything the Communists can offer."[2] Senator Kennedy's explanation to the assembly of Friends summarized the rationale for American involvement in Indochina as it was to stand for the next 16 years:

> Vietnam represents the cornerstone of the Free World in Southeast Asia, the keystone to the arch, the finger in the dike. Burma, Thailand, India, Japan, the Philippines obviously Laos and Cambodia are among those whose security would be threatened if the red tide of communism overflowed into Vietnam. . . . Her economy is essential to the economy of all of Southeast Asia; and her political liberty is an inspiration to those seeking to obtain or maintain their liberty in all parts of Asia — and indeed the world. . . .
>
> Vietnam represents a proving ground of democracy in Asia. However we may choose to ignore it or deprecate it, the rising prestige and influence of Communist China in Asia are unchallengeable facts. Vietnam represents the alternative to Communist dictatorship. . . . The United States is directly responsible for this experiment — it is playing an important role in the laboratory where it is being conducted. We cannot afford to permit that experiment to fail. . . .
>
> And in somewhat similar fashion, Vietnam represents a test of American responsibility and determination in Asia. If we are not the parents of little Vietnam, then surely we are the godparents. We presided at its birth, we gave assistance to its life, we have helped to shape its future. American influence has steadily grown. This is our offspring — we cannot abandon it, we cannot ignore its needs. And if it falls victim to any of the perils that threaten its existence — communism, political anarchy, poverty and the rest — then the United States, with some justification, will be held responsible; and our prestige in Asia will sink to a new low.[3]

When President Kennedy came to the Vietnam question, therefore, his beliefs were already well defined and, in general, they conformed to the prevailing concept of America's interests in the non-Western world and Southeast Asia. President Kennedy was aware, however, that the Diem regime had not conformed to the image one expects in a supposed proving ground for democracy. Between 1955 and 1961 Diem's control of the South had become more and more repressive. In late 1956, a Western observer described South Vietnam as a "quasi-police state characterized by arbitrary arrests and imprisonment, strict censorship of the press and the absence of an effective political opposition."[4] By 1959 Diem had abolished most local government at the village level and carried out a program of land reform that did little or nothing to break the hold of large and absentee land owners. Finally, in 1959, ordinances were passed that gave Diem's military courts very nearly complete latitude and the people no right to appeal from the courts' decisions.[5]

As a result of these circumstances, Diem was soon confronted with a thriving indigenous insurgency. Organized opposition to Diem emerged in 1957 and 1958 but did not have the support of the communists in the North. Indeed, Radio Hanoi repeatedly attacked this new South Vietnam Liberation Front comprised of Viet Cong, southern Viet Minh from the struggle against the French, and the newly disaffected. The communists in the North apparently feared, throughout 1958 and 1959, that this new political force in the South, though articulating an avowedly communist program of action, nevertheless constituted a threat to any subsequent reunification effort. Furthermore, the primary concern of the North at this time seems to have been their own internal economic reconstruction and development, not fomenting revolution in the South. By 1960, however, the Southern opposition to Diem was threatening to move totally beyond the control of Hanoi. Thus, in September 1960, the Northern leaders moved to endorse the activities of the Southern insurgents. Nevertheless, "[t]he socialist revolution in the North was to be regarded as the 'most decisive task for the development of the whole Vietnamese revolution for the cause of national reunification,' but the Southerners were now encouraged to take direct and militant action."[6] By the end of 1960 and into early 1961, the insurgency had escalated. Political assassinations, terrorism, and large battalion-sized battles were not infrequent. Contrary to what the American government would claim subsequently, observers at the time noted: "the insurrection is Southern rooted; it arose at Southern initiative in response to Southern demands."[7]

Upon assuming office, Kennedy sent Vice President Lyndon Johnson to Southeast Asia in May 1961 to evaluate the situation and recommend a course of action. The crux of Johnson's report was that:

> The basic decision in Southeast Asia is here. We must decide whether to help these countries to the best of our ability or throw in the towel in the area and pull back our defenses to San Francisco and a "Fortress America" concept. More important, we would say to the world in this case that we don't live up to treaties and don't stand by our friends. This is not my concept. I recommend that we move forward promptly with a major effort to help these countries defend themselves.[8]

Thus Johnson conceived of the war in Vietnam in terms not unlike those that ran through Truman's mind as he flew back to Washington from Independence, Missouri, in June 1950.

During the spring and summer of 1961, Kennedy increased the American military presence in South Vietnam by some 400 special forces troops and an additional 100 other advisers. In addition, a special mission was sent to Saigon to aid Diem in establishing a strategic hamlet program, which would remove South Vietnamese peasants from insecure areas and relocate them in more centralized and easily protected areas. Finally, in the fall, Kennedy dispatched his chairman of the Joint Chiefs, General Maxwell Taylor, and White House adviser Walt W. Rostow to South Vietnam for yet another evaluation of the situation. By November 1961, Taylor had returned and was recommending to the president that there be an increase of American ground combat strength immediately. Secretary of Defense McNamara and Secretary of State Rusk agreed with this proposal and urged the president to accept Taylor's position that the United States "commit itself to the clear objective of preventing the fall of South Vietnam to Communism."[9] Echoing Johnson (as well as Eisenhower, Dulles, and Truman), the secretaries argued:

> The loss of South Vietnam would make pointless any further discussion about the importance of Southeast Asia to the free world; we would have to face the near certainty that the remainder of Southeast Asia and Indonesia would move to a complete accommodation with Communism, if not formal incorporation with the Communist bloc.
>
> The loss of South Vietnam to Communism would not only destroy SEATO but would undermine the credibility of American commitments elsewhere.[10]

Like Korea a decade earlier, the loss of a country on the periphery would not only undercut regional security and "involve the transfer of a nation of 20 million people from the free world to the communist bloc,"[11] it would also undermine the entire structure of global containment. Moreover, warned McNamara and Rusk, there was yet another Korean ghost abroad in Southeast Asia: the "loss of South Vietnam would stimulate bitter domestic controversies in the United States and would be seized upon by extreme elements to divide the country and harass the Administration."[12] In sum, Kennedy's year-long review of the situation confirmed Eisenhower and Dulles's domino theory of aggression in Southeast Asia. Furthermore, Kennedy's advisers emphasized that at the end of the row of international dominoes was what Leslie Gelb, one of the authors of the *Pentagon Papers,* would later term the "essential domino," American public opinion.[13] It seemed to Kennedy — a man who had been elected by less than one percentage point, stained by the disaster at the Bay of Pigs, again tarnished by the construction of the Berlin wall following the difficult Vienna Conference, and confronted with an even more rapidly deteriorating situation in Laos than in Vietnam — that there was really no choice; he would have to stay.

The next year and a half provided some apparent basis for optimism. The strategic hamlet program had an apparently successful initiation as American troop strength went over 10,000. Secretary of Defense McNamara would report that "Every quantitative measurement we have shows that we're winning this war."[14] Taylor had called in the previous year for both a troop increase as well as the bombing of the North. Kennedy had given him some of the personnel but had refused to initiate the bombing, and it seemed by early 1963 that Kennedy's limited response was working well. Indeed, by 1963 McNamara had initiated planning for U.S. troop withdrawals and, on paper at least, was able to show a 1000-man reduction in force in December 1963. In the meantime, however, apparent success turned decidedly sour.

The Collapse of the Diem Regime

The sense of movement associated with the American build-up in 1962 had provided a deceptive image of progress. The strategic hamlets proved a disaster, as Diem used the program to disrupt traditional Vietnamese society in an effort to extend his authority. A program designed to increase security became, ironically, a contribution to the potential pool of insurgents. Within the South Vietnamese army the situation was actually worsening. Government weapons losses increased and Viet Cong terrorism increased dramatically, thereby demonstrating Diem's loss of control throughout the country. In May 1962, the resentment among the nation's Buddhist majority toward the Catholic minority symbolized by Diem and his brother, Ngo Dinh Nhu, broke into the open. During a demonstration in Hue, on May 8, government troops fired into a crowd of demonstrating Buddhists. Demonstrations escalated as Diem refused to compromise his stand against religious demonstrations. During the fall of 1962 and the summer of 1963 the demonstrations took a grisly turn as seven Buddhist monks committed suicide by public self-immolation, an act of protest sarcastically characterized by Nhu's wife as a "barbecue show."[15] Finally, in August, Nhu ordered government troops to raid major Buddhist pagodas throughout the country and arrest the Buddhist leadership; schools were closed, and the public suicides continued.

By September 1963, things were clearly out of control. Kennedy sent McNamara to South Vietnam with instructions to Diem that reforms must be forthcoming or U.S. assistance would be reduced. In the meantime, the U.S. embassy learned of a conspiracy within the army to overthrow Diem. Orders went out from Washington that the coup was not to be interfered with and in fact should be encouraged and supported if the plan showed likelihood of success. By November, after one false start, the planning for the coup was completed with assistance from the CIA and the American embassy, notably Ambassador Lodge, and was carried out on November 1, 1963. Diem and his brother were assassinated, and an unstable Military Revolutionary Council took over.[16]

By late 1963 the situation in South Vietnam had turned murky. Kennedy was increasingly ambivalent:

> In the final analysis, it is their war. They are the ones who have to win it or lose it. We can help them, we can give them equipment, we can send our men out there as advisers, but they have to win it — the people of Vietnam — against the Communists. . . . [A]ll we can do is help, and we are making it very clear.[17]

"But," cautioned Kennedy, "I don't agree with those who say we should withdraw. That would be a great mistake."[18] As evidence of this conviction, American personnel reached 15,000 in November. Moreover, American complicity in the coup had complicated any decision to withdraw.

At the same time, however, Kennedy intimates have reported that the president, fearing that the war was becoming an American war, was moving toward a decision in 1963 to end American involvement in 1965. The immediate restraining factor was, of course, the presidential election of 1964, the last time Kennedy would have to face the electorate. In the spring of 1963, Kennedy informed Senator Mike Mansfield, who, though an early supporter of Diem, now called for a complete American withdrawal, that he (Kennedy) now agreed, "But I can't do it until 1965 — after I'm reelected."[19] Kenneth O'Donnell, a confidant of the president, recalled:

> After Mansfield left the office, the President told me that he had made up his mind that after his reelection he would take the risk of unpopularity and make a complete withdrawal of American forces from Vietnam. "In 1965, I'll be damned everywhere as a Communist appeaser. But I don't care. If I tried to pull out completely now, we would have another Joe McCarthy red scare on our hands, but I can do it after I'm reelected. So we had better make damned sure that I *am* reelected."[20]

The country would never learn whether Kennedy's decision was a firm one, for he was himself assassinated three weeks after Diem. Lyndon Johnson came into office with the knowledge that the situation in the South was rapidly disintegrating. As McNamara would report in December 1963:

> The situation is very disturbing. Current trends, unless reversed in the [next] 2–3 months, will lead to neutralization at best and more likely to a Communist controlled state.
> The new government is the greatest source of concern. It is indecisive and drifting. . . .
> Vietcong progress has been great during the period since the coup, with my best guess being that the situation has in fact been deteriorating in the countryside . . . to a far greater extent than we realized because of our undue dependence on distorted Vietnamese reporting. . . . We should watch the situation very carefully, running scared, hoping for the best, but preparing for more forceful moves if the situation does not show early signs of improvement.[21]

McNamara's closing recommendation would prove to be a prophetic description of American policy for the next 4 years. The situation would never show more than illusory signs of improvement, especially during 1964, when seven South Vietnamese governments moved in and out of Saigon, and Lyndon Johnson became increasingly fearful of a resurgent Republican right wing in the November 1964 elections.

Transforming the War into an American War

Throughout early 1964 the United States steadily escalated the scale of American involvement in a covert war against North Vietnam in the hope that collapse of the South Vietnamese government could be staved off. The authors of the *Pentagon Papers* characterize Johnson's decision making at this time as being one of pursuing "noncommitting" actions. However, the continuing decline of the situation in the South, the president's impending election campaign, and his own adherence to the view that South Vietnam must remain noncommunist made escalation a certainty. The covert war involved clandestine raids and attacks inside North Vietnam, air strikes in Laos, and destroyer patrols in the Gulf of Tonkin. Most important in the view of the authors of the *Pentagon Papers*, this covert war "carried with it an implicit symbolic and psychological intensification of the U.S. commitment. . . . A firebreak had been crossed."[22]

Significantly, almost no one in the Johnson administration at this time believed that these covert actions would be in themselves sufficient to prevent the loss of the South. Accordingly, in January 1964, proposals for a further escalation of the war to include the bombing of North Vietnam were developed by the Joint Chiefs of Staff.[23] And in May, William P. Bundy prepared a scenario for the escalation of American involvement culminating in an all-out bombing campaign against the North. Included in the proposal was a draft congressional resolution that would give to the president the authority "to use all measures, including the commitment of armed forces" to ensure the survival of South Vietnam.[24] Thus by midyear 1964, Johnson had secretly developed a plan for the escalation of American involvement in Southeast Asia even as he was executing a clandestine low-level war against the North and in Laos.

In spite of a steadily deteriorating situation in South Vietnam, Johnson shelved the proposed escalation temporarily. The president had already moved into the 1964 campaign against Senator Barry Goldwater and was portraying himself to the American people as a man who would not pursue a rash escalation of the war because it would undercut his pursuit of the Great Society at home. Goldwater, in contrast, was calling for an escalation of force in Southeast Asia including the bombing of the North, with nuclear weapons if necessary. Johnson retorted that such a step would dangerously widen the war, perhaps bringing the Chinese or Russians into the conflict; it might also require the commitment of American ground troops to the war, a step that Johnson had scorned during the campaign: "We are not going to send American boys nine or ten thousand miles away from home to do what Asian boys ought to be doing for themselves."

Privately, however, Johnson was approving the very steps that he was publicly attacking Goldwater for recommending. On September 7, 1964, the general conclusion was reached within the administration that bombing of the North would have to begin. As in the previous decisions to initiate covert actions against the North, the measure was rationalized as a limited means to prevent collapse of the political situation in the South. The president could not begin the bombing immediately in view of the position he was taking in the presidential campaign. In the meantime, however, he was able to get the Southeast Asia Resolution passed in August as the result of extremely confusing and uncertain August naval engagements in the Gulf of Tonkin. The purported North Vietnamese attacks came in the wake of a provocative covert naval action against the North approved earlier in the year by the president. Moreover, Assistant Secretary of Defense John McNaughton suggested after the Tonkin "attacks," President Johnson's air strikes in retaliation, and the hurried congressional passage of the open-ended Tonkin Gulf Resolution, that yet

another incident might be staged later as a part of a "provocation strategy" to provide a pretext for the initiation of additional bombing of the
North.[25]

The impression of deceit surrounding the Tonkin Gulf Resolution has,
of course, been intensified by revelations subsequent to the events of
August 1964. It is now apparent that there was considerable confusion and
uncertainty surrounding the purported attacks on the *Maddox* and *C.
Turner Joy*.[26] The *causis belli* for sending fighter bombers to bomb and
strafe North Vietnam was said to be a second North Vietnamese attack on
American warships in 48 hours. The administration maintained the ships
were on "routine" patrol on the high seas and the "attacks" were "piracy."
But the vessels, as Anthony Austin points out in his account, "were not
engaged in 'routine' sea patrol . . . but in a special espionage mission that
took the ships well within North Vietnamese waters. . . . The *Maddox*
[was] running in and out of territorial waters" before the first real attack
by North Vietnam, and 24 hours after the *Maddox* was found by the
Turner Joy on the night of August 3 and 4, the *Maddox* again attempted
to "excite" North Vietnamese radar. There was, in Austin's words, "considerable evidence that one objective of the patrol was to provoke the
North Vietnamese and bloody them if they responded."[27]

Just after the attack, Captain Herrick flashed a cable:

> Review of the action makes many radar contacts and torpedo fuel seemed
> doubtful. Freak weather effects and overeager sonarman may have ac-
> counted for many reports. No actual visual sightings by Maddox. Suggest
> complete evaluation before further action.[28]

Apparently, however, a complete evaluation would have stalled a
bureaucracy eager to bring American power against the North, and dis-
confirming evidence that indicated that an attack never took place was all
but ignored. With the publication of the *Pentagon Papers* it became evident that one of the purposes was also to provide support for the secret
South Vietnamese navy's sallies against the North. These "A34" assaults
could easily have been interpreted as hostile acts by the North Vietnamese. But most of the evidence now seems to indicate that the second
alleged attack by North Vietnam just did not take place.

A White House official in a "position to know," confided to *The New
York Times* columnist Tom Wicker "that the President had been carrying
around the text of the resolution 'in his pocket' long before the Tonkin
episode gave him the right opportunity to lay it before Congress."[29] When
opportunity knocked, the secretary of defense hurriedly sent American
fighter bombers over North Vietnam, bombing oil storage and port facili-

ties. Secretary McNamara could report to the president that the "retalia-tory" air strikes were a huge success. "Smoke was observed rising to 14,000 feet," he declared. Johnson was elated. One reporter heard him gloat, "I didn't just screw Ho Chi Minh; I cut his pecker off."[30] The Tonkin resolution was then brought out of Johnson's pocket to be used as the basis for legitimizing the planned expansion of the war — all that had been needed was an event to set things in motion. Publication of the *Pentagon Papers* makes the claims put forward in support of the resolution patently transparent. The *Papers* themselves and the documents published with them make it clear that from February to August 1964 the United States was consciously pursuing a policy of escalating the conflict in Southeast Asia by overt and covert means. With the election safely behind him, President Johnson moved to the crucial decisions on the escalation and transformation of the war. Detailed plans for initiating a bombing cam-paign against the North were tentatively approved in early December. For the time being, however, the president gave final approval only to increased, but secret, bombing of the infiltration routes in Laos.

By the end of 1964 American aircraft had been shot down over South Vietnam, domestic political chaos had increased in Saigon, and the South Vietnamese army seemed on the verge of collapse. Furthermore, much of the intelligence community was now warning the president that the increased U.S. military action envisioned in the bombing proposal could not save the situation on the ground in South Vietnam. Early 1965 was, therefore, a critical decision point, perhaps the most crucial period in the evolution of American policy in Southeast Asia. The administration was confronted with the undeniable fact that previous efforts had not halted the decline in the South. Although the president displayed some caution in late 1964, by January and February 1965 he was prepared to initiate the bombing in the North. When the Vietcong struck an American installation at Pleiku in February, Johnson ordered the initiation of Operation Rolling Thunder, the sustained bombing of strategic targets in the North which would continue for the next 3 years. It is important to note that this was probably not the only option available to the United States at this time, for Hanoi had initiated peace feelers during December and January. The view from Washington was, however, that negotiations at a time when circumstances in the South were so obviously bad would have the appear-ance of negotiating from weakness, therefore talks should be avoided until more military pressure could be brought to bear on the North.

The bombing of the North, including areas surrounding Hanoi, came as Soviet Premier Aleksei Kosygin arrived in North Vietnam. The Soviet Premier was widely reported as a moderate, and many Western intelli-gence analysts saw his visit as a means of dampening the war and reasserting Russian influence in the area against Chinese ambitions. But while Kosygin was in Hanoi the bombs fell. The Soviet Premier bitterly told Kissinger and Nixon some 8 years later, "I shall never forget it."[31] David Halberstam relates a story that indicated it was not the attack on Pleiku that prompted American reprisal* but rather that it was an opportune moment to head off negotiation and increase the pace of the war:

> A few days after the bombing campaign had begun, a White House reporter came across Bundy in the White House barbershop. Bundy was sitting there being lathered, and since he could not easily escape, the reporter thought it was a good time to ask Bundy something that had been bothering him since the incident. "Mac," he said, "what was the difference between Pleiku and the other incidents?"
> Bundy paused and then answered, "Pleikus are like streetcars" (i.e., there's one along every ten minutes).[32]

However, the bombing could not prevent the next decision facing Johnson. The South Vietnamese Army was collapsing, and bombing the North was not going to reverse this trend any more than covert raids and incremental increases of U.S. advisers had stopped the growth of the Viet Cong during the preceding 2 to 3 years. The authors of the *Pentagon Papers* underscore the dilemma:

> Once set in motion, however, the bombing effort seemed to stiffen rather than soften Hanoi's backbone, as well as the willingness of Hanoi's allies, particularly the Soviet Union, to work toward compromise. . . .
> Official hopes were high that the Rolling Thunder program would rapidly convince Hanoi that it should agree to negotiate a settlement to the war in the South. After a month of bombing with no response from the North Vietnamese, optimism began to wane. . . .
> The U.S. was presented essentially two options: (1) to withdraw unilaterally from Vietnam leaving the South Vietnamese to fend for themselves, or (2) to commit ground forces in pursuit of its objectives.[33]

On April 1, 1965, President Johnson ordered that American troops would be used in offensive action in South Vietnam. In a National Security Action Memorandum issued on April 6, 1965, the president approved: an 18,000 to 20,000 man increase in U.S. forces; the deployment of two marine battalions in northern South Vietnam; and a change of mission for all marine battalions in South Vietnam "to permit their more active

*The attack occurred on February 7, 1965. The Pleiku barracks housed American military advisers. The night attack killed 8 and wounded 126 and was the long awaited provocation the administration had sought.

use."[34] The memorandum also cautioned, "The President desires that with respect to the actions ..., premature publicity be avoided by all possible precautions."[35]

"I Want to Leave the Footprints of America There"[36]

On April 7, 1965, in a speech at Johns Hopkins University, the president sought to explain why the war must be fought. The reasons given were familiar ones:

> We are ... there because there are great stakes in the balance. Let no one think for a moment that retreat from Vietnam would bring an end to conflict. The battle would be renewed in one country and then another. The central lesson of our time is that the appetite of aggression is never satisfied. To withdraw from one battlefield means only to prepare for the next. We must say in Southeast Asia — as we did in Europe — in the words of the Bible: "Hitherto shalt thou come, but no further."[37]

Vietnam was in fact no different from Europe before World War II, Johnson implied. Furthermore, Hanoi was analogous to Nazi Germany, for "the first reality is that North Vietnam has attacked the independent nation of South Vietnam. Its object is total conquest."[38] This was no civil war; indeed:

> Over this war — and all Asia — is another reality: the deepening shadow of Communist China. The rulers in Hanoi are urged on by Peiping. This is a regime which has destroyed freedom in Tibet, which has attacked India, and has been condemned by the United Nations for aggression in Korea. It is a nation which is helping the forces of violence in almost every continent. The contest in Vietnam is part of a wider pattern of aggressive purposes.[39]

The rationale for action put before the American people was, therefore, the same that had been advanced for almost 2 decades. There was a hint of the decision already secretly taken and of what was to come: "We know that air attacks alone will not accomplish all of these purposes."[40] By the end of the year there would be 184,314 American troops in South Vietnam.

In April 1965 the director of the Central Intelligence Agency, John McCone, had argued that

> I believe our proposed track offers great danger of simply encouraging Chinese Communists and Soviet support of the DRV [North Vietnam] and VC cause, if for no other reason than the risk for both will be minimum. ...

In effect, we will find ourselves mired down in combat in the jungle in a military effort that we cannot win, and from which we will have extreme difficulty in extracting ourselves.[41]

In June and July 1965, those opposed to further escalation of the war marshalled their arguments, which had been passed over at the time the April decisions to commit American ground troops had been made. McCone had argued for an increased air effort to avoid ground combat in this jungle quagmire. By mid-1965 the "doves" insisted that even with an increase in the air war, McCone's prophecy would be fulfilled. But on July 28, 1965, President Johnson announced that "We did not choose to be the guardians at the gate, but there is no one else. . . . [W]e learned from Hitler at Munich that success only feeds the appetite of aggression. . . . I have asked the commanding general, General Westmoreland, what more he needs to meet this mounting aggression. He has told me. We will meet his needs. . . . Additional forces will be needed later, and they will be sent as requested."[42]

This was clearly not a decision made in the absence of any debate or indication of what might come. There was full awareness on the part of the administration that they were now embarked on a new course. They chose, however, to hide that awareness from the American people. Thus during a July 28, 1965, press conference, the president was asked:

Q. Mr. President, does the fact that you are sending additional forces to Vietnam imply any change in the existing policy of relying mainly on the South Vietnamese to carry out offensive operations and using American forces to guard installations and to act as emergency backup?

A. It does not imply any change in policy whatever. It does not imply any change of objective.[43]

The Pentagon analysts who prepared the 3000-page analysis of the Vietnam War provide the best summation of these private mid-1965 decisions.

The major participants in the decision knew the choices and understood the consequences. . . . [The mid-July decision to approve forty-four maneuver battalions] was perceived as a threshold — entrance into an Asian land war. The conflict was seen to be long, with further U.S. deployments to follow. The choice at that time was not whether or not to negotiate, it was not whether to hold on for a while or let go — the choice was viewed as winning or losing South Vietnam. . . . This was sanctioned implicitly as the only way to achieve the U.S. objective of a noncommunist South Vietnam.

The acceptance of the search and destroy strategy . . . left the United States commitment to Vietnam open-ended. The implications in terms of manpower and money are inescapable.

Final acceptance of the desirability of inflicting defeat on the enemy rather than merely denying him victory opened the door to an indeterminate amount of additional force.[44]

American policymaking now assumed a kind of tragic predictability. On July 2, 1965, McNaughton requested of the Joint Chiefs an estimate of "the forces required to win in South Vietnam."[45] But it was soon apparent that no one knew, and Washington deferred to Westmoreland's estimate of what he said he needed. In July 1965 he requested an additional 100,000 men; in November 1965 an additional 154,000; in December 1965 Westmoreland requested a total of 443,000 troops by the end of 1966; in January 1966 he increased his 1966 figure to 459,000 men; and in August 1966 Westmoreland requested 542,588 men by the end of 1967. The war would be over, he said, by the end of 1967; 1968 was, of course, an election year.[46]

As American escalation of the ground war continued throughout 1966, the air war followed a similar pattern as previously untouched petroleum, oil, and lubricant supplies were hit and destroyed. Nevertheless, the North continued to match each American escalation; and by the fall of 1966 a special report of the Institute for Defense Analysis commissioned by the Department of Defense concluded that:

1. As of July 1966 the U.S. bombing of North Vietnam (NVN) had had no measurable direct effect on Hanoi's ability to mount and support military operations in the South at the current level. . . .

The available evidence clearly indicates that Hanoi has been infiltrating military forces and supplies into South Vietnam at an accelerated rate during the current year. Intelligence estimates have concluded that North Vietnam is capable of substantially increasing its support.[47]

Finally, the report concluded with the observation:

There is currently no adequate basis for predicting the levels of U.S. military effort that would be required to achieve the stated objectives — indeed, there is no firm basis for determining if there is *any* feasible level of effort that would achieve these objectives.[48]

In October McNamara went to Vietnam for another evaluation of the war, and upon returning to Washington reported to Johnson that he was in substantial agreement with the institute's conclusions. This report by McNamara in October was accompanied by his recommendation that the United States set a limit to its troop levels and shift the pattern of American bombing away from the Hanoi-Haiphong area to infiltration routes in preparation for a negotiated settlement of the conflict. This recommendation sparked an intense debate within the administration, with the Joint Chiefs standing in opposition to McNamara. The Johnson administration was now split as to the future course of the war. The president compromised by allowing McNamara to cut the military's requested troop level to 469,000 by the end of 1968, but approving yet another step up in the air war despite CIA findings that 80 percent of the casualties in North Vietnam during 1965 and 1966 were civilians. In February 1967, Johnson approved an increase in B-52 sorties from 60 to 800 monthly.[49]

Midway into 1967 the debate within the administration was at its peak and was intensified by General Westmoreland's request for 200,000 troops, or an ultimate troop strength of more than 670,000 troops by mid-July 1968. Moreover, pressure from within the military began to rise for unlimited bombing, an invasion of Cambodia, Laos, or even North Vietnam, as well as attacks on the port of Haiphong.[50] Johnson continued to resist the pressure for an expansion of the war on land. At the same time the preconditions he attached to any peace overtures offered the North Vietnamese were such as to preclude real negotiations. These prior conditions were little changed from those Johnson offered in 1965 and 1966 when the president ordered bombing pauses while offering that if the North Vietnamese and the Viet Cong would concede that they were the aggressors in the war and stop their infiltration of the South, then the United States would end its bombing and begin negotiations. The entire position was rooted in the contention that the war was not a civil war, a position that was unacceptable and hence nonnegotiable to the North. The fighting continued.

By late 1967, disaffection with the war had begun to swell in the United States. Draft resistance increased during 1966 and 1967, and during these same years the War on Poverty turned into a skirmish because of the budgetary demands of the war and widespread rioting became almost commonplace in black ghettoes. Radical politics seemed to be the norm on many college campuses. And within Congress, the bipartisan consensus of foreign policy disintegrated as congressional doves led by Senator Fulbright and other liberal members of the Foreign Relations Committee openly challenged the administration's policies in Southeast Asia. Indeed, by the end of 1967 there was virtually no communication between the Foreign Relations Committee and the administration. Public opinion remained uneasily behind the president. But as the nation approached the 1968 elections, polls found growing opposition to American policy in Indochina, especially the bombing of the North and the refusal of the Johnson administration to facilitate negotiations.

In the face of this disintegrating domestic base, Johnson reiterated the now worn justifications for the war, increased secret domestic surveillance on American antiwar dissidents, and brought General Westmoreland before the Congress to extol progress and eminent success in the war. It would all be over in 2 years, the General said, if, of course, he got the necessary forces. But Johnson would not go this far; instead, there would be more bombing and greater use of indiscriminate firepower as ever-larger areas of South Vietnam were declared "free fire zones." Anyone found in these areas was assumed to be the "enemy" and therefore subject, in the jargon of the day, to being "blown away," or "wasted." By one estimate, one-third to one-half of the people of Southeast Asia had become refugees.[51] Vast areas of land had been defoliated by American herbicide and weed killers. Between 1961 and 1971 the United States dropped more than 100 million pounds of herbicide on South Vietnam (six pounds of herbicide for every man, woman, and child in South Vietnam). Dioxin, one of the ingredients of the defoliant, Agent Orange, is now known to cause genetic mutation, liver damage, and cancer, according to a National Academy of Science study completed in February 1975. About one-seventh of the territory of South Vietnam was sprayed in order to destroy crops and jungle canopy which supposedly sheltered the Viet Cong. The 1925 Geneva treaty on chemical and biological warfare prohibits the deployment of gases and toxins. Just the same, some 36 percent of the mangrove swampland — the breeding ground of the staples of fish and rice of the Vietnamese diet — had been destroyed by 1974. The seventeen scientists commissioned to study the effect of these toxins estimated that it could take over 100 years for the swamps to recover.[52] Moreover, by the late 1970s and early 1980s this campaign would produce a grim irony as the United States government faced suits from American veterans of the war who had been exposed to the defoliants and were experiencing abnormally high rates of cancer. The damages claimed in the suits could run into the billions of dollars.

Between 1965 and 1971 the enormous quantity of ordnance expended in Indochina as a whole represented some 142 pounds of explosives per acre of land and 584 pounds per person. "The average rate of detonation was 118 pounds per second," which equaled, in terms of explosive power, the equivalent of 450 Hiroshima-type atomic bombs.[53] Craters filled with water, causing mosquito populations to intensify and malaria to spread. Unexploded shells killed and maimed those who dared remain to work the land. The timber industry was wiped out. Workers attempting to cut wood with power saws risked being hit from shrapnel buried in the wood. The rubber industry was ruined, and the landscape of the once rich Mekong Delta became, according to observers, "gray porridge . . . torn as if by an angry giant." Senator Gaylord Nelson noted that "There is nothing in the history of warfare to compare with [it]. A 'scorched earth' policy has been a tactic . . . throughout history, but never has a land been so massively altered and mutilated."[54]

By the end of 1967 more bombs had been dropped on Vietnam than in the entirety of Europe during World War II. McNamara now began to testify openly that the air war had failed to stop the infiltration of men and supplies into the South and the destruction inflicted on the North could not be said to have broken Hanoi's will to go on. It was a remarkable departure for the secretary of defense to contradict publicly and powerfully the Joint Chiefs. But McNamara had changed. Previously, students at Harvard had nearly overturned his car when he made one of his last public addresses in defense of what was once known as McNamara's War. Then he shouted, "I'm tougher than you. I was tougher in World War II and I'm tougher now!" But his doubts grew. He commissioned the Pentagon Papers. When the papers were handed to him, he confessed to a friend, "You know they could hang people for what's in there."[55] McNamara's son began turning up at peace demonstrations and became a prominent figure in the antiwar movement. McNamara's behavior, once so controlled, determined, and calculating, became "erratic."[56] In the end, he was given to public weeping. He was the third secretary of defense in less than 25 years to break in office.

On January 31, 1968, the start of the Buddhist Tet holiday, the communists launched large-scale attacks throughout South Vietnam. Communist forces penetrated to the heart of every major city in the South, including Saigon. Hue was captured, and it was only after weeks of fighting and the literal destruction of most of the ancient and culturally important city that it was retaken. Parts of Saigon and other cities could be saved only by calling destructive and indiscriminate air strikes down on them. The communists took enormous casualties, and the Pentagon claimed a major battlefield victory, but in fact Tet marked the end of the open-ended American war in South Vietnam. If, after almost 3 years of steady escalation and expansion of the effort, the communists could launch an attack of the magnitude of the Tet offensive, then it was clear that a change in policy was necessary.

The crucial decision was made by Clark Cifford, who had replaced McNamara as secretary of defense in February 1968. Faced with a new Westmoreland request for 206,000 additional troops, Clifford recommended that it be denied. Moreover, the new secretary of defense asked on March 5, 1968, that the chairman of the Joint Chiefs of Staff evaluate a proposal from the Department of State that the bombing in the North be curtailed or halted, implying that he (Clifford) favored such a move.

The domestic domino began wobbling as an avowed peace candidate, Senator Eugene McCarthy, claimed a moral victory in the New Hampshire primary with 40 percent of the Democratic vote. Then the American casualty figures were released. They numbered 139,801 — exceeding the overall Korean War losses. At the same moment, an emergency meeting of European and American bankers was held in Washington to stem a run on gold as the price soared. And on March 13 Senator Robert Kennedy announced that he would seek the Democratic party nomination for president in 1968. The day Senator Kennedy announced he would run, Johnson rejected Westmoreland's troop request. Within a week, the president recalled the general to become army chief of staff.[57]

The Tet offensive simply could not be ignored, for it ran completely against the years of deceptively optimistic official reporting. As Kissinger wrote in 1968:

> The Tet offensive marked the watershed of the American effort.... [T]he prevalent strategy could no longer achieve its objectives in a period or with force levels politically acceptable to the American people.[58]

The president was forced to reconsider the entire course of the war. On March 25 Johnson convened a Senior Informal Advisory Group, which consisted of former members of the foreign and defense policy community and was informally headed by Dean Acheson. Almost without exception these were men who had been hawks for years; many of them, such as Acheson and Omar Bradley, traced their service back to the immediate postwar period.[59] After a 2 day review of the situation, this group, informally known as the "wise men," dramatically recommended that the president reverse course and deescalate the war. The president, according to the authors of the *Pentagon Papers,* was stunned by the position now taken by this group, which in previous years had recommended escalation. On March 31, 1968, the president announced that he was cutting back on the bombing. Moreover, he announced that in order to facilitate the search for peace he would not seek the presidential nomination in 1968. The domestic domino had fallen.

In his 1965 Johns Hopkins speech Johnson had stated a desire to bring a $1 billion economic assistance program to Vietnam. "The vast Mekong River," he said, "can provide food and water and power on a scale to dwarf even our own TVA." He also noted that "we often say how impressive power is. But I do not find it impressive at all. The guns and bombs, the rockets and the warships, are all symbols of human failure . . . [t]hey are witness to human folly."[60]

UNDERSTANDING THE QUAGMIRE
AND THE STALEMATE MACHINE

A combination of a misperception of the nature of the revolutionary conflict in Vietnam, the relationship of that conflict to America's broader world role, and presidential politics set a framework within which we might understand America's (and Vietnam's) Vietnamese tragedy. At the confluence of these streams lies the swamp into which American foreign policy was knowingly carried during during the 1960s. John Kennedy was murdered even as he seemed to recognize the peril confronting his administration. Lyndon Johnson's administration died in the swamps as he tried to extricate himself from that quagmire first through violence and then through negotiations.

The International Costs of "Losing"

Those who have tried to grasp and explain America's deadly fascination with and involvement in Vietnam have frequently employed the image of a man floundering helplessly in a quagmire into which he had inadvertently slipped.[61] Other careful students of American policy have argued to the contrary, that American presidents have in no way stumbled into the Vietnamese swamp. Rather they in most instances entered knowingly into the bog. There may have been times, such as early and mid-1965, that the intense desire for victory made the wish seem a real possibility. But for the most part American policy makers were aware that the actions they were taking at a particular moment would at best allow them to hold their position on what seemed eternally shifting and treacherous grounds, and at worst would probably require subsequent additional commitment.[62] As Leslie Gelb has argued:

> Vietnam was indeed a quagmire, but most of our leaders knew it. Of course there were optimists and periods where many were genuinely optimistic. But those periods were infrequent and short-lived and were invariably followed by periods of deep pessimism. Very few, to be sure, envisioned what the Vietnam situation would be like by 1968. Most realized, however, that "the light at the end of the tunnel" was very far away — if not finally unreachable.[63]

If in their frantic effort to press on and/or extricate themselves from the swamp, Kennedy, Johnson, and the "best and the brightest" who made up their administrations maimed and killed other creatures who lived in the swamp, the Americans should not be blamed, guilt should not be apportioned, for American intentions were good. It was necessary, or so it seemed to Truman, Eisenhower, Kennedy, and Johnson, that we be in Vietnam, not because Vietnam itself was so vital to American security, but because if we were not willing to go in and stay there, "our word" and reputation would suffer. "We are there," said Johnson, "because we have a promise to keep. . . . We are also there to strengthen the world order. Around the globe from Berlin to Thailand are people whose well-being rests . . . on the belief that they can count on us."[64]

Assistant Secretary of Defense McNaughton put matters in perspective in a memo he wrote laying out American war objectives as the Johnson administration approached the fateful escalation decisions in late 1964 and early 1965. American aims should be:

> 70 pct. — To avoid a humiliating U.S. defeat (to our reputation as a guarantor).
>
> 20 pct. — To keep SVN (and then adjacent) territory from Chinese hands.
>
> 10 pct. — To permit the people of SVN to enjoy a better, freer way of life.
>
> Also — To emerge from crisis without unacceptable taint from methods used.
>
> [American aims should] not [be] — To "help a friend," although it would be hard to stay in if asked out.[65]

McNaughton went further: even if the Viet Cong were not defeated, American involvement "would demonstrate that the U.S. was a 'good doctor' willing to keep promises, be tough, take risks, get bloodied and hurt the enemy badly."[66]

Now, we do not mean to suggest that every president had such a quantified apportionment of American aims before him at all times. On the other hand, the McNaughton ranking of American priorities does suggest a plausible set of benchmarks against which the employment of American means were evaluated, otherwise one would have to argue that the Kennedy and Johnson administrations were filled with willful sadistic monsters. If the well-being of one's ally is evaluated on the order of magnitude of 10 percent out of a hundred, whereas the avoidance of a "humiliating defeat" stands at or near 70 percent, then clearly the figurative and quite literal destruction of one's ally is a small price to pay if "humiliation" is avoided. If, as a doctor, you believe that your worth to the larger society will be evaluated primarily in terms of your cool willingness to enter a potentially bloody operating room, then it does not matter much that the patient be disabled, disfigured, or die a horrible and lingering death.

Johnson's desire that the United States leave behind in Vietnam that which he regarded as truly "impressive" — schools, dams, a better life — is more understandable in this light. There is no reason to doubt that the president set forth in all honesty and with deep conviction this image of what Indochina could be. What is more important, however, was his belief that first "we must deal with the world as it is, if it is ever to be as we wish." The building of the world that we wish must be deferred as we deal with and contain the perceived threats and disorder of the contemporary system. In this vision, if the road be painful, so be it: "this nation [must] hazard its ease, its interest, and its power." Ultimately, however, we must do so not primarily, as Johnson implied, "for the sake of a people so far away," but rather because our particular vision of the political and economic order of the world demands it. The difficulty and danger for those people "so far away" is, however, that the pursuit of that vision, as in Vietnam, frequently requires that *they* hazard *their* ease, *their* interest, and *their* power so that the American vision might be realized.

In one sense, therefore, the quagmire metaphor is useful. Kennedy and Johnson, but especially Johnson, did behave as if they were men in a swamp. That part of the swamp in which they found themselves, Vietnam, was but a part of a much larger morass — a quagmire created and sustained, it was believed, by the flow of Chinese and Soviet communism. If that source of aggression threatened to turn the entire international system into a swamp, then it was essential that the United States try to dam up Asian and Soviet communism. If that meant in turn that the United States must stay in the swamp indefinitely, then it was, nevertheless, essential.

The persistence of Kennedy, Johnson, and subsequently Richard Nixon, once in the swamp, is understandable in terms of their fears of the international consequences of losing Vietnam. Given the perceived all-encompassing nature of the threat, to lose once is to lose everything. It does not follow, as Dulles used to insist, that one must win finally and definitely. But one must certainly not lose. All American presidents faced with the problem of Vietnam have desired the final defeat of the Viet Cong and North Vietnamese. Yet the larger international imperatives demanded at a minimum that the American client not be defeated. Thus, when Johnson found that, to avoid such a defeat, the commitment of American troops was necessary, he proceeded with the escalation of the war. And once in, of course, it was now not only the American client who was at stake; rather it was the United States itself. Indeed, the client was only a symbol of the higher stakes of battle. As Kissinger readily confessed in print in January 1969, Vietnam may not have been important intrinsically, but "the commitment of five hundred thousand Americans . . . settled the issue of the importance of Vietnam." Kissinger continued:

> For what it involved now is confidence in American promises. However fashionable it is to ridicule the terms "credibility" or "prestige," they are not empty phrases; other nations can gear their actions to ours only if they can count on our steadiness. . . . In many parts of the world — the Middle East, Europe, Latin America, even Japan — stability depends on confidence in American promises.[67]

In 1965, 1966, and early 1967, Johnson believed that the United States could have final victory. Certainly events in the Dominican Republic in 1965, even as he was escalating the Vietnam War, might have suggested as much to him. In that case when an American-backed regime was "deserted by everyone"[68] and subsequently attacked by leftists and conservatives, Johnson landed the marines and imposed order. The original pretense was the protection of Americans in Santo Domingo, but subsequently the United States published a hastily drawn and largely inaccurate list of communists and "Castroite leaders who were purportedly active in the revolution." A stable conservative government was installed.

The thrust of this policy was repeated throughout Latin America as Lyndon Johnson's new assistant secretary of state for inter-American affairs, Thomas Mann, redirected much of what was left of the Alliance of Progress to military governments, such as that established in Brazil in 1964 following a coup that overthrew a liberal-leftist regime. Moreover, American aid was increasingly tied to the purchase of expensive American goods, thereby subsidizing in many instances noncompetitive American exporters. The American balance of payments was undoubtedly aided by such a program; Latin American aid was, however, correspondingly reduced.[69] Nevertheless, Johnson's policies in Latin America seemed to prevent the appearance of any more Castros, and insofar as they did so, they fulfilled their primary objectives.

The apparent success of these efforts and especially the Dominican intervention may also have reinforced Johnson's propensities to escalate the scale of military involvement in Vietnam. Arthur Schlesinger speculates that Johnson also "found it viscerally inconceivable that what Walt Rostow kept telling him was 'the greatest power in the world' could not dispose of a collection of nightriders in black pajamas."[70] Further, insofar as the Dominican intervention was carried out without much negative public outcry in the United States, it is not inconceivable that Johnson might have concluded that his domestic base was strong and supportive. On the other hand, Johnson's behavior before the 1964 election suggests more complex conclusions.

Presidential Politics and the Cost of Losing

In contrast to Johnson's bold escalation of the fighting and American participation in it after 1965, there was the covert war, secret preparation for the escalation, and the outright public deception of 1964. These facts suggest that there was more than the fear of the international consequences of a loss or overconfidence concerning U.S. power at work. In short, more than one stream was feeding the swamp. Presidents have indeed been afraid of losing in Vietnam because of the international implications of such a loss, but they have also been preoccupied with its domestic consequences. Moreover, this concern and preoccupation with losing to communists or looking "soft" when confronted with a communist challenge has extended to more than Vietnam. We have noted the import of this factor on the Truman and Eisenhower administrations previously. John Kennedy's emotional and bellicose reaction to the Bay of Pigs disaster was perhaps due in some part to his fear that he would suffer during the next election or because he perceived the American people chastising him not for the blatant illegality of the act but for his failure. Similarly, the Cuban missile crisis over a year later seems to have been fed in some measure by this same anticipation of a popular backlash to a posture more conducive to a negotiated resolution of the conflict.

These fears were clearly at work throughout the Vietnam escalation. For Kennedy and Johnson the war could not be lost if they and their administrations were to survive. We have seen that Kennedy may have decided by late 1963 that he would have to reverse course, but he did not see his way clear to do so until after the 1964 election. The choice for Lyndon Johnson was even more complex. Johnson could no more "lose" the war before the 1964 election than the murdered Kennedy; and then Johnson could not lose the war after the election either, because he hoped to face the electorate again in 1968. At the same time, during the 1964 campaign, Johnson sought to maintain an image of a calm moderate on the war so as to set himself apart from Goldwater's bellicose proposals. To save the situation on the ground in Vietnam was difficult, for Johnson and his advisers knew that matters were disintegrating rapidly. Thus the covert war, actually conceived in the Kennedy administration, was employed to hold the situation until November 1964. In the meantime, Johnson was planning secretly to do what Goldwater was proclaiming publicly that the United States should be doing.

Underlying this balancing act by Johnson was a perception of the American people with which Kennedy could have agreed:

> I knew our people well enough to realize that if we walked away from Vietnam and let Southeast Asia fall, there would follow a divisive and de-

structive debate in our country. . . . A divisive debate about "who lost Viet-nam" would be, in my judgment, even more destructive to our national life than the argument over China had been.[71]

In Johnson's view this debate would in turn undercut the capacity of the United States to play its global role:

Our allies . . . throughout the world would conclude that our word was worth little or nothing. . . . [Moscow and Peking] could not resist the opportunity to expand their control into the vacuum of power.[72]

Thus the two streams converged precisely where the president of the United States stood. For Lyndon Johnson as well as his predecessors and his successor, the only way to survive in the midst of the cross-currents was to avoid a loss in Vietnam. Or, as Daniel Ellsberg has argued, the end of policy became the production and maintenance of a stalemate.[73]

The problem after the 1964 election was no less complex, for by then the situation in Vietnam had become desperate as governments came and went and the South Vietnamese army fought indifferently. If the situation was to be held for another 4 years, it was clear that the Americans would have to do it. Now, however, Johnson sought a middle way along the escalatory path he had chosen. On one side were the doves who demanded withdrawal. The latter could be placated, at least in the short run, with breathless bombing pauses and peace initiatives. The hawks could be bought off by dribbling out the troop escalations that everybody knew were coming and inching up the bombing campaign while warning of the dangers of Chinese or Soviet intervention if the escalation went too fast or too violently. Finally, to maintain the support of that large number of confused and disoriented people in the middle, Johnson carefully avoided for as long as possible taking those steps that would significantly disrupt the lives of the average American. Thus he resisted tax increases and a call-up of the reserves until 1967 and maintained draft deferments for college-age males as long as possible.[74]

At the same time, however, the incremental escalation necessitated by this approach simplified the problem of matching the escalation on the part of the North Vietnamese. There can be little doubt that Hanoi was quite aware of the nature of Johnson's domestic circumstance and sought to exploit it:

American public opinion was the essential domino. Our leaders knew it. Hanoi's leaders knew it. Each geared its strategy — both the rhetoric and the conduct of the war — to this fact.

> Hanoi adopted what seems to have been a . . . strategy to cause U.S. withdrawal from Vietnam by playing on American domestic politics. The . . . aim was to try to convince Americans that unless U.S. forces withdrew, the killing of Americans would never end.[75]

The *Pentagon Papers* seemed to confirm that Johnson and his advisers were quite aware of Hanoi's appeal to the American public. Moreover, Johnson also knew that the course he had chosen would be arduous and long: "Johnson . . . knew that the intelligence analysts offered little promise of victory ever, while no one (except, most of the time, Walt Rostow) promised it quickly."[76] But the president also knew (or thought he knew) what the American people would do if he caved in. Thus he was compelled to hang on and hope that something would turn up. These judgments fated him to play out the scenario presented to him by Undersecretary of State George Ball, perhaps the leading dove in the Johnson Administration, who argued for no further escalation and lost in mid-1965:

> The South Vietnamese are losing the war to the Viet Cong. No one can assure you that we can beat the Viet Cong or even force them to the conference table on our terms, no matter how many hundred thousand white, foreign (U.S.) troops we deploy. . . . The decision you face now, therefore, is crucial. Once large numbers of U.S. troops are committed to direct combat . . . [and] once we suffer large casualties, we will have started a well-nigh irreversible process. Our involvement will be so great that we cannot — without national humiliation — stop short of achieving our complete objectives. Of the two possibilities I think humiliation would be more likely than the achievement of our objectives — even after we have paid terrible costs.[77]

Negotiating in Quicksand

After the Tet offensive and the collapse of his political career, Johnson was more or less personally free of presidential politics. These pressures remained for his party and his vice president, who would become the Democratic party candidate. Nevertheless, after March 1968 the American public, which had been hawkish earlier, no longer had any stomach for the war. In short, the opportunities for a negotiated settlement in Vietnam seemed better than at any time since the 1950s. The North Vietnamese, in responding to Johnson's limited bombing halt of March 1968, agreed to discuss only the full cessation of the bombing at the outset; if there was to be only a limited bomb suspension, they would engage in only limited talks. They probably concluded that time was on their side, for as the elections drew closer, the Americans might become more forthcoming. There was some risk in this strategy, however, for if they delayed too long they might be confronted with a new president who would escalate the war. Thus they had to be willing to engage in some compromise in their position although central questions of the war, unification and the illegitimacy of the Saigon regime, remained nonnegotiable issues.

In the meantime, however, Johnson refused to take the minimum steps necessary to move the talks to the level of true negotiations. Throughout April, May, and most of June 1968, the United States insisted that the bombing could completely stop only if the North Vietnamese demonstrated some restraint on the battlefield. The North Vietnamese refused any concession to the American demand, for to do so would be an indirect admission that they were aggressors in South Vietnam. Since the North Vietnamese refused to concede that South Vietnam existed and insisted that the United States was in fact the aggressor against Vietnam, there could be no *formal* and *public* concession of this most fundamental of points.

During June, July, and August 1968, however, the Viet Cong and North Vietnamese drastically reduced their offensive action, and the North Vietnamese reportedly withdrew more than 80,000 of their troops as a gesture to the Americans. Johnson refused to respond, however, apparently believing that further concessions could be gained by the continued application of force. Furthermore, he was now under pressure from Saigon to make no concession that in any way recognized the Viet Cong; they should not be given any recognition at formal negotiations. To do so, argued President Nguyen Van Thieu of South Vietnam, would be to concede the point of the entire war. Saigon understood Hanoi's position even if Johnson continued to believe it was negotiable.

In late July and early August the administration took the position that the informal signals from the North were no longer adequate. There would have to be a formal statement or assurance of what the North Vietnamese would do in the way of a response if the United States stopped the bombing. In effect, the United States had not modified its original hard position. The United States would maintain its military presence and pressure, thereby protecting the Thieu regime, but the North would have to withdraw — then true negotiations could begin. From the perspective of the North this U.S. demand was tantamount to saying that the North must surrender what the United States had not been able to win on the battlefield, then negotiations could begin.[78] The North refused and promptly reescalated the violence in the South, with rocket attacks against major cities and the partial overrunning of Tay Ninh City in the northern part of South Vietnam. By early autumn 1968, American casualties rose dramatically after the marked decline during the lull of the preceding months.

By mid-October, with the election deadline closing fast but Hubert Humphrey lagging seriously, Johnson finally made a major concession which went to the heart of the 20-year war. In an effort to move the informal talks to the level of full negotiations, he offered to allow the National Liberation Front (the South Vietnamese communists) full representation at the conference, thereby extending tacit recognition of the communists. In return, the North Vietnamese would accept a representative of Saigon. Johnson got around the question of bombing by not requiring a formal concession from Hanoi. Johnson merely stated that he would halt the bombing and not resume it unless the demilitarized zone was violated or the communists attacked southern cities. The president announced the proposal publicly on October 31, 1968, less than a week before the elections, and the North Vietnamese and the NLF accepted immediately.[79]

Now, however, the South Vietnamese exercised what amounted to a veto. They simply refused to sit down with the United States, the North Vietnamese, and the NLF. For 2 months they argued over any arrangements that implied recognition of the NLF, with the shape of the conference table becoming the symbolic issue over which the procedural wrangling continued. In the meantime, a surge of Humphrey support in the wake of the announcement that formal negotiations might be getting under way petered out just before election day as the delays by the Saigon regime created confusion. Only after president-elect Richard Nixon urged the Saigon regime to begin negotiations did the South Vietnamese reluctantly go along. Formal negotiations began on January 24, 1969, 4 days after Nixon had become president.[80]

Conclusion

With the end of the Johnson administration, the second major phase of the Vietnam war also came to an end. Negotiations had begun. And the Nixon administration entered office intimating it had a secret plan to end the war. It would soon become apparent that the secret plan would consist of a largely secret effort in 1971 and 1972 to negotiate a cease fire, the return of American prisoners of war, and the conditions of postwar political processes in the South. In the meantime, however, the fighting would continue for 4 more years: there would be secret bombing[81] and subsequent invasions of Cambodia and Laos by American and South Vietnamese troops, massive bombing of Hanoi and the mining of Haiphong harbor, and the Nixon administration would initiate and carry out a program of Vietnamization in which American troops were withdrawn incrementally as the South Vietnamese army received the latest American equipment and training neglected for the most part during the American-ized portion of the war.

In conclusion, we should emphasize the persistence and, in at least one narrow respect, the success of the Johnson administration's policy of stalemate. The Johnson administration never formally recognized communist claims in South Vietnam, and the Viet Cong flag was not run up over Saigon during its years in office. With respect to the broader and more important aspects of that policy, however, the outcomes are more problematic. First, Johnson's pursuit of stalemate cost him his administration, not only with respect to his foreign policy but his domestic policy as well, in that the important programs of the Great Society had to be sacrificed to support the war effort. Second, it is not clear that Johnson succeeded ultimately in demonstrating for the future America's will to resist leftist revolution in the third world. This observation is based on the fact that the enormous American effort in Southeast Asia never touched the core of the revolution underway for 20 years in Vietnam. The entire effort employed modalities of conflict designed to stop international and conventionally militarized aggression. So while the Johnson administration succeeded in that mode of combat, it failed in countering and even exacerbated the social and economic revolution that was always the crux of the issue in Southeast Asia.

There is a paradox in this; for as we have seen, the Kennedy and Johnson administrations began with a prodigious intellectual effort to anticipate unconventional war. What was lacking, however, was the full acceptance of the implications of Bernard Fall's observations even as the Johnson administration was undertaking the conventional militarized Americanization of the war in 1965:

> The "kill" aspect, the military aspect, definitely always remain[s] the minor aspect. The political, administrative, ideological aspect is the primary aspect. . . . by its very nature, the insurgency problem is military only in a secondary sense, and political, ideological, and administrative in a primary sense. Once we understand this we will understand more of what is actually going on in Vietnam or in some other places affected by [revolutionary war].[82]

Kennedy may have approached an understanding of this point, but if Johnson did, he never acted on that realization. Indeed, no American president who believed in the necessity of containment and stalemating international communism's advance could act upon such a realization, for it would involve concessions to and acceptance of much of the revolutionary's position. That is to say, one would have to recognize the corruption and repression of a Diem, which was the source and sustenance of much non-Western revolutionary activity.

Failing such a realization or willingness to act upon it, the Johnson administration was committed to the course of escalation and frustration. The upshot was the maiming of Vietnam as well as the spirit of the American people. Insofar as America's conception of world order is maintained by the willingness of the United States, its people, and its leaders to commit its resources to a global effort, then the Vietnam War during the Kennedy and Johnson administrations undercut that willingness. Thus, by 1969, the implementation of stalemate in Vietnam had undermined the very will that the commitment was ostensibly to demonstrate.

SAVING THE STALEMATE MACHINE

The Nixon administration entered office with a dual problem. First, the Tet offensive had demonstrated to many, perhaps most, Americans the futility of incremental escalation of and continued American involvement in the war. The beginnings of talks with the North Vietnamese had raised expectations that meaningful negotiations might be possible which could bring to an end the years of frustrating carnage. Moreover, Nixon had during his campaign exploited the cumulating frustrations of the American people to help fashion his marginal victory over Hubert Humphrey. Thus Nixon was confronted with a nebulous, rather inarticulate desire, encouraged by him during the campaign, that the war be ended. If he did not do this or show considerable progress in this direction, his own reelection in 1972 might be endangered.

On the other hand, Nixon maintained the belief that the American right wing remained a potent force. If the ending of the war took on the appearance of what he termed a "bug out," the country and his administration might be ravished by that McCarthyite segment of public opinion which, of course, he, as much if not more than any American, had nourished and exploited throughout his public career. Therefore the domestic domino was no less important to the Nixon administration than to those of his predecessors. Indeed, Henry Kissinger saw the domestic danger as not unlike the unraveling of Weimar Germany he had experienced as a boy.[83]

The new president's problem in dealing with this fact of political life was complicated by the second dimension of the overall problem confronting his administration. For although Nixon had attacked Johnson's policies in Vietnam, he nevertheless accepted the broad premises upon which they rested. That is to say, he accepted the general notion that the United States must maintain its "special place in the world."[84] Or as Henry Kissinger would argue a decade later:

> As the leader of democratic alliances we had to remember that scores of countries and millions of people relied for their security on our willingness to stand by allies, indeed in our confidence in ourselves. No serious policy-maker could allow himself to succumb to the fashionable debunking of "prestige" or "honor" or "credibility." For a great power to abandon a small country to tyranny simply to obtain a respite from our own travail seemed to me — and still seems to me — profoundly immoral and destructive of our efforts to build a new and ultimately more peaceful pattern of international relations.[85]

On the other hand, Nixon and Kissinger were prepared to accept the proposition that "the postwar period in international relations has ended."[86] But the Nixon administration still felt that "there are those who would threaten our vital interests," and "American weakness could tempt would-be aggressors to make dangerous miscalculations."[87] He neverthe-less felt there were new opportunities for "negotiations" and the end of confrontation, especially with the Chinese and the Soviets who were no longer viewed as functionally monolithic. This new situation implied the possibility of reducing somewhat the American global presence. In sum, retrenchment was now a possibility, although retreat was out of the question.

Nixon sought therefore to maintain America's global role but to do it in such a manner that what appeared to be opportunities for a stable order could be maximized. At the same time this process of fashioning what he termed a "new strategy for peace" had to be done on the debris of the Vietnam-shattered domestic foreign policy consensus. This latter con-straint dictated the minimalist rhetoric of the Nixon Doctrine. But Nixon and Kissinger knew that rhetoric would not, in itself, save the essential domino — the Nixon presidency. The two dimensions of his foreign policy problem were, therefore, joined in Vietnam: Nixon's own perception of the risks and opportunities in the international system required that he pursue the old objectives of a salient, even dominant American world role, which seemed to imply in turn that Vietnam not appear to be "lost." Simultaneously, however, Americans had to be withdrawn from the swamp in such a manner that Nixon was not cut with either edge of domestic political opinion. The direction of the movement was to be different from that of the Kennedy and Johnson years, but the dangers were the same.[88]

Buying Time

The Nixon administration's effort involved a multitracked process of talking and fighting which the president characterized as the pursuit of "peace with honor." The fighting dominated most of the first 2½ years after Nixon's election. There was, however, an important difference from the 1960s. In early June of 1969 Nixon met with President Thieu on Midway Island and announced that the United States would begin withdrawing American troops from the South. The withdrawal would continue over the next 4 years in irregular increments. In the meantime, the scale of violence, especially in the air war, was increased in time as virtually all target restrictions were removed and reports of American air attacks on civilian targets proliferated. Moreover, a secret air war was opened against North Vietnamese supply areas in Cambodia, the reporting of which by the White House and Defense Department to the Congress and the American people was systematically distorted and covered up so as to hide its existence.

The land war was also expanded before American troop levels were reduced to levels that would be prohibitive of offensive ground action. Most spectacular was the invasion of Cambodia by American and South Vietnamese in the spring of 1970. This was followed by an invasion of southern Laos by South Vietnamese troops with American air support in February 1971. The Cambodian invasion could claim some tactical success in that significant North Vietnamese and Viet Cong supplies were captured. On the other hand, the much-heralded command headquarters for the communist military effort in the South was not found, and large concentrations of communist troops were not located and destroyed.

North Vietnamese and Viet Cong capacity for waging offensive war in the South appeared to have been weakened somewhat by the communists' Tet casualties and Nixon's actions, but their capacity to continue the war was by no means broken by these efforts. It appears that the communist reaction during this period of expanded American military activity was not unlike that which they had exercised in the past. When the military pressure increased, they would simply avoid contact as much as possible. Indeed, it was clear that it was only a matter of time before an active American ground effort would be precluded by reduced American troop levels. It was also apparent that the antiwar sentiment in the United States was undiminished. In fact, the antiwar movement was at its height during the first 2 years of the Nixon administration, with massive demonstrations in Washington and sometimes violent protest throughout the United States. These protests culminated in the tragic and cathartic events following the Cambodian invasion as 4 students were shot to death by the Ohio National Guard at Kent State University, followed by an assault on a dormitory at Jackson State University in Mississippi in which two students were killed. Following these events militant antiwar activity did drop off, although there was a notable increase in general antiwar sentiment nationwide. By early and mid-1971 sizeable portions of the American people — in excess of 60 percent — could be found consistently opposed to the war, now believing that it had been a mistake in the first place, and not believing that the Nixon administration was being truthful concerning plans for ending the fighting.[89] As Leslie Gelb noted in early 1972, "At bottom, President Nixon's credibility gap has the same sources as President Johnson's — promises of an end to a war that does not end."[90]

On the other hand, Nixon's expansion of the war did accomplish the end of neutralizing criticism of him from the right insofar as he had taken actions that they had advocated throughout the mid and late 1960s. Furthermore, Nixon allowed ongoing protective reaction air strikes against the North and approved the undertaking of a dramatic but fruitless raid on the Son Tay POW camp in North Vietnam. This kind of escapade had marginal impact on the military situation, but as the White House saw it, it was great "theater" and held a feared segment of public opinion at bay.[91]

By roughly the middle of his first term, therefore, Nixon seemed to be holding his own with public opinion. He had mollified the right with his willingness to employ and even escalate the level of violence in Vietnam. The costs were enormous as American battle deaths continued to rise, though at a slower rate, toward the the 50,000 mark. Vietnamese casualties and refugees increased by hundreds of thousands, and yet another Southeast Asian society and political system — Cambodia — disintegrated under the impact of an expanded war. By 1975 some 700,000 Cambodians had died and more than 250,000 tons of bombs had been dropped. From 1970 to 1975, nearly half the Cambodian population, some 3,389,000 people, had been made homeless by the war; which, to use Nixon's words of July 1, 1970, was waged in order to secure "Cambodia's chances of surviving as a neutral country."[92] Nixon was able, however, to defuse pressure from the left somewhat by changing and eventually ending the Selective Service System while initiating aggressive disruptive action against the antiwar left including surveillance, infiltration, and the use of the Justice Department under Attorney General John Mitchell to initiate numerous conspiracy cases against the leadership of the antiwar movement. None of these cases were ever won by the Justice Department. Nevertheless, as long as the antiwar left was tied up in litigation, it was not in the streets. Antiwar sentiment was rising in the Congress, but the slowness and incremental nature of congressional action directed against the war gave Nixon room and time for maneuver. Finally Nixon's "middle America" seemed numb and willing to wait. They would not wait forever, however, and 1972 was approaching.

"Peace with Honor"

By the end of 1970 it was not inconceivable that the fighting could remain indefinitely stalemated. American ground forces were approaching a level one-half of that of January 1969, or about 270,000 to 300,000 men. This reduction in American offensive military capability had been offset somewhat by increased air power; thus the South Vietnamese army and remaining but declining American land forces could probably hold their own indefinitely. However, Nixon had set in motion a process of withdrawal that would be virtually impossible to stop or reverse in terms of his domestic support. Moreover, continued escalation of American air power was not an indefinitely viable posture, for the North Vietnamese air defense system guaranteed that the number of American prisoners of war would increase.

But there was no certainty as to whether the South Vietnamese could stand without American support. Vietnamization was receiving optimistic evaluations, but vast uncertainty remained. The problem, then, was to extricate the remaining American forces yet to leave behind a politico-military framework that would allow the South Vietnamese an opportunity to survive. At a minimum, Nixon would need a "decent interval" between the time the United States withdrew and a communist takeover in the South occurred. That is to say, assuming the worst, the "loss" of the Saigon regime, it was essential that it not appear that the United States was responsible. If it could be argued that the good doctor had done all that he could and the patient died anyway, the expected international losses could be minimized. If the death could be delayed until after the 1972 elections, it would not matter domestically. If the patient lived, this would be a bonus from the standpoint of American policy, but it was not essential. All that was essential was that America's international interests and the Nixon administration live.

The obvious way to go about building a real or at least an apparent continuation of stalemate by proxy or at a minimum a decent interval was through the Paris negotiations. However, the talks had been deadlocked since 1969. The United States was calling for a cease fire in place, a timetable for withdrawal of all foreign forces from the South, and the release of American POWs. Hanoi, on the other hand, refused to acknowledge that it had forces in the South and demanded as a precondition the removal of the Thieu regime in Saigon.[93] In other words, little had changed since Nixon entered office.

In May 1971 Kissinger sought to initiate movement on the diplomatic track in elaborately arranged and protracted secret talks with the North Vietnamese. The new American position, in secret, was that the United States would agree to a deadline for U.S. withdrawal in exchange for the release of American POWs. In public Nixon was dramatically refusing to set any deadline until all POWs had been released. Moreover, the president was emphasizing "mutual withdrawals," but in private Kissinger was ambiguous on this issue. As Tad Szulc notes, "This may have been his free trial balloon — a hint of a fundamental concession if Hanoi were responsive in other ways — notably in dropping its insistence on the removal of the Thieu regime."[94] None of these maneuvers were reported to the South Vietnamese. The North Vietnamese did not reject the proposal out of hand and continued the secret contacts throughout the summer of 1971. In September, however, they rejected the proposal. The United States responded with further secret proposals, which included having Thieu step down just before new elections were held in the South. The elections were to be supervised by an independent body. Finally, the NLF would be represented in the oversight of the elections.

By this time, however, the North Vietnamese were far along in the planning for a new military offensive in the South in the spring of 1972. Consequently, the year ended without any agreement. Nixon was now entering the election year with American forces significantly reduced but no peace agreement. To counter anticipated pressure from the left concerning his lack of peace efforts, he made a dramatic television revelation in January 1972 of the secret talks and the American proposals. The Nixon speech opened a round of public and private invective between the United States and the North Vietnamese. Nevertheless, the secret contacts were reestablsihed even as the North launched their Easter offensive, which succeeded in capturing the northernmost province of South Vietnam and seriously threatening Hue. During the battles that broke all over South Vietnam, it became clear that the South Vietnamese army was not yet fully able to stand before the North Vietnamese without massive U.S. air support.

Nixon and Kissinger now turned to the use of other secret channels to the North, specifically the Russians. In a secret meeting with Brezhnev in April, Kissinger "produced what probably was the first major turning point in the history of Vietnam negotiations."[95] Kissinger informed Brezhnev that the United States was willing to allow the North Vietnamese to keep in South Vietnam those forces that were there prior to the Easter offensive. At the same time, however, Kissinger linked the offer to a North

Vietnamese agreement not to demand the removal of Thieu prior to any agreement. During these negotiations, Nixon's public stance on these questions remained ambiguous. Moreover, the United States was once again making major and explicit concessions without consulting the South Vietnamese.

In the meantime Nixon decided, despite the upcoming summit meeting with the Russians concerning strategic arms limitations, to punish the North Vietnamese for their spring offensive by resuming massive bombing of the North and, on May 8, 1972, mining Haiphong harbor. It was a serious gamble, for it was not inconceivable that the Russians would cancel the summit and the excruciating process of negotiating the SALT agreement would be lost. The decision split the White House, but the Russians did not break off their negotiations with the United States. It was clear that their own interests came before those of their socialist brothers in Hanoi, and in fact they might be willing to help their common capitalist adversary out of the Vietnam swamp if the United States could provide needed trade and technology.

During the summit of late May 1972, Kissinger made two more concessions to the North Vietnamese position: aggreement to the establishment of an electoral commission with Viet Cong representation and the suggestion that the air action over North Vietnam could be called off before all American POWs were returned. The United States was simultaneously pounding the North Vietnamese with the stick of American air power and offering them concessions that very nearly brought the American position in line with that of the North Vietnamese. Only the problem of the survival of the Thieu regime remained, and Kissinger took this up with Chou En-Lai during his secret visit to Beijing in mid-June. Chou was reluctant to press Hanoi, but according to one report, there were indications that the Chinese passed the word to the North Vietnamese that they should not be so adamant about the removal of Thieu prior to an agreement.[96]

Kissinger was now confronted with the problem of informing Thieu that he had been bargaining over his destiny for the preceding year without consulting him. The meeting was held in mid-August. Kissinger insists that he provided Thieu with a full disclosure of the negotiations rather than the vague description of the talks with the North Vietnamese that critics of the Nixon administration suggest were given to Thieu. Kissinger notes that he "played with the idea" of a diversionary invasion of the North, but asserts that both he and Thieu recognized that this was "a gimmick, not a strategy."[97] Other analysts claim that these talks were a throwback to the end of the Korean War 20 years earlier with Kissinger making extravagant but gossamer promises to Thieu to the effect that after

Richard Nixon had been reelected it would be a different story. Any concessions that the United States might be making were, he implied, necessary because of the domestic political situation. The United States, he said, "would not hesitate to apply all its power to bring North Vietnam down to its knees,"[98] including the suggestion that Thieu begin preparations for an invasion of the North.

Perhaps Thieu was not "nonplussed" and baffled[99] by all this as some have reported. But even Kissinger concedes that very little was clarified by the negotiations. Confusion, he insists, was the result of diametrically different domestic positions now occupied by Thieu and Nixon: the former needing a continued and open-ended American presence; the latter committed to ending such a commitment. Moreover, Kissinger now feels that there were unbridgeable cultural gaps between the allies. In any event, he stated

> [Thieu] and I had engaged in a minuet, stately in its careful avoidance of the real issues, courtly in its pretense of continued partnership, inherently inconclusive in confining itself to traditional, now irrelevant, patterns. Thieu certainly complicated matters by never making his objections explicit. Instead . . . he fought with characteristic Vietnamese opaqueness and with a cultural arrogance compounded by a French Cartesianism that defined any deviation from abstract, unilaterally proclaimed principles as irreconcilable error.
>
> I left Saigon with a false sense of having reached a meeting of the minds.[100]

Kissinger, for his part, probably did intend leaving Thieu in as strong a position militarily as possible, but he was prepared to go forward with negotiations with Hanoi whether Thieu agreed or not. On the return flight to Washington Kissinger reportedly remarked to his staff: "One thing is for sure: we cannot stand another four years of this. . . . So let's finish it brutally once and for all."[101]

Negotiations proceeded secretly with the North Vietnamese, and it was clear that agreement was within reach as Hanoi accepted the ideas advanced by Kissinger and Nixon secretly through Moscow and Peking. The bad news now had to be broken to Saigon, and General Alexander Haig was dispatched to tell Thieu about the electoral commission. Thieu adamantly opposed any such arrangement, fearing that it could become a coalition government that would undermine his position. Kissinger, desiring to maintain momentum, decided to press on without Thieu's concurrence, and in October achieved a breakthrough with the North Vietnamese, who nevertheless insisted that the agreements be initialed before the American election. The North Vietnamese, undoubtedly remembering the events of 1954 and 1955, sought to ensure the American commitment, fearing that after the election the Americans might renege. Kissinger agreed, but insisted that he would have to get Saigon's approval first.

Kissinger now flew to Saigon and met with Thieu between October 19 and 23. Thieu's fury was upon occasion unrestrained, and he refused to agree to the arrangements worked out by Kissinger. Kissinger was compelled, therefore, to cancel his planned trip to Hanoi for the signing of the agreement and returned to the United States. However, presidential politics remained paramount. Therefore Kissinger announced on October 26 that "peace is at hand," although he and Nixon knew full well that this was simply not the case. If anything, it seemed farther away than ever. In the meantime Hanoi, fearing that it was being used by the Nixon administration for domestic political purposes, announced publicly the terms of the agreement.

Pressure was applied to Thieu again on November 9, with no effect. Kissinger then returned to Paris with a list of South Vietnamese objections, which he read into the record. Kissinger insists that this was done primarily for appearance's sake, but he probably underestimated the North Vietnamese sensitivity to the delay even as he had underestimated Thieu's recalcitrance. By December 1972, the North Vietnamese began to display reluctance to proceed. They suggested changes in the agreement in mid-December, and Kissinger publicly denounced their action as "perfidy." Two days later Nixon ordered "Operation Linebacker II," which included massive bombing of Hanoi and the rest of North Vietnam. The bombing continued throughout Christmas and New Year's, turning large areas of Hanoi into a wasteland.

> Flying in groups of three, the B-52 dropped their bombs . . . with the payload falling in a rectangular pattern . . . a mile long and a half mile wide. Each plane could carry about two dozen five hundred pound bombs and more than forty-seven hundred and fifty pound bombs. About one hundred of the big strategic bombers and five hundred . . . fighter bombers flew round the clock raids. . . .[102]

William Saxbe, Republican Senator from Ohio and soon to become Nixon's fourth attorney general, guessed, along with many others, that Nixon had "lost his senses."[103] Reports of civilian casualties occupied the front pages of the world's newspapers,[104] but the attacks continued. The Kalbs report one of their sources who reviewed the situation later as saying:

Look, we were in an embarrassing situation. Could we suddenly say we'll sign in January what we wouldn't in October? We had to do something. So the bombing began . . . [it] creat[ed] the image of a defeated enemy crawling back to the peace table to accept terms demanded by the U.S. Maybe the bombing had some effect . . . but the B-52's weren't critical.[105]

And on January 13, 1973, the North Vietnamese agreed to sign the agreements reached in principle months earlier. Thieu, now satisfied that the North had been seriously weakened and mollified by the American show of force, finally went along, and the negotiations were concluded on January 27, 1973.

Concluding Observations on Leaving Swamps

In reviewing this final phase and termination of direct American combat involvement in Vietnam, one is taken back to 1953 when the United States sought to extricate itself from another Asian war fought to preserve the concept of containment largely at the expense of the specific country being defended. In both instances, the final agreement confirmed an existing stalemate. In both instances the final agreement was delayed and very nearly precluded because of the actions of America's client. And in both instances American firepower brutally savaged the negotiating adversary partner during the denouement of the bargaining process. In the Vietnamese case this fact is especially tragic, for the Christmas 1972 bombings of Hanoi resulted only in part from anything the North Vietnamese had done. In no small measure, Hanoi was attacked because Henry Kissinger misjudged Thieu's willingness to accept cavalier treatment at the hands of the United States. It is hard to escape Tad Szulc's judgment:

> One is left with the impression that Nixon and Kissinger took advange of Hanoi's political hesitations in December 1972 to inflict the greatest possible damage on North Vietnam so that Thieu would be able to accept the agreement.
>
> The Christmas bombings, therefore, were designed to induce Thieu to sign the Paris Agreement, the price being the "brutalizing" of the North. But, at the same time, this was the price that had to be paid for Kissinger's miscalculation of Thieu's responses . . . the proposals on which he was never adequately, if at all, consulted.[106]

The question of whether the 1972 Christmas bombings could have been avoided raised the question of whether, for that matter, the violence of the preceding 4 years could have been avoided. In effect, could the agreement of 1973 have been reached in 1968 or 1969? It must have been known, for example, that the North Vietnamese would never leave the South. Why should they surrender in negotiations that which they had not been forced to surrender on the battlefield? The negotiation of peace treaties and postwar settlements seldom do more than ratify what has been wrought by the course of battle. If this is the case, then it would follow that Nixon continued fighting for many of the reasons the United States entered the conflict in the first place.

That is to say, the Nixon administration knew that North Vietnam and the NLF could not be defeated, that they could only be stalemated. But Nixon and Kissinger also believed that if an approximation of the Paris Agreements of 1973 had been signed in 1969, the Saigon regime would have fallen quickly, thereby threatening the Nixon administration, the security of which we have since learned (if we had not known before) was an ultimately all-consuming obsession. The Nixon administration felt it could no more afford to "lose" Vietnam than its predecessors. The survival of the Nixon administration is properly emphasized, we think, because, by their own perception and prescription concerning the international system, many if not most of the conditions of international politics that required a display of will and commitment in 1961 through 1965–1966 were no longer relevant in 1969. The Nixon administration heralded the advent of a new era of negotiations in 1969; why, then, not negotiate in 1969? The answer would seem to lie in Nixon's fear of the domestic consequences of the Viet Cong flag going up over Saigon while he was running for reelection in 1972. For this reason, then, the land and people of Vietnam were pulverized for 4 more years.

The style of the diplomacy leading to the Paris Agreement is revealing and supportive of this general conclusion. Throughout the process Nixon maintained a public position that was at best ambiguous and at worst contrary to the position adopted in private by Kissinger. To have revealed the positions being set forth by Kissinger would not only have enraged Saigon, which like the American people was kept in the dark, it would also have enraged those McCarthyites whom Nixon was so responsible for and yet so afraid of. Nixon was after all bargaining away many of the points over which the war had been stalemated for years. In the end, Thieu was enraged anyway, but his anger could be assuaged with the Christmas bombing of the North and the promise of increased military and economic assistance. The remnants of the McCarthyite segment of American public opinion could not, it was thought, be so easily bought off.

In fairness to the Nixon administration, it should be emphasized that they may also have feared that the appearance of a "loss" in Vietnam could severely limit their freedom of action in pursuing the other dimensions of the Nixon Doctrine. The opening of relations with China and the negotiation of significant arms control agreements with the Soviets was undoubtedly seen as requiring a good deal of support from the American people. If the potential for a right-wing backlash was as great as the Nixon administration seemed to fear, then a bitter national debate over who "lost" Vietnam had to be avoided if the other pressing business of building Nixon's vision of world order was to go forward. Thus the larger vision of world order could be used to justify the further destruction of Vietnam, and gave the insurance, if brutally purchased, that Nixon thought he needed.

There may be one additional tragic irony in all of this. In view of the large body of opinion against the war by the middle of the Nixon administration, one wonders whether the potential for the backlash was real, or if real, as substantial as Nixon seemed to imagine. If, as Gelb suggests, domestic opinion had turned decisively against the war, then the much-feared backlash was a figment of the imagination of an administration which, as the Watergate affair demonstrates, was almost paranoid about its public image. To the extent that the 4 years of war under Richard Nixon were conceived and prosecuted to anticipate a public opinion threat that existed primarily in the mind of Richard Nixon, these were the cruelest years of the war.

Thus, as it began, the direct involvement of the United States in Vietnam ended with Vietnam and the Vietnamese people being used as pawns in a much larger game. There was a new international system to be ordered and maintained. The dynamics of strategic weapons development set in motion by the Cuban missile crisis were culminating in 1969 through 1972 in a relationship of rough strategic parity between the United States and the Soviet Union. The SALT talks were by and large an effort to institutionalize this parity and set predictable limits on the future growth of the duopolists' strategic arms stockpiles. The Sino-Soviet split seemed irremediable, and opened up possibilities for a new kind of balance of power diplomacy. Finally, the emergence of new and barely understood transnational economic forces could not be ignored. Tad Szulc reports that at that time during the negotiations of the Paris Agreements when the Vietnamese problem came into conflict with Nixon's dual negotiations with Moscow and China in the spring of 1972, "a senior White House official remarked . . . (that) Vietnam was a 'cruel side show' in the Administration's new world wide policies."[107] It was nevertheless part of the main show in the administration's domestic priorities.

For a short while the war in Southeast Asia receded from the American consciousness, replaced by the drama of Nixon trying desperately to save his presidency from the spreading stain of Watergate. (Many of the Watergate horrors, ironically, came about as a result of Nixon's efforts to protect his policy in Southeast Asia from domestic dissent.) The military situation remained stalemated throughout 1974. By early 1975, however, the new Ford administration was calling for emergency assistance from Congress as signs of increasing North Vietnamese pressure began to appear. In mid-March, the South Vietnamese undertook a poorly planned and poorly executed withdrawal from the strategic central highlands and thereby initiated massive panic and refugee flights into the Saigon area and the loss of hundreds of millions of dollars worth of equipment. In the meantime in Cambodia, Communist-led Khmer Rouge forces completely surrounded and cut off the Cambodian capital of Phnom Penh, and on April 17, 1975, the American-backed government surrendered. Four days later President Thieu resigned in Saigon and angrily denounced the United States for reneging on secret promises made by the Nixon administration at the time of the Paris agreements. Thieu (with a sizeable sum of American dollars reportedly on deposit) went into exile in Taiwan.

A week later Vietnam's agony ended as the surrender of Saigon was negotiated between South Vietnamese officials and the communists. For the United States, however, the last week of the American presence was marked by the tense withdrawal, often under North Vietnamese fire, of thousands of Americans from Tan Son Nhut Air Base, as South Vietnamese who had associated themselves with and/or profited from the American war effort desperately sought a way out of the country. By April 29, 1975, the air base had been closed, and 1000 remaining Americans and 5500 South Vietnamese whose lives were assumed to be in danger because of their cooperation and association with the Americans, had to be evacuated by helicopter from the grounds of the U.S. embassy to aircraft carriers in the South China Sea. In the process yet another four American marines lost their lives, the body of one being left behind in the frantic last moments of the evacuation.

Ironically, at home, the long-feared wave of recrimination did not occur. The American people met the final unravelling of South Vietnam with an almost fatalistic detachment and some skepticism concerning the arrival of thousands of South Vietnamese refugees in the United States. Indeed, if there were signs of recrimination they came from the Ford administration, as it tried to shift responsibility for the final collapse of Vietnam to Congress.[108] But even though one additional Southeast Asian domino — Laos — fell and Thailand and the Philippines seemed to wobble noticeably as they announced a reassessment of their relationship with the Asian communist powers in mid-1975, there was no hysteria or, for that matter, outward concern on the part of the American people. After all, the Nixon Doctrine itself was based on a similar reassessment and, even more important, as public opinion analyses during the early 1970s revealed, the American citizenry was not the fickle, belligerent, and vengeful monster prophesied in the conventional wisdom of the foreign policy elite that had managed the cold war. Rather, the American people were in many ways more open to change than the foreign policy community.[109]

NOTES

1. We are indebted for this metaphor to Carl Oglesby, "The Vietnamese Crucible," in Carl Oglesby and Richard Schaull, *Containment and Change* (New York: Macmillan Company, 1967), p. 3.
2. From John Galloway (ed.), *The Kennedys and Vietnam* (New York: Facts on File, 1971), citing speech of June 1, 1956, p. 13. Reprinted by permission.
3. Ibid., pp. 14–15.
4. William Henderson, "South Vietnam Finds Itself," *Foreign Affairs*, Vol. 35 (January 1957), p. 285.
5. George McT. Kahin and John W. Lewis, *The United States in Vietnam*, rev. ed. (New York: Delta Books, 1969), pp. 100–102.
6. "Resolution of the Third National Congress of the Vietnam Workers' Party on the Tasks and Line of the Party in the New Stage," quoted in ibid., p. 115.
7. Ibid., p. 119.
8. "Report by Vice President Johnson on His Visit to Asian Countries," in *The Pentagon Papers* (New York: Bantam Books for The New York Times, 1971), p. 129, Hereafter cited as *Pentagon Papers.*
9. "Conclusions of McNamara on Report by General Taylor," *Pentagon Papers*, p. 148.
10. "1961 Rusk-McNamara Report to Kennedy on South Vietnam," *Pentagon Papers*, p. 150.
11. Ibid.
12. Ibid.
13. Leslie H. Gelb, "The Essential Domino: American Politics and Vietnam," *Foreign Affairs*, Vol. 50 (April 1972), pp. 459–475.
14. Arthur Schlesinger, Jr., *A Thousand Days* (Boston: Houghton Mifflin Company, 1965), p. 549.
15. Cited in Walter LaFeber, *America, Russia, and the Cold War, 1945–1971*, 2nd ed. (New York: John Wiley & Sons, 1972), p. 244.
16. See Kahin and Lewis, op. cit., pp. 143–146 and *The Pentagon Papers*, pp. 158–233.
17. CBS Interview of September 2, 1963, *Department of State Bulletin*, Vol. XLIX, No. 1266 (September 30, 1963), pp. 498–499.
18. Ibid., p. 499.
19. Quoted by Kenneth O'Donnell in "LBJ and the Kennedys," *Life*, Vol. 69, No. 6 (August 7, 1970), p. 51.
20. Ibid. (emphasis in the original), pp. 51–52.
21. "McNamara Report to Johnson on the Situation in Saigon in '63," *Pentagon Papers*, pp. 271, 272, 274.
22. Neil Sheehan, "The Covert War and Tonkin Gulf: February–August, 1964," quoting the authors of the *Pentagon Papers*, p. 240.
23. " '64 Memo by Joint Chiefs of Staff Discussing Widening of the War," in *Pentagon Papers*, pp. 274–277, esp. p. 277.

24. "Draft Resolution for Congress on Actions in Southeast Asia," in *Pentagon Papers*, pp. 286–288, esp. p. 287.
25. Neil Sheehan, citing authors of the *Pentagon Papers*, p. 240.
26. Anthony Austin, *The President's War* (Philadelphia: J. B. Lippincott Co., 1971), pp. 182–183. See U.S. Congress, Senate Committee on Foreign Relations, *Hearings: The Gulf of Tonkin, the 1964 Incidents*, 90th Congress, 2nd Session, 1968.
27. Austin, op. cit., pp. 182–183.
28. Ibid., pp. 205, 292–293.
29. Tom Wicker, *J. F. K. and L. B. J.: The Influence of Personality upon Politics* (Baltimore: Penguin Books, 1972), pp. 224–225.
30. David Halberstam, *The Best and the Brightest* (New York: Random House, 1972), p. 414.
31. Tad Szulc, "Behind the Vietnam Cease-Fire Agreement," *Foreign Policy*, No. 15, (Summer 1974), p. 42.
32. Halberstam, op. cit., pp. 533–534.
33. Neil Sheehan, "The Launching of the Ground War: March–July 1965," quoting *Pentagon Papers*, p. 383.
34. "National Security Action Memorandum 328, April 6, 1965," in *Pentagon Papers*, pp. 442–443.
35. Ibid., p. 443.
36. *The New York Times*, August 27, 1966, p. 10.
37. Lyndon B. Johnson, "Pattern for Peace in Southeast Asia," *Department of State Bulletin*, Vol. 41, No. 1348 (April 26, 1965), p. 607.
38. Ibid., pp. 606–607.
39. Ibid., p. 607.
40. Ibid., p. 608.
41. "McCone Memo to Top Officials on Effectiveness of the Air War," in *Pentagon Papers*, p. 441.
42. Press Conference of July 28, 1965, in *Public Papers of the Presidents, Lyndon B. Johnson, 1965*, Vol. II (Washington, D.C.: U.S. Government Printing Office, 1966), pp. 796 and 797.
43. Ibid., p. 801.
44. Sheehan, "Launching of the Ground War," quoting the *Pentagon Papers*, pp. 416–417.
45. McNaughton Memo to Goodpaster on "Forces Required to Win," in *Pentagon Papers*, pp. 455–456.
46. See Fox Butterfield, "The Buildup: July 1965–September 1966," in *Pentagon Papers*, pp. 459–485.
47. "The Effects of U.S. Bombing on North Vietnam's Ability to Support Military Operations in South Vietnam: Retrospect and Prospect," August 29, 1966, quoted in *Pentagon Papers*, pp. 502–504.
48. Ibid., pp. 506–507.
49. Hedrick Smith, "Secretary McNamara's Disenchantment: October 1966–May 1967," in *Pentagon Papers*, pp. 510–541.
50. Ibid., pp. 524–535.
51. U.S. Congress, Senate Committee on the Judiciary, Hearings Before the Subcommittee to Investigate Problems Connected with Refugees and Escapees, *War-Related Problems in Indochina, Part 1, Vietnam*, 92nd Congress, 1st Session, 1971, pp. 1–3.
52. *The New York Times*, February 22, 1974.
53. Arthur Westin and E. W. Pfeiffer, "The Cratering of Indochina," in Herbert F. York,

Arms Control: Readings from Scientific American (New York: W. H. Freeman and Co., 1973), p. 329.

54. Ibid., p. 338.
55. Halberstam, op. cit., p. 633.
56. Ibid., pp. 632–634.
57. E. W. Kenworthy, "The Tet Offensive and the Turnaround," in *Pentagon Papers*, pp. 589–612.
58. Henry Kissinger, "The Vietnam Negotiations," in *American Foreign Policy: Three Essays* (New York: W. W. Norton & Company, 1969), p. 107.
59. The list of wise men comprised a "Who's Who" of U.S. foreign policy. They included General Omar Bradley, McGeorge Bundy, Arthur Dean (Eisenhower's negotiator in Korea), Douglas Dillon, Associate Justice Abe Fortas, former Justice Arthur Goldberg, Henry Cabot Lodge, John J. McCloy, former diplomat Robert Murphy, General Matthew Ridgeway, Maxwell Taylor, former Deputy Defense Secretary Cyrus Vance, and George Ball. The best accounts of the Great Reversal are in *The New York Times*, March 6, 1969, and March 7, 1969 in stories filed by Hedrick Smith and William Beecher.
60. Johnson, op. cit. p. 609.
61. See Arthur Schlesinger, Jr., *The Bitter Heritage: Vietnam and American Democracy, 1941–1966* (Boston: Houghton Mifflin Company, 1968).
62. Daniel Ellsberg, *Papers on the War* (New York: Simon & Schuster, 1972), pp. 42–135; and Leslie Gelb, "Vietnam: The System Worked," *Foreign Policy*, No. 3 (Summer 1971), pp. 140–167. Gelb's analysis of the war has been expanded in his 1979 book written with the assistance of Richard K. Betts, *The Irony of Vietnam: The System Worked* (Washington, D.C.: Brookings Institution, 1979).
63. Gelb, "The System Worked," p. 140.
64. Johnson, op. cit., p. 607.
65. Quoted in *Pentagon Papers*, p. 255.
66. Ibid.
67. Kissinger, op. cit., p. 112.
68. LaFeber, op. cit., p. 255.
69. Ibid., pp. 254–255.
70. Arthur Schlesinger, Jr., "The Quagmire Papers (Continued)," *New York Review of Books*, December 16, 1971, p. 41, also cited by Ellsberg, op. cit., p. 124.
71. Lyndon B. Johnson, *Vantage Point* (New York: Holt, Rinehart and Winston, 1971), pp. 151–152.
72. Ibid.
73. Ellsberg, op. cit., pp. 100–127.
74. See Gelb's discussion of this point in "The Essential Domino," pp. 463–466.
75. Ibid., pp. 459–460.
76. Ellsberg, op. cit., p. 124.
77. *Pentagon Papers* (original), Vol. IV, pp. 615–616, quoted by Ellsberg, op. cit., p. 124.
78. See the editorial in *The New York Times*, May 15, 1968, and Kahin and Lewis, op. cit., pp. 379–390.
79. Kahin and Lewis, op. cit., pp. 386–388.
80. After the election there were reports that Nixon had communicated through Mrs. Anna Chenault to the South Vietnamese that they should delay their participation until after the election. This could achieve what in fact happened during the last week of the campaign, confusion in the minds of those undecided voters who might have

been moving toward Humphrey because of apparent movement toward peace. Presumably the *quid pro quo* from Nixon would have been a promise from Nixon to Saigon that they would get a better "deal" from his administration than from Humphrey's. Theodore H. White, *The Making of the President, 1968* (New York: Atheneum Publishers, 1969), pp. 380–381, p. 383. Much of this speculation was subsequently confirmed by Mrs. Chenault in her memoirs, *The Education of Anna* (New York: Times Books, 1980). See also the review by Robert Shaplan, "A Somewhat Naive Dragon Lady," *The New York Times Book Review*, February 3, 1980, p. 12.

81. A bitterly critical account and analysis of this bombing and all of American policy towards Cambodia is William Shawcross, *Sideshow: Kissinger, Nixon and the Destruction of Cambodia* (New York: Pocket Books, 1979). Kissinger defends himself in *White House Years* (Boston: Little, Brown, Co., 1979), chapters 7 and 12. An account of the extent to which Kissinger wrote portions of his memoirs in response to Shawcross's attack can be found in Wolfgang Saxon, "Kissinger Revised His Book More Than He Reported," *New York Times*, October 31, 1979.

82. Bernard Fall, "The Theory and Practice of Insurgency and Counterinsurgency," *Naval War College Review*, April 1965, Reprinted in Mark E. Smith, III, and Claude J. Johns, Jr. (eds.), *American Defense Policy*, 2nd ed. (Baltimore: Johns Hopkins University Press, 1968), p. 272.

83. Kissinger, *White House Years*, pp. 229–230. For other indications of the administration's concern about domestic opinion as well as the constraints imposed by the bureaucracy, see pp. 260–261 and 282.

84. Richard Nixon, *U.S. Foreign Policy for the 1970's: A New Strategy for Peace* (Washington, D.C.: U.S. Government Printing Office, 1970), p. 2.

85. Kissinger, *White House Years*, p. 228 and pp. 226–235, for Kissinger's initial appraisal of the problem before the Nixon Administration as it entered office.

86. Nixon, *U.S. Foreign Policy for the 1970's: A New Strategy for Peace*, p. 4.

87. Ibid., p. 4.

88. Gelb, "The Essential Domino," pp. 471–472.

89. See Gallup Polls for February through August of 1971.

90. Gelb, "The Essential Domino," p. 473.

91. Tad Szulc, op. cit., p. 33. Szulc uses this term with respect to the peace talks during 1971 and 1972, but the concept clearly applies here as well.

92. Statistics and Nixon quote cited by Anthony Lewis, "A Successful Operation," *The New York Times*, February 6, 1975. See also Shawcross, *passim*.

93. Szulc, op. cit., p. 25, and Kahin and Lewis, op. cit., pp. 392–405. The following analysis is based primarily on Szulc's essential analysis of the development of the 1973 Vietnam peace agreement and Kissinger's *White House Years*.

94. Szulc, op. cit., p. 27.

95. Ibid., p. 36.

96. Ibid., p. 45.

97. Kissinger, pp. 1321–1324, esp. 1324.

98. Szulc, p. 46.

99. Ibid.

100. Kissinger, pp. 1325–1326.

101. Szulc, p. 47. Kissinger's memoirs are silent on this point.

102. Marvin Kalb and Bernald Kalb, *Kissinger* (Boston: Little, Brown and Company, 1974), pp. 415–416.

103. For a summary of some domestic and foreign press comment see ibid., pp. 416–417. But it is important to note that the bombing policy was Kissinger's as much as Nixon's. It was a version of the good cop–bad cop routine, wherein a criminal gets brutally harassed by one man and then his partner comes into the interrogation room and offers the dazed man a cigarette and says, "If you cooperate I'll see to it that the despicable first interrogator doesn't return."

104. A less damning account of the bombing — and one favorably cited by Kissinger — is Guenter Lewy, *America in Vietnam* (New York: Oxford University Press, 1978), pp. 413–414.

105. Kalb & Kalb, p. 422.

106. Szulc, op. cit., p. 67.

107. Ibid., p. 35.

108. See, for example, "CBS News Excerpts," in *Congressional Quarterly Weekly Report*, Vol. 33, No. 17 (April 26, 1975), esp. pp. 853–854.

109. See Murrey Marder, "Public Called Wary on Foreign Policy," *Washington Post*, September 11, 1975, p. A 2; Leslie H. Gelb "Poll-Takers Say Most Americans Oppose Isolationism," *The New York Times*, September 11, 1975, p. 18.

Chapter 10
The Nixon Doctrine and Beyond

The Nixon-Kissinger stewardship of foreign policy represents something of a paradox. On the one hand, Nixon liquidated the major source of domestic criticism for American foreign policy — Vietnam; but he did not relinquish American global commitments, and Vietnam was the logical result of extended commitments. The Nixon Doctrine did not repudiate the premise of American policy since World War II but rather sought not to get caught with the results of the logic of those premises — intervention on a grand scale. Maintaining the means and rebuilding the will to uphold commitments and sustain order while not succumbing to sustained conventional combat intervention was the preoccupation of the Nixon administration. In short, the Nixon Doctrine is not unlike the new look which sought to conserve containment but at a lower cost.

THE NIXON-KISSINGER DOCTRINE: CONTAINMENT AND MANAGEMENT

The paradoxical nature of the Nixon Doctrine is heightened by the fact that Nixon heralded its promulgation with the assertion that the "postwar period in international relations had ended."[1] Purportedly there were new opportunities for negotiation and the movement of Soviet-American relations to a basis other than the bitter and frequently awesome confrontations that marked the cold war. Yet the president insisted that the United States would not abandon its commitments — commitments incurred during the period of confrontation. There was a new era of international politics, but threats to American interests persisted although the nature of these threats was never clearly delineated.

Moreover, Nixon saw the continued need for the "defense and development of allies and friends."[2] Now, however, the effort would be part of a system of shared responsibilities:

> The United States will participate in the defense and development of allies and friends, but . . . America cannot — and will not — conceive *all* the plans,

design *all* the programs, execute *all* the decisions and undertake *all* the defense of the free nations of the world. We will help where it makes a real difference and is considered in our interest.[3]

Indeed, the concept of "interests" moved to the center of American policy during the Nixon years: "We are not involved in the world because we have commitments; we have commitments because we are involved. Our interests must shape our commitments, rather than the other way around."[4]

But what were American interests? None of Nixon's four major statements on U.S. foreign policy defined these in terms other than in Wilsonian rhetoric concerning a "generation of peace." There was reference to the "creative possibilities of a pluralistic world," but are we to assume that this meant the free play of American and communist ideology with their fundamentally antithetical views of the human condition and potentiality?[5] "We seek a new and stable framework of international relationships," Nixon said; a framework

which reflects the contributions and reconciles the aspirations of nations.
which is cemented by the shared goal of coexistence and the shared practice of accommodation.
which liberates countries and continents to realize their destinies free from the threat of war.
which promotes social justice and human dignity.[6]

The framework of international relationships that emerged was far more traditional than this Wilsonian rhetoric implied. Nixon forswore mere balance of power politics as the ultimate form and substance of U.S. foreign policy.[7] But in the absence of the more stable order that his rhetoric referred to and the persistence of perceived threats to American interests, it remained the only prudent course, in his view. The policy framework that emerged in the time before the collapse of the Nixon administration into the Watergate crisis and the onset of the Ford interregnum consisted of several elements. They were designed to both balance and constrain Soviet strategic power but also to pull the Soviets into a detente or easing of tensions within which the Soviets might be schooled in the behavior, expectations, and obligations of great powers.

At least three major elements of the policy framework developed by Nixon and his special assistant for national security affairs and later secretary of state, Henry Kissinger, require close analysis. First, there were direct negotiations with the Soviets to salvage and institutionalize the

THE NIXON-KISSINGER DOCTRINE 369

balance of strategic power between the United States and the Soviet Union that they found when they entered office. Second, there was an historic opening of relations with the People's Republic of China which, when combined with the extraction of the United States from Vietnam, eased the military demands on the U.S. in Asia. More important, however, Sino-Soviet animosities could be used by the United States to apply diplomatic pressure on the Soviets. Finally, there was to be the notion of detente itself. The Soviets were to be offered recognition of their status as a great power as well as access to American capital, technology, and agricultural assistance if they would in turn relax their revolutionary impulses and support for those in the third world who pursued revolutionary change. At a minimum it was hoped that a relaxation of tensions would allow for minimal strategic arms control.

Strategic Arms Control

The Nixon administration's approach to strategic arms control negotiations with the Soviets was conditioned by two concerns: (1) a perceived deteriorioation in the strategic balance and (2) the relationship between that balance and what was feared to be declining American political capability. There was concern for stabilizing the arms race and perhaps ultimately even reducing the high levels of strategic arms possessed by the United States and the Soviet Union. The overriding concern of the Nixon administration, however, was that any arms control negotiations and agreements with the Soviets be consistent with and serve the broader strategic concept defined by Henry Kissinger:

> Throughout history the political influence of nations has been roughly correlative to their military power. While states might differ in the moral worth and prestige of their institutions, diplomatic skill could augment but never substitute for military strength. In the final reckoning weakness has invariably tempted aggression and impotence brings abdication of policy in its train. ... The balance of power, a concept much maligned in American political writing — and rarely used without being preceded by the perjorative "outdated" — has in fact been the precondition of peace. A calculus of power, of course, is only the beginning of policy; it cannot be its sole purpose. The fact remains that without strength even the most elevated purpose risks becoming overwhelmed by the dictates of others.[8]

Thus Kissinger's conception of the relationship between military power and diplomacy remained consistent with what he had set forth during the debate over Eisenhower's new look more than a decade earlier. Furthermore, as in the late 1950s, Kissinger was troubled by the seeming disjunction of military power and political influence in a nuclear age. Finally, the dilemma was seen as being made more complex because its resolution would have to be undertaken by the Nixon administration in a domestic context of intense upheaval and "... at a moment when technology, combined with earlier deliberate decisions, was altering the nature of the strategic balance."[9]

The earlier decisions alluded to by Kissinger had been made during the Johnson administration in the mid-1960s. Specifically, then Secretary of Defense Robert McNamara had concluded that the buildup in strategic forces initiated by the Soviet Union in the wake of the Cuban missile crisis made it inevitable that they would achieve a degree of strategic parity with the United States. That is, no matter what the United States did, the Soviet Union, once it had begun to increase its numbers of land-based intercontinental ballistic missiles (ICBMs) and expand its fleet of submarine launched ballistic missile (SLBM) carrying submarines, would achieve, perhaps within a decade, the capacity to devastate the United States in a nuclear war even if the United States struck the Soviet Union first. Similarly, if the Soviet Union attacked the United States first, the United States would be able to retaliate with devastating effects on Soviet society destroying perhaps one-fourth to one-third of the Soviet population and two-thirds of Soviet industry.

McNamara decided that in the face of this inevitable parity it made little sense to keep expanding the number of ICBMs and SLBMs in the American force structure. McNamara reasoned[10] that once the United States and the Soviet Union had achieved "mutual assured destruction" (MAD) capability, it was wasteful to continue expanding their respective strategic force structures. Accordingly, the United States unilaterally stopped deploying ICBMs and SLBMs after 1967, thereby sustaining a strategic force structure of 1054 ICBMs and 656 SLBMs as well as several hundred B-52 bombers. Presumably such a step by the United States would offer the Soviets an incentive to halt their force structure expansion and provide a basis for a more stable strategic relationship.

At the same time, however, the Johnson administration, in response to bureaucratic pressures[11] within the defense establishment and political pressures from Congress, went forward with research, development and testing of two new weapons technologies that could serve as hedges against an uncertain future. The first technology was an antiballistic missile defense system (ABM) designed to disable nuclear warheads launched against the United States. The Soviet Union had begun to deploy a limited and, according to American analysis, easily penetrated ABM system around Moscow in the mid-1960s. The pressure to emulate the Soviets

grew into what one observer has described as "a wave of ABM hysteria."[12]
The Johnson administration responded with a decision to deploy a limited
system, although McNamara justified deployment primarily in terms of a
defense against what was thought to be an emerging Chinese ICBM capability. The second technological development involved increasing the
number of nuclear warheads that each American ICBM and SLBM could
launch towards separate targets. These multiple independently targeta-
ble reentry vehicles or MIRVs would, therefore, significantly increase the
destructive capability of the American strategic forces although the number of missiles or launch vehicles comprising those forces remained fixed
at the number which existed in 1967. Thus, for example, a portion of the
ICBM fleet — ultimately 550 — would carry three MIRVs and some 496
of the SLBMs would be capable of carrying from ten to fourteen warheads.

Either of the new technologies, once incorporated into the Soviet or
American force structures, would complicate the accomplishment and
maintenance of the strategic stability to which McNamara aspired. ABM
was the more immediate problem, however, for if an ABM system could
be made to work, then the side deploying the system would be able to
remove the threat to its population posed by the other side's strategic
forces. In the calculus of deterrence developed in the United States, this
could be destabilizing because the retaliatory threat of the non-ABM state
would be neutralized leaving it open to blackmail or attack by the side
deploying ABM. Moreover, some deterrence theorists and planners feared
that the side that saw itself falling behind in the race to develop and
deploy an ABM might well decide to use its strategic capability *before* the
other side deployed its ABM.

MIRVs were rationalized in the Defense Department in part as a
counter to the Soviet ABM. Thus, it was argued, the deployment of hundreds if not thousands of additional warheads by the United States would
allow the United States to overwhelm any ABM system that the Soviets
might deploy. On the other hand, if the United States began testing and
ultimately deployed MIRVs, was it reasonable to assume that the Soviets
could accept a strategic relationship in which they did not also have their
own MIRVs? Perhaps, therefore, MIRVs, and thus a further escalation of
offensive arms development, could be headed off by an agreement to ban
the deployment of ABM. In fact, the Johnson administration initiated
negotiations with the Soviet Union on precisely this point in early 1967
and again at the meeting between President Johnson and Premier Kosygin at Glasboro, New Jersey. The Soviet invasion of Czechoslovakia in
early 1968 led to the termination of these initial attempts at strategic arms
limitations talks (SALT) and the development of the American ABM and

the testing of MIRVs, went forward, leaving to the Nixon administration the decisions concerning their deployment and the future of SALT.

For the Nixon administration, however, the primary question to be addressed was the appearance of a deteriorating strategic balance of forces between the Soviet Union and the United States resulting from the decision by the Johnson administration not to expand the number of American ICBMs and SLBMs even as the Soviet buildup continued. By 1969 the quantitative parity projected by McNamara was fast becoming a reality (see Table 10-1). Notwithstanding the successful flight-test of MIRVs in 1968 which, when deployed, would expand significantly the capability of American launch vehicles, the fixed number of American launchers standing in contrast to a rapidly expanding Soviet force was a strong preoccupation of Nixon and Kissinger. Moreover, they were concerned that if the numbers of larger Soviet launch vehicles continued to grow significantly beyond the parity point of 1968–1969, and those launchers were subsequently augmented by Soviet MIRVs, then some portion of the American retaliatory capacity might conceivably become vulnerable. Finally, apart from MIRV, there was little the United States could do to redress the image of a deterioriating quantitative balance except to build more of the smaller (though technologically superior) Minuteman missiles, given the fact that the development of a new American ICBM would take years to develop, test, and deploy.

By early 1969, the Nixon administration was confronted by growing pressure, especially in the Senate, for a unilateral American decision against the deployment of ABM. Popular opinion in those cities picked in 1967 to be deployment sites for ABM was running against deployment, and scientific opinion on the feasibility of the system was deeply divided. But Nixon and Kissinger did not want to give up the ABM without some concession from the Russians in return. Thus the Nixon administration, though shifting the deployment of the ABM to defense of ICBM sites

TABLE 10-1. HISTORICAL CHANGES IN STRATEGIC FORCES, 1962–1970

		1962	1963	1964	1965	1966	1967	1968	1969	1970
USA	ICBM	294	424	834	854	904	1054	1054	1054	1054
	SLBM	144	224	416	496	592	656	656	656	656
	Bombers	600	630	630	630	630	600	545	560	400
USSR	ICBM	75	90	190	224	292	570	858	1028	1513
	SLBM	some	107	107	107	107	107	121	196	304
	Bombers	190	190	175	160	155	160	155	145	140

Source: The Military Balance 1975–1976; 1977–1978; 1979–1980; 1980–1981 (London: International Institute for Strategic Studies, 1975, 1977, 1978, 1979, and 1980). Reprinted by permission.

(generally located in the less populated areas of the Midwest), announced that the United States would go forward with the system — a decision sustained by a one-vote margin in the Senate when authorization for the system was voted on in August of 1969. The administration had begun, therefore, to regard ABM and MIRV as bargaining chips to be used in the upcoming SALT negotiations, which the Russians had agree to resume in November of 1969.

The Nixon administration's concept of SALT was grounded, therefore, in the view that a strategic arms control agreement with the Soviets might accomplish a slowing of the momentum of Soviet strategic force expansion and perhaps establish a more predictable and stable strategic relationship with the Soviet Union. Kissinger's negotiating strategy was to offer to limit ABM deployment in exchange for a freeze on further strategic force expansion during the life of the agreement, which was to run for 5 years. By the time the agreement was completed in 1972, the Soviets had achieved higher force levels than the United States in both ICBMs and SLBMs. But the superior quality of American strategic forces and the very large number of long-range bombers in the American arsenal were viewed as off-setting the quantitative advantages of the Soviet Union. The American advantage with respect to MIRV was crucial in this accounting, since the ability of the United States to place accurate multiple warheads on its missiles meant that despite the greater number of Soviet missiles allowed under the agreement, the United States retained a significant advantage in the number of more effective warheads.

No less important than the force levels negotiated in the agreement, however, the Nixon administration was able to guarantee that the Soviets would not deploy any more strategic weapons than they had been planning to deploy as of 1972.[13] At the same time, the United States was not required to sacrifice any of its programs directed at offensive force expansion. The Soviets for thier part, retained the option to develop MIRVs in the future and, perhaps most important of all, achieved formal recognition by the United States that they had indeed reached a degree of parity with the United States.

Critics of SALT in the United States insisted that the Soviets had achieved a great deal more as well. Senator Henry Jackson (D., Wash.) quickly became the leader of a large group of hard-line Senate critics of SALT who insisted that the agreement confirmed in its freeze on the force structures in place in mid-1972, a substantial Soviet superiority, especially in a class of very large Soviet ICBMs known as the SS-9. Although the agreement on limiting offensive weapons froze the number of SS-9s allowed the Soviets at approximately 300, Senator Jackson argued that if and when these large ICBMs were eventually married to accurate MIRVs, they might well make vulnerable the smaller number of American ICBMs. Thus the quantitative advantages in large ICBMs and SLBMs conceded to the Soviets merely institutionalized the appearance of greater Soviet dynamism — a condition that, in the view of Jackson and a growing number of critics in the Congress and among conservative defense analysts, would ultimately be used by the Soviets for their political advantage. Accordingly, Jackson demanded during the Senate debate on the agreements that the administraton negotiate equal ceilings on strategic systems as well as pursuing limitations on qualitative developments. The latter objective was already a primary element on the administration's agenda and, together with Jackson's demands, became the core of the next round of negotiations.

A second comprehensive agreement proved impossible to complete as Watergate plagued and truncated the second Nixon term. Gerald Ford was able, however, to initial an agreement with the Russians at Vladivostok in November of 1974, which did incorporate the principle of equal ceilings on strategic delivery vehicles (a common ceiling of 2400) and the number of those vehicles that could be MIRVed (a common ceiling of 1320). By that time, however, newer technologies developed by the two sides impinged on the negotiations, leading to a stalemate during the waning months of the Ford administration. SALT II, as it was now being referred to would become, therefore, the first item on the agenda of Soviet-American relations during the Carter administration.

In the meantime the SALT process became the most tangible evidence of the Nixon administration's approach to preserving America's preeminent global role in the face of expanding Soviet strategic power and an American public grown ambivalent about an activist global role. SALT became, therefore, a process pursued not because it promised an end to or reversal of the dynamic of strategic arms development and certainly not because it promised any diminution of the American global role. Rather, the process promised a modicum of order and predictability in the ongoing relationship of Soviet and American strategic power and their mutual politico-military superiority with respect to the overall international system.

The Opening to China

The restructuring of political and military order from American hegemony to a kind of duopolistic Soviet-American managed global balance was a continuing process. It required the muting of strident ideological themes so that American power and interest could face Soviet power and interest in a context uncluttered by emotionalism. Moreover, to the extent that a Soviet threat persisted, it was to be contained by drawing the Soviets' other rival, China, into a diplomatic and even strategic tripolar relationship. The administration's complex effort assumed that once the American presence on the Asian mainland was reduced, America would be less of an anathema to Beijing than the Soviets were. During the late 1960s, the Soviets became the main enemy to the Chinese. The Soviets, in turn, found the Chinese to be a formidable ideological and diplomatic rival within the communist and third world, with enormous territorial claims against the Soviet Union. Indeed, during the spring and summer of 1969, these territorial claims became a pretext for a series of Sino-Soviet border clashes along the Sinkiang province border with the Soviet Union and in the Amur River valley. A buildup of Soviet forces along these areas of the Chinese border undoubtedly deepened the Chinese sense of fear but also strengthened the hand of those within China who desired an opening towards the United States. The Nixon administration's response was in turn an attempt to enlist the Chinese in its structure of world balance.

At the same time, however, improving Soviet-American relations could not help but concern the Chinese. For example, Soviet-American agreement on troop reductions in Europe could release Soviet military forces for the Sino-Soviet border. But insofar as the Chinese became more preoccupied with their northern borders they would be less likely to fish in troubled waters beyond their southern and eastern boundaries. The American burden in Asia might then be transferred to others in the region. Brezhnev's summer 1973 journey to the United States was undoubtedly seen by the Chinese as a measure implicitly directed toward China. Did this trip mean, asked the Chinese, that the Soviets and the Americans had reached an agreement about the "Asian security treaty" long advocated by the Soviets — a treaty to limit the Chinese sphere of influence? The Nixon policy, therefore, was in part to use the great Sino-Soviet dispute to retain American political, economic, and even military access in East, Southeast, and South Asia. Kissinger recalls:

> We did not consider our opening to China as inherently anti-Soviet. Our objective was to purge our foreign policy of all sentimentality. . . . We moved toward China not to expiate liberal guilt over our China policy of the late 1940s but to shape a global equilibrium. It was not to collude against the Soviet Union but give us a balancing position to use for constructive ends — to give each Communist power a stake in better relations with us. Such an equilibrium could assure stability among the major powers, and even eventual cooperation, in the Seventies and Eighties.[14]

The opening itself was developed over the course of the first 2 years of the Nixon administration, initially through indirect contacts with the Chinese in Europe and then through more direct contacts such as the trip by an American table tennis team to China in the spring of 1971. In the interim both governments had been signaling one another through relaxation of trade restrictions and other indirect contacts.[15] Finally, on April 21, 1971, the Chinese extended a secret invitation to the United States asking that a personal envoy of the president be sent to Beijing to prepare the way for a formal reestablishment of contact between the United States and the People's Republic. Kissinger made the trip and within a year President Nixon visited China for talks with Mao and Chou En-lai.

In a communique at the end of the visit the United States affirmed that Taiwan was part of China and indicated that it was American policy to withdraw ultimately from the island. Moreover, the United States acknowledged that the peaceful resolution of the relationship bewteen Taiwan and the People's Republic was a matter that they must decide for themselves. From the Chinese standpoint, however, these statements by the United States were not all that they might have hoped for. Substantively, the issue of American recognition of Taiwan remained, and this meant that from Peking's perspective the crux of the problem of Sino-American relations also remained.

The Nixon administration, especially once the debilitating effects of Watergate set in, could never respond satisfactorally to this Chinese demand. The political support for full normalization was simply not available to a president fighting for his survival within 18 months of the visit. Moreover, his successor, Gerald Ford, found himself locked in a bitter struggle for nomination with a representative of the right wing of the Republican party, Ronald Reagan, whose support for Taiwan was unqualified. Thus apart from the psychological impact of the initiative itself — which was significant — there was always an air of unsubstantiality about the China opening. It was, in a sense, all diplomatic nuance and no substance. But from the administration's perspective this nuance was sufficient:

> Triangular diplomacy, to be effective, must rely on the natural incentives and propensities of the players. It must avoid the impression that one is "using" either of the contenders against the other; otherwise one becomes vulnerable to retaliation or blackmail. The hostility between China and the Soviet Union served our purposes best if we maintained closer relations with each side than they did with each other. The rest could be left to the dynamic of events.[16]

The Difficulties of Detente

The third element of the Nixon administration's foreign policy framework was ostensibly to complement the China opening. For if the presidential visit to China was to serve as a stick to prod the Russians towards a more accomodating posture, the offer of detente was a carrot offered in reward for the move. Thus as the SALT negotiations proceeded and were ultimately completed in 1972, the United States proffered agricultural sales (which proved disruptive to American food prices), credits, and the prospect of significantly increased trade. The latter inducements could not be delivered by the Nixon administration, however, for those in the Congress suspicious of detente attached conditions to any trade liberalization that made the measures unacceptable to the Soviets. Specifically, Senator Jackson and others in the Senate and House were able to pass amendments to trade legislation that required the Soviets to liberalize Jewish immigration from the Soviet Union, before Moscow could benefit from more U.S. trade. Predictably the Soviets regarded such conditions as interference in their internal affairs and consequently the trade dimension of detente was never fully developed.

On the other hand, Soviet security concerns in Eastern Europe were given grudging recognition by the United States. In part, this was forced on the administration by West German acceptance of the Central European status quo as the probably permanent outcome of World War II. After Chancellor Willy Brandt's formal recognition of the Oder-Neisse line, East Germany, and the renunciation of claims in Poland in 1972, it made little sense for the Nixon administration to sustain a tone of illegitimacy toward the Eastern European governments or the Soviet position in Eastern Europe.

However, this accommodation was granted reluctantly and incompletely. Something more than echoes of "liberation" and "rollback" lingered in Nixon's actions toward Eastern Europe. Thus the Nixon visit to Rumania in 1969 left the Soviets furious for a year and probably stalled SALT negotiations.[17] And American diplomats continued saying that United States relations with Eastern European countries had nothing to do with the Soviet Union, [18] making it apparent that clear acknowledgment of the Soviet position in Eastern Europe was far from complete. Similarly, funds for Radio Liberty and Radio Free Europe were sought at around $40 million a year. The existence of these organizations undoubtedly reflected bureaucratic politics, but they also suggested a less than complete acceptance of the internal structure of the Soviet empire. More direct evidence of this ongoing American reluctance to accept finally the outcome of World War II was to be found in the conditions the United

States would impose on the comprehensive European security agreement sought by the Soviets during the 1970s and partially achieved in 1975, in the Helsinki Accords. Specifically, the United States insisted that Eastern Europe be opened to Western cultural access. Such conditions were clearly unacceptable to a Soviet leadership that crushed the "Prague spring" and suffer Rumanian eccentricities only as long as Rumanian domestic life remains comfortably neo-Stalinist.

It was where spheres and interests overlapped outside Europe, however, that Soviet-American detente encountered greatest difficulty. For its part, the Nixon administration used American power and diplomacy boldly in order to obviate any speculation that America was developing a "reputation for unsteadiness" or that the United States was becoming in Nixon's words, a "pitiful helpless giant." For example, North Vietnam was bombed and its harbors mined as part of a systematic escalation of violence to force American peace terms on a nominal ally of the Soviet Union and China. The boldness of the act was underscored by the fact that even as their ally was being pummelled, the Soviets and Chinese were being used as interlocutors between Washington and Hanoi.[19]

Again in May of 1975, as the American tragedy of Vietnam was ending, the Ford administration responded to the seizure of the American freighter *Mayaguez* by Cambodia with a dramatic show of force. Air attacks were initiated against Cambodia, and marines were landed on Koh Tang Island in the Gulf of Siam where, incorrectly, it was assumed the American crew was being held. In contrast with the regular resort to diplomatic means when American fishing vessels have been seized, their crews beaten and even shot at off Ecuador, no diplomatic channels were used until after the show of force was completed. It mattered little, however, for the entire incident seemed a useful pretext to demonstrate that the United States would, in Henry Kissinger's words, maintain its "reputation for fierceness."[20]

Perhaps the most dramatic cases of colliding Soviet-American interests occurred in the Middle East. In that area the Soviets were held responsible for disruptions of international order while at the same time the U.S. tried to minimize Soviet influence. The schooling of the Soviet Union in the limitations of influence to be accorded to them by the United States was forceful and frequently undertaken without consultation with or the consent of America's allies, the Congress, and in one instance, the Joint Chiefs of Staff.

In September 1970 American military might was displayed in an impressive effort to force the Russinas to withdraw support from the Syrians when they moved tanks into Jordan to help the Palestinians against King Hussein. American troops were mobilized to intervene, but no congressional advice was sought and objections of the Joint Chiefs of Staff, who opposed intervention on both political and military grounds, were overridden. No allies could be found to give American-based C-130's landing rights on their way to the Middle East. The Turks and the Germans told Nixon that the planes could land only if they were on a humanitarian mission. The Spanish were unwilling to be a stopping area as they had been for the 1958 invasion of Lebanon, and Britain was unwilling to allow Malta to be used. But the Russians were warned of "the gravest consequences"[21] if the Syrian tanks did not desist. Kissinger told a tense, frightened Soviet diplomat, "The last time you told me that the Syrians would send no more troops."[22] The Russian minister councilor complained, "We didn't know the Syrians would cross the border, our own military advisers stopped at the border and went no further."[23] Kissinger retorted, "Your client started it, you have to end it."[24]

The episode has been described as another link in the chain of U.S.–Soviet confrontations, and the "management" of the "crisis" has been compared to Cuba.[25] The latter is perhaps overdrawn, inasmuch as Cuba involved a direct U.S.–Soviet confrontation. In contrast, the Nixon administration in this instance was instructing the Soviets in how to manage their clients and maintain stability. These kinds of lessons may be seen as part of an emerging Soviet-American relationship where the great powers manage their conflicting interests without disorder and so that the global structure of peace is maintained. Presumably China was to be incorporated as well, but in the meantime:

Nixon saw the situation in its broadest implications. Jordan to him was a microscopic spot on the map and yet he viewed it as having far-reaching implications on the world-wide stage and on American relations with the Soviet Union.

The idea that Soviet-American relations must be viewed as a chain with each link representing a test of the validity of relations as a whole, was ... uppermost in the President's mind.[26]

Once again in 1973, during the Yom Kippur War, Henry Kissinger pronounced 2 days after Egyptian and Syrian units moved on Israeli-occupied territory that "we shall resist aggressive foreign policies. Detente cannot survive irresponsibility in the Middle East."[27] The news that the Soviet Union was actively encouraging other Arab states to join the conflict, that Soviet cargo planes were resupplying the Arab belligerents, and that Russian officers were leading Syrian tank columns, again prompted the Nixon administration to point to the delicate linkages of detente. The expansion of trade and technological transfer crucial to the Soviets' pursuit of detente were pegged to their acting responsibly in restraining themselves from an urge to expand influence in the Middle East. American diplomats were given instructions that were unmistakable injunctions for the Soviets to realize the imperatives of detente. As one aide remembered, "We were told to tell the Soviets we hold them responsible for everything the Arabs do."[28]

But American pressure was by no means confined to diplomatic remonstrances. As initial Arab military successes were checked by the Israelis in both the Sinai and on the Golan Heights between Syria and Israel, the Soviets proposed joint Soviet-American diplomatic and military intervention. The United States was prepared to undertake the former but not the latter because Kissinger feared that participation in the joint Soviet-American military force proposed by the Soviets would lead to a reestablishment of a strong Soviet presence in the region. Thus the United States joined the Soviets in advancing a cease-fire resolution in the United Nations. The cease-fire did not hold and the Soviet-backed Arab position began to deteriorate rapidly, prompting the Soviets to warn Washington that the Soviet Union was prepared unilaterally to prevent an Arab catastrophe. The United States reacted by placing American forces around the globe on alert and sternly warned the Soviets that the introduction of any troops into the area was unacceptable to the United States. The Soviets quickly backed away from the imminent confrontation with the United States; accepted a UN emergency force; and more importantly, acceded to and ultimately lent some support to Kissinger's personal diplomatic effort to establish a cease-fire and develop a basis for some sort of permanent settlement of the Middle Eastern situation.

The Arab members of the Organization of Petroleum Exporting Countries (OPEC) introduced a new sense of urgency into the crisis by imposing an embargo on oil to Europe, Japan, and the United States, and demanding that Arab positions on the Arab-Israeli dispute be adopted in the West. The international oil distribution system insured that the economic effects of the embargo did not affect any single importer inordinantly. Nonetheless, the Europeans and Japanese, being more dependent upon Middle Eastern oil than the United States, shifted to a more accomodating position vis-a-vis the Arabs and by and large have remained so. By the late 1970s this development would serve to introduce significant strains in the Atlantic alliance. In the shorter run, however, the major effects of the embargo were economic.

In the meantime, Kissinger not only succeeded in bringing about a cease-fire and disengagement of Arab and Israeli forces, but through weeks of shuttling back and forth between Arab capitals and Israel in late

1973 and again in the spring of 1974, Kissinger firmly established the United States as the only mediator acceptable to the major parties to the Middle Eastern conflict. The Syrians remained dependent on the Soviets for military assistance but were nonetheless prepared to work with Kissinger in developing the cease-fire and disengagement agreements of June 1974. The Egyptians, having borne the brunt of four wars with Israel, became active and supportive participants in Kissinger's "shuttle" diplomacy. Kissinger's so-called step-by-step approach of dealing with immediate military problems and avoiding the deeper and more contentious issues of the establishment of a Palestinian state ultimately bogged down. In the meantime, however, a further recourse to military means was avoided; the United States was firmly positioned as interlocutor between Egypt, the largest of the Arab states, and Israel; and perhaps more important from the perspective of the Soviet-American relationship, the United States seized the diplomatic initiative and consigned the Soviets to the sidelines.

By the same token, however, the Soviets were prepared to move in support of anti-American forces in Black Africa when the opportunity presented itself in southern Africa during the latter part of the Ford administration. From the outset of the Nixon administration, American policy had been predicated on the assumption that the Portuguese colonial presence and the white regimes in Rhodesia and South Africa were likely to be permanent fixtures in the region. By 1974, however, the Portuguese presence had collapsed, a black nationalist regime had come to power in Mozambique and civil war among competing nationalist groups raged in Angola. By 1975 a Soviet and Cuban-backed group had emerged as the likely victor in the Angolan conflict. The Ford administration tried to extend U.S. assistance to competing insurgents, but was decisively blocked by overwhelming congressional votes against any further U.S. assistance to pro-Western Angolan insurgent groups. By early 1976, a Marxist regime was consolidating control of Angola. Meanwhile, Kissinger could only warn the Soviets that the structure of Soviet-American relations was endangered by Soviet abuses of detente.

The Ambiguities
of the Nixon-Kissinger Balance

Thus the Nixon administration's effort to define a balance of power managed by means of Soviet-American condominial power, influence, and responsibility was asymmetrical at best; for it prohibited expansion of Soviet power and presence while demanding active Soviet cooperation. Indeed, the Soviets were in some instances faced with the actual diminution of their influence, for in the case of the Middle East, Kissinger's diplomacy was more or less successfully directed at undermining altogether what remained of Soviet influence in the area.

The Kissinger-Nixon policy in Asia was a variation on the theme of responsibility and order played in the Middle East. To no small extent the Vietnam war was an effort to force the Chinese to control their purported clients, the NLF and Hanoi. The Chinese refusal to extend responsible authority south was a significant motivation for the American Vietnam adventure. As Undersecretary of State George Ball said in a major address on January 30, 1966:

> The Soviet Union, having grown powerful, has begun to have a stake in the
> *status quo.* The purpose of the forcible containment of Communist China
> is to induce a similar change in its outlook ... This is the issue in Vietnam.
> This is what we are fighting for. This is why we are there.[29]

It was often observed that the Chinese did not control North Vietnam or the Viet Cong. Nonetheless, the American position was that China should be responsible for confederates within its sphere of interest. Under the Nixon administration, this ambition that the Chinese exert a conservative regional influence received some fulfillment. As a key member of the United States team that negotiated with the North Vietnamese, William H. Sullivan, pointed out:

> When President Nixon decided to put the mines into the harbors of North
> Vietnam on May 8, it produced a situation in which North Vietnam became
> one hundred per cent dependent upon China for the provision of its equip-
> ment. Everything coming from the Soviet Union had to transit Chinese
> territory. Nothing could go through the waters and come into Haiphong ...
> This means that China's preoccupation with Soviet encirclement came into
> play. This means that China's feeling that it would rather have four Balkan-
> ized States in Indochina rather than an Indochina that was dominated by
> Hanoi and possibly susceptible to Moscow, came into play.[30]

And, by early 1974, Chinese Premier Chou En Lai was publicly proclaiming the end of Chinese assistance to insurgencies in Southeast Asia and was fretting in public about Soviet influence in North Vietnam and among Thai insurgents.

A large part of the intellectual framework of this approach to foreign policy is found in the writings and thoughts of Nixon's and then Ford's principal adviser, Henry Kissinger. Professor Kissinger's major research was into the political prerequisites of international stability. To Special Assistant for National Security Affairs and Secretary of State Kissinger it remained a universal principle that stability, not peace, is the hallmark of successful diplomacy.

> Those ages which in retrospect seem most peaceful were least in search of peace. Those whose quest for it seems undying appear least able to achieve tranquility. Whenever peace — conceived as the avoidance of war — has been the primary objective of a power or a group of powers, the international system has been at the mercy of the most ruthless member of the international community. Whenever the international order has acknowledged that certain principles could not be compromised even for the sake of peace, stability based on an equilibrium of forces was at least conceivable.[31]

To Kissinger, the greatest contributors to international instability have been revolutionary powers: Napoleonic France in the nineteenth century, the Soviet Union in the twentieth. Revolutionary powers upset the established norms of governance because they refuse to accept the "legitimacy" of the international order, based on familar, essentially conservative approaches to both international and domestic political life: order, stability, even hierarchy as the framework "which promotes social justice and human dignity." Yet now it appeared that although the "Soviet Union is the greatest menace to peace," it could also be drawn into the international order. In short, revolutionary Russia could be instructed to become a status quo power as Britain was in the nineteenth century and as America has claimed itself to be in the cold war.

As Kissinger explains:

> We are at a point where we can redefine the American position with respect to the world, where, for whatever reasons, it may be that even the Soviet Union has come to a realization of . . . the limits of . . . its ideological fervor.
> But none of these possibilities can be realized except by an American government that is confident that it knows what it is doing, that can respond to its best judgment, and by an American public that has enough confidence in its leaders so that they are permitted the modicum of ambiguity that is sometimes inseparable from a situation in which you cannot at the beginning of a process, know completely what all the consequences are.[32]

A status quo power can be counted on to respond to the limited, rational demands of the balance of power. A status quo power can be enlisted in the worldwide maintenance of order. In either condominium or balance, the emphasis is to enlist the Soviets in achieving American ambitions, which, it is argued in good Wilsonian fashion, are in fact the "interests" of all.

But was all of this an accurate reading of Soviet interests and policy? Skeptics argued that the Soviets could never accept such a vision. In this dour view, the Soviets regard the American pursuit of SALT as but a demonstration that the historical "correlation of forces" is moving against the West and that the West's pursuit of detente is only an admission of the fact. From a Soviet standpoint, detente might have the advantage of allowing them to consolidate these gains, but in time they could be expected to continue exploiting the advantages conceded them under SALT I and to redouble their support for revolutionary forces in the third world.[33]

Howsoever the Soviets might perceive the historical dynamic, they did indeed take advantage of the latitude allowed them under SALT (as did the United States). Moreover, when the opportunity presented itself through a combination of internal developments in southern Africa and an American government distracted by Watergate and an anti-interventionist reaction to Vietnam, the Soviets moved to support anti-Western forces with military assistance or through their Cuban proxies. In this, however, their behavior was consistent with American action in the Middle East.

Detente was characterized by this fundamental ambiguity: It was heralded by Nixon as a relaxation of tensions tantamount to a new era of international politics. But rhetoric aside, relations with the Soviet Union remained essentially competitive, and when, in time, the competitive essence of the relationship reemerged in the Middle East and in Africa, public disillusionment invariably followed. Moreover, at that juncture those who had been arguing all along that the SALT process was itself pernicious gained new credibility. Finally, when Ford was confronted with a political challenge from the right wing of his own party as he sought nomination in 1976, he felt compelled to move toward the policy positions of his adversaries. In the process, Ford pointedly abjured the use of even the word detente by members of his administration.

THE LIMITS OF TRIANGULAR BALANCE

The long-run vision of the international system that might emerge from the application of the Nixon-Kissinger and then Ford diplomacy was framed in the classic metaphors of diplomatic equilibrium and balance of power. As President Nixon remarked in early 1972, echoing Dr. Kissinger's doctoral thesis:

We must remember that the only time in the history of the world that we have had any extended periods of peace is when there has been a balance of power. It is when one nation becomes infinitely more powerful in relation to its potential competitor that the danger of war arises. So I believe in a world in which the United States is powerful. I think it would be a safer world and a better world if we have a strong, healthy United States, Europe, Soviet Union, China and Japan, each balancing the other, an even balance.[34]

The U.S.–Soviet–Chinese dimensions of this vision were, as we have seen, assiduously developed by the president and Kissinger. Europe and Japan on the other hand never achieved comparable status in the "triangular diplomacy" of the Nixon Doctrine. There were other problems as well. The developing world is also conspicuous by its absence in the framework of policy that developed, although — as was evident in Chile and Iran — the United States was prepared to intervene to destroy its ideological adversaries and support those who were prospective surrogates for American power. Moreover, the instruments of force encompassed by this concept of world order were and are increasingly problematic in their applicability. And, finally, there were domestic limits to the entire process.

Europe and Japan

There may be a Europe in the future that can control nuclear weapons and serve as a meaningful balance between the Soviets and America. There might be a nuclear Japan that could do the same. In the meantime, American policy did not push for the independence of Europe; the NATO alliance structure, its commitments, and obligations, stood. The American-European relationship remained essentially one in which the Europeans were dependent on America for their security and open to U.S. economic access. How this political, military, and economic dependence could inspire a separate, credible, and presumably nuclear-armed European pole in the global balance was not explained.

Furthermore, not all Europeans seemed overly anxious to shed their military dependence for more strategic autonomy. Weapons technology is expensive, and the Americans have always been willing, even aggressive merchants. The economies of Europe would be seriously distorted if they had to pay for large standing armies and significant production of military equipment. Indeed, to try and maintain the level of social services provided by most European governments as well as shoulder the added burden of a full defense budget would contribute disastrously to already painful European tax levels.

A credible European nuclear deterrent is at least conceivable, for both the French and English possess a minimum of nuclear systems. But they are somewhat incompatible technologically. More important, such a common defense policy would require that Europe's national forces first be merged and then managed by a political organization representing a "Europe" that does not yet exist. Finally, the thought of Germany with nuclear weapons or strong, more autonomous conventional forces, which would be a highly likely consequence of a militarily independent Europe, would be enough to give Europeans — East and West — considerable pause.

But even if a nascent Europe with marginal political and strategic independence is emerging, its interests will probably remain narrow and inner-directed, too much so for the foreseeable future for Europe to serve as much more than a regional power. The task of political and economic integration is an immensely complex task. To be sure, many of the prerequisites of a European political economy are already in place, but others — a banking system, a European system of taxation, control of corporations, a European system of social welfare services, and above all, a strong, common political vision — are not present. Moreover, the continuing global economic crisis brought on by the Arab exercise of their "petro-power" in late 1973 and early 1974 demonstrated the vulnerability of European political and economic institutions, which are dependent upon external sources for more than 75 percent of their energy needs. One suspects, therefore, that the concerns of Europe will not be Asia or Latin America or the Indian subcontinent, at least not in the sense that a fully dimensionalized balance of power anticipates. The global powers with global interest would still be the Soviet Union and the United States.

Neither could Japan function as an independent and autonomous global power with global interests. Japan's increasingly global economic presence proved even more vulnerable than the Europeans, for in Japan's case more than 90 percent of its energy needs must be met with imports of petroleum from the Persian Gulf. By the mid-1970s it was apparent, therefore, that previous forecasts of an emerging political and economic East Asian "superstate"[35] required reevaluation.

Japan's global military capacity is, to say the least, problematic. A nation that is constitutionally prohibited from using force as an instrument of policy is ill-suited to be a point of countervailing power to the Soviets, Americans, Europeans, or Chinese. However, the Nixonian vision of a new balance of power sought to alter this situation. Even though Japan's geographical insularity gives her relative security from "conventional" aggression, Japan was increasingly encouraged to expand the definitions of her interest under pressure from the Nixon administration.

The Japanese had relied on the American nuclear umbrella and conformed to the rigid American policy toward mainland China despite much internal opposition and historic interest. When Nixon reversed American policy on China with virtually no prior consultation with the Japanese, it was not only taken as an insult but also read as a humiliating incentive for Japan to elaborate an independent course toward China. A similar shock occurred when the Nixon administration sought unilaterally to force the Japanese to reverse their trading position with America by realigning the value of her currency. The heavy-handed import tariffs, quotas, and embargoes combined with the decline of the dollar as a medium of international liquidity was seen as another indication to the Japanese that they should start to make their own way. American policy, under Nixon, undermined the paternalistic relationship that had evolved from Japan's wartime defeat. The rather brusque treatment of Japan — a country where "face" is a national priority — has, however, served to vitiate the surety of the American "nuclear umbrella." As Osgood relates: "Official statements suggest that Japan's nuclear abstention was contingent upon a confidence in the credibility of America's nuclear deterrence, which it no longer automatically takes for granted."[36]

The American effort to draw out the Japanese political and economic presence was designed to present both China and Russia with countervailing power in the Pacific — power that would not be directed against American interest in Asia. It remains a complex, ambiguous, and delicate effort. The extrusion of Japan could make her considerably less friendly toward the United States, and yet Japan's refusal to be so drawn could involve the Americans more than ever in guaranteeing stability in Asia and the Pacific. The consequence of commitments in Asia, pursued by the encouragement of expanding Japanese power and a new relationship with China, is a problematic strategy undertaken in response to the costs of hegemonial power. The alternative of reexamining commitment and responsibilities in Asia seems to have been examined unwillingly if at all.

The Third World

The uncertainties surrounding the position of the third world in the world balance were no less than those relating to Europe and Japan. If, for example, the third world was to be stabilized by American management, then the evidence of the Nixon-Kissinger-Ford years is at best mixed.

In the case of the Indo-Pakistani War of 1971, for example, the policy of great power management under American direction failed in almost every respect. In 1971 India had reversed her policy of nonalignment and signed a mutual assistance treaty with Russia aimed at the Chinese. In response, the Pakistanis and the Chinese became increasingly close; for both now feared the implied expansion of Indian power. It was also a time when the Americans were wooing China into a tripolar relationship. In this context, Pakistan, India's old rival, experienced a massive upheaval in her Eastern wing which was 1000 miles from dominant Western Pakistan. East Pakistan exploded. An election that voted independence for the East was rescinded and Western Pakistani troops started to slaughter Eastern Pakistani civilians in a barely concealed ethnic war. In spite of an attempt to appear neutral, America sent arms to Pakistan, which was a member of the now defunct SEATO. A unified Pakistan was supported by the United States. The rebellion was not considered by the United States as merely an internal affair of Pakistan, but rather in terms of the regional and global balance of power. Although India was inundated with millions of refugees, American aid for refugee relief was little and late. Kissinger, on his way to China, stopped in Delhi and told the Indians that if they moved into Pakistan, China would move on India and that the Americans would not help defend the Indians against the Chinese as they did in the Sino-Indian war of 1962.

Faced with the burden of supporting 10 million refugees and tales of horror about the fate of the ethnically kindred people of Bangladesh, the Indians marched against Pakistan. It was India's opportunity to see that her old antagonist would be permanently weakened by a separation of its eastern province. Washington counted on the Soviets to restrain their new Indian clients. However, in spite of America's calculations, the Pakistani-Chinese and Indian-Russian balance served not to inhibit the conflict but to free India to move against Pakistan. The Nixon administration then proceeded to condemn the Indians in the UN for aggression and sent the nuclear carrier *Enterprise* in a barely disguised "tilt" against India. The move failed. India achieved a spectacular military victory capturing 70,000 West Pakistani troops and secured the independence of Bangladesh and the reduction of Pakistani power on her frontiers.[37]

Protestations by Nixon and Kissinger of their acceptance of "uncertainty or even turmoil . . . in the political flux which is likely to accompany growth"[38] in Africa have proved no less problematic. The catalyst for greater American involvement in Africa[39] was the collapse of the Portuguese colonial presence and increasing pressure on the white regimes in Rhodesia and South Africa all within the context of increasing Russian activism in the area. During 1976, internal security within Rhodesia became increasingly tenuous as guerilla activity expanded markedly. The

South Africans, becoming alarmed at the growing threat to their north, proved supportive of an American-British diplomatic initiative in the late summer of 1976. Kissinger sought to replicate his Middle Eastern shuttle diplomacy successes by establishing himself as a mediator between the white regimes and the black governments in the region who were supporting black liberation efforts in Rhodesia. Kissinger tried to develop a framework for a gradual transfer of power from the white Rhodesian regime of Prime Minister Ian Smith to a black majority government. Despite some initial success — including the establishment of a Kissinger plan (comprising a multilateral conference, an interim government in which whites would maintain control of key ministerial portfolios including defense, internal security and the courts, and agreement by the whites to transfer power within two years)—the initiative eventually died as the Ford administration was defeated for reelection and black resistance to the scope of white control during the proposed transitional period overwhelmed the negotiations in early 1977.

We can not know, of course, whether a second Ford administration with Henry Kissinger as secretary of state would have proved more successful in southern Africa in resolving the fundamental political and racial issues that rent the region than Kissinger's diplomacy had been earlier in the Middle East. What is clear is that Kissinger's activism and diplomatic virtuosity were brought to bear only after the Soviet-American competition had become salient in the region. Moreover, Kissinger's declaration that American policy was designed to "achieve the great goals of national independence, economic development and racial justice" and that "white South Africa must recognize that the world will continue to insist that the institutionalized separation of the races must end" came only as a previous policy of support for European colonial rule and indifference or, at most, extreme gradualism towards ending white rule in South Africa, was collapsing under the pressures of the black African liberation struggles.

In Chile, the administration was confronted with a constitutionally elected Marxist-socialist government under President Salvadore Allende. Because Allende had not received an absolute majority of the presidential vote in September of 1970 (he received a plurality of 36 percent) his election by the Chilean Congress was dismissed by Kissinger as a "fluke."[40] It was assumed that because he was a Marxist he would set about the irreversible dismemberment of the Chilean democracy. Kissinger has argued that:

> In any circumstances, Allende's election was a challenge to our national interest. We did not find it easy to reconcile ourselves to a second Communist state in the Western Hemisphere. We were persuaded that it would soon

be inciting anti-American policies, attacking hemisphere solidarity, making common cause with Cuba, and sooner or later establishing close relations with the Soviet Union.[41]

Exactly what the United States did about this situation has been a matter of intense debate.[42] Kissinger concedes that the United States attempted to influence votes in the Chilean congress to prevent Allende's election but justifies the action as merely the continuation of the policies of past administrations at the time of the 1964 Chilean elections. More controversial is the extent to which the administration supported the attempts of International Telephone and Telegraph to bring down the government or whether the United States, after Allende's election, encouraged an invisible blockade of Chile through a tightening-up on Export-Import Bank loans and other forms of economic assistance. Money already authorized before Allende's election continued to flow to Chile, but new support from either the United States, private bankers, or international agencies was restricted. On the other hand, the Allende regime's administrative capacity has been called into question as the basis for the development of internal conditions which made the country a poor credit risk for both governmental and nongovernmental financial institutions. It is worth noting, however, that poor administrative performance has not proved a sufficient basis for U.S. support to be withdrawn in other cases where the regimes in question were pro-American, such as the Mobutu regime in Zaire or the succession of American sponsored regimes in Vietnam.

In any event economic conditions deteriorated within Chile throughout 1971 and 1972 and in September of 1973, Allende was overthrown in a violent coup to be replaced by a military junta. Allende was killed — the junta has claimed, by his own hand — and Chilean democracy was aborted. Subsequently the junta's leadership has undertaken an international campaign of assassination of former officials of the Allende regime, including the car-bomb murder of Orlando Letelier, Allende's foreign minister, as Letelier drove along the streets of Washington, D.C. in 1976.

The character of American involvement in the descent of Chile into right-wing dictatorship remains somewhat obscure. Nonetheless, Kissinger has observed that "presidents of both parties have felt the need for covert operations in the gray area between formal diplomacy and military intervention throughout the postwar period."[43] Furthermore, he has insisted:

> I cannot accept the proposition that the United States is debarred from acting in the gray area between diplomacy and military intervention, a shadow world in which our adversaries have as instruments a political party,

their own infinitely greater foreign resources, and innumerable front organizations to mask their role.[44]

Presumably, therefore, whatever the role of the United States in Chile,
activity in this gray area remained an essential element of the Nixon
administration's new framework for international order.

The involvement of the Nixon-Kissinger-Ford administrations with
the regime of Shah Mohammed Reza Pahlavi was a continuation of what
had developed over the preceding three administrations. The Shah was
regarded in Kissinger's words as "a friend of our country and a pillar of
stability in a turbulent and vital region."[45] In sum, his regime was viewed
as a surrogate for American power in the region and it became the policy
of the Nixon administration to provide the Shah with all the military
assistance he thought he required for the pursuance of that role. Thus by
1973 the Shah had placed orders, primarily with the United States, which
would provide him with almost 400 modern fighter-bombers, including
the F-14 fighter, over 600 helicopters, more than 50 long-range transport
aircraft, as well as maritime patrol aircraft. By 1974–1975, the Shah was
placing orders for the most modern United States Navy destroyers, hundreds of armored fighting vehicles, and still more fighter aircraft from the
United States. By 1975 the Shah had spent in excess of $15 billion on arms
purchases and had proclaimed a security mission for Iran that included
prevention of the region as well as responsibility for maintaining order in
the northwestern Indian Ocean.[46]

Internally, the United States provided technical assistance and support for the Shah's secret police, Savak. In return, the United States received permission to establish intelligence sites along the Iran-Soviet
border, which provided significant access to Soviet missile testing as well
as tactical weapons test ranges. But these benefits were not without their
costs, for when OPEC began escalating the price of oil dramatically in
1975, the American dependency on its surrogate proved decisive. Indeed,
by the late 1970s allegations had become common that Kissinger had
either tacitly accepted or had been blackmailed into accepting the price
increases being proposed by America's ostensible ally, the Shah. The oil
revenues were clearly necessary to pay for the massive arms imports.
Moreover, the threat of closing down American assets in Iran were also
available to Tehran. In any event, it is reported that Kissinger refused to
support Saudi Arabian attempts to restrain the 1975 price increases.[47]

Thus the pattern of American involvement in the third world and its
place in the larger framework developed during the Nixon-Ford years is
uneven, but nonetheless, closely related to the larger concern with Soviet-
American relations. That is, the countries of the third world remained

what they had traditionally been in American postwar policy: objects in a larger game, episodically important, but only insofar as they impinged upon the traditional focus of the Nixon Doctrine. Yet as has so often been the case since World War II, events on the periphery have proved crucial to the development of American policy: Korea in the 1950s, Vietnam in the 1960s, and the Middle East in the 1970s.

The Limits of Force and Diplomacy

A further difficulty of the Nixon approach to a balanced world order was the problem of adapting force as instrument of that policy. The difficulty with the use of force to maintain a balanced world order in the 1970s was that the consequences of large-scale intervention using conscript personnel had been shown to be unsuccessful and politically intolerable, especially in conflict situations requiring long-term, open-ended, and escalating commitment, such as counterrevolutionary war. Projecting force by symbolic means — the use of nuclear blackmail — has become increasingly unpalatable and problematic, especially with respect to countering revolutionary activity in the third world. Hanoi knew that the United States possessed nuclear weapons, but continued to fight anyway. As Bernard Fall noted some time ago, revolutionary war is essentially a political, not a military phenomenon, and must be dealt with accordingly.[48]

How, then, can the end of stability based on military power be attained? If policy is based on power whose persuasive potential is equated with the implied threat of force, how and at what levels is the force to be employed? The answer of the Nixon administration was that each state has a responsibility for order. Within each region that is not a sphere of influence there would be a balance of power. The Nixonian vision held that access to each region should be open to American power in case stability or balances break down. For such breakdowns, although possibly unimportant in themselves, affect the overall global equilibrium and, most important, the Soviet-American relationship. But the employment of force was recognized to be difficult, so it was deemed best that local powers, such as Iran — with American military assistance which reached perhaps its highest levels during the Nixon-Kissinger years — fend for themselves to enforce stability.

However, the problem remains of what to do in the event that this proves inadequate. The issue has been posed succinctly by Earl Ravenal, "The basic question is whether the Nixon Doctrine is an honest policy that will fully fund the worldwide and Asian commitments it proposes to maintain, or whether it conceals a drift toward nuclear defense or an acceptance of greater risk of local defeat."[49] The Nixon administration's effort to incorporate the Chinese into its system of global order suggests that the problem in Asia was mitigated somewhat, at least to the extent that the Nixon administration abjured the close-in containment of the People's Republic. Nevertheless, the dilemma remained, and one cannot escape the inference that the gap between conventional force and the use of nuclear weapons was compressed. Indeed, the nuclear threat seemed the only solution to the quandary of how to keep commitments and keep American ground forces out of ground combat. If forces were to be committed to combat, then they would have to be professionals, and not draftees. But would there be enough of them for *global* commitments?

But the Nixon Doctrine was marked by almost impenetrable ambiguity. On the one hand, we have the rhetoric of retrenchment and a "reduced profile," but the implementation of American strategy and diplomacy during the early 1970s suggests that there was no fundamental reduction of American objectives. The Nixon policy seems to have been one of keeping a high degree of policy latitude, especially with respect to the use of nuclear weapons: "[H]aving a full range of options does not mean that we will necessarily limit our response to the level or intensity chosen by an enemy. Potential enemies must know that we will respond to whatever degree is required to protect our interests."[50]

The Nixon-Kissinger variation on John Foster Dulles's theme of nuclear retaliation was fraught with all the problems and dangers of the original doctrine. That the new version could achieve the kind of flexibility appropriate to the world of the 1970s, especially in the face of Soviet-American parity, was nowhere clearly demonstrated. Kissinger himself acknowledged the difficulties of the notion of limited or flexible application of strategic and tactical nuclear weapons.[51] Other experts have commented on the illusory nature of this approach:

> The trouble with this concept is that it rests on faulty assumptions (for example, that civilian casualties and collateral damage can be kept to low levels); it ignores a basic lesson that the leaders of the U.S. Government in all cold war crises have learned — that when faced with the decision to start a nuclear war, almost any other alternative looks better; and it is too risky to serve as the foundation for a preferred strategy.[52]

Domestic Constraints

Finally, there were important domestic implications to the Nixon-Kissinger policies which warrant at least passing mention. First, there was the problem of control. Balance of power politics with shifting alignments was possible in previous centuries when a few men were stewards of foreign policy. Modern states, however, are complex organizations no matter how centralized the foreign policy apparatus might be. As Graham Allison and Morton Halperin have noted, there are inherent bureaucratic interests of the military and other foreign policy bureaucracies that can be reconciled only by compromises.[53] If control were to be achieved by a single will, as in the Kissinger management of the National Security Council, there is little assurance that these practices could continue or be institutionalized by succeeding administrations. Indeed, insofar as Kissinger succeeded in personalizing the formulation and conduct of American diplomacy, he completed the task of enfeebling the State Department begun by Senator Joseph McCarthy more than 20 years earlier. The Kissinger control of foreign policy has proved to be a hard act to follow.

Second, the old diplomacy, on which much of the Nixon-Kissinger approach was based, was secret and insulated from domestic politics. Foreign policy was a game of sovereigns, not nations. The representative of the state achieved glory for his prince and the people were left, until the Napoleonic revolution and the rise of popular sovereignty, to the role of disinterested spectator. Arms were borne by mercenaries. Wars were financed with booty or the spoils of colonial exploration. Military adventure was expensive but had real compensation. Yet in the twentieth century there is little possibility of insulating foreign and domestic politics. As Stanley Hoffmann observes:

> [I]n balance of power diplomacy, national interests were defined in terms that took only small account of domestic politics: secrecy, continuity and the primacy of foreign affairs were prerequisites. Today ... [a]ny statesman, however shrewd a negotiator or profound a philosopher of history, who miscalculates the domestic effects of his moves here or abroad, will be in trouble.[54]

Nixon and Kissinger sought insulation of themselves and their diplomacy from domestic political constraints. Nixon was quite willing to use the flash and swirl of foreign affairs to buttress his eroding domestic position. Nevertheless, both he and Kissinger protested efforts to limit their freedom of maneuver. But if freedom of maneuver requires illegal surveillance (wire tapping), deceit, and the other distortions of democratic values that were the essence of the Watergate crisis, one is entitled to ask whether a democracy can afford a new balance based on the old rules.[55]

Summary

Clearly, there are problems with this vision of a newly balanced world political and military order. Nevertheless, Dr. Kissinger's virtuosity in extricating the United States from Vietnam, SALT, his development and manipulation of the Soviet-American and Sino-American dimensions of the balance, and his short-term success with "step-by-step" diplomacy in the Middle East were significant achievements. At the same time, however, as Kissinger assumed the sole stewardship of American foreign policy after Nixon's resignation, it was apparent that there were new forces at work in world politics.[56] The massive transfer of wealth to the Arabs and a handful of other third world countries resulting from the oil embargo and escalating prices in 1975 was perhaps the most salient of these challenges to the prevailing conception of world political reality. But there were other anomalies: the enormous growth and expansion of transnationally mobile private economic power — the multinational corporations — based in the industrialized world, the deep and simultaneous crises of the domestic and international economic systems of the industrialized world, and the rapid onset of widespread malnutrition and famine in much of the third world.

Kissinger is reported to have once remarked, "I am not interested in, nor do I know anything about, the southern portion of the world from the Pyrenees down."[57] Whether or not the words were actually uttered, the sentiment expresses the practical effect of Kissinger's world view; indeed it is a fair characterization of the outlook of much of U.S. statecraft from the onset of the cold war. But new political, military, and economic realities are increasingly apparent. It is difficult, for instance, to think of foreign politics as merely a matter of armed force meeting force, or of billiard balls colliding. Rather, foreign policy is a mix of domestic and international factors — a close-knit interaction of economies, societies, organizations, and statesmen. And unlike the late 1940s, 1950s, and early 1960s, American foreign economic policy is now something more than an instrument to be used in an overarching political and military confrontation. The American economy, in an interdependent world, has become subject to a gossamer international confidence, and the United States is no longer completely master of its economic and hence political destiny. The Nixon administration's policy of balance to maintain global commitments became shaken by the international effects of domestic politics and international economics in a way that Bismarck or Castlereagh could never have imagined. Herein lies perhaps, a fundamental inadequacy of the old classic vision of international reality.

THE LIMITS
OF POWER AND POLICY
IN AN INTERDEPENDENT WORLD

From the end of World War II until the early 1970s two dimensions of international relations have interacted, with one — the security or politico-military dimension — assuming dominance over the other — the politico-economic dimension. In recent years the politico-military and strategic issues so long the preoccupation of American and other statesmen have become increasingly diffused. Instruments of policy such as alliances, threats of military action, and military force have been found increasingly uncertain in their effect and costly in use. Moreover, the formerly dominant sphere of foreign and national security policy is now penetrated by international and transnational economic issues.[58] The breakdown in the international hierarchy of the late 1940s, 1950s and 1960s; the emergent salience of nonsecurity issues; and the problematic applicability of force are the result of this interpretation of security and nonsecurity issues. Understanding the nature of the linkage of politics and economics is critical to how these new phenomena impinge on the traditional notions of force, power, and influence.

The Collapse of the Bretton Woods System[59]

Economic considerations have occupied a dual position in American foriegn policy. At the end of World War II and under the strong influence of the United States, a particular conception of the international economic order was developed and institutionalized at the Bretton Woods Conference in 1944. By and large it was a system that looked to the reconstruction of the world's economy and an institutionalization of conditions amenable to orderly growth and prosperity. Free enterprise, free trade, and the free movement of private capital in accordance with a capitalist conception of economic rationality were to be the basic structural elements of this system. Moreover, it was widely assumed that such an international economic order was absolutely necessary to the establishment and preservation of a stable political and military order commensurate with American national interests.

Thus, the building and maintenance of world economic order, conceived at Bretton Woods, was a primary objective of American foreign policy. At the same time, American foreign economic policy was frequently conceived of in an instrumental manner. American trade and foreign assistance programs (and in the case of East-West relations, their denial) became major instruments of American policy during the 1940s,

1950s, and 1960s. The persistent and growing American balance of payments deficits of these years were not thought of within the context of the Bretton Woods system, as deficits that ultimately would have to be adjusted. Rather, they were seen as simply the price the United States was paying to establish the political and military preconditions of international order. Moreover, it was argued that the American deficits were a kind of international resource in that they provided an international money for a system that was desperately short of liquidity necessary for recovery and growth.

By the mid-1960s, however, this flow of American dollars under changed international conditions, especially in Europe, was no longer viewed as an unalloyed blessing. The Europeans and the French in particular began to demand that the inflation-stimulating dominance of the dollar in the European economy be somehow reduced. Temporary measures followed. By the end of the decade, however, the American export of dollars was, in fact, increasing under the pressure of Vietnam-related military spending and growing U.S. private investment abroad. American corporate investment exacerbated this outflow of dollars while simultaneously benefiting from the easily available credit growing out of the huge concentration of Eurodollars in European banks. By the early 1970s, European economies were experiencing inflation in excess of 15 to 20 percent, American corporations were expanding their presence in Europe, and European currencies came under heavy speculative pressure. It was apparent to all that the international supply of dollars ($60 to $100 billion in Europe alone) far exceeded the capacity of the United States to back them with gold.

The Nixon administration's response was initially a policy of benign neglect. During 1969, 1970, and much of 1971 the Nixon administration refused to concede that there was a problem. The Nixon administration's political need as 1972 approached was for a booming domestic economy which required in turn an inflating of the economy.[60] Moreover, American dollars, it was repeated, provided liquidity for the system, and it did not matter that there was no gold to back the dollars. If the Europeans did not want to hold the dollars, they could spend them on American goods (thereby helping the U.S. balance of payments) or revalue their own currencies upward against the dollar (which would also help the American balance of payments because American goods would then become cheaper vis-à-vis European goods). In short, the Nixon administration told European governments that whether they liked it or not, the dollar and not gold was the basis of the international monetary system. The United States would not change the foreign policy that had made it so, nor would the U.S. government significantly restrain American multinational corporations that were taking advantage of the fact, nor, finally, would the United States significantly deflate its domestic economy (with attendant unemployment in an election year) to soothe European concerns.

In the short run at least, European governments were faced with having to accept the American position. Private holders of dollars were not, however, and began selling dollars for stronger currencies such as the German mark. The upshot was, of course, the threat of more inflation in already inflated economies and, additionally, a further drawdown of American gold reserves. By mid-1971 the dwindling stock of American gold had become intolerable, and Nixon acted by suddenly and without warning ending the convertability of dollars into gold and imposing an import surcharge of 10 percent on foreign goods. Months of speculation followed as the dollar sank on world currency markets, generally to the competitive detriment of other currencies. Finally, in December 1971, at a conference held in Washington at the Smithsonian Institution, the United States officially devalued the dollar, but refused to restore convertability. International economic order was not restored, however, and yet another devaluation occurred in 1972 along with initial European efforts to construct some kind of monetary bloc to protect their own currencies. European economies remained glutted with American dollars, but now, with the second U.S. devaluation, (and, therefore, an improved competitive position) the Europeans were not only forced to hold American dollars but also to absorb the consequences of a deteriorating world trade position. Previously they were forced to import American inflation. Now they had the inflation plus the potential for increasing unemployment in national economies acutely sensitive to a drop in exports.

By March of 1973, the remnants of the Smithsonian Agreement had vanished. Worldwide inflation and currency speculation continued and by early spring, all governments had retreated from fixed exchange rates — the core of the Bretton Woods system —and were allowing market forces to determine the value of their currencies. Some central bank and private bank intervention was employed to avoid total collapse of the financial structure negotiated at the Smithsonian, but increasingly it was clear that governments and especially the United States were surrendering leadership. Some encouragement could be taken from the fact that there was no return to the nationalistic protectionism of the 1930s. Indeed, there was established within the International Monetary Fund a Committee on Reform of the International Monetary System and Related Issues, or as it was commonly known, the Committee of Twenty, comprised of representatives from the major industrialized powers of the West as well as representatives from the third world. The committee's charge was to develop guidelines for a comprehensive reform of the international monetary system. But before the committee's work could be completed, the system was overwhelmed by the international oil crisis growing out of the Yom Kippur War in October of 1973.

The Exercise of "Petropower"

On October 16, 1973, as military events were beginning to turn against the Arabs, the Arab members of the Organization of Petroleum Exporting Countries (OPEC) imposed an embargo on shipments of oil to the United States and other industrialized countries. Simultaneously, OPEC increased the per barrel price of oil such that when added to increases earlier in the year meant that the price of oil increased $2.50 per barrel to $11.65 per barrel by early 1974. Thus an already disorganized industrialized world economy was confronted with an even more complex challenge. Apart from the immediate problem of how the vast sums of money implied in the price increase were going to be recycled from the industrialized countries to the oil exporters, there were the inflationary implications of the price increases.

The price of virtually everything produced in the industrialized world surged dramatically, but oil-dependent industrialized economies were now confronted with enormous debt stemming from oil import bills that were now four times higher than they had been a year earlier. Italy, France, and Britain faced bankruptcy; Japan, importing virtually all of its oil from the Middle East, was faced with a payments deficit. The United States, because it was less dependent upon OPEC oil imports, fared somewhat better and, along with the Germans and the Swiss, benefited from the fact that much of the oil wealth surplus now accumulating in the Middle East was deposited in their banks. The Germans were also able to handle their oil debts better than their European neighbors because of the strong surplus position they had developed before the crisis. In fact, the Germans loaned the Italians $2 billion to deal with their short-term deficit and assumed a more activist role in Common Market attempts to negotiate with the United States some form of industrialized world financial response to the crisis. By early 1975 a $6 billion loan facility had been established within the IMF to aid countries in dealing with their oil debts. However, the immediate financial crisis was managed primarily by the private banking system of the industrialized world, which accepted deposits from the oil-producing nations and reloaned the money to the oil-importing countries in the industrialized countries and third world.

The governments of the West, on the other hand, continued their desultory pursuit of monetary reform. Apart from ad hoc consultations among central bankers and marginal interventions in the floating exchange markets, there was no real management of the system. By late 1975, the West Europeans under French and German leadership had convinced the United States that the prevailing drift in national policies and lack of international coordination was sufficiently dangerous that a more systematic effort had to be made to reconstitute international monetary order. Accordingly, at the IMF meetings in September and at a summit conference in November of 1975 talks were begun. The talks culminated in a conference in Jamaica in 1976, which focused on the issues of international economic management and monetary reform. That the summit conferences would be so focused is testament to the new priorities imposed on Western leadership by interdependence.

In the final analysis, however, the Jamaica Conference could not produce reform of the system. Rather, the participants agreed that floating exchange rates were to remain the central feature of the international monetary system although a return to fixed exchange rates by all countries, or the Europeans regionally, was not precluded. At the same time, multilateral management of the system was furthered insofar as finance ministers and central bankers agreed to consult closely concerning exchange rate developments and interventions in the currency markets. Nonetheless, by the end of the Nixon and Ford administrations all that remained of the old international economic order was a weak consensus that some form of management was a necessity, although leadership toward that goal remained uncertain. The Bretton Woods system had been obliterated,[61] and those who beheld this new and extraordinary set of circumstances could discern no self-evident course for the future. Indeed, the very nature of power and order or the relationship between the two seemed even more problematic than in the past. In something less than a year during 1973 and 1974, the foreign ministries of the developed countries and the politico-military superpowers had to grant new status to a group of "petropowers." The concessions were not always made willingly as some, notably the United States, made threatening noises concerning the use of military force in response to the exercise of economic coercion in the Middle East.[62] In the end, however, the industrialized world turned to the uncertain international financial implications of the dramatic shift in economic power represented by the 1973–1974 oil crisis.

In spite of short-term fears that the transfer of wealth to the oil exporting countries from the industrialized and non–oil exporting developing countries would prove unmanageable, the mid-1970s saw a reasonably orderly adjustment to the problems of recycling and oil debt management throughout the international monetary system.[63] The amounts of money accumulating in the oil exporting countries were indeed impressive. From 1973 to 1974 the current account surpluses of the major oil exporters (Algeria, Indonesia, Iran, Iraq, Libya, Nigeria, Oman, Qatar, Saudi Arabia, the United Arab Emirates, and Venezuela) surged from $6.2 billion to $67.4 billion, with some estimates of projected OPEC financial accumulations in excess of $400 billion by the early 1980s. In contrast, the industrial countries experienced a swing in their current account balances from an $11.1 billion surplus in 1973 to an $11.1 billion deficit in 1974,[64] with no less impressive deficits emerging in the less developed world.

The management of the financial difficulties posed by transfers of this magnitude was facilitated by a number of factors. First, the dramatic increase in the price of oil in addition to stimulating additional international inflation also pushed the international economy into recession, including the first calendar year decline in the volume of the world trade since 1958.[65] The recession led in turn in a reduction in demand for oil in the industrialized world, thereby slowing the growth of exporting countries' surpluses. In fact between 1974 and 1975, the aggregate surpluses on current account of the oil exporting countries dropped from $67.4 billion to $34.7 billion. Simultaneously, the oil exporting countries were initiating substantial development programs which required imports from the industrialized world. In a few instances, notably Iran, these imports included billions of dollars in arms from the United States and Western Europe. According to the International Monetary Fund: "More than two thirds of the drop in the surplus can be attributed to the import expansion, while the remainder was due chiefly to the cyclical downturn in the demands for oil in the importing countries, to economies of fuel consumption in response to the 1973–1974 price increases, and to official measures of oil conservation."[66]

At the same time, more than 90 percent of the oil exporting countries' surplus in 1975 was concentrated in Saudi Arabia, Kuwait, the United Arab Emirates, and Qatar, none of which had the capacity or, given their small size and considerable wealth, the need for massive imports from the industrialized world. During 1974 most of the surplus accruing to these countries was placed in Eurocurrency bank deposits and other short-term government securities where the money was then loaned back out to industrialized and less developed countries to finance their oil deficits. By 1976, however, these same oil exporting countries were diversifying their holdings rapidly with more than half of their investments now being placed in long-term and less liquid investments such as real property and long-term government securities in the industrialized world, especially the United States, Britain, and Germany.[67]

Finally, the immediate financial consequences of the oil crisis were found manageable because the vast network of essentially private international financial institutions proved able to serve as intermediaries in the recycling process. Private banks in the United States, Britain, and elsewhere in Europe became essential brokers in the transfer process by serving as willing receptors of oil exporting countries' investments for relending to the oil importing countries or managers of long-term investment by the oil exporters. Perhaps the most remarkable loan operations had to do with the non–oil exporting third world countries who borrowed heavily in 1974 and 1975 to finance their oil payment deficits. As the world economic recession deepened and industrial activity in the industrialized world slackened, it was this group of primary raw material exporting countries that suffered under the greatest burden of the contraction of world trade. With their earnings thus reduced they were compelled to engage in unprecedented borrowing from private sources in the industrialized world. Indeed, during 1974 and 1975 the non–oil producing, developing countries borrowed more from private sources than they had borrowed from all other sources in any other year prior to 1974.[68]

The worst fears concerning the political and economic consequences of the oil crisis and the emergence of the petropowers were not, therefore, realized. On the other hand, it was clear that the distribution of world political and economic capability had changed significantly as the result of the crisis. By the end of the Nixon-Ford administration this fact was reflected in the increasing status and institutional role accorded the OPEC states, especially Saudi Arabia, in the International Monetary Fund and other international financial institutions. Moreover, OPEC's biannual meetings in which the member states negotiated oil prices assumed an importance and attracted Western media attention previously reserved for Soviet-American summit meetings.

The crisis and its aftermath also underscored the importance that large concentrations of private economic power now played in the world's political economy. Multinational corporations (MNCs) had been a fixture in the international economy since the early 1960s, when American corporations began moving in considerable numbers and with significant economic and political effect into Western Europe. Furthermore, for decades the most common and pervasive form of the American presence of the political economies and even the cultures of the developing world, especially in Latin American, had been the American corporation. And, of course, American interests in the Middle East had always been tied to the fortunes of the international oil cartel, most of which was American. The oil crisis demonstrated that in many instances the MNCs are by no means as autonomous as some had argued and feared. When faced with OPEC and other forms of petropower action, the international oil companies were revealed to be essentially "tax collectors" (who nevertheless took their cut) for the oil producing countries.[69] Finally, there was some evidence that by the mid-1970s many third world countries had begun to approach more systematically — either individually or, in some instances, miltilaterally — the problem of balancing, if not actually controlling, the MNCs in their midst.

Nonetheless, an international political economy in which MNCs control tens of billions of dollars and hundreds of subsidiaries throughout the world, and in which much of the world's trade flows among the MNCs, is a rather different world political economy than that envisaged at Bretton Woods. Furthermore, when this vast private activity is undergirded and facilitated by an essentially private international financial system through which hundreds of billions of dollars and other currencies can move for the most part beyond the immediate control of governments, the very concept of international economic management developed in the postwar period becomes questionable. Not only does such activity challenge the international financial instruments of governments, but as the rapidly transmitted inflation of the early 1970s suggests, the management of domestic economies is affected decisively by international economic activity. Indeed, by the end of the Nixon-Ford years the increasing sensitivity and vulnerability of major sectors of American industry to the combination of increasing foreign competition, MNC exploitation of third world labor markets, and raw materials price inflation, was giving rise to demands for protection that threatened the internationalist economic orthodoxy of the post–World War II era.

Finally, a survey of the contemporary political economic system requires a refinement of our conception of the less developed world. In particular, it is necessary to recognize that there are some important distinctions to be drawn among third world countries. In the first place, the onset of worldwide food shortages in the mid-1970s points up the existence of a "fourth world" — a group of nations almost totally dependent upon others for their survival. The combination of low productivity, short-term crop failures due to climate change, and overpopulation raises the spectre of tens of millions starving within the next decade. Indeed, international food and relief experts began to take seriously the prospect of a kind of international system of *triage* in which those peoples who are beyond saving are simply allowed to perish, while limited international resources are directed to those for whom survival seems more likely.[70]

A second group at the bottom of any measure of world power and development are those traditionally thought of as "developing." These are nations that seem able to achieve some growth as measured by traditional economic indices such as GNP. What is less clear, however, is whether this constitutes development in any holistic sense of social, economic, and political development. The answer is not obvious; for, in spite of positive changes in aggregate economic indicators, some observers argue that these changes mask the persistence of enormous social and political inequities. The latter are frequently viewed as the necessary price that must be paid for economic development. But these inequities can also be seen as the by-product of the "development of underdevelopment" necessary to the preservation of an essentially exploitive relationship between the developed and underdeveloped world, a relationship within which the MNC serves as a kind of autonomous middle man.[71]

The success of the petropowers in exploiting their control of petroleum gave rise to much speculation that other less-developed countries could replicate the petropowers' leap to instant economic and political power.[72] In fact, however, the unique combination of dependence of the industrialized world on petroleum and a mutually perceived threat that could mobilize joint action (in the Middle Eastern case, Israeli military power and the Palestinian question) simply did not exist elsewhere. Moreover, and ironically, the very success of OPEC may have made less likely its replication simply because the greatest burden of debt generated by its action fell on the third world and drove the latter into even greater financial dependency on the private and intergovernmental financial institutions of the industrialized world. Nevertheless, the persistent and militant call during the mid-1970s by the third world for a "new international economic order" embodying a radical redistribution of world wealth and the means whereby that wealth was distributed caused many to worry that the future of the international political economy was unlikely to include much order.[73]

BEYOND THE NIXON DOCTRINE

There were a number of advantages to the Nixon-Kissinger approach to establishing and maintaining world order. First, it represented a breach with 50 years of viewing the Soviet Union as an international leper, an abnormality with interests that were rational only in the context of a perverse dogma. The dogma was still viewed as perverse; the scabrous condition of communism and leftist revolution still existed, but the Russian pariah was seen as recovering if not cleansed. In this sense, therefore, these changes represented an abandonment of the vision of politics epitomized by Dulles, which held international politics as a contest between the forces of light and the forces of darkness. Second, the normalization of relations with China, and the treatment of China as a great power, released the United States from a pathological illusion that the People's

Republic had been an imperialist or expansionist power. China has been, if anything, the soul of caution, painfully aware of its backwardness and weakness. The rhetoric of "people's war," though interpreted in the West to be the framework for Asian aggression, was always an essentially defensive doctrine of warfare.[74] Third, the ability to deal with great powers as if they are normal and understandable, subject to logic and a calculus of interest and accommodation as well as force, allowed negotiations to proceed on both political and military issues.

Nixon, Kissinger, and Ford sought, with some success, to adjust American policy to what they saw as the new realities of the Soviet-American relationship, especially the conditions and implications of strategic parity. In this Nixon and Kissinger were in fact confronting a reality over which they had little control. A Soviet strategic capacity that is essentially equivalent to the capacity of the United States was a condition that was bound to persist throughout the 1970s. SALT was aimed, therefore, at establishing an accomodation to this situation acceptable to both sides. There was, however, a price: institutionalizing the very bureaucracies, arms development, and deployment dynamic that they sought to restrain. In fashioning a new triangular balance of power incorporating China, Kissinger once again succeeded in finally suppressing American phobias that his two superiors (Nixon and Ford) had done so much to foster and take advantage of during their political careers. It remains to be seen, however, whether the trilateral balance that Kissinger tried to construct will truly aid the United States in containing Soviet power, or whether the United States will find itself drawn into conflict with the Soviet Union as the Chinese play their new American card in pursuit of their interests.

In the Middle East, Kissinger's tactical virtuosity was at its height as the United States succeeded in projecting itself into the position of mediator between the contending parties. The accomplishment was significant, for it also entailed a diminution of Soviet leverage. It should not be forgotten, however, that in the end this breakthrough could be exploited no further than could be allowed by the fundamental issue of Israeli security concerns in the face of an Arab demand for recognition of Palestinian rights. Kissinger's shuttle and step-by-step diplomacy could get him no further than a necessary but ultimately insufficient disengagement of the combatants. And perhaps most important of all, American policy during the 1973 Yom Kippur War contributed directly to what may prove to be the most important event of the Nixon presidency, the 1973–1974 oil crisis and its consequences for the world political economy, which still reverberate through the international politics of the early 1980s.

For one thing, the Arab oil boycott supplied the *coup de grace* to a Bretton Woods system then in its death throes. It is important to note that the oil boycott laid bare what many had come to suspect by 1973: American capacity and willingness to manage unilaterally the world's political economy was a thing of the past. In this respect, Nixon's economic policies of mid-1971 started what the Arabs finished in October of 1973. In the immediate wake of the boycott, the Europeans and the Japanese established a pattern of behavior which had emerged spasmodically during the 1960s and would become the norm during the latter 1970s: a decided tendency to pursue their own interests notwithstanding American appeals for unity and joint action, a posture rendered disingenuous if not absurd by American economic nationalism during the years leading up to the oil crisis. Thus as Kissinger tried in the months after the embargo to establish an international energy agency and oil-sharing arrangement, the Europeans and the Japanese, much more dependent on Middle Eastern oil, also went their own way and developed separate arrangements with OPEC. Moreover, it was the Europeans, especially the French, who urged that the United States and the other industrialized powers engage in a formal dialog with the developing nations. The Europeans once again assumed the initiative in moving the United States and the Japanese towards the Jamaica Conference in early 1976.

In fairness it must be said that, by the time that the Nixon administration came to office, management of the international system solely by the United States may no longer have been possible. Parity was, by 1969, a virtual reality, and the Bretton Woods system was already burdened to the breaking point by the international costs associated with the last great but failing effort by the United States to manage and direct events in the third world. But the administration that confronted this situation, though expressing satisfaction with the onset of a new era of international relations — such as in President Nixon's initial State of the World message or Kissinger's conciliatory statement to the third world before the United Nations in 1974[75] — nonetheless, sought to preserve an international order in many respects antithetical to the change its rhetoric welcomed.

NOTES

1. Richard M. Nixon, *U. S. Foreign Policy for the 1970's: A New Strategy for Peace* (Washington, D.C.: U.S. Government Printing Office, 1970), p. 2.
2. Ibid., p. 6
3. Ibid.
4. Ibid., p. 7.

5. See Richard M. Nixon, *U.S. Foreign Policy for the 1970's: Building for Peace* (Washington, D.C.: U.S. Government Printing Office, 1971), p. 6.
6. Ibid.
7. Richard M. Nixon, *U.S. Foreign Policy for the 1970's: Shaping a Durable Peace* (Washington, D.C.: U.S. Government Printing Office, 1973), p. 232.
8. Henry Kissinger, *White House Years* (Boston: Little, Brown and Co., 1979), p. 195.
9. Ibid., p. 196.
10. See W. W. Kaufmann, *The McNamara Strategy* (New York: Harper and Row, 1964) and Robert McNamara, *The Essence of Security* (New York: Harper and Row, 1968).
11. Morton Halperin, "The Decision to Deploy the ABM," *World Politics,* Vol. 25 (October 1972).
12. John Newhouse, *Cold Dawn: The Story of SALT* (New York: Holt, Rinehart and Winston, 1973), p. 101.
13. For estimates of Soviet deployment rates at this time see J. I. Coffey, "The Savor of SALT," *Science and Public Affairs* (May 1973), p. 11.
14. Kissinger, op. cit., pp. 191–192.
15. Ibid., pp. 684–712.
16. Ibid., p. 712.
17. Rowland Evans and Robert Novak, *Nixon in the White House: The Frustration of Power* (New York: Random House, Vintage, 1972), pp. 100–101.
18. See Deputy Secretary of State Kenneth Rush's statements, *The New York Times,* July 10 and July 13, 1973.
19. See Tad Szulc, "Behind the Vietnam Cease-Fire Agreement," *Foreign Policy,* No. 15 (Summer 1974), pp. 21–69.
20. William Safire, "Puppet as Prince," *Harper's Magazine,* Vol. 250, No. 1498 (March 1975), p. 12.
21. Henry Brandon and David Schoenbrun, "Jordan: The Forgotten Crisis," *Foreign Policy,* No. 10 (Spring 1973), p. 172.
22. Ibid., p. 168
23. Ibid.
24. Ibid.
25. Evans and Novak, op. cit. p. 265.
26. Brandon and Schoenbrun, op. cit., p. 170.
27. *The New York Times,* October 11, 1973.
28. *Newsweek,* October 22, 1973, p. 93.
29. *The New York Times,* February 1, 1966.
30. "Meet the Press," Vol. 17, No. 3 (Sunday, January 28, 1973), Merkle Press, Inc., Washington, D.C.
31. Henry Kissinger, *A World Restored* (Boston: Houghton Mifflin Company, 1957), p. 1.
32. Text of a background briefing in New Orleans, August 14, 1970, p. 16, cited by David Landau, *Kissinger: The Uses of Power* (Boston: Houghton Mifflin Company, 1973), p. 128.
33. For an elaboration of this analysis based on an examination of Soviet writings see, R. Judson Mitchell, "A New Brezhnev Doctrine: The Restructuring of International Relations," *World Politics,* Vol. 30, No. 3 (April 1978).
34. *Time,* January 3, 1972.
35. Herman Kahn, *The Emerging Japanese Superstate: Challenge and Response* (Englewood Cliffs, N.J.: Prentice-Hall, 1970).

36. *The New York Times,* February 11, 1975, p. 15. See also his *The Weary and the Wary: U.S. and Japanese Security Policies in Transition* (Baltimore: Johns Hopkins University Press, 1972).
37. See, U.S. Congress, Senate Committee on the Judiciary, Subcommittee to Investigate Problems Connected with Refugees and Escapees, *The Tilt: American Views of South Asia,* 93rd Congress, 2nd Session, 1973, p. 183.
38. Nixon, *A New Strategy for Peace,* p. 87.
39. For the background of Kissinger's policies in Africa, see Anthony Lake, *The "Tar Baby" Option: American Policy Toward Southern Rhodesia* (New York: Columbia University Press, 1976).
40. Kissinger, *White House Years,* p. 654.
41. Ibid.
42. See for example Paul E. Sigmund, "The 'Invisible Blockade' and the Overthrow of Allende," *Foreign Affairs,* Vol. 52, No. 2 (January 1974), and Elizabeth Farnsworth, "More Than Admitted," and Sigmund, "Less Than Charged," both in *Foreign Policy,* No. 16 (Fall 1974),
43. Kissinger, *White House Years,* p. 658.
44. Ibid., p. 677.
45. Ibid., p. 1258.
46. For a survey of the Shah's military purchases during this period see *Strategic Survey 1973* and *Strategic Survey 1975* (London: International Institute for Strategic Studies, 1974 and 1976).
47. Among the more insistent advocates of this argument has been journalist Jack Anderson. See for example, "How the Oil Mess Got That Way," *Parade Magazine,* August 26, 1979, pp. 4–8. However, among Anderson's quoted sources are James Adkins, U.S. ambassador to Saudi Arabia at this time, and Secretary of the Treasury William Simon.
48. Bernard Fall, "The Theory and Practice of Insurgency and Counterinsurgency," *Naval War College Review,* April 1965.
49. Earl C. Ravenal, "The Nixon Doctrine and Our Asian Commitments," *Foreign Affairs,* Vol. 49 (January 1971), pp. 206–207.
50. Nixon, *Building for Peace,* p. 179.

Moreover, as Nixon left office, the full logic of strategic sufficiency came to the fore as the "unthinkable" became thinkable again after more than a decade of suppression. In 1970 and again in 1973 Nixon's first two secretaries of defense could be found saying that "the President has made it perfectly clear that we do not intend to develop counter-force capabilities which the Soviets could construe as having a first strike potential" (Secretary of Defense Melvin Laird, cited in *Congressional Record,* Vol. 116, Prt. 19 (July 29, 1970), 26386 and

> The President has also stated that the numbers, characteristics, and deployments of U.S. strategic forces should be such that the Soviet Union cannot reasonably interpret them as intended to threaten a disarming attack. Such a threat would be inconsistent with the U.S. desire to maintain a stable strategic balance and, thereby, reduce the likelihood of nuclear war (U.S. Congress, Hearings before the Senate Committee on the Armed Services, *Fiscal Year 1974 Authorization for Military Procurement, Research and Development, Construction Authorization for the Safeguard ABM, and Active Duty and Selected Reserve Strengths,* 93rd Congress, 1st Session, 1973, p. 313).

But in his "Posture Statement" on the Fiscal Year 1975 Defense Budget, Secretary of Defense James R. Schlesinger stated elliptically:

Assured destruction must remain an essential ingredient in our overall deterrent strategy. However, under certain hypothetical circumstances, if the use of U.S. strategic capability were required in response to an act of aggression we might well reserve our assured destruction forces so as to deter attacks against the American and other free world cities into the wartime period–what we call intrawar deterrence.

The emphasis in the new retargeting doctrine is to provide a number of options, selectivity, and flexibility, so that our response, regardless of the provocation, is appropriate rather than disproportionate to the provocation. I think that understanding of this will serve to shore up deterrence. (Secretary of Defense James R. Schlesinger, Hearings on *Military Posture and H.R. 12564, Department of Defense Authorization for Appropriations for Fiscal Year 1975,* before House Committee on Armed Services, 93rd Congress, 2nd Session, 1974, p. 14.)

In short, the secretary of defense sought to recoup some of the flexibility lost at the lower end of the spectrum of force by building greater "flexibility" and "options" into the strategic nuclear arsenal of the United States. However, some have suggested that such flexibility already existed due to improvements in American command and control capability allowing for almost unlimited and immediate retargeting of American strategic forces [See John C. Baker, "Flexibility: The Imminent Debate," *Arms Control Today,* Vol. 4, No. 1 (January 1974), p. 2.] Also, it has been argued that the United States has possessed for some time the capacity to attack some Soviet missile silos; hence, any significant increase in U.S. capacity to attack the Soviet ICBM force would of necessity be viewed as provocative by them. [See the colloquy between Morton Halperin and Robert Ellsworth in "Should We Develop Highly Accurate Missiles and Emphasize Military Targets Rather than Cities?" *The Advocates* (Boston: WGBH, February 12, 1974), pp. 28–29, and Herbert Scoville, Jr., "Flexible MADness," *Foreign Policy,* No. 14 (Spring 1974), pp. 168–170.] The provocativeness of the step proposed by Schlesinger is undoubtedly heightened in the eyes of Soviet defense planners when viewed in conjunction with the accelerated U.S. ASW [antisubmarine warfare] program.

All in all, as Scoville demonstrates (see Scoville, pp. 171–174) it is extremely difficult to conceive of any *strategic* scenario in which increased hard-target killing capability on the part of the United States contributes to strategic deterrence. Indeed, quite the opposite conclusion pushed to the fore: "No matter how often we disclaim it, the development of improved silo-killing missiles must inevitably look to the Russians like an attempt to acquire a firststrike counterforce capability against their ICBMs. Similar Soviet programs for getting high-yield MIRVs have been viewed here in exactly such alarming terms." (see Scoville, p. 170.)

51. Kissinger, *White House Years,* pp. 217–220.
52. Alain C. Enthoven and K. Wayne Smith, "What Forces for NATO? And From Whom?" *Foreign Affairs,* Vol. 48, No. 1 (October 1969), p. 82.
53. Graham Allison, *Essence of Decision* (Boston: Little, Brown and Company, 1971); Morton Halperin, *Bureaucratic Politics and Foreign Policy* (Washington, D.C.: Brookings Institution, 1974).
54. Stanley Hoffmann, "A New Foreign Policy: Is It Possible? Do We Need It?" prepared statement before U.S. Congress, House Committee on Foreign Affairs, Hearings and Symposium Before the Subcommittee on National Security Policy and Scientific De-

velopment, *National Security Policy and the Changing World Power Alignment,* 92nd Congress, 2nd Session, 1972, p. 33.

55. For a more extended discussion of the analysis in this section see James A. Nathan and James K. Oliver, *Foreign Policymaking in the American Political System* (Boston: Little Brown and Co., 1981).

56. Seyom Brown, *New Forces in World Politics* (Washington, D.C.: Brookings Institution, 1974).

57. Gabriel Garcia Marquez, "The Death of Salvador Allende," *Harper's Magazine,* Vol. 248, No. 1486, p. 46.

58. Richard N. Cooper, "Trade Policy Is Foreign Policy," *Foreign Policy,* No. 9 (Winter 1972–1973).

59. The following section is drawn from Robert Stevens, *A Primer on the Dollar in the World Economy,* pp. 142–150, and David P. Calleo and Benjamin M. Rowland, *America and the World Political Economy* (Bloomington, Ind: University of Indiana Press, 1974), pp. 87–117. and Joan Spero, *The Politics of International Economic Relations* (New York: St. Martin's Press, 1977). Also useful is Robert Solomon, *The International Monetary System, 1945–1976: An Insider's View* (New York: Harper and Row, 1977).

60. See Edward R. Tufte, *Political Control of the Economy* (Princeton: Princeton University Press, 1978), for an analysis of presidential manipulation of the economy in election years.

61. See Robert Triffin, "Jamaica: 'Major Revision' or Fiasco?" In Edward M. Bernstein *et. al.,* "Reflections on Jamaica," *Essays in International Finance,* No. 115 (Princeton: International Finance Section, Department of Economics, Princeton University, 1976).

62. "Kissinger on Oil, Food, and Trade," *Business Week,* (January 13, 1975), pp. 66–76.

63. The following discussion, unless otherwise noted, is drawn from: the *Annual Reports* of the International Monetary Fund for 1976 and 1977 (Washington, D.C.: International Monetary Fund, 1977 and 1978 respectively); Thomas D. Willet, "The Oil-Transfer Problem and International Economic Stability," *Essays in Internation Finance,* No. 113 (Princeton: International Finance Section, Department of Economics, Princeton, University, 1975); Spero, op. cit.; and Raymond Vernon, ed., *The Oil Crisis* (New York: Norton, 1976).

64. *IMF Annual Report, 1977,* p. 14.

65. *IMF Annual Report, 1976,* pp. 9–12.

66. Ibid., pp. 14–15.

67. *IMF Annual Report, 1977,* p. 14, and Willet, *passim.*

68. *IMF Annual Report, 1976,* pp. 20–21.

69. See M. A. Adelman, "Is the Oil Shortage Real?" *Foreign Policy,* No. 9 (Winter 1972–1973), pp. 69–107.

70. Walter Sullivan, "Computer 'Model' of World Sought to Cope with Food Shortage," *The New York Times,* August 10, 1974, pp. 31–46.

71. For a succinct statement of this argument see Osvaldo Sunkel, "Big Business and 'Dependencia': A Latin American View," *Foreign Affairs,* Vol. 50 (April 1972), pp. 517–531; also James D. Cockcroft, Andre Gunder Frank, and Dale L. Johnson, *Dependence and Underdevelopment: Latin America's Political Economy* (Garden City, N.Y.: Doubleday, Anchor, 1972). For a critique of this view, see Benjamin J. Cohen, *The Question of Imperialism: The Political Economy of Dominance and Dependence* (New York: Basic Books, 1973).

72. See the exchange of views, "One, Two, Many OPEC's . . .?" in *Foreign Policy,* No. 14 (Spring 1974), pp. 57–90.

73. Robert Tucker, *The Inequality of Nations* (New York: Basic Books, 1976), *passim.*
74. See Arthur Huck, *The Security of China: Chinese Approaches to Problems of War and Strategy* (New York: Columbia University Press, 1970).
75. "Challenges of Interdependence," Address by Secretary of State Henry A. Kissinger before the Sixth Special Session of the United Nations General Assembly, New York, New York, April 15, 1974 (Washington, D.C.: Department of State, Bureau of Public Affairs, 1974).

Chapter 11
"Commitments in Search of a Roost"

Like movie goers who saw the recent science fiction thriller, "Alien," observers of the Carter administration's foreign policy have been presented with a creature whose inexorable and seemingly inexplicable transmogrifications both amuse and terrify. If those ill-fated astronauts of the film set in the year 2039 always had the option of abandoning ship, the American public did not. Opinion polls found in the American mood only a resignation to the worst, as the public contemplated an administration that came to office proclaiming its differences from its predecessors but which, in time, returned to all the old themes.

Policy formulation was to be more "open" and imbued with a new moral tone. Human rights, a new relationship with the third world, a reconstituted Atlantic alliance, the control of nuclear proliferation and the transfer of conventional arms to other countries, and strategic arms limitations and even disarmament were all policy objectives. But within months, even supporters of the administration had begun calling for a clearer sense of direction and priorities among the many but sometimes conflicting objectives.[1] By midterm, "confusion," "incoherence," and "inconsistency" were terms being applied to the administration's actions. And as his reelection campaign began, Carter had to go to the nation, not with an ambitious policy agenda completed, but with a strategic arms control agreement he could not get ratified in the United States Senate, Middle East peace negotiations that had deadlocked after a promising start, and fifty-three American hostages in Iran seemingly irretrievable after an embarrassingly failed rescue attempt and the refusal of America's European and Japanese allies to go through with strong economic and diplomatic sanctions against a revolutionary Iranian regime that had overthrown one of America's closest allies in the Middle East. No less important, relations with the Soviet Union had descended to perhaps their lowest point in more than a decade after the Soviets invaded Afghanistan in late 1979 and the United States called for — with mixed success — a boycott of the Olympic Games held in Moscow. The Afghanistan invasion contributed to the largest peacetime military buildup since the early Kennedy administration with some projections of U.S. military expenditures during the first half of the 1980s running to a trillion dollars. The cold war — so fervently exorcised by part of the Carter foreign policy apparat for nearly 3 years yet so feverishly conjured by others — had resurfaced.

INTERDEPENDENCE AND CONTAINMENT

The Carter administration was forced to confront the implications of the two unifying ambitions of postwar U.S. foreign policy. Foremost, of course, has been the attempt to contain Soviet expansion. A necessarily more elusive but no less avidly pursued policy has been the attempt, as Carter's special assistant for national security affairs, Zbigniew Brzezinski, has been fond of putting it: "to make the world congenial to ourselves" and "to prevent America from being lonely."[2] In order to escape from solitude and to confine Soviet influence, few places have been immune from American concern. Throughout the cold war, formal guarantees were issued to over forty countries. But it was clear, after the Korean War, that America's security perimeter was defined not merely by treaty but also by events. The Soviet's involvement in all this was viewed in more sophisticated terms than in the past. It was understood that they did not instigate every coup, insurrection or international disturbance. Still, there has always been a central policy tenet that the Soviet Union gleaned profit from upheaval. The consistent positing of a cosmology — variously labeled "domino theory," "linkage," or the "spreading arc of crisis" — implied, at the least, the necessity for unfailing American vigilance lest there begin a changing rhythm of history. For in any retreat, there might be a gathering of miscalculations about American determination. Ultimately, then, the nuclear card itself might have to be played through inadvertence or as a desperate signal of American will.

But a resort to an overtly threatening posture dependent upon American strategic superiority was an option of limited credibility. In fact, strategic superiority was a thing of the past and the Carter administration could initially find no alternative to the strategic arms limitations process initiated by the Nixon administration. Furthermore, the resort to lower levels of military capability as a response to revolutionary instability was deemed no less inappropriate in view of the Vietnam experience. Moreover, it was little solace to the many members of the Carter administration who had criticized the Nixon and Ford administrations that they were now compelled to confront dilemmas that emerged and were, in some measure, exacerbated by those earlier administrations. The strategic arms limitations approach to the problems of strategic parity had been shaped by Carter's predecessors. The constraints — both political and material — on the use of force had been established in the preceding decade as had the decline of American economic hegemony. And American dependence on regional surrogates such as the Shah of Iran was the result of the Nixon-Kissinger-Ford pursuit of stability in the third world without a substantial American military presence or capability. Nonetheless, it seemed that the worst fears of those who argued for the necessity of preserving some relationship between force and diplomacy (lest policy paralysis result from their divorce)[3] were met at the threshold of the Carter administration.

"Interdependence" as Policy

The response of the Carter administration to these problems was frequently ambivalent; at worst, almost inexplicably incoherent and unpredictable. Much of this inconsistency can be traced to contending and ultimately irreconcilable policy perspectives within the Carter foreign policy establishment.

One part of the administration sought to make a virtue of the dilemmas presented by the apparently limited utility of American military capability. Proponents of the position argued that the growing interdependence of the international system provided unique opportunities for the United States. These new conditions meant, for example, that economic transactions and issues within the industrialized world and between the West and the third world now defined the crucial arenas of world politics. The cold war Soviet-American confrontation was, therefore, decreasingly relevant. If ideological questions remained important, they were not the old issues of Soviet communism versus American capitalism. The new issues concerned the third world's aspirations for national dignity and a greater measure of autonomy in its relationship with the industrialized west. The third world recognized that the relationship is necessary, because its aspirations for development required access to Western capital, technology, markets, and technical assistance. It was argued by many in the Departments of State and Treasury, and with particular force by Andrew Young, Carter's United Nations ambassador, that in such a world, the United States possessed an enormously varied, appropriate, and readily applied set of economic and technical instrumentalities.[4]

In contrast, the Soviets had little to offer. Their influence on the development of an international economic order for the industrialized West was nonexistent. Moreover, Soviet influence on the more volatile conditions of the third world was greatest where revolutionary conflict was underway. Young — who was appointed to the UN post because of his presumed sensitivity for and appeal to the non-West — and others argued that the United States should be less supportive of its traditional antirevolutionary clients and more responsive to the aspirations of those seeking change. Where violent change implied inordinate Soviet influence, such as in Southern Africa, then American policy should anticipate those circumstances through diplomatic efforts designed to facilitate the emergence of change-oriented, nationalistic, but pragmatic regimes. In some instances this might require deferring to the United Nations or the diplomacy of other Western allies, such as the successful British mediation of the revolutionary situation in Zimbabwe in 1979–1980. In other cases, such as Nicaragua in 1978 and 1979, this approach would require at least a passive U.S. stance even though a former U.S. client, Anastasio Somoza, was threatened with ouster. In either case, it was argued, the United States would be well positioned to advance its interests in the postrevolutionary situation. Indeed, Young was prepared to assert publicly, to the administration's embarrassment, the heretical position that Soviet intervention in Africa or elsewhere via its Cuban surrogates need not be regarded as necessarily a bad thing if it contributed to the termination of revolutionary turmoil and the onset of circumstances in which the need for Western developmental assistance came to preoccupy a particular third world country's foreign policy, as in Angola, or in the Nicaraguan revolutionary government's turn to the United States rather than Cuba for assistance.

At the outset, therefore, some within the Carter administration seemed to accept the end of the cold war pronounced by Nixon in 1969 and baptized in Helsinki as the great *given* of contemporary history. The problem in formulating policy in a "post cold war environment," as Leslie Gelb, then at the State Department's Bureau of Politico-Military Affairs, explained in 1977, was that "fewer and fewer things had to do with the Soviet-American connection."[5] The question of how to proceed with Soviet-American relations since outstanding issues were seen as either settled or marginal to the larger course of history (a history which did not include an especially bright prospect for the Russians), was uncertain. Nonetheless, American capabilities in such an environment were far superior to those of the Soviet Union. Though the context of foreign policy would likely prove constraining for the old means and ends of American policy, there was considerable reason to believe that a new set of means and ends commensurate with these changed conditions, could prosper.

Brzezinski Speaks
to Realpolitik . . . and Interdependence

On the other hand, there was in the Carter administration another conception of the appropriate American response to these new conditions, a position forcefully articulated and advanced by Carter's special assistant for national security affairs, Zbigniew Brzezinski. Carter came to office with little background in foreign policy save his participation in the Trilateral Commission, a collection of political, economic, and academic notables from throughout the industrialized world (the United States, Canada, Western Europe, and Japan) under the leadership of David Rockefeller. The commission's executive director during Carter's association with it had been Brzezinski. Moreover, his secretary of state, Cyrus Vance, was usually heralded as more of a technician in negotiations than a conceptualizer. Thus whatever coherent view of the world that eventually emerged in the Carter administration would be heavily, even primarily, influenced by Brzezinski. He was, after all, as Carter explained, "the eyes through which I view the world."[6]

Brzezinski's views were not, at least superficially, totally inconsistent with the arguments advanced by those who saw an interdependent world potentially more responsive to American diplomacy than Soviet power. The world had entered a "technotronic age," according to Brzezinski, one in which "technology and electronics — particularly in the area of computers and communications" were now the dominant shapers of domestic and international society.[7] Simultaneously, "[g]lobal politics are becoming egalitarian rather than libertarian, with demands from more politically activated masses focussing predominantly on material equality than on spiritual or legal liberty."[8]

There were in these conditions great dangers for the United States, especially if it adopted what Brzezinski called a "siege mentality," setting itself intransigently against these conditions and especially demands for greater equality. Preferable, said Brzezinski in an essay published during the bicentennial year, was

> ... an America that is cooperatively engaged in shaping new global relations, both despite and because of the rising global egalitarian passions. . . . America still provides to most people in the world the most attractive social *condition* (even if not the *model*) and that remains America's special strength. The Soviet Union is not even a rival in this respect. But that strength can only be applied if American foreign policy is sympathetically sensitive to the significant shift in global emphasis toward a value [egalitarianism] which has not been central to the American experience. This need not entail an embrace of egalitarianism as the supreme virtue. . . . But it does imply a policy that does not ignore (nor reciprocate with doctrinal hostility) the global pressures for reform of existing international arrangements.[9]

At the same time, however, Brzezinski departed from the interdependence perspective in that he persisted in the more traditional American preoccupation with the Soviet Union and especially its presence in Eastern Europe. But he took great pains to distinguish his outlook and methods from those of the previous 8 years. On the eve of the signing of the Helsinki accords, for example, when Carter was but a distant gleam in his eye, Brzezinski gave a remarkably candid assessment of his differences with the "Ford/Kissinger approach" to detente "which seeks to perpetuate the status quo" in Europe "with all that entails."[10] For Brzezinski, the whole purpose of Helsinki and the latter years of Kissinger's tenure was ill-conceived and ahistorical:

> ... the anachronistic division of Europe ... is the source of instability. If we contribute to its legitimation in the form of some security declaration, we are not contributing to European security but to its opposite.[11]

Brzezinski's plan for the future of the Soviet Union was as fissiparous as it was for Eastern Europe. As he confessed to a Radio Free Europe interrogator:

> ... realistic encouragement of pluralism via nationalism and separatism may be our best answer to the Soviet challenge on the ideological front ... [A]fter the disappearance of the communist state, a combination of residual socialism and internationalism would mitigate the power-oriented ambitions of extreme Russian nationalism ...[12]

For President Carter's soon-to-be-appointed national security advisor, the Soviets could be treated in a fundamentally different fashion from the status finally accorded to them by Kissinger and Ford. To Brzezinski, the Soviets' internal regime could be publicly questioned and loudly proclaimed illegitimate, irrelevant, and even pernicious to the tide of progress sweeping the globe. A "truly *comprehensive* [emphasis his] detente" would be "a challenge to [the Soviet Union's] legitimacy and thus ... their very existence, and I must say their fears [would be] justified."[13] Carter echoed this theme when he told members of the Magazine Publishers Association:

> My own inclination ... is to aggressively challenge ... the Soviet Union and others for influence in areas of the world that we feel are crucial to us now or potentially crucial in 15 or 20 years from now.[14]

All this could not help but abrade the Soviets at their most irritable spots. When Carter visited Poland and Rumania early in his administration, Brzezinski was not unaware of the implications, "[I]t was," he explained, "a gesture which underlines our interests in pluralism in Eastern Europe."[15] Brzezinski elaborated Carter's reversal of American accession to Helsinki in his address to the Foreign Policy Association on December 20, 1978: ". . . We do not believe that our relations with Eastern Europe should be subordinate to our relationship with Moscow. . . ."[16] It was not widely noticed, but in his first budget request, Carter asked for a doubling of broadcast capability of Radio Free Europe and Radio Liberty. VOA broadcasts to the Soviet Union were increased by 25 percent.[17]

Brzezinski (as well as many of those he brought to the National Security Council) was not, therefore, insensitive to either the constrained condition of American military power or the complex interdependence that contributed to that condition. Furthermore, he seemed to accept that the emerging new age of world politics was potentially more amenable to a reformed American view of world order and new American instrumentalities (largely political and economic, but also American ideals in the form of an almost militant emphasis on human rights) than it was to Soviet power and policy. However, Brzezinski was not prepared more or less to ignore Soviet power and international presence. Soviet strategic power had to be checked as a necessary condition of world order, but presumably this could be achieved by arms control agreements and the continued mobilization of American technological sophistication and superiority. Even more important, Brzezinski was prepared to engage — not merely coexist with — the Soviets within the context of the new interdependence, using American advantages and leverage to contribute to Soviet difficulties internally and especially within their East European empire.

Here, then, was a crucial difference, not only in Brzezinski's position with respect to many of his colleagues within the Carter administration, but compared with his Republican predecessors as well. A Soviet Union beset by internal weaknesses and dubious prospects for long-term successful participation in the new era of world politics was not to be merely accepted as a kind of junior partner. Rather, wherever possible its problems and difficulties were to be exacerbated. Its need for Western capital and technology was not to be approached as an opportunity to pull it gradually into a moderating web of detente but as a vulnerability to be exploited so as to hasten its decline. Soviet sensitivity to Chinese potential on its Asian border was not to be subtly and carefully manipulated through diplomatic maneuver, but rather prodded and even inflamed through indirect and direct military assistance to the Chinese.

The ambivalence and indecision that many observers have attributed to the Carter years can be traced in considerable measure to these warring policy perspectives within the Carter administration. The media often explained things in terms of an intense personal and institutional clash between, on the one hand, Brzezinski and his National Security Council staff, and on the other hand Secretary of State Vance and his department, a clash culminating in Vance's resignation in early 1980. Though there were clearly elements of such a struggle permeating Carter administration policy, it is important to recognize that the two men represented subtly but consequentially different views of the world, American interests, the specific options available, and the means to be used.[18] Furthermore, to the extent that American policy in the late 1970s can be seen as having drifted towards the pole represented by Brzezinski, that outcome was made more likely by the president's desire to make human rights a centerpiece of his foreign policy.

Human Rights

In his inaugural address, Carter told the American people and the world: "Because we are free we can never be indifferent to the fate of human beings elsewhere . . . our commitment to human rights must be absolute." In March of 1977, he told the United Nations: "No member of the United Nations can claim that the mistreatment of its citizens is solely its own business."[19] Nonetheless, the specific meaning and application of the policy remained unclear and, upon examination, proves problematical.

The NSC spent innumerable hours in 1977 and 1978 attempting to assess what human rights means to Islamic, Latin, and Oriental societies. One participant at these meetings despaired: "It's a hard problem for a bureaucracy to come to grips with. It's a hard subject for people to discuss collectively."[20] Early on, the Carter administration discovered that if it is difficult to discuss what constitutes human rights with people of the same cultural-political-ethnic backgrounds, it is downright confounding to discuss the matter of judicial torture and wholesale murder with representatives of other cultures that are often in revolutionary contexts.

The problem of cultural variability of human rights as an absolute principle of foreign policy stems from the necessarily indiscriminate nature of an absolute commitment to human rights. To most people educated in Judeo-Christian principles, humans have rights. If, then, their rights are violated and abused, how is one to express concern? If one manifests concern wherever there are abuses, then one must be prepared to identify an enormous array of circumstances and activities that are, by most American's standards, obnoxious. But what, then, is one to *do?* Dealing with the problem implies a willingness to intervene in some fashion in the internal affairs of another society. Presumably, one should be prepared to chastise and even dispatch leadership if the abuses are gross enough. But also, if one's policy is to have significant moral force, its application would have to be consistent. But should moral opprobrium and intervention be directed at the Saudis, South Koreans, or the Shah of Iran? Were the Chinese to be the object of moral condemnation even as the Carter administration sought to complete a *de facto* alliance with the Chinese to contain the Soviets?

One could, in theory at least, rank one's interests from the most important to the least important, trading lesser interests to safeguard the more serious. But how can one rank or differentiate the objects of great and absolute principles? Does sacrificing some segment of a principle weaken it altogether? One can compromise competing interests, but compromising with morality is a visible sin. The policy now seems to have been foredoomed, whether it was an "absolute principle" of foreign policy as Carter proclaimed, or "absolute in principle but flexible in application" as one of the president's NSC assistants explained to one of the present authors.[21]

The American public's sentiment that Carter perceived and sought to respond to with his pronouncements concerning human rights is, nonetheless, difficult to exaggerate and easy to underestimate. But among some Europeans and the Soviets, there was incomprehension and even hostility to Carter's concern for those who suffered abridgment of liberty or dignity. Among the Germans especially, there were fears that open letters to dissidents in the Soviet Union and the reception of Soviet exiles in the White House would jeopardize a decade of detente. Carter found it "surprising" that the Soviets would have an "adverse reaction." His policy had, he would in time confess, "provided a greater obstacle to . . . common goals, like SALT, than I had anticipated."[22]

If Carter had not suspected that the Soviets would be taken aback by his professions of sympathy for Soviet dissidents, his national security adviser might have pointed to the words that he and his associate, Samuel Huntington, authored as early as 1962. The main source of danger to the stability of the Soviet political system, wrote Brzezinski and Huntington, is

> any decline in the ideological and political monopoly of the ruling party. If tomorrow the Soviet Union were to open its frontiers to foreign books, newspapers and criticism of the system, the effect could be politically dramatic. . . .[23]

But as we have seen, such a politically dramatic effect was, for Brzezinski, the most desirable of outcomes for American policy in the complexly interdependent world confronting the United States. Thus Carter's emphasis on human rights was congruent with Brzezinski's conception of American policy. At the same time, however, this convergence of views merely underscored the traditional foci of American policy in the late 1970s. That is, notwithstanding much rhetoric and some policy initiatives that reflected awareness of interdependence, there was in the moralistic thrust of Carter's human rights emphasis a throwback to the globalism of Truman and even beyond that, to Wilson. To the extent that this moralism came into focus with Brzezinski's approach to the new age on continued confrontation with the Soviet Union, this moralism was subject to becoming indistinguishable from NSC-68. In the short run, these irreconciled tensions between interdependence and containment complicated an already deteriorating Soviet-American relationship. In the longer run, they were reflected in most other aspects of the Carter administration's foreign policy as well.

CARTER AND THE WORLD

The context of Soviet-American relations for the Carter administration was considerably more complicated than that confronting the last Democratic president who assumed office after a Republican ascendancy. John Kennedy found the cold war oppressively in place in 1961. Indeed, he all but exulted in the challenge to the American purpose presented by that stony prospect. Jimmy Carter, on the other hand, inherited a relationship still in the process of redefinition following the radical changes accompanying America's post-Vietnam retrenchment and the Soviet Union's achievement of strategic parity with the United States. SALT negotiations were moving forward, but Soviet-American consensus on relations beyond arms control was lacking. Furthermore, American domestic support for either SALT or more importantly, detente, was extremely fragile. In addition, there was the now chronic dependence on Middle Eastern oil and the nagging sense that that region was once again headed for war unless the diplomatic momentum of the period after the 1973 war could be regained. But notwithstanding the desire of many in the Carter administration to refocus American diplomacy on these and other interdependence issues, the Soviet-American nexus could not be displaced.

There seemed to be a general desire for better Soviet-American relations and especially an extension of the SALT process, but there was also an undercurrent of skepticism as to whether the detente atmosphere of the early 1970s could be regenerated or was even worth the effort. Continuing Soviet activism in Africa made it clear that they entertained a different conception of detente than the United States. Furthermore, there was growing concern about the balance of Soviet-American military capability, as critics of SALT and the balance of forces in central Europe warned ominously of Soviet superiority within a decade, a superiority that would surely be used to extract advantages from the United States. Such criticism was especially intense in the Senate where, of course, any SALT II treaty would have to be ratified and could be blocked by a coalition of conservative Democrats and Republicans numbering only thirty-four — a number deemed well within the grasp of Senator Jackson, who was regarded as the leader of the anti-SALT and antidetente forces in the Senate. Apart from whatever uncertainties, ambivalence, or conflicting policy approaches there were in the Carter administration, these domestic political factors served as powerful and active constraints on the development of Carter's policies.

SALT

There were, as we have seen, important differences in perspective coexisting within the new administration. On the question of strategic arms control, however, there was a degree of consensus — the Carter administration wanted to move rapidly to conclude a SALT II agreement. Such a step was consistent with the president's oft-repeated desire for arms reductions and defense expenditure cuts. Like Kissinger and Nixon before him, SALT seemed the only readily available means to limit Soviet force structure expansion. In addition, the SALT I agreement was due to expire in October of 1977. Finally, the Ford administration had left behind fifty pages of draft treaty text already agreed to by the Soviets. In fact, it was widely believed that the only issues left to negotiate were problems associated with the Soviet's newly developed "Backfire" bomber — thought by some in the West to possess strategic capability — and the Americans' cruise missiles which, because of technological developments since Vladivostok, could now be deployed in considerable numbers on virtually any air, land, or sea-based platform. They might also be easily deployed by the United States in Europe or transferred to the West Europeans for their own use. Finally, their small size presented significant verification problems given their easy concealment.

By late March the administration was prepared to reopen negotiations on SALT II.[24] However, when Secretary of State Vance met with the Soviets in Moscow, the United States proposed a much more far-ranging agreement than had been negotiated within the Vladivostok guidelines. The Vladivostok guidelines placed equal ceilings on strategic delivery vehicles and MIRVed launchers at the relatively high levels already programmed by or acceptable to the Soviet and American military establishments. In contrast, the new Carter comprehensive package called for significant cuts in total forces and MIRVed launchers, but also proposed ceilings on MIRVed ICBM launchers that would have cut deeply into the muscle of Soviet forces. The Carter administration's proposal has been judged to have been a major departure in the strategic arms limitations process.[25] For the first time a proposal was advanced that would have meant significant reductions in the capability of both sides as well as limiting the modernization of strategic arsenals. The Soviet Union, however, brusquely dismissed the plan, charging that with its proposed deep cuts in ICBM numbers, the proposal was designed to extract unilateral advantage for the United States, since it was precisely by means of ICBM numbers and the size of Soviet warheads that the Soviet Union had achieved strategic parity with the United States. The Soviets insisted that negotiations return to the framework developed during the preceding 5 years.

In May the United States brought forth another suggestion that sought to break the new impasse that had emerged. First the United States would accept a treaty to run until 1985, based on the Vladivostok ceilings as a starting point, though the United States made it clear that it would pursue lower levels. Second, the two sides would develop a protocol to the treaty that would run for 3 years and cover all the systems and issues, such as cruise missiles, Backfire bombers, limits on new ICBMs such as mobile ICBMs, and qualitative restraints which the two sides could not negotiate into the treaty itself. Finally, a set of mutually agreed principles would be negotiated to apply to subsequent talks; in effect, agreeing in advance on the agenda for SALT III. It was recognized that the October deadline was not likely to be met, but the two sides agreed to observe the ceilings imposed under the 1972 agreement, and proceeded with what would prove to be a laborious 2½-year process of negotiations culminating in a treaty and protocol signed by Presidents Carter and Brezhnev at Vienna on June 18, 1979.

The treaty signed at Vienna was in fact much closer to the American comprehensive package than might have been expected in March of 1977. The overall ceilings were higher than those desired by the United States: 2250 strategic delivery vehicles, 1320 of which could be MIRVed. However, subceilings on MIRVed ICBMs and SLBMs were agreed to, and many of the issues that had been thought likely to be included in the protocol for subsequent negotiations (such as modernization controls, new ICBM developments, and qualitative limits, e.g., limits on the number of warheads that could be deployed on MIRVed launch vehicles) were actually incorporated into the treaty. Only some of the issues involving the cruise missile and the Backfire bomber remained outside the treaty but within the protocol or other understandings incorporated under the Vienna package.

Yet when the treaty and protocol were submitted to the Senate for ratification in the summer of 1979, it was clear that the treaty was in deep trouble. Notwithstanding an elaborate public relations campaign undertaken by the Carter administration, the hearings before the Senate Foreign Relations Committee revealed substantial opposition to the agreements. Objections included the familiar arguments that SALT II, like SALT I before it, did nothing to eliminate the Soviet lead in large ICBMs; doubts about whether the United States could verify key provisions of the treaty in view of the loss of intelligence facilities resulting from the fall of the Shah's regime in Iran in early 1979; and concern that acceptance of the treaty would lull the American people into complacency about what many Senators saw as the growing threat of Soviet strategic superiority.

The administration responded to these questions on the treaty. But in the course of the hearings and debate, it was revealed by the administration that intelligence data suggested the presence in Cuba of about 2600 Soviet combat troops with their equipment. Even staunch supporters of SALT II demanded that the president do something about the situation, although it was generally known that Soviet troops had been on the island for the preceding 17 years, and it was not clear how a brigade of less than 3000 men with no amphibious transport constituted a threat to the United States. The fact that such an issue could command such attention, bring the treaty ratification process to a virtual halt, and require a presidential address to the nation was an indication that far more than a strategic arms control agreement was being debated in the United States in late 1979.

The Final Decline of Detente

Signs of trouble were apparent at the very outset of the Carter administration, as the Soviets complained privately and then publicly about the human rights policy of the administration. The president professed not to be concerned and wrote a sympathetic letter to the most well-known Soviet dissident, Andrei Sakharov. The week before the Moscow meeting in which the comprehensive SALT II package was to be presented, however, Brezhnev complained that the tone and thrust of the administration's policies constituted interference in Soviet internal affairs. The Soviet rejection of the administration's SALT package was undoubtedly based on objections to the proposal's contents, especially when they seemed to deviate so markedly from what had been negotiated previously. Nonetheless, the atmosphere surrounding a deteriorating detente had clearly not improved with the arrival of the new administration.

In the meantime, events in Africa continued as an irritant in Soviet-

American relations. In February 1977, a Marxist regime seized control of Ethiopia and, while seeking assistance from the Russians, undertook full scale war against Somalia over the latter's territorial claims in the Ogaden region of Ethiopia. The Soviets were initially in a difficult position, for they had previously supported the Somalis, but by the fall of the year the Soviets had aligned themselves with the Ethiopians and had begun providing military assistance, including the dispatch of thousands of Cuban troops. Earlier, in March, both Fidel Castro and then Soviet President Podgorny had visited the southern African "front-line states" and Castro visited Ethiopia and Somalia as well. Also in March, Zaire's resource rich Shaba province was invaded by a rebel group operating out of Angola. The invasion was turned back after the insertion of some 1500 Moroccan troops and additional U.S. military assistance.

By early 1978, however, relations had become even more strained, not only regarding Africa but also with respect to Carter's human rights policy. Early in the year the United States and the Soviet Union exchanged warnings concerning each other's actions, with the Soviets asserting that the U.S. attitude on arms control and other issues was unhelpful, and the United States responding that Soviet actions in Africa threatened relations. In May, yet another invasion of Zaire was launched from Angola, with the president charging that Cubans were involved. The United States responded with an airlift of French, Belgian, and Moroccan troops, and by June the situation was once again calm. Simultaneously, however, the Soviets had placed on trial a number of prominent dissidents, all of whom were convicted and sentenced to prison terms. Congress passed joint resolutions deploring the trials as Carter announced that Soviet-American exchange programs would be reevaluated and the sale of high technology to the Soviet Union would receive closer scrutiny and be subjected to tighter controls than in the past. In mid-July 1978, as two American newspapermen were being convicted of having libeled Soviet television and ordered to pay fines, the president canceled the sale of computer equipment to the Soviet Union.

Undoubtedly even more alarming from a Soviet perpective, however, was the culmination of the American-Chinese rapprochment begun by Nixon. In late May, after Soviet attempts to improve relations with the Chinese had broken down, Brzezinski visited China to discuss SALT and normalization. Upon his return to Washington, the sale of technology (in this case infra-red scanning equipment) previously denied the Russians was approved for the Chinese. Throughout the remainder of the year, a parade of high U.S. officials went to China to discuss scientific exchanges and assistance, energy, and agriculture. Finally, in December 1978, after the Chinese had provided assurances to the United States concerning the future status of Taiwan, normal diplomatic relations were established and official ties with Taiwan broken, including the Mutual Defense Treaty between the United States and Taiwan. By early spring of 1979 Deputy Prime Minister Deng Xiaoping was visiting Washington to sign scientific and cultural agreements but, more provocatively from a Soviet standpoint, issuing stern lectures to American audiences concerning the threat posed by Soviet imperialism and "hegemonism."

Midway through Carter's term, therefore, there was little left of the detente that the Nixon administration had sought to construct. The demise of detente was well underway by the time Carter came to the White House, but by mid-1978 he was warning the Soviets in language reminiscent of an earlier time: "The Soviet Union can choose either confrontation or cooperation. The United States is prepared to meet either choice."[26] In fact very little remained except the common interest in a SALT agreement. Against a backdrop of increasingly cool relations along virtually every other dimension of contact, the last details of the treaty were worked out in early 1979 and the treaty submitted to the Senate at mid-year. By that time, however, SALT had become the last salient vestige and symbol of a policy of detente that was — in the minds of many, perhaps a majority, in the Senate — a thoroughly discredited approach to dealing with Soviet power. Moreover, for many of these same skeptics and opponents of SALT and detente, the debate and ratification vote were nothing less than a vote on the Carter administration itself.

The domestic reaction against Carter's stewardship of American policy set in almost immediately upon his assuming office. Carter had, of course, come to the presidency promising to reduce defense spending and he immediately cut the Ford defense budget by about $2.8 billion. However, he also announced that he wanted to reevaluate the need for procuring the new B-1 strategic bomber, which was nearing completion of its development. His appointment of Paul Warnke, a noted advocate of detente and arms control as his chief SALT negotiator, also provoked the more hard-line critics of American policy. But perhaps even more important was the president's apparent willingness to adopt a restrained posture towards Soviet policy in Africa, even as Ambassador Young articulated in forceful language his heretical views concerning the character of third world revolutionary activity.

In addition, Carter's seeming inconsistencies lent support to the growing impression among those who wanted a harder and more uncompromising line towards the Soviet Union, that this president was not the man for the job. Thus in early 1978, after urging the West Europeans to accept deployment of the enhanced radiation or neutron bomb, Carter reversed course and deferred a production decision. For those Europeans, such as Prime Minister Helmut Schmidt in Germany, who had expended considerable political capital building support for the weapon, the reversal was a rude shock. For those in the United States who wanted to see a buildup of U.S. military capability, the decision was very nearly outrageous, especially when combined with what were deemed by them to be overly limited increases in defense spending by the United States. Moreover, Carter even took the unusual step in August of 1978 of vetoing a Defense Department appropriation authorization bill when Congress included in it funds for a nuclear powered aircraft carrier that the president had not requested.

The severing of relations with Taiwan necessary for the reestablishment of normal relations with the People's Republic and the playing of the China card against the Russians further incensed conservative critics of the administration. Conservatives and long-time supporters of Nationalist China refused to accept the president's rationale that the step was but the culmination of Richard Nixon's geopolitical balancing of Soviet power. No less galling to most conservatives was Carter's advocacy, signing, and active support in the Senate for treaties to return the Panama Canal Zone back to the sovereignty of Panama. The United States retained operating rights over the canal and as the result of understandings and reservations to the agreements increased its security access to the canal; but to its opponents, the treaties were a giveaway of what Republican presidential hopeful Ronald Reagan insisted upon calling "our canal." Here again, the president's view—that the treaty was the fulfillment of a diplomatic initiative originally undertaken in the Johnson administration, pursued by his Republican successors, and, in any event, was essential to establishing a more sensitive and responsive relationship with Latin America — was to no avail.

The Camp David Summit:
An Ambiguous Breakthrough

President Carter was able to deflect, for a time, this building resentment with his temporarily successful mediation of the Egyptian-Israeli peacemaking process at Camp David in late 1978. But even here, the initiative was not the president's and the results proved far less certain than the president's rhetoric at the signing of the agreements suggested.

There was initially, in the Middle East, an attempt by the Carter administration to draw the Soviets into the negotiating process between Israel and its neighbors. The negotiating framework proposed was multilateral negotiations in Geneva co-chaired by the United States and the Soviet Union. The Carter administration reasoned that no settlement would be lasting if the Soviets could always act the role of spoiler. The explicit tone of Kissinger's policy, which was designed to expel the Soviets from the Middle East, would, therefore, be reshaped. The melody that the Carter administration now whistled beckoned the Soviets back into the region in an effort to make their would-be proxies and clients in the Arab world — especially the Syrians, Libyans, and the Palestine Liberation Organization — more susceptible to an accord. But the lyrics of the song did not speak of any rewards to the Soviets apart from those of the psyche: mere acknowledgement of some residual Russian interests and influence by the Americans, who would continue to hold most of the cards. In sum, as in the early Nixon years, the Soviets were once again called to be of assistance in their own containment.

The astonishing announcement and subsequent trip of President Anwar Sadat of Egypt to Jerusalem in November 1977 for the purpose of opening a direct dialogue between Egypt and Israel, unhinged American policy. Sadat, fearing precisely a superpower designed and imposed settlement, moved to establish a negotiating process in which he would have maximum control of the agenda, minimum Soviet involvement, and, by encouraging American intermediation, the benefit of whatever credits he had accumulated in Washington following his dramatic ouster of the Soviets in 1972 and his generally pro-American stance since the 1973 war and Kissinger's shuttle diplomacy. Sadat would thereby represent not only his own interests, but if successful, would seize leadership of the Arab camp. In the meantime, the rest of the Arab world reacted with dismay and hostility as the largest Arab state set out on its own, ostensibly in pursuit of common interests, but initially proposing a permanent end to Egyptian-Israeli hostilities and hence, though Sadat would deny it repeatedly, pursuing a separate peace with Israel.

The Soviets would be pushed not only away from center stage but almost out of the theater. Sadat, was, however, perilously poised, extending himself like some over-aged trapeze artist to an initially confused and even indifferent American assistant. The Carter administration, like much of the rest of the world, was knocked off stride by Sadat's initiative. Their planning had all reflected a great-power solution. But Sadat initiative had its advantages — Soviet displacement — and its desired effect: the road toward a Middle East settlement via Geneva and Soviet participation was abandoned.

The American grip was breathtakingly late. But once in hand, a new "island of stability" — at a cost of up to $10 billion in economic and military assistance to Egypt — was to be established. There were other diplomatic costs, however, for in supporting what other Arab states regarded as treasonous behavior on Sadat's part, American diplomatic credibility in the region was diminished. Apparently, however, the Carter administration reasoned that if by using the opportunity presented by Sadat's boldness, a settlement could be reached, the rest of the Arabs, the Palestinians, and even the Russians, confronted with a *fait accompli,* would in time accept.

After months of negotiations between Sadat and Israeli Prime Minister Menachem Begin produced no diplomatic breakthroughs, however, President Carter in early September 1978, convened a tripartite summit at Camp David, Maryland.[27] For eight days between September 5th and 13th, the president, with the assistance of Secretary of State Vance, served as a personal mediator trying to narrow differences for an Egyptian-Israeli peace treaty and what came to be known as a "Framework for Peace in the Middle East" within which detailed negotiations on the Palestinian issue might proceed. As always, the issue of Palestinian rights proved most difficult and very nearly led to the collapse of the talks. In the final analysis, however, President Carter's persistence won a compromise on the Palestinian issue with which Sadat and Begin could live: (1) provisions for the establishment of some form of elected self-governing Palestinian authority, (2) withdrawal of the Israeli occupation forces on the West Bank, and (3) negotiations concerning the final status of whatever Palestinian political entity was eventually formed out of the West Bank and Gaza.

Leaving aside the drama surrounding the negotiations and the fanfare with which the peace treaty and "framework for peace" were announced, it is important to underscore that nothing final was settled at Camp David. Rather it was at most an attempt to get serious negotiations under way. Apart from whatever short-term domestic benefits accrued to President Carter, the ultimate success of the Camp David process would depend on the diplomatic follow-up to the summit.

Moreover, though the Camp David improvisation was masterful and courageous, it was also expensive and fraught with dangers. For by excluding the Russians yet again in an area of traditional concern to them, it pinned the most radical Middle Eastern groups and states closer than ever to the Soviets. It is also not unlikely that the Soviet's worst fears concerning the Carter administration's acceptance of the Soviet Union's new international status were confirmed by the diplomatic maneuvering in 1977–1978. The reaction was summarized by State Department Soviet expert Dr. Marshall Shulman in October of 1979:

> The action of President Sadat in going to Jerusalem and the development of a bilateral negotiations between Egypt and Israel has had the practical effect of excluding the Soviet Union from effective participation in the negotiating process. They bear this very resentfully and have spoken of it quite sharply many times. . . . It clearly is the situation that the Soviet position in

the Middle East has deteriorated compared to what it was. That has been the outcome of diplomatic efforts on our part.[28]

But if the Soviets had been shoved aside once again, American diplomacy, as in 1973 and 1974, proved insufficient in itself to bring about a resolution of the Arab-Israeli dispute. Carter, like Kissinger before him, found it easier to get agreement and action by Israel and Egypt concerning territorial questions associated with their bilateral peace treaty, such as Israeli withdrawal from most of the Sinai still held by the Israelis after the 1973-1974 round of negotiations, return of oil producing facilities in the Sinai and the Red Sea to the Egyptians, return of the Gaza area with its large Palestinian refugee population to Egyptian sovereignty, and the reestablishment of normal diplomatic relations between Cairo and Tel Aviv. But on the central question of a Palestinian homeland and its political status, there was little progress.

The framework for negotiating some measure of Palestinian autonomy developed at Camp David proved to be a point of diplomatic contention rather than an agreed agenda for action. Notwithstanding more or less constant American intermediation as well as direct Egyptian-Israeli talks throughout 1979 and early 1980, agreement proved elusive. Indeed, the Begin government, in the face of increasingly militant West Bank Palestinian reaction to the Camp David accords and continuous Jewish settlement in previously Arab areas, reaffirmed and expanded its support of Jewish settlement by groups of Jewish militants who denied any legitimate Arab rights on the West Bank. By mid-1980, open clashes between West Bank Arabs and these Jewish militants were becoming common place, and disagreements within the Begin government concerning settlement policy and the negotiations had broken into the open. Foreign Minister Moshe Dayan and Defense Minister Ezer Weizmann — both regarded as moderates on the Palestine question — resigned from the Begin government. Israeli-Egyptian talks stalemated, agreed deadlines for beginning the autonomy process passed, and with the stalemate, the Carter administration was confronted with the possibility that the West Europeans were about to launch their own diplomatic initiative for a resolution of the Middle East situation. Such a move would further emphasize the disarray in the alliance and the lack of European confidence in Carter's leadership. It was also widely assumed that given European dependence upon Arab oil and the West European contention that no lasting settlement could be reached without Palestinian participation in negotiations, whatever proposals the Europeans might advance would likely be far more pro-Palestinian than could be acceptable to a Carter administration facing a difficult presidential election season.

Thus as Carter's reelection effort began, what he had hoped could be advanced as decisive proof of his diplomatic skill — a genuine Middle East peace — seemed as far away as ever. He now found himself positioned between two weakening and hence, inflexible partners within the region: the Begin government, torn internally by reaction to its West Bank settlement policy and the raging Israeli inflation fed in large measure by military spending; and Sadat, who found himself more and more isolated as he and his American benefactors proved unable to deliver the diplomatic breakthrough assumed to have been inherent in Sadat's courageous Jerusalem pilgrimage and the Camp David process. Furthermore, the entire structure of American policy was now being subjected to pressure from a new quarter: the West Europeans, concerned about their own economic interests in the region and the seeming inability of American diplomacy to protect those interests.

A return to Egyptian-Israeli belligerence seemed unlikely. The removal of Egyptian military capability from any potential Arab military coalition and the realignment of the Egyptians with the United States was an important, even fundamental change in the Middle Eastern strategic situation. Moreover, war between Iraq and Iran and military confrontation between Syria and Jordan at the end of 1980 further underscored the Moslem world's inability to unite to meet the Israeli nemesis. But Carter's rhetoric after Camp David seemed to promise much more than the continued isolation of the Soviets from the region and ambiguous geopolitical shifts in the Middle Eastern strategic equation. Furthermore, the uncertainties rather than accomplishments were underscored by the caveat that nearly everyone attached to analysis of the Camp David process: Consolidation of what had been achieved and progress within the Camp David process depended largely on Sadat's retention of power in Egypt — a condition that could prove increasingly problematical unless the Camp David process yielded both the international and internal developmental benefits foreseen and promised by Sadat when he undertook his momentous 1977 trip to Jerusalem.

One could not be sure that the Camp David framework was itself sufficient. For even if a major breakthrough in Egyptian-Israeli negotiations could be achieved, it was always unclear how the Palestinians and Arab states were to be incorporated into the agreement. In this respect the initial position of the Carter administration in 1977 may have made more sense. For in its diplomatic overtures to the Palestinians and its apparent commitment to multilateral negotiations that would have included Palestinian representation at Geneva in some form, Carter was developing a framework that might have been more readily perceived as legitimate by all parties in the region. The Camp David process, in addition to cutting the Soviets out of the action, seemed to preclude this necessary contact with the Palestinians and other Arabs.

Finally, in addition to the Palestinian homeland/autonomy question, there remained the issue of Jerusalem's status. That Jerusalem should be again free of Israeli control seemed crucial to the Saudi Arabians and all other Arab states. However, their aspirations seemed unlikely to be fulfilled as the Israeli Knesset passed legislation in mid-1980 to make Jerusalem the permanent capital of Israel. Moreover, as these and other issues (such as outstanding territorial issues regarding Jordan, Syria and even Lebanon) dragged on, no one in the Carter administration (or among his political adversaries) could offer ideas as to the next step. And, of course, the longer the impasse persisted, the more likely it became that Arab West Bank militancy would continue to develop in the direction of more of the violence that had emerged by the end of the 1970s. Indeed, by mid-1980, the spectre of PLO *and* extremist Israeli nationalist terrorism appeared as Arab attacks on Israeli settlements elicited extremist Israeli retaliations in the form of attacks on West Bank Arab leaders. If such violence escalated the United States could find itself caught between Sadat's rhetorical support for the Palestinians and the Israeli need to suppress the violence. Moreover, such instability could provide opportunities for increased Russian influence. The signing of a 20-year friendship treaty by Syrian President Assad and the Russians in late 1980, for example, provided access for the Russians. The Soviet Union, it seemed, almost like some adolescent Romeo, was available to any client who would accept its advances. And overarching the entire situation remained the possibility of some reapplication of the oil weapon with all that that implied not only for the American economy but the political economy of the NATO alliance and the industrialized world.

Nicaragua and Iran

Whatever domestic political respite Carter received for undertaking this tactically impressive act of summit diplomacy was brief, for long-standing American clients on opposite sides of the world were toppling. In 1978 and 1979, in Nicaragua Anastazio Somoza's regime grudgingly and then violently gave way before a coalition of Marxist revolutionaries, the Sandinista National Liberation Front, in coalition with a broad-based collection of opposition groups within the country. The American posture was to withhold support for Somoza and push him towards a mediated settlement. The effort failed and after another 6 months of fighting, the Somoza regime collapsed in mid-1979, with the Carter administration moving quickly to recognize the new revolutionary government and support with economic assistance its efforts to achieve economic viability.

The refusal to support Somoza represented something of a departure in American policy in Latin America. But though it conformed to the policy approach preferred by interdependence advocates, it was disturbing to traditionalists. The collapse of the 25-year American investment in Iran was even more dramatic evidence, for those longing for the more simple era of pre-Vietnam and preparity American hegemony, of the bankruptcy of the Carter administration's foreign policy.

Throughout 1978 what had been assumed to be the unshakeable regime of Shah Mohammed Reza Pahlavi and, hence, the surrogate for American interests in the Persian Gulf area, slowly disintegrated in the face of increasingly violent demonstrations and rioting. Beneath the religious rhetoric concerning the immorality of the modernization programs pursued by the Shah was deep and intense resentment of a regime that was perceived as illegitimate and only the extension and instrument of American control. By the fall, the religious leader, the Ayatollah Ruhollah Khomeini, exiled from Iran for 15 years, was calling from Paris for demonstrations to bring down the Shah and for the institution of an Islamic Republic that would expel the United States and its influence. Strikes shut down the oil industry in November, and by the end of the year virtually all sectors of the economy were paralyzed in response to the Ayatollah's urging. By early January 1979 the Shah was expressing his willingness to take a "vacation" once a new government appointed by him was in power. Within a week the United States government — after considering a coup d'etat[29] — endorsed his leaving, and on January 16 the Shah departed on a desultory journey that would take him to Egypt, Morocco, the Bahamas, Mexico, Panama, and finally Egypt again, in search of a place of exile. In the meantime, the Ayatollah returned to Tehran and despite the existence of a civilian government, he and his Revolutionary Council assumed power.

Within Iran months of revolutionary turmoil ensued as the religious militants consolidated their control of the revolution and, in the face of rebellions among Kurds, Baluchis, and other ethnic minorities, prepared for parliamentary elections and the promulgation of an Islamic constitution. American policy at this juncture was ambivalent. There did seem to be a willingness on the part of the Carter administration to wait for a subsiding of the revolutionary disorder and in the interim try to work with whatever government emerged while maintaining contact with presumably the most pro-American elements on the Iranian scene. Thus, for example, in early October the Defense Department announced that it was resuming the shipment of spare parts for American aircraft previously sold to the Shah.

This American search for a moderate center proved to be a profound misunderstanding of what was occurring within Iran. The religious hierar-chy with its deep hatred and resentment of the Shah and his American benefactors was in control of the revolution despite the presence of a government that seemed to give the impression of working towards more normal relations with the United States. The magnitude of this misunder-standing of the internal situation in Iran became dramatically apparent in late October when President Carter, reportedly yielding to pressure from former Secretary of State Henry Kissinger and David Rockefeller, admit-ted the Shah to the United States for cancer treatment.

The effect inside Iran was electric. On November 4, militant students seized the U.S. embassy in Tehran and made hostages of some sixty Ameri-cans in the embassy compound. They would be released, the militants told the world through the hundreds of media representatives that converged to cover the seizure and the massive demonstrations that accompanied it, only if the Shah and the wealth he had taken from Iran were returned. Subsequently, the militants released the women and black hostages, but insisted that the remainder would be held until their demands were met and/or the Ayatollah ordered otherwise. The Ayatollah, however, gave full support to the militants and threatened to put the hostages on trial.

With the Ayatollah and his militant Revolutionary Council now in control, the Carter administration found it virtually impossible to carry out negotiations. A United Nations Security Council resolution and Inter-national Court of Justice ruling that the seizure was illegal and demanding the immediate release of the hostages were obtained. Moreover, a United Nations mediation attempt was undertaken under the secretary general's auspice even as some economic and diplomatic sanctions were being ap-plied. None of the efforts gained anything, however, but the Islamic Republic's defiance and a reiteration of the demands for the Shah's return. Finally, on April 24–25 (to the dismay of Secretary of State Cyrus Vance, who was trying to negotiate even more stringent economic sanctions with the Common Market countries and Japan against Iran — a condition of which was that the United States would not use force), Carter ordered a rescue attempt involving helicopters, C-130 aircraft, and commandoes from a special antiterrorist unit. The rescue attempt failed disastrously as equipment failures at the desert strike base led to a decision to abort the mission, followed by the collision of a helicopter and a C-130 aircraft. Eight crewmen died, their bodies then ghoulishly displayed by the Irani-ans. The United States government and people could only wonder in frustrated consternation what, if any, instruments of power could now be brought to bear.

Apart from the collapse of the Pahlavi regime itself, what outraged conservatives in the United States was the seeming reluctance and then inept use of American military power by Carter in support of the Shah and afterwords. Whether military capability was relevant to the crisis is an issue to which we will turn below. However, Carter's performance during the crisis was noteworthy for its apparent indecisiveness. When the crisis broke, the president was not prepared to extend unequivocal support to a man he had earlier toasted as an "island of stability" and for the remarkable "respect and admiration and love which your people give to you." In fact, he mixed public statements of support with ambivalence concerning the positioning of a naval task force in the region. Later, Carter sent the task force, but when the Shah suggested his own withdrawal, the administration seemed to encourage him. Finally, of course, there was the embarrassing failure of the rescue mission itself. For those who had come to question the president's leadership it was the quintessential example of what one proponent of using military force in the region called an "America in decline."[30] The president, however, as his poll ratings declined, asserted that matters were now under "better control" and returned to the campaign activities he had earlier forsworn until the hostages were returned.

Another Decade . . . Another Doctrine

By the end of the decade, therefore, policies that the President liked to characterize as involving "a combination of adequate American strength, of quiet self-restraint in the use of it, of a refusal to believe in the inevitability of war and of a patient and persistent development of all the peaceful alternatives . . .,"[31] were being rejected by a vocal and increasingly influential segment of the policy establishment. Indeed, that organ of the establishment, *Foreign Affairs,* gave the lead article of its retrospective evaluation of 1979 to a critic who judged Carter foreign policy to have been a "failure" burdened by its "self-inflicted wounds."[32] Moreover, as the decade turned into an election year, the president was confronted by poll after poll which showed diminishing popular confidence in his foreign policy leadership and the likelihood that if the election had been held in mid-1980, he would have lost to his Republican adversary.

Confronted with these political facts the president had already begun to move toward his critics' position. As it became apparent, for example, that the SALT treaty was in trouble, Mr. Carter expressed a willingness to increase defense spending at both the conventional and strategic levels. Furthermore, when in November, the U.S. embassy in Tehran was seized, the president, while rejecting the immediate use of force, increased the American naval presence in the Indian Ocean and began planning a permanent military presence in the region. By early 1980 more than twenty naval vessels, including two aircraft carriers, were stationed in the Arabian Sea. However, it was not the hostage crisis or the travails of SALT alone that led to the crystallization of a new posture on the part of the Carter administration. Rather, on December 26, 1979, the Soviet Union launched an invasion by upwards of 80,000 men into Afghanistan in support of a pro-Soviet coup directed against a Marxist regime whose leader, Hafizullah Amin, was proving both unable to control an Islamic insurgency but also pursuing an increasingly independent line from that preferred by Moscow. By the 27th of December 1979, Amin was dead and it was apparent within the next few weeks that the Soviets intended to stay in Afghanistan in force until a pro-Soviet regime was firmly in place. The reaction in Washington recalled the deep days of crisis in the 5 years after World War II.

The SALT treaty was withdrawn by the president. Though there were ritual references to the need to pass the treaty, the administration's rhetoric was now predominantly that of confrontation. The last orphan of detente was to be consigned to the attic, its presence too embarrassing for a president who now asserted that the United States ". . . must pay whatever price is required to remain the strongest nation in the world."[33] Just before the Afghanistan invasion, the secretary of defense had warned, "We must decide now whether we intend to remain the strongest nation in the world. Or we must accept now that we will let ourselves slip into inferiority, into a position of weakness in a harsh world where principles unsupported by power are victimized, and that we will become a nation with more of a past than a future."[34] Afterwards, in his State of the Union Address, Carter claimed that in "a world of major power confrontation . . . We have a new will at home to do what is required to keep us the strongest nation on earth."[35] What was "required" in Carter's view was a defense budget some 5 percent larger than the previous year and proposed future spending on defense that would lead to about 5 percent per year through the middle of the decade.[36]

No less important, the security interests and commitments to which these resources were to be committed had now grown. There remained, of course, the traditional European and Asian commitments which, in the president's words, "would be automatically triggered." Now, however, there was the Persian Gulf and its oil:

> The denial of these oil supplies — to us or to others — would threaten our security and provoke an economic crisis greater than that of the Great Depression 50 years ago, with a fundamental change in the way we live.
>
> Twin threats to the flow of oil — from regional instability and now potentially from the Soviet Union — require that we firmly defend our vital interests when threatened.[37]

Accordingly, the administration established a rapid deployment force to be capable, when fully developed at middecade, to move anywhere from a few ships to as many as 100,000 men anywhere in the world, but especially into the Persian Gulf region. Much of their equipment was to be pre-positioned on storage ships permanently stationed in the Indian Ocean. The troops, if and when needed, would be rapidly deployed by air into bases access to which was to be negotiated with countries in the region. Finally in the fall of 1980, as war raged between Iraq and Iran at the head of the Persian Gulf, the Carter administration responded to a Saudi Arabian request for aid by deploying an AWACS air defense aircraft and ground support personnel in Saudi Arabia. In addition, the American naval presence in the Persian Gulf itself was increased. A Carter Doctrine was born and baptized.

Nor was the buildup to be concentrated solely on the Persian Gulf. Modernization of NATO was to proceed, including the introduction of a new main battle tank for U.S. forces, a new fighter aircraft, the F-16, and an expansion of the ability of NATO to launch nuclear weapons against the Soviet Union in the form of a new Pershing II missile to be supplemented by ground launched cruise missiles. Strategically, the MX missile, a mobile ICBM with three times the number of warheads and throwweight and twice the accuracy of the Minuteman III, and the new Trident SLBM and submarines would all be fully deployed by the end of the decade, giving the United States the capacity to threaten the Soviets ICBMs where some 70 percent of their deliverable warheads were deployed in 1980. Talk of "nuclear war fighting" and "victory" in a nuclear war became commonplace. Subsequently, a new American targeting doctrine was announced which officially confirmed the intention of the United States to attack hardened Soviet targets. Finally, and perhaps most ominously from a Soviet standpoint, observers of the evening news were treated to the extraordinary sight at midyear of a Chinese communist defense official standing shoulder-to-shoulder with an American secretary of defense in the halls of the Pentagon and announcing that the United States would begin the sale of "nonlethal" military hardware to the Chinese. Combat equipment, the Chinese official noted, would not be made available "at this time."

FACING THE LIMITS

In its initial formulation, therefore, the Carter Doctrine had about it the kind of open-ended and globalist character that the first of the many cold war doctrines contained. In Southwest Asia the pledge as well as the region to which it was directed were filled with uncertainties. "You are not alone," Brzezinski told refugees at the Kyber Pass in early 1980. Facing

Soviet-occupied Afghanistan with an automatic weapon in hand, he exhorted, "You will go back to your villages and your mosques. Your cause is just. God is on your side."[38] The Almighty, the Americans, and the disaffected Afghan mountain people might form a league against atheistic Southwest Asian communism. But neither the petropowers nor the middle-range powers of Europe or even Pakistan were eager to be enlisted in the new crusade. All the more reason to be grimly steadfast. For as a stern Brzezinski lectured television audiences during the latter half of 1980, Southwest Asia was now regarded as of no less strategic importance than had been Europe and East Asia during the early cold war years:

> I think it is important to remember that since WW II there first emerged the central strategic zone of Western Europe. The second central strategic zone for us was the Far East. In both places we have permanently stationed American forces. The third central strategic zone is southwest Asia, the Persian Gulf.... Iran, Turkey, to some extent Pakistan, Afghanistan as a buffer were the protective shield. That shield is now being pierced. As a consequence, our friends in the region and our vital interest in the third central strategic zone are beginning to be threatened. This is why this is becoming a strategic problem.[39]

Though Brzezinski recognized the need for using a different mix of foreign policy instruments in this new central strategic zone than had been employed elsewhere, America's buildup of military capability was the primary evidence of its new commitment. Moreover Brzezinski predicted that American involvement in the region would be prolonged, stretching for at least two or three decades into the future.[40] Thus the hard ground of confrontation stretched toward a horizon beyond vision. And if Brzezinski's rhetoric on the Afghan border is translated into policy, then rollback and liberation may be conjoined with the newly invigorated nuclear threat. Carter and Brzezinski seemed to have found John Foster Dulles 300 miles from the Indian Ocean.

The Limits of Military Instruments

One reason that the Carter Administration turned towards a reemphasis of security policy was the fear that the visible presence of American firepower was fast becoming about as welcome and as valuable as a Susan B. Anthony dollar: a discounted coin of uncertain value would have to be either withdrawn from circulation or given special emphasis. This was clearly the case in the long Iranian ordeal, when American arms seemed irrelevant and when American promoted reform seemed a proximate (but certainly, in fact, not the only) cause of the Shah's collapse. As the one who once warmed the Peacock Throne flew off to exile, a pivotal assumption of at least the Kissinger years was challenged: American clients, no matter how well stocked militarily, could not be counted to remain semiautonomous agents of American interests. They could even become a foreign policy nemesis.

A defining characteristic of the Iranian crisis was the hesitance of American policy makers to use force or even to broach the subject openly. The gestures of support that were offered seemed out of a comic opera. A carrier force was ordered to the Persian Gulf from Subic Bay in the Philippines and then, after barely reaching the Straits of Malacca, directed to steam around in a desultory fashion. Equally frustrating was the fact that some of the United States' most dependable European clients refused to allow their NATO air bases to be used as staging areas for even a rescue squadron for the evacuation of American personnel.

American reluctance to use force and the unwillingness of its allies to even contemplate abetting its efforts is not understandable merely in terms of military incapacity. It can neither be simply attributed to a frayed post-Vietnam consensus or explained by a fear of Soviet intervention. A comprehensive explanation for American restrained, albeit clumsy, behavior must also include the realization that, quite simply, nobody in or outside the Carter administration could see what bearing force had to the political, religious, and social tensions tearing at the Pahlavi regime. Even if a quick strike team had entered Iran, no one could offer a reasonable scenario of what they might accomplish once they had arrived. In early 1978, as Iran sank into chaos, Secretary Brown despondently ruminated: "We are as yet unsure of the utility of U.S. military power in Persian Gulf contingencies."[41]

The Enlistment of Economic Interdependence

In part, in response to the obvious uncertainty concerning the relevance of military responses and the unmanageable elements of Carter's human rights campaigns, the administration turned to economic coercion. Perhaps, it was felt, economic preponderance could do what armies and threats could not. Ironically, however, this use, or misuse, of economic power came at the nadir of America's relative economic strength in this century. That is to say, the Carter administration had been unsuccessful in leading the industrialized world to the establishment of a comprehensive new international economic order. Much had been made of the initial attempt of the Carter administration to promote a series of economic summit conferences among the industrialized powers to coordinate their domestic economic policies. This reflected acceptance of the fact that these economies were now inextricably linked but also vulnerable to one another. However, within months it had become apparent that none of the industrialized powers were prepared to accept readily the kind of political risks that such coordination implied.

In the United States, for example, the Carter administration was confronted with a number of powerful economic interests demanding protection from, not an increase in, interdependence. The automobile industry — both management and labor — the steel industry, and portions of the home appliance industry were all pressuring the Carter administration to impose new quotas and/or tariffs to protect them from Japanese and European competition. The Europeans and Japanese, in turn, were critical of the inability or unwillingness of the United States to move decisively against its domestic inflation and thereby restore confidence in the dollar. And, of course, suffusing all of this international economic anxiety was the persistent vulnerability of developed and developing economies alike to rising prices for their energy imports from OPEC.

In short, interdependence had served to emphasize the conflicting needs and vulnerabilities of those caught in its web. This suggested in turn the need for sensitive and systematic coordination of policies. But for a Carter administration increasingly preoccupied with the Soviet-American and Iranian crises, a traditional emphasis on using economic relationships as instruments of coercion gradually assumed dominance. The irony of this was doubly intense because this administration had come to office rejecting such an approach to economic interdependence. Moreover, those officials responsible for the attempted enlistment of economic interdependence as an instrumentality of American confrontation with the Soviet Union and Iran, had been, in some instances, among the most forceful proponents of a new and more cooperative approach to managing interdependence before they assumed public office. Now, however, they were called upon to design and administer a kind of economic cold war. In truth, as many of them understood, economic warfare was an existential act: more a symbol of pique and a sop to domestic critics on the right than a realistic instrument to affect events.

In the case of the Soviet Union, it was argued that even if a cut-off of wheat, high technology, or phosphates hurt Americans as much as it did the Soviets, it was all for the better. For any step that involved a trivial cost to the United States would be treated unseriously by the Russians. Yet there were almost no specific commodities for which the United States was the most important supplier. In dollar terms, most American exports to the Soviet Union were agricultural. Even if the Russians could not find enough grain on the open market, there was little reason to believe they would not be able to survive the contretemps. In the end, they would obtain most of the grains they need from others or simply do without. And, there was no evidence that Europeans and Japanese suppliers and creditors would treat the Soviets in any manner other than business-as-usual.

If a convincing argument could be made that the Soviet Union and Eastern Europe had reached a point of strategic vulnerability *vis-a-vis* technological imports from the West, it still remained unclear how or whether such a vulnerability could be manipulated. Restraining credits would, at best, reduce the subsidy Western governments give their businesses to export to the Soviet Union. Tighter controls — if obtainable — would only increase the cost to the Russians of their own modernization. It would neither prevent it nor significantly retard it. And, attempts to restrict exports of some oil and gas equipment and technology would, at best, reduce the energy generating capacity of the Soviet Union, and perhaps give a kind of ironic incentive to any Russian urge to increase their stake in the Middle East. Further, a cutback on United States or European oil-related technology might leave Eastern Europe without Russian oil supplies and would force bloc countries to import more oil from OPEC; thereby further undermining Eastern Europe's hard currency–credit reserves as well as drawing down scarce financial resources necessary to purchase Western technology.

In the Iranian case, as well, there were important questions concerning the American use of economic leverage unanswered by an administration attempting to substitute economic warfare for military coercion. Clearly the boycott of Iranian oil was an effort to prevent Iran from blackmailing the United States over the hostages. But the application of financial pressure on Iran, begun with a freeze on Iranian financial assets in the West, could not be effective unless the rest of the industrialized world was enlisted in the American designed and led economic warfare. At the onset of the crisis with Iran, reports circulated that the Europeans might participate in limited measures, including even a slowing of trade with the Iranians. But they were reluctant to go much further. The Japanese were accused by American officials of moving with "unseemingly haste" to buy on the spot market Iranian oil previously intended for the United States. The Ohira government, having narrowly survived a parliamentary crisis during the fall of 1979, resisted having the almost totally import-dependent Japanese economy drafted into the American economic war against Iran. With about 15 percent of Japanese daily imports coming from Iran (in early 1980), Japanese sensitivity was or should have been predictable. Moreover, since the Japanese had been the primary target of the Ford and Carter administrations' attempts to get the rest of the industrialized world to relent in its export pressure on the American market, one suspects that there were not all that many American credits left in Tokyo. Moreover, disruption of the overall United States–Japanese economic relations seems scarcely worth the gains of economic warfare. Indeed, one wonders whether at some point American pressures on the Japanese to act against their economic self-interests, presaged by the "Nixon shocks" of the early 1970s, does not risk setting off a syndrome of Japanese hostility similar to that of the interwar period.

The Europeans Resist Conscription

The Carter administration's almost frantic attempts to fashion a new doctrine incorporating some combination of military and economic instruments raised a final and disturbing set of questions concerning the traditional core of American policy — the Atlantic community. The cold war, after all, had begun because of the fate of Europe and had been centered there for the most part. Throughout the period of European economic reconstruction, American ends and means had been ultimately — though sometimes reluctantly — accepted by the Europeans. By the late 1970s, however, European leaders, especially in the largest countries of the European community, were often brutal in their rejection and defiance of American leadership. Only with respect to the military dimensions of the alliance was there acceptance of American conceptions. But as the SALT process moved through the 1970s, there was an undercurrent of European worry that the United States' strategic concerns were ultimately not their own. By the onset of the 1980s, the Europeans had insisted upon and won from the Carter administration an American commitment to place in Europe a new generation of intermediate range nuclear weapons that could threaten the Soviet Union from Europe. Presumably this would counter the Soviets new tactical theater nuclear weapons, especially the SS-20 missile. It was understood that this step would complicate subsequent strategic arms limitations talks and negotiations concerning force reductions in central Europe. But in the late 1970s there seemed to be diminishing prospect that such negotiations would lead to significant results in any event. In the larger sense, however, the nagging fear persisted that at some point American strategic concerns and policy would be decoupled from Europe's.

On other matters the decoupling seemed already to have occurred, largely at European initiative. Thus the American attempt to conscript the Europeans into economic warfare against the Iranians and diplomatic isolation of the Russians was met with resistance and then outright defiance. Slowly and painfully throughout early 1980 the Common Market countries and Japan negotiated a series of economic sanctions that they might bring to bear on Iran. Perhaps in fear that unless they participated in some form of economic warfare, the Americans would attempt what, from a European perspective, would be a dangerously provocative use of military force in a region upon which they were vitally dependent for oil. But after the United States attempted precisely such an intervention, even this rationale for cooperation vanished. The British government of Prime Minister Margaret Thatcher could not command the support of even its own Conservative party, and the common European-Japanese position disintegrated. An independent European initiative on the Middle East was discussed within the European Community. The French lectured the new American secretary of state, Edmund Muskie, about the lack of coordination of diplomacy within the alliance and then, with studied cynicism, undertook their own unannounced summit with the Russians.

Reports circulated that throughout Europe there was a mixture of condescension and despair concerning the Carter administration's leadership capacity and the prospect of submitting the alliance to the winner of a Carter-Reagan presidential contest. An American reporter in Europe felt that the European mood was captured by a French satirical magazine which portrayed the differences between the likely American presidential contestants in terms of cross-sectional views of Reagan's and Carter's heads showing the former as empty and latter containing only a small peanut.

European concern and skepticism about the wisdom and constancy of American diplomacy was not new. The 1970s, however, saw somewhat greater willingness and capacity to articulate policies often in conflict with those of the United States. Certainly one would not view the institutional mechanisms of the European Community as being yet equal to the task of fashioning and sustaining a truly "European" diplomacy. At the same time, however, coordinated and coherent alliance policy on anything except perhaps elements of security policy, seemed a thing of the past. Even here difficulties seemed likely to multiply, especially if the major European states — France, Great Britain, and Germany — set out on some form of quasi-coordinated military cooperation involving the British and French nuclear forces coupled with cruise missile technology. Finally, if the next decade sees the continuation of the decline of American economic and diplomatic preponderance and the arrested state of development of European-wide institutions, then it is not inconceivable that the larger European political economies might well feel compelled to seek their independent resolution of the tensions of interdependence.

Conclusion

One by one, the means by which the Carter administration had, at first, wished to turn aside from the cold war proved vulnerable to the apparent immutability of the Soviet-American contest and the doctrines and commitments that have surrounded that conflict. By the beginning of 1980, the Soviet Union — once placed in an equivalent station with other global issues — reemerged as the pivotal focus of the Carter administration. With the Afghan crisis, an even more expansive series of undertakings was contemplated and formal overtures were tendered to an embarrassingly coquettish constellation of would-be satrapies in the Persian Gulf region. It could not be argued that Oman, Yemen, or Somalia were outposts of liberal values. But the cold war quandary of aligning with regimes of low repute and military advantage had, after all, been customary to just about everyone but Carter and some of his younger State Department advisors. Perhaps, after Afghanistan, the reproduction of personal animus in Soviet-American relations made it easier to yield scruple to necessity. Moreover, tired critics of an undifferentiated definition of American interests seemed to have spent their energies as cold war policy routines, shaped in an era when American power had been little contested, reappeared. It seemed reasonably clear that early advocates of interdependence and world order policies no longer controlled much of the Carter administration's image of international reality. On the other hand, it was by no means clear whether the attempt to marry somehow the more traditional conception of American interests with the ambiguous conditions of contemporary interdependence could serve as a guide for policy either.

In the tenth century, foreign ambassadors used to be called to Constantinople in order that they might be impressed with the military splendor of an enervated empire. There were, as Harold Nicholson once described:

> interminable reviews at which the same troops emerging from one of the gates and entering by another, came round and round again carrying different kinds of armour. In order to dazzle . . . [by] glamour and mystery, mechanical devices caused the lions on the steps of [the Emperor's] throne to roar terribly.[42]

By early 1980, one had the feeling that the American Empire, like that of Byzantium, was also largely held together with smoke and mirrors. Not that firepower was unavailable — rather, the real question was whether any volume or type of coercion could now service extended American commitments.

NOTES

1. See for example Stanley Hoffmann's two essays: "The Hell of Good Intentions," *Foreign Policy*, No. 29 (Winter 1977–78), pp. 3–26 and "A View from At Home: The Perils

of Incoherence," *Foreign Affairs, America and the World 1978,* Vol. 57, No. 3, pp. 463–491.

2. See his interview with James Reston, *New York Times,* December 31, 1978 and again in the *New York Times,* March 30, 1980.

3. See for example, Henry Kissinger, *White House Years* (Boston: Little, Brown and Co., 1979), esp. pp. 54–70 and 195–225; also Robert Tucker, "America in Decline: The Foreign Policy of 'Maturity,' " *Foreign Affairs, America and the World 1979,* Vol. 58, No. 3, pp. 449–484 and "A New International Order?" *Commentary,* Vol. 59 (February 1975).

4. Among the many analyses of the sort outlined here see Robert O. Keohane and Joseph Nye, Jr., *Power and Interdependence: World Politics in Transition* (Boston: Little Brown and Co., 1977); C. Fred Bergsten and Lawrence Krause, eds., *World Politics and International Economics* (Washington, D.C.: Brookings Institution, 1975); Seyom Brown, *New Forces in World Politics* (Washington, D.C.: Brookings Institution, 1974) and Brown, "The Changing Essence of Power," *Foreign Affairs,* Vol. 51 (January 1973); Richard Cooper, *The Economics of Interdependence* (New York: McGraw-Hill, 1968); and Ed Morse, *Modernization and the Transformation of International Relations* (New York: Free Press, 1976). Nye, Bergsten, Cooper, and Morse all became part of the Carter administration.

5. Leslie Gelb, cited by *U.S. News and World Report,* January 20, 1980, p. 24.

6. Cited by James Wooten, "Here Comes Zbig," *Esquire,* November 1979, p. 120.

7. Zbigniew Brzezinski, *Between Two Ages: America's Role in the Technetronic Era* (New York: Penguin Books, 1970), p. 9.

8. Brzezinski, "America In A Hostile World," *Foreign Policy,* No. 23 (Summer 1976), p. 65.

9. Ibid.

10. From a remarkably revealing interview in March of 1975, found in G. R. Urban, ed., *Detente* (New York: Universe Books, 1976), p. 263.

11. Ibid.

12. Ibid., pp. 278–279.

13. Ibid., p. 264.

14. Cited by Joseph Kraft, *Washington Post,* June 17, 1977.

15. Speech of November 21, 1977, Department of State, Bureau of Public Affairs, Washington, D.C., 1977.

16. Ibid.

17. *New York Times,* March 23, 1977.

18. See for example, Vance's Harvard Commencement Address on June 5, 1980 in *New York Times,* June 6, 1980, p. A12.

19. "Human Rights: Selected Documents," No. 5, n.d. (Washington, D.C.: Department of State, Bureau of Public Affairs).

20. Elizabeth Drew, "Reporter at Large: Human Rights," *The New Yorker,* July 18, 1977, p. 54.

21. For similar comments see ibid., *passim.*

22. Ibid., p. 56.

23. Brzezinski and Samuel Huntington, *Political Power: USA/USSR* (New York: Viking Books, 1964), p. 424.

24. Excellent surveys of the development of the Carter administration's SALT II positions and the negotiations themselves can be found in Strobe Talbot, *Endgame: The Inside Story of SALT II* (New York: Harper and Row, 1979), and Thomas W. Wolfe, *The SALT Experience* (Cambridge, Mass.: Ballinger Publishing Co., 1979). Useful documentary sources are Roger P. Labrie, ed., *SALT Handbook: Key Documents and Issues 1972–*

1979 (Washington, D.C.: American Enterprise Institute, 1979) and U.S., Department of State, *SALT II Agreement,* Selected Documents No. 12A (Washington, D.C.: Bureau of Public Affairs, June 1979).

25. Wolfe, op. cit., pp. 222–223.
26. Presidential address to the graduating class at the United States Naval Academy, June 7, 1978, *New York Times,* June 8, 1978.
27. For a review of the Camp David Summit and American policy during this period see, John C. Campbell, "The Middle East: The Burden of Empire," *Foreign Affairs, America and the World 1978,* pp. 613–632. Documentary materials may be found in U.S., Department of State, *The Camp David Summit, September 1978* (Washington, D.C.: Bureau of Public Affairs, 1978).
28. Testimony given at a hearing before the Subcommittee on Europe and the Middle East of the Committee on Foreign Affairs, House of Representatives, 96th Cong., 1st Sess., October 16, 1979.
29. See the article by the former American ambassador, William H. Sullivan, "Dateline Iran: The Road Not Taken," *Foreign Policy,* No. 40 (Fall 1980), pp. 175–186.
30. Tucker, "America in Decline," op. cit.
31. Address at the United States Naval Academy, op. cit.
32. Tucker, op. cit., pp. 468ff.
33. State of the Union Message, *New York Times,* January 22, 1980.
34. *New York Times,* December 14, 1979.
35. State of the Union Message, op. cit.
36. See U.S. Department of Defense, *FY 1981 DOD Report* (Washington, D.C.: Government Printing Office, 1980).
37. State of the Union Message, op. cit.
38. CBS Sunday Night News, February 4, 1980. See also *Washington Post,* February 4, 1980. Brzezinski's more studied analysis of this event was revealed in an interview with television commentator Bill Moyers; "Bill Moyers' Journal: A Conversation with Zbigniew Brzezinski," Public Broadcasting System, November 16, 1980.
39. "National Security Adviser Brzezinski Interviewed on 'Issues and Answers,' " *Department of State Bulletin,* Vol. 80, No. 2039 (June 1980), p. 49.
40. *McNeil/Lehrer Report,* Public Broadcasting System, October 15, 1980.
41. *Washington Post,* January 27, 1978.
42. Harold Nicholson, *The Evolution of Diplomacy* (New York: Collier Brooks, 1954), p. 41.

Chapter 12
Conclusion

By the late 1940s it had become clear that world politics could never again be of episodic significance to the United States. Indeed, because of America's emergence as a great power, the Soviet presence in Europe, and the impact of nuclear weapons, foreign affairs would become very nearly transcendent. It was realized that there was more to international political life than Soviet-American relations. But since only the Russians and the Americans possessed both nuclear weapons and the semblance of a coherent foreign policy design reaching far beyond their respective frontiers, it was not illogical to suggest that their antagonistic relationship was central and gave a bipolar structure to international society. The notion implied, in the words of one of the patriarchs of contemporary international studies, a "worldwide balance of which the United States and the Soviet Union are the main weights, placed on opposite scales."[1] The ancient balance of power in Europe and the politics of the Near and Far East "shared the fate of the general European system. They have become functions of the new worldwide balance, mere 'theaters' where the power contest between the two great protagonists is fought out."[2]

AMERICAN POWER AND
THE DYNAMICS OF THE COLD WAR

This portrayal of a cosmic struggle found resonance in NSC-68. Here it was explained how total were the stakes, how irrelevant the specific day-to-day issues, how consuming the struggle, and how brutally the battle must be fought:

> What is new, what makes the continuing crisis, is the polarization of power which now inescapably confronts [a] slave society with the free.... The assault ... is world wide, and in the context of the present polarization of power a defeat ... anywhere is a defeat everywhere....[3]

If there were to be negotiations, they would have to occur well past the mid-1950s — and then, the report concluded, they should be only a means

447

for recording a favorable outcome for American power, not accommodating Soviet interests. Hence, American objectives were to

> ... promote the gradual retraction of Soviet power.... To encourage the development ... of the national life of groups evidencing the ability ... to achieve and maintain national independence ... [and to] promote ... the emergence of satellite countries as entities independent of the USSR.[4]

In short, the description was of a world divided by a Manichean struggle in which the Soviet Union had few if any legitimate interests. The only means of obviating the contest was to gain the upper hand and then demand a withdrawal by the Soviet Union to a position of such reduced circumstances that the Soviet, no matter what its ultimate designs, would be forever limited in its means.

Technically, the American strategy was less incongruent with international and Soviet-American reality than, perhaps, it is now. That is, the Soviet Union was, by all accounts, a relatively weak although highly militarized society with limited means beyond those in place by 1948. In fact, for much of the postwar period, the world described by planners and professors was neither militarily equilibrated nor was it balanced in any other way. The Soviets, from the late 1940s to the mid-1960s, could pose no realistic military threat to the United States. At the end of World War II, although the Soviets had the largest armed force in the world, less than 50 percent of their transport was motorized, the rest was drawn by man and horse. And in 1962, at the time of the Cuban missile crisis, the Russians had few operational ICBMs, and they may well have been vulnerable to an American first strike. It is true that the Soviets could threaten Europe, probe at the frontiers of their empire, and, in that sense, held those areas hostage. But there was always a ramshackle bluster attendant to each Soviet performance that belied the fears in American military planning documents and academic descriptions regarding the dimensions of the Soviet challenge.

The Soviets were, therefore, a massive, potential counterweight, largely isolated from international politics. To some extent their exclusion was self-imposed. Just as much, it was a product of the heroic scale of the American engagement in world affairs. Zbigniew Brzezinski's characterization of most of the years of the cold war rings true:

> ... more than a million American troops stationed on some 400 major and almost 300 minor United States military bases scattered all over the globe. [There were] more than forty-two nations tied to the United States by security pacts, American military missions training the officers and troops of

many other national armies, and the approximately two hundred thousand United States civilian government employees in foreign posts all makes for striking analogies to the great classical imperial systems.[5]

This position of preeminence was basically unchanged until the 1970s. Yet most of the cold war was also marked by the growing complexity of international society as this American hegemony gradually deteriorated. And once American hegemony was lost and bipolarity became a more empirical portrait, those earlier strategies constructed around the hegemonial reality became less plausible.

A DECLINING PROSPECT FOR ORDER?

For the first 20 years there was a series of intense but, from an American standpoint, manageable, spasms of change that undulated over global politics. Middle range powers gained access to nuclear weapons, but whatever form the professions of independence the nascent nuclear powers of Europe, China, and Israel took, their weapons inventories were no threat to the United States. On the contrary, they were almost invariably targeted on the Soviet Union.

In the former colonial areas, nationalist upheavals were as common as Marxist rhetoric, but if America's European associates were embarrassed by a declining capacity to monopolize the profit and politics of third world states, America hardly suffered from the process of decolonization. Although uncomfortable with both nationalism and collectivist ideologies, American business nonetheless moved with alacrity to fill the opportunities presented by rising demands for modernization and diminished European vigor. By the mid-1970s, notwithstanding a spurt of Soviet activity in the late 1950s and occasional abortive efforts on the Europeans to retain vestiges of the past, decolonization was complete. And nowhere in what was now called the Third World were American and Western capital and technology unwelcomed; at worst, conditions were attached. When it mattered — in providing the means for international liquidity, managerial techniques, technology, or arms — American goods and services still had a leg up on the rest. The world had been, in Brzezinski's words, "filled by the more pervasive but less tangible [than military power] influence of American economic presence and innovation. . . ."[6]

By the 1970s, then, the reach of the United States — even its access — was no less and perhaps as great as at any time in the postwar era. However, the capacity to control events and determine outcomes had, nevertheless, been vitiated. In part, this resulted from circumstances over which the United States had little control. In other respects, the diminution of American hegemony has resulted from the playing-out — sometimes in an unforeseen manner and with unintended consequences — of policies consciously set in motion by the United States at the height of its international preeminence.

Perhaps the most fundamental change to affect the structure and dynamics of world politics in the 1970s has been the emergence of real Soviet military power that approximates the image of its power that existed in the early cold war years. Whereas its power was more hypothetical and potential than real and immediate in the late 1940s, 1950s, and most of the 1960s, by those early standards of the cold war, the Soviet Union is now a great power. They have a flexible nuclear capability, competent conventional arms, and adequate logistics, if not to sustain a global presence at great distance from the Soviet Union, then at least sufficient to complicate such a projection of power by the United States. Moreover, through the employment of proxies and surrogates such as the Cubans or East Germans, the Soviets can now conjure a more favorable correlation of forces, which, in the view of some Western observers, allows for the development of a new

> Soviet strategy ... to help Communist parties gain state power. Then, via friendship treaties, arms aid and Soviet, Cuban or East European advisors, the Soviets will help the local communists hold onto and consolidate power. Ultimately, the aim of this strategy is to establish a new alliance system for the Russians in Africa and Asia, a looser eastern version of the Warsaw Pact.[7]

Short of preemptive war, the United States had few if any means available to it to prevent the Soviet Union achieving strategic parity. But the loss of nuclear supremacy has meant that American foreign and national security policies predicated on the threat and/or use of military force have become more problematic when applied to the Soviet Union. Though retaining a measure of deterrent utility and perhaps defensive efficacy should deterrence fail, nuclear weapons are hard to relate to any other purposeful activity. Few objectives really seem worth the costs associated with carrying out a nuclear threat. To remain credible, the brandishing of nuclear weapons must be ever more forceful "the next time." But a policy so poised seems loud, dangerous, and, ultimately, paralyzed.[8]

Nor are the constraints on the use of force confined to the domain of nuclear weapons. If there are observers to write a century or so hence, they may well record the 1970s and 1980s a watershed in the history of weapons. Innovations in weapons technology have allowed for miniaturization and the exponential multiplication of missile warheads deliverable with near perfect accuracy and thus the capacity to extirpate any target, once acquired. Consequently technological change may have doomed any serious attempt to monitor nuclear or conventional weapons stocks, fix the number of nuclear warheads, control the dispersion of inventories, and, equally distressing, may have eroded the functional distinction between the effects of nuclear and conventional weapons.

For example, former Secretary of Defense James Schlesinger pointed out in 1974, that air-breathing cruise missiles, when armed with highly accurate conventional warheads, might crack a Soviet silo almost as effectively as a nuclear weapon. And while there might be theoretical ABM defensive systems against ballistic missiles, American defense planners have insistently noted that the burden of defending against cruise missiles is immensely greater. Cruise missiles will, in the near future, fly to their targets at almost ground level (hence thwarting most radar), with accuracies of within thirty feet or less. Their numbers are, moreover, difficult to verify given their small size and their warheads can be MIRVed. MIRV and cruise missile technologies, then, whatever the intentions of the Soviets and Americans in the early 1970s when their development was accelerated, may well have spelled the end of meaningful arms control.

Then, too, there is the revolutionary increase in the defense capacity of conventional weapons inspired by the advent of precision guided, "one shot — one kill" weapons.[9] When these weapons spread to less advanced countries, the coercive capabilities of even superpowers against the weak will be constrained. Any future military planner contemplating military intervention will have to consider putting ships, planes, even tanks and armored personnel carriers at the risk of being disabled by foot soldiers toting simple, cheap, precision-guided weapons.

Finally, American policy must operate within an international system in which this diffusion of military capability encompasses nuclear as well as conventional weapons. In not many years, states that have abutted one another in hostility for years will gain access to nuclear weapons. Yet their technical ability to manage any meaningful control or viable command of these weapons, even in peacetime, may not be as extensive as the explosive power they can project into a territory that is the locus of ancient hatreds. Of those states that arms control experts expect to have viable nuclear delivery systems by 1990, many are in the third world and perhaps as many as seven have direct interest in the future of the Persian Gulf/Indian Ocean area. Insofar as antagonistic neighbors have had some tendency to bloody one another, it is not hard to understand why most observers are not hopeful about the future of a proliferated world.

Some have argued, however, that an extended "domino effect" of future conflict implicit in these arguments was discredited by the experience of the United States in Vietnam. But the example may be poorly chosen. For Vietnam's effects were isolable, it could be argued, because of an eccentric confluence of events and circumstances: a domestic political paralysis in the United States and an international stalemate produced by the emerging triangular Sino-Soviet-American relationship and Soviet-American strategic parity. But what of an international environment in which — as may be the case now — diplomacy has fallen into low repute among the most significant actors, and military technology has begun to proliferate? Moreover, to the extent that the idea that peace is indivisible has prevailed, the notion itself has probably constrained interstate violence. Ironically, however, success in isolating Vietnam, not to mention a succession of Mideast wars, the Indo-Pakistani War, or the Sino-Vietnamese War, may have called into question the understanding that peace is a seamless web. War, especially in the non-West, may now be becoming more comfortably contemplated.

Of course, one cannot be sure. Some suggest, for example, that even if proliferation occurs it need not follow that war is inevitable between nuclear armed neighbors within a region. Or, if conflict occurs, it need not follow that it will be comprehensive and inevitably implicate the United States and the Soviet Union. Thus it may well be that deterrence dynamics will come to dominate the relationships of the *nouveau* nuclear powers and their relations with the superpowers even as deterrence has come to define so much of mutual superpower affairs.[10] But even if the latter condition does come about, other global interdependencies seem likely to insure persistent vulnerabilities, tension, and conflict. And these are conditions likely to implicate the United States given the magnitude of its international economic involvement and dependency.

This is especially ironic, for if there was one set of conditions that the United States thought it could control after World War II, it was international economic interaction within the Western world. Weapons diffusion may have proceeded with unforeseen consequences in spite of an American attempt to use arms transfers as an instrument of policy. However, American initiative and resources for international economic reconstruction after World War II constituted a virtual monopoly. Presumably, therefore, an American vision would obtain.

In a certain sense it has. American policy was conceived within a context of economic ideas that held that if the economies of Western Europe and Japan could be reconstructed within an interdependent framework of monetary stability and free trade, both prosperity and peace would result. The benefits of interdependence, it was hoped, would constrain the nationalism that had ripped the world system to shreds during the first half of the twentieth century. Moreover, American planners believed that prosperity based on such interdependence was a necessary condition for the containment of Soviet power and the world economic growth necessary for the development of the third world.

The Bretton Woods System, Marshall Plan, and the dependencies of the third world on the industrial West for capital and markets are in a sense the fulfillment of the vision. On the other hand, the United States has not been able to escape the implications of this interdependence. For the decline of American strategic hegemony has been paralleled by the decline of its economic hegemony as well. The rise of European and Japanese centers of economic and hence, political power — in part by American design — impinges on American freedom of diplomatic maneuver internationally and, no less painfully, penetrates American society through economic competition that threatens formally secure markets and jobs. Similarly, formerly pliant energy producers in the third world now whipsaw the industrialized world's economy through the exercise of a kind of economic power unimagined at the dawn of the cold war. In short, the United States and the rest of the world have come to realize what Rousseau knew: that interdependence and propinquity are as likely to produce conflict as peace.

Although the international politics of the late twentieth century does not therefore conform to a vision of an exclusively American century, the United States is, nevertheless, in a position of considerable potential leverage on the future. American resource scarcities and economic and military dependencies are linked to the financial, technological, investment, and security dependencies of others including America's adversaries. The sheer size and scope of America's military capability and economy and their centrality to the security of both the industrialized and the less developed world insures that, as Helmut Schmidt has put it, ". . . it is hard to achieve anything fundamental without the cooperation of the United States."[11] There are now others in international politics whose cooperation is no less essential, but, in a word, the United States, though no longer a hegemonial power, remains, nonetheless, a preponderant power.

The United States finds itself, therefore, at that point where most of the vulnerabilities and interdependencies of the rest of the world intersect. That position means that the United States will likely incur significant and probably increasing costs in its foreign and national security policies. But it also means that the United States is a necessary participant if successful international adjustment to the difficulties of interdependence is to come about. Dictating outcomes — a capability that the United States fleetingly possessed after World War II — is no longer within American grasp. But to the extent that very little that is creative can be done without it, the United States retains considerable capacity to influence and shape the relationships that will determine its international position and fortunes. As a power to be reckoned with and as a compelling voice, it could revert to some of the traditions of mediation and arbitration that characterized American diplomacy in the early nineteenth and then, again, in the early twentieth century. This would require a retreat from a sense of American mission and exceptionalism; a return to some diplomatic formalism, tolerance, and patience; and the forswearing of the short-term advantages that sometimes accrue to the manipulation of national security issues and fears in domestic politics. But real American security could be enhanced. And that alone should give sufficient warrant to the effort.

THE ROAD TAKEN?

As the United States entered the 1980s, however, the Carter administration persisted in defining American interests in the same way as administrations that preceded it: in terms of an American-inspired international order. That order, it has been believed, is held together by power — not an equilibrium of power, but an overall position of preeminence. Beyond a rational worry about the sum of deliverable warheads, alliances, and the distribution of bases, there continues to be the overarching concern with a psychological intangible: the malevolent intentions of the Soviet Union to feed on international chaos and the questioned capability of Americans to face the worst and stay the course. Hence, traditional criteria of evaluating interests such as geography, raw materials, markets, and armaments are placed alongside considerations of image, perceptions, prestige and credibility at home and abroad. The result is to blur distinctions between one American interest and another. For the means to cast the "shadow of power," as Acheson once put it, has come to imply that American steadfastness must seem convincing on virtually a global scale. It is not surprising, therefore, that American interests remain in undiminished and undifferentiated definition or that the United States still concerns itself with the internal social structure and stability of states that have little tangible relationship to American security.

Brzezinski's words as he left office could have been spoken by Dulles, Eisenhower, Rusk, McNamara, or Truman without hesitation over anything but syntax: Power, he suggested, "has to be sustained, cultivated and, when need be, applied so that others find it credible." "[O]ur willingness to cooperate with the Soviets," he warned, "must be carefully balanced with our willingness to compete assertively."[12] Similarly, when Brzezinski and Vice President Mondale publicly polished old commitments lest any hint of tarnished doubt remain and added new commitments in the Middle East, there was always a sense that, whatever understandings there might have been as "new global political and economic arrangements . . . reflect new realities," the American response is fundamentally unchanged. American commitments remain extended like one of those financial empires of Billy Sol Estes, Bernard Cornfeld, or the Hunt brothers — offering ever new and shiny prospectuses, and living in dread of the auditors. The alternative of reexamining the structure and assumptions and techniques used to buttress the enterprise goes untried, lest the attention itself seem to lead to a panic which neither the United States nor its associates could withstand.

An especially deep pathos attached to the Carter administration, torn so many ways from itself and facing its reelection ordeal. This was an administration, it will be recalled, that came to office proclaiming new perspectives and sensitivities to the international position of the United States. Moreover, the American electorate, though undoubtedly skeptical, seemed, nonetheless, tolerant of an attempt to develop policies predicated on new perspectives and a sensitivity to a changed international environment. The 1976 Carter campaign, lest we forget, was based on an underscoring of its proclaimed differences from its predecessors who, especially in the figure of Henry Kissinger, represented the old approach to the world — and the electorate chose Carter, not Ford and Kissinger.

The Carter administration had, therefore, great opportunities. It could have used a moral appeal to ask Americans to contribute generously to a soothing of North-South issues instead of letting the issue become a battering ram for the left and right. It could have used the Kissinger legacy of a resurgence of diplomacy and treated as juridical/diplomatic equivalents the Soviets, Chinese, Vietnamese, Cambodians, and even the Rhodesians, instead of measuring them in terms of their moral validity.[13] It could have attempted to open a sensible dialogue about the nature of American commitments and interests instead of insisting that all were equivalent and beyond reexamination.

Carter could have dealt with the revolutionary third world in terms other than simply a Soviet-Cuban cabal. There were, of course, some steps in this direction in Central America and southern Africa. But Carter's contribution to the trivial question of Soviet troops in Cuba was a half-hearted compromise that pointed to the nub of the administration's problem: Carter conceded that there was no security threat in troops that had been stationed in Cuba for over 17 years. Yet at the same time he gave in to pressures to make parallel military arrangements with the Chinese, to examine yet again the question of bludgeoning the Soviets with economic weapons only marginally at America's disposal, and reopened the lid on a repertoire of military responses that have proved problematic and whose relevance to contemporary conditions seems more distant than ever. All this was *before* the Afghanistan crisis begot the Carter Doctrine that threatened to seal Soviet-American relations at the frigid plateau to which they had been diving since the Ford administration abandoned detente in the face of partisan thunder from the right.

Cuba, SALT, and Afghanistan became the vehicles for moving off the fence. No longer could the Carter administration contend that it would keep the interests and commitments of an imperial power and point to the logic and requirements of interdependence at the same time. That issue had been settled. The United States would dampen the rhetoric of human rights, redistributive equality, and arms control and would yield to the language of military superiority.

With military policy ascendant once again, any contemplated bold diplomatic overtures to the third world would be necessarily eclipsed, subsidiary to the question of the 1950s: "Which side are you on?" But if global politics had assumed a new rigidity, and coercion a new centrality, it did not mean that force had found a new utility. Force and diplomacy are two different tracks; sometimes they parallel one another; sometimes one leads into the other. As Averell Harriman once observed, "Nobody negotiates while being beaten on the head." The act of giving such a thrashing may serve short-term or even domestic interests, but it involves costs that successful and sustained diplomatic relations might have avoided. Force is diplomacy's nemesis; it serves best when it stands mutely behind a negotiator.

Yet in much American thought on international relations and strategic studies, and in much current political discussion, coercion and diplomacy have become synonymous. Force, even nuclear war, it is widely held, are instruments capable of a kind of choreography in which the manipulation of threats of violence and the use of violence itself in dealing with crisis has been defined as a kind statecraft. Let us recall, however, that a diplomacy of violence has been tested and found wanting. Not the least, because Americans became aware of the difficulties in rearranging their domestic institutions to meet the needs of a diplomacy of force, or, for that matter, imposing democratic institutions on others by dint of firepower. Yet, the drum marshalling another attempt to fashion a liberal world order has been beaten ever more forcefully in recent years. "Never," George Kennan despaired recently, since World War II has there been so far-reaching a militarization of thought and discourse in the capital. An unsuspecting stranger, plunged into its midst, could only conclude that the last hope of peaceful, nonmilitary solutions had been exhausted — that from now on only weapons, however used, could count. . . . We are now in the danger zone. I can think of no instance in modern history where such a breakdown of political communication and such a triumph of unstrained military suspicions as now marks Soviet-American relations has not led, in the end, to armed conflict.[14]

How such force and conflict could be made relevant to the task of world order in the contemporary environment has not yet been explained. Force could, to be sure, serve to inhibit the Soviets from embarking on a course of precipitous military action against states with whom Americans have associated themselves by reason of treaty, trade, or sentiment. Beyond that, however, military power has not seemed to be able to stave off revolutionary change. The spread of collectivist ideologies antithetical to liberal procedural values has proceeded. Nor has military power seemed very relevant to a policy designed to promote human rights. And, finally, military power has seemed only tangentially, and perhaps even harmfully, to touch upon the increasing salience of international economic issues.

The relevance of military power is most apparent if the world is portrayed as anarchical and encompassing a zero-sum, bipolar Soviet-American relationship. As Brzezinski told Elizabeth Drew:

[I]t gets down to a simple proposition: They would like to become number one, like we did. It's better to become number one from the number two position than to be toppled from number one . . . there's no way of knowing where you will stop once you get going downhill.[15]

Years ago, with another colleague at Harvard, Brzezinski put it more chillingly:

. . . peaceful coexistence of the nations peopling the world presupposes the destruction of totalitarian dictatorships. Since, according to their own loudly proclaimed professions, their system must be made worldwide, those who reject the system, have no alternative but to strive for its destruction.[16]

That was an unabashed call for the refutation of compromise. And with the abandonment of the diplomatic enterprise, only force remains. In a sense this is in keeping with a fashionable view of the diplomatic profession. Today, diplomacy is widely seen as but a glittering remnant of another era. As Brzezinski explained in 1970:

> ... to be a diplomat is to be part of a sociological category. . . .[T]hey occupy anachronistic jobs. . . . The Secretary of State [heads] an increasingly irrelevant bureaucracy.[17]

But if the irrelevance of diplomacy is coupled with generalized conditions inhospitable to American power, then the United States could realize its worst fears: expensively armed with inappropriate instruments but still vulnerable to careening events.

NOTES

1. Hans J. Morgenthau, *Politics Among Nations,* 1st ed. (New York: Knopf, 1949), p. 149.
2. Ibid.
3. NSC-68, p. 51.
4. Ibid., p. 62.
5. Zbigniew Brzezinski, *Between Two Ages: America's Role in the Technotronic Era* (New York: Viking, 1970), p. 34.
6. Ibid., p. 35.
7. Donald Zagoria, "New Soviet Alliances," *Foreign Affairs*, Vol. 57 No. 4 (Spring 1979), p. 738.
8. This is not to say that there are not many who assert that a rational and credible strategy of nuclear weapons use against the Soviet Union cannot be developed. For example, see: Colin Gray, "Nuclear Strategy: A Case for a Theory of Victory," *International Security*, Vol. 4, No. 1 (Summer 1979), pp. 54–87, and Gray and Keith Payne, "Victory is Possible," *Foreign Policy*, No. 39 (Summer 1980), pp. 14–27. For a more restrained view of the utility of force see, Robert J. Art, "To What Ends Military Power?" *International Security*, Vol. 4, No. 4 (Spring 1980), pp. 3–35.
9. James F. Digby, "Precision-Guided Weapons," *Adelphi Papers*, No. 118 (London: International Institute for Strategic Studies, 1975) and Richard Burt, "New Weapons Technologies: Debate and Directions," *Adelphi Papers*, No. 126 (London: International Institute for Strategic Studies, 1976).
10. For an elaboration of this projection, see John J. Weltman, "Nuclear Devolution and World Order," *World Politics*, Vol. 32, No. 2 (January 1980), pp. 169–193.
11. *New York Times*, August 25, 1974.
12. See Richard Burt, "Brzezinski Calls Democrats Soft Toward Moscow," *New York Times*, November 30, 1980, and Michael Getler, "A Balanced Foreign Policy 'Much Needed,' Brzezinski Says," *Washington Post*, November 30, 1980.
13. For an early gesture in this direction see Under Secretary of State Warren Christopher's speech at Occidental College, "Normalization of Diplomatic Relations," June 11, 1977.

14. *New York Times,* "Op Ed", February 1, 1978.
15. "Reporter at Large," *New Yorker,* May 1, 1980, p. 111.
16. Carl J. Friedrich and Zbigniew Brzezinski, *Totalitarian Dictatorship and Autocracy* (Cambridge, Mass.: Harvard Univ. Press, 1956), p. 68.
17. Cited in *Newsweek,* International Edition, July 6, 1970 and *Washington Post,* July 5, 1970.

Index

Acheson, Dean, 62–63, 156
  and Berlin blockade, 94, 95
  and Chinese revolution, 103–104
  and Congress, 68–69
  and H-bomb, 105–106
  and Marshall Plan, 72
  and NATO, 97, 98
  and NSC-68, 109–112, 118–119, 122
  on Soviet Union, 158
Adenauer, Konrad, 227
Afghanistan, 436
Africa, 238–239. *See also specific names and subjects*
Alliance for Progress, 259, 262–265
Allende, Salvador, 389–390
Angola, 381
Antiballistic missile (ABM), 370–371, 373
Arbenz Guzman, Jocobo, 188–190
Armas, Carlos Castillo, 189–190
Aswan dam, 212
Atomic Energy Commission, 105–106
Atomic weapons policy
  and Baruch's formulation, 59
  and Korea, 146, 173
  and H-bomb, 105–106
  policy rethinking of, 218–220
  Soviet testing of, 99, 100
  and Taiwan Strait crisis, 192, 194–196

Baghdad Pact, 211–212
Baldwin, Hanson, 125
Ball, George, 345
Balance of payments deficit, 306–314
  and Bretton Woods system, 396–399
Bank of England, 215
Bao Dai, 185, 186
Barr, David, 103
Baruch, Bernard, 59
Bay of Pigs, 256–258
Begin, Menachim, 429
Bell, Coral, 158

Benes, Eduard, 83
Berlin blockade, 90–95
Berlin crisis (1961), 274, 275–278
Bohlen, Charles, 111, 169, 170, 200–201, 230
Bowie, Robert, 178–179
Bretton Woods system, collapse of, 396–399
Brezhnev, Leonid, 354–355
Brzezinski, Zbigniew, 299–300
  and East-West interdependence, 415–419
Brussels Pact, 84

Cambodia, 179–180, 185, 347, 351, 352, 361, 378
Camp David, 225
Carter administration, 412–444
  and Camp David summit, 427–432
  and detente, 424–427
  and East-West interdependence, 414–419
  and Europe, 442–443
  and human rights, 419–421
  and Iranian Revolution, 433–435
  and military power, 438–439
  and SALT, 422–424, 436
Castro, Fidel, 239, 256–257
Chamberlain, Neville, 19
Chemical warfare, and Vietnam War, 336
Chiang Kai-Shek, 58, 101, 103, 104, 123, 131, 193
  and Taiwan Strait crisis, 192–196
Chile, 389–391
China, People's Republic of, 425–426
  Communist revolution in, 100–104
  and Korea, 120, 122–123, 139–148, 156–157, 172–174
  and Nixon administration, 374–376
  and Soviet Union, 156–157, 222, 252–253

China, People's Republic of
  (*continued*)
  and Taiwan Strait crisis, 192–196
  and Third World, 253–256
  post–World War II, 58–59, 68–69
Chou En-Lai, 139
Churchill, Winston, 62–63
  and Iron Curtain, 56–57
  and Stalin's death, 199
  and World War II, 22–32
CIA
  and Bay of Pigs, 257
  and Guatemala, 189–190, 191
  and Iran, 187, 191–192
  and U-2 incident, 229, 232
  and Vietnam, 326
Clay, Lucius, 84, 91
Clifford, Clark, 337
Colby, Bainbridge, 16–17
Cold war. *See also* Detente; Soviet
  Union
  economic impact of, 306–314
  onset of, 56–77
    and atomic weapons policy,
      59–60
    and Kennan telegram, 57
    and Marshall Plan, 70–77
    and public opinion, 61–64
    and Truman Doctrine, 64–70
  prelude to, 11–48
    and pre–World War II period,
      18–20
    and Russian Revolution, 11–17
    and World War II, 20–33
  and Stalin's death, 196–202
Cominform, 74
Common Market, 309–310
Congo, 238–239
Congress
  and Chinese Revolution, 102, 104
  and defense policy, 132–133
  and NATO, 96–99
  and 1950 elections, 152–153
  and Truman Doctrine, 65, 67–68
  and Vandenberg Resolution, 84–85
  and Vietnam War, 352–353
Connally, Thomas, 119–120
Crisis management, central tenets of,
  286–287
Cuba, and Bay of Pigs, 256–258

Cuban missile crisis
  and American military, 298–299
  and American self-image, 299–300
  and American "toughness," 295–
    297
  and domestic politics, 291–292
  effects of, 303–306, 314–315
  historical views of, 288
  and illusion of control, 290–291
  Soviet motives in, 293–295
Cutler, Robert, 171
Czechoslovakia, 13–14
  coup in, 83–84

Davies, John Paton, 169–170
Defense spending
  and balance of payments, 306–314
  and Eisenhower administration, 175–
    179
  and Kennedy administration, 265–
    270, 276–277
  and Korean War, 130
  after "massive retaliation" policy,
    220–221
  and NSC-68, 107–108, 110
  post–World War II, 85–87
  and Soviet-American summits, 226–
    227, 233
Dennis v. *U.S.* (1951), 159
Detente
  decline of, 424–427
  and Khrushchev-Eisenhower sum-
    mits, 223–234
  and Nixon administration, 377–381,
    384
  and Stalin's death, 196–202
Diem, Ngo Dinh, 185–186, 322–323,
  325–326
Dien Bien Phu, 181, 182
Dillon, C. Douglas, 228
Disarmament
  and Carter administration, 374, 422–
    424
  and Eisenhower administration, 202–
    203
  and Ford administration, 374
  and Johnson administration, 371–372
  and Kennedy administration, 370
  and Nixon administration, 369–370,
    372, 384

post–World War II, 59–60
SALT, 436
Dominican Republic, 263, 342
Domino theory, 67, 182
Draft, 130
Dulles, Allen, 27, 191
Dulles, John Foster, 124, 191
  containment policies of, 176–177
  death of, 223
  and French-Indochina war, 182,
    184
  and Geneva Conference, 202–204
  illness of, 214
  and McCarthyism, 169–170
  "massive retaliation" policy of, 178–
    179
  and Mideast, 186, 187
  political background of, 168
  and Stalin's death, 197, 199
  and Suez crisis, 212–217
  and Taiwan Strait crisis, 193–196

East Berlin, riots in, 177
Eastern Europe. *See also specific names
    and subjects*
  and Truman administration, 82–85
East Germany, 227–228
Eden, Anthony, 183, 211, 212
Egypt
  and Camp David summit, 427–432
  and Suez crisis, 211–216
Eisenhower, Dwight D., 25–26. *See also*
    Eisenhower administration
  background on, 167
  farewell address of, 236–237
  on French-Indochina war, 181–182
  illness of, 211
Eisenhower administration, 8
  and defense strategy, 220–221
  economic policies of, 179
  and Geneva Conference, 202–204
  and Guatemala, 188–190, 191
  international outlook of, 174–177
  and Korean truce, 172–175
  last phase of, 234–236, 238–240
  and "massive retaliation" policy,
    177–179, 218–219
  and Mideast, 186–188, 191–192
  overview of, 236–238
  and Republican right wing, 167–191

and Soviet-American summit, 223–
  224
and Stalin's death, 196–202
and Suez crisis, 211–217
and Taiwan Strait crisis, 192–196
and Vietnam, 179–186
world views of, 179–181, 190, 191
Elections
  1952, 153–154
  1960, 240
  1964, 328, 343
  1968, 335–336, 338, 343–344, 347
Ellsberg, Daniel, 302
Europe. *See individual names and sub-
    jects;* Eastern Europe; Western Eu-
    rope

Fall-out shelters, 273–274
Feiss, Herbert, 74, 93
Food supply, 403
Ford administration. *See also* Kissinger,
    Henry
  accomplishments of, 405–406
  and SALT, 374
  and Vietnam, 361
Foreign policy. *See specific names and
    subjects*
France, 71, 72
  and Indochina, 181–184
  and Soviet-American summits, 226–
    227
  and Suez crisis, 212–215
  and West German statehood, 88, 93
Fulbright, J. William, 233

Gaither, H. Rowan, 220
Geneva Conference, 181–184, 202–204
Germany. *See also* East Germany; West
    Germany
  and Stalin, 18–20
Global deterrence, and Dulles, 176–177
Goldwater, Barry, 328
Great Britain, 182, 183
  and Iran, 186, 188
  and Soviet Union, 19
  and Suez crisis, 211–216
  and World War II, 22–23
Greece, and Truman Doctrine, 64–69
Guatemala, coup in, 188–190

Haiphong harbor, 355
Halle, Louis, 138
Hammarskjold, Dag, 239
Harriman, Averell, 27, 143
Herter, Christian, 226, 231
Hinton, Harold, 139
Hitler, Adolf, and Stalin, 18
Ho Chi Minh, 181, 182
Humphrey, Hubert, 185, 346, 347
Hungarian Revolt, 214
Huntington, Samuel, 261
Hydrogen bomb, 105–106, 131, 177

ICBMs, 265–268
Inchon, Korea, 137–138
Inflation, 61, 62
Iran, 30, 31, 58, 60, 65, 391
  and Eisenhower administration, 186–
    188, 191–192
  revolution in, 433–435
Iraq, 211
Israel
  and Camp David summit, 427–432
  and Suez crisis, 213–216

Jackson, Henry, 373–374
Jackson State incident, 352
Japan, 386–387
Jessup, Philip, 124
Johnson, Louis, 98–99
Johnson, Lyndon B., *See also* Johnson
    administration
  and 1968 election, 338
  on Vietnam, 323–324
Johnson administration. *See also* Viet-
    nam War
  economic policy of, 312
  and SALT, 371–372
  and Vietnam War, 327–347, 348
Jordan, 217, 221, 378–379

Kennan, George F., 21–22, 57–58, 73,
    74, 75–76, 124, 204, 236, 294, 297
  and H-bomb, 105, 106
  and NSC-68, 111, 112
Kennedy, John F., 185. *See also* Ken-
    nedy administration
  election of, 240
  world views of, 240–241, 250
Kennedy, Robert, 338

and Cuban missile crisis, 288–289,
    290, 294, 296, 298
Kennedy administration
  and Bay of Pigs, 256–258
  and Berlin crisis, 274, 275–278
  challenge to, 251
  and Cuban missile crisis, 287–300
  defense strategy of, 265–270
  economic policy of, 312–313
  overview of, 278–280
  and Sino-Soviet dispute, 250–253
  Third World policies of, 255–265
  transition to, 240–241
  and Vienna Conference, 272–275
  and Vietnam, 323–327
Kent State incident, 351–352
Khomeini, Ayatollah Ruhollah, 433–
    434
Khrushchev, Nikita, 120
  and Berlin crisis, 274, 275–278
  and Cuban missile crisis, 294–297
  and 1960 election, 240
  rise of, 200–202, 204
  and Soviet-American summits, 223–
    234
  and Third World, 253–255
  at UN, 239
  and Vienna Conference, 272–275
Kissinger, Henry, 8, 273, 293. *See also*
    Nixon administration
  accomplishments of, 404–406
  and Chile, 389–391
  and China, 374–375
  and detente, 379–380
  and nuclear-age diplomacy, 218–219
  policies summarized, 395
  and SALT, 370, 372, 373
  shuttle diplomacy of, 380–381
  and Vietnam War, 338, 341–342, 349,
    350, 354, 355–357, 358, 359
  world view of, 382–383
Korean War, 113
  and domestic politics, 126–130, 139
  evaluation of, 155–159
  military outline of, 137–138, 140–
    145
  outbreak of, 125–126
  prelude to, 118–125
  truce, 172–175
Kosygin, Aleksei, 330–331

Laos, 179–180, 271–272, 274, 330, 347, 351, 361
and SEATO, 185
League of Nations, 12
Lebanon, 221
Lenin, Nikolai, 12–13
Liberation, of Communist countries, 176–177
Lippman, Walter, 15, 230, 233
London Conference, 89–90
Luce, Henry R., 299
Lumumba, Patrice, 238–239, 272

MacArthur, Douglas
dismissal of, 149–152
and Korean War, 123, 125, 126, 137–142, 155
vs. Truman, 142–149, 151–152
McCarran Act, 159
McCarthy, Eugene, 338
McCarthy, Joseph, 149
anticommunism of, 129–130, 153
and Eisenhower administration, 169–170
McCleod, Scott, 169
McCone, John, 332–333
MacMillan, Harold, 222, 226
McNamara, Robert, 256, 266–270, 290, 291, 292, 372
and Vietnam, 324–327, 330, 334–335, 337
Malenkov, Georgi M., 196, 199–202
Mansfield, Mike, 185, 326
Mao Zedong, 58–59, 101, 104
Marshall, George C., 23, 72
and Chinese Revolution, 101–102
Marshall Plan, 70–77
and NATO, 96–97
as politico-economic concept, 87–89
Martin, Joseph, 148–149
"Massive retaliation" policy, 178–179
demise of, 218–219
Matsu, 195
Mayaguez, 378
Mendes-France, Pierre, 183
Mexico, 12
Mideast. *See also specific names and subjects*

and Camp David summit, 427–432
and Suez crisis, 211–217
Middle East Resolution, 216
Mobutu, Joseph, 239
Molotov, Vyacheslav, 24–25, 73, 74
Mossadegh, Mohammed, 186–187
Multinational corporations, 402–403, 404
Mutual Defense Assistance Program (MDAP), 97–99

Nasser, Gamal Abdel, 221
and Suez crisis, 211–213
National Security Council, 171
Nation-building, 259–265, 278–279
NATO
formation of, 94–100
and Suez crisis, 214–216
New Frontier. *See* Kennedy administration
Nicaragua, 432–433
Nitze, Paul, 105, 106, 111, 130
Nixon, Richard M., 149, 170, 194, 291–292. *See also* Nixon administration
and Checkers speech, 153–154
Nixon administration
accomplishments of, 404–406
and balance of payments, 397–399
and China, 374–376
and detente, 377–381
doctrine of, 367–369
and domestic politics, 393–394
and force-diplomacy relationship, 392–393
and Japan, 386–387
and Third World, 387–392
and Vietnam War, 347, 349–362
and Watergate, 360–361
NSC-68, 104–105, 106–113, 176–176
Nuclear Weapons and Foreign Policy (Kissinger), 218–219

Oil
embargo on, 380
and Iranian Revolution (1953), 186–188
and "petropower," 399–404
OPEC, 380, 399–404
Osgood, Robert F., 95–96

Pahlavi, Shah Mohammed Reza, 391
  fall of, 433–435
Pakistan, 387–388
Pearl Harbor, 24
Pentagon Papers, 327, 329, 331, 333–
  334, 337, 345
Peurifoy, John E., 189, 190
Poland, 19–20
  and World War II, 28–33
Polish Americans, 28, 30
Powers, Francis Gary, 225, 228–
  234

Quemoy, 193, 195

Radford, Admiral Arthur, 177, 182
Republican party, 30–31
  and Chinese Revolution, 101–102,
    104
  and cold war onset, 62–64
  and Eisenhower administration, 167–
    172
  and Korean War, 127
  and McCarthyism, 129
Rhee, Syngman, 119, 123–124, 193
  and Korean truce, 174
Rhodesia, 388–389
Ridgeway, Matthew, 147
Roosevelt, Franklin D., 21, 24, 27–28,
  30–31, 32
Roosevelt, Kermit, 187–188, 192
Ropacki, Adam, 22
Ruhr Valley, 93
Rusk, Dean, 255–257
  and Vietnam, 324
Russian Revolution, American inter-
  vention in, 12–17

Sadat, Anwar, and Camp David sum-
  mit, 428–429
Schelling, Thomas, 156, 159
Schlesinger, Arthur, Jr., 262, 263, 267,
  268, 290, 299
Seventh Fleet, 173, 192
Singer, J. David, 273–274
Smith, Margaret Chase, 130
Smith, Walter Bedell, 187, 191
Somozo, Anastazio, 432–433
Sorensen, Theodore, 292–293

Soviet Union. See also Cold war; Detente; Khrushchev, Nikita; Stalin,
  Josef
  and Carter "interdependence" pol-
    icy, 414–419
  and detente, 377–381
  and human rights, 419–420
  and Korean War, 120, 122
  and Marshall Plan, 73–74
  military buildup in, 300–301
  and pre–World War II period, 18–20
  and Sino-Soviet relations, 59, 222,
    252–253
  and Stalin's death, 196–200
  and Suez crisis, 211–212
  and Vietnam War, 354–355
  and World War II, 20–33
South Africa, 388–389
Southeast Asia Treaty Organization,
  (SEATO), formulation of, 184–185
Spanish Civil War, 18
Sputnick, 217, 218
Stalin, Josef
  and China, 59, 157
  death of, 173, 196–200
  and Eastern Europe, 82–84
  and Hitler, 18
  and Iran, 58
  and Korean War, 120
  post–World War II philosophy of, 56
  and West German statehood, 89–95
  and World War II, 20–22
Stevens, Robert, 313
Stevenson, Adlai, 153, 232, 297
Stimson, Henry L., 60
Strategic Arms Limitation Treaty. See
  Disarmament, SALT
Stress, and crisis management, 288–289
Suez Canal Users Association (SCUA),
  213
Syria, 217, 378–379

Tachen Island, 193
Taft, Robert A., 177
  on defense, 131–132
  and McCarthyism, 129
  and Korean War, 143
  and NSC-68, 119
Taiwan Strait, 192–196, 222

Taylor, Maxwell
  and "massive retaliation" policy, 218
  and Vietnam, 324, 325
Tet Offensive, 337, 338
Thailand, 180
Thieu, Nguyan Van, 355–358, 361
Third World
  and nation-building, 259–265
  and Nixon administration, 387–388
  and wars of revolution, 253–256
Tito, Josep B., 82–83
Tonkin Gulf Resolution, 328–330
Trade Expansion Act (TEA), 312
Truman, Harry S., 24, 256
  and General MacArthur, 123, 142–149
  and 1952 election, 152–153
  Truman Doctrine, 64–70
Truman administration
  atomic weapons policy of, 59–66
  and Berlin blockade, 90–95
  and China, 58–59, 100–104
  compared with Eisenhower administration, 175–176
  and defense spending, 85–87
  and H-bomb
  and Iran, 186
  and Korean War, 119–152
  and Marshall Plan, 70–77
  and Mideast, 58
  and NSC-68, 106–113
  and public opinion, 61–64
  and Truman Doctrine, 64–70
Tucker, Robert, 155
Turkey, 158
  and Truman Doctrine, 64–69

Ulam, Adam, 120–121
Unemployment, 61
United Fruit Company, 188–190, 191
United Nations, 68
  and Khrushchev, 239
  and Korean War, 125, 126, 139, 157–158
United States. *See specific names and subjects*
U-2 incident, 225, 228–234

Vandenberg Resolution, 84–85
Vienna Conference, 272–275

Viet Minh, 181
Vietnam. *See also* Vietnam War
  and Eisenhower administration, 179–180, 181–186
  and Geneva Convention, 182–185
Vietnam War
  Americanization of, 327–332
  analysis of, 339–342
  and chemical warfare, 336
  destruction in, 336–337
  and domestic politics, 343–345, 349
  end of, 361
  and Kennedy administration, 323–327
  in 1950s, 322–323
  Nixon takeover of, 349–350
  observations on, 358–362
  opposition to, 335, 351–353
  peace negotiations on, 330, 345–347, 353–358
  rationale for, 332, 340
  roots of, 179–180, 184–186
  and Tet Offensive, 337
  turning point in, 337–338
  U.S. ground troops enter, 333–334
  withdrawals from, 351, 353
Vincent, John Carter, 169–170

Wallace, Henry, 58
Warsaw Pact, 201
Watergate, 360–361, 394
Wechsler, James, 295
Wedemeyer, Albert, 101
Western Europe
  and Marshall Plan, 70–77
  outlook for, 385–386
West Germany, 227
  and Marshall Plan, 71–74
  rearmament of, 199, 200, 201, 222
  statehood for, 87–95
Westmoreland, William, 338
Wills, Gary, 170, 171
Wilson, Woodrow, and cold war origins, 11–17
World War II, and Soviet-Western relations, 20–33

Yalta Conference, 32–33
Yom Kippur War, 379–381
Yugoslavia, 82–83, 91